The **Dread** of Difference

Texas Film and Media Studies Series
Thomas Schatz, Editor

Edited by

Barry Keith

Grant

The **Dread**

f Difference

Gender

and the Horror Film

University of Texas Press, Austin

Fifth paperback printing, 2005

Requests for permission to reproduce material
from this work should be sent to Permissions,
University of Texas Press, Box 7819, Austin,
TX 78713-7819.

www.utexas.edu/utpress/about/bpermission.html

⊗ The paper used in this publication meets the
minimum requirements of American National
Standard for Information Sciences—Permanence
of Paper for Printed Library Materials,
ANSI Z39.48-1984.

Library of Congress
Cataloging-in-Publication Data

The dread of difference :
gender and the horror film /
edited by Barry Keith Grant.

p.   cm. — (Texas film studies series)

Includes bibliographical references and index.

ISBN 0-292-72794-1 (pbk : alk. paper).

1. Horror films—History and criticism.

2. Sex role in motion pictures.

3. Women in motion pictures.

I. Grant, Barry Keith, 1947–

II. Series.

PN1995.9.H6D74   1996

791.43′616—dc20   96-11099

Acknowledgments

I would like to thank the University of Texas Press for working with me yet again, particularly Betsy Williams, for her initial endorsement of the project, Tayron Tolley Cutter and Carolyn Wylie, for seeing the book through to completion, and Alison Tartt, once more, for her careful reading of the manuscript. Thanks are also due to both Dr. John Sivell, dean of humanities at Brock University, and Professor Joan Nicks, chair of the Department of Film Studies, Dramatic and Visual Arts, for their generous support of my research. The Photocopy Queen is one of a kind. No thanks are offered the folks at New Line Cinema, who refused to allow me to include any illustrations from the *Nightmare on Elm Street* films because they did not want Freddy Krueger, apparently more sensitive than any of us thought, "to be associated with such a project."

Berenstein, Rhona J. "'It Will Thrill You, It May Shock You, It Might Even Horrify You': Gender, Reception, and Classic Horror Cinema" is a slightly revised and somewhat shorter version of chapter 3 of *Attack of the Leading Ladies: Gender, Sexuality, and Spectatorship in Classic Horror Cinema* (New York: Columbia University Press, 1995). Copyright © 1995 by Columbia University Press. Used with permission of Columbia University Press and the author.

Clover, Carol J. "Her Body, Himself: Gender in the Slasher Film" originally appeared in *Representations,* no. 20 (Fall 1987): 187–228. Copyright © 1987 by the Regents of the University of California. Reprinted by permission of the University of California Press and the author.

Conlon, James. "The Place of Passion: Reflections on *Fatal Attraction*" originally appeared in *Journal of Popular Film and Television* 16, no. 4 (Winter 1989): 148–154. Reprinted by permission of the Helen Dwight Reid Educational Foundation. Published by Heldref Publications, 1319 Eighteenth St. N.W., Washington, D.C. 20036-1802. Copyright © 1989.

Creed, Barbara. "Horror and the Monstrous-Feminine: An Imaginary Abjection" originally appeared in *Screen* 27, no. 1 (January–

Sharrett, Christopher. "The Horror Film in Neoconservative Culture" is a revised version of an article that appeared originally in *Journal of Popular Film and Television* 21, no. 3 (Fall 1993): 100–110. Copyright © 1993 by Christopher Sharrett. Used with permission of the author.

Sobchack, Vivian. "Bringing It All Back Home: Family Economy and Generic Exchange" appeared originally in *American Horrors: Essays on the Modern American Horror Film*, edited by Gregory A. Waller (Urbana and Chicago: University of Illinois Press, 1987), pp. 175–194. Copyright © 1987 by the University of Illinois Press. Reprinted with permission of the University of Illinois Press and the author.

Williams, Linda. "When the Woman Looks" appeared in *Re-Vision: Essays in Feminist Film Criticism*, edited by Mary Ann Doane, Patricia Mellencamp, and Linda Williams (Frederick, Md.: University Publications/American Film Institute, 1983), pp. 83–99. Copyright © 1983. Reprinted by permission of the author and the American Film Institute.

Williams, Tony. "Trying to Survive on the Darker Side: 1980s Family Horror." Used with permission of the author.

Wood, Robin. "Burying the Undead: The Use and Obsolescence of Count Dracula" originally appeared in *Mosaic* 16, nos. 1–2, *Film/Literature* special issue (Winter/Spring 1983): 175–187. Copyright © 1983 by *Mosaic*. Reprinted by permission of *Mosaic* and the author.

Young, Elizabeth. "Here Comes the Bride: Wedding Gender and Race in *Bride of Frankenstein*" originally appeared in *Feminist Studies* 17, no. 3 (Fall 1991): 403–437. Copyright © 1991 by Feminist Studies, Inc. Reprinted by permission of the publisher, *Feminist Studies,* Inc., c/o Women's Studies Program, University of Maryland, College Park, MD 20742, and the author.

Zimmerman, Bonnie. "*Daughters of Darkness:* The Lesbian Vampire on Film" originally appeared as "*Daughters of Darkness:* Lesbian Vampires" in *Jump Cut*, nos. 24–25 (1981): 23–24. Copyright © 1981 by *Jump Cut*. Reprinted by permission of *Jump Cut* and the author. Excerpt from "Vampire" by Karen Lindsey reprinted from *The Second Wave* 2, no. 2 (1972): 36.

WITCHCRAFT, Music by Cy Coleman, Lyric by Carolyn Leigh
Copyright 1957 Renewed and Assigned to Notable Music Co., Inc., and Morley Music Co.
All rights on behalf of Notable Music Co., Inc., administered by WB Music Corp.
All Rights Reserved   Used by Permission
WARNER BROS. PUBLICATIONS U.S. INC., Miami, FL 33014

Stills courtesy of Museum of Modern Art Film Stills Archive, New York; Jerry Ohlinger's Movie Shop, New York; and the author's personal collection.

For Lila and Habib

Contents

Introduction *1*

Part One

1   When the Woman Looks
    Linda Williams *15*

2   Horror and the Monstrous-Feminine:
    An Imaginary Abjection
    Barbara Creed *35*

3   Her Body, Himself: Gender in the Slasher Film
    Carol J. Clover *66*

Part Two

4   "It Will Thrill You, It May Shock You,
    It Might Even Horrify You": Gender,
    Reception, and Classic Horror Cinema
    Rhona J. Berenstein *117*

5   Bringing It All Back Home:
    Family Economy and Generic Exchange
    Vivian Sobchack *143*

6   Trying to Survive on the Darker Side:
    1980s Family Horror
    Tony Williams *164*

7   Genre, Gender, and the *Aliens* Trilogy
    Thomas Doherty *181*

8 Taking Back the *Night of the Living Dead:*
George Romero, Feminism, and the Horror Film
Barry Keith Grant 200

9 Gender, Genre, Argento
Adam Knee 213

10 "Beyond the Veil of the Flesh": Cronenberg
and the Disembodiment of Horror
Lianne McLarty 231

11 The Horror Film in Neoconservative Culture
Christopher Sharrett 253

Part Three

12 Horror, Femininity, and Carrie's Monstrous Puberty
Shelley Stamp Lindsey 279

13 The Monster as Woman: Two Generations of Cat People
Karen Hollinger 296

14 Here Comes the Bride: Wedding Gender
and Race in *Bride of Frankenstein*
Elizabeth Young 309

15 *King Kong:* The Beast in the Boudoir—
or, "You Can't Marry That Girl, You're a Gorilla!"
Harvey Roy Greenberg 338

16 *The Stepfather:* Father as Monster
in the Contemporary Horror Film
Patricia Brett Erens 352

17 Burying the Undead:
The Use and Obsolescence of Count Dracula
Robin Wood 364

18 *Daughters of Darkness:*
    The Lesbian Vampire on Film
    Bonnie Zimmerman 379

19 From Dracula—with Love
    Vera Dika 388

20 The Place of Passion:
    Reflections on *Fatal Attraction*
    James Conlon 401

21 Birth Traumas: Parturition
    and Horror in *Rosemary's Baby*
    Lucy Fischer 412

    Selected Bibliography *433*

    Notes on Contributors *439*

    Index *443*

And I've got no defense for it
the heat is too intense for it
what good would common sense for it do?
'Cause it's witchcraft, wicked witchcraft,
and although I know it's strictly taboo
when you arouse the need in me
my heart says yes indeed in me
proceed with what you're leading me to . . .

—"Witchcraft"

The **Dread** *of Difference*

Introduction

Near the beginning of *Matinee* (1993), Joe Dante's affectionate homage to B horror movies of the 1950s, independent horror director Lawrence Woollsey, pausing for a rest while driving through Florida on a promotional tour for his newest movie, unexpectedly finds inspiration in a small roadside sculpture of an alligator. Always looking for an angle to exploit, Woollsey (openly modeled on the period's self-styled schlockmeister of horror, William Castle) immediately begins to muse on the title of his next work: "Manigator . . . ali-man; she-gator . . . gator-girl." Then, after a pause, he announces triumphantly, as if this constituted a significant improvement, "Gal-igator!" The scene, like all good comedy, is at once witty and wise, for it acknowledges an essential truth about the genre of the horror film: the extent to which it is preoccupied with issues of sexual difference and gender.

Even a casual glance at the titles of actual horror movies reveals the genre's marked emphasis on gender. There are, to be sure, some genderless monsters—the blobs, parasites, gremlins, and so forth—but gender-specific monsters clearly predominate: *Weird Woman* (1944) and *She Freak* (1966); *The Wolf Man* (1941) and *The Ape Man* (1943); and, of course, the legions of Dracula's sons and daughters of darkness. In many horror movies the politics of sexual difference is immediately signaled as an issue by the title, as in *Bride of Frankenstein* (1935), *The Monster and the Girl* (1941), *Jesse James Meets Frankenstein's Daughter* (1966), and *Jack's Wife* (1972). Think of *He Knows You're Alone* (1980) with a feminine pronoun instead of the masculine, and the importance of gender to the genre becomes clear.

Of course, many of the horror films that do not foreground difference explicitly, either in their names or in the physical design of the monster, also share the same concerns. *The Entity* (1982), to take an oft-cited example, would seem to be a genderless monster, but as a supernatural force that sexually victimizes a female character, it clearly embodies a monstrous masculinity. Horror movies of psychological disturbance, such as *Psycho* (1960) and *Homicidal* (1961), usually offer a vague psychoanalytic explanation locating the cause of madness in the character's earlier developing sense of sexual identity. One subgenre, the rape revenge film, more often than not hinges on sexual difference. So, too, does another clearly delineated subgenre, the lesbian vampire film. (And let us remember that during the cinema's silent period the term "vamp," shortened from "vampire," referring to a woman who exploited her sexual allure, escaped the confines of the genre and entered common discourse.) It is not insignificant that in another cannily humorous look at the genre, the horror parody episode of *Everything You Always Wanted to Know about Sex . . .* (1973), Woody Allen has his mad scientist, played by the redoubtable John Carradine, terrorize the countryside with a monstrously enlarged breast. The casting of Carradine is a self-conscious gesture on the director's part to indicate that the sequence is intended as a commentary on the genre's history; and, indeed, it may be possible to see the entire genre on one level as about patriarchy and the challenges to it.

In 1986 Constance Penley wrote that "science fiction film as a genre—along with its evil twin, the horror film—is now more hyperbolically concerned than ever with the question of difference."[1] Certainly she is correct in her observation about the genre's concerns, although her use of the temporal qualifier ("now") is perhaps somewhat misleading, for such a treatment has tended to characterize the genre throughout its history. Most obvious are the horror movies made in the postwar 1950s, a period when popular culture was emphatically repositioning women within domestic space. The threat to masculinity in movies like *The Incredible Shrinking Man* (1957) and *Attack of the 50-Foot Woman* (1958) is graphically clear. (It is hardly surprising that in the 1970s the shrinking person is reinterpreted as a female who, instead of fighting a spider over territory, is caught in the kitchen drain along with the garbage that swamps her domestic existence, or that in the backlash of the

Hyperbolic imagery of sexual difference: publicity poster for *Attack of the 50-Foot Woman* (1958).

1990s the fifty-foot woman returns, into our very living rooms in a made-for-TV version, in the statuesque form of Darryl Hannah.) During the same period, the threats of incorporation and lack of differentiation evinced by such movies of the period as *Them!* (1954), *Invasion of the Body Snatchers* (1956), and *The Blob* (1958), although they have most often been discussed as articulating fears of communism, late capitalism, or both, also address these anxieties.

Indeed, perhaps the most frightening moment in any of these films—for heterosexual male viewers, at least—is the close-up of Dana Wynter's face in *Invasion of the Body Snatchers* as she responds dispassionately to Kevin McCarthy's ardent kiss. Director Don Siegel has pinpointed the nature of the fear expressed in this scene in his observation that McCarthy tries "to kiss her awake in a delicious non-pod way but she's a limp fish and he knows immediately that she is a pod. In my life, I am sorry to say, I have kissed many pods." [2] Here the director, like so much of horror cinema generally, disavows the possibility of his own inadequacy and projects it onto the woman as Other. But of course the images these movies conjure are hardly subtle; indeed, they verily shout the fact that men were, in the apposite words of Peter Lehman, "running scared." [3] Surely these movies are as hyperbolic, if not as hysterical, as any of today's overblown science fiction action movies which, with their excessive display of masculine hardbodies, are the opposite side of the same coin.

Psychoanalysis has provided the most common critical approach to the horror film, as well as having proven thus far the most profitable. As Andrew Tudor puts it, the genre is most often conceived "as a kind of collective dreamworld requiring analysis by methods derived from one or another tradition of psychoanalysis." [4] For Robin Wood, who has been so influential in defining the terms by which we have come to understand the horror film, "the true subject of the horror genre is the struggle for recognition of all that our civilization *re*presses or *op*presses." [5] As Tudor has shown, from the 1970s on, "madness" as a kind of transcendent evil is redefined as "psychosis," secular in origin, and almost always having its roots in "perverse" sexuality. [6] While this approach also involves issues of race and class, it is the various forms of repressed sexual energy, particularly within the site of the nuclear family, that has received the most critical attention.

In films of monster horror, the common interpretation has been an orthodox Freudianism. The monster is usually understood as, in Wood's terms, the "return of the repressed," the outward, distorted projection as Other of the protagonist's unacknowledged desire. Both Margaret Tarratt and Frank McConnell, for example, explain the conventional narrative of so many of these movies as ideological endorsements of patriarchal, heterosexual monogamy wherein the monster (desire) must be defeated (negotiated through the superego) by the male hero in order for him to succeed in winning the hand (metonymically speaking) of the attractive daughter of the scientist (the Father).[7] And those films that T. J. Ross calls the "psychological thriller" and that Charles Derry dubs "horror of personality" movies are most frequently understood as variations of the Jekyll-Hyde paradigm of the beast within, often defined in terms of desire.[8]

Some critics have extended the psychoanalytic approach beyond the texts themselves to account for the spectatorial pleasures of watching horror. Walter Evans, for example, interprets the classic monsters of the Universal films of the 1930s as addressing issues of sexual identity in ways that are "uniquely tailored to the psyches of troubled adolescents," particularly in their coded concerns with the "rites of initiation" involving puberty—masturbation and menstruation.[9] James Twitchell, similarly, sees horror as a ritualistic form that serves to conduct the viewer through the passage from adolescent onanism to mature reproductive sexuality.[10]

Probably the most common image in horror movies, whatever the subgenre—from *The Cabinet of Dr. Caligari* (1919) to *Candyman* (1992), and even before that in Gothic art (perhaps most notably Henry Fuseli's *The Nightmare* [1781])—is what Harvey Roy Greenberg, in his essay on *King Kong* (1933) in this volume, calls the beast in the boudoir. Most often in such scenes (but not always—a point to which I shall return shortly), the monster is coded as male, the victim female. Typically, her vulnerability and sexuality are heightened because she is a comely maiden "wearing a night-gown or a wedding-dress or some other light-coloured garment."[11] Steve Neale, building on John Ellis's notion of an individual film's "narrative image," discusses what he terms "the generic image" that helps to set the "labels, terms and expectations which will come to characterize the genre as a whole."[12] Surely the beast in the boudoir constitutes this image for horror, for the sexual tensions that resonate in this scenario vividly evoke the genre's dominant themes.

Of course, the horror evoked by such images of monstrous penetration of the bedroom also articulates, on one level, the generalized fear, at least in western culture, that monsters are bred by the sleep of reason. To be in the state of sleep is, in effect, to surrender one's identity—a fundamental fear exploited by the horror film (consider, again, that memorable scene in *Invasion of the Body Snatchers*)—and hence to be in a position of extreme vulnerability, as in the shower. Such fears have informed many of the sweeping assertions made about the genre. Horror films have been seen as nothing less than grand metaphysical morality plays that embody the residual manifestation of ancient religious thinking in the age of science[13] or that bring us to an acceptance

I Walked with a Zombie (1943): an example of the generic image of horror films.

of the inevitability of death.[14] Certainly horror films are about such great themes, but the experience of horror in the cinema is almost always grounded in the visual representation of bodily difference.

Some contemporary critics have tended to modify such universalizing claims by seeking to connect various cycles of horror and significant individual films to historical contexts. This approach begins, of course, with Siegfried Kracauer, who argued in his famous "From Caligari to Hitler" thesis in 1947 that the collapse of the Weimar Republic and the German people's disposition toward authority was both anticipated by and reflected in *Caligari* and subsequent German expressionist films, many of which employed elements of horror. The premises of his argument can be detected in such later assertions as those of T. J. Ross, who makes the more general claim that "the monster belongs to our age of moral and ecological chaos" or the more specific explanation of the rise of the "horror of personality" film in the context of the violent events, including a number of widely publicized multiple murders, that filled the news headlines in the early 1960s.[15]

Such analyses have provided much insight into horror movies, both their textual operations and spectatorial appeal. Critics such as James Twitchell and Mark Jancovich, for example, have persuasively linked the development of horror to the rise of the bourgeoisie and the dialectic of class.[16] Certainly it is true that one cannot fear the violation of the boudoir's privacy until one has attained the capital to acquire a room of one's own. Similarly, it makes perfect sense to understand a film such as, say, *King Kong* in the context of the Great Depression,[17] or *Night of the Living Dead* (1968) in terms of the social unrest in the United States in the 1960s. Yet whether one prefers to examine horror films in terms of universal fears or historically determined cultural anxieties, issues of gender remain central to the genre. For gender, as recent theory has argued, is, like horror itself, both universal and historical, biological and cultural.

Until recently, though, the genre was assumed to be a uniformly masculine discourse, just as its audience was said to be predominantly male. Derry, for example, emphasizes the importance in classic horror of the physical form of the monster as something "abstracted from man"—and he employs the masculine form here not simply as a linguistic convention to mean "human beings," for all his examples clearly refer to the masculine.[18] The tag line of Universal's *The Wolf Man*, "even a man who is pure at heart," unambiguously expressed this assumption that operated in both the cultural and critical sphere, much like the tautological "a man's gotta do what a man's gotta do" has served for the western and various subgenres of the (male) action/adventure film. Similarly, the overlapping genre of science fiction, until recently, almost always centered on men going where no one had gone before; if women accompanied them, they tended to be represented, as Thomas Doherty puts it in his article on the *Aliens* trilogy, as "space bimbos." Even while Steve Neale concurs that the horror film is "centrally concerned with the fact and the effects of difference," he nevertheless argues that the genre's discourse, particularly in its depiction of the monster, is structured around the disavowal of castration anxiety.[19] However, in making this claim he fails to account for the interest the genre holds for female spectators—an appeal which, as Rhona Berenstein demonstrates here in her essay on the marketing strategies of classic horror films, is quite pronounced. Indeed, women have been central to the production of horror as well as its consumption, from the Gothic novel to the contemporary bestsellers of Anne Rice. Significantly, while women have found it difficult throughout the history of the cinema to become directors, they are noticeably prominent in contemporary horror film production. Following upon the earlier work of Stephanie Rothman (*The Velvet Vampire* [1971], *Terminal Island* [1973]) and Amy Jones's take on the slasher film, *Slumber Party Massacre* (1982, written by Rita Mae Brown), more recent examples include Kathryn Bigelow's *Near Dark* (1987), Katt Shea Ruben's two *Stripped to Kill* movies (1987, 1989) and *Poison Ivy* (1992), Mary Lambert's two *Pet Sematary* movies (1989, 1992), Kristine Peterson's *Body Chemistry* (1990), and Fran Rubel Kuzui's *Buffy, the Vampire Slayer* (1992).

It is not surprising, therefore, that the treatment of gender in the horror genre is in fact markedly heterogenous. Nor that, consequently, the genre has been of such consistent concern to film theory and criticism—for horror texts possess great potential for widely divergent readings. The generic image of the beast in the boudoir may offer a startlingly vivid representation of patriarchal control, or a critique of it. Horror is hardly the simplistic, limited genre Andrew Tudor claims it to be.[20] Indeed, quite the contrary, it is simply too versatile and complex to be contained by any one theory or interpretation. As Stephen King aptly puts it, "the horror genre is extremely limber, extremely adaptable, extremely *useful*."[21] It is no accident, then, that today, in the age of political correctness, the genre should focus so emphatically on the body as sight/site of horror. The genre, now more than ever, is proving "useful" in addressing the dilemmas of difference, dilemmas so consciously acute that films like the recent thriller *Disclosure* (1995) would wish us to escape our bodies entirely in favor of virtual reality. Like the epic and the war film, horror is currently one of the most profitable genres for such analysis.

Thus a collection of essays on the horror film focusing specifically on issues of gender is both likely and timely. The writings gathered here provide examples of the various theoretical models and critical methods that have gained currency in the analysis of the genre. As well, they offer a balance of theoretical generalizations about the genre with close readings of particular films. Collectively they include discussions of many of the important films and directors known for their work in the genre.

The book begins with three landmark accounts of the horror film in the context of gender that have influenced the scope of contemporary critical debate, including much of the subsequent work included in this volume. Collected in Part One, these three essays, following upon Laura Mulvey's groundbreaking 1975 essay "Visual Pleasure and Narrative Cinema," share a concern with the gendered dynamics of looking in the horror film. Linda Williams's "When the Woman Looks" examines Mulvey's notion of narrative film as articulating a controlling male gaze in the context of the horror film specifically. Her suggestion that there is a sympathetic alignment between the monster's gaze and that of the female spectator is echoed by Barbara Creed, who employs Julia Kristeva's notion of abjection as it relates to the horror film, especially in terms of monstrous images of the maternal. Carol Clover reexamines those assumptions concerning the supposed masculine essence of horror in the context of the slasher subgenre. Her emphasis on the fluidity of point of view and spectator identification is informed by more recent theory that has moved beyond the binary gender determinism of Mulvey's model and argues that these movies, which previously had been understood as particularly misogynist, might indeed hold some value for feminism.

The essays comprising Part Two examine specific periods of horror film production or the work of particular directors. Some of these essays build upon the theoretical ideas discussed in the preceding essays, others take issue with them. The section begins with Rhona Berenstein's analysis of the gendered marketing strategies of 1930s horror. Next, in her examination of modern horror cinema, Vivian Sobchack focuses on the representation of the child in relation to patriarchy and considers horror's connections with the related genres of science fiction and melodrama. Tony Williams, in his overview of family horror films in the 1980s, argues that these movies generally articulate a forceful conservatism and patriarchal backlash, to the extent that they cannot be theorized as possessing any politically progressive potential. Thomas Doherty's analysis of the first three *Aliens* movies shows how the series engages with the changing boundaries of gender representations that characterized the 1980s. My own contribution applies a feminist analysis within an auteurist framework, examining the pronounced critique of patriarchy in the work of George Romero, one of the most important directors of modern horror. Adam Knee claims that the films of Dario Argento problematize the conventional representations of gender in the horror genre, embodying a kind of postmodern rejection of traditional binary oppositions. Lianne McLarty approaches the work of David Cronenberg (a contentious figure ever since Robin Wood placed him squarely within the genre's "reactionary wing") from a similar perspective, showing how the director's work has evolved from the conventional yoking of the monstrous with the feminine to a critique of the masculine worldview that is responsible for generating such representations in the first place. McLarty's critique of postmodernism's avoidance of political commitment is forcefully reiterated in this section's final essay by Christopher Sharrett, who similarly attacks what he calls the neoconservative politics of so many recent horror movies.

Part Three offers a series of readings of important horror films. In her persuasively close reading of *Carrie* (1976), Shelley Stamp Lindsey examines the female monster within the constraints of patriarchy. Karen Hollinger compares both versions of *Cat People* (1942, 1982) within the context of feminist gaze theory. Her consideration of the different representation of the female monster in the two films places them within the historical and cultural constraints that informed their production, an approach explored in greater detail by Elizabeth Young in her analysis of *Bride of Frankenstein* (1935). Young's further yoking of issues of racial representation with those of gender and sexuality is also addressed in Harvey Roy Greenberg's classic Freudian analysis of *King Kong*. Patricia Brett Erens, in her feminist reading of *The Stepfather* (1987), extends the analysis of masculine sexuality to a deliberate critique of patriarchy that is only implicit in Greenberg's much earlier essay. Then follow three takes on the vampire, perhaps the most overtly sexual of classic movie monsters. In one of his lesser-known pieces on horror, Robin Wood discusses Dracula as a cultural icon of our sexual fears by comparing the treatment of the monster and female sexuality in Bram Stoker's source novel and two important film adaptations—by F. W. Murnau (1922) and John Badham (1979). In an early instance of queer reading, Bonnie Zimmerman seeks to find in female vampire films representations of lesbian desire and pleasure that might escape containment by the controlling masculine gaze. If Wood finds the undead aristocratic vampire, at this historical moment, to be an inappropriate embodiment of the return of the repressed, Vera Dika reads him anew, arguing that in *Bram Stoker's Dracula* (1992) Francis Coppola and Gary Oldman have created a postmodern "neomythification" of Dracula that subverts the classic vampire story's traditional ideology of sexuality and gender. Passion is also central to James Conlon's reading of *Fatal Attraction* (1987). He argues that the film is a fable about western culture's traditional fear of desire, wherein the independent woman becomes, in effect, the man's monstrous Other. The section concludes with Lucy Fischer's discussion of *Rosemary's Baby* (1968) and its horrifying representation of the discourses surrounding childbirth.

Together, the readings collected in this volume attest to the central importance that themes of gender have had in the horror film. However, it is not my intention to suggest that all horror films must be read in the context of issues of sexuality and gender. I would agree with Noel Carroll who, even while seeking to establish universal principles of horror, emphasizes that no single approach can accommodate the range of horror narratives. As he notes specifically about gender in the genre, "There are horror fictions that will elude charges of sexism insofar as they have neither women characters, nor are the monsters characterized by means of (culturally derived) feminine imagery nor is their lack of women characters worked into any detectable derogation of women." [22]

There are, for example, signs that issues of race—another kind of difference—are becoming increasingly important in horror. Race had emerged as a theme in the genre only occasionally, in such movies as *White Zombie* (1932), *I Walked with a Zombie* (1943), and, more recently, *Night of the Living Dead;* as in most Hollywood genre movies, race in the horror film has been a decidedly marginal issue. Just as the genre film (with melodrama and the musical as the exceptions that proved the rule) was assumed to be masculine in form and content, so it was, again like most popular movie genres, understood as made by and addressed to white viewers. But with movies such as *Nightbreed* (1990), *The People under the Stairs* (1991), and *Candyman,* race has emerged with a new forcefulness in horror. After the Los Angeles riot that followed upon the Rodney King verdict, action thrillers such as *Trespass* (1993) exploited the white middle-class fear of the inner city, often presented as a hellish landscape. *Judgment Night* (1994) employs the metaphor of the mobile home as lack of bourgeois stability, an idea borrowed directly from the earlier supernatural horror film *Race with the Devil* (1975).[23]

Nevertheless, as several of the contributions in this volume insist, gender is central to the horror film, in large part because it inevitably involves other ideological issues as well. But the very adaptability that has given the genre such durability and made it so interesting for theorists and fans alike also exacerbates the difficulties of critical understanding—a state of affairs reflected by the internal disagreements the reader will find within this collection. So, for example, Clover's attempt to read films positively for women spectators, while central to the developing dialogue on the relations of horror and gender, is challenged here by Tony Williams. At the more specific level of textual interpretation, Dika and Sharrett offer directly opposing views about *Bram Stoker's Dracula*. The discerning reader will find many such tensions in this collection.

Bruce Kawin tells us that "A good horror film takes you down into the depths and shows you something about the landscape."[24] Landscape, of course, accommodates multiple perspectives. In the end, the differences of critical opinion in this book mirror the confusion over difference itself that informs our culture at this point in history. Yet at the same time this critical difference reveals the health and vitality that has been characteristic of the horror film and our thinking about it for the last thirty years. Today gender roles are being tested, challenged, and redefined everywhere, and until such time as difference is no longer dreaded, this crucial aspect of the horror film will remain very important for us.

Notes

1. Constance Penley, introduction to *Close Encounters: Film, Feminism, and Science Fiction,* ed. Constance Penley, Elizabeth Lyon, Lynn Spigel, and Janet Bergstrom (Minneapolis: University of Minnesota Press, 1991), p. vii.

2. Quoted in Stuart Kaminsky, *Don Siegel, Director* (New York: Curtis Books, 1974), p. 106.

3. Peter Lehman, *Running Scared: Masculinity and the Representation of the Male Body* (Philadelphia: Temple University Press, 1993).

4. Andrew Tudor, *Monsters and Mad Scientists: A Cultural History of the Horror Movie* (Cambridge, Mass.: Basil Blackwell, 1989), p. 2.

5. Robin Wood, "An Introduction to the American Horror Film," in *American*

Nightmare: Essays on the Horror Film, ed. Robin Wood and Richard Lippe (Toronto: Festival of Festivals, 1979), p. 10.

6. Tudor, *Monsters and Mad Scientists,* p. 57.

7. Margaret Tarratt, "Monsters from the Id," *Films and Filming* 17, no. 3 (December 1970): 38–42; and no. 4 (January 1971): 40–42; reprinted in *Film Genre Reader II,* ed. Barry Keith Grant (Austin: University of Texas Press, 1995), pp. 330–349. Frank D. McConnell, *The Spoken Seen: Film and the Romantic Imagination* (Baltimore and London: Johns Hopkins University Press, 1975), pp. 135–146.

8. T. J. Ross, introduction to *Focus on the Horror Film,* ed. Roy Huss and T. J. Ross (Englewood Cliffs, N.J.: Prentice-Hall, 1972), pp. 1–10; Charles Derry, *Dark Dreams: The Horror Film from Psycho to Jaws* (Cranbury, N.J.: A. S. Barnes, 1977).

9. Walter Evans, "Monster Movies and Rites of Initiation," *Journal of Popular Film* 4, no. 2 (1975): 354; Evans, "Monster Movies: A Sexual Theory," *Journal of Popular Film* 2, no. 4 (Fall 1973): 353–365.

10. James Twitchell, *Dreadful Pleasures: An Anatomy of Modern Horror* (New York: Oxford University Press, 1985), p. 68.

11. S. S. Prawer, *Caligari's Children: The Film as Tale of Terror* (New York: Da Capo, 1980), p. 39.

12. Steve Neale, *Genre* (London: British Film Institute, 1980), p. 49.

13. Ivan Butler, *Horror in the Cinema* (New York and London: A. S. Barnes/Zwemmer, 1970), p. 10; Carlos Clarens, *An Illustrated History of the Horror Film* (New York: Capricorn, 1968), p. xiii.

14. R. H. W. Dillard, "Even a Man Who Is Pure at Heart: Poetry and Danger in the Horror Film," in *Man and the Movies,* ed. W. R. Robinson (Baltimore: Penguin, 1974), pp. 60–96.

15. Ross, introduction, p. 3; Derry, *Dark Dreams,* p. 18.

16. Twitchell, *Dreadful Pleasures;* Mark Jancovich, *Horror* (London: Batsford, 1992).

17. Noel Carroll, "*King Kong:* Ape and Essence," in *Planks of Reason: Essays on the Horror Film,* ed. Barry Keith Grant (Metuchen, N.J.: Scarecrow Press, 1984), pp. 215–244.

18. Derry, *Dark Dreams,* p. 17.

19. Neale, *Genre,* p. 43.

20. Andrew Tudor, *Image and Influence: Studies in the Sociology of Film* (New York: St. Martin's Press, 1975), pp. 208–209.

21. Stephen King, *Danse Macabre* (New York: Everest House, 1981), p. 138.

22. Noel Carroll, *The Philosophy of Horror, or Paradoxes of the Heart* (New York and London: Routledge, 1990), p. 197.

23. See my "*Race with the Devil:* A Brief Vacation on the Open Road," *Jump Cut,* nos. 10–11 (1976): 20.

24. Bruce Kawin, "Children of the Light," in *Film Genre Reader,* ed. Barry Keith Grant (Austin: University of Texas Press, 1986), p. 237.

Part One

When the Woman Looks

Linda Williams

Whenever the movie screen holds a particularly effective image of terror, little boys and grown men make it a point of honor to look, while little girls and grown women cover their eyes or hide behind the shoulders of their dates. There are excellent reasons for this refusal of the woman to look, not the least of which is that she is often asked to bear witness to her own powerlessness in the face of rape, mutilation, and murder. Another excellent reason for the refusal to look is the fact that women are given so little to identify with on the screen. Laura Mulvey's extremely influential article on visual pleasure in narrative cinema has best defined this problem in terms of a dominant male look at the woman that leaves no place for the woman's own pleasure in seeing: she exists only to be looked at.[1]

Like the female spectator, the female protagonist often fails to look, to return the gaze of the male who desires her. In the classical narrative cinema, to see is to desire. It comes as no surprise, then, that many of the "good girl" heroines of the silent screen were often figuratively, or even literally, blind.[2] Blindness in this context signifies a perfect absence of desire, allowing the look of the male protagonist to regard the woman at the requisite safe distance necessary to the voyeur's pleasure, with no danger that

15

she will return that look and in so doing express desires of her own. The relay of looks within the film thus duplicates the voyeuristic pleasure of the cinematic apparatus itself—a pleasure that Christian Metz and Laura Mulvey have suggested to be one of the primary pleasures of film viewing: the impression of looking in on a private world unaware of the spectator's own existence.[3]

But even when the heroine is not literally blind, the failure and frustration of her vision can be the most important mark of her sexual purity. An illuminating example of this failed vision occurs in D. W. Griffith's 1911 two-reeler, *Enoch Arden*.[4] A remarkable illustration of the pleasures of voyeurism the cinema could offer audiences of that time, the film is entirely structured as a series of romantic or domestic scenes which are spied upon by two successive male voyeurs.

In a small fishing village Enoch Arden and Phillip Ray are rivals for Annie Lee's affections. After separate shots that introduce each of them, Enoch in the background spies upon what he presumes to be the happy love of Phillip and Annie Lee. Soon after the shot is repeated, but this time with Phillip as the outsider spying on Annie Lee and Enoch. A title provides Tennyson's lines, "Phillip looked, and in their eyes and faces read his doom."[5] The decision as to which of these rivals "gets" the girl is based on the abdication of an unseen onlooker who believes he "reads" the true desires of the couple. But since Enoch and Phillip have each read the same desire in the couple which excludes them, it becomes apparent that what matters is not so much the desire of the couple but the sad and jealous look of the outsider-voyeur who imagines—and thus constitutes—a happiness that must exclude him. Through this process Enoch wins Annie.

After some years of marriage, Enoch is forced to leave his happy home and family to go to sea. Annie Lee stands on the beach waving to Enoch's ship as it disappears in the distance, watching "to the last dip of the vanishing sail." The frustration of her look is emphasized by the spyglass she brings with her and through which she vainly peers for the next twenty years as she awaits Enoch's return.[6]

What Annie strains to see but cannot, Griffith's parallel editing permits us to see clearly: Enoch's shipwreck and long vigil on a desert island, scanning the horizon for the ship that will bring him home. Throughout their long separation Griffith is careful to maintain consistent screen direction in both Enoch and Annie Lee's looks "off." Annie always looks screen left, Enoch on his island looks screen right, thus preserving the spectator's hope that their gazes, and their paths, might one day meet. This is especially acute when Enoch is on the ship transporting him home. Throughout his long absence

Annie has steadfastly resisted Phillip's renewed advances. Although she finally gives in to his offer of marriage "for the children's sake," she still refuses his embrace and remains loyal to Enoch by continuing to look out her window in the "correct" direction—away from Phillip and toward the absent Enoch.

But just as parallel editing informs us that Enoch is about to arrive home, an intertitle, for which we have had no visual preparation, informs us that "when her new baby came, then Phillip was her all and all." Given the visual evidence of Annie's rejection of Phillip's advances and her persistent watch out the window for Enoch, this baby comes as rather a surprise. It does not seem possible for it to have arisen out of any sexual desire for Phillip on Annie Lee's part. Griffith uses this baby, which will soon become the visual proof of Annie's happiness with Phillip *in Enoch's eyes,* as the proper maternal justification of Annie finally turning *her eyes* from the window and toward her new family now headed by Phillip. The baby thus functions as cause, rather than effect, of Annie's desire for Phillip. This remarkable reversal of the usual logic of cause and effect allows the narrative to deny Annie a look of desire in *both* directions—at both Enoch and Phillip. The film ends as it began, with the look of the male voyeur (this time a literal voyeur) as the long-lost Enoch creeps up to the window to spy on the happy family scene from which he is now excluded. Once again he "reads" their happiness and his own "doom."

Let us take *Enoch Arden* as one paradigm for the frustration of the woman's "look" in the silent melodrama. It is a frustration necessary for the male regime of voyeuristic desire already clearly articulated by 1911. Given this paradigm, we can go on to examine the exceptions to it: those moments (still in the silent film) when the woman in the text not only tries to look, but actually sees.

The bold, smouldering dark eyes of the silent screen vamp offer an obvious example of a powerful female look.[7] But the dubious moral status of such heroines, and the fact that they must be punished in the end, undermine the legitimacy and authentic subjectivity of this look, frequently turning it into a mere parody of the male look.[8] More instructive are those moments when the "good girl" heroines are granted the power of the look, whether in the woman's film, as discussed by Mary Ann Doane, or in the horror film as discussed below. In both cases, as Doane suggests, "the woman's exercise of an active investigating gaze can only be simultaneous with her own victimization."[9] The woman's gaze is punished, in other words, by narrative processes that transform curiosity and desire into masochistic fantasy.

The horror film offers a particularly interesting example of this punishment in the woman's terrified look at the horrible body of the monster. In what follows I will examine the various ways the woman is punished for looking in both the classic horror film and in the more recent "psychopathic" forms of the genre. I hope to reveal not only the process of punishment but a surprising (and at times subversive) affinity between monster and woman, in the sense in which her look at the monster recognizes their similar status within patriarchal structures of seeing.

In F. W. Murnau's *Nosferatu* (1922), for example, Nina's ambiguous vigil by the sea is finally rewarded, not by the sight of her returning husband, who arrives by land in a carriage, but by the vampire's ship toward which a wide-eyed Nina in a trancelike state reaches out her arms.[10] Later, from the windows of facing houses, Nina and the vampire stare at one another until she finally opens the window. When the vampire's shadow approaches, she again stares at him in wide-eyed terror until he attacks.

There are several initial distinctions to be made between what I have characterized above as the desiring look of the male-voyeur-subject and the woman's look of horror typified by Nina's trancelike fascination. First, Nina's look at the vampire fails to maintain the distance between observer and observed so essential to the "pleasure" of the voyeur. For where the (male) voyeur's properly distanced look safely masters the potential threat of the (female) body it views, the woman's look of horror paralyzes her in such a way that distance is overcome; the monster or the freak's own spectacular appearance holds her originally active, curious look in a trancelike passivity that allows him to master her through *her* look. At the same time, this look momentarily shifts the iconic center of the spectacle away from the woman to the monster.

Rupert Julian's 1925 version of *The Phantom of the Opera,* starring Lon Chaney and Mary Philbin, offers another classic example of the woman's look in the horror film. Christine, an aspiring young opera singer, is seduced by the voice of the Phantom speaking to her through the walls of her dressing room at the Paris Opera. She follows "her master's voice" by stepping through the mirror of her dressing room. Her first glimpse of the masked Phantom occurs as she turns to respond to the touch of his hand on her shoulder. Thus her look occurs *after* the film audience has had its own chance to see him—they are framed in a two-shot that has him standing slightly behind her; only when she turns does she see his masked face.

Similarly, in the famous unmasking scene, Christine first thrills to the sound of the organ music the Phantom plays ("Don Juan Triumphant"), then sneaks up behind him and hesitates several times before finally pulling the string that will drop his mask. Since both he and Christine face the camera in a two-shot (with Christine situated behind him), we again see the Phantom's

The Phantom of the Opera (1925): the monster as biological freak doubles for woman.

face, this time unmasked, before Christine does. The audience thus receives the first shock of the horror even while it can still see the curiosity and desire *to see* on Christine's face.[11]

Everything conspires here to condemn the desire and curiosity of the woman's look. Our prior knowledge of what she will see encourages us to judge her look as a violation of the Phantom's privacy. Her unmasking of his face reveals the very wounds, the very lack, that the Phantom had hoped her blind love would heal. It is as if she has become responsible for the horror that her look reveals, and is punished by not being allowed the safe distance that ensures the voyeur's pleasure of looking. "Feast your eyes, glut your soul, on my accursed ugliness!" cries the Phantom as he holds her face up close to his.

When the men in this film look at the Phantom, the audience first sees the man looking, then adopts his point of view to see what he sees. The audience's belated adoption of the woman's point of view undermines the usual audience identification and sympathy with the look of the cinematic character. But it may also permit a different form of identification and sympathy to take place, not between the audience and the character who looks, but between the two objects of the cinematic spectacle who encounter one another in this look—the woman and the monster.

In *The Phantom of the Opera* Christine walks through her mirror to encounter a monster whose face lacks the flesh to cover its features. Lon Chaney's incarnation of the Phantom's nose, for example, gives the effect of two large holes; the lips fail to cover a gaping mouth. Early in the film women dancers from the corps de ballet argue excitedly about his nose: "He had no nose!" "Yes he did, it was enormous!" The terms of the argument suggest that the monster's body is perceived as freakish in its possession of too much or too little. Either the monster is symbolically castrated, pathetically lacking what Christine's handsome lover Raoul possesses ("He had no nose!"), or he is overly endowed and potent ("Yes he did, it was enormous!"). Yet it is a truism of the horror genre that sexual interest resides most often in the monster and not the bland ostensible heroes like Raoul who often prove powerless at the crucial moment. (*The Phantom of the Opera* is no exception. Raoul passes out when most needed, and Christine's rescue is accomplished by her accidental fall from the Phantom's racing carriage.)

Clearly the monster's power is one of sexual difference from the normal male. In this difference he is remarkably like the woman in the eyes of the traumatized male: a biological freak with impossible and threatening appetites that suggest a frightening potency precisely where the normal male would perceive a lack. In fact, the Phantom's last act of the film is to restage the drama of the lack he represents to others. Cornered by a crowd more bestial than he has ever been, a crowd that wants to tear him apart, the Phantom pulls back his hand as if threatening to detonate an explosive device. The crowd freezes; the Phantom laughs and opens his hand to reveal that it contains . . . nothing at all.

It is this absence, this nothing at all so dramatically brandished by the Phantom, that haunts a great many horror films and often seems the most effective element of their horror. It may very well be, then, that the power and potency of the monster body in many classic horror films—*Nosferatu, The Phantom of the Opera, Vampyr* (1931), *Dracula* (1931), *Freaks* (1932), *Dr. Jekyll and Mr. Hyde* (1931, 1941), *King Kong* (1933), *Beauty and the Beast* (1945)—should not be interpreted as an eruption of the normally repressed animal sexuality of the civilized male (the monster as double for the male viewer and characters in the film), but as the feared power and potency of a different kind of sexuality (the monster as double for the women).

As we have seen, one result of this equation seems to be the difference between the look of horror of the man and of the woman. The male look expresses conventional fear at that which differs from itself. The female look—

Bette Davis and Joan Crawford as horror objects in *Whatever Happened to Baby Jane?* (1962).

a look given preeminent position in the horror film—shares the male fear of the monster's freakishness, but also recognizes the sense in which this freakishness is similar to her own difference. For she too has been constituted as an exhibitionist-object by the desiring look of the male. There is not that much difference between an object of desire and an object of horror as far as the male look is concerned. (In one brand of horror film this difference may simply lie in the age of its female stars. The Bette Davises and the Joan Crawfords considered too old to continue as spectacle-objects nevertheless persevere as horror objects in films like *Whatever Happened to Baby Jane?* [1962] and *Hush . . . Hush, Sweet Charlotte* [1965].) The strange sympathy and affinity that often develops between the monster and the girl may thus be less an expression of sexual desire (as in *King Kong, Beauty and the Beast*) and more a flash of sympathetic identification.

In Carson McCullers's *The Member of the Wedding*, Frankie fears that the carnival freaks look at her differently, secretly connecting their eyes with hers, saying with their look "We know you. We are you!"[12] Similarly, in *The Phantom of the Opera,* when Christine walks through a mirror that ceases to reflect her, it could very well be that she does so because she knows she will encounter a true mirror in the freak of the Phantom on the other side. In other words, in the rare instance when the cinema permits the woman's look, she not only sees a monster, she sees a monster that offers a distorted reflection of her own image. The monster is thus a particularly insidious form of the many mirrors that patriarchal structures of seeing hold up to the woman. But there are many kinds of mirrors; and in this case it may be useful to make a distinction between beauty and the beast in the horror film.

Laura Mulvey has shown that the male look at the woman in the cinema involves two forms of mastery over the threat of castration posed by her "lack" of a penis: a sadistic voyeurism which punishes or endangers the woman through the agency of an active and powerful male character; and fetishistic overvaluation, which masters the threat of castration by investing the woman's body with an excess of aesthetic perfection.[13]

Stephen Heath, summarizing the unspoken other side of Mulvey's formulation, suggests that the woman's look can only function to entrap her further within these patriarchal structures of seeing: "If the woman looks, the spectacle provokes, castration is in the air, the Medusa's head is not far off; thus, she must not look, is absorbed herself on the side of the seen, seeing herself seeing herself, Lacan's femininity."[14] In other words, her look even here becomes a form of not seeing anything more than the castration she so exclusively represents for the male.

If this were so, then what the woman "sees" would only be the mutilation of her own body displaced onto that of the monster. The destruction of the monster that concludes so many horror films could therefore be interpreted as yet another way of disavowing and mastering the castration her body represents. But here I think it may be helpful to introduce a distinction into Mulvey's, Heath's, and ultimately Freud's notion of the supposed "mutilation" of the "castrated" woman that may clarify the precise meaning of the woman's encounter with a horror version of her own body.

A key moment in many horror films occurs when the monster displaces the woman as site of the spectacle. In *King Kong,* Kong is literally placed on stage to "perform" before awed and fearful audiences. In *The Phantom of the Opera,* the Phantom makes a dramatic, show-stopping entrance at the Masked Ball as the Masque of the Red Death, wearing a mask modeled on the absences of his own face beneath. Count Dracula, in both the Murnau and the Browning versions, makes similarly show-stopping performances. Tod Browning's *Freaks* begins and ends with the sideshow display of the woman who has been transformed by the freaks into part bird, part woman. These spectacular moments displaying the freakish difference of the monster's body elicit reactions of fear and awe in audiences that can be compared to the Freudian hypothesis of the reaction of the male child in his first encounter with the "mutilated" body of his mother.

In her essay "Pornography and the Dread of Woman," Susan Lurie offers a significant challenge to the traditional Freudian notion that the sight of the mother's body suggests to the male child that she has herself undergone castration. According to Lurie, the real trauma for the young boy is not that the mother is castrated but that she *isn't:* she is obviously *not* mutilated the way he would be if his penis were taken from him. The notion of the woman as a castrated version of a male is, according to Lurie, a comforting, wishful fantasy intended to combat the child's imagined dread of what his mother's very real power could do to him. This protective fantasy is aimed at convincing himself that "women are what men would be if they had no penises—bereft of sexuality, helpless, incapable."[15]

I suggest that the monster in the horror film is feared by the "normal" males of such films in ways very similar to Lurie's notion of the male child's fear of this mother's power-in-difference. For, looked at from the woman's perspective, the monster is not so much lacking as he is powerful in a different way. The vampire film offers a clear example of the threat this different form of sexuality represents to the male. The vampiric act of sucking blood, sapping the life fluid of a victim so that the victim in turn becomes a vampire, is similar to the female role of milking the sperm of the male during intercourse.[16] What the vampire seems to represent then is a sexual power whose threat lies in its difference from a phallic "norm." The vampire's power to make its victim resemble itself is a very real mutilation of the once human victim (teeth marks, blood loss), but the vampire itself, like the mother in Lurie's formulation, is not perceived as mutilated, just different.

Thus what is feared in the monster (whether vampire or simply a creature whose difference gives him power over others) is similar to what Lurie says is feared in the mother: not her own mutilation, but the power to mutilate and transform the vulnerable male. The vampire's insatiable need for blood seems a particularly apt analogue for what must seem to the man to be an insatiable sexual appetite—yet another threat to his potency. So there is a sense in which the woman's look at the monster is more than simply a punishment for looking or a narcissistic fascination with the distortion of her own image in the mirror that patriarchy holds up to her; it is also a recognition of their similar status as potent threats to a vulnerable male power. This would help explain the often vindictive destruction of the monster in the horror film and the fact that this destruction generates the frequent sympathy of the women characters, who seem to sense the extent to which the monster's death is an exorcism of the power of their own sexuality. It also helps to explain the conventional weakness of the male heroes of so many horror films (e.g., David Manners in *Dracula,* Colin Clive in *Frankenstein* [1931]) and the extreme excitement and surplus danger when the monster and the woman get together.

Thus I suggest that, in the classic horror film, the woman's look at the monster offers at least a potentially subversive recognition of the power and potency of a nonphallic sexuality. Precisely because this look is so threatening to male power, it is violently punished. In what follows I would like to look closely at a different kind of horror film that offers a particularly self-conscious and illuminating version of the significance of the woman's look in the horror genre. And then, lest we get carried away with enthusiasm, I shall look at two other, more typically exploitative examples of the recent evolution of the genre.

Michael Powell's *Peeping Tom* (1960) is a self-conscious meditation on the relations between a sadistic voyeur-subject and the exhibitionist objects he murders. Along with *Psycho* (1960), it marked a significant break in the structure of the classic horror film, inaugurating a new form of psychological horror. In these two films, a physically normal but psychologically deranged monster becomes the central figure of the narrative. For better or worse (we will see later just how bad it can be), the audience is now asked to identify with the monster's point of view, and even to sympathize with the childhood traumas that produced his deranged behavior. In *Peeping Tom,* the first images we see are through the lens of Mark's 16mm camera as he murders a prostitute with a knife concealed in a leg of his tripod. We learn in the opening credits that Mark is a killer whose only apparent sexual gratification comes while watching from the womblike safety of his dark projection room the murders he commits in his own movies.

Peeping Tom suggests that Mark's obsession evolved as a protection against his father's voyeuristic experimentation upon him as a young child. We see home movies showing the young Mark terrified by lizards placed in his bed, probed with lights and coldly spied upon by his father's camera. It becomes clear that Mark's only defense was to master the very system that had turned him into an exhibitionist object of scientific spectacle. In one of the home movies we see Mark receive a camera from his father and turn it, weaponlike, back upon the world, mastering his own victimization by gaining the means to victimize others.

Where Mark's father represents the sadistic power of the voyeur-scientist to scrutinize his subjects safe from any involvement with them, Mark's own manipulation is on a different level: he is the voyeur as romantic artist. His home movies are a desperate attempt to capture on film the perfect expression of the terror of his victims—a terror that might match his own. As Mark is a classic voyeur, any actual contact with his victims disrupts the distance so necessary to his sadistic pleasure. It is precisely this distance that Helen, an artist herself (she has a book of stories about a "magic camera" that she wants Mark to illustrate), disrupts. Helen intrudes upon the inner sanctum of his screening room, watches the home movies of Mark as a child, demands an explanation ("I like to understand what I'm shown!"), and eventually switches on the projector to view his latest murder. Her own autonomous looking, her ambitious sense of herself as a creator of images in her own right, and her instinctive distrust of Mark's dependence on his camera to avoid contact with the world, force him to see her not as another victim, but as a subject with her own power of vision. All his other victims, a prostitute, a movie stand-in, and a pornographer's model, have willingly accepted their positions as exhibitionist spectacles for his camera.

Helen's power of vision becomes dramatically evident in her ability to refuse the mirror-snare that ultimately gives this film its greatest horror. For Mark not only films his victims as he stabs them, the artist in him wants to perfect this image of their terror. To do this, he holds up before them, while filming and stabbing, a concave mirror that reflects the hideous distortion of their faces. Thus what Mark films is his victim at the moment of death looking at her own distorted reflection and not, as in the conventional look of horror, back at the monster. Our own awareness of this mirror is withheld until near the end when Mark finally turns the apparatus on himself, running on the knife as he looks into the distorting mirror, uniting voyeur and exhibitionist in a one-man movie of which he is both director and star.

In the classic horror film, the woman encountered a monster whose deformed features suggested a distorted mirror-reflection of her own putative lack in the eyes of patriarchy, although this supposed lack could also be construed as a recognition of the threat both beauty and the beast presented to this patriarchy. In *Peeping Tom,* however, the woman's look is literally caught up in a mirror reflection that does not simply suggest an affinity with the monster in the eyes of patriarchy, but attempts to lure her into the false belief that she is the monster. Mark's self-reflective cinematic apparatus uses its mirror effect to haunt the woman with her own image, to trap her in an attitude of exhibitionism and narcissism that has traditionally been offered as the "natural" complement to the voyeur's sadistic pleasure.

The point of the film, of course, is to show that the woman is *not* the monster. Mark's attempt to convince her that she is, is simply a way of alienating her from her own look, of forcing her into a perverse reenactment of his own

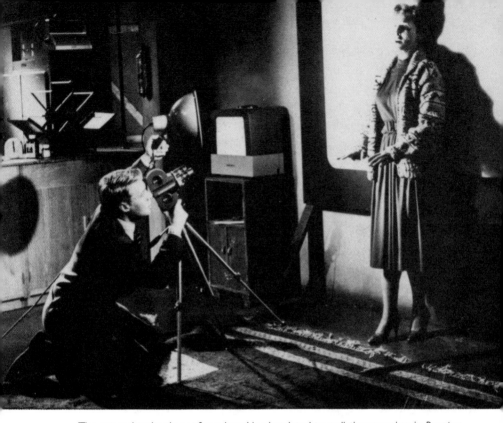

The art and technology of moviemaking is related to sadistic voyeurism in *Peeping Tom* (1960).

traumatic experience of being looked at. In making his films (the mise-en-scène of which is murder) Mark assumes the role of his sadistic father, mastering his own terror by becoming the victimizer himself. Then in watching his films he can relive his original experience of terror at a safe distance, identify with his own victims, and repossess his own look of terror from a safer aesthetic distance.

Throughout the film we are invited to equate the art and technology of moviemaking with the sadist-voyeur's misuse of the female body. Mark lures the women he kills into exhibitionist performances—the prostitute's come-on, the stand-in's frenetic jazz dance, the pornographic model's pose—which he captures with his camera-mirror-weapon and then punishes. Yet this punishment is clearly only a substitute for the revenge on his dead father that he can never accomplish. Ultimately he will turn the weapon back on himself and exult in his own terror as he dies before the distorting mirror.

Mark's regression to his original position of victim occurs when Helen refuses to occupy that same position herself. Helen is not transfixed by the mirror Mark holds up to her; she sees it for the distortion it is and has the power to turn away, to reject the image of woman as terrified victim and monster proffered by the male artist.

Helen's refusal of the mirror marks an important moment in the history of the woman's look in the horror film: in a rare instance her look both sees and understands the structure of seeing that would entrap her; her look is not paralyzed by the recognition of the horror she represents, and she therefore refuses the oppressive lie of the narcissistic mirror that the cinematic apparatus holds up to her.

Peeping Tom thus lays bare the voyeuristic structure of cinema and that structure's dependence on the woman's acceptance of her role as narcissist. Both Mark and his victims are trapped in a perverse structure of seeing that is equated throughout the film with the art of making "true-to-life" movies. Yet it is also true that Helen's ability to refuse the mirror is simply a result of her status as a nonsexual "good girl." As played by Anna Massey, Helen is the stereotypical "girl next door." She mothers Mark, feeds him, tells him not to work so hard, and gives him a chaste goodnight kiss which he later, and much more erotically, transfers to the lens of his camera.

Helen's refusal of narcissism also turns out to be a refusal of the only way patriarchal cinema has of representing woman's desire. If she has the power to recognize and refuse the mirror-trap, it is because she is portrayed as ignorant of sexual desire altogether. She is like the one virginal babysitter who survives the attacks of the monster in *Halloween* (1978), or like Lila, Marion Crane's "good girl" sister in *Psycho,* who survives Norman Bates's final attack, or even like Helen's blind mother in *Peeping Tom* who immediately "sees"—in the tradition of the blind seer—the turbulence in Mark's soul. In other words, in most horror films the tradition of the power of the woman "pure of heart" is still going strong: the woman's power to resist the monster is directly proportional to her absence of sexual desire.[17] Clarity of vision, it would seem, can exist only in this absence.

If *Peeping Tom* can be privileged as a progressive horror film, not so much for sparing the life of its "good girl" heroine as for exposing the perverse structures of seeing that operate in the genre, then we might compare two much more popular horror films in the same mode: Alfred Hitchcock's *Psycho* (made in the same year as *Peeping Tom*) and Brian de Palma's *Psycho*-inspired *Dressed to Kill* (1980). Both films offer insidious and much more typical forms of the narcissistic trap that frustrates the woman's look of desire.

Psycho has been the model for the new form of the "psycho at large" horror films that began to emerge in the early 1960s and which now dominate the market. There is no more convincing proof of the influence of this model

Woman as both victim (Angie Dickinson) and monster (Michael Caine) in *Dressed to Kill* (1980).

than de Palma's flagrant imitation of it in *Dressed to Kill*. In both *Psycho* and *Dressed to Kill,* the primary female stars are killed off early by knife-wielding murderers who appear, to both their victims and the audience, to be female. In both films the snooping of a second heroine, who is similarly endangered but not killed, corrects the original vision: the attacking she is a he. But also in both films the psychoanalytic voice of reason revises this vision as well: although the body of the attacker might appear to be male, it is really the woman in this man who kills.

In other words, both films offer yet another form of the look of recognition between the woman and the monster. The monster who attacks both looks like and, in some sense, *is* a woman. But unlike *Peeping Tom,* which exposes the lie of the female victim's encounter with her own horror in the mirror image that Mark holds up to her, *Psycho* and *Dressed to Kill* perpetuate this lie, asking us to believe that the woman is both victim and monster.[18]

In *Psycho* we learn that the mother did it. As the psychiatrist explains at the end of the film, Norman Bates had been dominated by his demanding and clinging mother whom he eventually killed. Not able to bear the crime of matricide, he maintains the fiction that she lives by dressing in her clothes and speaking in her voice. Each time he feels sexual desire for a woman, the mother he has killed rises up in him to murder the cause of this betrayal of her son's affections. Thus Norman, the matricide and killer of several other women, is judged the victim of the very mother he has killed.

Marion Crane is punished for sexual desires which put her in the wrong place at the wrong time. Yet her decision to return the money and go back to face the consequences of her theft makes her subsequent murder seem all the more gratuitous. One of the more insidious changes in Brian de Palma's reworking of the *Psycho* plot in *Dressed to Kill* is that Kate, the Angie Dickinson character who replaces Janet Leigh's Marion, is a sexually frustrated middle-aged woman whose desperate search for satisfaction leads directly to her death. Not only does a "woman" commit the crime but the female victim asks for it.[19]

In this and other ways de Palma's film *Dressed to Kill* extends *Psycho*'s premise by holding the woman responsible for the horror that destroys her. Here too the psychiatrist explains at the end that it was the woman in the man who killed—in this case the female, "Bobbie" half of Kate's schizophrenic therapist, Dr. Elliot. Bobbie wants the doctor to undergo a sex change operation so that "she" will become dominant. Bobbie kills Kate when she discovers that Kate's sexual desires have aroused the very penis that Bobbie would like to eradicate. But this time the murder is clearly meant to be seen as the fault of the sex-hungry victim who, in the words of the detective who solves the case, was "*looking* to get killed."

The film begins with a form of interior "looking": with Kate's violent sexual fantasy of being attacked in the shower. This fantasy, which begins with the blurring of Kate's vision by the steam of the shower, condenses Hitchcock's illicit love-in-a-motel-room scene with the famous shower sequence, encouraging us to believe that Kate's desire is to be the victim of male aggression. The rest of the film will give her what she "wants."

A second instance of Kate's desiring look occurs during a therapy session with Dr. Elliot. She discusses her sexual frustrations with her husband and her unwillingness to confess her lack of satisfaction: "I moaned with pleasure at his touch, isn't that what every man wants?" The doctor assures her that the problem must lie in her husband's technique; she is perfectly attractive so there could be nothing wrong with *her*. The film thus assumes that sexual satisfaction must be given by the aggressive man to the passive and sufficiently attractive woman; there is no route to achieving it herself. This lesson is borne out by Kate's very next act: her aggressive proposition to Dr. Elliot leads not to sexual satisfaction but to humiliation and death.

Proof follows in an elaborate cat-and-mouse chase in the labyrinthine art museum where Kate tentatively pursues a strange man.[20] Throughout the sequence Kate's look and pursuit of the man is continually frustrated and outmaneuvered by his look and pursuit of her. It is as if the game for him consists in hiding from her look in order to surprise her with his.

Once again the camera adopts Kate's subjective point of view only to demonstrate her failure to see, while the objective shots reveal the many times she fails to look in the right direction to see the lurking figure of the man she seeks and whom we so easily see. Repeatedly, her look of expectation encounters thin air. She only encounters him when vision can give her no warning, as when she turns at the sudden touch of his hand, wearing her dropped glove; or outside the museum when he waves her lost glove, symbol of his triumph, at her from a cab.

When she thanks him for the glove, he pulls her into the cab, aggressively undresses her, and performs cunnilingus. Her ecstasy is mixed with the humiliation of watching the cab driver adjust his rear-view mirror to get a better view. Later, in the stranger's apartment, she encounters a second humiliating punishment for the dubious pleasure she has just received: a public health record attesting to the fact that the stranger has venereal disease. But these humiliations are only teases for the real punishment to come: the revenge of Bobbie, the tall blond in sunglasses, who slashes her to pieces in the elevator, spoiling her pretty white suit.

Bobbie wreaks her revenge on Kate as a substitute for the castration she has not yet been able to have performed on her male half. The film stresses the gory details of the transsexual operation in no uncertain terms when Liz the hooker explains to Peter, Kate's son, just how a "penectomy" is performed. In *Psycho* the dead mother-villain was guilty of an excessive domination that figuratively castrated her son, eventually turning him into her entirely. In *Dressed to Kill* this figurative castration by the woman in the man becomes a literal possibility, and the desiring look of the female victim becomes a direct cause of the sexual crisis that precipitates her own death.

"If the woman looks, the spectacle provokes, castration is in the air."[21] Kate's crime is having tried to look, having actively sought the satisfaction of her desires. The film teaches that such satisfaction cannot be actively sought; it must be received, like rape, as a gift from the gods. And if Kate dies while Liz, the hooker and ostensibly promiscuous woman, survives (much as Marion Crane's "good girl" sister survives in *Psycho*), it is because Kate's desires have made disturbing demands on the male that Liz does not make.

Thus, although the film gives the impression of reversing the conventions by which the "good girls" are saved and the promiscuous ones punished, it actually reinforces the convention by redefining the "good girl" as the professional sex machine who knows how to satisfy but makes no demands of her own.

The film leaves us with one last, nagging "insight" as to the nature of woman's desire: Liz's dream of the return of Bobbie to murder her as she steps out of the shower that was the scene of Kate's original fantasy. She awakens from the dream and is comforted by Peter as the film ends. But there can be no comfort for the female spectator, who has been asked to accept the truth of a masochistic female imagination that envisions its own punishment at the hands of the sick man whose very illness lies in the fact that he wants to become a woman.

In the decades since *Psycho* and *Peeping Tom* began the new horror tradition of the psychopathic hero, one of the most significant changes in the genre has been the deepening of the woman's responsibility for the horror that endangers her. We have seen that in the classic horror film the woman's sexually charged look at the monster encounters a horror version of her own body. The monster is thus one of many mirrors held up to her by patriarchy. But, as I have tried to suggest, she also encounters in this mirror at least the possibility of a power located in her very difference from the male.

In the more recent psychopathic horror films, however, the identification between woman and monster becomes greater, the nature of the identification is more negatively charged, and women are increasingly punished for the threatening nature of their sexuality. *Peeping Tom* is both exception and rule to this in its self-conscious exploration of the male monster's need to shift responsibility for her victimization to the woman. For *Peeping Tom* exposes the male aggressor's need to believe that his female victims are terrified by their own distorted image. It thus reveals the process by which films themselves ask women to believe that they have asked for it.

Much more typical are *Psycho, Dressed to Kill,* and a host of vastly inferior exploitation films—what Roger Ebert calls the new brand of "woman-in-danger" films—including *He Knows You're Alone* (1980), *Prom Night* (1980), *Terror Train* (1979), and *Friday the 13th* (1980).[22] Ebert points out that in these films we rarely see the psychopathic murderer whose point of view the audience nevertheless adopts. This "non-specific male killing force" thus displaces what was once the subjective point of view of the female victim onto an audience that is now asked to view the body of the woman victim as the only visible monster in the film. In other words, in these films the recognition and affinity between woman and monster of the classic horror film gives way to pure identity: she *is* the monster, her mutilated body is the only visible horror.

These films are capitalizations—and vulgarizations—of currently popular formulae begun with *Psycho* and *Peeping Tom*. There are, of course, obvious differences of technical and aesthetic quality between these exploitative women-in-danger films and a film like *Dressed to Kill*. Ebert suggests that the distinction lies in the "artistry . . . and inventive directional point-of-view" of such films as *Halloween, Dressed to Kill,* and *The Texas Chainsaw Massacre* (1974) over *Friday the 13th* and the rest. The former films endow their villains with characters, while in the exploitative films they are faceless noncharacters whose point of view the audience is forced to adopt.[23]

Although we must be deeply indebted to Ebert for identifying and condemning the onslaught of these offensive films (and for doing so on public television), the argument that the greater artistry and characterization of the more "artistic" films exonerate them from the charge of gratuitously punishing their female heroines rings false. The real issue (to continue the argument in Ebert's terms of false or nonexistent characterization) is that the *women* in these films are nonexistent fantasies. *Dressed to Kill* is a male horror fantasy in drag; the film attributes a whole slew of inauthentic fantasies to an ostensible female subject who is never really there in the first place. While supposedly about Bobbie's desire to castrate her male half, what the film actually shows is not this mutilation but another: the slow-motion slashing of Kate's body as substitute for the castration Bobbie cannot yet perform on Dr. Elliot. In this light, Bobbie's vengeance on Kate can be viewed not as the act of a jealous woman eliminating her rival, but as acting out the *male* fantasy that woman is castrated, mutilated, "what men would be if they had no penises—bereft of sexuality, helpless, incapable."[24] Thus the mutilation of Kate should be properly viewed as a form of symbolic castration on a body that is frightening to the male precisely because it cannot be castrated, has none of his own vulnerability. The problem, in other words, is that she is not castrated; the fantasy solution of the male psychopath and the film itself is symbolically to prove that she is.

It is crucial for women spectators to realize the important change that is taking place before our very eyes, but which habits of viewing, not to mention habits of *not* viewing, of closing our eyes to violence and horror in general, may keep us from seeing. We are so used to sympathizing, in traditional cringing ways, with the female victims of horror that we are likely not to notice the change, to assume that films such as these have maintained this sympathy while simply escalating the doses of violence and sex. What we need to see is that in fact the sexual "freedom" of such films, the titillating attention given to the expression of women's desires, is directly proportional to the violence perpetrated against women. The horror film may be a rare example of a genre that permits the expression of women's sexual potency and desire and that associates this desire with the autonomous act of looking, but it does so in these more recent examples only to punish her for this very act, only to demonstrate how monstrous female desire can be.

Notes

1. Laura Mulvey, "Visual Pleasure and Narrative Cinema," *Screen* 16, no. 3 (Autumn 1975): 6–18. See also John Berger's description of the different "social presence" of the woman in western painting and advertisement in *Ways of Seeing* (London: Penguin, 1978), 46–47. Berger argues that where the man in such works simply "surveys" the woman before acting toward her, the woman is split into a "surveyor" and a "surveyed." In other words, she is constantly aware of being looked at, even as she herself looks. Mary Ann Doane similarly notes the woman's status as spectacle rather than spectator and goes on to make a useful distinction between primary and secondary identifications within these structures of seeing in "Misrecognition and Identity," *Cine-Tracts,* no. 11 (Fall 1980): 25–31.

2. The pathetic blind heroine is a cliché of melodrama from D. W. Griffith's *Orphans of the Storm* (1921) to Chaplin's *City Lights* (1936) to Guy Green's *A Patch of Blue* (1965).

3. Mulvey, "Visual Pleasure." Also Christian Metz, "The Imaginary Signifier," *Screen* 16, no. 2 (Summer 1975): 14–76.

4. *Enoch Arden* is a two-reel remake of Griffith's earlier one-reeler entitled *After Many Years* (1908). Both are adaptations of Tennyson's 1864 poem "Enoch Arden." The earlier version is often cited as Griffith's first integrative use of the close-up and as his first radical use of spatial discontinuity. The 1911 version is usually cited as his first expansion into the two-reel length. Lewis Jacobs, *The Rise of the American Film* (New York: Teachers College Press, 1967), pp. 103–104.

5. The intertitle is quoted verbatim from Tennyson's poem.

6. In Tennyson's poem Annie Lee fails to catch even this last sight of Enoch. Enoch had assured her that she could prolong their farewell by looking at him through a spyglass—the same spyglass that Griffith uses to emphasize her inability to see in subsequent scenes. In the poem Annie fails to operate the glass properly and thus misses her last look at Enoch.

7. It could very well be that the tradition of the fair-haired virgin and the dark-haired vamp rests more upon this difference in the lightness or darkness of the eyes than in hair color. The uncanny light eyes of many of Griffith's most affecting heroines—Mae Marsh, Lillian Gish, and even his wife Linda Arvidson, who plays Annie Lee—contribute to an effect of innocent blindness in many of his films. Light eyes seem transparent, unfocused, easy to penetrate, incapable of penetration themselves, while dark eyes are quite the reverse.

8. Mae West is, of course, one "master" of such reversals.

9. Mary Ann Doane, "The 'Woman's Film': Possession and Address," in *Re-vision: Essays in Feminist Film Criticism,* ed. Mary Ann Doane, Patricia Mellencamp, and Linda Williams (Frederick, Md.: University Publications of America/American Film Institute, 1984), p. 72.

10. Miriam White points out that the film's visuals suggest that Nina is really awaiting the Count, not her husband, even though the film's intertitles construe Nina's behavior only in relation to her husband. "Narrative Semantic Deviation: Duck-Rabbit Texts of Weimar Cinema" (paper presented at the Center for Twentieth-Century Studies Conference on Cinema and Language, University of Wisconsin–Milwaukee, March 1979).

11. I am indebted to Bruce Kawin for pointing out to me the way in which the audience receives the first shock of this look at the Phantom.

12. Leslie Fiedler refers to this passage in *Freaks: Myths and Images of the Secret Self* (New York: Simon and Schuster, 1978), p. 17.

13. Mulvey, "Visual Pleasure," pp. 10–16.

14. Stephen Heath, "Difference," *Screen* 19, no. 3 (Autumn 1978): 92.

15. Susan Lurie, "Pornography and the Dread of Woman," in *Take Back the Night,* ed. Laura Lederer (New York: William Morrow, 1980), pp. 159–173. Melanie Klein, in *Psycho-Analysis of Children* (London: Hogarth Press, 1932), has written extensively of the child's terror of being devoured, torn up, and destroyed by the mother, although for Klein these fears derive from a pre-Oedipal stage and apply to both male and female infants.

16. According to Stan Brakhage, the word "nosferatu" itself means "splashed with milk" in Transylvanian. A Rumanian legend tells how a servant woman frightened by Count Dracula spilled a pitcher of milk on him. Brakhage thus suggests that the word connotes a homosexual allusion of "sucking for milk." *Film Biographies* (Berkeley: Turtle Island, 1977), p. 256.

17. *The Book of the Vampires,* as quoted in Murnau's *Nosferatu,* states that only a woman "pure in heart," who will keep the vampire by her side until the first cock crows, can break his spell.

18. Henry Herrings's as yet unpublished comparison of these two films, "The Endurance of Misogyny: *Psycho* and *Dressed to Kill,*" points out the way in which the woman is both cause and perpetrator of the violence against her in both films.

19. Andrew Sarris, one of the few critics to call the film on this issue, writes: "In de Palma's perhaps wishful world, women do not just ask for it, they are willing to run track meets for it." *Village Voice,* September 17, 1980, p. 44.

20. This is another of de Palma's Hitchcock allusions—this one to *Vertigo* (1958)—in which the Kim Novak character sits pretending to be entranced before the portrait of her supposedly dead former self. Sarris correctly points out with respect to such borrowings that de Palma "steals Hitchcock's most privileged moments without performing the drudgery of building up to these moments as thoroughly earned climaxes." Ibid.

21. Heath, "Difference," p. 92.

22. Roger Ebert, "Why Movie Audiences Aren't Safe Anymore," *American Film* 6, no. 5 (March 1981): 54–56.

23. Ibid., p. 56.

24. Lurie, "Pornography," p. 166.

2

Horror and the Monstrous-Feminine:
An Imaginary Abjection

Barbara Creed

Horror and Abjection

Mother is not herself today.

—Norman Bates, *Psycho*

All human societies have a conception of the monstrous-feminine, of what it is about woman that is shocking, terrifying, horrific, abject. "Probably no male human being is spared the terrifying shock of threatened castration at the sight of the female genitals," Freud wrote in his paper "Fetishism" in 1927.[1] Joseph Campbell, in his book *Primitive Mythology,* noted that "there is a motif occurring in certain primitive mythologies, as well as in modern surrealist painting and neurotic dream, which is known to folklore as 'the toothed vagina'—the vagina that castrates. And a counterpart, the other way, is the so-called 'phallic mother,' a motif perfectly illustrated in the long fingers and nose of the witch."[2] Classical mythology also was populated with gendered monsters, many of which were female. The Medusa, with her "evil eye," head of writhing serpents, and lolling tongue, was queen of the pantheon of female monsters; men unfortunate enough to look at her were turned immediately to stone.

It is not by accident that Freud linked the sight of the Medusa to the equally horrifying sight of the mother's genitals, for the concept of the monstrous-feminine, as constructed within and by a patriarchal and phallocentric ideology, is related intimately to the problem of sexual difference and castration. In 1922 he argued that the "Medusa's head takes the place of a representation of the female genitals."[3] If we accept Freud's interpretation, we can see that the Perseus myth is mediated by a narrative about the *difference* of female sexuality as a difference which is grounded in monstrousness and which invokes castration anxiety in the male spectator. "The sight of the Medusa's head makes the spectator stiff with terror, turns him to stone."[4] The irony of this was not lost on Freud, who pointed out that becoming stiff also means having an erection. "Thus in the original situation it offers consolation to the spectator: he is still in possession of a penis, and the stiffening reassures him of the fact."[5] One wonders if the experience of horror—of viewing the horror film—causes similar alterations in the body of the male spectator. And what of other phrases that apply to both male and female viewers—phrases such as "It scared the shit out of me"; "It made me feel sick"; "It gave me the creeps"? What is the relationship between physical states, bodily wastes (even if metaphoric ones), and the horrific—in particular, the monstrous-feminine?

Julia Kristeva's *Powers of Horror* provides us with a preliminary hypothesis for an analysis of these questions. Although this study is concerned with literature, it nevertheless suggests a way of situating the monstrous-feminine in the horror film in relation to the maternal figure and what Kristeva terms "abjection," that which does not "respect borders, positions, rules," that which "disturbs identity, system, order."[6] In general terms, Kristeva is attempting to explore the different ways in which abjection, as a source of horror, works within patriarchal societies as a means of separating the human from the non-human and the fully constituted subject from the partially formed subject. Ritual becomes a means by which societies both renew their initial contact with the abject element and then exclude that element.

Through ritual, the demarcation lines between human and nonhuman are drawn up anew and presumably made all the stronger for that process. One of the key figures of abjection is the mother who becomes an abject at that moment when the child rejects her for the father who represents the symbolic order. The problem with Kristeva's theory, particularly for feminists, is that she never makes clear her position on the oppression of women. Her theory moves uneasily between explanation of, and justification for, the formation of human societies based on the subordination of women.

Kristeva grounds her theory of the maternal in the abject, tracing its changing definitions from the period of the pagan or mother-goddess religions to the time of Judaic monotheism and to its culmination in Christianity. She deals with abjection in the following forms: as a rite of defilement in paganism; as a biblical abomination, a taboo, in Judaism; and as self-defilement, an interiorization, in Christianity. Kristeva, however, does not situate abjection solely within a ritual or religious context. She argues that it is "rooted historically (in the history of religions) and subjectively (in the structuration of the subject's identity), in the cathexis of maternal function—mother, woman, reproduction" (p. 91). Kristeva's central interest, however, lies with the structuring of subjectivity within and by the processes of abjectivity in which the subject is spoken by the abject through both religious and cultural discourses, that is, through the subject's position within the practices of the rite as well as within language.

> But the question for the analyst-semiologist is to know how far one can analyze ritual impurity. The historian of religion stops soon: the critically impure is that which is based on a natural "loathing." The anthropologist goes further: there is nothing "loathsome" in itself; the loathsome is that which disobeys classification rules peculiar to the given symbolic system. But as far as I am concerned, I keep asking questions. . . . Are there no subjective structurations that, within the organization of each speaking being, correspond to this or that symbolic-social system and represent, if not stages, at least *types* of subjectivity and society? Types that would be defined, in the last analysis, according to the subject's position in language . . . ? (p. 92)

A full examination of this theory is outside the scope of this article; I propose to draw mainly on Kristeva's discussion of abjection in its construction in the human subject in relation to her notions of (a) the "border" and (b) the mother-child relationship. At crucial points, I shall also refer to her writing on the abject in relation to religious discourses. This area cannot be ignored, for what becomes apparent in reading her work is that definitions of the monstrous as constructed in the modern horror text are grounded in ancient religious and historical notions of abjection—particularly in relation to the following religious "abominations": sexual immorality and perversions; corporeal alteration, decay, and death; human sacrifice; murder; the corpse; bodily wastes; the feminine body; and incest.

The place of the abject is "the place where meaning collapses" (p. 2), the place where "I" am not. The abject threatens life; it must be "radically excluded" (p. 2) from the place of the living subject, propelled away from the body and deposited on the other side of an imaginary border which separates the self from that which threatens the self. Kristeva quotes Bataille: "Abjection . . . is merely the inability to assume with sufficient strength the imperative act of excluding abject things (and that act establishes the foundations of collective existence)" (p. 56). Although the subject must exclude the abject, it must, nevertheless, be tolerated, for that which threatens to destroy life also helps to define life. Further, the activity of exclusion is necessary to guarantee that the subject take up his or her proper place in relation to the symbolic.

> To each ego its object, to each superego its abject. It is not the white expanse or slack boredom of repression, not the translations and transformations of desire that wrench bodies, nights and discourse; rather it is a brutish suffering that "I" puts up with, sublime and devastated, for "I" deposits it to the father's account (*verse au pere—pere-version*): I endure it, for I imagine such is the desire of the other. . . . On the edge of nonexistence and hallucination, of a reality that, if I acknowledge it, annihilates me. There, abject and abjection are my safeguards. The primers of my culture. (p. 2)

The abject can be experienced in various ways, one of which relates to biological bodily functions, the other of which has been inscribed in a symbolic (religious) economy. For instance, Kristeva claims that food loathing is "perhaps the most elementary and archaic form of abjection" (p. 2). Food, however, becomes abject only if it signifies a border "between two distinct entities or territories" (p. 75). Kristeva describes how, for her, the skin on the top of milk, which is offered to her by her father and mother, is a "sign of their desire," a sign separating her world from their world, a sign which she does not want. "But since the food is not an 'other' for 'me,' who am only in their desire, I expel *myself,* I spit *myself* out, I abject *myself* within the same motion through which 'I' claim to establish *myself*" (p. 3). Dietary prohibitions are, of course, central to Judaism. Kristeva argues that these are directly related to the prohibition of incests; she argues this not just because this position is supported by psychoanalytic discourse and structural anthropology but also because "the biblical text, as it proceeds, comes back, at the intensive moments of its demonstration and expansion, to that mytheme of the archaic relation to the mother" (p. 106).

The ultimate in abjection is the corpse. The body protects itself from bodily wastes such as feces, blood, urine, and pus by ejecting these substances just as it expels food that, for whatever reason, the subject finds loathsome. The body extricates itself from them and from the place where they fall, so that it might continue to live.

> Such wastes drop so that I might live, until, from loss to loss, nothing remains in me and my entire body falls beyond the limit—*cadere*, cadaver. If dung signifies the other side of the border, the place where I am not and which permits me to be, the corpse, the most sickening of wastes, is a border that has encroached upon everything. It is no longer I who expel. "I" is expelled. (pp. 3–4)

Within the biblical context, the corpse is also utterly abject. It signifies one of the most basic forms of pollution—the body without a soul. As a form of waste it represents the opposite of the spiritual, the religious symbolic: "Corpse fanciers, unconscious worshippers of a soulless body, are thus preeminent representatives of inimical religions, identified by their murderous cults. The priceless debt to great mother nature, from which the prohibitions of Yahwistic speech separates us, is concealed in such pagan cults" (p. 109).

In relation to the horror film, it is relevant to note that several of the most popular horrific figures are "bodies without souls" (the vampire), the "living corpse" (the zombie), and the corpse-eater (the ghoul). Here the horror film constructs and confronts us with the fascinating, seductive aspect of abjection. What is also interesting is that such ancient figures of abjection as the vampire, the ghoul, the zombie, and the witch (one of whose many crimes was that she used corpses for her rites of magic) continue to provide some of the most compelling images of horror in the modern cinema. The werewolf, whose body signifies a collapse of the boundaries between human and animal, also belongs to this category.

Abjection also occurs where the individual fails to respect the law and where the individual is a hypocrite, a liar, a traitor: "Any crime, because it draws attention to the fragility of the law, is abject, but premeditated crime, cunning murder, hypocritical revenge are even more so because they heighten the display of such fragility. He who denies morality is not abject; there can be grandeur in amorality. . . . Abjection, on the other hand, is immoral, sinister, scheming, and shady" (p. 4). Thus, abject things are those which highlight the "fragility of the law" and which exist on the other side of the border that separates out the living subject from that which threatens its extinction. But abjection is not something of which the subject can ever feel free—it is always there, beckoning the self to take up its place, the place where meaning collapses. The subject, constructed in and through language, through a desire for meaning, is also spoken by the abject, the place of mean-

inglessness—thus, the subject is constantly beset by abjection which fasci-
nates desire but which must be repelled for fear of self-annihilation. The crucial point is that abjection is always ambiguous. Like Bataille, Kristeva emphasizes the attraction, as well as the horror, of the undifferentiated:

> We may call it a border; abjection is above all ambiguity. Because, while
> releasing a hold, it does not radically cut off the subject from what
> threatens it—on the contrary, abjection acknowledges it to be in per-
> petual danger. But also because abjection itself is a composite of judge-
> ment and affect, of condemnation and yearning, of signs and drives.
> Abjection preserves what existed in the archaism of pre-objectal rela-
> tionship. . . . (pp. 9–10)

To the extent that abjection works on the sociocultural arena, the horror
film would appear to be, in at least three ways, an illustration of the work of
abjection. First, the horror film abounds in images of abjection, foremost of
which is the corpse, whole and mutilated, followed by an array of bodily
wastes such as blood, vomit, saliva, sweat, tears, and putrifying flesh. In terms
of Kristeva's notion of the border, when we say such-and-such a horror film
"made me sick" or "scared the shit out of me,"[7] we are actually foregrounding that specific horror film as a "work of abjection" or "abjection at work"
—in both a literal and metaphoric sense. Viewing the horror film signifies a
desire not only for perverse pleasure (confronting sickening, horrific images,
being filled with terror/desire for the undifferentiated) but also a desire, having taken pleasure in perversity, to throw up, throw out, eject the abject (from
the safety of the spectator's seat).

Second, there is, of course, a sense in which the concept of a border is
central to the construction of the monstrous in the horror film; that which
crosses or threatens to cross the "border" is abject. Although the specific nature of the border changes from film to film, the function of the monstrous
remains the same: to bring about an encounter between the symbolic order
and that which threatens its stability. In some horror films the monstrous
is produced at the border between human and inhuman, man and beast
(*Dr. Jekyll and Mr. Hyde* [1931, 1941], *Creature from the Black Lagoon* [1954],
King Kong [1933]); in others the border is between the normal and the supernatural, good and evil (*Carrie* [1976], *The Exorcist* [1973], *The Omen* [1976],
Rosemary's Baby [1968]); or the monstrous is produced at the border which
separates those who take up their proper gender roles from those who do not
(*Psycho* [1960], *Dressed to Kill* [1980], *Reflection of Fear* [1971]); or the border is

between normal and abnormal sexual desire (*Cruising* [1980], *The Hunger* [1983], *Cat People* [1942, 1982]).

In relation to the construction of the abject within religious discourses, it is interesting to note that various subgenres of the horror film seem to correspond to religious categories of abjection. For instance, blood as a religious abomination becomes a form of abjection in the "splatter" movie (*The Texas Chainsaw Massacre* [1974]); cannibalism, another religious abomination, is central to the "meat" movie (*Night of the Living Dead* [1968], *The Hills Have Eyes* [1977]); the corpse as abomination becomes the abject of ghoul and zombie movies (*The Evil Dead* [1982]; *Zombie Flesheaters* [1979]); blood as a taboo object within religion is central to the vampire film (*The Hunger*) as well as the horror film in general (*Bloodsucking Freaks* [a.k.a. *The Incredible Torture Show*, 1976]); human sacrifice as a religious abomination is constructed as the abject of virtually all horror films; and bodily disfigurement as a religious abomination is also central to the slash movie, particularly those in which woman is slashed, the mark a sign of her "difference," her impurity (*Dressed to Kill*, *Psycho*).

The Abject Mother

The third way in which the horror film illustrates the work of abjection refers to the construction of the maternal figure as abject. Kristeva argues that all individuals experience abjection at the time of their earliest attempts to break away from the mother. She sees the mother-child relation as one marked by conflict: the child struggles to break free but the mother is reluctant to release it. Because of the "instability of the symbolic function" in relation to this most crucial area—"the prohibition placed on the maternal body (as a defense against autoeroticism and incest taboo)" (p. 14)—Kristeva argues that the maternal body becomes a site of conflicting desires. "Here, drives hold sway and constitute a strange space that I shall name, after Plato (*Timeus*, 48–53), a *chora*, a receptacle" (p. 14). The position of the child is rendered even more unstable because, while the mother retains a close hold over the child, it can serve to authenticate her existence—an existence which needs validation because of her problematic relation to the symbolic realm.

It is a violent, clumsy breaking away, with the constant risk of falling back under the sway of a power as securing as it is stifling. The difficulty the mother has in acknowledging (or being acknowledged by) the symbolic realm—in other words, the problems she has with the phallus that her father or husband stands for—is not such as to help the future subject leave the natural mansion. (p. 13)

In the child's attempt to break away, the mother becomes an abject; thus, in this context, where the child struggles to become a separate subject, abjection becomes *"a precondition of narcissism"* (p. 13). Once again we can see abjection at work in the horror text where the child struggles to break away from the mother, representative of the archaic maternal figure, in a context in which the father is invariably absent (*Psycho, Carrie, The Birds* [1963]). In these films, the maternal figure is constructed as the monstrous-feminine. By refusing to relinquish her hold on her child, she prevents it from taking up its proper place in relation to the Symbolic. Partly consumed by the desire to remain locked in a blissful relationship with the mother and partly terrified of separation, the child finds it easy to succumb to the comforting pleasure of the dyadic relationship. Kristeva argues that a whole area of religion has assumed the function of tackling this danger:

> This is precisely where we encounter the rituals of defilement and their derivatives, which, based on the feeling of abjection and all converging on the maternal, attempt to symbolize the other threat to the subject: that of being swamped by the dual relationship, thereby risking the loss not of a part (castration) but of the totality of his living being. The function of these religious rituals is to ward off the subject's fear of his very own identity sinking irretrievably into the mother. (p. 64)

How, then, are prohibitions against contact with the mother enacted and enforced? In answering this question, Kristeva links the universal practices of rituals of defilement to the mother. She argues that within the practices of all rituals of defilement, polluting objects fall into two categories: excremental, which threatens identity from the outside, and menstrual, which threatens from within.

> Excrement and its equivalent (decay, infection, disease, corpse, etc.) stand for the danger to identity that comes from without: the ego threatened by the non-ego, society threatened by its outside, life by death. Menstrual blood, on the contrary, stands for the danger issuing from within identity (social or sexual); it threatens the relationship between the sexes within a social aggregate and, through internalization, the identity of each sex in the face of sexual difference. (p. 71)

Both categories of polluting objects relate to the mother: the relation of menstrual blood is self-evident; the association of excremental objects with the maternal figure is brought about because of the mother's role in sphincteral training. Here Kristeva argues that the subject's first contact with "authority" is with the maternal authority when the child learns, through interaction with the mother, about its body: the shape of the body, the clean and unclean, the proper and improper areas of the body. Kristeva refers to this process as a "primal mapping of the body" that she calls "semiotic." She distinguishes between maternal "authority" and "paternal laws": "Maternal authority is the trustee of that mapping of the self's clean and proper body; it is distinguished from paternal laws within which, with the phallic phase and acquisition of language, the destiny of man will take shape" (p. 72). In her discussion of rituals of defilement in relation to the Indian caste system, Kristeva draws a distinction between the maternal authority and paternal law. She argues that the period of the "mapping of the self's clean and proper body" is characterized by the exercise of "authority without guilt," a time when there is a "fusion between mother and nature." However, the symbolic ushers in a "totally different universe of socially signifying performances where embarrassment, shame, guilt, desire etc. come into play—the order of the phallus." In the Indian context, these two worlds exist harmoniously side by side because of the working of defilement rites. Here Kristeva is referring to the practice of public defecation in India. She quotes V. S. Naipaul, who says that no one ever mentions "in speech or in books, those squatting figures, because, quite simply, no one sees them." Kristeva argues that this split between the world of the mother (a universe without shame) and the world of the father (a universe of shame) would, in other social contexts, produce psychosis; in India it finds a "perfect socialization": "This may be because the setting up of the rite of defilement takes on the function of the hyphen, the virgule, allowing the two universes of *filth* and *prohibition* to brush lightly against each other without necessarily being identified as such, as *object* and as *law*" (p. 74).

Images of blood, vomit, pus, shit, and so forth, are central to our culturally/ socially constructed notions of the horrific. They signify a split between two orders: the maternal authority and the law of the father. On the one hand, these images of bodily wastes threaten a subject that is already constituted, in relation to the symbolic, as "whole and proper." Consequently, they fill the subject—both the protagonist in the text and the spectator in the cinema— with disgust and loathing. On the other hand, they also point back to a time when a "fusion between mother and nature" existed; when bodily wastes, while set apart from the body, were not seen as objects of embarrassment and shame. Their presence in the horror film may evoke a response of disgust from the audience, situated as it is within the symbolic, but at a more archaic level the representation of bodily wastes may evoke pleasure in breaking the taboo of filth—sometimes described as a pleasure in perversity—and a pleasure in returning to that time when the mother-child relationship was marked by an untrammeled pleasure in "playing" with the body and its wastes.

The modern horror film often "plays" with its audience, saturating it with scenes of blood and gore, deliberately pointing to the fragility of the symbolic order in the domain of the body which never ceases to signal the repressed world of the mother. This is particularly evident in *The Exorcist,* where the world of the symbolic, represented by the priest-as-father, and the world of the presymbolic, represented by woman aligned with the devil, clashes head on in scenes where the foulness of woman is signified by her putrid, filthy body covered in blood, urine, excrement, and bile. Significantly, a pubescent girl about to menstruate played the woman who is possessed—in one scene blood from her wounded genitals mingles with menstrual blood to provide one of the film's key images of horror. In *Carrie,* the film's most monstrous act occurs when the couple are drenched in pig's blood, which symbolizes menstrual blood—women are referred to in the film as "pigs," women "bleed like pigs," and the pig's blood runs down Carrie's body at a moment of intense pleasure, just as her own menstrual blood runs down her legs during a similar pleasurable moment when she enjoys her body in the shower. Here women's blood and pig's blood flow together, signifying horror, shame, and humiliation. In this film, however, the mother speaks for the symbolic, identifying with an order that has defined women's sexuality as the source of all evil and menstruation as the sign of sin. The horror film's obsession with blood, particularly the bleeding body of woman, where her body is transformed into the "gaping wound," suggests that castration anxiety is a central concern of the horror film—particularly the slasher subgenre. Woman's body is slashed and mutilated, not only to signify her own castrated state, but also the possibility of castration for the male. In the guise of a "madman" he enacts on her body the one act he most fears for himself, transforming her entire body into a bleeding wound.

Kristeva's semiotic posits a preverbal dimension of language that relates to sounds and tone and to direct expression of the drives and physical contact with the maternal figure: "it is dependent upon meaning, but in a way that is not that of *linguistic* signs nor of the *symbolic* order they found" (p. 72). With the subject's entry into the symbolic, which separates the child from the mother, the maternal figure and the authority she signifies are repressed. Kristeva argues that it is the function of defilement rites, particularly those relating to

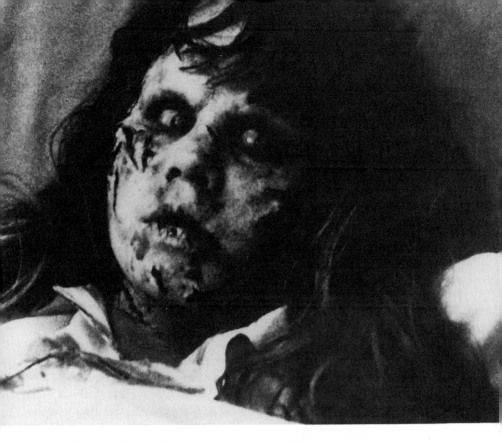

The Exorcist (1973): the world of the presymbolic represented by the foul, possessed female body (Linda Blair).

menstrual and excremental objects, to point to the "boundary" between the maternal semiotic authority and the paternal symbolic law:

> Through language and within highly hierarchical religious institutions, man hallucinates partial "objects"—witnesses to an archaic differentiation of the body on its way toward ego identity, which is also sexual identity. The *defilement* from which ritual protects us is neither sign nor matter. Within the rite that extracts it from repression and depraved desire, defilement is the translinguistic spoor of the most archaic boundaries of the self's clean and proper body. In that sense, if it is a jettisoned object, it is so from the mother. . . . By means of the symbolic institution of ritual, that is to say, by means of a system of ritual exclusions, the partial-object consequently becomes *scription*—an inscription of limits,

an emphasis placed not on the (paternal) Law but on (maternal) Authority through the very signifying order. (p. 73)

Kristeva argues that, historically, it has been the function of religion to purify the abject but with the disintegration of these "historical forms" of religion, the work of purification now rests solely with "that catharsis par excellence called art" (p. 17).

> In a world in which the Other has collapsed, the aesthetic task—a descent into the foundations of the symbolic construct—amounts to retracing the fragile limits of the speaking being, closest to its dawn, to the bottomless "primacy" constituted by primal repression. Through that experience, which is nevertheless managed by the Other, "subject" and "object" push each other away, confront each other, collapse, and start again—inseparable, contaminated, condemned, at the boundary of what is assimilable, thinkable: abject. (p. 18)

This, I would argue, is also the central ideological project of the popular horror film—purification of the abject through a "descent into the foundations of the symbolic construct." In this way, the horror film brings about a confrontation with the abject (the corpse, bodily wastes, the monstrous-feminine) in order, finally, to eject the abject and redraw the boundaries between the human and nonhuman. As a form of modern defilement rite, the horror film works to separate out the symbolic order from all that threatens its stability, particularly the mother and all that her universe signifies. In Kristeva's terms, this means separating out the maternal authority from paternal law.

As mentioned earlier, the central problem with Kristeva's theory is that it can be read in a prescriptive rather than a descriptive sense. This problem is rendered more acute by the fact that, although Kristeva distinguishes between the maternal and paternal figures when she speaks of the subject who is being constituted, she never distinguishes between the child as male or female. Obviously, the female child's experience of the semiotic *chora* must be different from the male's experience in relation to the way it is spoken to, handled, and so on. For the mother is already constituted as a gendered subject living within a patriarchal order and thus aware of the differences between the "masculine" and the "feminine" in relation to questions of desire. Thus, the mother might relate to a male child with a more acute sense of pride and pleasure. It is also possible that the child, depending on its gender, might find it more or less difficult to reject the mother for the father. Kristeva does not consider any of these issues. Nor does she distinguish between the relation of the adult male and female subject to rituals of defilement—for instance, menstruation taboos, where one imagines notions of the gendered subject would be of crucial importance. How, for instance, do women relate to rites of defilement such as menstruation rites, which reflect so negatively on them? How do women within a specific cultural group see themselves in relation to taboos that construct their procreative functions as abject? Is it possible to intervene in the social construction of woman as abject? Or is the subject's relationship to the processes of abjectivity, as they are constructed within subjectivity and language, completely unchangeable? Is the abjection of women a precondition for the continuation of sociality? Kristeva never asks questions of this order. Consequently her theory of abjection could be interpreted as an apology for the establishment of sociality at the cost of women's equality. If, however, we read it as descriptive, as one attempting to explain the origins of patriarchal culture, then it provides us with an extremely useful hypothesis for an investigation of the representation of women in the horror film.[8]

Alien and the Primal Scene

The science fiction horror film *Alien* (1979) is a complex representation of the monstrous-feminine in terms of the maternal figure as perceived within a patriarchal ideology. She is there in the text's scenarios of the primal scene, of birth and death; she is there in her many guises as the treacherous mother, the oral sadistic mother, the mother as primordial abyss; and she is there in the film's images of blood, of the all-devouring vagina, the toothed vagina, the vagina as Pandora's box; and finally she is there in the chameleon figure of the alien, the monster as fetish object of and for the mother. But it is the archaic mother, the reproductive/generative mother, who haunts the mise-en-scène of the film's first section, with its emphasis on different representations of the primal scene.

According to Freud, every child either watches its parents in the act of sexual intercourse or has fantasies about that act—fantasies that relate to the problem of origins. Freud left open the question of the cause of the fantasy but suggested that it may initially be aroused by "an observation of the sexual intercourse of animals."[9] In his study of "the Wolf Man," Freud argued that the child did not initially observe the parents in the act of sexual intercourse but rather witnessed the copulation of animals whose behavior the child then displaced onto the parents. In situations where the child actually witnesses sexual intercourse between its parents, Freud argued that all children arrive at the same conclusion: "They adopt what may be called a *sadistic view of coition*."[10] If the child perceives the primal scene as a monstrous act—whether in reality or fantasy—it may fantasize animals or mythical creatures as taking part in the scenario. Possibly the many mythological stories in which humans copulate with animals and other creatures (Europa and Zeus, Leda and the Swan) are reworkings of the primal scene narrative. The Sphinx, with her lion's body and woman's face, is an interesting figure in this context. Freud suggested that the Riddle of the Sphinx was probably a distorted version of the great riddle that faces all children—Where do babies come from? An extreme form of the primal fantasy is that of "observing parental intercourse while one is still an unborn baby in the womb."[11]

One of the major concerns of the science fiction horror film (*Alien, The Thing* [1951, 1982], *Invasion of the Body Snatchers* [1956, 1978], *Altered States* [1980]) is the reworking of the primal scene in relation to the representation of other forms of copulation and procreation. *Alien* presents various representations of the primal scene. Behind each of these lurks the figure of the archaic mother, that is, the image of the mother in her generative function—the mother as the origin of all life. This archaic figure is somewhat different from the mother of the semiotic *chora* posed by Kristeva in that the latter is the pre-Oedipal mother who exists in relation to the family and the symbolic order. The concept of the parthenogenic, archaic mother adds another dimension to the maternal figure and presents us with a new way of understanding how patriarchal ideology works to deny the "difference" of woman in her cinematic representation.

The first birth scene occurs in *Alien* at the beginning, where the camera/spectator explores the inner space of the mother-ship whose life support system is a computer aptly named "Mother." This exploratory sequence of the inner body of the Mother culminates with a long tracking shot down one of the corridors which leads to a womblike chamber where the crew of seven are woken up from their protracted sleep by Mother's voice monitoring a call for help from a nearby planet. The seven astronauts emerge slowly from their sleep pods in what amounts to a rebirthing scene that is marked by a fresh, antiseptic atmosphere. In outer space, birth is a well-controlled, clean, painless affair. There is no blood, trauma, or terror. This scene could be interpreted as a primal fantasy in which the human subject is born fully developed—even copulation is redundant.

The second representation of the primal scene takes place when three of the crew enter the body of the unknown spaceship through a "vaginal" opening: the ship is shaped like a horseshoe, its curved sides like two long legs spread apart at the entrance. They travel along a corridor that seems to be

Alien (1979): the vaginal openings of the alien space ship.

made of a combination of inorganic and organic material—as if the inner space of this ship were alive. Compared to the atmosphere of the *Nostromo,* however, this ship is dark, dank, and mysterious. A ghostly light glimmers, and the sounds of their movements echo throughout the caverns. In the first chamber, the three explorers find a huge alien life form that appears to have been dead for a long time. Its bones are bent outward as if it exploded from the inside. One of the trio, Kane, is lowered down a shaft into the gigantic womblike chamber in which rows of eggs are hatching. Kane approaches one of the eggs; as he touches it with his gloved hand, it opens out, revealing a mass of pulsating flesh. Suddenly the monstrous thing inside leaps up and attaches itself to Kane's helmet, its tail penetrating Kane's mouth in order to fertilize itself inside his stomach. Despite the warnings of Ripley, Kane is taken back on board the *Nostromo* where the alien rapidly completes its gestation processes inside Kane.

This representation of the primal scene recalls Freud's reference to an extreme primal-scene fantasy in which the subject imagines traveling back inside the womb to watch her or his parents having sexual intercourse, perhaps to watch her or his own conception. Here three astronauts explore the gigantic, cavernous, malevolent womb of the mother. Two members of the group watch the enactment of the primal scene in which Kane is violated in an act of phallic penetration—by the father or phallic mother? Kane himself is guilty of the strongest transgression; he actually peers into the egg/womb in order to investigate its mysteries. In so doing, he becomes a part of the primal scene, taking up the place of the mother, the one who is penetrated, the one who bears the offspring of the union. The primal scene is represented as violent and monstrous (the union is between human and alien), and is mediated by the question of incestuous desire. All restagings of the primal scene raise the question of incest, as the beloved parent (usually the mother) is with a rival. The first birth scene, in which the astronauts emerge from their sleep pods, could be viewed as a representation of incestuous desire par excellence: the father is completely absent; here the mother is sole parent and sole life support.

From this forbidden union, the monstrous creature is born. But man, not woman, is the "mother," and Kane dies in agony as the alien gnaws its way through his stomach. The birth of the alien from Kane's stomach plays on what Freud described as a common misunderstanding that many children have about birth: that the mother is somehow impregnated through the mouth— she may eat a special food—and the baby grows in her stomach from which it is also born. Here we have a third version of the primal scene.

A further version of the primal scene—almost a convention of the science fiction film[12]—occurs when smaller crafts or bodies are ejected from the mother ship into outer space, although the ejected body sometimes remains attached to the mother ship by a long lifeline or umbilical cord. This scene is presented in two separate ways: when Kane's body, wrapped in a white shroud, is ejected from the mother ship; and when the small space capsule, in which Ripley is trying to escape from the alien, is expelled from the under- belly of the mother ship. In the former, the "mother's" body has become hostile; it contains the alien whose one purpose is to kill and devour all of Mother's children. In the latter birth scene the living infant is ejected from the malevolent body of the "mother" to avoid destruction; in this scenario, the "mother's" body explodes at the moment of giving birth.

Although the "mother" as a figure does not appear in these sequences— nor indeed in the entire film—her presence forms a vast backdrop for the en- actment of all the events. She is there in the images of birth, the representa- tions of the primal scene, the womblike imagery, the long winding tunnels leading to inner chambers, the rows of hatching eggs, the body of the mother ship, the voice of the life-support system, and the birth of the alien. She is the generative mother, the pre-phallic mother, the being who exists prior to knowledge of the phallus.

In explaining his difficulty in uncovering the role of the mother in the early development of infants, Freud complained of the almost "prehistoric" remoteness of this "Minoan-Mycenaean" stage: "Everything in the sphere of this first attachment to the mother seemed to me so difficult to grasp in analysis—so grey with age and shadowy and almost impossible to revivify—that it was as if it had succumbed to an especially inexorable repression."[13] Just as the Oedipus complex tends to hide the pre-Oedipal phase in Freudian theory, the figure of the father, in the Lacanian rewriting of Freud, obscures the mother-child relationship of the imaginary. In contrast to the maternal figure of the Lacanian imaginary, Kristeva posits another dimension to the mother—she is associated with the preverbal or the semiotic and as such tends to disrupt the symbolic order.[14]

I think it is possible to open up the mother question still further and posit an even more archaic maternal figure, to go back to mythological narratives of the generative, parthenogenetic mother—that archaic figure who gives birth to all living things. She exists in the mythology of all human cultures as the mother-goddess who alone created the heavens and earth. In China she was known as Nu Kwa, in Mexico as Coatlicue, in Greece as Gaia (literally meaning "earth"), and in Sumer as Nammu. In "Moses and Monotheism," Freud attempted to account for the historical existence of the great mother-goddesses: "It is likely that the mother-goddesses originated at the time of the curtailment of the matriarchy, as a compensation for the slight upon the mothers. The male deities appear first as sons beside the great mothers and only later clearly assume the features of father-figures. These male gods of polytheism reflect the conditions during the patriarchal age."[15] Freud proposed that human society developed through stages from patriarchy to matriarchy and finally back to patriarchy. During the first, primitive people lived in small hordes, each one dominated by a jealous, powerful father who possessed all the females of the group. One day the sons, who had been banished to the outskirts of the group, overthrew the father—whose body they devoured—in order to secure his power and to take his women for themselves. Overcome by guilt, they later attempted to revoke the deed by setting up a totem as a substitute for the father and by renouncing the women whom they had liberated. The sons were forced to give up the women, whom they all wanted to possess, in order to preserve the group, which otherwise would have been destroyed as the sons fought among themselves. In "Totem and Taboo," Freud suggests that here "the germ of the institution of matriarchy" may have originated.[16] Eventually, however, this new form of social organization, constructed upon the taboo against murder and incest, was replaced by the reestablishment of a patriarchal order. He pointed out that the sons had "thus created out of their filial sense of guilt the two fundamental taboos of totemism, which for that very reason inevitably corresponded to the two repressed wishes of the Oedipus complex." [17]

Freud's account of the origins of patriarchal civilization is generally regarded as mythical. Lévi-Strauss points out that it is "a fair account not of the beginnings of civilization, but of its present state" in that it expresses "in symbolical form an inveterate fantasy"—the desire to murder the father and possess the mother. [18] In her discussion of "Totem and Taboo," Kristeva argues that a "strange slippage" (p. 56) has taken place in that, although Freud points out that morality is founded on the taboos of murder and incest, his argument concentrates on the first to the virtual exclusion of the latter. Yet, Kristeva argues, the "woman—or mother—image haunts a large part of that book and keeps shaping its background" (p. 57). She poses the question:

> Could the sacred be, whatever its variants, a two-sided formation? One aspect founded by murder and the social bond made up of a murderer's guilt-ridden atonement, with all the projective mechanisms and obsessive rituals that accompany it; and another aspect, like a lining, more secret and invisible, non-representable, oriented toward those uncertain spaces of unstable identity, toward the fragility—both threatening and fusional—of the archaic dyad, toward the non-separation of subject/object, on which language has no hold but one woven of fright and repulsion? (pp. 57–58)

From the above, it is clear that the figure of the mother in both the history of human sociality and in the history of the individual subject poses immense problems. Freud attempts to account for the existence of the mother-goddess figure by posing a matriarchal period in historical times while admitting that everything to do with the "first attachment to the mother" is deeply repressed—"grey with age and shadowy and almost impossible to revivify." Nowhere does he attempt to specify the nature of this matriarchal period and its implications for his own psychoanalytical theory, specifically his theory of the Oedipus complex, which, as Lacan points out, "can only appear in a patriarchal form in the institution of the family." [19] Kristeva criticizes Freud for failing to deal adequately with incest and the mother questions while using the same mystifying language to refer to the mother; the other aspect of the sacred is "like a lining," "secret and invisible," "non-representable." In his rereading of Freud, Lacan mystifies the figure of woman even further: "the woman is not-all, there is always something with her which eludes discourse."[20] Further, all three writers conflate the archaic mother with the mother of the dyadic and triadic relationship. They refer to her as a "shadowy" figure (Freud); as "non-representable" (Kristeva); as the "abyss of the female organ from which all life comes forth" (Lacan),[21] then make no clear attempt to distinguish this aspect of the maternal imago from the protective/suffocating mother of the pre-Oedipal or the mother as object of sexual jealousy and desire as she is represented in the Oedipal configuration.

The maternal figure constructed within and by the writings of Freud, Lacan, and Kristeva is inevitably the mother of the dyadic or triadic relationship, although the latter figure is more prominent. Even when she is represented as the mother of the imaginary, of the dyadic relationship, she is still constructed as the pre-Oedipal mother—that is, as a figure about to "take up a place" in the symbolic, as a figure always in relation to the father, the representative of the phallus. Without her "lack," he cannot signify its opposite—lack of a lack or presence. But if we posit a more archaic dimension to the mother—the mother as originating womb—we can at least begin to talk about the maternal figure as *outside* the patriarchal family constellation. In this context, the mother-goddess narratives can be read as primal-scene narratives in which the mother is the sole parent. She is also the subject, not the object, of narrativity.

For instance, in the Spider Woman myth of the North American Indians, there was only the Spider Woman, who spun the universe into existence and then created two daughters from whom all life flowed. She is also the Thought Woman or Wise Woman who knows the secrets of the universe. Within the Oedipus narrative, however, she becomes the Sphinx, who also knows the answers to the secret life, but here her situation has been changed. She is no longer the subject of the narrative; she has become the object of the narrative of the male hero. After he has solved her riddle, she will destroy herself. The Sphinx is an ambiguous figure; she knows the secret of life and is thereby linked to the mother-goddess, but her name, which is derived from "sphincter," suggests she is the mother of toilet training, the pre-Oedipal mother who must be repudiated by the son so that he can take up his proper place in the symbolic. It is interesting that Oedipus has always been seen to have committed two horrific crimes: patricide and incest. But his encounter with the Sphinx, which leads to her death, suggests he is also responsible for another horrific crime—that of matricide. For the Sphinx, like the Medusa, is a mother-goddess figure; they are both variants of the same mythological mother who gave birth to all life. Lévi-Strauss has argued that a major issue in the Oedipus myth is the problem of whether man is born from woman. This myth is also central to *Alien:* "Although the problem obviously cannot be solved, the Oedipus myth provides a kind of logical tool which relates the original problem—born from one or born from two?—to the derivative problem: born from different or born from same?"[22]

The Medusa, whose head signifies, according to Freud, the female genitals in their terrifying aspect, also represents the procreative function of woman. The blood that flows from her severed head gives birth to Pegasus and Chrysaor. Although Neptune is supposed to be the father, the nature of the birth once again suggests the parthenogenetic mother. Teresa de Lauretis argues that "to say that narrative is the production of Oedipus is to say that each reader—male or female—is constrained and defined within the two positions of a sexual difference thus conceived: male-hero-human, on the side of the subject; and female-obstacle-boundary-space, on the other."[23] If we apply her definition to narratives that deal specifically with the archaic mother—such as the Oedipus and Perseus myths—we can see that the "obstacle" relates specifically to the question of origins and is an attempt to repudiate the idea of woman as the source of life, woman as sole parent, woman as archaic mother.

Roger Dadoun, also referring to this archaic maternal figure, describes her as

> . . . a maternal thing situated on this side of good and evil, on this side of all organized form, on this side of all events—a totalizing, oceanic mother, a "mysterious and profound unity," arousing in the subject the anguish of fusion and of dissolution; the mother prior to the uncovering of the essential *béance* [gap], of the *pas-de-phallus,* the mother who is pure fantasm, in the sense that she is posed as an omnipresent and all-powerful totality, an absolute being, only in the intuition—she does not have a phallus—which deposes her . . . .[24]

Dadoun places emphasis on her "totalizing, oceanic" presence. I would stress her archaism in relation to her generative powers—the mother who gives birth all by herself, the original parent, the godhead of all fertility, and the origin of procreation. What is most interesting about the mythological figure of woman as the source of all life (a role taken over by the male god of monotheistic religions) is that, within patriarchal signifying practices, particularly the horror film, she is reconstructed and represented as a *negative* figure, one associated with the dread of the generative mother seen only as the abyss, the monstrous vagina, the origin of all life threatening to reabsorb what it once birthed. Kristeva also represents her in this negative light: "Fear of the uncontrollable generative mother repels me from the body; I give up cannibalism because abjection (of the mother) leads me toward respect for the body of the other, my fellow man, my brother" (pp. 78–79).

In this context it is interesting to note that Freud linked the womb to the *unheimlich,* the uncanny:

> It often happens that neurotic men declare that they feel that there is something uncanny about the female genital organs. This *unheimlich* place, however, is the entrance to the former *Heim* [home] of all human beings, to the place where each one of us lived once upon a time and in the beginning. There is a joke saying that "Love is home-sicknesses"; and whenever a man dreams of a place or a country and says to himself, while he is still dreaming: "this place is familiar to me, I've been here before," we may interpret the place as being his mother's genitals or her body.[25]

Freud also supported, and elaborated upon, Schelling's definition of the uncanny as "something which ought to have remained hidden but has come to light."[26] In horror films such as *Alien,* we are given a representation of the female genitals and the womb as uncanny—horrific objects of dread and fascination. Unlike the mythological mother narratives, here the archaic mother, like the Sphinx and the Medusa, is seen only in a negative light. But the central characteristic of the archaic mother is her total dedication to the generative, procreative principle. She is outside morality and the law. Ash's eulogy to the alien is a description of this mother: "I admire its purity; a survivor unclouded by conscience, remorse or delusions of morality."

Clearly, it is difficult to separate out completely the figure of the archaic mother, as defined above, from other aspects of the maternal figure—the maternal authority of Kristeva's semiotic, the mother of Lacan's imaginary, the phallic woman, the castrated woman. While the different figures signify quite separate things about the monstrous-feminine, as constructed in the horror film, each one is also only part of the whole—a different aspect of the maternal figure. At times the horrific nature of the monstrous-feminine is totally dependent on the merging together of all aspects of the maternal figure into one—the horrifying image of woman as archaic mother, phallic woman, and castrated body represented as a single figure within the horror film. However, the archaic mother is clearly present in two distinct ways in the horror film.

First, the archaic mother—constructed as a negative force—is represented in her phantasmagoric aspects in many horror texts, particularly the science fiction horror film. We see her as the gaping, cannibalistic bird's mouth in

The Giant Claw (1957); the terrifying spider of *The Incredible Shrinking Man* (1957); the toothed vagina/womb of *Jaws* (1975); and the fleshy, pulsating womb of *The Thing* and *Poltergeist* (1982). What is common to all of these images of horror is the voracious maw, the mysterious black hole that signifies female genitalia as a monstrous sign threatening to give birth to equally horrific offspring as well as threatening to incorporate everything in its path. This is the generative archaic mother, constructed within patriarchal ideology as the primeval "black hole." This, of course, is also the hole that is opened up by the absence of the penis, the horrifying sight of the mother's genitals—proof that castration can occur.

However, in the texts cited above, the emphasis is not on castration; rather it is the gestating, all-devouring womb of the archaic mother that generates the horror. Nor are these images of the womb constructed in relation to the penis of the father. Unlike the female genitalia, the womb cannot be constructed as a "lack" in relation to the penis. The womb is not the site of castration anxiety. Rather, the womb signifies "fullness" or "emptiness" but always it is its *own point of reference*. This is why we need to posit a more archaic dimension to the mother. For the concept of the archaic mother allows for a notion of the feminine that does not depend for its definition on a concept of the masculine. The term "archaic mother" signifies woman as sexual difference. In contrast, the maternal figure of the pre-Oedipal is always represented in relation to the penis—the phallic mother who later becomes the castrated mother. Significantly, there is an attempt in *Alien* to appropriate the procreative function of the mother, to represent a man giving birth, to deny the mother as signifier of sexual difference—but here birth can exist only as the other face of death.

Second, the archaic mother is present in all horror films as the blackness of extinction—death. The desires and fears invoked by the image of the archaic mother, as a force that threatens to reincorporate what it once gave birth to, are always there in the horror text—all-pervasive, all-encompassing—because of the constant presence of death. The desire to return to the original oneness of things, to return to the mother/womb, is primarily a desire for nondifferentiation. If, as Georges Bataille argues, life signifies discontinuity and separateness, and death signifies continuity and nondifferentiation,[27] then the desire for and attraction of death suggests also a desire to return to the state of original oneness with the mother. As this desire to merge occurs after differentiation—that is, after the subject has developed as separate, autonomous self—then it is experienced as a form of psychic death. In this sense, the confrontation with death, as represented in the horror film, gives rise to a terror of self-disintegration, of losing one's self or ego—often represented cinematically by a screen that becomes black, signifying the obliteration of self, the self of the protagonist in the film and the spectator in the cinema. This has important consequences for the positioning of the spectator in the cinema.

One of the most interesting structures operating in the screen–spectator relationship relates to the sight/site of the monstrous within the horror text. In contrast to the conventional viewing structures working within other variants of the classic text, the horror film does not constantly work to suture the spectator into the viewing processes. Instead, an unusual phenomenon arises whereby the suturing processes are momentarily undone while the horrific image on the screen challenges the viewer to run the risk of continuing to look. Here I refer to those moments in the horror film when the spectator, unable to stand the images of horror unfolding, is forced to look away, to not-look, to look anywhere but at the screen. Strategies of identification are temporarily broken, as the spectator is constructed in the place of horror, the place where the sight/site can no longer be endured, the place where pleasure in looking is transformed into pain and the spectator is punished for his or her voyeuristic desires. Perhaps this should be referred to as a *fifth* look operating alongside the other "looks" that have been theorized in relation to the screen–spectator relationship.[28]

Confronted by the sight of the monstrous, the viewing subject is put into crisis. Boundaries, designed to keep the abject at bay, threaten to disintegrate, collapse. According to Lacan, the self is constituted in a process which he called the "mirror phase," in which the child perceives its own body as a unified whole in an image it receives from outside itself. Thus, the concept of identity is a structure that depends on identification with another. Identity is an imaginary construct, formed in a state of alienation, grounded in misrecognition. Because the self is constructed on an illusion, Lacan argues that it is always in danger of regressing:

> Here we see the ego, in its essential resistance to the elusive process of Becoming, to the variations of Desire. This illusion of unity, in which a human being is always looking forward to self-mastery, entails a constant danger of sliding back again into the chaos from which he started; it hangs over the abyss of a dizzy Assent in which one can perhaps see the very essence of Anxiety.[29]

The horror film puts the viewing subject's sense of a unified self into crisis, specifically in those moments when the image on the screen becomes too threatening or horrific to watch, when the abject threatens to draw the viewing subject to the place "where meaning collapses," the place of death. By not-looking, the spectator is able momentarily to withdraw identification from the image on the screen in order to reconstruct the boundary between self and screen and reconstitute the self that is threatened with disintegration. This process of reconstitution of the self is reaffirmed by the conventional ending of the horror narrative in which the monster is usually "named" and destroyed.[30]

Fear of losing oneself and one's boundaries is made more acute in a society which values boundaries over continuity and separateness over sameness. Given that death is represented in the horror film as a threat to the self's boundaries, symbolized by the threat of the monster, death images are most likely to cause the spectator to look away, to not-look. Because the archaic mother is closely associated with death in its negative aspects, her presence is marked negatively within the project of the horror film. Both signify a monstrous obliteration of the self and both are linked to the demonic. Again Kristeva presents a negative image of the maternal figure in her relationship to death: "What is the demoniacal—an inescapable, repulsive, and yet nurtured abomination? The fantasy of an archaic force, on the near side of separation, unconscious, tempting us to the point of losing our differences, our speech, our life; to the point of aphasia, decay, opprobrium, and death?" (p. 107).

Alien collapses the image of the threatening archaic mother, signifying woman as "difference," into the more recognized figure of the pre-Oedipal mother.[31] This occurs in relation to two images of the monstrous-feminine: the oral-sadistic mother and the phallic mother. Kane's transgressive disturbance of the egg/womb initiates a transformation of its latent aggressivity into an active, phallic enemy. The horror then played out can be read in relation to Kristeva's concept of the semiotic *chora*. As discussed earlier, Kristeva argues that the maternal body becomes the site of conflicting desires (the semiotic *chora*). These desires are constantly staged and restaged in the workings of the horror narrative where the subject is left alone, usually in a strange, hostile place, and forced to confront an unnameable terror, the monster. The monster represents both the subject's fears of being alone, of being separate from the mother, and the threat of annihilation—often through reincorporation. As oral-sadistic mother, the monster threatens to reabsorb the child she once nurtured. Thus, the monster, like the abject, is ambiguous; it both repels and attracts.

In *Alien*, each of the crew members comes face to face with the alien in a scene whose mise-en-scène is coded to suggest a monstrous, malevolent maternal figure. They watch with fascinated horror as the baby alien gnaws its way through Kane's stomach; Dallas, the captain, encounters the alien after he has crawled along the ship's enclosed, womblike air ducts; and the other three members are cannibalized in a frenzy of blood in scenes that emphasize the alien's huge razor-sharp teeth, signifying the monstrous oral-sadistic mother. Apart from the scene of Kane's death, all the death sequences occur in dimly lit, enclosed, threatening spaces reminiscent of the giant hatchery where Kane first encounters the pulsating egg. In these death sequences the terror of being abandoned is matched only by the fear of reincorporation. This scenario, which enacts the conflicting desires at play in the semiotic *chora,* is staged within the body of the mother-ship, the vessel that the space travelers initially trust, until Mother herself is revealed as a treacherous figure programmed to sacrifice the lives of the crew in the interests of the company.

The other face of the monstrous-feminine in *Alien* is the phallic mother. Freud argued that the male child could either accept the threat of castration, thus ending the Oedipus complex, or disavow it. The latter response requires him to mitigate his horror at the sight of the mother's genitals—proof that castration can occur—with a fetish object that substitutes for her missing penis. For him, she is still the phallic mother, the penis-woman. In "Medusa's Head" Freud argued that the head with its hair of writhing snakes represents the terrifying genitals of the mother, but that this head also functions as a fetish object: "The hair upon the Medusa's head is frequently represented in works of art in the form of snakes, and these once again are derived from the castration complex. It is a remarkable fact that, however frightening they may be in themselves, they nevertheless serve actually as a mitigation of horror, for they replace the penis, the absence of which is the cause of horror." [32] Freud noted that a display of the female genitals makes a woman "unapproachable and repels all sexual desires." He refers to the section in Rabelais which relates "how the Devil took flight when the woman showed him her vulva." [33] Perseus' solution is to look only at a reflection, a mirror image of her genitals. As with patriarchal ideology, his shield reflects an "altered" representation, a vision robbed of its threatening aspects. The full difference of the mother is denied; she is constructed as other, displayed before the gaze of the conquering male hero, then destroyed. [34] The price paid is the destruction of sexual heterogeneity and repression of the maternal signifier. The fetishization of the mother's genitals could occur in those texts where the maternal figure is represented in her phantasmagoric aspects as the gaping, voracious vagina/womb. Do aspects of these images work to mitigate the horror by offering a substitute for the penis?

Roger Dadoun argues very convincingly that the Dracula variant of the vampire movie is "an illustration of the work of the fetish function": [35]

. . . against the primitive identification with the mother, a phallus; against the anguish of psychotic break-down, sexuality; against spatio-temporal disorganization, a ritual—and this is what is fabricated, we could say, on the positive slopes of fetishism, a sexualized phallic object, it is as rigid and impressive as it is fragile and threatened, where we will perhaps have the pleasure of recognizing one of the familiar figures of horror film, Count Dracula.[36]

Dadoun argues that the archaic mother exists as a "non-presence . . . signify-ing an extremely archaic mode of presence."[37] Signs of the archaic mother in the Dracula film are the small, enclosed village; the pathway through the for-est that leads like an umbilical cord to the castle; the central place of enclo-sure with its winding stairways, spiderwebs, dark vaults, worm-eaten stair-cases, dust, and damp earth—"all elements which come back to the *imago* of the bad archaic mother."[38] At the center of this, Dracula himself materializes. With his black cape, pointed teeth, rigid body—carried "like an erect phal-lus"—piercing eyes, and "penetrating look,"[39] he is the fetish form, "a sub-stitute of the maternal phallus."[40]

It is clear, nevertheless, since the threat comes from the absent maternal phallus, that the principal defense is sex. The vampire, markedly fasci-nated by the maternal *pas-de-phallus* and identifying himself with the ar-chaic mother for lack of having a phallus, becomes phallus; he transfers a default of *having* to the plan of an illusory *being*.[41]

As he emerges in Dadoun's argument, the Dracula figure is very much act-ing on behalf of the mother—he desires to be the phallus for the mother. When he is finally penetrated by the stake, his heart is "revealed as hollow, a gash, or a gaping wound—it is castration made flesh, blood and *béance*. . . ."[42] However, it is possible that we could theorize fetishism differently by asking: For whom is the fetish-object a fetish? The male or female subject? In gen-eral, the fetishist is usually assumed to be male, although Freud did allow that female fetishism was a possibility.[43] The notion of female fetishism is much neglected, although it is present in various patriarchal discourses.

Mary Kelly argues that "it would be a mistake to confine women to the realm of repression, excluding the possibility, for example, of female fetishism":

When Freud describes castration fears for the woman, this imaginary scenario takes the form of losing her loved objects, especially her chil-

Winding staircases, spiderwebs, and dankness signify the archaic mother in *Dracula* (1931).

dren; the child is going to grow up, leave her, reject her, perhaps die. In order to delay, disavow that separation she has already in a way acknowledged, the woman tends to fetishise the child: by dressing him up, by continuing to feed him no matter how old he gets, or simply by having another "little one."[44]

In *The Interpretation of Dreams,* Freud discusses the way in which the doubling of a penis symbol indicates an attempt to stave off castration anxieties.[45] Juliet Mitchell refers to doubling as a sign of a female castration complex: "We can see the significance of this for women, as dreams of repeated number of children—'little ones'—are given the same import."[46] In this context, female fetishism represents an attempt by the female subject to continue to "have" the phallus, to take up a "positive" place in relation to the symbolic.

Female fetishism is clearly represented within many horror texts—as instances of patriarchal signifying practices—but only in relation to male fears and anxieties about women and the question What do women want? *(The Birds, Cat People, Alien, The Thing).* Women as yet do not speak their own "fetishistic" desires within the popular cinema—if, indeed, women have such desires. The notion of female fetishism is represented in *Alien* in the figure of the monster. The creature is the mother's phallus, attributed to the maternal figure by a phallocentric ideology terrified at the thought that women might desire to have the phallus. The monster as fetish object is not there to meet the desires of the male fetishist, but rather to signify the monstrousness of woman's desire to have the phallus.

In *Alien* the monstrous creature is constructed as the phallus of the negative mother. The image of the archaic mother—threatening because it signifies woman as difference rather than constructed as opposition—is, once again, collapsed into the figure of the pre-Oedipal mother. By relocating the figure of woman within an Oedipal scenario, her image can be recuperated and controlled. The womb, even if represented negatively, is a greater threat than the mother's phallus. As phallic mother, woman is again represented as monstrous. What is horrific is her desire to cling to her offspring in order to continue to "have the phallus." Her monstrous desire is concretized in the figure of the alien, the creature whose deadly mission is represented as the same as that of the archaic mother—to reincorporate and destroy all life.

If we consider *Alien* in the light of a theory of female fetishism, then the chameleon nature of the alien begins to make sense. Its changing appearance represents a form of doubling or multiplication of the phallus, pointing to the mother's desire to stave off her castration. The alien is the mother's phallus, a fact made perfectly clear in the birth scene when the infant alien rises from Kane's stomach and holds itself erect, glaring angrily around the room, before screeching off into the depths of the ship. But the alien is more than a phallus; it is also coded as a toothed vagina, the monstrous-feminine as the cannibalistic mother. A large part of the ideological project of *Alien* is the representation of the maternal fetish object as an "alien" or foreign shape. This is why the body of the heroine becomes so important at the end of the film.

Much has been written about the final scene, in which Ripley (Sigourney Weaver) undresses before the camera, on the grounds that its voyeurism undermines her role as successful heroine. A great deal has also been written about the cat. Why does she rescue the cat and thereby risk her life, and the lives of Parker and Lambert, when she has previously been so careful about quarantine regulations? Again, satisfactory answers to these questions are provided by a phallocentric concept of female fetishism. Compared to the horrific sight of the alien as fetish object of the monstrous-feminine, Ripley's body is pleasurable and reassuring to look at. She signifies the "acceptable" form and shape of woman. In a sense the monstrousness of woman, represented by Mother as betrayer (the computer/life-support system) and Mother as the uncontrollable, generative, cannibalistic mother (the alien), is controlled through the display of woman as reassuring and pleasurable sign. The image of the cat functions in the same way; it signifies an acceptable, and in this context, a reassuring fetish object for the "normal" woman.[47] Thus, Ripley holds the cat to her, stroking it as if it were her "baby," her "little one." Finally, Ripley enters her sleep pod, assuming a virginal repose. The nightmare is over and we are returned to the opening sequence of the film where birth was a pristine affair. The final sequence works, not only to dispose of the alien, but also to repress the nightmare image of the monstrous-feminine, constructed as a sign of abjection within the text's patriarchal discourses.

Kristeva's theory of abjection, if viewed as description rather than prescription, provides a productive hypothesis for an analysis of the monstrous-feminine in the horror film.[48] If we posit a more archaic dimension to the mother, we can see how this figure, as well as Kristeva's maternal authority of the semiotic, are both constructed as figures of abjection within the signifying practices of the horror film. We can see its ideological project as an attempt to shore up the symbolic order by constructing the feminine as an imaginary other that must be repressed and controlled in order to secure and protect the social order. Thus, the horror film stages and restages a constant repudiation of the maternal figure.

But the feminine is not a monstrous sign *per se;* rather, it is constructed as such within a patriarchal discourse that reveals a great deal about male desires and fears but tells us nothing about feminine desire in relation to the horrific. When Norman Bates remarked to Marion Crane in *Psycho* that "Mother is not herself today," he was dead right. Mother wasn't herself. She was someone else—her son Norman.

Notes

1. Sigmund Freud, "Fetishism," in *On Sexuality,* Pelican Freud Library, vol. 7 (1977; reprint, Harmondsworth: Penguin, 1981), p. 354.

2. Joseph Campbell, *The Masks of God: Primitive Mythology* (New York: Penguin, 1969), p. 73.

3. Sigmund Freud, "Medusa's Head," in *The Standard Edition of the Complete Works of Sigmund Freud,* ed. and trans. James Strachey (London: Hogarth Press, 1964), 18: 273–274.

4. Ibid., p. 273.

5. Ibid.

6. Julia Kristeva, *Powers of Horror: An Essay on Abjection* (New York: Columbia University Press, 1982), p. 4. Subsequent references are cited parenthetically in the text.

7. For a discussion of the way in which the modern horror film works upon its audience, see Philip Brophy, "Horrality—the Textuality of Contemporary Horror Films," *Screen* 27, no. 1 (January–February 1986): 2–13.

8. For a critique of *Powers of Horror,* see Jennifer Stone, "The Horrors of Power: A Critique of Kristeva," in *The Politics of Theory,* ed. F. Barker et. al. (Colchester: University of Essex, 1983), pp. 38–48.

9. Sigmund Freud, "From the History of an Infantile Neurosis," in *Case Histories II,* Pelican Freud Library, vol. 9 (1979; reprint, Harmondsworth: Penguin, 1981), p. 294.

10. Sigmund Freud, "On the Sexual Theories of Children," in *On Sexuality,* Pelican Freud Library, vol. 7 (1977; reprint, Harmondsworth: Penguin, 1981), p. 198.

11. Sigmund Freud, "The Paths to the Formation of Symptoms," in *Introductory Lectures on Psychoanalysis,* Pelican Freud Library, vol. 1 (1973; reprint, Harmondsworth: Penguin, 1981), p. 417.

12. Daniel Dervin argues that this structure does deserve the status of a convention. For a detailed discussion of the primal-scene fantasy in various film genres, see his "Primal Conditions and Conventions: The Genres of Comedy and Science Fiction," *Film/Psychology Review* 4, no. 1 (Winter–Spring 1980): 115–147.

13. Sigmund Freud, "Female Sexuality," in *On Sexuality,* Pelican Freud Library, vol. 7 (1977; reprint, Harmondsworth: Penguin, 1981) p. 373.

14. For a discussion of the relation between the "semiotic" and the Lacanian "imaginary," see Jane Gallop, *The Daughter's Seduction: Feminism and Psychoanalysis* (Ithaca, N.Y.: Cornell University Press, 1983), pp. 124–125.

15. Sigmund Freud, "Moses and Monotheism," in *Standard Edition,* 23: 83.

16. Sigmund Freud, "Totem and Taboo," in *The Origins of Religion,* Pelican Freud Library, vol. 13 (Harmondsworth, Penguin, 1985), p. 206.

17. Ibid., p. 205.

18. Quoted in Georges Bataille, *Death and Sensuality: A Study of Eroticism and the Taboo* (New York: Walker and Co., 1962), p. 200.

19. Quoted in Anthony Wilden, ed. and trans., *The Language of Self* (Baltimore: Johns Hopkins University Press, 1970), p. 126.

20. Quoted in Stephen Heath, "Difference," *Screen* 19, no. 3 (Autumn 1978): 59.

21. Quoted in ibid., p. 54.

22. Claude Lévi-Strauss, *Structural Anthropology,* trans. C. Jacobson and B. G. Schoepf (New York: Doubleday, 1976), p. 212.

23. Teresa de Lauretis, *Alice Doesn't: Feminism, Semiotics, Cinema* (Bloomington: Indiana University Press, 1984), p. 121.

24. Roger Dadoun, "Fetishism in the Horror Film," *Enclitic* 1, no. 2 (1977): 55–56.

25. Sigmund Freud, "The Uncanny," in *Standard Edition,* 17: 245.

26. Ibid., p. 225.

27. Bataille, *Death and Sensuality.*

28. For a discussion of cinema and the structures of the "look," see Paul Willemen, "Letter to John," *Screen* 21, no. 2 (Summer 1980): 53–66.

29. Jacques Lacan, "Some Reflections on the Ego," *International Journal of Psychoanalysis* 34 (1953): 15.

30. For a discussion of the relationship between the female spectator, structures of looking, and the horror film, see Linda Williams, "When the Woman Looks," in this volume.

31. Dadoun refers to a similar process when he speaks of the displacement of the large "omnipresent mother" into the small "occulted mother." "Fetishism in the Horror Film," p. 55.

32. Sigmund Freud, "Medusa's Head," p. 105.

33. Ibid., p. 106.

34. For a fascinating discussion of the place of woman as monster in the Oedipal narrative, see de Lauretis, *Alice Doesn't,* chap. 5.

35. Dadoun, "Fetishism in the Horror Film," p. 40.

36. Ibid., p. 42.

37. Ibid., p. 53.

38. Ibid., p. 64.

39. Ibid., p. 57.

40. Ibid., p. 56.

41. Ibid., pp. 59–60.

42. Ibid., p. 60.

43. Sigmund Freud, "An Outline of Psychoanalysis," *Standard Edition,* 23: 202: "This abnormality, which may be counted as one of the perversions, is, as is well known, based on the patient (who is *almost always* male) not recognizing the fact that females have no penis" (my emphasis).

44. Mary Kelly, "Woman-Desire-Image," *Desire* (London: Institute of Contemporary Arts, 1984), p. 31.

45. Sigmund Freud, *The Interpretation of Dreams,* Pelican Freud Library, vol. 4 (1976; reprint, Harmondsworth: Penguin, 1982).

46. Juliet Mitchell, *Psychoanalysis and Feminism* (Harmondsworth: Penguin, 1974), p. 84.

47. The double bird images of Hitchcock's *The Birds* (1963) function in the same way: the love birds signify an "acceptable" fetish, the death birds a fetish of the monstrous woman.

48. For an analysis of the horror film as a "return of the repressed," see Robin Wood, "Return of the Repressed," *Film Comment* 14, no. 4 (July–August 1978): 25–32; and "Neglected Nightmares," *Film Comment* 16, no. 2 (March–April 1980): 24–32.

3

Her Body, Himself:
Gender in the Slasher Film

Carol J. Clover

The Cinefantastic and Varieties of Horror

On the high side of horror lie the classics: F. W. Murnau's
Nosferatu (1922), *King Kong* (1933), *Dracula* (1931), *Frankenstein*
(1931), and various works by Alfred Hitchcock, Carl Theodor
Dryer, and a few others—films that by virtue of age, literary
ancestry, or fame of director have achieved reputability within
the context of disreputability. Farther down the scale fall the
productions of Brian de Palma, some of the glossier satanic films
(*Rosemary's Baby* [1968], *The Omen* [1976], *The Exorcist* [1973]),
certain science fiction hybrids (*Alien* [1979], *Aliens* [1986], *Blade
Runner* [1982]), some vampire and werewolf films (*Wolfen* [1981],
An American Werewolf in London [1981]), and an assortment of
other highly produced films, often with stars (*Whatever Happened to Baby Jane?* [1962], *The Shining* [1980]). At the very bottom, down in the cinematic underbrush, lies—horror of horrors—the slasher (or splatter or shocker) film: the immensely
generative story of a psycho killer who slashes to death a string
of mostly female victims, one by one, until he is himself subdued
or killed, usually by the one girl who has survived.

Drenched in taboo and encroaching vigorously on the pornographic, the slasher film lies by and large beyond the purview of the respectable (middle-aged, middle-class) audience. It has also lain by and large beyond the purview of respectable criticism. Staples of drive-ins and exploitation houses, where they "rub shoulders with sex pictures and macho action flicks," these are films that are "never ever written up."[1] Books on horror film mostly concentrate on the classics, touch on the middle categories in passing, and either pass over the slasher in silence or bemoan it as a degenerate aberration.[2] The one full book on the category, William Schoell's *Stay Out of the Shower,* is immaculately unintelligent.[3] Film magazine articles on the genre rarely get past technique, special effects, and profits. The Sunday *San Francisco Examiner* relegates reviews of slashers to the syndicated "Joe Bob Briggs, Drive-In Movie Critic of Grapevine, Texas," whose low-brow, campy tone ("We're talking two breasts, four quarts of blood, five dead bodies . . . . Joe Bob says check it out") establishes what the paper and others like it deem the necessary distance between their readership and that sort of film.[4] There are of course the exceptional cases: critics or social observers who have seen at least some of these films and tried to come to grips with their ethics or aesthetics or both. Just how troubled is their task can be seen from its divergent results. For one critic, *The Texas Chainsaw Massacre* (1974) is "the *Gone With the Wind* of meat movies."[5] For another it is a "vile little piece of sick crap . . . nothing but a hysterically paced, slapdash, imbecile concoction of cannibalism, voodoo, astrology, sundry hippie-esque cults, and unrelenting sadistic violence as extreme and hideous as a complete lack of imagination can possibly make it."[6] Writes a third: "[Director Tobe] Hooper's cinematic intelligence becomes more apparent in every viewing, as one gets over the initial traumatizing impact and learns to respect the pervasive felicities of camera placement and movement."[7] The Museum of Modern Art bought the film in the same year that at least one country, Sweden, banned it.

Robin Wood's tack is less aesthetic than anthropological: "However one may shrink from systematic exposure to them [slasher films], however one may deplore the social phenomena and ideological mutations they reflect, their popularity . . . suggests that even if they were uniformly execrable they shouldn't be ignored."[8] We may go a step farther and suggest that the qualities that locate the slasher film outside the usual aesthetic system—that indeed render it, along with pornography and low horror in general, the film category "most likely to be betrayed by artistic treatment and lavish production values"[9]—are the very qualities that make it such a transparent source for (sub)cultural attitudes toward sex and gender in particular. Unmediated by otherworldly fantasy, cover plot, bestial transformations, or civilized routine, slasher films present us in startlingly direct terms with a world in which male and female are at desperate odds but in which, at the same time, masculinity and femininity are more states of mind than body. The premise of this essay, then, is that the slasher film, not despite but exactly because of its crudity and compulsive repetitiveness, gives us a clearer picture of current sexual attitudes, at least among the segment of the population that forms its erstwhile audience, than do the legitimate products of the better studios.

Before we turn to the generic particulars, however, let us review some of the critical and cinematic issues that attend the study of the sensation genres in general and horror in particular. We take as our point of departure not a slasher film but Brian de Palma's art-horror film *Body Double* (1984). The plot—a man witnesses and after much struggle solves the mysterious murder of a woman with whom he has become voyeuristically involved—concerns us less than the three career levels through which the hero, an actor named Jake, first ascends and then descends. He aspires initially to legitimate roles (Shakespeare), but it becomes clear during the course of a method-acting class that his range of emotional expression is impaired by an unresolved childhood fear. For the moment he has taken a job as vampire in a "low-budget, independent horror film," but even that job is threatened when, during a scene in which he is to be closed in a coffin and buried, he suffers an attack of claustrophobia and must leave the set. A plot twist leads him to the underworld of pornography, where he takes on yet another role, this time in a skin flick. Here, in the realm of the flesh with a queen of porn, the sexual roots of Jake's paralysis—fear of the (female) cavern—are exposed and finally resolved. A new man, he returns to *A Vampire's Kiss* to master the burial scene, and we are to understand that Shakespeare is the next stop.

The three cinematic categories are thus ranked by degree of sublimation. On the civilized side of the continuum lie the legitimate genres; at the other end, hard on the unconscious, lie the sensation or "body" genres, horror and pornography, in that order. For de Palma, the violence of horror reduces to and enacts archaic sexual feelings. Beneath Jake's emotional paralysis (which emerges in the "high" genre) lies a death anxiety (which is exposed in the burying-alive of horror), and beneath *that* anxiety lies a primitive sexual response (which emerges, and is resolved, in pornography). The layers of Jake's experience accord strikingly, and perhaps not coincidentally, with Freud's archaeology of "uncanny" feelings. "To some people," Freud wrote, "the idea of being buried alive by mistake is the most uncanny thing of all. And yet psycho-analysis has taught us that this terrifying phantasy is only a transformation of another phantasy which originally had nothing terrifying about it at all, but was qualified by a certain lasciviousness—the phantasy, I mean, of intra-uterine existence [*der Phantasie vom Leben im Mutterleib*]."[10] Pornography thus engages directly (in pleasurable terms) what horror explores at one remove (in painful terms) and legitimate film at two or more. Beneath the "legitimate" plot of *The Graduate* (1967), in which Ben must give up his relationship with a *friend's* mother in order to marry and take his proper social place, lies the plot of *Psycho* (1960), in which Norman's unnatural attachment to his *own* mother drives him to murder women to whom he is attracted; and beneath *that* plot lies the plot of the porn film *Taboo* (1980), in which the son simply has sex with his mother ("Mom, am I better than Dad?"). Pornography, in short, has to do with sex (the act) and horror with gender.

It is a rare Hollywood film that does not devote a passage or two—a car chase, a sex scene—to the emotional/physical excitement of the audience. But horror and pornography are the only two genres specifically devoted to the arousal of bodily sensation. They exist solely to horrify and stimulate, not always respectively, and their ability to do so is the sole measure of their success: they "prove themselves upon our pulses."[11] Thus in horror-film circles, "good" means scary, specifically in a bodily way (ads promise shivers, chills, shudders, tingling of the spine; Lloyds of London insured audiences of *Macabre* [1958] against death by fright);[12] and *Hustler's Erotic Film Guide* ranks pornographic films according to the degree of erection they produce (one film is ranked a "pecker popper," another "limp"). The target is in both cases the body, our witnessing body. But *what* we witness is also the body, another's body, in experience: the body in sex and the body in threat. The terms "flesh film" ("skin flicks") and "meat movies" are remarkably apt.

Cinema, it is claimed, owes its particular success in the sensation genres (witness the early and swift rise of vampire films) to its unprecedented ability to manipulate point of view. What written narrative must announce, film can accomplish silently and instantaneously through cutting. Within the space of seconds, the vampire's first-person perspective is displaced by third-person or documentary observation. To these simple shifts can be added the variables of distance (from the panorama of the battlefield to the close-up of an eyeball), angle, frame tilt, lighting effects, unsteadiness of image, and so on—again, all subject to sudden and unannounced manipulation.[13] *Friday the 13th* (1980) locates the I-camera with the killer in pursuit of a victim; the camera is hand-held, producing a jerky image, and the frame includes in-and-out-of-focus foreground objects (trees, bushes, window frames) behind which the killer (I-camera), is lurking—all accompanied by the sound of heartbeats and heavy breathing. "The camera moves in on the screaming, pleading victim, 'looks down' at the knife, and then plunges it into the chest, ear, or eyeball. Now that's sick."[14]

Lagging behind practice is a theoretical understanding of effect. The processes by which a certain image (but not another) filmed in a certain way (but not another) causes one person's (but not another's) pulse to race finally remains a mystery—not only to critics and theorists but even, to judge from interviews and the trial-and-error (and baldly imitative) quality of the films themselves, by the people who make the product. The process of suture is sensed to be centrally important in effecting audience identification, though just how and why is unclear.[15] Nor is identification the straightforward notion some critics take it to be.[16] Where commentators by and large agree is in the importance of the "play of pronoun function."[17] If the fantastic depends for its effect on an uncertainty of vision, a profusion of perspectives and a confusion of subjective and objective, then cinema is preeminently suited to the fantastic. Indeed, to the extent that film can present "unreal" combinations of objects and events as "real" through the camera eye, the "cinematic process itself might be called fantastic."[18] The "cinefantastic" in any case succeeds, far more efficiently and effectively and on a far greater scale than its ancestral media, in the production of sensation.

The fact that the cinematic conventions of horror are so easily and so often parodied would seem to suggest that, individual variation notwithstanding, its basic structures of apperception are fixed and fundamental. The same is true of the stories they tell. Students of folklore or early literature recognize in the slasher film the hallmarks of oral story: the free exchange of themes and motifs, the archetypal characters and situations, the accumulation of sequels, remakes, imitations. This is a field in which there is in some sense no original, no real or right text, but only variants; a world in which, therefore, the meaning of the individual example lies outside itself. The "art" of the horror film, like the "art" of pornography, is to a very large extent the art of rendition, and it is understood as such by the competent audience.[19] A particular example may have original features, but its quality as a horror film lies in the ways it delivers the cliché. James B. Twitchell rightly recommends an "ethnological approach, in which the various stories are analyzed as if no one individual telling really mattered. . . . You search for what is stable and repeated; you neglect what is 'artistic' and 'original.' This is why, for me, auteur criticism is quite beside the point in explaining horror. . . . The critic's first job in explaining the fascination of horror is not to fix the images at their every appearance but, instead, to trace their migrations to the audience and, only then, try to understand why they have been crucial enough to pass along."[20] That auteur criticism is at least partly beside the point is clear from interviews with such figures as John Carpenter (*Halloween* [1978], *The Fog* [1980])—interviews that would seem to suggest that, like the purveyors of folklore, the makers of film operate more on instinct and formula than conscious understanding. So bewildered was Hitchcock by the unprecedented success of *Psycho* that he approached the Stanford Research Institute about doing a study of the phenomenon.[21]

What makes horror "crucial enough to pass along" is, for critics since Freud, what has made ghost stories and fairy tales crucial enough to pass along: its engagement of repressed fears and desires and its reenactment of the residual conflict surrounding those feelings. Horror films thus respond to interpretation, as Robin Wood puts it, as "at once the personal dreams of their makers and the collective dreams of their audiences—the fusion made possible by the shared structures of a common ideology."[22] And just as attacker and attacked are expressions of the same self in nightmares, so they are expressions of the same viewer in horror film. Our primary and acknowledged identification may be with the victim, the adumbration of our infantile fears and desires, our memory sense of ourselves as tiny and vulnerable in the face of the enormous Other; but the Other is also finally another part of ourself, the projection of our repressed infantile rage and desire (our blind drive to annihilate those toward whom we feel anger, to force satisfaction from those who stimulate us, to wrench food for ourselves if only by actually devouring those who feed us) that we have had in the name of civilization to repudiate. We are both Red Riding Hood *and* the Wolf; the force of the experience, the horror, comes from "knowing" both sides of the story—from giving ourselves over to the cinematic play of pronoun functions. It is no surprise that the first film to which viewers were not admitted once the theater darkened was *Psycho*. Whether Hitchcock actually meant with this measure to intensify the "sleep" experience is unclear, but the effect both in the short run, in establishing *Psycho* as the ultimate thriller, and in the long run, in altering the cinema-going habits of the nation, is indisputable. In the current understanding, horror is the least interruptable of all film genres. That uninterruptability itself bears witness to the compulsive nature of the stories it tells.

Whatever else it may be, the slasher film is clearly "crucial enough to pass along." Profits and sequels tell much of the story. *Halloween* cost $320,000 to make and within six years had grossed over $75,000,000; even a highly produced film like *The Shining* has repaid itself tenfold.[23] *The Hills Have Eyes* (1977), *The Texas Chainsaw Massacre,* and *Alien* (a science fiction/slasher hybrid) are [as of 1987] at Part Two. *Psycho* and *A Nightmare on Elm Street* are at Part Three. *Halloween* is at Part Four, and *Friday the 13th* is at Part Six. These are better taken as remakes than sequels; although the subsequent part purports to take up where the earlier part left off, it in most cases simply duplicates with only slight variation the plot and circumstances—the formula—of its predecessor. Nor do different titles indicate different plots; *Friday the 13th* is set at summer camp and *Halloween* in town, but the story is much the same, compulsively repeated in those ten films and in dozens like them under different names. The audience for that story is by all accounts largely young and largely male—most conspicuously groups of boys who cheer the killer on as he assaults the victims, then reverse their sympathies to cheer the survivor on as she assaults the killer.[24] Our question, then, has to do with that particular audience's stake in that particular nightmare, with what in the story is "crucial" enough to warrant the price of admission and what the implications are for the current discussion of women and film.

The Slasher Film

The immediate ancestor of the slasher film is Hitchcock's *Psycho* (1960). Its elements are familiar: the killer is the psychotic product of a sick family but still recognizably human; the victim is a beautiful, sexually active woman; the location is not-home, at a Terrible Place; the weapon is something other than a gun; the attack is registered from the victim's point of view and comes with shocking suddenness. None of these features is original, but the unprecedented success of Hitchcock's particular formulation, above all the sexualization of both motive and action, prompted a flood of imitations and variations. In 1974, a film emerged that revised the *Psycho* template to a degree and in such a way as to mark a new phase: *The Texas Chainsaw Massacre,* directed by Tobe Hooper. Together with *Halloween,* it engendered a new spate of variations and imitations.

The plot of *The Texas Chainsaw Massacre* is simple enough: five young people are driving through Texas in a van; they stop off at an abandoned house and are murdered one by one by the psychotic sons of a degenerate local family; the sole survivor is a woman. The horror, of course, lies in the elaboration. Early in the film the group picks up a hitchhiker, but when he starts a fire and slashes Franklin's arm (having already slit open his own hand), they kick him out. The abandoned house they subsequently visit, once the home of Sally's and Franklin's grandparents, turns out to be right next door to the house of the hitchhiker and his family: his brother Leatherface; their father; an aged and only marginally alive grandfather; and their dead grandmother and her dog, whose mummified corpses are ceremonially included in

Leatherface pursues Sally in *The Texas Chainsaw Massacre* (1974).

the family gatherings. Three generations of slaughterhouse workers, once proud of their craft but now displaced by machines, have taken up killing and cannibalism as a way of life. Their house is grotesquely decorated with human and animal remains—bones, feathers, hair, skins. The young people drift apart in their exploration of the abandoned house and grounds and are picked off one by one by Leatherface and Hitchhiker. Last is Sally. The others are attacked and killed with dispatch, but Sally must fight for her life, enduring all manner of horrors through the night. At dawn she manages to escape to the highway, where she is picked up by a passing trucker.

Likewise, the nutshell plot of *Halloween:* a psychotic killer (Michael) stalks a small town on Halloween and kills a string of teenage friends, one by one; only Laurie survives. The twist here is that Michael has escaped from the asylum in which he has been incarcerated since the age of six, when he killed his sister minutes after she and her boyfriend parted following an illicit interlude in her parents' bed. That murder, in flashback, opens the film. It is related entirely in the killer's first person (I-camera) and only after the fact is the identity of the perpetrator revealed. Fifteen years later, Michael escapes his prison and returns to kill Laurie, whom he construes as another version of his sister (a sequel clarifies that she is in fact his *younger* sister, adopted by another family at the time of the earlier tragedy). But before Michael gets to Laurie, he picks off her high school friends: Annie, in a car on her way to her boyfriend's; Bob, going to the kitchen for a beer after sex with Lynda; Lynda, talking on the phone with Laurie and waiting for Bob to come back with the beer. At last only Laurie remains. When she hears Lynda squeal and then go silent on the phone, she leaves her own babysitting house to go to Lynda's. Here she discovers the three bodies and flees, the killer in pursuit. The remainder of the film is devoted to the back-and-forth struggle between Laurie and Michael. Again and again he bears down on her, and again and again she either eludes him (by running, hiding, breaking through windows to escape, locking herself in) or strikes back (once with a knitting needle, once with a hanger). In the end, Dr. Loomis (Michael's psychiatrist in the asylum) rushes in and shoots the killer (though not so fatally as to prevent his return in the sequels).

Before we turn to an inventory of generic components, let us add a third, more recent example: *The Texas Chainsaw Massacre, Part 2* (1986). The slaughterhouse family (now named the Sawyers) is the same, though older and, owing to their unprecedented success in the sausage business, richer.[25] When Mr. Sawyer begins to suspect from her broadcasts that a disk jockey named Stretch knows more than she should about one of their recent crimes, he dispatches his sons Leatherface and Chop Top (Hitchhiker in the earlier film) to the radio station late at night. There they seize the technician and corner Stretch. At the crucial moment, however, power fails Leatherface's chainsaw. As Stretch cowers before him, he presses the now still blade up along her thigh and against her crotch, where he holds it unsteadily as he jerks and shudders in what we understand to be orgasm. After that the sons leave. The intrepid Stretch, later joined by a Texas Ranger (Dennis Hopper), tracks them to their underground lair outside of town. Tumbling down the Texas equivalent of a rabbit hole, Stretch finds herself in the subterranean chambers of the Sawyer operation. Here, amidst all the slaughterhouse paraphernalia, the Sawyers live and work. The walls drip with blood. Like the decrepit mansion of the first film, the residential parts of the establishment are quaintly decorated with human and animal remains. After a long ordeal at the hands of the Sawyers, Stretch manages to scramble up through a culvert and beyond that up onto a nearby pinnacle, where she finds a chainsaw and wards off her final assailant. The Texas Ranger evidently perishes in a grenade explosion underground, leaving Stretch the sole survivor.

The spiritual debt of all the post-1974 slasher films to *Psycho* is clear, and it is a rare example that does not pay a visual tribute, however brief, to the ancestor—if not in a shower stabbing, then in a purling drain or the shadow of a knife-wielding hand. No less clear, however, is the fact that the post-1974 examples have, in the usual way of folklore, contemporized not only Hitchcock's terms but also, over time, their own. We have, in short, a cinematic formula with a twenty-six-year history, of which the first phase, from 1960 to 1974, is dominated by a film clearly rooted in the sensibility of the 1950s, while the second phase, bracketed by the two *Texas Chainsaw* films of 1974 and 1986, responds to the values of the late sixties and early seventies. That the formula in its most recent guise may be in decline is suggested by the campy, self-parodying quality of *The Texas Chainsaw Massacre, Part 2,* as well as the emergence, in legitimate theater, of the slasher satire *Buckets of Blood* (1991). Between 1974 and 1986, however, the formula evolved and flourished in ways of some interest to observers of popular culture, above all those concerned with the representation of women in film. To apprehend in specific terms the nature of that mutation, let us, with *Psycho* as the benchmark, survey the genre by component category: killer, locale, weapons, victims, and shock effects.

Killer. The psychiatrist at the end of *Psycho* explains what we had already guessed from the action: that Norman Bates had introjected his mother, in life a "clinging, demanding woman," so completely that she constituted his other, controlling self. Not Norman but "the mother half of his mind" killed Marion—*had* to kill Marion—when he (the Norman half) found himself aroused by her. The notion of a killer propelled by psychosexual fury, more particularly a male in gender distress, has proved a durable one, and the progeny of Norman Bates stalk the genre up to the present day. Just as Norman wears his mother's clothes during his acts of violence and is thought, by the screen characters and also, for a while, by the film's spectators to *be* his mother, so the murderer in the *Psycho* imitation *Dressed to Kill* (1980), a transvestite psychiatrist, seems until his unveiling to be a woman; like Norman, he must kill women who arouse him sexually. Likewise, in muted form, Hitchhiker/Chop Top and Leatherface in the *Texas Chainsaw* films: neither brother shows overt signs of gender confusion, but their cathexis to the sick family—in which the mother is conspicuously absent but the preserved corpse of the grandmother (answering the treated body of Mrs. Bates in *Psycho*) is conspicuously present—has palpably arrested their development. Both are in their twenties (thirties, in the later film), but Hitchhiker/Chop Top seems a gangly kid and Leatherface jiggles in baby fat behind his butcher's apron. Like Norman Bates, whose bedroom displays his childhood toys, Hitchhiker/Chop Top and Leatherface are permanently locked in childhood. Only when Leatherface "discovers" sex in *The Texas Chainsaw Massacre, Part 2* does he lose his appetite for murder. In *Motel Hell* (1980), a sendup of modern horror with special reference to *Psycho* and *The Texas Chainsaw Massacre,* we are repeatedly confronted with a portrait of the dead mother, silently presiding over all manner of cannibalistic and incestuous doings on the part of her adult children.

No less in the grip of boyhood is the killer in *The Eyes of Laura Mars* (1978). The son of a hooker, a hysterical woman gone for days at a time, the killer has up to now put his boyish anger to good use in police work—the film makes much of the irony—but the sight of Laura's violent photographs causes it to be unleashed in full force. The killer in *Hell Night* (1981) is the sole member of his family to survive, as a child, a murderous rampage on the part of his father; the experience condemned him to an afterlife as a murderer himself. In *Halloween* the killer *is* a child, at least in the first instance: Michael, at the age of six, is so enraged at his sister (evidently for her sexual relations with her boyfriend) that he stabs her to death with a kitchen knife. The remainder of the film details his return rampage at the age of twenty-one, and Dr. Loomis, who has overseen the case in the interim, explains that although Michael's body has attained maturity, his mind remains frozen in infantile fury. In *It's Alive* (1974), the killer is literally an infant, evidently made monstrous through intrauterine apprehension of its parents' ambivalence (early in the pregnancy they considered an abortion).

Even killers whose childhood is not immediately at issue and who display no overt gender confusion are often sexually disturbed. The murderer in *A Nightmare on Elm Street* is an undead child molester. The killer in *Slumber Party Massacre* (1982) says to a young woman he is about to assault with a power drill: "Pretty. All of you are very pretty. I love you. Takes a lot of love for a person to do this. You know you want it. You want it. Yes." When she grasps the psychodynamics of the situation in the infamous crotch episode of *Texas Chainsaw, Part 2,* Stretch tries a desperate gambit: "You're really good, you really are good," she repeats; indeed, immediately after ejaculation Leatherface becomes palpably less interested in his saw. The parodic *Motel Hell* spells it out. "His pecker don't work; you see when he takes off his overalls—it's like a shrivelled prune," Bruce says of his killer-brother Vincent when he learns of Terry's plans to marry him. Terry never does see, for on her wedding night he attempts (needless to say) not sex but murder. Actual rape is practically nonexistent in the slasher film, evidently on the premise—as the crotch episode suggests—that violence and sex are not concomitants but alternatives, the one as much a substitute for and a prelude to the other as the teenage horror film is a substitute for and a prelude to the "adult" film (or the meat movie a substitute for and prelude to the skin flick).[26] When Sally under torture (*The Texas Chainsaw Massacre*) cries out, "I'll do anything you want," clearly with sexual intention, her assailants respond only by mimicking her in gross terms; she has profoundly misunderstood the psychology.

Female killers are few and their reasons for killing significantly different from men's. With the possible exception of the murderous mother in *Friday the 13th,* they show no gender confusion. Nor is their motive overtly psychosexual; their anger derives in most cases not from childhood experience but from specific moments in their adult lives in which they have been abandoned or cheated on by men (*Strait-Jacket* [1964], *Play Misty for Me* [1971], *Attack of the 50–Foot Woman* [1958]). (Films like *Mother's Day* [1980], *Ms. 45* [1980], and *I Spit on Your Grave* [1978] belong to the rape-revenge category.) *Friday the 13th* is something of an anomaly. The killer is revealed as a middle-aged woman whose son, Jason, drowned years earlier as a consequence of negligence on the part of the camp counselors. The anomaly is not sustained in the sequels (Parts Two to Six), however. Here the killer is Jason himself, not dead after all but living in a forest hut. The pattern is a familiar one; his motive is vengeance for the death of his mother, his excessive attachment toward whom is manifested in his enshrining of her severed head. Like Stretch in the crotch episode of *Texas Chainsaw, Part 2,* the girl who does final combat with Jason in *Friday the 13th Part 2* (1981) sees the shrine, grasps its significance (she's a psych major), and saves herself by repeating in a commanding tone, "I am your mother, Jason; put down the knife." Jason, for his part, begins to see his mother in the girl (I-camera) and obeys her.

In films of the *Psycho* type (*Dressed to Kill, The Eyes of Laura Mars*), the killer is an insider, a man who functions normally in the action until, at the end, his other self is revealed. *The Texas Chainsaw Massacre* and *Halloween* introduced another sort of killer: one whose only role is that of killer and one whose identity as such is clear from the outset. Norman may have a normal half, but these killers have none. They are emphatic misfits and emphatic outsiders. Michael is an escapee from a distant asylum; Jason subsists in the forest; the Sawyer sons live a bloody subterranean existence outside of town. Nor are they clearly seen. We catch sight of them only in glimpses—few and far between in the beginning, more frequent toward the end. They are usually large, sometimes overweight, and often masked. In short, they may be recognizably human, but only marginally so, just as they are only marginally visible—to their victims and to us, the spectators. In one key aspect, however, the killers are superhuman: their virtual indestructibility. Just as Michael (in *Halloween*) repeatedly rises from blows that would stop a lesser man, so Jason (in the *Friday the 13th* films) survives assault after assault to return in sequel after sequel. Chop Top in *Texas Chainsaw, Part 2,* is so called because of a metal plate implanted in his skull in repair of a head wound sustained in the truck accident in the earlier film. It is worth noting that the killers are normally the fixed elements and the victims the changeable ones in any given series.

Terrible Place. The Terrible Place, most often a house or tunnel in which the victims sooner or later find themselves, is a venerable element of horror. The Bates mansion is just one in a long list of such places—a list that continues, in the modern slasher, with the decaying mansion of *The Texas Chainsaw Massacre,* the abandoned and haunted mansion of *Hell Night,* the house for sale but unsellable in *Halloween* (also a point of departure for such films as *Rosemary's Baby* and *The Amityville Horror* [1979]), and so on. What makes these houses terrible is not just their Victorian decrepitude but the terrible families—murderous, incestuous, cannibalistic—that occupy them. So the Bates mansion enfolds the history of a mother and son locked in a sick attachment, and so the mansion/labyrinth of the *Texas Chainsaw* movies shelters a lawless brood presided over by the decaying corpse of the grandmother. Jason's forest hut (in the *Friday the 13th* sequels) is no mansion, but it houses another mummified mother (or at least her head), with all the usual candles and dreadful paraphernalia. The terrors of the *Hell Night* mansion stem, we learn, from an early owner's massacre of his children. Into such houses unwitting victims wander in film after film, and it is the conventional task of the genre to register in close detail those victims' dawning understanding, as they survey the visible evidence, of the human crimes and perversions that have transpired there. That perception leads directly to the perception of their own immediate peril.

In *The Texas Chainsaw Massacre, Part 2,* house and tunnel elide in a residential labyrinth underground, connected to the world above by channels and culverts. The family is intact, indeed it thrives, but for reasons evidently having to do with the nature of their sausage business has moved residence and slaughterhouse underground. For Stretch, trying desperately to find a way out, it is a ghastly place: dark, full of blind alleys, walls wet with blood. Likewise the second basement of the haunted mansion in *Hell Night:* strewn with decaying bodies and skeletons, lighted with masses of candles. Other tunnels are less familial: the one in *Body Double* that prompts Jack's claustrophobic faint, and the horror-house tunnel in *He Knows You're Alone* (1980) in which the killer lurks. The morgue episode in the latter film, certain of the hospital scenes in *Halloween II* (1981), and the bottom-cellar scenes from various films may be counted as Terrible Tunnels: dark, labyrinthine, exitless, usually underground and palpably damp, and laced with heating ducts and plumbing pipes. In *Hell Night,* as in *Texas Chainsaw, Part 2,* Terrible House (the abandoned mansion) and Terrible Tunnel (the second basement) elide.

The house or tunnel may at first seem a safe haven, but the same walls that promise to keep the killer out quickly become, once the killer penetrates them, the walls that hold the victim in. A phenomenally popular moment in post-1974 slashers is the scene in which the victim locks herself in (a house, room, closet, car) and waits with pounding heart as the killer slashes, hacks, or drills his way in. The action is inevitably seen from the victim's point of view; we stare at the door (wall, car roof) and watch the surface break with first the tip and then the shaft of the weapon. In Hitchcock's *The Birds* (1963), it is the birds' beaks we see penetrating the door. The penetration scene is commonly the film's pivot moment; if the victim has up to now simply fled, she has at this point no choice but to fight back.

Weapons. In the hands of the killer, at least, guns have no place in slasher films. Victims sometimes avail themselves of firearms, but like telephones, fire alarms, elevators, doorbells, and car engines, guns fail in the squeeze. In some basic sense, the emotional terrain of the slasher film is pretechnological. The preferred weapons of the killer are knives, hammers, axes, icepicks, hypodermic needles, red-hot pokers, pitchforks, and the like. Such implements serve well a plot predicated on stealth, the unawareness of later victims that the bodies of their friends are accumulating just yards away. But the use of noisy chainsaws and power drills and the nonuse of such relatively silent means as bow and arrow, spear, catapult, and even swords would seem to suggest that closeness and tactility are also at issue.[27] The sense is clearer if we include marginal examples like *Jaws* (1975) and *The Birds,* as well as related werewolf and vampire genres. Knives and needles, like teeth, beaks, fangs, and claws, are personal, extensions of the body that bring attacker and attacked into primitive, animalistic embrace.[28] In *I Spit on Your Grave,* the heroine forces her rapist at gunpoint to drop his pants, evidently meaning to shoot him in his genitals. But she changes her mind, invites him home for what he all too readily supposes will be a voluntary follow-up of the earlier gang rape. Then, as they sit together in a bubble bath, she castrates him with a knife. If we wondered why she threw away the pistol, now we know: all phallic symbols are not equal, and a hands-on knifing answers a hands-on rape in a way that a shooting, even a shooting preceded by a humiliation, does not.[29]

Beyond that, the slasher evinces a fascination with flesh or meat itself as that which is hidden from view. When the hitchhiker in *The Texas Chainsaw Massacre* slits open his hand for the thrill, the onlookers recoil in horror—all but Franklin, who seems fascinated by the realization that all that lies between the visible, knowable outside of the body and its secret insides is one thin membrane, protected only by a collective taboo against its violation. It is no surprise that the rise of the slasher film is concomitant with the development of special effects that let us see with our own eyes the "opened" body.

Victims. Where once there was one victim, Marion Crane, there are now many: five in *The Texas Chainsaw Massacre,* four in *Halloween,* fourteen in *Friday the 13th Part III* (1982), and so on. (As Schoell puts it, "Other filmmakers figured that the only thing better than one beautiful woman being gruesomely murdered was a whole series of beautiful women being gruesomely murdered."[30]) Where once the victim was an adult, now she is typically in her teens (hence the term "teenie-kill pic"). Where once she was female, now she is both girl and boy, though most often and most conspicuously girl. For all this, her essential quality remains the same. Marion is first and foremost a sexual transgressor. The first scenes show her in a hotel room dressing at the end of a lunch hour, asking her lover to marry her. It is, of course, her wish to be made an honest woman that leads her to abscond with $40,000, an act that leads her to the Bates motel in Fairvale. Here, just as we watched her dress in the opening sequences, we now watch her undress. Moments later, nude in the shower, she dies. A classic publicity poster for *Psycho* shows Janet Leigh with a slightly uncomprehending look on her face sitting on the bed, dressed in a bra and half-slip, looking backward in such a way as to outline her breasts. If it is the task of promotional materials to state in one image the essence of a film, those breasts are what *Psycho* is all about.

In the slasher film, sexual transgressors of both sexes are scheduled for early destruction. The genre is studded with couples trying to find a place beyond purview of parents and employers where they can have sex, and immediately afterwards (or during) being killed. The theme enters the tradition with the Lynda-Bob subplot of *Halloween.* Finding themselves alone in a neighborhood house, Lynda and Bob make hasty use of the master bedroom. Afterwards, Bob goes downstairs for a beer. In the kitchen he is silently dispatched by the killer, Michael, who then covers himself with a sheet (it's Halloween), dons Bob's glasses, and goes upstairs. Supposing the bespectacled ghost in the doorway to be Bob, Lynda jokes, bares her breasts provocatively, and finally, in irritation at "Bob's" stony silence, dials Laurie on the phone. Now the killer advances, strangling her with the telephone cord, so that what Laurie hears on the other end are squeals she takes to be orgasmic. *Halloween II* takes the scene a step farther. Here the victims are a nurse and orderly who have sneaked off for sex in the hospital therapy pool. The watching killer, Michael again, turns up the thermostat and, when the orderly goes to check it, kills him. Michael then approaches the nurse from behind (she thinks it's the orderly) and strokes her neck. Only when he moves his hand toward her bare breast and she turns around and sees him does he kill her.

Other directors are less fond than John Carpenter of the mistaken-identity twist. Denise, the English vamp in *Hell Night,* is simply stabbed to death in bed during Seth's postcoital trip to the bathroom. In *He Knows You're Alone,* the student having the affair with her professor is stabbed to death in bed while the professor is downstairs changing a fuse; the professor himself is stabbed when he returns and discovers the body. The postcoital death scene is a staple of the *Friday the 13th* series. Part Three offers a particularly horrible variant. Invigorated by sex, the boy is struck by a gymnastic impulse and begins walking on his hands; the killer slices down on his crotch with a machete. Unaware of the fate of her boyfriend, the girl crawls into a hammock after her shower; the killer impales her from below.[31] Brian de Palma's *Dressed to Kill* presents the infamous example of the sexually desperate wife, first seen masturbating in her morning shower during the credit sequence, who lets herself be picked up later that day in a museum by a man with whom she has sex first in a taxi and later in his apartment. On leaving his place in the evening, she is suddenly attacked and killed in the elevator. The cause-and-effect relationship between (illicit) sex and death could hardly be more clearly drawn. *All* of the killings in *Cruising* (1980) occur during (homo)sexual encounters; the difference here is that the killer is one of the participants, not a third party.

Killing those who seek or engage in unauthorized sex amounts to a generic imperative of the slasher film. It is an imperative that crosses gender lines, affecting males as well as females. The numbers are not equal, and the scenes not equally charged; but the fact remains that in most slasher films after 1978 (following *Halloween*), men and boys who go after "wrong" sex also die. This is not the only way males die; they also die incidentally, as girls do, when they get in the killer's way or try to stop him, or when they stray into proscribed territory. The victims in *Hell Night,* and in the *Texas Chainsaw Massacre* and *Friday the 13th* films are, respectively, those who trespass in Garth Manor, those who stumble into the environs of the slaughterhouse family, and those who become counselors at a cursed camp, all without regard to sex. Boys die, in short, not because they are boys but because they make mistakes.

Some girls die for the same mistakes. Others, however, and always the main one, die—plot after plot develops the motive—because they are female. Just as Norman Bates's oedipal psychosis is such that only female victims will do, so Michael's sexual anger toward his sister (in the *Halloween* series) drives him to kill her—and after her a string of sister surrogates. In much the same way, the transsexual psychiatrist in *Dressed to Kill* is driven to murder only those women who arouse him and remind him of his hated maleness. In *The Eyes of Laura Mars,* the killer's hatred of his mother drives him to prey on women specifically—and, significantly, one gay male. *He Knows You're Alone* features a killer who in consequence of an earlier jilting preys exclusively on brides-to-be.

But even in films in which males and females are killed in roughly even numbers, the lingering images are inevitably female. The death of a male is always swift; even if the victim grasps what is happening to him, he has no time to react or register terror. He is dispatched and the camera moves on. The death of a male is moreover more likely than the death of a female to be viewed from a distance, or viewed only dimly (because of darkness or fog, for example), or indeed to happen offscreen and not be viewed at all. The murders of women, on the other hand, are filmed at closer range, in more graphic detail, and at greater length. The pair of murders at the therapy pool in *Halloween II* illustrates the standard iconography. We see the orderly killed in two shots: the first at close range in the control room, just before the stabbing, and the second as he is being stabbed, through the vapors in a medium-long shot; the orderly never even sees his assailant. The nurse's death, on the other hand, is shot entirely in medium close-up. The camera studies her face as it registers first her unwitting complicity (as the killer strokes her neck and shoulders from behind), then apprehension, and then, as she faces him, terror; we see the knife plunge into her repeatedly, hear her cries, and watch her blood fill the therapy pool. This cinematic standard has a venerable history, and it remains intact in the slasher film. Indeed, "tits and a scream" are all that is required of actresses auditioning for the role of victim in *Co-Ed Frenzy,* the fictive slasher film whose making constitutes the frame story of *Blow Out* (1981). It is worth noting that none of the actresses auditioning has both in the desired amount and that the director must resort to the use of doubles: one for the tits, one for the screams.

Final Girl. The image of the distressed female most likely to linger in memory is the image of the one who did not die: the survivor, or Final Girl. She is the one who encounters the mutilated bodies of her friends and perceives the full extent of the preceding horror and of her own peril; who is chased, cornered, wounded; whom we see scream, stagger, fall, rise, and scream again. She is abject terror personified. If her friends knew they were about to die only seconds before the event, the Final Girl lives with the knowledge for long minutes or hours. She alone looks death in the face; but she alone also finds the strength either to stay the killer long enough to be rescued (ending A) or to kill him herself (ending B). She is inevitably female. In Schoell's words: "The vast majority of contemporary shockers, whether in the sexist mold or not, feature climaxes in which the women fight back against their attackers— the wandering, humorless psychos who populate these films. They often show more courage and levelheadedness than their cringing male counterparts."[32] Her scene occupies the last ten to twenty minutes (thirty in the case of *The Texas Chainsaw Massacre*) and constitutes the film's emphatic climax.

The sequence first appears in full-blown form (ending A) in *The Texas Chainsaw Massacre* with Sally's spirited self-defense and eventual rescue. Her brother and companions were dispatched suddenly and uncomprehendingly, one by one, but Sally survives the ninth round—long enough to see what has become of her fellows and what is in store for her, long enough to meet and even dine with the whole slaughterhouse family, long enough to undergo all manner of torture (including the ancient grandfather's effort to strike a fatal hammer blow on the temple as they bend her over a washtub), and long enough to bolt and rebolt, be caught and recaught, plead and replead for her life, and eventually escape to the highway. For nearly thirty minutes of screen time—a third of the film—we watch her shriek, run, flinch, jump through windows, and sustain injury and mutilation. Her will to survive is astonishing; in the end, bloody and staggering, she finds the highway, Leatherface and Hitchhiker in pursuit. Just as they bear down on her, a truck comes up and crushes Hitchhiker. Minutes later a pickup driver plucks Sally up and saves her from Leatherface. The final shots show us Leatherface from her point of view (the bed of the pickup): standing on the highway, wounded (having gashed open his abdomen during the truck episode) but upright, waving the chainsaw crazily over his head.

Halloween's Final Girl is Laurie. Her desperate defense is shorter in duration than Sally's but no less fraught with horror. Limping from a knife wound in the leg, she flees to a garden room and breaks in through the window with a rake. Neighbors hear her scream for help but suspect a Halloween prank and shut the blinds. She gets into her own babysitting house—by throwing a potted plant at a second-story window to rouse the children—just as the killer descends. Minutes later he comes through the window and they grapple; she manages to fell him with a knitting needle and grabs his butcher knife— but drops it when he seems dead. As she goes upstairs to the children, the killer rises, takes the knife, and goes after her. She takes refuge in a closet, lashing the two doorknobs together from the inside. As the killer slashes and stabs at the closet door—we see this from her inside perspective—she bends a hanger

Laurie Strode (Jamie Lee Curtis), the terrorized Final Girl in *Halloween* (1978).

into a weapon and, when he breaks the door down, stabs him in the eye. Again thinking him vanquished, she sends the children to the police and sinks down in pain and exhaustion. The killer rises again, but just as he is about to stab her, Dr. Loomis, alerted by the children, rushes in and shoots the killer.

Given the drift in just the four years between *The Texas Chainsaw Massacre* and *Halloween*—from passive to active defense—it is no surprise that the films following *Halloween* present Final Girls who not only fight back but do so with ferocity and even kill the killer on their own, without help from the outside.[33] Valerie in *Slumber Party Massacre* (a film directed by Amy Jones and scripted by Rita Mae Brown) takes a machete-like weapon to the killer, striking off the bit from his drill, severing his hand, and finally impaling him. Alice assaults and decapitates the killer of *Friday the 13th*. Pursued by the killer in *Hell Night,* Marti pries the gate key from the stiff fingers of a corpse to let herself out of the mansion grounds to safety; when the car won't start, she repairs it on the spot; when the car gets stuck in the roadway, she inside and killer on top, she releases it in such a way as to cast the killer on the gate's upper spikes. The grittiest of the Final Girls is Nancy of *A Nightmare on Elm*

Street. Aware in advance that the killer will be paying her a visit, she plans an elaborate defense. When he enters the house, she dares him to come at her, then runs at him in direct attack. As they struggle, he springs the contraptions she has prepared; he is stunned by a swinging sledgehammer, jolted and half incinerated by an electrical charge, and so on. When he rises yet again, she chases him around the house, bashing him with a chair.[34] In *The Texas Chainsaw Massacre, Part 2,* the Final Girl sequence takes mythic measure. Trapped in the underground slaughterhouse, Stretch repeatedly flees, hides, is caught, tortured (at one point forced to don the flayed face of her murdered technician companion), and nearly killed. She escapes with her life chiefly because Leatherface, having developed an affection for her after the crotch episode, is reluctant to ply his chainsaw as the tyrannical Mr. Sawyer commands. Finally Stretch finds her way out, leaving the Texas Ranger to face certain death below, and clambers up a nearby pinnacle, Chop Top in pursuit. At the summit she finds the mummified grandmother, ceremoniously enthroned in an open-air chamber, and next to her a functional chainsaw. She turns the saw on Chop Top, gashing open his abdomen and tossing him off the precipice. The final scene shows her in extreme long shot, in brilliant sunshine, waving the buzzing chainsaw triumphantly overhead. (It is a scene we are invited to compare to the final scene of the first film, in which the wounded Leatherface is shown in long shot at dawn, staggering after the pickup on the highway waving his chainsaw crazily over *his* head.) In the 1974 film the Final Girl, for all her survivor pluck, is, like Red Riding Hood, saved through male agency. In the 1986 sequel, however, there is no male agency; the figure so designated, the Texas Ranger, proves so utterly ineffectual that he cannot save himself, and much less the girl. The comic ineptitude and failure of would-be "woodsmen" is a repeated theme in the later slasher films. In *Slumber Party Massacre,* the role is played by a woman—though a butch one (the girls' basketball coach). She comes to the slumber party's rescue only to fall victim to the drill herself. But to focus on just who brings the killer down, the Final Girl or a male rescuer, is—as the easy alternation between the two patterns would seem to suggest—to miss the point. The last moment of the Final Girl sequence is finally a footnote to what went before, to the quality of the Final Girl's fight, and more generally to the qualities of character that enable her, of all the characters, to survive what has come to seem unsurvivable.

The Final Girl sequence too is prefigured, if only rudimentarily, in *Psycho's* final scenes, in which Lila (Marion's sister) is caught reconnoitering in the Bates mansion and nearly killed. Sam (Marion's boyfriend) detains Norman at the motel while Lila snoops about (taking note of Norman's toys). When she perceives Norman's approach, she flees to the basement. Here she encounters the treated corpse of Mrs. Bates and begins screaming in horror. Norman bursts in and is about to strike when Sam enters and grabs him from behind. Like her generic sisters, then, Lila is the spunky inquirer into the Terrible Place—the one who first grasps, however dimly, the past and present danger, the one who looks death in the face, and one who survives the murderer's last stab.

There the correspondences end, however. The *Psycho* scene turns, after all, on the revelation of Norman's psychotic identity, not on Lila as a character— she enters the film midway and is sketchily drawn—and still less on her self-defense. The Final Girl of the slasher film is presented from the outset as the main character. The practiced viewer distinguishes her from her friends minutes into the film. She is the girl scout, the bookworm, the mechanic. Unlike her girlfriends (and Marion Crane), she is not sexually active. Laurie (*Halloween*) is teased because of her fears about dating, and Marti (*Hell Night*) explains to the boy with whom she finds herself sharing a room that they will have separate beds. Although Stretch (*Texas Chainsaw, Part 2*) is hardly virginal, she is not available, either; early in the film she pointedly turns down a date, and we are given to understand that she is, for the present, unattached and even lonely. So too Stevie of Carpenter's *The Fog*, like Stretch a disk jockey. Divorced mother and a newcomer in town, she is unattached and lonely but declines male attention. The Final Girl is also watchful to the point of paranoia; small signs of danger that her friends ignore she takes in and turns over. Above all, she is intelligent and resourceful in extreme situations. Thus Laurie even at her most desperate, cornered in a closet, has the wit to grab a hanger from the rack and bend it into a weapon; Marti can hot-wire her getaway car, the killer in pursuit; and the psych major of *Friday the 13th Part 2,* on seeing the enshrined head of Mrs. Voorhees, can stop Jason in his tracks by assuming a stridently maternal voice. Finally, although she is always smaller and weaker than the killer, she grapples with him energetically and convincingly.

The Final Girl is boyish, in a word. Just as the killer is not fully masculine, she is not fully feminine—not, in any case, feminine in the ways of her friends. Her smartness, gravity, competence in mechanical and other practical matters, and sexual reluctance set her apart from the other girls and ally her, ironically, with the very boys she fears or rejects, not to speak of the killer himself. Lest we miss the point, it is spelled out in her name: Stevie, Marti, Terry, Laurie, Stretch, Will. Not only the conception of the hero in *Alien* and *Aliens* but also her name, Ripley, owes a clear debt to slasher tradition.

With the introduction of the Final Girl, then, the *Psycho* formula is radically altered. It is not merely a question of enlarging the figure of Lila but of absorbing into her role, in varying degrees, the functions of Arbogast (investigator) and Sam (rescuer) and restructuring the narrative action from beginning to end around her progress in relation to the killer. In other words, *Psycho*'s detective plot, revolving around a revelation, yields in the modern slasher film to a hero plot, revolving around the main character's struggle with and eventual triumph over evil. But for the femaleness, however qualified, of that main character, the story is a standard one of tale and epic.

Shock. One reason that the shower sequence in *Psycho* has "evoked more study, elicited more comment, and generated more shot-for-shot analysis from a technical viewpoint than any other in the history of cinema" is that it suggests so much but shows so little.[35] Of the forty-odd shots in as many seconds that figure the murder, only a single fleeting one actually shows the body being stabbed. The others present us with a rapid-fire concatenation of images of the knife-wielding hand, parts of Marion, parts of the shower, and finally the bloody water as it swirls down the drain. The horror resides less in the actual images than in their summary implication.

Although Hitchcock is hardly the first director to prefer the oblique rendition of physical violence, he may, to judge from current examples, be one of the last. For better or worse, the perfection of special effects has made it possible to show maiming and dismemberment in extraordinarily credible detail. The horror genres are the natural repositories of such effects; what can be done is done, and slashers, at the bottom of the category, do it most and worst. Thus we see a head being stepped on so that the eyes pop out, a face being flayed, a decapitation, a hypodermic needle penetrating an eyeball in close-up, and so on.

With this new explicitness also comes a new tone. If the horror of *Psycho* was taken seriously, the "horror" of the slasher films is of a rather more complicated sort. Audiences express uproarious disgust ("Gross!") as often as they express fear, and it is clear that the makers of slasher films pursue the combination. More particularly, spectators fall silent while the victim is being stalked, scream out at the first stab, and make loud noises of revulsion at the sight of the bloody stump. The rapid alternation between registers—between something like "real" horror on one hand and campy, self-parodying Horror on the other—is by now one of the most conspicuous characteristics of the tradition. In its cultivation of intentionally outrageous excess, the slasher film intersects with the cult film, a genre devoted to such effects. Just what this self-ironizing relation to taboo signifies, beyond a remarkably competent audience, is unclear—it is yet another aspect of the phenomenon that has lain beyond criticism—but for the time being it stands as a defining characteristic of the lower genres of popular culture.

The Body

On the face of it, the relation between the sexes in slasher films could hardly be clearer. The killer is with few exceptions recognizably human and distinctly male; his fury is unmistakably sexual in both roots and expression; his victims are mostly women, often sexually free and always young and beautiful ones. Just how essential this victim is to horror is suggested by her historical durability. If the killer has over time been variously figured as shark, fog, gorilla, birds, and slime, the victim is eternally and prototypically the damsel. Cinema hardly invented the pattern. It has simply given visual expression to the abiding proposition that, in Poe's famous formulation, the death of a beautiful woman is the "most poetical topic in the world." [36] As slasher director Dario Argento puts it, "I like women, especially beautiful ones. If they have a good face and figure, I would much prefer to watch them being murdered than an ugly girl or a man." [37] Brian de Palma elaborates: "Women in peril work better in the suspense genre. It all goes back to the *Perils of Pauline.* . . . If you have a haunted house and you have a woman walking around with a candelabrum, you fear more for her than you would for a husky man." [38] Or Hitchcock, during the filming of *The Birds:* "I always believe in following the advice of the playwright Sardou. He said 'Torture the women!' The trouble today is that we don't torture women enough." [39] What the directors do not say, but show, is that "Pauline" is at her very most effective in a state of undress, borne down upon by a blatantly phallic murderer, even gurgling orgasmically as she dies. The case could be made that the slasher films available at a given neighborhood video rental outlet recommend themselves to censorship under the Dworkin-MacKinnon guidelines at least as readily as the hardcore films the next section over, at which that legislation is aimed; for if some victims are men, the argument goes, most are women, and the women are brutalized in ways that come too close to real life for comfort. But what this line of reasoning does not take into account is the figure of the Final Girl. Because slashers lie for all practical purposes beyond the purview of legitimate criticism and, to the extent that they have been reviewed at all, have been reviewed on an individual basis, the phenomenon of the female victim-hero has scarcely been acknowledged.

It is, of course, "on the face of it" that most of the public discussion of film takes place—from the Dworkin-MacKinnon legislation to Siskel's and Ebert's reviews to our own talks with friends on leaving the movie house. Underlying that discussion is the assumption that the sexes are what they seem; that screen males represent the Male and screen females the Female; that this identification along gender lines authorizes impulses toward sexual violence in males and encourages impulses toward victimization in females. In part because of the massive authority cinema by nature accords the image, even academic film criticism has been slow—slower than literary criticism— to get beyond appearances. Film may not appropriate the mind's eye, but it certainly encroaches on it; the gender characteristics of a screen figure are a visible and audible given for the duration of the film. To the extent that the possibility of cross-gender identification has been entertained, it has been in the direction female-with-male. Thus some critics have wondered whether the female viewer, faced with the screen image of a masochistic/narcissistic female, might not rather elect to "betray her sex and identify with the masculine point of view."[40] The reverse question—whether men might not also, on occasion, elect to betray their sex and identify with screen females—has scarcely been asked, presumably on the assumption that men's interests are well served by the traditional patterns of cinematic representation. Then too there is the matter of the "male gaze." As E. Ann Kaplan sums it up: "Within the film text itself, men gaze at women, who become objects of the gaze; the spectator, in turn, is made to identify with this male gaze, and to objectify the women on the screen; and the camera's original 'gaze' comes into play in the very act of filming."[41] But if it is so that all of us, male and female alike, are by these processes "made to" identify with men and "against" women, how are we then to explain the appeal to a largely male audience of a film genre that features a female victim-hero? The slasher film brings us squarely up against a fundamental question of film analysis: where does the literal end and the figurative begin; how do the two levels interact and what is the significance of the particular interaction; and to which, in arriving at a political judgment (as we are inclined to do in the case of low horror and pornography), do we assign priority?

A figurative or functional analysis of the slasher begins with the processes of point of view and identification. The male viewer seeking a male character, even a vicious one, with whom to identify in a sustained way has little to hang on to in the standard example. On the good side, the only viable candidates are the schoolmates or friends of the girls. They are for the most part marginal, undeveloped characters; more to the point, they tend to die early in the film. If the traditional horror film gave the male spectator a last-minute hero with whom to identify, thereby "indulging his vanity as protector of the helpless female,"[42] the slasher eliminates or attenuates that role beyond any such function; indeed, would-be rescuers are not infrequently blown away for their efforts, leaving the girl to fight her own fight. Policemen, fathers, and sheriffs appear only long enough to demonstrate risible incomprehension and incompetence. On the bad side, there is the killer. The killer is often unseen, or barely glimpsed, during the first part of the film, and what we do see, when we finally get a good look, hardly invites immediate or conscious empathy. He is commonly masked, fat, deformed, or dressed as a woman. Or "he" *is* a woman: woe to the viewer of *Friday the 13th* who identifies with the male killer only to discover, in the film's final sequences, that he was not a man at all but a middle-aged woman. In either case, the killer is himself eventually killed or otherwise evacuated from the narrative. No male character of any stature lives to tell the tale.

The one character of stature who does live to tell the tale is of course female. The Final Girl is introduced at the beginning and is the only character to be developed in any psychological detail. We understand immediately from the attention paid it that hers is the main story line. She is intelligent, watchful, levelheaded; the first character to sense something amiss and the only one to deduce from the accumulating evidence the patterns and extent of the threat; the only one, in other words, whose perspective approaches our own privileged understanding of the situation. We register her horror as she stumbles on the corpses of her friends; her paralysis in the face of death duplicates those moments of the universal nightmare experience on which horror frankly trades. When she downs the killer, we are triumphant. She is by any measure the slasher film's hero. This is not to say that our attachment to her is exclusive and unremitting, only that it adds up and that in the closing sequence it is very close to absolute.

An analysis of the camerawork bears this out. Much is made of the use of the I-camera to represent the killer's point of view. In these passages—they are usually few and brief, but powerful—we see through his eyes and (on the sound track) hear his breathing and heartbeat. His and our vision is partly obscured by bushes or window blinds in the foreground. By such means we are forced, the argument goes, to identify with the killer. In fact, however, the relation between camera point of view and the processes of viewer identification are poorly understood; the fact that Steven Spielberg can stage an attack in *Jaws* from the shark's point of view (underwater, rushing upward toward the swimmer's flailing legs) or Hitchcock an attack in *The Birds* from the bird's-eye perspective (from the sky, as they gather to swoop down on the streets of Bodega Bay) would seem to suggest either that the viewer's identificatory powers are unbelievably elastic or that point-of-view shots can sometimes be pro forma.[43] But let us for the moment accept the equation point of view = identification. We are linked, in this way, with the killer in the early part of the film, usually before we have seen him directly and before we have come to know the Final Girl in any detail. Our closeness to him wanes as our closeness to the Final Girl waxes—a shift underwritten by story line as well as camera position. By the end, point of view is hers: we are in the closet with her, watching with her eyes the knife blade stab through the door; in the room with her as the killer breaks through the window and grabs at her; in the car with her as the killer stabs through the convertible top; and so on. With her, we become if not the killer of the killer then the agent of his expulsion from the narrative vision. If, during the film's course, we shifted our sympathies back and forth and dealt them out to other characters along the way, we belong in the end to the Final Girl; there is no alternative. When Stretch eviscerates Chop Top at the end of *Texas Chainsaw, Part 2,* she is literally the only character left alive, on either side.

Audience response ratifies this design. Observers unanimously stress the readiness of the "live" audience to switch sympathies in midstream, siding now with the killer and now, and finally, with the Final Girl. As Schoell, whose book on shocker films wrestles with its own monster, "the feminists," puts it:

Social critics make much of the fact that male audience members cheer on the misogynous misfits in these movies as they rape, plunder, and murder their screaming, writhing female victims. Since these same critics walk out of the moviehouse in disgust long before the movie is over, they don't realize that these same men cheer on (with renewed enthusiasm, in fact) the heroines, who are often as strong, sexy, and independent as the [earlier] victims, as they blow away the killer with a shotgun or get him between the eyes with a machete. All of these men are said to be identifying with the maniac, but they enjoy *his* death throes the most of all, and applaud the heroine with admiration.[44]

What filmmakers seem to know better than film critics is that gender is less a wall than a permeable membrane.[45]

No one who has read "Red Riding Hood" to a small boy or participated in a viewing of, say, *Deliverance* ([1972], an all-male story that women find as gripping as men) or, more recently, *Alien* and *Aliens,* with whose space-age female Rambo, herself a Final Girl, male viewers seem to engage with ease, can doubt the phenomenon of cross-gender identification.[46] This fluidity of engaged perspective is in keeping with the universal claims of the psychoanalytic model: the threat function and the victim function coexist in the same unconscious, regardless of anatomical sex. But why, if viewers can identify across gender lines and if the root experience of horror is sex blind, are the screen sexes not interchangeable? Why not more and better female killers, and why (in light of the maleness of the majority audience) not Pauls as well as Paulines? The fact that horror film so stubbornly genders the killer male and the principal victim female would seem to suggest that representation itself is at issue—that the sensation of bodily fright derives not exclusively from repressed content, as Freud insisted, but also from the bodily manifestations of that content.

Nor is the gender of the principals as straightforward as it first seems. The killer's phallic purpose, as he thrusts his drill or knife into the trembling bodies of young women, is unmistakeable. At the same time, however, his masculinity is severely qualified: he ranges from the virginal or sexually inert to the transvestite or transsexual, is spiritually divided ("the mother half of his mind"), or even equipped with vulva and vagina. Although the killer of *God Told Me To* (a.k.a. *Demon* [1979]) is represented and taken as a male in the film text, he is revealed, by the doctor who delivered him, to have been sexually ambiguous from birth: "I truly could not tell whether that child was male or female; it was as if the sexual gender had not been determined . . . as if it were being developed." [47] In this respect, slasher killers have much in common with the monsters of classic horror—monsters who, in Linda Williams's formulation, represent not just "an eruption of the normally repressed animal sexual energy of the civilized male" but also the "power and potency of a *non-phallic* sexuality." To the extent that the monster is constructed as feminine, the horror film thus expresses female desire only to show how monstrous it is. [48] The intention is manifest in *Aliens,* in which the Final Girl, Ripley, is pitted in the climactic scene against the most terrifying "alien" of all: an egg-laying Mother.

Nor can we help noticing the "intrauterine" quality of the Terrible Place, dark and often damp, in which the killer lives or lurks and whence he stages his most terrifying attacks. "It often happens," Freud wrote, "that neurotic men declare that they feel there is something uncanny about the female genital organs. This *unheimlich* place, however, is an entrance to the former *Heim* [home] of all human beings, to the place where each one of us lived once upon a time and in the beginning. . . . In this case too then, the *unheimlich* is what once was *heimisch,* familiar; the prefix *'un'* ['un-'] is the token repression." [49] It is the exceptional film that does not mark as significant the moment that the killer leaps out of the dark recesses of a corridor or cavern at the trespassing victim, usually the Final Girl. Long after the other particulars have

Amy (Caitlin O'Heaney) is attacked in the morgue in *He Knows You're Alone* (1980).

faded, the viewer will remember the images of Amy assaulted from the dark halls of a morgue (*He Knows You're Alone*), Sally or Stretch facing dismemberment in the ghastly dining room or underground labyrinth of the slaughterhouse family (the *Texas Chainsaw* films), or Melanie trapped in the attic as the savage birds close in (*The Birds*). In such scenes of convergence the Other is at its bisexual mightiest, the victim at her tiniest, and the component of sadomasochism at its most blatant.

The gender of the Final Girl is likewise compromised from the outset by her masculine interests, her inevitable sexual reluctance (penetration, it seems, constructs the female), her apartness from other girls, sometimes her name. At the level of the cinematic apparatus, her unfemininity is signaled clearly by her exercise of the "active investigating gaze" normally reserved for males and hideously punished in females when they assume it themselves. Tentatively at first and then aggressively, the Final Girl looks *for* the killer, even tracking him to his forest hut or his underground labyrinth, and then *at* him, therewith bringing him, often for the first time, into our vision as well.[50] When, in the final scene, she stops screaming, looks at the killer, and reaches for the knife (sledgehammer, scalpel, gun, machete, hanger, knitting needle, chainsaw), she addresses the killer on his own terms. To the critics' objection that *Halloween* in effect punished female sexuality, director John Carpenter responded: "They [the critics] completely missed the boat there, I think. Because if you turn it around, the one girl who is the most sexually uptight just keeps stabbing this guy with a long knife. She's the most sexually frustrated. She's the one that killed him. Not because she's a virgin, but because all that repressed energy starts coming out. She uses all those phallic symbols on the guy. . . . She and the killer have a certain link: sexual repression."[51] For all its perversity, Carpenter's remark does not underscore the sense of affinity, even recognition, that attends the final encounter. But the "certain link" that puts killer and Final Girl on terms, at least briefly, is more than "sexual repression." It is also a shared masculinity, materialized in "all those phallic symbols"—and it is also a shared femininity, materialized in what comes next (and what Carpenter, perhaps significantly, fails to mention): the castration, literal or symbolic, of the killer at her hands. His eyes may be put out, his hand severed, his body impaled or shot, his belly gashed, or his genitals sliced away or bitten off. The Final Girl has not just manned herself; she specifically unmans an oppressor whose masculinity was in question to begin with. By the time the drama has played itself out, darkness yields to light (often as day breaks) and the close quarters of the barn (closet, elevator, attic, basement) give way to the open expanse of the yard (field, road, lakescape, cliff). With the Final Girl's appropriation of "all those phallic symbols" comes the quelling, the dispelling, of the "uterine" threat as well. Consider again the paradigmatic ending of *Texas Chainsaw, Part 2.* From the underground labyrinth, murky and bloody, in which she faced saw, knife, and hammer, Stretch escapes through a culvert into the open air. She clambers up the jutting rock and with a chainsaw takes her stand. When her last assailant comes at her, she slashes open his lower abdomen—the sexual symbolism is all too clear—and flings him off the cliff. Again, the final scene shows her in extreme long shot, standing on the pinnacle, drenched in sunlight, buzzing chainsaw held overhead.

The tale would indeed seem to be one of sex and parents. The patently erotic threat is easily seen as the materialized projection of the dreamer's (viewer's) own incestuous fears and desires. It is this disabling cathexis to one's parents that must be killed and rekilled in the service of sexual autonomy. When the Final Girl stands at last in the light of day with the knife in her hand, she has delivered herself into the adult world. Carpenter's equation of the Final Girl with the killer has more than a grain of truth. The killers of *Psycho, The Eyes of Laura Mars, Friday the 13th,* Parts Two through Six, and *Cruising,* among others, are explicitly figured as sons in the psychosexual grip of their mothers (or fathers, in the case of *Cruising*). The difference is be-

Slumber Party Massacre (1982): abject terror is gendered feminine.

tween past and present and between failure and success. The Final Girl enacts in the present, and successfully, the parenticidal struggle that the killer himself enacted unsuccessfully in his own past—a past that constitutes the film's backstory. She is what the killer once was; he is what she could become should she fail in her battle for sexual selfhood. "You got a choice, boy," says the tyrannical father of Leatherface in *Texas Chainsaw, Part 2,* "sex or the saw; you never know about sex, but the saw—the saw is the family."

But the tale is no less one of maleness. If the early experience of the oedipal drama can be—is perhaps ideally—enacted in the female form, the achievement of full adulthood requires the assumption and, apparently, brutal employment of the phallus. The helpless child is gendered feminine; the autonomous adult or subject is gendered masculine; the passage from childhood to adulthood entails a shift from feminine to masculine. It is the male killer's tragedy that his incipient femininity is not reversed but completed (castration) and the Final Girl's victory that her incipient masculinity is not thwarted but realized (phallicization). When de Palma says that female frailty is a predicate of the suspense genre, he proposes, in effect, that the lack of the phallus, for Lacan the privileged signifier of the symbolic order of culture, is itself simply horrifying, at least in the mind of the male observer. Where pornography (the argument goes) resolves that lack through a process of fetishization that allows a breast or leg or whole body to stand in for the missing member, the slasher film resolves it either through eliminating the woman (earlier victims) or reconstituting her as masculine (Final Girl). The moment at which the Final Girl is effectively phallicized is the moment that the plot halts and horror ceases. Day breaks, and the community returns to its normal order.

Casting psychoanalytic verities in female form has a venerable cinematic history. Ingmar Bergman has made a career of it, and Woody Allen shows signs of following his lead. One immediate and practical advantage, by now presumably unconscious on the part of makers as well as viewers, has to do with a preestablished cinematic "language" for capturing the moves and moods of the female body and face. The cinematic gaze, we are told, is male, and just as that gaze "knows" how to fetishize the female form in pornography (in a way that it does not "know" how to fetishize the male form),[52] so it "knows," in horror, how to track a woman ascending a staircase in a scary house and how to study her face from an angle above as she first hears the killer's footfall. A set of conventions we now take for granted simply "sees" males and females differently.

To this cinematic habit may be added the broader range of emotional expression traditionally allowed women. Angry displays of force may belong to the male, but crying, cowering, screaming, fainting, trembling, begging for mercy belong to the female. Abject terror, in short, is gendered feminine, and the more concerned a given film with that condition—and it is the essence of modern horror—the more likely the femaleness of the victim. It is no accident that male victims in slasher films are killed swiftly or offscreen, and that prolonged struggles, in which the victim has time to contemplate her imminent destruction, inevitably figure females. Only when one encounters the rare expression of abject terror on the part of a male (as in *I Spit on Your Grave*) does one apprehend the full extent of the cinematic double standard in such matters.[53]

It is also the case that gender displacement can provide a kind of identificatory buffer, an emotional remove, that permits the majority audience to explore taboo subjects in the relative safety of vicariousness. Just as Bergman came to realize that he could explore castration anxiety more freely via depictions of hurt female bodies (witness the genital mutilation of Karin in *Cries and Whispers* [1972]), so the makers of slasher films seem to know that sadomasochistic incest fantasies sit more easily with the male viewer when the visible player is female. It is one thing for that viewer to hear the psychiatrist intone at the end of *Psycho* that Norman as a boy (in the backstory) was abnormally attached to his mother; it would be quite another to see that attachment dramatized in the present, to experience in nightmare form the elaboration of Norman's (the viewer's own) fears and desires. If the former is playable in male form, the latter, it seems, is not.

The Final Girl is, on reflection, a congenial double for the adolescent male. She is feminine enough to act out in a gratifying way, a way unapproved for adult males, the terrors and masochistic pleasures of the underlying fantasy, but not so feminine as to disturb the structures of male competence and sexuality. Her sexual inactivity, in this reading, becomes all but inevitable; the male viewer may be willing to enter into the vicarious experience of defending himself from the possibility of symbolic penetration on the part of the killer, but real vaginal penetration on the diegetic level is evidently more femaleness than he can bear. The question then arises whether the Final Girls of slasher films—Stretch, Stevie, Marti, Will, Terry, Laurie, and Ripley—are not boyish for the same reason that the female "victims" in Victorian flagellation literature—"Georgy," "Willy"—are boyish: because they are transformed males. The transformation, Steven Marcus writes, "is itself both a defense against and a disavowal of the fantasy it is simultaneously expressing"—namely, that a "little *boy* is being beaten . . . by another man."[54] What is represented as male-on-female violence, in short, is figuratively speaking male-on-male sex. For Marcus, the literary picture of flagellation, in which *girls* are beaten, is utterly belied by the descriptions (in *My Secret Life*) of real-life episodes in which the persons being beaten are not girls at all but "gentlemen" dressed in women's clothes ("He had a woman's dress on tucked up to his waist, showing his naked rump and thighs. . . . On his head was a woman's cap tied carefully round his face to hide whiskers") and whipped by prostitutes. Reality, Marcus writes, "puts the literature of flagellation out of the running . . . by showing how that literature is a completely distorted and idealized version of what actually happens."[55] Applied to the slasher film, this logic reads the femaleness of the Final Girl (at least up to the point of her transformation) and indeed of the women victims in general as only apparent, the artifact of heterosexual deflection. It may be through the female body that the body of the audience is sensationalized, but the sensation is an entirely male affair.

At least one director, Hitchcock, explicitly located thrill in the equation victim = audience. So we judge from his marginal jottings in the shooting instructions for the shower scene in *Psycho*: "The slashing. An impression of a knife slashing, as if tearing at the very screen, ripping the film."[56] Not just the body of Marion is to be ruptured, but also the body on the other side of the film and screen: our witnessing body. As Marion is to Norman, the audience of *Psycho* is to Hitchcock; as the audiences of horror film in general are to the directors of those films, female is to male. Hitchcock's "torture the women" then means, simply, torture the audience. De Palma's remarks about female frailty likewise contemplate a male-on-"female" relationship between director and viewer. Cinefantastic horror, in short, succeeds in the production of sensation to more or less the degree that it succeeds in incorporating its spectators as "feminine" and then violating that body—which recoils, shudders, cries out collectively—in ways otherwise imaginable, for males, only in nightmare. The equation is nowhere more plainly put than in David Cronenberg's *Videodrome* (1983). Here the threat is a mind-destroying video signal and the victims television viewers. Despite the (male) hero's efforts to defend his mental (and physical) integrity, a deep, vaginalike gash appears on his lower abdomen. Says the media conspirator as he thrusts a videocassette into the victim's gaping wound, "You must open yourself completely to this."

If the slasher film is "on the face of it" a genre with at least a strong female presence, it is in these figurative readings a thoroughly strong male exercise, one that finally has very little to do with femaleness and very much to do with phallocentrism. Figuratively seen, the Final Girl is a male surrogate in things oedipal, a homoerotic stand-in, the audience incorporate; to the extent she "means" girl at all, it is only for purposes of signifying phallic lack, and even that meaning is nullified in the final scenes. Our initial question—how to square a female victim-hero with a largely male audience—is not so much answered as it is obviated in these readings. The Final Girl is (apparently) female not despite the maleness of the audience, but precisely because of it. The discourse is wholly masculine, and females figure in it only insofar as they "read" some aspect of male experience. To applaud the Final Girl as a feminist development, as some reviews of *Aliens* have done with Ripley, is, in light of her figurative meaning, a particularly grotesque expression of wishful thinking.[57] She is simply an agreed-upon fiction, and the male viewer's use of her as a vehicle for his own sadomasochistic fantasies an act of perhaps timely dishonesty.

For all their immediate appeal, these figurative readings loosen as many ends as they tie together. The audience, we have said, is predominantly male; but what about the women in it? Do we dismiss them as male-identified and account for their experience as an "immasculated" act of collusion with the oppressor?[58] This is a strong judgment to apply to large numbers of women; for while it may be that the audience for slasher films is mainly male, that does not mean that there are not also many female viewers who actively like such films, and of course there are also women, however few, who script, direct, and produce them. These facts alone oblige us at least to consider the possibility that female fans find a meaning in the text and image of these films that is less inimical to their own interests than the figurative analysis would have us believe. Or should we conclude that males and females read these films differently in some fundamental sense? Do females respond to the text (the literal) and males the subtext (the figurative)?[59]

Some such notion of differential understanding underlies the homoerotic reading. The silent presupposition of that reading is that male identification with the female as female cannot be, and that the male viewer/reader who adjoins feminine experience does so only by homosexual conversion. But does female identification with male experience then similarly indicate a lesbian conversion? Or are the processes of patriarchy so one-way that the female can identify with the male directly, but the male can identify with the female only by transsexualizing her? Does the Final Girl mean "girl" to her female viewers and "boy" to her male viewers? If her masculine features qualify her as a transformed boy, do not the feminine features of the killer qualify him as a transformed woman (in which case the homoerotic reading can be maintained only by defining that "woman" as phallic and retransforming her into a male)? Striking though it is, the analogy between the Victorian flagellation story's Georgy and the slasher film's Stretch falters at the moment that Stretch turns on her assailant and unmans him. Are we to suppose that a homoerotic beating fantasy suddenly yields to what folklorists call a "lack-liquidated" fantasy? Further, is it simple coincidence that this combination tale—trials, then triumph—bears such a striking resemblance to the classic (male) hero story? Does the standard hero story featuring an anatomical female "mean" differently from one featuring an anatomical male?

As Marcus perceived, the relationship between the Georgy stories of flagellation literature and the real-life anecdote of the Victorian gentleman is a marvelously telling one. In his view, the maleness of the latter must prove the essential or functional maleness of the former. What his analysis does not come to full grips with, however, is the clothing the gentleman wears—not that of a child, as Marcus's "childish" reading of the scene contemplates, but explicitly that of a woman.[60] These women's clothes can of course be understood, within the terms of the homoerotic interpretation, as a last-ditch effort on the part of the gentleman to dissociate himself from the (incestuous) homosexuality implicit in his favored sexual practice. But can they not just as well, and far more economically, be explained as part and parcel of a fantasy of literal femaleness? By the same token, cannot the femaleness of the gentleman's literary representatives—the girls of the flagellation stories—be understood as the obvious, even necessary, extension of the man's dress and cap? The same dress and cap, I suggest, haunt the margins of the slasher film. This is not to deny the deflective convenience, for the male spectator (and film-maker), of a female victim-hero in a context so fraught with taboo; it is only to suggest that the femaleness of that character is also conditioned by a kind of imaginative curiosity about the feminine in and of itself.

So too the psychoanalytic case. These films do indeed seem to pit the child in a struggle, at once terrifying and attractive, with the parental Other, and it is a rare example that does not directly thematize parent-child relations. But if Freud stressed the maternal source of the *unheimlich,* the Other of our films is decidedly androgynous: female/feminine in aspects of character and place (the "intrauterine" locale) but male in anatomy. Conventional logic may interpret the killer as the phallic mother of the transformed boy (the Final Girl), but the text itself does not compel such a reading. On the contrary, the text at every level presents us with hermaphroditic constructions—constructions that draw attention to themselves and demand to be taken on their own terms.

For if we define the Final Girl as nothing more than a figurative male, what do we then make of the context of the spectacular gender play in which she is emphatically situated? In his essay on the uncanny, Freud rejected out of hand Jentsch's theory that the experience of horror proceeds from intellectual uncertainty (curiosity?)—feelings of confusion, induced by an author or a coincidence, about who, what, and where one is.[61] One wonders, however, whether Freud would have been quite so dismissive if, instead of the mixed materials he used as evidence, he were presented with a coherent story corpus—forty slashers, say—in which the themes of incest and separation were relentlessly played out by a female character, and further in which gender identity was repeatedly thematized as an issue in and of itself. For although the factors we have considered thus far—the conventions of the male gaze, the feminine constitution of abject terror, the value for the male viewer of emotional distance from the taboos in question, the special horror that may inhere, for the male audience, in phallic lack, the homoerotic deflection—go a long way in explaining why it is we have Pauline rather than Paul as our victim-hero, they do not finally account for our strong sense that gender is simply being played with, and that part of the thrill lies precisely in the resulting "intellectual uncertainty" of sexual identity.

The "play of pronoun function" that underlies and defines the cinefantastic is nowhere more richly manifested than in the slasher; if the genre has an aesthetic base, it is exactly that of a visual identity game. Consider, for example, the by now standard habit of letting us view the action in the first person long before revealing who or what the first person *is.* In the opening sequence of *Halloween,* "we" are belatedly revealed to ourselves, after committing a murder in the cinematic first person, as a six-year-old boy. The surprise is often within gender, but it is also, in a striking number of cases, across gender. Again, *Friday the 13th,* in which "we" stalk and kill a number of teenagers over the course of an hour of screen time without even knowing who "we" are; we are invited, by conventional expectation and by glimpses of "our" own bodily parts—a heavily booted foot, a roughly gloved hand—to suppose that "we" are male, but "we" are revealed, at film's end, as a woman. If this is the most dramatic case of pulling out the gender rug, it is by no means the only one. In *Dressed to Kill,* we are led to believe, again by means of glimpses, that "we" are female—only to discover, in the denouement, that "we" are a male in drag. In *Psycho,* the dame we glimpse holding the knife with a "visible virility quite obscene in an old lady" is later revealed, after additional gender teasing, to be Norman in his mother's clothes.[62] *Psycho II* (1983) plays much the same game. *Cruising* (in which, not accidentally, transvestites play a prominent role) adjusts the terms along heterosexual/homosexual lines. The tease here is whether the originally straight detective assigned to the string of murders in a gay community does or does not succumb to his assumed homosexual identity; the camerawork leaves us increasingly uncertain as to his (our) sexual inclinations, not to speak of his (our) complicity in the crimes. Even at film's end we are not sure who "we" were during several of the first-person sequences.[63]

The gender-identity game, in short, is too patterned and too pervasive in the slasher film to be dismissed as supervenient. It would seem instead to be an integral element of the particular brand of bodily sensation in which the genre trades. Nor is it exclusive to horror. It is directly thematized in comic terms in the recent "gender benders" *Tootsie* ([1982], in which a man passes himself off as a woman) and *All of Me* ([1984], in which a woman is literally introjected into a man and affects his speech, movement, and thought). It is also directly thematized, in the form of bisexual and androgynous figures and relations, in such cult films as *Pink Flamingos* (1973) and *The Rocky Horror Picture Show* (1975). (Some version of it is indeed enacted every few minutes on MTV.) It is further thematized (predictably enough, given their bodily concerns) in such pornographic films as *Every Woman Has a Fantasy* (1954), in which a man, in order to gain access to a women's group in which sexual fantasies are discussed, dresses and presents himself as a woman. (The degree to which "male" pornography in general relies for its effect on cross-gender identification remains an open question; the proposition makes a certain sense of the obligatory lesbian sequences and the phenomenal success of *Behind the Green Door* (1972), to pick just two examples.[64]) All of these films, and others like them, seem to be asking some version of the question: what would it be like to be, or to seem to be, if only temporarily, a woman? Taking exception to the reception of *Tootsie* as a feminist film, Elaine Showalter argues that the success of "Dorothy Michaels" (the Dustin Hoffman character), as far as both plot and audience are concerned, lies in the veiling of masculine power in feminine costume. *Tootsie*'s cross-dressing, she writes,

> is a way of promoting the notion of masculine power while masking it. In psychoanalytic theory, the male transvestite is not a powerless man; according to the psychiatrist Robert Stoller, in *Sex and Gender,* he is a "phallic woman" who can tell himself that "he is, or with practice will become, a better woman than a biological female if he chooses to do so." When it is safe or necessary, the transvestite "gets great pleasure in revealing that he is a male-woman. . . . The pleasure in tricking the unsuspecting into thinking he is a woman, and then revealing his maleness (e.g., by suddenly dropping his voice) is not so much erotic as it is proof that there is such a thing as a woman with a penis." Dorothy's effectiveness is the literal equivalent of speaking softly and carrying a big stick.[65]

By the same literalistic token, then, Stretch's success must lie in the fact that in the end, at least, she "speaks loudly" *even though* she carries *no* "stick." Just as "Dorothy's" voice slips serve to remind us that her character really is male, so the Final Girl's "tits and scream" serve more or less continuously to remind us that she really is female—even as, and despite the fact that, she in the end acquits herself "like a man."[66] Her chainsaw is thus what "Dorothy's" skirt is: a figuration of what she *does* and what she *seems,* as opposed to—and the films turn on the opposition—what she *is.* The idea that appearance and behavior do not necessarily indicate sex—indeed, can misindicate sex—is predicated on the understanding that sex is one thing and gender another; in practice, that sex is life, a less-than-interesting given, but that gender is theater. Whatever else it may be, Stretch's waving of the chainsaw is a moment of high drag. Its purpose is not to make us forget that she is a girl but to thrust that fact on us. The moment, it is probably fair to say, is also one that openly mocks the literary/cinematic conventions of symbolic representation.

It may be just this theatricalization of gender that makes possible the willingness of the male viewer to submit himself to a brand of spectator experience that Hitchcock designated as "feminine" in 1960 and that has become only more so since then. In classic horror, the "feminization" of the audience is intermittent and ceases early. Our relationship with Marion's body in *Psycho* halts abruptly at the moment of its greatest intensity (slashing, ripping, tearing). The considerable remainder of the film distributes our bruised sympathies among several lesser figures, male and female, in such a way and at such length as to ameliorate the Marion experience and leave us, in the end, more or less recuperated in our (presumed) masculinity. Like Marion, the Final Girl is the designated victim, the incorporation of the audience, the slashing, ripping, and tearing of whose body will cause us to flinch and scream out in our seats. But unlike Marion, she does not die. If *Psycho,* like other classic horror films, solves the femininity problem by obliterating the female and replacing her with representatives of the masculine order (mostly but not inevitably males), the modern slasher solves it by regendering the woman. We are, as an audience, in the end "masculinized" by and through the very figure by and through whom we were earlier "feminized." The same body does for both, and that body is female.

The last point is the crucial one: the same *female* body does for both. The Final Girl (1) undergoes agonizing trials and (2) virtually or actually destroys the antagonist and saves herself. By the lights of folk tradition, she is not a heroine, for whom phase 1 consists in being saved by someone else, but a hero, who rises to the occasion and defeats the adversary with his own wit and hands. Phase 1 of the story sits well on the female; it is the heart of heroine stories in general (Red Riding Hood, Pauline), and in some figurative sense, in ways we have elaborated in some detail, it is gendered feminine even when played by a male. Odysseus's position, trapped in the cave of the Cyclops, is after all not so different from Pauline's position tied to the tracks or Sally's trapped in the dining room of the slaughterhouse family. The decisive moment, as far as the fixing of gender is concerned, lies in what happens next: those who save themselves are male, and those who are saved by others are female. No matter how "feminine" his experience in phase 1, the traditional hero, if he rises against his adversary and saves himself in phase 2, will be male.

What is remarkable about the slasher film is that it comes close to reversing the priorities. Presumably for the various functional or figurative reasons we have considered in this essay, phase 1 wants a female: on that point all slashers from *Psycho* on are agreed. Abject fear is still gendered feminine, and the taboo anxieties in which slashers trade are still explored more easily via Pauline than Paul. The slippage comes in phase 2. As if in mute deference to a cultural imperative, slasher films from the seventies bring in a last-minute male, even when he is rendered supernumerary by the Final Girl's sturdy defense. By 1980, however, the male rescuer is either dismissably marginal or dispensed with altogether; not a few films have him rush to the rescue only to be hacked to bits, leaving the Final Girl to save herself after all. At the moment that the Final Girl becomes her own savior, she becomes a hero; and the moment that she becomes a hero is the moment that the male viewer gives up the last pretense of male identification. Abject terror may still be gendered feminine, but the willingness of one immensely popular current genre to re-represent the hero as an anatomical female would seem to suggest that at least one of the traditional marks of heroism, triumphant self-rescue, is no longer strictly gendered masculine.

So too the cinematic apparatus. The classic split between "spectacle and narrative," which "supposes the man's role as the active one of forwarding the story, making things happen," is at least unsettled in the slasher film.[67] When the Final Girl (in films like *Hell Night, Texas Chainsaw, Part 2,* and even *Splatter University* [1985]) assumes the "active investigating gaze," she exactly reverses the look, making a spectacle of the killer and a spectator of herself. Again, it is through the killer's eyes (I-camera) that we saw the Final Girl at the beginning of the film, and through the Final Girl's eyes that we see the killer, often for the first time with any clarity, toward the end. The gaze becomes, at least for a while, female. More to the point, the female exercise of scopic control results not in her annihilation, in the manner of classic cinema, but in her triumph; indeed, her triumph *depends* on her assumption of the gaze. It is no surprise, in light of these developments, that the Final Girl should show signs of boyishness. Her symbolic phallicization, in the last scenes, may or may not proceed at root from the horror of lack on the part of audience and maker. But it certainly proceeds from the need to bring her in line with the epic laws of western narrative tradition—the very unanimity of which bears witness to the historical importance, in popular culture, of the literal representation of heroism in male form—and it proceeds no less from the need to render the reallocated gaze intelligible to an audience conditioned by the dominant cinematic apparatus.

It is worth noting that the higher genres of horror have for the most part resisted such developments. The idea of a female who outsmarts, much less outfights—or outgazes—her assailant is unthinkable in the films of de Palma and Hitchcock. Although the slasher film's victims may be sexual teases, they are not in addition simple-minded, scheming, physically incompetent, and morally deficient in the manner of these filmmakers' female victims. And however revolting their special effects and sexualized their violence, few slasher murders approach the level of voluptuous sadism that attends the destruction of women in de Palma's films. For reasons on which we can only speculate, femininity is more conventionally elaborated and inexorably punished, and in an emphatically masculine environment, in the higher forms—the forms that *are* written up, and not by Joe Bob Briggs.

That the slasher film speaks deeply and obsessively to male anxieties and desires seems clear—if nothing else from the maleness of the majority audience. And yet these are texts in which the categories masculine and feminine, traditionally embodied in male and female, are collapsed into one and the same character—a character who is anatomically female and one whose point of view the spectator is unambiguously invited, by the usual set of literary-structural and cinematic conventions, to share. The willingness and even eagerness (so we judge from these films' enormous popularity) of the male viewer to throw in his emotional lot, if only temporarily, with not only a woman but a woman in fear and pain, at least in the first instance, would seem to suggest that he has a vicarious stake in that fear and pain. If the act of horror spectatorship is itself registered as a "feminine" experience—that the shock effects induce bodily sensations in the viewer answering the fear and pain of the screen victim—the charge of masochism is underlined. This is not to say that the male viewer does not also have a stake in the sadistic side; narrative structure, cinematic procedures, and audience response all indicate that he shifts back and forth with ease. It is only to suggest that in the Final Girl sequence his empathy with what the films define as the female posture is fully engaged, and further, because this sequence is inevitably the central one in any given film, that the viewing experience hinges on the emotional assumption of the feminine posture. Kaja Silverman takes it a step farther: "I will hazard the generalization that it is always the victim—the figure who occupies the passive position—who is really the focus of attention, and whose subjugation the subject (whether male or female) experiences as a pleasurable repetition from his/her own story," she writes. "Indeed, I would go so far as to say that the fascination of the sadistic point of view is merely that it provides the best vantage point from which to watch the masochistic story unfold." [68]

The slasher is hardly the first genre in the literary and visual arts to invite identification with the female; one cannot help wondering more generally whether the historical maintenance of images of women in fear and pain does not have more to do with male vicarism than is commonly acknowledged. What distinguishes the slasher, however, is the absence or untenability of alternative perspectives and hence the exposed quality of the invitation. As a survey of the tradition shows, this has not always been the case. The stages of the Final Girl's evolution—her piecemeal absorption of functions previously represented in males—can be located in the years following 1978. The fact that the typical patrons of these films are the sons of marriages contracted in the 1960s or even early seventies leads us to speculate that the dire claims of that era—that the women's movement, the entry of women into the workplace, and the rise of divorce and woman-headed families would yield massive gender confusion in the next generation—were not entirely wrong. We may prefer, in the eighties, to speak of the cult of androgyny, but the point is roughly the same. The fact that we have in the killer a feminine male and in the main character a masculine female—parent and Everyteen, respectively—would seem, especially in the latter case, to suggest a loosening of the categories, or at least of the equation sex = gender. It is not that these films show us gender and sex in free variation; it is that they fix on the irregular combinations, of which the combination masculine female repeatedly prevails over the combination feminine male. The fact that masculine males (boyfriends, fathers, would-be rescuers) are regularly dismissed through ridicule or death or both would seem to suggest that it is not masculinity per se that is being privileged, but masculinity in conjunction with a female body— indeed, as the term "victim-hero" contemplates, masculinity in conjunction with femininity. For if "masculine" describes the Final Girl some of the time and in some of her more theatrical moments, it does not do justice to the sense of her character as a whole. She alternates between registers from the outset; before her final struggle she endures the deepest throes of "femininity"; and even during that final struggle she is now weak and now strong, now flees the killer and now charges him, now stabs and is stabbed, now cries out in fear and now shouts in anger. She is a physical female and a characterological androgyne: like her name, not masculine but either/or, both, ambiguous.[69]

Robin Wood speaks of the sense that horror, for him the by-product of cultural crisis and disintegration, is "currently the most important of all American [film] genres and perhaps the most progressive, even in its overt nihilism."[70] Likewise Vale and Juno say of the "incredibly strange films," mostly low-budget horror, that their volume surveys: "They often present unpopular—even radical—views addressing the social, political, racial, or sexual inequities, hypocrisy in religion or government."[71] And Tania Modleski rests her case against the standard critique of mass culture (stemming from the Frankfurt School) squarely on the evidence of the slasher, which does *not* propose a spurious harmony; does *not* promote the "specious good" (but indeed often exposes and attacks it); does *not* ply the mechanisms of identification, narrative continuity, and closure to provide the sort of narrative pleasure constitutive of the dominant ideology.[72] One is deeply reluctant to make progressive claims for a body of cinema as spectacularly nasty toward women as the slasher film is, but the fact is that the slasher does, in its own perverse way and for better or worse, constitute a visible adjustment in the terms of gender representation. That it is an adjustment largely on the male side, appearing at the farthest possible remove from the quarters of theory and showing signs of trickling upwards, is of no small interest.

Notes

I owe a special debt of gratitude to James Cunniff and Lynn Hunt for criticism and encourage-ment. Particular thanks to James (not Lynn) for sitting with me through not a few of these movies.

1. Morris Dickstein, "The Aesthetics of Fright," *American Film* 5, no. 10 (September 1980): 34.

2. "Will Rogers never met a man he didn't like, and I can truly say the same about the cinema," Harvey R. Greenberg says in his paean to horror, *The Movies on Your Mind* (New York: Dutton/Saturday Review Press, 1975); yet his claim does not extend to the "plethora of execrable imitations [of *Psycho*] that debased cinema" (p. 137).

3. William Schoell, *Stay Out of the Shower: Twenty-Five Years of Shocker Films Beginning with Psycho* (New York: Dembner, 1985).

4. "Joe Bob Briggs" was evidently invented as a solution to the *Dallas Time Herald's* problem of "how to cover trashy movies." See Calvin Trillin's "American Chronicles: The Life and Times of Joe Bob Briggs, So Far," *New Yorker,* December 22, 1986, pp. 73–88.

5. Lew Brighton, "Saturn in Retrograde; or, The Texas Jump Cut," *Film Journal* 2, no. 4 (1975): 25.

6. Stephen Koch, "Fashions in Pornography: Murder as Cinematic Chic," *Harper's,* November 1976, pp. 108–109.

7. Robin Wood, "Return of the Repressed," *Film Comment* 14, no. 4 (July–August 1978): 30.

8. Robin Wood, "Beauty Bests the Beast," *American Film* 8, no. 10 (September 1983): 63.

9. Dickstein, "Aesthetics of Fright," p. 34.

10. Sigmund Freud, "The Uncanny," in *Standard Edition of the Complete Psychological Works of Sigmund Freud,* ed. and trans. James Strachey (London: Hogarth Press, 1964), 17: 244.

11. Steven Marcus, *The Other Victorians: A Study of Sexuality and Pornography in Mid-Nineteenth-Century England* (New York: Basic Books, 1964), p. 278.

12. William Castle, *Step Right Up! I'm Gonna Scare the Pants Off America* (New York: Pharos Books, 1992), p. 262.

13. Given the number of permutations, it is no surprise that new strategies keep emerging. Only a few years ago, a director hit upon the idea of rendering the point of view of an infant through the use of an I-camera at floor level with a double-vision image (Larry Cohen, *It's Alive*). Nearly a century after technology provided a radically different means of telling a story, filmmakers are still uncovering the possibilities.

14. Mick Martin and Marsha Porter, *Video Movie Guide: 1987* (New York: Ballantine, 1987), p. 690. Wood, "Beauty," p. 65, notes that the first-person camera also serves to preserve the secret of the killer's identity for a final surprise—crucial to many films—but adds: "The sense of indeterminate, unidentified, possibly supernatural or superhuman Menace feeds the spectator's fantasy of power, facilitating a direct spectator-camera identification by keeping the intermediary character, while signified to be present, as vaguely defined as possible." Brian de Palma's *Blow Out* opens with a parody of just this cinematic habit.

15. On this widely discussed topic, see Kaja Silverman, *The Subject of Semiotics* (New York: Oxford University Press, 1983), pp. 194–236; and Lesley Stern, "Point of View: The Blind Spot," *Film Reader*, no. 4 (1979): 214–236.

16. In this essay I have used the term "identification" vaguely and generally to refer both to primary and secondary processes. See Mary Ann Doane, "Misrecognition and Identity," *Ciné-Tracts*, no. 11 (1980): 25–32; and Christian Metz, "The Imaginary Signifier," *The Imaginary Signifier: Psychoanalysis and the Cinema* (Bloomington: Indiana University Press, 1982).

17. Mark Nash, "*Vampyr* and the Fantastic," *Screen* 17, no. 3 (Autumn 1976): 37. Nash coins the term "cinefantastic" to refer to this play.

18. Rosemary Jackson, *Fantasy: The Literature of Subversion* (London and New York: Methuen, 1981), p. 31.

19. As Dickstein puts it, "The 'art' of horror film is a ludicrous notion since horror, even at its most commercially exploitative, is genuinely subcultural like the wild child that can never be tamed, or the half-human mutant who appeals to our secret fascination with deformity and the grotesque." "Aesthetics," p. 34.

20. James B. Twitchell, *Dreadful Pleasures: An Anatomy of Modern Horror* (New York: Oxford University Press, 1985), p. 84.

21. Donald Spoto, *The Dark Side of Genius: The Life of Alfred Hitchcock* (Boston and Toronto: Little, Brown, 1983), p. 421.

22. Wood, "Return of the Repressed," p. 26. In Wes Craven's *A Nightmare on Elm Street* (1985), it is the nightmare itself, shared by the teenagers who live on Elm Street, that is fatal. One by one they are killed by the murderer of their collective dream. The one girl who survives does so by first refusing to sleep and then, at the same time that she acknowledges her parents' inadequacies, by conquering the feelings that prompt the deadly nightmare. See, on the topic of dream/horror, Dennis L. White, "The Poetics of Horror," *Cinema Journal* 10, no. 2 (Spring 1971): 1–18. Reprinted in *Film Genre: Theory and Criticism*, ed. Barry K. Grant (Metuchen, N.J.: Scarecrow Press, 1977), pp. 124–144.

23. It is not just the profit margin that fuels the production of low horror. It is also the fact that, thanks to the irrelevance of production values, the initial stake is within the means of a small group of investors. Low horror is thus for all practical purposes the only way an independent filmmaker can break into the market. Add to this the filmmaker's unusual degree of control over the product, and one begins to understand why it is that low horror engages the talents of such people as Stephanie Rothman, George Romero, Wes Craven, and Larry Cohen. As V. Vale and Andrea Juno put it, "The value of low-budget films is: they can be transcendent expressions of a single person's individual vision and quirky originality. When a corporation decides to invest $20 million in a film, a chain of command regulates each step, and no person is allowed free rein. Meetings with lawyers, accountants, and corporate boards are what films in Hollywood are all about." *Incredibly Strange Films*, ed. V. Vale and Andrea Juno (San Francisco: ReSearch #10, 1986), p. 5.

24. Despite the film industry's interest in demographics, there is no in-depth study of the composition of the slasher-film audience. Twitchell, *Dreadful Pleasures*, pp. 69–72 and 306–307, relies on personal observation and the reports of critics, which are re-

markably consistent over time and from place to place; my own observations concur. The audience is mostly between the ages of twelve and twenty, disproportionately male. Some critics remark on a contingent of older men who sit separately and who, in Twitchell's view, are there "not to be frightened, but to participate" specifically in the "stab-at-female" episodes. Roger Ebert and Gene Siskel corroborate the observation.

25. The development of the human-sausage theme is typical of the back-and-forth borrowing in low horror. *The Texas Chainsaw Massacre* hints at it; *Motel Hell* turns it into an industry ("Farmer Vincent's Smoked Meats: This is it!" proclaims a local billboard); and *The Texas Chainsaw Massacre, Part 2* expands it to a statewide chili-tasting contest.

26. "The release of sexuality in the horror film is always presented as perverted, monstrous, and excessive, both the perversion and the excess being the logical outcome of repressing. Nowhere is this carried further than in *The Texas Chainsaw Massacre*. Here sexuality is totally perverted from its functions, into sadism, violence, and cannibalism. It is striking that there is no suggestion anywhere that Sally is the object of an overtly sexual threat; she is to be tormented, killed, dismembered, and eaten, but not raped." Wood, "Return of the Repressed," p. 31.

27. With some exceptions—for example, the speargun used in the sixth killing in *Friday the 13th, Part III*.

28. Stuart Kaminsky, *American Film Genres: Approaches to a Critical Theory of Popular Film* (Dayton, Ohio: Pflaum, 1974), p. 107.

29. The shower sequence in *Psycho* is probably the most echoed scene in all of film history. The bathtub scene in *I Spit on Your Grave* (not properly speaking a slasher, though with a number of generic affinities) is to my knowledge the only effort to reverse the terms.

30. Schoell, *Stay Out of the Shower*, p. 35. It may be argued that *Blood Feast* (1963), in which a lame Egyptian caterer slaughters one woman after another for their bodily parts (all in the service of Ishtar), provides the serial-murder model.

31. This theme too is spoofed in *Motel Hell*. Farmer Vincent's victims are two hookers, a kinky couple looking for same (he puts them in room 1 of the motel), and Terry and her boyfriend Bo, out for kicks on a motorcycle. When Terry (allowed to survive) wonders aloud why someone would try to kill them, Farmer Vincent answers her by asking pointedly whether they were married. "No," she says, in a tone of resignation, as if accepting the logic.

32. "Scenes in which women whimper helplessly and do nothing to defend themselves are ridiculed by the audience, who find it hard to believe that anyone—male or female—would simply allow someone to kill them with nary a protest." Schoell, *Stay Out of the Shower*, pp. 55–56.

33. *Splatter University* (1984) is a disturbing exception. Professor Julie Parker is clearly established as a Final Girl from the outset and then killed just after the beginning of what we are led to believe will be the Final Girl sequence (she kicks the killer, a psychotic priest-scholar who keeps his knife sheathed in a crucifix, in the groin, runs for the elevator—and then is trapped and stabbed to death). So meticulously are the conventions observed, and then so grossly violated, that we can only assume sadistic intentionality. This is a film in which (with the exception of an asylum orderly in the preface) only females are killed and in highly sexual circumstances.

34. This film is complicated by the fact that the action is envisaged as a living dream. Nancy finally kills the killer by killing her part of the collective nightmare. See note 22 above.

35. Spoto, *Dark Side of Genius,* p. 454. See also William Rothman, *Hitchcock: The Murderous Gaze* (Cambridge: Harvard University Press, 1982), pp. 246–341.

36. Edgar Allan Poe, "The Philosophy of Composition," *Selected Prose, Poetry and Eureka* (San Francisco: Rhinehart Press, 1950), p. 425.

37. Quoted in Schoell, *Stay Out of the Shower,* p. 56.

38. Quoted in ibid., p. 41.

39. Spoto, *Dark Side of Genius,* p. 483.

40. Silvia Bovenschen, "Is There a Feminine Aesthetic?" *New German Critique* 10 (Winter 1977): 114. See also Doane, "Misrecognition and Identity."

41. E. Ann Kaplan, *Women and Film: Both Sides of the Camera* (New York and London: Methuen, 1983), p. 15. The discussion of the gendered "gaze" is lively and extensive. See, above all, Laura Mulvey, "Visual Pleasure and Narrative Cinema," *Screen* 16, no. 3 (Autumn 1975): 6–18; also see Christine Gledhill, "Recent Developments in Feminist Criticism," *Quarterly Review of Film Studies* 3, no. 4 (Fall 1978): 458–493.

42. Wood, "Beauty Bests the Beast," p. 64.

43. The locus classicus in this connection is the view-from-the-coffin shot in Carl Dreyer's *Vampyr* (1932), in which the I-camera sees through the eyes of a dead man. See Nash, "*Vampyr* and the Fantastic," esp. pp. 32–33. The 1986 remake of *The Little Shop of Horrors* (originally a low-budget horror film, made the same year as *Psycho* in two days) lets us see the dentist from the proximate point of view of the patient's tonsils.

44. Two points in this paragraph deserve emending. One is the suggestion that rape is common in these films; it is in fact virtually absent, by definition (see note 26 above). The other is the characterization of the Final Girl as "sexy." She may be attractive (though typically less so than her friends), but she is with few exceptions sexually inactive. For a detailed analysis of point-of-view manipulation, together with a psychoanalytic interpretation of the dynamic, see Steve Neale, "*Halloween:* Suspense, Aggression, and the Look," *Framework* 14 (1981): 25–29; reprinted in *Planks of Reason: Essays on the Horror Film,* ed. Barry Keith Grant (Metuchen, N.J.: Scarecrow Press, 1984), pp. 331–345.

45. Wood is struck by the willingness of the teenage audience to identify "against" itself, with the forces of the enemy of youth: "Watching [*The Texas Chainsaw Massacre*] recently with a large, half-stoned youth audience, who cheered and applauded every one of Leatherface's outrages against their representatives on the screen, was a terrifying experience" ("Return of the Repressed," p. 32).

46. "I really appreciate the way audiences respond," Gail Anne Hurd, producer of *Aliens,* is reported to have said in the *San Francisco Examiner Datebook,* August 10, 1986, p. 19. "They buy it. We don't get people, even rednecks, leaving the theatre saying, 'That was stupid. No woman would do that.' You don't have to be a liberal ERA supporter to root for Ripley." *Time,* July 28, 1986, p. 56, suggests that Ripley's maternal impulses (she squares off against the worst aliens of all in her quest to save a little girl) give the audience "a much stronger rooting interest in Ripley, and that gives the picture resonances unusual in a popcorn epic."

47. "When she [the mother] referred to the infant as a male, I just went along with it. Wonder how that child turned out—male, female, or something else entirely?" The birth is understood to be parthenogenetic, and the bisexual child, literally equipped with both sets of genitals, is figured as the reborn Christ.

48. Linda Williams, "When the Woman Looks," in *Re-Vision: Essays in Feminist Film Criticism,* ed. Mary Ann Doane, Patricia Mellencamp, and Linda Williams (Frederick, Md.: University Publications of America/American Film Institute, 1984), p. 90 (reprinted in this volume). Williams's emphasis on the phallic leads her to dismiss slasher killers as a "non-specific male killing force" and hence a degeneration in the tradition. "In these films the recognition and affinity between woman and monster of classic horror film gives way to pure identity: she *is* the monster, her mutilated body is the only visible horror" (p. 96). This analysis does justice neither to the obvious bisexuality of slasher killers, nor to the new strength of the female victim. The slasher film may not, in balance, be more subversive than traditional horror, but it is certainly not less so.

49. Freud, "The Uncanny," p. 245. See also Neale, "*Halloween*," esp. pp. 28–29.

50. "The woman's exercise of an active investigating gaze can only be simultaneous with her own victimization. The place of her specularization is transformed into the locus of a process of seeing designed to unveil an aggression against itself." Mary Ann Doane, "The Woman's Film: Possession and Address," in *Re-Vision,* p. 72.

51. John Carpenter, interviewed by Todd McCarthy, "Trick or Treat," *Film Comment* 16, no. 1 (January–February 1980): 23–24.

52. This is not so in traditional film or in heterosexual pornography, in any case. Gay male pornography, however, films some male bodies in much the same way that heterosexual pornography films female bodies.

53. Compare the visual treatment of the (male) rape in *Deliverance* (1972) with the (female) rapes in Hitchcock's *Frenzy* (1972), Craven's *Last House on the Left* (1972), or Bergman's *The Virgin Spring* (1959). The latter films study the victims' faces at length and in close-up during the act; the former looks at the act intermittently and in long shot, focusing less on the actual victim than on the victim's friend who must look on.

54. Marcus, *The Other Victorians,* pp. 260–261. Marcus distinguishes two phases in the development of flagellation literature: one in which the figure being beaten is a boy, and a second in which the figure is a girl. The very shift indicates, at some level, the irrelevance of apparent sex. "The sexual identity of the figure being beaten is remarkably labile. Sometimes he is represented as a boy, sometimes as a girl, sometimes as a combination of the two—a boy dressed as a girl, or the reverse." The girls often have sexually ambiguous names as well. The beater is a female but, in Marcus's reading, a phallic one—muscular, possessed of body hair—representing the father.

55. Ibid., pp. 125–127.

56. "Suspense is like a woman. The more left to the imagination, the more the excitement. . . . The perfect 'woman of mystery' is one who is blonde, subtle, and Nordic. . . . Movie titles, like women, should be easy to remember without being familiar, intriguing but never obvious, warm yet refreshing, suggest action, not impassiveness, and finally give a clue without revealing the plot. Although I do not profess to be an authority on women, I fear that the perfect title, like the perfect woman, is difficult to find." Quoted in Spoto, *Dark Side of Genius,* p. 431.

57. This would seem to be the point of the final sequence of de Palma's *Blow Out,* in which we see the boyfriend of the victim-hero stab the killer to death but later hear the television announce that the woman herself vanquished the killer. The frame plot of the film has to do with the making of a slasher film (*Co-Ed Frenzy*), and it seems clear that de Palma means his ending to stand as a comment on the Final Girl formula of the genre. De Palma's (and indirectly Hitchcock's) insistence that only men can kill men, or protect women from men, deserves a separate essay.

58. The term is Judith Fetterly's. See her *The Resisting Reader: A Feminist Approach to American Fiction* (Bloomington: Indiana University Press, 1978).

59. On the possible variety of responses to a single film, see Norman N. Holland, "I-ing Film," *Critical Inquiry* 12 (Summer 1986): 654–671.

60. Marcus, *The Other Victorians,* p. 127. Marcus contents himself with noting that the scene demonstrates a "confusion of sexual identity." In the literature of flagellation, he adds, "this confused identity is also present, but it is concealed and unacknowledged." But it is precisely the femaleness of the beaten figures that does acknowledge it.

61. Freud, "The Uncanny," esp. pp. 219–221 and 226–227.

62. Raymond Durgnat, *Films and Feelings* (London: Faber and Faber, 1967), p. 216.

63. Not a few critics have argued that the ambiguity is the unintentional result of bad filmmaking.

64. So argues Susan Barrowclough: the "male spectator takes the part not of the male but of the female. Contrary to the assumption that the male uses pornography to confirm and celebrate his gender's sexual activity and dominance, is the possibility of his pleasure in identifying with a 'feminine' passivity or subordination." "*Not a Love Story,*" *Screen* 23, no. 5 (November–December 1982): 35–36. Alan Soble seconds the proposal in his *Pornography: Marxism, Feminism, and the Future of Sexuality* (New Haven: Yale University Press, 1986), p. 93. Porn/sexploitation filmmaker Joe Sarno: "My point of view is more or less always from the woman's point of view; the fairy tales that my films are based on are from the woman's point of view; I stress the efficacy of women for themselves. In general, I focus on the female orgasm as much as I can." Quoted in Vale and Juno, eds., *Incredibly Strange Films,* p. 94. "Male identification with women," Kaja Silverman writes, "has not received the same amount of critical attention [as sublimation into professional 'showing off' and reversal into scopophilia], although it would seem the most potentially destabilizing, at least as far as gender is concerned." See her discussion of the "Great Male Renunciation" in "Fragments of a Fashionable Discourse," in *Studies in Entertainment: Critical Approaches to Mass Culture,* ed. Tania Modleski (Bloomington: Indiana University Press, 1986), p. 141.

65. Elaine Showalter, "Critical Cross Dressing: Male Feminists and the Woman of the Year," *Raritan* 3 (Fall 1983): 138.

66. Whatever its other functions, the scene that reveals the Final Girl in a degree of undress serves to underscore her femaleness. One reviewer of *Aliens* remarks that she couldn't help wondering why in the last scene, just as in *Alien,* "we have Ripley wandering around clad only in her underwear. A little reminder of her gender, lest we lose sight of it behind all that firepower?" Christine Schoefer, *East Bay Express,* September 5, 1986, p. 37.

67. Mulvey, "Visual Pleasure and Narrative Cinema," p. 12.

68. Kaja Silverman, "Masochism and Subjectivity," *Framework* 12 (1979): 5. Needless to say, this is not the explanation for the girl hero offered by the industry. *Time,* July 28, 1986, p. 44, on *Aliens:* "As director Cameron says, the endless 'remulching' of the masculine hero by the 'male-dominated industry' is, if nothing else, commercially shortsighted. 'They choose to ignore that 50% of the audience is female. And I've been told that it has been proved demographically that 80% of the time it's women who decide which film to see.'" It is of course not Cameron who established the female hero of the series but Ridley Scott (in *Alien*), and it is fair to assume, from his careful manipulation of the formula, that Scott got her from the slasher film, where she has flourished for some time among audiences that are heavily male. Cameron's analysis is thus both self-serving and beside the point.

69. If this analysis is correct, we may expect horror films of the future to feature Final Boys as well as Final Girls. Two recent figures may be incipient examples: Jesse, the pretty boy in *A Nightmare on Elm Street, Part 2: Freddy's Revenge* (1985), and Ashley, the character who dies last in *The Evil Dead* (1983). Neither quite plays the role, but their names, and in the case of Jesse the characterization, seem to play on the tradition.

70. For the opposite view (based on classic horror in both literary and cinematic manifestations), see Franco Moretti, "The Dialectic of Fear," *New Left Review,* no. 136 (1982): 67–85.

71. Vale and Juno, eds., *Incredibly Strange Films,* p. 5.

72. Tania Modleski, "The Terror of Pleasure: The Contemporary Horror Film and Postmodern Theory," in *Studies in Entertainment,* pp. 155–166. (Like Modleski, I stress that my comments are based on many slashers, not all of them.) This important essay (and volume) appeared too late for me to take it into full account here.

Part Two

"It Will Thrill You, It May Shock You, It Might Even Horrify You": Gender, Reception, and Classic Horror Cinema

Rhona J. Berenstein

Setting the Stage

*How do you do? Mr. Carl Laemmle feels that it would be a little un-
kind to present this picture without just a word of friendly warning. . . .
It is one of the strangest tales ever told. It deals with the two great mysteries of Creation: Life and Death. I think it will thrill you. It may
shock you. It might even horrify you. So . . . if you feel that you do not
care to subject your nerves to such a strain, now's your chance to—Well
. . . we warned you. . . .*

—Edward Van Sloan,
Prologue to *Frankenstein* (1931)

Before viewers were drawn into the story proper of James
Whale's *Frankenstein* in 1931, they were treated to Edward Van
Sloan's ominous introductory remarks. Van Sloan—who plays
Frankenstein's medical mentor, Dr. Waldman, in the movie—
steps out from behind a curtain to greet the film's audience. In
his movement from backstage to onstage, Van Sloan bridges
diegetic and theatrical worlds and attempts to provide some
guidance to the film's prospective spectators.

Yet Van Sloan's monologue can be understood as much more

than helpful advice. For in addition to letting viewers know that they can escape from the theater if his warning proves too terrifying, he articulates the
promise of horror cinema: "It will thrill you. It may shock you. It might even
horrify you." That Van Sloan expects spectators to subject themselves willingly to thrills, shocks, and horrors is implicit in his stilted phrase—"now's
your chance to"—and in his immediate transition to these chilling words:
"Well, we warned you."

While it is possible to interpret Van Sloan's speech at face value—that is, as
the result of Carl Laemmle's concern that spectators be forewarned of the terrors soon to be portrayed onscreen—the prologue is better read as a publicity
ploy, an effort to heighten the emotional upheaval that awaits viewers. But
who, according to Van Sloan, will be experiencing those thrills, shocks, and
horrors? To whom does he address his warning?

Van Sloan's target audience is, it seems, a genderless mass, a group of spectators expected to respond in unison to the film's affective lures and threats.
This streamlining of the audience by Van Sloan is a counterpoint to popular
assumptions about horror cinema—that it is a male form of filmmaking and
one that, until recently, has been characterized by genre critics as home to
male sadism and the victimization of women.[1] Yet Van Sloan's targeting of *all*
spectators in his monologue suggests that gender polarization was—if not absent in the 1930s—not mobilized in every form of spectatorial address.

This article will use Van Sloan's opening comments as a starting point to
underscore the degree to which some contemporary critics avoided gender
stratification in their discussion of horror films in the 1930s. But I also begin
with Van Sloan's words in order to use them as a foil of sorts. For in the pages
that follow I will detail a range of studio marketing devices, local exhibitor
ploys, and film reviews that played with, appealed to, and made fascinating
assumptions about the genre's gender address during the thirties. That all
viewers were expected, as Van Sloan assumes, to enjoy the thrills, shocks, and
horrors of films like *Frankenstein* is something I take for granted. But, as I will
argue, spectators' enjoyment and affective experiences were also characterized in often contrasting, usually compelling, and very instructive ways when
it came to gender.

Horror cinema, like melodrama, is a genre that has been the subject of fairly
rigid, gendered assumptions when it comes to spectatorship. Whereas the
principal viewers for melodrama are assumed to be women, according to
most scholarly accounts, horror's spectators are usually cast as sadistic (or,
more recently, masochistic) men, while the presence of women in the audience has either been underestimated or assumed to be nonexistent. My interest in studying the marketing and reception of 1930s horror, the period that

has been deemed the classic era of the genre, is to highlight the precarious-
ness of the genre's reputed spectator demographic. In an effort to draw out
the complexities of classic horror spectatorship, then, I summarize the address
to male and female viewers in marketing strategies and emphasize the reception context as it pertains to women. My focus on women spectators throughout this article is, then, a corrective approach to genre analysis, an effort to
highlight the ways in which women were, like men, quite actively recruited
to attend, enjoy, and engage with horror films in the 1930s.

How To Be a Horror Viewer

Take the girl friend and by the middle of the first reel she'll have
both arms around your neck and holding on for dear life.

James E. Mitchell, review of *Doctor X* (1932)

What did a man have to do to be a good horror viewer in the 1930s? According to James E. Mitchell in his review of *Doctor X* for the *Los Angeles Ex-*
aminer, he had to take his girlfriend to the movies and subject himself to her
hysterical clutches. Like the traditional model of film and horror spectatorship, Mitchell casts men as the genre's brave patrons, while women cower in
their seats and hold on to their dates as if their lives depend on it. In the dark
of the theater, Mitchell seems to suggest, horror movies provide women with
a socially sanctioned reason to grab on to their boyfriends, to hold tight with
all their might.

But was holding a quivering woman the only thing a man had to do to be
a horror viewer in the 1930s? Not quite. In an effort to offer a conventional
portrait of horror spectatorship, I pre-empted Mitchell's words at a crucial
moment: "Take the girl friend and by the middle of the first reel she'll have
both arms around your neck and holding on for dear life. *And you'll be giggling*
hysterically, too, trying to convince her you are not scared to death, either" (emphasis
added).[2] Mitchell's direct address to horror's male viewer not only relies on
traditional gender dynamics—women are terrified and men are called upon
to be brave—but confirms that gender traits can be performed. Just as social
mandates invited women to cling to men while screening horror movies in
the thirties, thus encouraging them to display conventionally feminine behavior as a means of garnering male attention, so too did the male viewer, at
least according to Mitchell, use female fear, as well as his own traditional display of bravery, to disguise *his* terror behind a socially prescribed behavior.

Mitchell's recognition that male spectators perform conventional gender traits adds an important element to any consideration of horror spectatorship. For, according to Mitchell, not only is male courage acted out in the dark of the movie theater, so too are the traditional ground rules for heterosexual coupling. Mitchell's 1932 commentary reinforces the findings of Norbert Mundorf, James Weaver, and Dolf Zillman, who note in their recent study that contemporary horror movies offer prime arenas for teenagers of both sexes to play out the conventional mandates of gender roles and heterosexual coupling.[3]

The socially prescribed behaviors that Mitchell details in his review of *Doctor X* are, then, markers of the degree to which traditional gender traits can be mobilized in a specific social setting—such as a movie theater, and for particular cultural purposes—such as abiding by gender expectations, performing heterosexual dating rituals as expected. Whether as gender play, dating ploy, or both, the performance of bravery on the part of the male spectator to whom Mitchell addresses his review underscores the degree to which conventional signs of masculinity and heterosexual coupling can be constructed.

What gender dynamics were played out in horror's reception during the 1930s? How were expectations about socially desirable gender traits mobilized in marketing the genre to exhibitors and viewers alike? How was gender portrayed in a manner that highlights both the pervasiveness as well as the theatricality of conventionalized behavior? I want to explore these questions with a view to addressing the marketing and reception of classic horror cinema as modes of negotiation and contradiction. With that goal in mind, what follows is not a comprehensive study of classic horror's historical configurations, but rather a selective, primarily urban analysis of the genre's appeal to audiences in the 1930s.

My intent is to present and situate original documents both as a means of tracing the historical twists and turns of classic horror reception—as it pertains specifically to gender—as well as as a vehicle for suggesting that theatrical role-play was elicited by studio and theater marketing ploys and in film reviews in the 1930s. Thus, I will suggest that cinematic spectatorship, at least when it comes to classic horror cinema, has a performative dimension, especially when viewership is framed in historical terms.

My focus on the gender dynamics of popular film reviews and marketing tactics derives from my belief that the textual and extratextual levels of classic horror movies should be studied as parallel forms of expression, as meaning systems that toyed with gender repeatedly and appealed to assumptions about appropriate gender behavior as a selling ploy. Whether the parallels between horror's onscreen and offscreen representations of gender were intended by those who produced them in the 1930s (such as publicity departments and directors) is of less interest to me than is tracing the genre's address to viewers on the basis of gender expectations. Offscreen mentions of horror's appeal to women or its ability to terrify them, for example, found parallel representations in movies that portrayed heroines who were positively transformed while under a monster's sway (e.g., Francis Drake's Mina in *Dracula* [1931]) or who swooned when faced with terrors too horrible to bear (e.g., Elizabeth Allan's Irena in *Mark of the Vampire* [1935]). Horror movies are particularly intense sites of negotiation and contradiction when it comes to their portrayals of and assumptions about gender, both male and female.

Believing that the textual and extratextual levels are connected, however, is not the same as pinpointing the exact impact of their convergence on viewers. Much as I would like to claim that the gender behaviors that appeared or are promoted onscreen and offscreen *fully* determined spectators' interpretations of classic horror, doing so would be an exercise in analytic projection, not precision. As Janet Staiger comments vis-à-vis notions of a coherent reader: "They derive from assuming something about texts (e.g., that texts are coherent), from confusing what might be 'in' a text with what a reader might do with the details of a text, and from believing that the primary obligation of readers is creating a logical interpretation rather than, for instance, developing a coherent self in opposition to the text or finding pleasure in dispersion and contradiction."[4] Staiger's points are well suited to classic horror, a genre whose films rarely offered coherent narratives. While viewers may have tried to make sense of story lines, they were often confronted with confusing plot twists, inconsistent character portrayals, sudden shifts of tone between horror and comedy, and narrative loose ends that went unexplained. As one *Variety* reviewer remarked of James Whale's *The Old Dark House* (1932) and horror in general: "There are sundry inanities throughout, but as with the horror school . . . the audience seemingly doesn't expect coherence, and so everything goes by the boards."[5] As this comment suggests, not only were horror movies filled with incoherent inanities, but viewers expected them as well. Taking the opinion of *Variety*'s reporter as a guide, classic horror's ideal is not a viewer who searches for coherence, but one who accepts its absence.

Staiger's suggestion that readers respond to and find pleasure in dispersion and contradiction is in any case a more preferable model for cinematic spectatorship than one that relies on an ideal/coherent viewer. By the same token, however, to assume that viewing is entirely free-form and owes nothing to textual and extratextual meanings is to locate *all* signification in the act of spectatorship. Instead, as Staiger notes, reception studies need to "recognize the

Conventions abound in *The Old Dark House* (1932): Gloria Stuart as the frightened female.

dialectics of evidence and theory, and . . . take up a critical distance on the *relations* between spectators and texts."[6] As a result, I look at reception with a focus on gender and the genre's address to female patrons in this essay. My intention is to outline the reception climate for horror in the early 1930s with a view to highlighting the ways in which the industry's promotional efforts opened up viewership to a wide spectrum of patrons and an even wider range of affective responses to the genre.

Taking Staiger's comments as my guide, I cannot possibly know *exactly* how male and female viewers responded to horror in the 1930s. What I do know is that their reactions were contested in reviews, hoped for and promoted in pressbooks, and overtly manipulated in exhibition ploys. How men and women were believed to react to horror movies was given contradictory attention by reviewers and promoters. Precisely what spectators did with those diverse messages remains a matter of speculation—my guess is that they responded with a matching dose of contradiction and complexity, at least when inside theater doors.

Like Van Sloan's address to *Frankenstein*'s audience in the film's prologue, many horror reviews from the thirties addressed spectators in terms that were not gender specific. Reporters used gender-neutral language such as "horror fans" and "audiences." As Mordaunt Hall remarked of *Dracula:* "It is a production that evidently had the desired effect upon many in the audience yesterday afternoon, for there was a general outburst of applause when Dr. Van Helsing produced a little cross that caused the dreaded Dracula to fling his cloak over his head and make himself scarce."[7] Edwin Schallert was convinced that *Frankenstein* elicited a range of affective responses from spectators when the film ran at the RKO Orpheum in 1932, but the audience remained a similarly genderless mass for him: "This weird shiver feature . . . seems to cause the audience not only to experience the spinal chills, but also to laugh, cry and otherwise express hysteria of the moment."[8] While Louella O. Parsons gave viewership a more dramatic flair in her review of *King Kong* (1933), she was equally vague when it came to gender: "Breathless with suspense, nervous with suppressed emotion and thrilled with continued horrors, the audience greeted *King Kong* at the Chinese Theatre last night, as something entirely new in the way of motion picture entertainment."[9] This lack of gender specification in so many reviews is instructive, for it suggests that while assumed differences in male and female spectatorship are crucial to more recent scholarship on horror cinema, they were of less concern to contemporary critics of classic horror. What mattered most consistently to reporters was whether films were "good" and whether they were suitable for children.

Despite the focus on other criteria, gender was referenced in a number of reviews. Critics usually offered one of three perspectives: (1) they remarked upon the terrors endured by both men and women in the audience; (2) they were surprised or convinced that women responded well to horror movies; and (3) they suggested that male and female viewers appreciated different aspects of films.[10] Leo Meehan's 1931 review of *Frankenstein* in the *Motion Picture Herald* is a good example of the first critical perspective on gender: "Women come out trembling, men exhausted. I don't know what it might do to children, but I wouldn't want my kids to see it."[11] One reviewer for Warner Bros.'s *Mystery of the Wax Museum* (1933) painted an almost identical portrait of spectatorship two years later: "Adults of both sexes will find more than enough in the way of startling excitement to interest them, but because of its gruesomeness, *Wax Museum* is a little too strong for juvenile patronage."[12] As late as 1935, when the first horror cycle neared its end, reviewers continued to emphasize horror's draw to men, women, and children: "In *Bride of Frankenstein,* Boris Karloff comes again to terrify the children, frighten the women and play a jiggling tune upon masculine spines."[13]

Like the other critics cited, *Time*'s reporter responded to *White Zombie* in 1932 by affirming that men, like women, are scared of monsters, but went a step farther by critiquing the star's performance: "Bela Lugosi . . . looks like a comic imbecile, [and] can make his jawbones rigid and show the whites of his eyes. These abilities qualify him to make strong men cower and women swoon."[14] The anonymous reviewer's critical tone suggested disdain not only for the movie and its star, but also for patrons who responded with fear in spite of Lugosi's botched performance. In fact, *White Zombie* is an excellent example of a horror movie that fared poorly among critics but well with the public. As Michael Price and George Turner note, "*White Zombie* opened on Broadway at the Rivoli Theatre. No movie ever received a more thorough critical scourge, although the public loved it and it brought in a great deal of money."[15] *White Zombie* is a reminder that thirties reviews are limited gauges of spectatorship. Since classic horror films were released during an era when audience studies were scarce, historical research can describe the environment for spectatorship but not the minutiae of viewer reactions.[16]

The second approach to gender evidenced by reporters—surprise or conviction that horror movies delighted female patrons—was articulated in a *Variety* review of *Dracula* in 1931: "Here was a picture whose screen fortunes must have caused much uncertainty as to the femme fan reaction. As it turns out all the signs are that the woman angle is favorable and that sets the picture for better than average money at the box office."[17] Universal had a hand in eliciting female interest in the film. The studio released *Dracula* with an explicitly romantic campaign targeted at women. The movie opened in New York City on February 14, 1931—Valentine's Day—accompanied by suggestive cutlines: "The Story of the Strangest Passion Ever Known"; "The Strangest Love Story of All"; and "The Strangest Love a Man Has Ever Known."[18]

The assumption that women might have a romantic stake in vampire movies may not have been surprising at the time, given that fiends often sweep heroines off their feet. But the same *Variety* reporter thought female patrons hooked on *Frankenstein* as well: "Appeal is candidly to the morbid side and the screen effect is up to promised specifications. Feminine fans seem to get some kind of emotional kick out of this sublimation of the bedtime ghost story done with all the literariness of the camera." Although the reporter did not elaborate upon why he or she thought women were drawn to James Whale's movie, a more general viewer profile was provided: "The audience for this type of film is probably the detective story readers and the mystery yarn radio listeners."[19]

Who were those detective readers and mystery listeners? The *Variety* reporter did not say. Yet clues appeared in two industry magazines geared toward exhibitors: the *Motion Picture Herald* (*MPH*) and its predecessor, the *Exhibitors Herald-World* (*EHW*). In a 1933 issue of *MPH*, the following headline appeared: "Girls Want Mystery; Boys War Pictures." The brief article announced the results of an Edinburgh, Scotland, study of children's spectatorial preferences. The gender lines were drawn between mystery and war movies but, noted the report, neither group liked romance films.[20] The column went on to suggest that girls will, eventually, become women with a continued investment in mysteries. That they might also grow up to crave romance was an assumption made by the motion picture industry at the time.

That assumption was articulated in a 1930 article in *EHW* entitled "B.O. Explodes Idea That Women Dislike War and Crook Pictures. Feminine Attendance at Four Productions Classed as Lacking in Love or Romantic Interest Averages 61 Per Cent of Total at Matinees and 59 Per Cent at Night." Although the films cited were war and gangster pictures, the unconventional results predicted female horror attendance—*Dracula* debuted and was a box office success only five months later. "Smashing a traditional theory of the box office," the article continued, "investigation has brought to light some pertinent facts to disprove the idea that women, who decide the fate of motion pictures, object as a rule to war pictures, crook dramas and films in which the love or romantic interest is conspicuous by its absence."[21] While the percentage of men attending matinees increased in the early part of the 1930s due to rising unemployment rates, women remained a significant viewing force. Thus, the study's announcement of female interest in gangster and war films was also a promising sign of horrific things to come.

Although the *EHW* article encouraged exhibitors to quell their anxieties about female attendance at rough-and-tumble movies, classic horror marketing rarely took women for granted. Films often included romance at the narrative level, which was promoted as a selling point to women viewers. McCarthy's review of *The Mummy* (1932) in *MPH,* for example, articulated the gender divide assumed in spectator tastes: "It has that type of romance, which, although far-fetched and entirely visionary, is nevertheless fascinating to feminine patrons, while the mystic unrealism should provide the men folk something new."[22] Men and women may have enjoyed horror movies, McCarthy claimed, but their pleasures were found in divergent aspects of the films. (Furthermore, McCarthy thought that the source of fascination for women was decidedly unimpressive—"far-fetched" romance.)

Not surprisingly, though, given the goal of as wide a viewership as possible, classic horror movies were made and marketed with a general audience in

Thriller plus romance: Miriam Hopkins and Fredric March in *Dr. Jekyll and Mr. Hyde* (1931).

mind. As the *MPH* review noted of *King Kong* in 1933, the film "has everything—romance, drama, spectacle, unrealism, thrill, terror and 'love interest.'"[23] The same combination of disparate themes was proclaimed in a 1931 *MPH* advertisement for *Dr. Jekyll and Mr. Hyde*. As the cutline notes: "Paramount Brings You the THRILLER OF ALL THRILLERS!—plus a great love story." Diverse promotional possibilities were emphasized later in the same advertisement: "Swell cast; great director and a fascinating story. Mystery and horror! Heart-warming romance and intense drama! Everything! Its appeal is unlimited."[24] Just in case that appeal was divided along gender lines, *Variety* ran what David J. Skal calls a "split-personality review"—a sidebar commentary entitled "The Woman's Angle" recast some of the film's supposed failures in the horror department as draws for female spectators: "Classic shocker loses much of its stark horror and consequent unpleasantness for women, by growing logical with psychoanalytical motivation and daringly presented sex appeal. Latest version made enticing instead of repellent to the girls."[25]

Along the same lines, one exhibitor of Paramount's film literally split his lobby display in two and separated the horror from romance theme. As *MPH* reported:

In connection with one of the recent so-called "Horror" pictures, *Dr. Jekyll and Mr. Hyde,* contrasting lobby displays were most effectively used by George Laby, manager of the Washington Street Olympia Theatre, Boston, Mass.; so effectively, in fact, that the displays were thought to be a contributing factor obtaining the highest weekly gross over the period of the year. The accompanying photo speaks for itself. At the left, now the famous "Doctor" in characteristic poses of himself and other self, treated from the "horror" angle. At the right are featured characters representing the romantic side of the picture.[26]

The romantic side consisted of a poster of actresses Miriam Hopkins and Rose Hobart flanking heartthrob Fredric March, who starred in the eponymous role. The dual-focus display parallels the film's dual theme and highlights exhibitor assumptions about male and female spectatorial preferences. Thus, although some reviewers claimed that women and horror were a fine match, others believed that female patrons had to be courted with romance themes and promotional stunts.

Acting Scared

The associations . . . of the theater with femininity are old ones in Western culture.
Women are felt to be on the side of the inauthentic and the spectacular.

Tania Modleski, *The Women Who Knew Too Much*

Classic horror's promotional gimmicks took various forms, including updating techniques from the silent era. The ambulance parked outside the theater door, for example, was a popular ploy in the 1920s and was refurbished by exhibitors in the next decade. As *MPH* reports, the following sign was displayed in front of the Princess Theatre in Aurora, Mississippi, for performances of *Bride of Frankenstein* in 1935: "No parking here, space reserved for ambulance."[27] Holden Swinger, manager of the Palace Theatre in Akron, Ohio, went a step farther—he "stationed an ambulance at his curb during his *Bride of Frankenstein* date with lobby easel and sign on ambulance calling attention to the free emergency service for those who 'couldn't take it.'"[28]

Both stunts, used earlier in the decade for *Frankenstein,* are variations on a ploy listed by John F. Barry and Epes W. Sargent in their 1927 guide to exhibitors, *Building Theatre Patronage: Management and Merchandising.* Barry and Sargent had clear ideas about the appeals of the ambulance to motion picture theater managers and, by extension, to spectators: "A standard comedy stunt is the ambulance parked in front of the theatre to carry out those who may be overcome with laughter. The ambulance may be paraded through the streets with signs to the effect that the occupant is being rushed to the hospital because he nearly died laughing at the named comedy. If you can get a man who can laugh naturally and infectiously, it will not hurt to have him stagger from the house, and be helped into the ambulance, laughing all the way."[29] While the ideal comedy stunt participant, according to Barry and Sargent, was a man whose laughter is infectious, horror exhibitors preferred women for exploitation purposes in the thirties. For example, in order to draw as many patrons to *Mark of the Vampire* as possible, a first-aid stretcher was placed in the lobby of the Loew's Colonial Theatre in Reading, Pennsylvania. The in-house stunt was accompanied by advertisements in the town's daily newspapers addressed to "women who are not afraid." The notices recounted the film's story line and challenged female viewers to attend a screening. As the copy for the ad suggests, the contest winner was expected to respond *against* her conventional gender role—by being brave.[30] A year later, the Wicomico Theatre in Salisbury, Maryland, devised a tie-in prize for *The Invisible Ray,* which targeted women again. A free permanent was offered by the town's leading beauty salon to any woman willing to sit alone in the theatre and watch the film at midnight. According to *MPH,* there were twenty applicants for the stunt and "crowds gathered at the theatre to watch the gal enter."[31] Both exhibitor efforts used women as prototypical viewers, drew upon stereotypes assuming that female patrons would be frightened by watching horror, and invited women to defy those stereotypes as a means of garnering prizes and proving their prowess as spectators.

In an analysis of the relationship between women and early exhibition tactics, Diane Waldman mentions that the manager of New York's Rialto Theatre took pride in promoting horror movies to a predominantly male clientele. Waldman uses the manager's claim as a springboard to analyze horror's sadistic address to women in the early 1940s:

If other theatres showing horror films were anything like the Rialto, one piece of exploitation aimed at women takes on ominous tones: a theatre exhibiting Universal's *Frankenstein Meets the Wolf Man* (1943) offered a prize to any woman who would sit through the midnight show alone. It is not clear whether the danger was supposed to derive from the terrors of the screen or from the other patrons of the theatre. This stunt, then, made explicit the connection between horror films and the terrorizing of women, capitalizing on one of women's most common experiences: fear of harassment when alone, especially at night, in a public place heavily frequented by men.[32]

While Waldman is right to take note of the midnight terrors endured by women in American society, she reduces the Rialto stunt to vulgar sexism and assumes that it fully encapsulates horror's relationship to women. Waldman is not far off in claiming that the choice of a female patron resulted from conventional assumptions about women in a patriarchal culture, but she is wrong to assert that the choice only connoted attack and harassment.

Women were classic horror's central stunt participants because they were thought to personify the genre's favored affect: fear. The upshot was that if women could survive the viewing of a horror film and, moreover, if they could respond bravely, then other patrons, meaning *men,* could do the same. While Waldman's claim has some validity, it was not exhibitors' primary motivation. Given that the woman chosen was expected to view *Frankenstein Meets the Wolf Man* alone in the theater, harassment by men was not part of the contest's requirements, but solitary bravery was. Female responses to horror were used by exhibitors to prove that the films should and could be seen by all patrons and to highlight the performative elements of terror. For if women were asked over and over again to *act* out or refuse to act out their fears in front of crowds or to garner prizes, their gender roles—though conventional and promoted—were also highly theatricalized.

Take the efforts of the Loew's Majestic Theatre in Bridgeport, Connecticut, for instance. During screenings of *Mark of the Vampire* in 1935 "a woman was planted in the audience at each show to scream and faint, after which she was carried out to an ambulance parked in front of the theatre and whisked away."[33] While the female scream is a popular onscreen trope in the horror genre, it was also promoted heavily as a horror gimmick, a performance intended to incite viewer response. So powerful was the female scream for audiences that Marquis Busby claimed it sparked his reaction to *Dracula* at the beginning of the decade: "I wasn't really scared until some lady in the audience let out a piercing scream. Maybe it was just a pin, but it was disconcerting to the rest of the audience."[34] Maybe it *was* just a pin, maybe she was a plant, maybe the viewer was terrified, or maybe she pretended to be. Whichever explanation holds true, the sound of a woman's scream promoted fear, guaranteed the genre's effectiveness, and linked female gender behavior to an overwrought performance.[35]

While some theaters addressed female patrons with tame ploys—for example, the Capitol in Dallas premiered Universal's *The Black Cat* (1934) with a contest for the most beautiful cat[36]—others tried to create as large a ruckus as possible. Owners of the Palace Theatre in Chicago, for example, placed advertisements in newspapers that noted: "Emotion Test Hits on [*Bride of*] *Frankenstein.*" The exhibitors remodeled a lie detector exam to register the affective roller-coaster experienced by viewers. The prototypical spectators chosen for the stunt were two female subjects, age five and twenty-five respectively, who were hooked up to the contraption as they screened the film.[37] A first-aid booth was placed in the lobby to dramatize the health hazards of horror viewing. The promotional efforts were rounded out by a tie-up with the Loop department store, which utilized "a professional mannikin modeling evening gowns, surrounded by color enlargements from the picture."[38] As was true of other stunts, female responses to horror were promoted vociferously and used to gauge the genre's ability to frighten, amuse, and satisfy patrons.

Although department store tie-ins were initiated by local theater managers, they were also suggested in pressbooks. The promotional materials distributed for *Mystery of the Wax Museum,* for instance, include a full-page game plan for linking the film to a local department store. Exhibitors were advised to approach a store as follows: "Here is a tie-up that is a natural for any store that uses the finer grade of lifelike wax models for gown displays. Offer to furnish the store with such equipment, the services of an experienced gown model, and one that in general dimensions, sizes up to the wax models to be used."[39] The idea was for the store to announce a window fashion show, at which time the live model would pose with the wax figurines, stand frozen for a few moments, and surprise the audience by smiling and bowing. The logic ran as follows: exhibit beautiful gowns at local department stores to pique women's interest in the latest horror film, and they will arrive at the next showing with their dates, friends, and families in tow.

Although the exhibition ploys mentioned thus far appealed to women as prototypical horror viewers and consumers of feminine wares, other promotional tactics were developed. One popular technique was to link women with monstrosity as well as suggest their desire for a fiend. The RKO Theatre in Los Angeles, for example, sent masked women into the streets to hand out "Beware" notices announcing the premiere of *The Invisible Man* (1934).[40] While the announcements targeted male as well as female patrons, women were used to promote the picture as fiendish doubles—like that of the film's monster, their identities remained hidden. *MPH* added yet another dimension in its advice to exhibitors for the same film: "There are a million more [exploitation angles] you can concoct, not the least of which are those that can be applied to women to stir their curiosity. How would they like to be

Kathleen Burke as Lota, the Panther Woman, and Charles Laughton as Dr. Moreau in *Island of Lost Souls* (1932).

embraced, kissed, by an invisible lover . . . ?"[41] Here *MPH* urged managers to address women in terms of their desire *for* the invisible man and not their resemblance to him.

The publicity ploys for *Island of Lost Souls* (1932) also targeted female patrons in dual terms. Prior to the release of the movie, Paramount conducted a nationwide search for the Panther Woman of America. Basing the competition on the female monster in Erle C. Kenton's screen adaptation of H. G. Wells's 1895 novel *The Island of Dr. Moreau,* the search gained public attention and boosted prerelease interest in the film. Paramount chose a winning entrant for each state and decided on a national victor amid fanfare in Chicago. The winner received a prize, the Panther Woman of America title, and the promise that Charles Laughton, who played the mad doctor in Kenton's film, would turn her into a beast.[42] The contest was mentioned in newspapers across the country and *Photoplay* hinted at it in a review: "A thriller of thrillers. . . . Among the monstrosities created is *Lota,* the much publicized 'Panther Woman.'"[43]

The movie's pressbook is filled with references to Kathleen Burke's prize-winning portrayal of the Panther Woman. Theater managers were advised to plant stories regarding her contest travails in local newspapers two days before the film's release. Proposed headlines included: "A Star Before She Starts! 'Panther Woman' Achieves New Overnight Film Success" and "Wins 60,000 to One Shot! Office Girl Captures 'Panther Woman' Role."[44]

Other publicity materials for *Island of Lost Souls* tempered the horror theme through an appeal to stardom. In the February 1933 issue of *Photoplay,* a three-page story was devoted to Laughton. The profile, which included glossies of Laughton in and out of costume, and a still of him posing with his thespian wife Elsa Lanchester in a moment of supposed conjugal bliss, presented him to *Photoplay*'s readership as a character actor of great versatility and a husband of exceeding warmth. This piece appeared in the same month that *Island of Lost Souls* was reviewed and advertised in the magazine. Laughton may have played a horrid man in the film, fans were told in the advertisements, but he was a gentleman in real life, according to the star profile.[45]

A full-page advertisement for *Island of Lost Souls* appeared near the beginning of the same *Photoplay* issue. Depicting a drawing of a partially clad woman surrounded by wild animals, the cutline intoned: "He took them from his mad menagerie . . . Nights were horrible with the screams of tortured beasts . . . From his House of Pain they came re-made. . . . His masterpiece—the Panther Woman—throbbing to the hot flush of love."[46] The publicity simultaneously positioned the mad doctor as a sadist, a passion-inspiring figure, and a man capable of transforming women in terrifying and desirable ways. *Photoplay*'s readers were invited to view Lota, the monstrous Panther Woman, as both tortured and positively transformed by Laughton, her equally monstrous creator.

The doubling of heroines and fiends persisted in publicity for other films as well. A striking poster for *Svengali* (1931) appeared in *Photoplay* in July of 1931 and positioned John Barrymore, who played the title role, as a simultaneous object of fear and desire for Marian Marsh's Trilby, as well as a double for her: "HE is genius-madman-lover! His hypnotic spell reaches out of darkness controlling love-hate—life itself. SHE is the beauty who had all Paris at her feet—who wins men with a smile—who hates Svengali the sinister love-maker—until his magic spell forces even *her* to beat to his *manufactured love!*"[47] In a mimicry of Svengali's hypnotic abilities, Trilby, the advertisement proclaimed, is not only subject to the fiend's control but exhibits her own brand of hypnosis—she has Paris at her feet and wins men with a smile.

Like *Photoplay*'s presentation of *Island of Lost Souls* two years later, this advertisement banks on multiple modes of address to, primarily, female readers.

The cutline aligns fiend with heroine, suggests they desire each other, *and* introduces stardom into the mix. Across the center of the layout, in capital letters, were the following words: "JOHN BARRYMORE as 'SVENGALI' The Hypnotist." The typeface was largest for the actor's last name—the word "BARRYMORE" literally slices the advertisement in half and draws the most visual attention.

The Masquerade of Stardom

Stars are incomplete images outside the cinema: the performance of the film is the moment of completion of images in subsidiary circulation, in newspapers, fanzines, etc. . . . The star is at once ordinary and extraordinary.

John Ellis, "Stars as Cinematic Phenomenon"

Fan magazines mediated the relationships between viewers and stars in a paradoxical manner during the 1930s. *Photoplay,* in particular, presented its predominantly female readership with a complex portrait of stardom. Writing of the interactions between women and star magazines during the twenties, Gaylyn Studlar notes: "Instead of automatically reinforcing female powerlessness and marginalization before a patriarchal system, [fan magazines] explored, albeit in ideologically contradictory terms, the historically specific locus of women in American cinema, culture and society." [48] The contradictory ideologies that Studlar mentions found form in a multiple address to women readers in the thirties as well. As they were represented in print and publicity stills, stars promised fans both an adherence to traditional mores and the transgression of familiar values.

From 1930 to 1934, for instance, *Photoplay*'s letters to the editor highlighted a heated debate between proponents of Greta Garbo versus those of Marlene Dietrich. Each side consisted of missives from female fans who made vehement claims regarding the superiority, power, and attractiveness of each actress. "Garbo carries us away from our modern, humdrum existence to a dream world," wrote Thelma Holland of Ann Arbor, Michigan, in one such printed debate. Holland's adoration was balanced by a letter from Betty Ferguson of Brooklyn, New York, who sang Dietrich's praises: "Dietrich is superior to Garbo in everything. She has twice the looks, twice the acting ability and an utterly charming talking and singing voice that Garbo can never aspire to." [49] In a fascinating display of the contradictory negotiations put into play between viewers and stars, the debate elicited the passions of female fans who unleashed their feelings for female performers, stars who each connoted traditional notions of beauty, as well as independence, androgyny, and danger to men.

According to Studlar, critics are mistaken to assume that the investment of female readers in fan discourses represents their loss of identity and their overinvestment in fantasies of Hollywood glamor: "Instead, what is evoked by both the tone and content of fan magazines is more on the order of an identification with stardom as a kind of 'masquerade,' a play with identity. . . . bringing elements of make believe and pretense into play—on both sides of the screen. Such a masquerade . . . would have elicited the understanding of many women . . . who themselves were engaged in an attempt to resituate themselves in relation to changing concepts of female social and sexual identity." [50] Studlar's use of disguise as a means of describing viewers' relationships to stars and images is important. Studlar's version of masquerade makes viewing a playful negotiation, an engagement of spectators in a game of fantasy. Studlar asserts that viewers have interpretive power in their relationships with actors—performers and fans masquerade for each other.

But how does the spectator-star masquerade take form in horror? One means of conceptualizing this rapport is to accept viewers' abilities to interpret films, and the publicity which surrounded them, in a complex manner. Quite possibly, spectators recognize the interplay between the fiction of roles and the different but related fiction of extratextual discourses. In fact, magazines and pressbooks promoted the conflation of contradictory onscreen and offscreen personae, which complicated both the stability of character portrayals and star images in the 1930s.

The potential impact of this combination of elements in reference to classic horror is that actors may have portrayed sinister or helpless characters onscreen while being promoted as kind or capable stars offscreen. This representational paradox engages spectators as active agents in the construction and comprehension of the inherent contradictions and complexities of cinematic discourses. Viewers likely refused to interpret onscreen portrayals in a vacuum in the thirties and probably opted, instead, to infuse films, characters, and stars with diverse meanings. Maestro Svengali's monstrosity, then, existed alongside John Barrymore's heartthrob reputation. In 1931, for example, *Photoplay* ran a series of articles on Marian Marsh, *Svengali*'s heroine, which illustrates the multiple identities created for horror stars. "And Who Is This Girl?" was a story that included photos of Marsh and linked her to John Barrymore: "Surely the young lady [in the photo] on the left is Mrs. John Barrymore, Dolores Costello that was. And the girl on the right must certainly be either Constance or Joan Bennett. But the fact is that both girls are Marian Marsh, the child still in her 'teens who has been chosen to play *Trilby* to John Barrymore's *Svengali* in the Warner Brothers's talking version of that famous Du Maurier story."[51] Marsh's onscreen assignment was collapsed with an offscreen relationship to Barrymore in this article (she looks like his wife), while her resemblance to glamorous female stars was emphasized.

The following month *Photoplay* ran another article on Marsh that traded more thoroughly in fantasies of stardom. In "You Should See My Kid Sister," Marsh's motion picture debut was attributed to a sibling who coaxed her to a place where, "like Cinderella, in the fairy tale, she met Prince Charming. Only in this story, Prince Charming is John Barrymore—but nothing could have been more princely or more charming to Marian than Barrymore's acceptance of her for the role of Trilby."[52] Marsh's impending starring role is considered romantic and her casting deemed a matter of Barrymore's personal choice. The article smacks of a rags-to-riches tale of transformation in its associations with Cinderella and Sleeping Beauty. Romance connotations are reinforced by the conflation of Marsh's extrafilmic roles (ingénue and Barrymore's adoring waif) with her narrative position (Svengali's unwilling yet compliant object of desire). Given the range of messages circulated, Warner Bros.'s actual production of *Svengali* is but one discourse among many. Marsh's onscreen incarnation of a heroine subjected to the horrifying advances of Barrymore's devious maestro appeared simultaneously with articles proclaiming that she resembled Barrymore's wife, was discovered by him, and was well matched with the actor in her onscreen portrayal.

Throughout the decade *Photoplay* and other fan magazines ran stories on horror's heroines as they posed in the latest fashions and tendered advice on makeup, grooming, and romance. Fay Wray was especially popular, given her starring roles in a range of films, including classic horror and jungle-adventure movies such as *Doctor X, King Kong, The Most Dangerous Game* (1932), *Mystery of the Wax Museum,* and *The Vampire Bat* (1933). In February 1931, the year Michael Curtiz's *Doctor X* debuted in Technicolor, Wray was profiled in a number of publications. *Picture Play* detailed her efforts to control her star image: "Resolutely Fay Wray set about to overcome the handicap of being overpublicized as a swansdown heroine at the beginning of her career [in 1927]. So well has she succeeded by dint of hard work that now she's placed by critics among the select few."[53] The same month that *Picture Play* commented on her popularity with critics, *Screenland* asked readers to determine her stature: "There seems to be quite an argument over Fay Wray. Is she still a pleasant ingénue, or a real dramatic artist? Fay thinks she has grown up—do you agree with her?"[54] By the spring of 1931, Wray was offering tips to *Photoplay's* readers on how to steam their hair to "bring out the wave."[55] Whether ingénue or not, her publicity focused on a "good girl" image, the same image she projected as the heroine of Curtiz's film.[56]

Nearly two years later, *Photoplay* ran a publicity still for *King Kong* that focused again on Wray: "Introducing you to just one of Fay Wray's bad moments in that new hair-raiser, *King Kong*."[57] Although the image depicts Wray dangling precariously from Kong's paw, the casual tone of the description and her mention in other publications are striking counterpoints to the horror elements. For example, her ingénue demeanor was replaced by strength and an immunity to terror in a 1933 piece that claimed her athletic abilities.[58] And in a Lux soap advertisement that appeared in the *Los Angeles Examiner* upon the film's release, *King Kong's* star promised "A Thousand thrills . . . and hers the thrill of *Supreme Beauty*."[59] Wray's simian troubles on top of the Empire State Building are nothing compared to her thrilling loveliness, according to the cutline. The actress may look tormented onscreen, *Photoplay* still suggested, but her stardom and advertising appearances assured readers she was alive, beautiful, and athletic offscreen.

Heroes and monsters were also subject to scrutiny and adoration in fan magazines. Boris Karloff, who plays the fiend in movies like *Frankenstein* and *The Mummy,* was presented to *Photoplay's* fans as a skilled actor. In an article entitled "Meet the Monster!" readers were introduced to the man behind the masks. Ruth Rankin's descriptions of Karloff's rise to fame from "incredible hardship and frustration" are almost as dramatic as his film roles. Karloff's onscreen and offscreen personae were conflated by Rankin and marked by high drama, suffering, ambition, and dissimulation. For instance, Rankin highlights the tortures endured by Karloff during the hours of makeup application required of so many of his roles. Here is an actor who has to suffer in order to become a monster that makes others suffer, Rankin told her readers.[60] In the month following Rankin's piece, *Photoplay* published a personable glossy of Karloff with an ominous caption: "And now his bosses have issued orders that hereafter Boris Karloff is to be photographed only in character. So this is the last straight portrait you will see of *The Monster*."[61] *Photoplay* thus shifted from humanizing Karloff, as in Rankin's exposé, to confirming that his monstrous roles were paramount.

Other horror actors received acclaim in *Photoplay* as well. In the case of Fredric March, who plays the dual eponymous roles in Paramount's *Dr. Jekyll and Mr. Hyde* and who went on to win an Oscar for his monstrous thespian efforts, his hero and star status were reinforced in the magazine, while his links to monstrosity were downplayed. In one review, for example, March was praised in an intimate fashion: "Fred handles the difficult dual role superbly."[62] In other references to the film, he was presented as either a dashing star or hardworking actor whose efforts paid off.[63]

Photoplay's focus on Miriam Hopkins, the actress who plays the woman killed by the fiendish Mr. Hyde in the movie, similarly avoided the horror theme. A January 1932 production still depicted Hopkins's thespian travails. She is shown bare-shouldered under the covers of a bed. The shot is from an early scene in which the kindhearted Dr. Jekyll visits her boudoir. The following commentary framed the still: "Miriam Hopkins suffers. . . . Imagine having to lie in that soft bed all day while the director gives instructions. She makes the sacrifice so your lives will be brighter."[64] While in the film Hopkins endures the sustained abuse of a monstrous Fredric March—in her role as the working-class character named Ivy—the sarcastic caption announced that her cinematic sacrifices are primarily glamorous, not painful.

Photoplay's publicity ploys complicated horror's reception by contrasting narrative events—in this case Hopkins's onscreen torment—with innocuous star profiles. The net result of this and other promotional tactics was an environment for spectatorship that provided female patrons with a range of prospective responses to the genre: women were told that they are terrified of horror movies but crave romance with fiends. They were also informed that they resemble monsters but do not need to take the genre too seriously because its stars are only playacting. This combination of contradictory discourses disabled viewer efforts to streamline the genre's gender address. If male and female spectators saw classic horror as a purveyor of traditional values and roles, which I am sure some did, they did so *against the grain* of publicity discourses and against the narratives of some of the films as well.

In all likelihood spectators acted out that warning provided by Edward Van Sloan in his prologue to *Frankenstein:* "[Classic horror cinema] will thrill you, it may shock you, it might even horrify you." Whatever it did to its audience, classic horror did it with flair and, above all, with an attention to conventional gender roles as both powerful social identities and compelling modes of cultural performance. Male and female spectators were offered a range of publicity, exhibition, and critical discourses that invited them alternately to act in line with traditional gender mores and to act out unconventional gender roles.

So what did those male and female spectators do who watched horror films in the 1930s? Like obedient heterosexual male viewers, they may have protected their dates or bitten their lips, held their girlfriends close, or responded bravely. Like exemplary female patrons, they may have screamed or swooned, cowered or fainted. Or they may have taken the marketing contradictions at face value and let loose, growled if they were women, fainted if men, and put the cultural expectations of proper gender behaviors to shame in the very act of spectatorship.

Notes

1. Examples of this approach to horror cinema include David J. Hogan, *Dark Romance: Sexuality in the Horror Film* (New York: McFarland, 1986), and James B. Twitchell, *Dreadful Pleasures: An Anatomy of Modern Horror* (New York: Oxford University Press, 1985). Although she continues to privilege male spectatorship in the genre, Carol J. Clover more recently shifts the focus from sadism to masochism in *Men, Women, and Chain Saws: Gender in the Modern Horror Film* (Princeton, N.J.: Princeton University Press, 1992).

2. James E. Mitchell, "Mad Scientists, Cannibalism, Bodies—Gosh!" *Los Angeles Examiner*, August 12, 1932.

3. Norbert Mundorf, James Weaver, and Dolf Zillman, "Effects of Gender Roles and Self Perceptions on Affective Reactions to Horror Films," *Sex Roles* 20, no. 11 (1989): 655–673.

4. Janet Staiger, *Interpreting Films: Studies in the Historical Reception of American Cinema* (Princeton, N.J.: Princeton University Press, 1992), p. 30.

5. Abel, "*The Old Dark House*," *Variety*, November 1, 1932.

6. Staiger, *Interpreting Films*, p. 81.

7. Mordaunt Hall, "Bram Stoker's Human Vampire," *New York Times*, February 13, 1931, p. 21.

8. Edwin Schallert, "*Frankenstein* a Hit," *Los Angeles Times*, January 4, 1932, part J.

9. Louella O. Parsons, "Horror, Thrills, and Suspense Fill Picture," *Los Angeles Examiner*, March 25, 1933.

10. I found only one direct mention of horror's incompatibility with female patrons in my research, which appeared in a letter to the editor in the *Motion Picture Herald*. The letter read as follows: "THEY HAVE OVERLOOKED THE WOMEN. The producers find that in some of the larger cities where their overhead is highest, horror pictures, weird and gruesome pictures . . . have taken their fair sized grosses. From this as a beginning they have figured that the whole country wants this type of film fare. In this they are very erroneous . . . the women have been almost entirely overlooked." Letter to the Editor, *Motion Picture Herald* 111, no. 4 (April 22, 1933): 50. The glut of horror and gangster films produced during the early 1930s were, according to F. M. A. Litchard, the letter's author, drawing "large numbers of unemployed men who have nothing to do." They were not pulling in the more important urban *and* rural patrons, namely women. Although Litchard's letter is the only direct complaint I located on the topic of horror's lack of appeal to women, the polarization of gender in viewership was commented on in a review for *Murders in the Zoo* (1933), a Paramount mystery film. As McCarthy noted in *Motion Picture Herald*: "The men in the preview audience seemed to appreciate the ruthless Gorman and the comic Yates, with the animal element. The women, as could

be expected did the gasping, and according to their comments, they seemed to agree that it was a little too brutal for feminine appreciation." "*Murders in the Zoo*," *Motion Picture Herald* 110, no. 11 (March 11, 1933): 19. Of course, it is possible to read the responses of female patrons as ambiguous—their gasps may have indicated their appreciation of the film behind the guise of gender norms and their comments to the reviewer may have favored more conventional gender expectations while downplaying more complex affective responses.

11. Leo Meehan, "*Frankenstein*," *Motion Picture Herald* 105, no. 7 (November 14, 1931): 40.

12. McCarthy, "*Wax Museum*," *Motion Picture Herald* 110, no. 2 (January 7, 1933): 23.

13. "At the Roxy," *New York Times*, May 11, 1935, p. 21.

14. "*White Zombie*," *Time*, August 8, 1932.

15. Michael Price and George Turner, "*White Zombie*—Today's Unlikely Classic," *American Cinematographer* 69, no. 2 (February 1988): 36.

16. Although Leo Handel's audience studies in the 1940s suggest that men liked horror more than women, the variance in preferences was less significant than might be expected, given popular assumptions about the relationship between gender and generic tastes. On the whole, the research reported by Handel for a 1942 study suggested that neither women nor men counted horror among their top four choices when they were asked to rank story types they liked the most. Mystery and horror pictures were ranked as men's fifth favorite type, behind war pictures, adventure action pictures, musical comedies, and westerns. Women ranked mystery and horror movies (which were listed as a pair in the survey) seventh out of a possible twenty-one options, after love stories, musical comedies, serious dramas, war pictures, sophisticated comedies, and historicals and biographies. It should be noted, however, that when ranking story types according to their dislikes, horror and mystery films ranked second behind westerns for women (and tied with G-men and gangster movies), while men rated the genre as eighth most disliked (again, in a tie with G-men and gangster films). Noteworthy is that Handel's results also varied according to age—younger audiences (between twelve and twenty-nine) liked mystery and horror films far more than those viewers between thirty and forty-four years of age. Leo A. Handel, *Hollywood Looks at Its Audience: A Report of Film Audience Research* (Urbana: University of Illinois Press, 1950), p. 124.

17. Rush, "*Dracula*," *Variety*, February 18, 1931.

18. *Motion Picture Herald* 102, no. 2 (January 10, 1931): 39; Michael J. Murphy, *The Celluloid Vampire: A History and Filmography 1897–1979* (Ann Arbor, Mich.: Pierian Press, 1979), p. 21; Alan Frank, *Horror Movies: Tales of Terror in the Cinema* (London: Octopus Books, 1974), p. 14.

19. Rush, "*Frankenstein*," *Variety*, December 8, 1931.

20. Bernard Charman, "Girls Want Mystery; Boys War Pictures," *Motion Picture Herald* 111, no. 4 (April 22, 1933): 47.

21. Charles S. Aaronson, "B.O. Explodes Idea That Women Dislike War and Crook Pictures. Feminine Attendance at Four Productions Classed as Lacking in Love or Romantic Interest Averages 61 Per Cent of Total at Matinees and 59 Per Cent at Night." *Exhibitors Herald-World* 100, no. 10 (September 6, 1930): 24.

22. McCarthy, "*The Mummy*," *Motion Picture Herald* 109, no. 10 (December 3, 1932): 27.

23. McCarthy, "*King Kong,*" *Motion Picture Herald* 110, no. 9 (February 25, 1933): 37, 40.

24. *Motion Picture Herald* 105, no. 13 (December 26, 1931): 28.

25. David J. Skal, *The Monster Show: A Cultural History of Horror* (New York: W. W. Norton, 1993), p. 144; Rush, "*Dr. Jekyll and Mr. Hyde,*" *Variety,* January 5, 1932.

26. "Laby's Effective Lobby Display," *Motion Picture Herald* 106, no. 5 (January 30, 1932): 68.

27. "Don't Park Here Says Caldwell on *Frankenstein,*" *Motion Picture Herald* 120, no. 5 (August 3, 1935): 82.

28. "Swinger Offers First Aid," *Motion Picture Herald* 120, no. 11 (September 14, 1935): 64.

29. John F. Barry and Epes W. Sargent, *Building Theater Patronage: Management and Merchandising* (New York: Chalmers Publishing Co., 1927), p. 222. In an excellent study of early marketing stunts, Jane Gaines mentions Barry and Sargent's ambulance ploy and adds: "The ambulance was also used threateningly to convey the message that audiences attended horror films at their own risk." Since she footnotes only Barry and Sargent after this comment and since the exhibitors did not mention the usefulness of the ambulance for horror showings in their 1927 book, my guess is that Gaines's reference points forward to the 1930s when ambulances and medical care became a promotional staple for the genre. Jane Gaines, "From Elephants to Lux Soap: The Programming and 'Flow' of Early Motion Picture Exploitation," *Velvet Light Trap* 25 (Spring 1990): 36.

30. *Motion Picture Herald* 120, no. 1 (July 6, 1935): 99.

31. "Free Permanent Given for *Invisible Ray,*" *Motion Picture Herald* 124, no. 3 (July 18, 1936): 85.

32. Diane Waldman, "From Midnight Shows to Marriage Vows," *Wide Angle* 6, no. 2 (1984): 41.

33. "'When Will She Wake?' Rosy Asks Bridgeport," *Motion Picture Herald* 119, no. 13 (June 29, 1935): 91. The fainting female patron was, it seems, a fixture of classic horror stunts in the thirties. In some cases, however, she was an unintended by-product of exhibitor efforts. According to Maury Foladare, one of *King Kong*'s publicists, a female patron in the Pacific Northwest was so distraught by a stunt for the film that she fainted and sued for damages. As Foladare noted many years later: "I got a big guy and rented an ape costume from Western Costume. I had the big ape walk into the Wenatchee (WA) Department Store. This one woman fainted. Later, she sued me and the studio (RKO) for $100,000." Eventually, the matter was settled without payment. Beverly Beyette, "Dean of Hollywood Publicists, 79, Keeps Plugging Away Honest," *Los Angeles Times,* September 21, 1986.

34. Marquis Busby, "*Dracula* Better Film than Stage Play at Orpheum," *Los Angeles Examiner,* March 28, 1931.

35. In some instances it was less what women did than what they did *not* do vis-à-vis horror that was remarked upon. A reporter for the *New York World Telegram* had the following to say about *Doctor X* in 1932: "As far as the eyes of this conscientious reporter could detect, not one woman in the audience fainted." *New York World Telegram,* August 4, 1932.

36. "Louie Charnisky Stages Swell *Black Cat* Show," *Motion Picture Herald* 116, no. 2 (July 7, 1934): 74.

37. Despite reviewer warnings that children and youth should not attend these films, exhibitors encouraged their attendance quite enthusiastically by mid-decade.

38. "Emotion Test Hits on *Frankenstein*," *Motion Picture Herald* 119, no. 7 (May 18, 1935): 79.

39. *The Mystery of the Wax Museum* (Warner Bros., 1932) Pressbook (Library of Congress microfiche file, Washington, D.C.).

40. "Dick and Ken Speed Up on *Invisible Man*," *Motion Picture Herald* 114, no. 4 (January 20, 1934): 78.

41. McCarthy, *"The Invisible Man,"* *Motion Picture Herald* 113, no. 6 (November 4, 1933): 37.

42. Kurt Singer, *The Laughton Story: The Intimate Story of Charles Laughton* (Philadelphia: John C. Winston, 1954), p. 105.

43. "*Island of Lost Souls*," *Photoplay* 43, no. 3 (February 1933): 58.

44. *Island of Lost Souls* (Paramount, 1932) Pressbook (Library of Congress microfiche file, Washington, D.C.).

45. Barbara Barry, "Such a Naughty Nero," *Photoplay* 43, no. 3 (February 1933): 46–47, 95–96.

46. *Photoplay* 43, no. 3 (February 1933): 4.

47. *Photoplay* 40, no. 2 (July 1931): 7. Whether *Svengali* is a horror film has been debated for a number of years. Phil Hardy does not include it in his *Encyclopedia of Horror* (New York: Harper and Row, 1986), but William K. Everson contextualized it in relation to Hollywood's horror cycle in *The New School Program Notes,* June 26, 1973. The film has a strong link to vampire and zombie films, with its focus on hypnosis and the construction of the eponymous character as a fiend. *Svengali*'s status as a horror movie is merely assumed by Ellen Draper in her analysis of films in which fiends mesmerize heroines. According to Draper, *Svengali,* like the classic horror movie *White Zombie,* depicts the victimization of women so well that it proves Laura Mulvey right about the primacy of the sadistic male gaze in Hollywood narrative cinema. For Draper, however, *Svengali* and a number of other films go one step farther: they overstate female suffering to the point that patriarchy's misogynistic machinations are laid bare. Ellen Draper, "Zombie Women When the Gaze Is Male," *Wide Angle* 10, no. 3 (1988): 52–62.

48. Gaylyn Studlar, "The Perils of Pleasure? Fan Magazine Discourse as Women's Commodified Culture in the 1920s," *Wide Angle* 13, no. 1 (1991): 8.

49. *Photoplay* 34, no. 6 (May 1931): 8.

50. Studlar, "The Perils of Pleasure?" p. 15.

51. "And Who Is This Girl?" *Photoplay* 34, no. 4 (March 1931): 68.

52. "You Should See My Kid Sister," *Photoplay* 34, no. 5 (April 1931): 31.

53. *Picture Play* (February 1931). Fay Wray Scrapbook 1929–1933, p. 54, Fay Wray Collection, University of Southern California Cinema Archives, Los Angeles.

54. *Screenland* (February 1931). Fay Wray Scrapbook, p. 55.

55. *Photoplay* 34, no. 6 (May 1931): 18.

56. Wray's sweet reputation was reinforced by stories about her home life. For ex-

ample, one New York paper painted an affectionate portrait of Wray's relationship with her husband, John Monk Saunders. According to the piece, her husband's "pet nickname for her is Goofy. She is very proper and merely calls him John." Sidney Skolsky, "Tintypes," *New York News,* October 19, 1931. Fay Wray Scrapbook, p. 82.

57. "What Power Can Save Them?" *Photoplay* 43, no. 5 (April 1933): 30.

58. In one 1933 item entitled "No More Horror for Fay Wray," a reporter claimed: "She is one of the best girl athletes in pictures." Fay Wray Scrapbook, p. 22.

59. The Lux Toilet Soap advertisement appeared in the *Los Angeles Examiner* on March 27, 1933. Other horror starlets such as Mae Clarke, Marion Davies, Sidney Fox, Miriam Hopkins, Leila Hyams, Elsa Lanchester, Marian Marsh, and Lupe Velez graced *Photoplay*'s pages. Some modeled outfits, as was the case with Sidney Fox, star of *Murders in the Rue Morgue* (1932), who looked "girlish" wearing a "boyish suit." *Photoplay* 34, no. 5 (April 1931): 61. Mae Clarke, heroine of *Frankenstein,* was the subject of a rise-to-stardom piece; see Harry Lang, " 'I'll Have Vanilla,' " *Photoplay* 41, no. 2 (January 1932): 72, 115.

60. Ruth Rankin, "Meet the Monster!" *Photoplay* 43, no. 2 (January 1933): 60.

61. *Photoplay* 43, no. 3 (February 1933): 27.

62. *Photoplay* 41, no. 4 (March 1932): 8.

63. "Ask the Answer Man," *Photoplay* 41, no. 4 (March 1932): 86.

64. *Photoplay* 41, no. 2 (January 1932): 58–59.

Bringing It All Back Home:
Family Economy and Generic Exchange

Vivian Sobchack

Two very special babies were born to the American cinema in 1968: Rosemary's and Stanley Kubrick's. One was born in a horror film, the other in a science fiction film. One stared up from a cradle toward its earthly mother, the other down from space toward Mother Earth. Nonetheless, both the "devil's spawn" and the "starchild" condensed the *visible sight* of cultural difference, social change, and historical movement into the single and powerful figure of a child—one marked as an enigma by virtue of its strange eyes and estranged, alien vision.

Both infants also signaled the replacement of previous generic displacements. In their bodies and through their eyes, those far-off and imaginary spaces that once characterized and differentiated traditional horror and science fiction films were replaced to the homesite from whence they were first envisioned. The *visual site* of horrific attraction and repulsion, of utopian wonder and dystopian anxiety, was redirected back toward that domestic structure of social relations—the nuclear family. Thus, despite their reversed visual perspectives and differing generic locations, the two newborns figured in *Rosemary's Baby* and *2001: A Space Odyssey* had a good deal in common. Born at—and as—the end or final cause of the narratives in which they were conceived and (re)produced, both babies not only infused a new flow of representational energy into their respective genres, but also marked the beginning of an extremely interesting and historically situated generic convergence.

In this essay I explore the cultural meanings that the figure of the child narrativizes as it is exchanged and transformed between the contemporary horror and science fiction films, and as it creates an adherence between these two genres and a third—the newly revitalized family melodrama. In all three genres, by virtue of its implication of domestic space, generational time, and familial structure, the privileged figure of the child condenses and initiates a contemporary and pressing cultural drama. That drama emerges from the crisis experienced by American bourgeois patriarchy since the late 1960s and is marked by the related disintegration and transfiguration of the traditional American bourgeois family—an ideological as well as interpersonal structure characterized, as Robin Wood so frequently points out, by its cellular construction and institutionalization of capitalist and patriarchal relations and values (among them, monogamy, heterosexuality, and consumerism) and by its present state of disequilibrium and crisis.[1]

Although historically asymmetrical in their major periods of production and popularity, the traditional horror and science fiction films have tended toward a structurally symmetrical relationship marked by *opposition*. The two genres have been connected but differentiated by what seems a systemic and binary reversal of themes, iconographies, and conventions of narrative, dramatic, and visual representation. As I have elaborated elsewhere, both genres deal with a grand-scale chaos that threatens "the order of things," but the nature of that order is differentiated: "the horror film deals with moral chaos, the disruption of natural order (assumed to be God's order), and the threat to the harmony of hearth and home; the science fiction film, on the other hand, is concerned with social chaos, with the disruption of social order (manmade), and the threat to the harmony of civilized society going about its business."[2] As well, the two genres can be differentiated by the primary modality of their "dreamwork"—those processes of condensation, displacement, and secondary elaboration that metaphorically and metonymically constitute narrative momentum and iconographic imagery. Repression seems the dominant strategy of the traditional horror film. And, as we all know by now, what is repressed returns in condensed and displaced form to threaten and challenge and disrupt that which would deny it presence. On the other hand, sublimation seems the dominant strategy of the traditional science fiction film. Libidinal energy is transferred into the creation of wondrous special effects and is displayed and condensed into dramas of technological (re)production or grand-scale destruction or both. Contemporary examples of both genres,

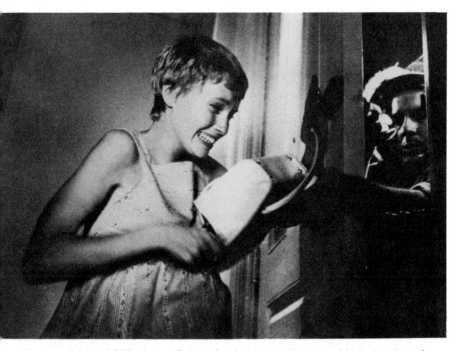

Rosemary's Baby (1968): the conflation of melodrama and horror with the invasion of familial space.

however, tend to deny the generally neat symmetrical opposition of their traditional cinematic ancestors. In the context of the ambivalent horror and wonder provoked by the social upheavals of the last two decades and by complementary upheavals in the entertainment industry, a convergence and conflation of generic difference has occurred.

Indeed, many recent horror and science fiction films have been marked as contemporary not only on the basis of their release dates, but also on the basis of their mutual spatial relocation to the American landscape and temporal relocation to the present, their mutual figuration of the Other as both the "same" as well as "different" from ourselves and somehow implicated in family life, and by their common and preconscious thematic recognition that the social world can no longer be conceptualized and dramatized as an opposition between private and public concerns and spheres of action.[3] Figures from the past and the future get into the house, make their homes in the closet, become part of the family, and open the kitchen and family room up to the horrific and wondrous world outside this private and safe domain. A man's home in bourgeois patriarchal culture is no longer his castle. In the age of television the drawbridge is always down; the world intrudes. It is no longer possible to avoid the invasive presence of Others—whether poltergeists, extraterrestrials, one's own alien kids, or starving Ethiopian children.

Since the 1960s, then, the events of family life and social life have been commonly and increasingly experienced as convergent. Thus, it is not surprising that contemporary generic articulations of horror and science fiction have tended to complement, rather than oppose, each other. Their previously binary relation has been transformed into an analogue that includes the family melodrama—a genre whose representations are governed not by the conventions of the fantastic, but by those of realism. In the currency of today's generic economy, the once markedly different representational registers of the fantastic and the realistic are more easily able to circulate and commensurably represent similar thematic and dramatic material. Thus, even as their distinction is seemingly still held sacred, the fantastic and the real pervade each other and insist on a closer and closer equivalence.

This triadic adherence of horror, science fiction, and family melodrama also entails a temporal and spatial exchange. The past, that temporal field usually grounding the horror film, is commensurable with the future, usually associated with the science fiction film—and both are commensurable with the present, usually the temporal field of the family melodrama. Correlatively, previously distinct narrative sites become contiguous or congruent. The exotic, decadent European world of the traditional horror film, the wondrous, alien outer space of the science fiction film, and the familiar, domestic, and traditionally American space of the family melodrama become closely associated. Exotic, decadent, and alien space geographically conflates with familiar and familial space. The displaced "There" has been replaced with "Here," and "Then" and "When" have been condensed as "Now." Thus, the time and place of horror and anxiety, wonder and hope, have been brought back into the American home. It is within the home and family that the institutionalization and perpetuation of the bourgeois social world begins—and ends. This is the common place, the present world, shared by horror films such as *The Exorcist* (1973), *Carrie* (1976), *The Fury* (1978), *The Amityville Horror* (1979), and *Poltergeist* (1982), and science fiction films like *Close Encounters of the Third Kind* (1977), *E.T.* (1982), and *Starman* (1984), and family melodramas like *Ordinary People* (1980) and *Shoot the Moon* (1982).

At a time when the mythology of our dominant culture can no longer resolve the social contradictions exposed by experience, the nuclear family has found itself in nuclear crisis. Rather than serving bourgeois patriarchy as a place of refuge from the social upheavals of the last two decades (many of which have been initiated by the young and by women), the family has become the site of them—and now serves as a sign of their representation. Not only has the bourgeois distinction between family members and alien Others, between private home and public space, between personal microcosm and sociopolitical macrocosm, been exposed as a myth, but also the family itself has been exposed as a cultural construction, as a set of signifying, as well as significant, practices. The family and its members are seen, therefore, as subject to the frightening, but potentially liberating, semiotic processes of selection and combination—and their order, meaning, and power are perceived as open to transformation, dissolution, and redefinition.

The contemporary genres of horror, science fiction, and family melodrama converge in their dramatization of these processes that test and represent the coherence, meaning, and limits of the family as it has been constructed in patriarchal culture. Historically asymmetrical in regard to their peak periods of production, each genre to some degree maintaining a discrete archetypal core of generic structures and motifs, the three have nonetheless come together in common response to their shared cultural context and the similar social malaise that surrounds and supports their current popularity.[4] Engaging in an urgent and dynamic exchange, whose goal is ultimately conservative, the three genres attempt to narratively contain, work out, and in some fashion resolve the contemporary weakening of patriarchal authority and the glaring contradictions that exist between the mythology of family relations and their actual social practice. In all three genres those contradictions are most powerfully condensed and represented in the problematic figure of the child.

I began this essay by invoking two newborns: Rosemary's baby and Kubrick's starchild. My interest is in their cinematic offspring: the babies, children, and childlike figures who have been born to the cinema in their generation and eventually transformed the cinematic shape of both patriarchy and the nuclear family. First, however, I must clarify the way in which I am using the concepts of *figure* and *figuration*.[5] Not simply "motifs," "symbols," or rhetorical "additions" to narrative discourse, figures visibly represent the origin and process of narrative. "Discussion of figures," Dudley Andrew tells us, "wants to flow back to the moment in which a particular meaning was shaped."[6] Figures coalesce, condense, embody, enact, and transform the trouble in the text, the narrative problematic. Their emergence and presence in the text serve not only to give visible form to the narrative problem, but also to alter it, to describe it differently from its previous visible articulations, to change its structure, its dynamic, and its meanings.

Figures, therefore, are metaphoric in function and event—if, as Andrew suggests, "metaphor is conceived of not as a . . . substitution but as a process resulting in the redescription of a semantic field."[7] The term "figuration" reminds us of this process. Figuration entails the figure actively engaged in transforming the text and being itself transformed through its work: adjusting the system of representation and the demands of the psyche and culture each to the other. The figure, then, is by nature and function unstable, problematic, and productive of new meanings and new interpretations. Following Paul Ricoeur, Andrew tells us that in its most vital work, the figure

> forces us to put into play all the possibilities of the sign and then leap to a new possibility, the one that will change the context itself and make us see it through the "improper and impertinent" sign. This is what produces a seismic shift in the contextual field. In politics we call such condensation "revolution," in psychoanalysis "transference," and in artistic and religious experience "insight." Figures are thus more than shortcuts by way of association and substitution; they have the power to disrupt the relation of context to sign and reorient not only the discursive event but the system itself which will never be the same afterwards.[8]

It is within this context that the production and emergence of the visible figure of the infant at—and as—the end of both *Rosemary's Baby* and *2001* can be said to have disrupted and reoriented not only the cultural meanings attached to representations of infants and children, but also the articulations, structure, and meanings of the two genres in which they appeared.

The secular baby and child have held a privileged place in bourgeois and patriarchal mythology since the nineteenth century. Infancy and childhood have been represented as the cultural site of such "positive" virtues as innocence, transparency, and a "pure" and wonderful curiosity not yet informed by sexuality. Representing these virtues, the baby has been culturally produced as a figure of poignant sweetness—helpless, vulnerable, and dependent not only because of its physical immaturity, but also because of its lack of the "corrupting" knowledge necessary for survival in the social world. This "lack," however, is represented as "hope" and "promise." Not yet having been *subjected to* the lessons of experience and history, the infant and child signify the *subject of* an experience and history still to be enacted and inscribed. In this way the child becomes the *signifier* of the future. But the child is also the *signified* of the past. Its familiar identity and family resemblance are produced as visible traces of the past's presence in the present and ensure the past's presence in a future safely contained and constrained by tradition and history. At best, it will carry the father's name forward—at least, his seed. Thus, in its representation of the infant and child, bourgeois mythology has constructed a sign of the future that is sweetly traditional and safely adventurous, open yet closed. The infant and child as sign evoke nostalgia. What seems a looking forward toward the possibilities of the future is a longing backward toward the promise once possessed by the past—a longing for inexperience, for potential rather than realized action, for an openness to the world based on a lack of worldliness.

Both *Rosemary's Baby* and *2001* ended up delivering infants to the screen who interrogated this mythology by their very presence, their bodies figuring a visible site of ambiguity, ambivalence, and contradiction.[9] The two newborns were as alien as they were human; calling up familiar and familial feelings by their "baby-ness," they were, nonetheless, not wholly the culture's own. Rosemary's emerged from the outer limits of bourgeois notions of time—from a historic coupling of primal, diabolic "negativity" with human being. Kubrick's emerged from the outer limits of bourgeois notions of space—from the "infinite and beyond," from a posthistoric coition of extraterrestrial openness with human being. Given their alien parentage (Satan in one instance, a transcendental and superior unknown in the other), the innocence and lack of knowledge of both babies were certainly questionable. Given the opacity of their eyes, their transparence and sweetness were also suspect. In addition, both newborns, while appearing vulnerable and dependent in their "baby-ness," clearly possessed special power and were not as helpless as their bodies suggested. An irrational, unthinkable past and an unimaginable future collapsed into their visible infantile presence; they evoked no nostalgia. Indeed, the children in these films threatened the mythology they represented and figured "childhood's end." In sum, the future these two children promised in their representation was not the safe future as traditionally envisioned and expected, but rather a radically transformed future, an apocalyptic and revolutionary future, an unimaginable future—perhaps no future at all. What they have delivered, however, is quite something other than radical.

Rosemary's baby has gone on to grow up in the horror film, inscribing dramas in which those negative aspects of childhood and parenthood repressed by bourgeois mythology are played out in ambivalent representations. Diachronically, this ambivalence can be bracketed between two generic declarations. "There's only one thing wrong with the Davis baby. It's alive!" pronounces the ad for *It's Alive* in 1974 (the same year that gave us the diabolic rage of the possessed but powerful Regan in *The Exorcist*). "Part of being a parent is trying to kill your kids," says the teenager in 1983's *Christine* (the same year that saw adults plotting to kill millions of American children in *Halloween III: Season of the Witch*). Over a ten-year period, the horror film has obliquely moved from the representation of children as terrors to children as terrorized. Unnatural natural infants or demonically possessed children become sympathetic victims whose special powers are justifiably provoked or venally abused. And, where once teenagers threatened an entire populace and its social regulation with their burgeoning sexuality and presumption to adulthood, in recent years they have been solipsistically annihilating each other in a quarantined and culturally negligible space. (Indeed, a subgenre solely devoted to teenagers watching and awaiting their own senseless annihilation emerged with *Halloween* in 1978 and *Friday the 13th* in 1980. These slasher movies seem to appeal to adolescent feelings of rage and helplessness—feelings always present but specifically articulated in apocalyptic terms in an age marked by generalized nuclear fear and the particularly brutal events of the 1960s youth and antiwar movements. These films abstract and ritualize adolescent isolation, rage, and helplessness, and it is particularly interesting to note how they rigorously repress the presence of parents and families, the latter's impotence and failure an absence that necessitates and structures the violence of the narratives.)

From the early to mid-1970s and coincident with bourgeois society's negative response to the youth movements and drug culture of the late 1960s and early 1970s, generic emphasis was on the child not as terrorized victim, but as cannibalistic, monstrous, murderous, selfish, sexual. The child was figured as an alien force that threatened both its immediate family and all adult authority that would keep it in its place—oppressed and at home. While runaway children provided the narrative impetus, but not the focus, for such precursors of the new family melodrama as *Joe* (1970) and *Taking Off* (1971), the horror film focused on children not run away but run amok. Their resentment, anger, destructiveness, aberrance, and evil were seen as unwarranted and irrational eruptions—extrafamilial and precivilized in origin. The bodies and souls of such children as appear in *The Other* (1972), *The Exorcist, The Omen* (1976), and *Audrey Rose* (1977) are "possessed" by demonic, supernatural, and ahistoric forces that play out apocalypse in the middle-class home—most often graphically represented by "special effects" that rage in huge and destructive temper tantrums across the screen. Thus, while these children are verbally articulated as "possessed" and "victims," they are visually articulated as in possession of and victimizing their households. Family resemblance notwithstanding, these kids are not their fathers' natural children. They are figured as uncivilized, hostile, and powerful Others who—like their extracinematic counterparts—refuse parental love and authority and mock the established values of dominant institutions. They are "changelings"—the horrifically familiar embodiment of difference.[10] Fascinating the culture that also found them abhorrent, these children collapsed the boundaries that marked off identity from difference and exercised a powerful deconstructive force dangerous to patriarchal bourgeois culture. Their figural presence and work on the screen and in the home restructured and redefined the semantic field of the generation gap—articulating it in vertiginous imagery, as *mise en abime*.[11]

In the mid-1970s, however, *Carrie* transfigures and softens the demonic and murderous child into a familiar Other whose difference is marked not only by her telekinetic power, but also by her relative innocence. Adolescent Carrie is a pitiable victim of her culture who evokes sympathy. She is a nerd whose outrage, however horrific and excessive its expression, is a response to a comprehensible betrayal.[12] Like Robin and Gillian who follow her (*The Fury*), Carrie's fury is as justified as it is frightening—irrational in its power and force, perhaps, but rationally motivated. While Damien and Regan grow up in possession of relatively predetermined sequels that continue to ascribe the cause of children's abuse of their parents and adult authority to extrafamilial, diabolic, and prehistoric forces, the apocalyptic destruction wrought by the likes of Carrie, Robin, and Gillian seem as much generated by familial incoherence and paternal weakness as the cause of it. They come from broken homes. They appear oppressed and vulnerable—exposed to harm and exploitation because of the apparent weakness and instability of the bourgeois family structure deemed responsible for their protection and nurturance. Their special powers are abused, and the apocalypse that follows from their provoked and childishly unselective fury is seen as somehow deserved.

Here it is pertinent to note that sandwiched between *Carrie* and *The Fury,* a 1979 family docu/melodrama made for television—*The Death of Richie*—plays out an opposed but also complementary narrative within the representational register of the realistic. As Leonard Maltin summarizes: "A family is torn apart by teenaged son's drug addiction. . . . straight-arrow father . . . brings himself to kill the boy."[13] Who is responsible for apocalypse here? Who destroys the family—child or parent? Although guilt is perceived as shared, *Richie* sympathetically stresses the anger and despair of the monstrous father rather than the monstrous child. Both structurally complementing and radically opposing *Carrie* or *The Fury,* this realistic melodrama presents a monstrous but sympathetic father who responds to betrayal by using his special power to annihilate his child.

Correlatively, we can see the horror film's earlier representation of parents as bewildered, foolish, and blindly trusting victims of their ungrateful and aberrant children and undergoing a transformation as the figures of those children change. From the terrifying Davis baby or Damien to the terrifying but terrorized Carrie, Robin, and Gillian, to the terrorized Danny (*The Shining* [1980]) or Carol Ann (*Poltergeist*), we can trace a visible shift in the ascription of responsibility for the breakdown of traditional family relations. That responsibility has been transferred from child to parent. As horror film children grow smaller, younger, and less adolescent, their special powers slowly diminish from apocalyptic fury to a relatively helpless insight (the "shining" of Danny's prescience or Carol Ann's "vital" innocence). What deserves note, however, is that this transference of apocalyptic familial fury is generically specific. Contradictory to the most popular contemporary family melodramas and contrary to certain trends in the science fiction film, the horror film moves either to quarantine helpless teenagers in the carnivalesque summer camps, holidays, and prom nights of slasher movies, or to single out Dad as the primary negative force in the middle-class family.

It is in the late 1970s that the genre begins to overtly interrogate paternal commitment and its relation to patriarchal power. In 1978, strong-jawed and iconic Kirk Douglas (playing Robin's natural father in *The Fury*) proves weak and ineffectual; he is unable to save his son from the unnatural father who would exploit him in the name of the law—except by killing the child and himself (albeit accidentally). The following year shows us a weak and possessed straight-arrow father taking to the axe and after his children. *The Amityville Horror* is figured not only as the haunted middle-class family home, but also as the haunted middle-class family Dad—who, weak, economically beleaguered, and under pressure from his corrupt and demanding dream house in a period of economic recession, terrorizes his children. (This corruption of paternal responsibility and perversion of paternal love follows a trajectory forward not only to the *Amityville* sequels in 1982 and 1983, but also to the ethically lax, real-estate salesman Dad whose willful ignorance of the ground of his business practice jeopardizes his children in 1982's *Poltergeist*.)[14]

The repressed in the genre is no longer the double threat found in the traditional horror film: an excessive will to power and knowledge as well as unbridled sexual desire. Rather, the repressed is patriarchal hatred, fear, and self-loathing. As the culture changes, as patriarchy is challenged, as more and more families no longer conform in structure, membership, and behavior to the standards set by bourgeois mythology, the horror film plays out the rage of paternal responsibility denied the economic and political benefits of patriarchal power. The figure of the child in the genre is problematic and horrific because it demands and generates the articulation of another figure. Father is the synchronic repressed who, first powerfully absenting himself, returns to terrify the family in the contemporary horror film. He is the one who, in 1968, willingly yields his paternity and patriarchal rite to Satan. He is the one whose absence powerfully marks the households of Regan and Carrie, who engenders these daughters' rage in their lack, but is not there to culturally

The mad face of patriarchy: Jack Nicholson as Jack Torrance in *The Shining* (1980).

constrain it within the Law of the Father.[15] Dad is also the one who—in the canny casting of John Cassavetes—carries his patriarchal pact with the devil (at Rosemary's and her baby's expense) forward into his surrogate and exploitative fatherhood of Robin and Gillian. By 1980 the return and figuration of the repressed Father become fully explicit—iconically realized in the leering, jeering, mad, child-abusive hatred of Jack Torrance in *The Shining*. Looking backward with the dull but still malevolent gaze of dead Jack, frozen in a labyrinth from which he could not escape, we can see in *Rosemary's Baby* the radical beginning of patriarchal failure: of paternity refused, denied, abandoned, hated; of patriarchy simultaneously terrified and terrorizing in the face of its increasing impotence; of patriarchy maddened by a paradoxical desire for its own annihilation. In the contemporary horror film the sins of the fathers are truly visited upon the sons—and daughters.

If the contemporary horror film dramatizes the terror of a patriarchy without power and refuses or perverts paternal responsibility when it is not rewarded with the benefits of patriarchal authority, the contemporary family melodrama plays out an uneasy acceptance of patriarchy's decline. The mode of the most popular films in the genre tends to be elegiac or comic. On the one hand, 1979 gave us *The Great Santini,* which found the exaggerated authoritarian power of its family patriarch excessively and pitiably inappropriate and impotent, but also celebrated its loss with a conservative nostalgia. On the other hand, the much more popular *Kramer vs. Kramer* gave us a father without practical authority, a father lovably and lovingly bumbling to an acceptance of paternity without traditional patriarchal benefit (which includes the surplus value of a wife/mother). Dustin Hoffman's Ted Kramer is—if I may pun—a "little" big man, hardly taller than his son: a son of fatherhood just barely intelligible to patriarchal law and hardly able to represent it. Any real rage Kramer may feel toward runaway mom, toward his dependent son, toward his loss of familial power and its benefits is as repressed in the text as his wife's past labor and those moments in which the adorable kid throws up or makes the bedroom look as if Regan has been there. If the horror film shows us the terror and rage of *patriarchy in decline* (savaged by its children or murderously resentful of them), then the popular family melodrama shows us a sweetly problematic *paternity in ascendance*.[16] The two genres exist in schizophrenic relation. Indeed, Greg Keeler brilliantly elaborates this relation by viewing the mad, murderous, bad father, Jack Torrance, as carrying out all of the negative patriarchal fury and paternal desire repressed by the nurturant "good father" in the previous year's *Kramer vs. Kramer*.[17]

It is also worth noting that *Ordinary People* wins the Academy Award in 1980, the year *The Shining* is considered a "disappointment." The good father in the uncomic melodrama of *Ordinary People* makes more explicit the patriarchal problematic of power, which demands a hierarchy of strength and weakness. If the good father in the family melodrama is now inscribed as not only caring *about* his child, but also as caring *for* it, in assuming what has been previously defined as a maternal function, he is ambivalently figured as soft and weak, if not servile.[18] Consistent with the systemic rules of patriarchal relation and its economy, the mother in the family melodrama becomes hard, strong, and selfish. From the tall, aristocratic, neurotic intelligence of Meryl Streep to the brittle yet steely coldness of Mary Tyler Moore (whose subsequent warmth as a single mother in 1982's *Six Weeks* is interestingly suspect in light of this previous role), the inability of patriarchy to cope with its loss of authority, to admit an equal distribution of familial power and responsibility, is inscribed in the opposition of bad mother and good father. Inverting the horror film, these two most popular family melodramas attribute the destruction of the nuclear family to Mom. It is she who goes on in later films to deprive Dad of his paternal right by taking off with his kids (*Hide in Plain Sight* [1980]) or to selfishly absent herself, abandoning her kids to the care of a father who comically tries to assume the role of what *Ms.* magazine used to call "Superwoman" (*Author! Author!* [1982]). *On Golden Pond* (1981), the only other extremely popular family melodrama of the period, resolves family tensions through a surrogate child and leaves Mom and Dad, doddering on the brink of death, elegiacally reassuring themselves that "the kids are all right."

The new family melodrama emerges right around the time when the horror film father begins his active and hostile return from the repressed, and the special powers of his furious and alienated children begin to weaken in the face of his paternal hostility. In direct contradiction to the horror film father, the most popular dads in the family melodrama-cum-comedy are little more than children themselves. When Mother is the "absent one," [19] these dads are given license to indulge themselves in feeling and ineptitude. They are innocents abroad in the home. But their bumbling ignorance, while endearing, is disempowering. Ted Kramer does not know how to make French toast. *Mr. Mom* (1983) is terrorized by a vacuum cleaner. In addition, their children conduct a running and critical, if finally indulgent, commentary on Dad's ineffective assumption of maternal labor.

The special power possessed by horror film children and deconstructively directed against their parents and adult authority is transformed and softened in the family melodrama. In the pathetic films, that special power becomes insight, making the child prescient and sensitive, but also vulnerable and fragile (as in *Ordinary People* and *Shoot the Moon*). In the comedic films, it becomes a cute, invincible precocity (as in *Kramer vs. Kramer, Author! Author!,* and innumerable contemporaneous television sit-coms). In both cases, however, it is the child who has the power to authorize the family, who evaluates Dad's abilities and performance, who denies or legitimates the particular family's existence as a viable structure. As Marina Heung points out: "What is striking in recent films . . . is the way . . . the child not only acts as humanizer, but also as the overseer of familial roles and responsibilities. Thus, the child is a contradictory blend of precocity and vulnerability, often helpless in controlling his own situation, but instrumental in influencing the actions of adults. In fact, his control over familial relationships is so great that it is practically parental." [20] All those "little adults" and insightful teenagers let Dad off the hook by themselves representing patriarchal law in the genre's families. And Dad, in giving up patriarchal power and authority to his children, in becoming merely paternal, is himself reduced—and liberated—to the status of a child.

As true of Calvin in *Ordinary People* as of more comically articulated fathers, Dad's figuration in the genre works to represent him as positively innocent, transparent, lacking in practical knowledge, and essentially unerotic. He thus becomes a figure of poignant sweetness—helpless, vulnerable, and dependent on his children not only because of his physical ineptitude in the home, but also because of his lack of corrupting knowledge necessary for his membership and survival in the exterior patriarchal bourgeois social world. If all this seems familiar, it is so because I have previously used these terms to characterize the privileged figure and positive lack of the infant and child in bourgeois mythology. Thus, an unresolvable paradox is figured in the genre. If Dad must become as an innocent child to represent the hope and promise of an imaginable future for patriarchy (which, in these versions of a single-parent family, accepts paternity), he must also give up his patriarchal power, his authority, to his children, retaining only its illusion, its image (and that at their indulgence).

But the horror film and the family melodrama play out scenarios that do not resolve the dilemmas faced by a contemporary patriarchy under assault. The former genre dramatizes patriarchal impotence and rage, the latter patriarchal weakness and confusion—both generated by the central and problematic figure of the child. If the child is figured as powerful at the expense of the father, then patriarchy is threatened; if father is figured as powerful at the expense of his child, then paternity is threatened. In both cases, the traditional and conceivable future is threatened—for if patriarchy is willfully destroyed by its children, no tradition will mark the future with the past and present, and if paternity is willfully denied by a patriarchy that destroys its children, then the future will not be conceived. This dilemma is more than Oedipal; in fact, it demonstrates a crisis of belief in the Oedipal model. Once conceived of as identical in bourgeois capitalist culture, patriarchy and paternity have been recently articulated as different—one powerful effect of white, middle-class feminist discourse. This difference, however, clearly poses a problem when patriarchy as a political and economic power structure and paternity as a personal and subjective relation both locate themselves in the same place (the home) and seek to constitute the same object (the child). Both genres cannot end happily—even when they are comedies; their dramatic victories are always Pyrrhic.

It is in one dominant strain of the contemporary science fiction film that patriarchy and paternity seek to happily resolve their relationship. The resolution is as ingenious as it is predictable and, finally, ingenuous. Rather than struggle for occupation of the same place (the home), they (temporarily) leave it; and rather than struggle to constitute the same object (the child), they (temporarily) become it. Before "phoning home," patriarchy and paternity conflate in a single figure that is both powerful and lovable: the innocent extraterrestrial who is at once childlike, paternal, and patriarchally empowered. It is in much recent science fiction that the good/weak father of the family melodrama attempts to regain his political power and patriarchal strength by moving *outside* or *beyond* the space of his natural family and being born again as an adorable child with the special power to again effect both familial and global events. Rather than the synchronic repressed who, first powerfully absenting himself, returns to the horror film to terrorize his family, Dad is the synchronic transformed of the science fiction film. And while he, too, seems at first to abandon and deny paternity and family, he—unlike his horror film counterpart—returns not to savage it, but to salvage it.

The figural development of the science fiction starchild took longer than its counterpart in the horror film. Nonetheless, in both genres, the figure of the child was first introduced as embodying a suspect miscegenation of alien and human characteristics. It bears remembrance that parallel to the birth of Rosemary's baby as the cinematic production of an ahistoric and demonic hallucination, the birth of the starchild was the cinematic production of a post-historic and "spaced-out" (drug) trip through the Star Gate. Although their delivery is delayed, the first science fiction babies are negative figures of the same generation as their horror film counterparts; born in the late 1970s, they are, nonetheless, hostile, threatening, and alien children of the late 1960s. The narrative cause for the child's negative (re)production is, of course, characteristic of science fiction: a powerful, dangerous, and cooperative science and technology are responsible for the child's alien-ation. Thus the petri-dish paternity of *Embryo* (1976), the computer conception of *Demon Seed* (1977), and even the retrograde cloning of *The Boys from Brazil* (1978).

Almost immediately, however, this negative imagery is overtaken by a more positive dramatization, which emerges from what I have suggested is bourgeois culture's attempts in the 1970s to reinterpret its ineffectiveness and failed aggressivity as childlike innocence and vulnerability. Initially, that movement toward the conflation of the American male adult with the child and alien is marked by the 1977 release of *Close Encounters of the Third Kind*. The film clearly valorizes the bourgeois myth of the little, innocent, vulnerable child and transcends and empowers it as a mythology of the little, innocent, benevolent alien, who is also awesomely powerful and invulnerable. By emphasizing its own vision as childlike and reveling in its own technology as do the aliens, *Close Encounters* also disavows alliance with traditional patriarchal institutions and traditional paternal behavior. The government and the military are viewed as deceitful and stupid, lacking in imagination and vision, and contemptuous of those they profess to protect. The traditional bourgeois family is seen in terms of failed paternity (this failure made even more painful in the special edition of the film).

In the Guiler family, Dad (like God) is dead. Jillian is a widow raising her son as a single parent. She is the first of a number of unattached mothers or mothers-to-be in the genre's contemporary films, including *E.T., Starman,* and *The Terminator* (1984).[21] (The single-parent family in current science fiction thus tends to reverse the structure of parental presence and absence found in the seriocomic family melodrama.) In the Neary family Dad literally abandons his paternal responsibility in an eventually successful attempt to regenerate his childhood. Misunderstood by his humorless wife and unappreciated by his conventional kids, Roy Neary's playfulness and curiosity are viewed as threatening and contemptible by his family; they are embarrassed by his childish behavior almost as much before his close encounter as after. Literally alien-ated from traditional family structure, Jillian and Roy join together in their complementary desire to relocate the innocent and playful child they have differently lost—and, in the process, they form a surrogate family unit, one "elevated as the counterpart and alternative to the biological family."[22] Nonetheless, the differences they represent, their opposing motives, signal the necessarily temporary nature of their union—for Jillian's journey to Devil's Tower is an assertion of maternity, while Roy's is a negation of paternity. Jillian wants to regain her child; Roy wants to regain his childhood.

These are irreconcilable differences insofar as they concern the hierarchical structure and function of the bourgeois family and its traditional relations of power. Nonetheless, the film reconciles them in the figure and mythology of the child, in the relocation of personal innocence and cultural simplicity. It is telling that both Jillian and Roy inhabit a world of material abundance encoded as overwhelming clutter, and in a world of communicative complexity encoded as jargon and noise. In their search, however, clutter yields to the wide-open, underdetermined, and undeveloped spaces of sky and western landscape. Jargon and noise are drowned out by a universal music of the spheres. (Indeed, Devil's Tower resembles the Tower of Babel painted by Brueghel the Elder. Upthrusting from the barren Wyoming landscape, its flattened top an aborted reach to the sky, it is an iconic figure that both represents and reverses the biblical narrative of failed communication.) Irreconcilable difference sublimated in their journey, Jillian and Roy's quest converges not only in their search for the innocence and wonder of childhood, but also in their flight from an incomprehensible, obstructive, overdeveloped, grownup world.

Thus, children unadulterated by sophistication and language, childlike purity and simplicity, innocence, wonder, transparency, and verbal inarticulateness are valorized by both the film and its central characters. And it is through the transcoding of the latter that the former is able to constitute equivalencies between the adult male father and the vulnerable and curious child, between the child and the powerful and curious alien, and between the vulnerable adult father and the childlike and patriarchally benevolent alien. By means of this transcoding, a further transformation is suggested—one whose teleology will find its major visible articulations in *Altered States* (1980), *E.T.*, and *Starman*. Incorporated as a child, an alien-ated and unadulterated patriachy reappropriates its power to reproduce the future as a nostalgic image of its bourgeois past.

The transformation of children into aliens, fathers and aliens into children, and adult males into alien fathers plays out a single patriarchal narrative, cinematically dramatized with greatest energy and force in the contemporary generic articulations of horror, family melodrama, and science fiction. In their figural and transformative work of spatially and temporally redescribing the structure and semantic field of the traditional patriarchal family, the three genres have exchanged and expended their representational energy dynamically and urgently—with the "politically unconscious" aim of seeking resolution, or at least absolution, for a threatened patriarchy and its besieged structure of perpetuation: the bourgeois family.[23] In sum, their mutual project has been (and is) aggressively regressive and conservative. Thus, however synchronic their intergeneric relations, the various transformations explored here seem to culminate diachronically in the current dominant popularity of the science fiction film—the genre that most visibly figures the grandest illusions of a capitalist and patriarchal cinema and that spatially liberates powerful male children from social, political, and economic responsibility for the past and to the present.

And yet that illusion cannot quite be maintained; it keeps dissolving in the context of present structural and cultural pressure. Despite all the representational energy and urgency that have linked and revitalized the three genres in a dramatic attempt to resolve patriarchal and familial crisis in relevant but conservative narratives, there seems no viable way for patriarchy to symbolically envision a satisfying future for itself. All it can do is deny the future. There is no narrative resolution for patriarchy in the horror film—except the denial or death of the father, finally impotent and subject to the present power of his own horrific past. The family melodrama also resolves nothing; in both its serious and comic modes, its final hopeful articulations are a celebration of algorithmic paralysis, of a patriarchal present that is on hiatus. And in the science fiction film (the most hopeful of the lot), there is no resolution of patriarchal crisis that is not patently fantastic—and no fantastic resolution that does not also annihilate any real imagination of the future in its nostalgic retreat to the outer space and other time of an impossible past. All these films symbolically enact the death of the future.

Focusing on the problematic figure of the child and its transformations leads us to a historicizing and dialectical criticism that reads across generic boundaries and through cultural and narrative time. What emerges from this reading is an understanding of intertextual relations that constitute "the very locus and model of ideological closure." [24] That is, the contemporary horror film, family melodrama, and science fiction film together map "the limits of a specific ideological consciousness" and mark "the conceptual points beyond which that consciousness cannot go, and between which it is condemned to oscillate." [25] Terrorized by its own past, not able to imagine and image its own presence in the future, American bourgeois patriarchy keeps getting trapped by its desire to escape the present. Nonetheless, this failure of symbolic imagination and the boredom its repetitions will eventually generate leads one to hope. Not only do we have an active and perversely popular marginal cinema that locates future outer space in the present inner city, but we also can look forward to the debilitating effects of a symbolic exhaustion so great that imaginative failure cannot be ignored. Theater previews at the time of this writing promise we shall shortly see a science fiction film blatantly called *Back to the Future*. [26] Surely this is ideological hysteria, the "political unconscious" of American bourgeois patriarchy teetering on the brink of babbling itself to consciousness and, perhaps, a cure.

Notes

1. See the following articles by Robin Wood: "Return of the Repressed," *Film Comment* 14, no. 2 (July–August 1978): 25–32; "Gods and Monsters," *Film Comment* 14, no. 5 (September–October 1978): 19–25; "The American Film Comedy: From *Meet Me in St. Louis* to *The Texas Chainsaw Massacre*," *Wide Angle* 3, no. 2 (1979): 5–11; "Neglected Nightmares," *Film Comment* 16, no. 2 (March–April 1980): 24–31; and his various pieces in *The American Nightmare: Essays on the Horror Film*, ed. Wood and Richard Lippe (Toronto: Festival of Festivals, 1979).

2. Vivian Carol Sobchack, *The Limits of Infinity: The American Science Fiction Film* (New York: A. S. Barnes, 1980), p. 30; revised as *Screening Space: The American Science Fiction Film* (New York: Ungar, 1987).

3. I would draw particular attention to my use here of the term "preconscious" rather than "unconscious." Indeed, the point is that in their traditional periods, both the horror and science fiction genres condensed and displaced their primary concerns and repressions so that the dramas centering around sexuality and kinship in the horror film and ontological identity and reproduction in the science fiction film were elaborately disguised and hidden. In contemporary examples of both genres, however, such dramas are more overtly played out and are more available to consciousness—even as such consciousness is directed to look elsewhere. Displacement becomes an act of *replacement* to primary sites of trauma, and condensation occurs in figures who *replicate* original sources of power: father, mother, child.

4. The horror film has probably been the most consistently popular of genres, but its contemporary period (dating from the 1960s) is particularly marked by a regular output with no peak years. Gaining particular force in 1977 (the year of both *Close Encounters* and *Star Wars*), the genre has gained in popularity and increased in number with the next two years (1983–1984) marking a new peak; at the moment of this writing (1986), the popularity and quantity of science fiction have an edge over that of the horror film—given box office reports, among other things. The contemporary family melodrama presents another history. The revitalization of the genre seems to be a result of the brief spate of liberal movies appearing in the mid-1970s, which attempted to respond to issues raised by the women's movement. From the initial focus on women protagonists the films moved to a concern with the effects of women's liberation on the family. Certainly the success of *Kramer vs. Kramer* in 1979 marks this shift of emphasis, and thus it is from about 1980 on (and *Ordinary People*) that the family melodrama engages public interest. Still, in popularity and quantity, it lags far behind the fantastic genres of horror and science fiction.

5. For an extremely clear and useful summary of these concepts and their importance to a "symptomatic reading of American culture" through an analysis of figures and figuration, see Dudley Andrew, *Concepts in Film Theory* (New York: Oxford University Press, 1984), pp. 157–171.

6. Ibid., p. 159.

7. Ibid., p. 167.

8. Ibid., p. 170.

9. It is striking that the infant does not figure at all in classic articulations of horror and science fiction before the 1960s (at least not in my memory). *The Bad Seed* (1956) seems singular not only in bringing horror into the domestic sphere through a child, but also in suggesting that infants might be evil. While young children have certainly figured in the science fiction films of the 1950s, they have generally served as unproblematic witness to—or dreamer of—alien threats (as in *The Day the Earth Stood Still* [1951], *Invasion of the Body Snatchers* [1956], and *Invaders from Mars* [1953]), or they have been unproblematically victimized by the threat (as in *Them!* [1954] or *The Monolith Monsters* [1957]). It is worth noting that the most figurally compelling and alien-ated children appear not in America but rather in British science fiction of the period: *Village of the Damned* (1960) and its sequel, *Children of the Damned* (1964).

10. By 1979 the "changeling" child is no longer the effect of extrafamilial and supernatural power. In *The Changeling* (1979), a natural father murders his chronically ill son to preserve the family inheritance and himself substitutes an/Other child for his son. The child in this film no longer victimizes his parent(s) but is victimized by them, his ghostly spirit left to seek retribution and justice from perfect strangers in a lonely, rented family house.

11. Although there has been an enormous and varied body of material on 1960s culture, I recommend Sohnya Sayres et al., *The Sixties without Apology* (Minneapolis: University of Minnesota Press, 1984).

12. It is interesting to note that *Carrie* has its comedic counterpart in *Revenge of the Nerds* (1984); another essay remains to be written about the nature and function of the generic economy and exchange between the contemporary horror film featuring teenagers as victims/victimizers and the contemporary teen revenge comedy.

13. Leonard Maltin, *TV Movies, 1985–86* (New York: Signet, 1984), p. 205.

14. A brilliant analysis of the contemporary horror film's dramatization of popular fear in the face of economic crisis with particular emphasis on *Poltergeist* can be found in Douglas Kellner, "Fear and Trembling in the Age of Reagan: Notes on *Poltergeist*," *Socialist Review* 69 (May–June 1983): 121–131.

15. Here, of course, I refer to Jacques Lacan's reading of Freud. Both *The Exorcist* and *Carrie* seem to me provocatively read in Lacanian terms; the female teenagers in these films—lacking both a phallus and the Phallus, or patriarchal law—have no access to the patriarchal symbolic. Unable to acquire the linguistic form of patriarchal discourse, their pubescent bodies seek expression through Other means, through menses. Indeed, the flow uncontained by the constraints of the Father, their physical and bloody rage is an apocalyptic feminine explosion of the frustrated desire to speak.

16. For a related discussion, see Dave Kehr, "The New Male Melodrama," *American Film* 8, no. 6 (April 1983): 42–47.

17. Greg Keeler, "*The Shining:* Ted Kramer Has a Nightmare," *Journal of Popular Film and Television* 8, no. 4 (Winter 1981): 2–8.

18. It is interesting to contrast Calvin's weakness in the 1980s family of *Ordinary People* with that of the father in *Rebel without a Cause* (1955). Both are figured as more "caring" and sensitive to their son's feelings than the films' mothers, but whereas the father in the latter film is clearly and negatively coded as henpecked (wearing an apron, for instance) by an unremittingly strident and strong wife, the father in the former is ambivalently coded. Not henpecked, he is figured as naive and ignorant of negative feelings; he is an innocent in the face of his wife's coldness and his son's anguish.

19. We might note that here the family melodrama does not symmetrically *oppose* the horror film. While Dad's absence is repressed in the latter genre until he returns as potential axe murderer, Mom's absence is explicitly and consciously addressed in the diegesis of the former.

20. Marina Heung, "Why E.T. Must Go Home: The New Family in American Cinema," *Journal of Popular Film and Television* 11, no. 2 (Summer 1983): 81. This exceptionally astute article describes contemporary family melodrama comedy as an attempt to redefine the structure of the American family and, toward the end, relates the concerns of these films to the figure of E.T. Unlike the present essay, however, it does not discuss the family in the horror film, nor does it make generic connections between the family melodrama and science fiction.

21. Her only predecessor is Mrs. Benson in the prescient and anomalous *The Day the Earth Stood Still*.

22. Heung, "Why E.T. Must Go Home," p. 82. The surrogate family is a central concern of Heung's article, but her discussion is primarily focused on the seriocomic family melodrama. Thus the surrogate family constituted in *E.T.* is offered as a singular culmination of a trend more generically developed elsewhere, rather than as a parallel generic figuration of the science fiction film. Nonetheless, Heung is particularly illuminating in her remarks about the distinction between the biological family and the family constituted "through circumstances or choice."

23. The reference here to the "political unconscious" is derived from Fredric Jameson's *The Political Unconscious: Narrative as a Socially Symbolic Act* (Ithaca, N.Y.: Cornell

University Press, 1981). The assertion of such a concept is based on the recognition that "nothing . . . is not social and historical—indeed, that everything is 'in the last analysis' political." Jameson's articulation of the "political unconscious" calls for this political analysis, this "unmasking of cultural artifacts as socially symbolic acts." (p. 20)

24. Ibid., p. 47.

25. Ibid.

26. *Back to the Future* was released in 1985 and achieved considerable commercial success. (Ed.)

6

Trying to Survive on the Darker
Side: 1980s Family Horror

Tony Williams

The 1980s decade was extremely disappointing for critics im-
pressed by the horror genre's brief 1970s renaissance. While the
1970s saw the emergence of radical works by directors such as
Larry Cohen, Wes Craven, and George Romero, the following
decade appeared to feature reductive exploitation films such
as the *Friday the 13th, Halloween,* and *Nightmare on Elm Street*
series—all highly dependent on spectacular special effects and
gory bloodbaths of promiscuous (mostly female) teenagers.[1]
As well as demonstrating, in this particular instance, one unar-
guable application of Foucault's "Death of the Author" thesis,
most 1980s films called into question Robin Wood's positive
evaluation of the horror genre. The horror film was far more
complex and contradictory.[2] While films such as *The Texas
Chainsaw Massacre* (1974), *It's Alive* (1974), *The Hills Have Eyes*
(1977), *Sisters* (1972), *Night of the Living Dead* (1968), and *Dawn
of the Dead* (1978) questioned the very nature of the nuclear
family and implicitly (though never coherently) argued for a
new form of society, their 1980s successors illustrated Lenin's
thesis of "One step forward—two steps backward." Patriarchal
avengers such as Michael Myers, Mrs. Voorhees, Jason Voorhees,
and Freddy Krueger slaughtered the youthful children of the

1960s generation, especially when they engaged in illicit activities involving sex and drugs. The whole decade appeared a cinematic wasteland.

In addition to retreating from radical social themes, 1980s Hollywood regressed stylistically and thematically to classical Hollywood narrative structures. The "same old story" (or Kaja Silverman's more appropriate "dominant fiction") reappeared with predictable story lines and rigid Oedipal narratives. For Silverman, the family is the central unit within this dominant fiction attempting to arouse conventional Oedipal desires and identifications within any subject.[3] Appearing in an era pathologically affirming conservative family values, most 1980s horror films brutally chastised those questioning or disobeying ideological norms.

However, "attempting" is the key word. Not all 1980s horror films resemble the *Friday the 13th* cycle. The decade also saw the appearance of the *Stepfather* films as well as related works such as *Flowers in the Attic* (1987) and *Parents* (1989), by no means supportive of the status quo. In fact, a meticulous examination of the period reveals a more contradictory, but never pleasant, picture. But most 1980s cinematic narratives, horror or otherwise, attempted to maintain dominant values.[4]

The decade also saw the development of a special effects industry, begun earlier by *The Exorcist* (1973) and *Star Wars* (1977), now operating excessively within the horror genre. Each *Friday the 13th* and *Nightmare* film saw special effects experts like Tom Savini out to beat preceding cinematic bloodbaths with more gore and spectacle. As well as resembling a perverted scenario of Guy Debord's *Society of the Spectacle,* these displays were remarkable for concealment as well as manifestation. Using Metz's still relevant psychoanalytical definition of a cinematic institution noted for its operations of disavowal, Steve Neale pertinently notes that contemporary special effects represent a concealing device veiling both the improbability of the representation and "genuine trauma."[5] This genuine trauma may have social and historical links which cinematic spectacle attempts to conceal and disavow.

As examples of an apocalyptic "crisis cinema" expressing despair, disbelief, and pessimistic retreat to outmoded past values, the infernoesque nature of the horror genre's reliance on special effects is by no means irrelevant to contemporary social and historical malaise. Christopher Sharrett's observations are also indicative of the *Friday the 13th, Halloween,* and *Nightmare on Elm Street* cycles: "It is precisely because the modern apocalypse is horrific that the horror film best represents its expression."[6] But rather than bemoan contemporary generic failure we should analyze and interrogate the various texts no matter how unpleasant and reactionary they appear. We may find significant links rather than definitive breaches with the past.

Most 1980s horror films represent texts in tension illustrating contradictory features paralleling Antonio Gramsci's insights into hegemonic and counterhegemonic operations.[7] Though we live in a similar but not identical situation to his, where reactionary forces appear predominant, a responsible use of his work is essential today. Rather than submit to some nihilistic features of postmodernist malaise and ahistorical theoretical speculation, it is highly important to examine these unartistic and reactionary generic manifestations to find inconsistencies and contradictions that may one day develop into more appropriate oppositional forms. In doing this we must be aware of relevant material dimensions affecting the text arising from salient social and historical factors. From this perspective, exclusively theoretical examinations of any genre is not enough.

Although Gramsci's work has currently been applied to "New Times" and "New Subjectivities," John Clarke notes the dangers of "accentuating the discursive constitution of subjects at the expense of other dimensions,"[8] especially the presence of supposedly *old* features within the new. These may involve "redundant" practices of close textual analysis, Marxist readings, psychoanalytic interpretations, and revealing social and historical background factors, supposedly regarded as obsolescent in neoconservative-influenced postmodernist interpretations, which still have much to offer toward interpreting certain cultural movements. In fact, contemporary generic formalistic devices involving spectacular play of special effects and supposedly progressive gender changes celebrating the "Final Girl" may actually be designed to conceal certain radical meanings associated with seventies horror, meanings now abhorrent to more conservative philosophies held by Hollywood studios and certain academic interpretations.

One major example of a new approach to horror is that of Carol J. Clover in *Men, Women, and Chain Saws* and in this volume. Her work argues against popular interpretations categorizing slasher films as works displaying male sadistic-voyeuristic desires against the female body. Instead, analyzing the recent nature of contemporary horror, despite a reluctance in making "progressive claims for a body of cinema as spectacularly nasty toward woman as the slasher film," Clover notes that this genre does "constitute a visible adjustment in the terms of gender representations."[9] While involving a conflict with the parental "Other," certain films, Clover believes, present more hermaphrodite constructions revealing an uncertain sense of sexual identity. At the conclusion of *Friday the 13th* (1979) we learn that the unseen assailant is "she," not "he." In succeeding films Jason inherits the mother's role as an incarnation of the destructive phallic woman. Instead of a victorious male, the slasher usually confronts a surviving female—the Final Girl. For Clover, this gender change is too pervasive to be dismissed as supervenient. She thus believes these films are really theatrical contests involving gender. The female protagonist is both active and passive, frightened by the monster's assault and vigorously defending herself. She thus takes on a male aggressive stance, defending herself while the predominantly male audience often passively submits to thrills and shock effects. Suffering fear and terror but eventually winning, this figure embodies a paradoxical gender spectatorship involving male spectators undergoing masochistic experiences via the cinematic female body. These particular forms of gender displacement oscillate between sadism and masochism. Clover's thesis attacks the usual binary oppositional definitions concerning spectatorship. Thus, it becomes possible for male viewers to continue submitting to a masochistic "feminizing" experience begun by *Psycho* (1960). While classical horror film audiences experienced an intermittent feminization, contemporary horror emphasizes this effect. Slasher films thus express obsessive male anxieties concerning gender. Though certainly not progressive, these films articulate the anxieties of a 1980s generation experiencing the effects of massive gender confusion.

Clover argues that most contemporary horror films reveal an obsession with feminism, displaying plots concluding with images of masculinized female power offering visual pleasures structured not according to a sadistic male gaze, but around a more radical victim-identified *point of view* involving particular masochistic pleasures. Clover thus believes that masochism, rather than sadism, is the dominant feature in horror cinema.

Clover's conclusions owe much to recent work in spectatorship theory recognizing more complex forms of audience motivations. Her emphasis on masochism follows recent redefinitions of it and further investigations into Freud's 1919 essay "A Child Is Being Beaten." This essay not only reveals the existence of oscillating subjective positions, often contradicting standard fixed gender definitions, but, more significantly, the presence of a feminine masochistic position open to the male subject. Within the fantasy scenario, the mother may even replace the father as the agent of the beating. Many critics regard this fantasy as revealing variable potentials within human subjectivity. As David Rodowick comments, "What must be stressed in Freud's essay is the structural complexity and fluidity of spectatorial activity, which may combine different mechanisms of defense (disavowal and repression) with intricate transactions between activity-passivity, sadism-masochism, and masculine or feminine identifications in both men and women."[10]

Undeniably, Clover's thesis has certain utopian functions. But it is highly doubtful whether the dysfunctional-family premises surrounding the beating fantasy and specific moments within horror films really justify the progressive conclusions drawn. Her thesis works almost exclusively at the level of the discursive. Despite masochism's supposedly progressive features, both Silverman and Paul Smith recognize masochism as subject to narrative containment within Hollywood cinema. This is certainly so within the normalizing operations of the dominant fiction, especially generic contemporary manifestations using special effects as suspense weapons to terrorize audiences.[11] The masochistic thesis is problematic. As Tania Modleski remarks, the Oedipal father may still lurk within the text (and Final Girl) as a hidden point of reference in any mainstream narrative.[12]

Furthermore, whatever oscillating subject positions may result, an act of patriarchal physical violence is being perpetuated. Whether actual or fantastic, it still involves a master-slave power relationship, one stemming from within the patriarchal family. We must also ask ourselves where Freud derives his case histories from. The answer is the patriarchal family. Despite Freud's attempts to disavow the various cases of actual child abuse discovered in his early work, the fact remains that his findings result from traumatic events within a specific social institution—the bourgeois family attempting to mold its subjects into acceptable gender positions. Even if he is correct about a feminine masochistic position available to the male child, this, nonetheless, is no utopian feature but the result of an act of patriarchal violence directed against the victimized child. If we follow Freud's conclusions and apply them to the horror film, the undeniable conclusion follows that all horror films, in one way or another, are family horror films. Some reveal the association more clearly than others. But the genre often depends upon sadistic-masochistic spectator mechanisms originally derived from situations of patriarchal violence. Most films deny the social-familial roots by recourse to the fetish device of special effects. Others reveal what is usually disavowed. In *Freddy's Dead: The Final Nightmare* (1991) Carlos, Jon, and Spencer discover that masochistic submission to a parental figure brings death, not liberation. The neglected *Psycho IV: The Beginning* (1990) reveals Norman's early victimization by a mother (Olivia Hussey) who sexually uses and abuses him. At one point, she even humiliates him masochistically by forcing him to wear her clothes and retreat into a closet. Like any abused adult child, the adult Norman (Anthony Perkins) masochistically denies the nature of his early family trauma. *Psycho IV* highlights a dysfunctional family's role in making Norman a monster. Clover's work ignores such revealing social and family dynamics, which contradict her argument that family horror has been dormant over the last few years.[13] Furthermore, her book neglects many films revealing the theme's survival over the past few years. Of the many instances that may be cited, the following are of interest. *Maniac* (1980), *Pieces* (1983), *Blood Splash*, and *Hollowgate* (both 1988) reveal adult monsters as products of abusive parents; *American Gothic* (1988) deals with a repressive patriarchal family attempting to keep its younger members in a state of permanent infancy, replaying motifs within *The Toolbox Murders* (1979); *The Boogeyman* (1980) explicitly presents children as either neglected or abused family victims. While not a traditional horror film (though usually found within the horror sections of video stores), *Diary of the Dead* (1976) depicts an affluent mother verbally abusing her low-income son-in-law. There is an urgent need to examine specific textual evidence and other examples ignored by Clover. Far from being affirmative, masochism, as derived from an authoritarian family situation, is extremely dangerous and has dubious claims as a positive feature within the genre.

There may not be any progressive bisexual influences inherent in Freud's "A Child Is Being Beaten," as Clover believes.[14] A child *is* being beaten by a parental figure. Even if we accept the nonrealistic, fantastic dimensions of this thesis, a parent still commits a brutal, authoritarian act upon a helpless victim. Furthermore, should we refuse the fantastic discourse and follow the arguments of Jeffrey Masson and Alice Miller concerning the possibility that Freud deliberately denied his earlier findings of the reality of child abuse in these case histories, then the "beaten" thesis becomes far more questionable.[15]

Assuming Freud is correct concerning the fluid nature of human subjectivity within his critical writing, the fact remains that the Oedipally defined "Law of the Father" aims at preventing the emergence of alternative personal structures. This process occurs within the authoritarian bourgeois family, an organization attempting to repress its subjects into being conformist products. Whenever this fails, the children become conveniently designated as monsters. As an authoritarian patriarchal structure, the family attempts to produce a convenient gendered product within capitalist society. Whenever this fails, the horror of difference results. As a product of the return of the repressed, the monster represents the alternative "No" to the family. Patrick McGrath's ironic short story, "The Boot's Tale," dealing with a dysfunctional family's retreat during a nuclear attack, ideally describes how these films function: "Herb, being a plumber, had seen to all the life-support systems necessary to maintain the family underground for the duration. Odd, then, that he had not factored in the psychic strains that were bound to arise—for the nuclear family is very much like a hydraulic machine, and unless it's adequately equipped with safety valves, pressure within the closed system may rise to dangerous levels."[16] It is thus not surprising that the patriarchal Reagan-Bush era, with its return to family values, saw the horror film developing into its most grotesque forms—the greater the social repression, the more monstrous the repressed, even against Clover's Final Girl.

Clover's supposedly progressive Final Girls are never entirely victorious at the end of certain films nor are they devoid of the recuperation into a male order of things that they are supposedly free of. Her argument needs to consider more detailed readings of individual scenes and other examples that contradict her thesis. In *Psycho,* Lila Crane needs Sam to save her from Norman as she submissively screams before his menacing figure. Dr. Loomis rescues Laurie Strode at the end of *Halloween.* The sequel sees Laurie submissive and terrified. Alice (Adrienne King) survives at the end of *Friday the 13th* to fall victim to Jason in the sequel's prologue after suffering traumatic nightmares, *Carrie*-style. Although *Friday the 13th*'s unseen assailant turns out to be a she rather than a he, Mrs. Voorhees does not act independently. The final battle reveals her as a split subject. She speaks in Jason's voice ("Kill her, Mummy. Kill her") and replies in her own, "I will! I will." Although eighties heroines may appear more masculinized than their predecessors, the conservative ideological dimensions of this gender change needs thorough investigation before we may safely regard it as progressive. The heroines of *Friday the 13th Part 2* (1981) and *Friday the 13th Part III* (1982) are alive at the end of the films but catatonic. In the former, Ginny temporarily adopts Mrs. Voorhees's authoritarian role to survive. Although circumstances necessitate this, she clearly uses the enemy's strategy to become a phallic mother herself. This posture really questions the positive image of the Final Girl. As the final image shows, the mother's decapitated (but still powerful) head survives as an enshrined totem. Indeed, the latter film's Final Girl is actually carried away on a stretcher calling in vain for her boyfriend in a definitely nonindependent manner, certainly not victorious! There is no Final Girl in *Friday the 13th—The Final Chapter* (1984). Young Tommy masquerades as Jason's mirror image, using a similar strategy to Ginny in the second film, before killing him. The film ends with Tommy's becoming Jason. In *Friday the 13th—A New Beginning* (1985), guilty parent Roy follows Mrs. Voorhees's vengeful trajectory in a film revealing the series' gradual changeover from dwelling excessively on teenage slaughter toward tentatively critiquing parental irresponsibility. Since Roy attempts displacing his guilt for neglecting his son onto violent revenge against teenagers, this also suggests an alternative reason for Mrs. Voorhees's original activities. Did she not, originally, neglect Jason and leave him to drown? *Friday the 13th Part VIII: Jason Takes Manhattan* (1989) indirectly suggests this, but this tantalizingly antihegemonic motif never receives full development. Although Megan actually saves Tommy at the end of *Friday the 13th,*

Part VI: Jason Lives (1986), this act occurs in a film that develops antifamily motifs absent from the earlier series.

As seventies horror revealed, critique of the family institution represented the genre's most progressive directions. As Engels showed long ago in "The Origins of the Family, Private Property, and the State," the family is a fundamental component of social conditioning for capitalist success—an argument conveniently neglected today by neoconservative academics championing retrograde tendencies within certain postmodernist and postfeminist ideologies. Freedom from "family values" is a fundamental axiom for progressive moments within horror films.

Both *Friday the 13th, Part VII—The New Blood* (1988) and *Part VIII: Jason Takes Manhattan* develop these themes in different ways, a potential lost in *Jason Goes to Hell: The Final Friday* (1993), which celebrates family values in reuniting a Final Father and Mother! The *Friday the 13th* films are not entirely identical; despite the repetitive elements, there are also some significant differences. Clover's analysis elevates the Final Girl into a rigid model. Her work does not closely examine relevant specific instances within each particular film that often question the validity of her thesis. Stretch may survive at the end of *The Texas Chainsaw Massacre, Part 2* (1986), but it is clearly at the cost of her sanity, like Sally in the earlier film. Grotesquely wielding Leatherface's chainsaw, she resembles less a surviving female victor than a nightmarishly phallic, castrating woman. She appears a mirror image of *Friday the 13th*'s Mrs. Voorhees and Mrs. Sawyer of *Leatherface: The Texas Chainsaw Massacre III* (1991).[17] It is only after 1986 that heroines really survive, due to historical factors that Clover ignores. This era saw a growing revelation of cases of child abuse and dysfunctional families, giving the lie to the Reagan family dream. At the same time, the developing Iran and Contragate revelations showed not only that Father did *not* know best but that, like a doddering grandfather, he was not even aware of what was going on in the White House. Later versions of the *Friday the 13th, Halloween,* and *Nightmare on Elm Street* films emphasized the role of dysfunctional families, showing the necessity of constant vigilance against supernatural patriarchal avatars and their real-life dysfunctional counterparts. It is the latter factor that distinguishes the real survival of the Final Girl in *Friday the 13th, Part VI, Friday the 13th, Part VII,* and *Jason Takes Manhattan,* all three films involving the survival of both male and female teenagers. These Final Girls differ in every film as a result of relevant historical, not discursively theoretical, factors.

Nor is there any real gender progression in the idea of males opening up. Steve Freeling does this in *Poltergeist II: The Other Side* (1986). But he is still the male head of the family, as his position at the climax shows—a "kinder,

Halloween (1978): the unfortunate result of familial dysfunction.

gentler" patriarch. Freddy Krueger opens up, absorbs bodies, and frequently changes sex during the various *Nightmare on Elm Street* films. He uses Jesse's body in a patriarchal, non-homoerotic revenge strategy in *A Nightmare on Elm Street, Part 2: Freddy's Revenge* (1985), emerging from a girl's chest in the climax; takes on female form as a high-school nurse in *A Nightmare on Elm Street 4: The Dream Master* (1989); and uses other fluid body strategies to attack his victims in other films. Like capitalism, Freddy constantly adapts and changes to eventually take over his victims. *Freddy's Dead* initially sees him as the Wicked Witch of the West from *The Wizard of Oz* (1939)—an appropriately dark maternal parallel to his patriarchal persona. He inhabits the body of Carlos's mother to trap him into parental submission. In his last moments of human life, Freddy opens up to the demonic Dream People, which shows that opening up does not necessarily have progressive implications. Here it represents another patriarchal terrorist tactic. Attack on gender is often used as an oppressive weapon, as various victims of totalitarian institutions such as Marine boot camp, prison, and concentration camps attest.

The discursive is not enough. We have to consider relevant historical and social factors influencing the films as well as relevant plot movements. In so doing we find that the family horror motif occurs throughout the 1980s, but it operates in a different manner from its 1970s predecessors in less utopian and more pessimistic directions. Although historians such as Stephanie Coontz reveal the presence of dysfunctional families and sexually/physically abused child victims within American society from the nineteenth century onward, the post-1986 era saw increasing attention to this issue.[18] Cracks within the Reaganite hegemony, Contragate, and the developing strains within the American social fabric brought these issues to public attention. Alert to any contemporary issues, various studios and screenwriters began developing films in response.[19] Among these were conscious plot motifs recognizing the monster/slasher figure as a product of a dysfunctional family, whether in *Manhunter* (1986) or *Confessions of a Serial Killer* (1989). The monstrous adult child product of a traumatic family situation existed in earlier decades, as works such as *Curse of the Cat People* (1944), *Psycho*, *The Strangler* (1963), *Lady in a Cage* (1964), *Marnie* (1964), *I Dismember Mama* (1972), *The Killing Kind* (1973), and *Don't Go in the House* (1979) show. Post-1986 works begin to emphasize the family's social creation of the serial killer monster. Shane Stevens's 1979 novel *By Reason of Insanity* also anticipates later Hollywood treatments. In *Psycho IV*, scenarist Joseph Stefano emphasized this element, left subtly ambiguous in the original version. Common knowledge of dysfunctional family creation of the adult monster leads to renewed attention to the monster's social origins. The family motif again becomes explicit. Eighties horror films serve as allegories to their adolescent audience stressing vulnerability to parents, the adult world, and monstrous punitive avatars whether Jason, Michael, or Freddy.

Many of these films thus contained themes highly relevant to audiences occupying marginal positions in society. They were not exclusively oriented toward decadent yuppie and upper-middle-class groups atavistically enjoying ritual slaughters of promiscuous females. For example, Wes Craven's *The People under the Stairs* (1991) opposed a preteen black ghetto hero against an incestuous and affluent white brother and sister engaging in kidnapping and child abuse. Informed as much by studio market research as intuition, Craven's comments concerning the *Nightmare on Elm Street* audience deserve attention since they describe a particular sociohistorical context overlooked by Clover's more theoretical approach:

It's an audience with a certain disposition. They're willing to look at things that are a lot more psychically challenging. They're a little bit more comfortable with crossing lines. I think that's why kids and minorities are more comfortable with horror films—because they're dealing more with primal issues, in confrontation with parents and authority figures,

Fool (Brandon Adams), the preteen black hero, and Leroy (Ving Rhames) in *The People under the Stairs* (1991): issues of race intersect with family horror.

being placed in personal danger. These things are familiar to kids and people in ghettos; they're not familiar to adults ensconced in a comfortable house, marriage or job. So the primary audience for horror seems to be either young or poor, but they're also essentially adventurous, bold and brave.[20]

Craven also defines the horror film as "boot camp for the psyche," envisaging Freddy Krueger as a "paradigm of the threatening adult: the savage side of male adulthood, the ultimate bad father." Obviously, with their marketing organization, the producers of the *Nightmare* series easily discerned the appeal of their films. While the series differs markedly from the more progressive developments within 1970s horror, concern with families and other authoritarian structures still appears. This concern possibly represents a dark reaction to the supposedly benevolent Reagan era, one in which the minority groups described above had no share in an illusionary "Morning in America." New Line head Robert Shayne, responsible for the *Nightmare* series, regards Freddy as the youthful generation's feared father figure. "He's the death-wheeling puritan, a kind of ultraconservative cultural bogeyman."[21] As the title song of *Jason Takes Manhattan* reveals, eighties horror films involve "Trying to Survive on the Darker Side," a side involving dysfunctional families and avenging supernatural patriarchal avatars.

The *Nightmare on Elm Street* series deserves examination in terms of these motifs. Neither Craven nor Shayne are auteurs in the commonly recognized sense of the word. The themes also exist in other contemporary horror films, such as the *Halloween* and *Friday the 13th* series. As Chuck Russell observes, "One of the messages is that you're on your own. Your parents don't believe you. They want you to go to sleep because it's supposed to be good for you. Only you and your fellow teenagers understand where the danger lies. Only you can defeat it for the first time. You can't rely on anybody else. That's a lot of truth for adolescents. It's what growing up is about."[22]

Despite fetishistic disavowal through supernatural overtones, dysfunctional family situations really structure the *Nightmare* series. Problematic family relationships often provide an avenue for Freddy's attacks. In the first film he avenges his death by punishing Elm Street children often, unconsciously, aided by undiscerning parents. Glenn's boorish father refuses to pass on Nancy's message and thus causes his son's death. By keeping silent over her role in Freddy's murder, Mrs. Thompson actually aids him. She tells Nancy, "I guess I should have told you about him. I wanted to protect you. I should have let you know. You face things. That's your nature. That's your gift. But sometimes you have to turn away." In *A Nightmare on Elm Street 3: Dream*

Warriors (1987), Nancy uses her skills to aid other victims of traumatic family situations, one of whom comments, "Great! Now it's my dick that's killing me!" The rejoinder is really significant since it rejects an over-theoretically Freudian castration, emphasizing instead the relevant material traumatic family circumstances structuring the whole series. In *A Nightmare on Elm Street 4: The Dream Master,* a mother indirectly causes her daughter's death by feeding her sleeping pills and leaving her vulnerable to Freddy's assault. Freddy also disciplines and punishes unruly children in *A Nightmare on Elm Street 5: The Dream Child* (1989). By the time of *Freddy's Dead,* surviving children are all outside the family living in a center for traumatically abused children.

The films all make clear that submission to any form of family authority results in death. At the climax of *Dream Warriors,* Freddy tricks Nancy by taking on the form of her deceased father. Yielding to dangerous desires for parental love, Nancy is ripped to shreds in her demonic father's embrace. Alice narrowly avoids the same fate in *The Dream Child* by escaping from Freddy's use of her deceased lover's body. By the time of *Freddy's Dead,* any desire for parental love and acknowledgement is dangerous and deadly masochistic. Jon's belief that Freddy is his father results in unawareness and submissive acceptance of death. Carlos masochistically submits to further physical abuse at the hands of his mother, who turns out to be Freddy in disguise. The final revelation reveals the social development of young Freddy showing him a victim of both family and society. Prior to killing his abusive stepfather (Alice Cooper), he masochistically punishes himself before embarking on his sadistic career.

This sequence clearly reveals the unity of both sadism and masochism within the patriarchal unconscious, the abused victim soon becoming the victimizer, a pattern also revealed in *Henry: Portrait of a Serial Killer* (1990). The *Nightmare* films clearly reveal masochism as a key structure within the patriarchal unconscious, producing generations of victims and future victimizers produced by the family. In this way, they parallel patterns within other contemporary horror films.[23]

Far from being gratuitously violent artifacts to be easily dismissed as deteriorating examples of the horror genre's decline, eighties works are far more complex. They do fall far below the achievements of their seventies predecessors in both quality and content, but this is no reason for neglecting them entirely. While affected by conservative values of the Reagan era, family values in these horror films are by no means entirely victorious. Works of the 1980s and 1990s stress hesitancy rather than opposition, a hesitancy undergoing several fluctuations in particular works. However, certain generic directions signified by Final Girls emphasize dubious bourgeois individual tendencies rather than collective solutions. Although recent theoretical approaches associated with Carol J. Clover provide interesting formal perspectives concerning contemporary movements, such analyses are clearly insufficient if they stress dubious theoretical premises at the expense of other relevant approaches. Eighties horror films have emerged from a particular set of historical and social circumstances and operate accordingly. Interrogating the textual content of each becomes important. The dominant ideology within each film may also recuperate the supposed utopian implications of a masochistic thesis. At the same time, there may be other elements concerning contemporary adolescent insecurity operating within these films needing elucidation. The masochistic thesis is, in itself, highly problematic. The theoretical and the discursive is not enough, being liable to recuperation. Unless these factors are recognized, horror films will remain an area where Father (still) Knows Best.

Notes

1. *Halloween* appeared in 1977 but, like *Rocky* (1976), it heralded the beginning of an onslaught of reactionary movies that would characterize the following decade. See Robin Wood, "80s Hollywood: Dominant Tendencies," *CineAction,* no. 1 (1985): 2–5; and Andrew Britton, "Blissing Out: The Politics of Reaganite Entertainment," *Movie,* nos. 31–32 (1986): 2–13.

2. See Robin Wood, *Hollywood from Vietnam to Reagan* (New York: Columbia University Press, 1986), pp. 70–134; Mark Jancovich, *Horror* (London: Batsford, 1992), p. 16.

3. Kaja Silverman, *Male Subjectivity at the Margins* (New York: Routledge, 1992), pp. 39–40.

4. For a contradictory argument see Douglas Kellner, "Film, Politics, and Ideology: Reflections on Hollywood Film in the Age of Reagan." *Velvet Light Trap,* no. 27 (1991): 9–24.

5. Steve Neale, "'You've Got to Be Fucking Kidding!': Knowledge, Belief, and Judgment in Science Fiction," in *Alien Zone: Cultural Theory and Contemporary Science Fiction,* ed. Annette Kuhn (London: Verso, 1990), p. 167. Recent extensions of Freud's disavowing fetish function toward a wider social definition may also explain the growth of special effects within horror films. Emerging within a ruthless conservative era, they attempt to disavow audience awareness from the material circumstances generating contemporary horror's excessive manifestations. Although never mentioning the genre, two recent works are extremely interesting here. See Laura Mulvey, "Some Thoughts on Theories of Fetishism in the Context of Contemporary Culture," *October,* no. 65 (1993): 3–20, and the various essays in *Fetishism as Cultural Discourse,* ed. Emily Apter and William Pietz (Ithaca, N.Y.: Cornell University Press, 1993).

6. Christopher Sharrett, "Apocalypticism in the Contemporary Horror Film: A Typological Survey of the Theme in Fantastic Cinema, Its Relationship to Cultural Tradition and Current Film Expression" (Ph.D. diss., New York University, 1983), p. 23.

7. See Antonio Gramsci, *Selections from the Prison Notebooks,* ed. and trans. Quintin Hoare and Geoffrey Nowell-Smith (New York: International Publishers, 1971); *Selections from Cultural Writings,* ed. David Forgacs and Geoffrey Nowell-Smith, trans. William Boelhower (London: Lawrence and Wishart, 1985).

8. John Clarke, *New Times and Old Enemies: Essays on Cultural Studies and America* (London: Harper Collins Academic, 1991), p. 173.

9. Carol J. Clover, *Men, Women, and Chain Saws: Gender in the Modern Horror Film* (Princeton, N.J.: Princeton University Press, 1992), p. 64.

10. D. N. Rodowick, *The Difficulty of Difference* (New York: Routledge, 1991), p. 82.

11. Silverman, *Male Subjectivity,* p. 416, n.48; Paul Smith, "Vas," *camera obscura* 17 (1988): 89–111.

12. Tania Modleski, *Feminism without Women* (New York: Routledge, 1991), p. 70. Masochism is a complex psychoanalytic mechanism, as Linda Williams recognizes in *Hard Core: Power, Pleasure, and the Frenzy of the Visible* (Berkeley: University of California Press, 1989). Arguing for a sadomasochistic trajectory within pornography, she criticizes utopian interpretations of masochism, which do not necessarily mean that mother and son are free from Oedipal power mechanisms (p. 213).

13. Clover, *Men, Women, and Chain Saws,* p. 236.

14. Ibid., pp. 214–218.

15. See Jeffrey Moussaieff Masson, *The Assault on Truth: Freud's Suppression of the Seduction Theory* (New York: Farrar, Straus and Giroux, 1984); *A Dark Science: Women, Sexuality, and Science in the Nineteenth Century* (New York: Farrar, Straus and Giroux, 1986); *Against Therapy: Emotional Tyranny and the Myth of Psychological Healing* (New York: Atheneum, 1988); Alice Miller, *For Your Own Good: Hidden Cruelty in Childrearing and the Roots of Violence* (New York: Farrar, Straus and Giroux, 1982); *Thou Shalt Not Be Aware: Society's Betrayal of the Child* (New York: Farrar, Straus and Giroux, 1984); *Banished Knowledge: Facing Childhood Injuries* (New York: Doubleday, 1990); *The Untouched Key: Tracing Childhood Trauma in Creativity and Destructiveness* (New York: Doubleday, 1990); and *Breaking Down the Wall of Silence: The Liberating Experience of Facing Painful Truth* (New York: Dutton, 1991). The only critic to have used Miller's ideas recently is Robin Wood. See "Theory vs. Experience: Alice Miller and the Status of Contemporary Psychoanalytic Theory," *CineAction,* nos. 19–20 (1990): 84–102.

16. Patrick McGrath, *Blood and Water and Other Tales* (New York: Ballantine Books, 1988), p. 185. I am grateful to Robert C. Cumbow for loaning me this book.

17. Referring to Clover's work, Williams significantly notes that when the woman looks at the monster, "she, too, becomes monstrous, as much a freak as he." This does not necessarily mean that a surviving woman presents the alternative image of being "*neither* male *nor* female" (*Hard Core,* p. 208). It may also denote her recuperation within the realm of the patriarchal unconscious. She further points out that, as in sadomasochistic pornography, the female victim "gains a power over the dominator that resembles the *momentary* power of the slasher film's victim-hero. Masochism thus deploys force and gains a modicum of power by turning punishment into pleasure" [italics added] (p. 209).

But we may ask what type of power and pleasure is involved? If dominated by patriarchal forces, the Final Girl's victory may be totally contaminated. Furthermore, assertions concerning the supposed progressiveness of the Final Girl are as problematic as those surrounding feminist interpretations of the comic strip figure, Tank Girl. For an excellent critique of the latter see Charlotte Raven, "Girl Crazy," *The Guardian* (U.K), May 25, 1995, sec. 2, pp. 6–7. Finally, Janet Staiger has furnished several examples from her current research seriously questioning some of Clover's arguments. "The Slasher, the Final Girl, and the Anti-Denouement: Appreciatively Revising Carol Clover" (paper presented at a conference of the Society for Cinema Studies, New York, New York, March 2, 1995).

18. Stephanie Coontz, *The Way We Never Were: American Families and the Nostalgia Trap* (New York: Basic Books, 1992); and *The Social Origins of Private Life* (London: Verso, 1988); Arlene Skolnick, *Embattled Paradise: The American Family in an Age of Uncertainty* (New York: Basic Books, 1993); Linda Gordon, *Heroes of Their Own Lives: The Politics and History of Family Violence, Boston 1880–1960* (New York: Viking, 1988); and Richard J. Gelles and Murray A. Straus, *Intimate Violence* (New York: Simon and Schuster, 1988).

19. Referring to these issues by no means implies accepting a reductive reflection theory of society's influence on the cinema. It does, however, recognize the ways in which the cinematic institution acts in rendering these issues ideologically as "harmless entertainment." For a definition of this latter term see Richard Maltby, *Harmless Entertainment: Hollywood and the Ideology of Consensus* (Metuchen, N.J.: Scarecrow Press, 1983).

20. Steve Biodrowski, "Wes Craven Alive and Shocking!" *Cinéfantastique* 22, no. 2 (October 1991): 11.

21. See Dan Gire, "Bye Bye Freddy: Elm Street Creator Quits Series," *Cinéfantastique* 18, no. 5 (July 1988): 10; and William Schoell and James Spencer, *The Nightmare Never Ends: The Official History of Freddy Krueger and the Nightmare on Elm Street Films* (New York: Citadel, 1992), p. 199.

22. Quoted in Schoell and Spencer, *The Nightmare Never Ends,* p. 52.

23. Director Rachel Talalay claims credit for developing the teenage survival motif throughout the final three *Nightmare* films, especially in the child-abuse subtext of *Freddy's Dead.* "We chose to have the subtext of child abuse with each of our kids; that is the general subtext of the whole film. It is related to Freddy as an abused child; to Maggie, the psychologist, as an abused child, and [to] every one of our kids." Quoted in Schoell and Spencer, *The Nightmare Never Ends,* p. 148.

There is definitely a campish side to Freddy's persona that youthful audiences respond to. However, this does not disavow the serious implications of certain actions behind the humor, which the text attempts to disavow. Recognizing this goes far beyond the issue of formal stylistic operations, a factor present in certain examinations. See Jeffrey Sconce, "Spectacles of Death: Identification, Reflexivity, and Contemporary Horror," in *Film Theory Goes to the Movies,* ed. Jim Collins, Hilary Radner, and Ava Preacher Collins (New York: Routledge, Chapman and Hall, 1993), pp. 103–119. There is certainly a generation gap in watching horror, but a youthful audience's campish tastes may represent a device of safe distancing. I am grateful to Barry K. Grant for bringing this article to my attention. A possible ending envisaged the Dream People descending on Freddy's successor—another abused child. According to screenwriter and executive producer Michael De Luca, "Originally, we had this idea about the cyclical nature of child abuse; then we came to the opinion that this is an inappropriate forum to bring up that issue, much less comment, and we cut it out." Quoted in Steve Biodrowski, "*Freddy's Dead* Post Mortem," *Cinéfantastique* 22, no. 4 (January 1992): 60. This proposed ending would have duplicated the climax of *Don't Go in the House,* where Donny's schizophrenic voices befriend another child suffering maternal abuse like Shane Stevens's Thomas Bishop.

Genre, Gender, and the *Aliens* Trilogy

Thomas Doherty

The science fiction–cum–horror–cum action adventure series comprised of *Alien* (Ridley Scott, 1979), *Aliens* (James Cameron, 1986), and *Alien*[3] (David Fincher, 1992) explores not only the impact of extraterrestrial parasites on human digestion but the frontiers of genre and gender in Hollywood narrative. Though the trilogy retains the core elements of the traditional science fiction film (futuristic hardware, space travel, alien beings), the old means are deployed to new ends. Technology challenges humanity, the vistas of space replicate the landscape of the human psyche, and the invasive alien violates the body to burst through the walls of sexual identity. The breakdown of once stable and secure realms—the conventions of motion picture genre and the barricades of gender—leaves a universe of unsettling possibilities. In the vacuum of space, the sheltering atmosphere of earthly verities collapses into a black hole.

As a rough index to contemporaneous obsessions, motion picture speculations about the future reflect a film's release date, not its chronological setting. True to generic form, the three *Aliens* films project the shape of the present onto things to come. Linking Hollywood with American history, the trilogy embodies three developments that, since the late 1960s, have sculpted the contours of the science fiction film: (1) the mushrooming prestige accorded a once juvenile genre, both in intellectual heft and studio financing; (2) the revolution in FX technology that spawned a frighteningly persuasive level of verisimilitude and visceral intensity in the depiction of futuristic worlds and extraterrestrial creatures; and (3) the changing status of women in American culture and hence American genre films. The convergence of youth-dominated demographics, the industrial light and magic of futuristic film technologies, and the arrival of feminism closed the curtain on the classical era of pods and blobs, bug-eyed monsters and brain eaters, fifty-foot women and space bimbos.

The shifting terrain of the time-obsessed genre was driven by another kind of postwar history. As the threat of nuclear war diminished in the second half of the Cold War, as mutually assured destruction locked the superpowers in a static balance of terror, alien invasion and human annihilation waned as the dominant themes of science fiction narratives.[1] Stanley Kubrick's *2001: A Space Odyssey* (1968) is the obvious line of demarcation between the traditional and the modern. As deep background to the postclassical science fiction film, its influence is hard to overstate. Where pre-*2001* science fiction was targeted at teens, low-budget, technically primitive, and intellectually stunted, post-*2001* science fiction was mass marketed, well financed, state of the art, and intellectually challenging, a genre of big budgets and big ideas. To be sure, huge sums had been lavished on a few fantasy adventures before *2001* (*20,000 Leagues under the Sea* [1954]; *Forbidden Planet* [1956]), but Kubrick's masterpiece—and later George Lucas's landmark *Star Wars* series (1977, 1979, 1981)—made a fringe genre mainstream and respectable. Its impact on narrative content was no less prophetic. In the post-*2001* universe, science fiction plotlines turned away from extraterrestrial menaces (what's out there after us?) and toward the enemy within (what's in here with us?). Don't watch the skies—watch the insides.

The realignment was abetted by the newly emergent technology pervading the office space of American culture: the threat/promise of the computer supplanting the threat/promise of atomic energy. In theme and imagery, science fiction traced a movement from nuclear to digital, from fear of extinction to intimations of obsolescence. Many of the important science fiction films of the post-*2001* era—*Colossus: The Forbin Project* (1970), *Demon Seed* (1977), *Blade Runner* (1981), *The Terminator* (1986), *Robocop* (1987), and *Terminator 2: Judgment Day* (1992)—tend to be built around the challenge of the computer to human uniqueness, either in the form of a Big Brotherly mainframe or its humanoid incarnation, the cyborg. For if, as western civilization has believed since Aristotle, the difference between human and animal life is the ability to reason, then the rational machine can lay claim to being human, uprooting our place as the crown of creation.

The usurpation of intelligence by the sentient machine is far more threatening to the male (defined by his ability to reason) than the female (defined by her body).[2] If the machine can steal what is most immutably man's (rationality), then his human status is no longer unique and privileged. In the era of artificial intelligence, woman retains her reproductive and generative prerogatives; man loses his intellectual superiority.[3] Hence the two pervasive and antagonistic impulses of science fiction cinema since *2001:* the movement of men to the periphery of the narrative and the containment and appropriation of women. In the male imagination, the true alien is always the female.

The *Aliens* trilogy can stand as a fair representative of the dominant tropes of post-*2001* science fiction cinema: each entry is a high-profile, high-tech, and sexually charged excursion into genre-gender dynamics. The intrinsic richness of at least two-thirds of the series and its present historical scope (1979–1992) make the three films an especially fertile template for the exploration of present-day meaning in science fiction tomorrowworlds—with two caveats. First, these remarks are based on the theatrical releases of each film, not the subsequent "director's cuts" and laser disc editions, which in the case of James Cameron's *Aliens* dislodges some of the maternal motif.[4] Second, for the present, the three *Aliens* are presumed to be a historically bound and narratively closed trilogy. Of course, given the box office value of a presold name brand, the series is ripe for reopening by Twentieth Century-Fox. Although the star of the series would seem to have been permanently and irrevocably eliminated in the finale of *Alien³*, foreclosing the likelihood of another sequel, a motion picture franchise dies hard. A fourth *Alien*—with or without Ripley, its heart and soul—is thus beyond the realm of narrative, but not commercial, possibility.[5]

A brief recapitulation of the basic plot outline of the trilogy, with a few comments on spectatorial experience and cinematic style, may be a helpful prelude. First, the three *Aliens* comprise an interconnected and progressive narrative. Unlike the three *Back to the Future* films (1985, 1989, 1990), the three *Robocop* films (1987, 1990, 1994), or the five *Nightmare on Elm Street* films (1984, 1985, 1987, 1988, 1989), the *Aliens* trilogy is a harmonious unity with a straight-through trajectory: growing organically, playing off one another, dependent on the previous episode for deep background and emotional wallop. For example, Ripley's terror on returning to LB426 in *Aliens* is felt by spectator and character alike but not the blithely ignorant marine invaders who precede her on the trail, a common *Alien* experience that cements identification and involvement. Likewise, the death of Newt and Hicks at the opening of *Alien*³ is a source of shared remorse because of the resonant memories of the mother and daughter reunion in *Aliens*. In truth, the *Aliens* audience had become so deeply invested in the maternal bond between Ripley and Newt and the romantic sparks between Ripley and Hicks that for *Alien*³ to wipe them away so cavalierly destroyed the whole meaning of the previous, beloved film. No wonder audiences howled betrayal and *Alien*³ failed commercially.

Alien

Appropriately for a nightmare vision of the future, all three films begin with an awakening from a deep sleep. *Alien* opens as the crew of the interplanetary cargo ship *Nostromo* arises stiffly from hypersleep. "Mother," the ship's automatic pilot and reigning computer, has buzzed them prematurely to respond to a distress signal from an uncharted planet. The crew's membership and hierarchy unfolds drowsily: an apparently stalwart captain, Dallas (Tom Skerritt); second in command Ripley (Sigourney Weaver); a prissy science officer, Ash (Ian Holm); navigator Lambert (Veronica Cartwright); an inscrutable officer named Kane (John Hurt); and a pair of below-the-line mechanics, Parker (Yaphet Kotto) and Brett (Harry Dean Stanton). Detaching itself from the cargo bay, the main ship descends to the purplish planet surface where the away team—Dallas, Lambert, and Kane—come upon a gigantic spaceship. They discover the distended cadaver of an alien goliath and, probing further down the vessel's intestinal underbelly, a seedling farm of womblike eggs.[6] A pulsating uterine form, breathing inside a pod, leaps out at Kane and attaches itself to his helmet. Brought back on board in violation of quarantine procedure and over Ripley's objections, Kane lies comatose, entangled by a crustacean creature that has wrapped itself onto his face, with one tentacle extended around his neck and another deep down into his throat. Mysteriously, he revives, none the worse for wear, the creature gone.

The dinner scene that follows is a cinematic ambush that ranks as one of the most jolting sequences in motion picture history. In its time, it was an unprecedented demonstration of the quantum leap in FX verisimilitude and explicit gore in the science fiction and horror genres. While eating his meal, Kane begins to gag, as if choking on his food. Writhing spasmodically, spitting blood, and shrieking in agony, he struggles supine on the dinner table as his comrades desperately try to control his contortions. To the sound of shredding flesh and crackling rib cage, Kane's torso ripples with blood, heaves upward, and—a creature bursts from his chest, spraying blood and entrails everywhere, hissing and rearing its head upward. The beastie pauses to scan the room before scurrying along the table out of sight. A reaction shot captures the stupefied crew, frozen like rabbits in a headlight, an apt reflection of the faces of moviegoers in multiplexes across North America.[7]

The search for the creature finds the hunters getting captured by the game, now transformed into a huge blackened dragon with extendable, metallic jaws. During a grisly process of character elimination, Ripley discovers Ash is a cyborg with a secret agenda: to recover the alien life form regardless of human body count ("crew expendable"). The last survivor, Ripley sets the *Nostromo* on automatic destruct and flees into an emergency escape shuttle, where the drooling alien waits to pounce. Stealthily, she dons a space suit and opens the hatch. The force of the vacuum of space sucks the creature outside the ship, Ripley blasts it with a rocket, and it cascades into oblivion. The dragon slain, Ripley, with Jonesy the cat, settles back into hypersleep.

Put down in coherent form, a plot synopsis of *Alien* fails to capture the unnerving unfolding of the narrative and the sheer shock that greets the rationed appearances of the shape-changing creature. The film's sound mix is muted and the dialogue muttered; exposition and orientation is scant; and the dreamscapes of LB426 and the *Nostromo* are surreal and haunting. A product of the collective unconscious of producer-designer Michael Seymour, art directors Les Dilley and Roger Christian, and alien designer H. I. Giger, the off-balance ambience alternates the antiseptic decor of computer consoles and medical laboratories with the underlit sarcophagal bowels of cargo bays and ventilation shafts. Parallel editing underscores the rupture between the spruced-up futurism of the ship's operational quarters and the medieval catacombs of the cavernous cargo areas and claustrophobic air shafts.[8] In embryo and adulthood, the alien is a realistic, lifelike creation, utterly persuasive and terrifying in its animate, sentient existence. Watching the alien in *Alien* requires not so much a willing suspension of disbelief as a periodic reminder of make-believe.

Aliens

Less a sequel to the first than an extension of it, Cameron's *Aliens* conjured a logical continuation that focused on the emotional wreckage of the burned-out heroine of *Alien*. Discovered drifting in space fifty-seven years after blasting the *Nostromo*'s stowaway to hell, Ripley is revived from hypersleep. She relates the plot of *Alien* to a board of inquiry convened by her corporate employers who, needing a fall guy for the loss of the ship and its cargo, discount her eyewitness report. A tormented survivor who awakes from nightmares

Aliens (1986): the sinewy woman warrior, Vasquez (Jenette Goldstein).

drenched in sweat, she nonetheless agrees to accompany a combat squad back to LB426, now an established mining outpost, and thereby face her demons down.

Again a space crew awakes from hypersleep, only this group is far more simpatico and convivial than the late members of the *Nostromo*. Except for the smarmy company man Burke (Paul Reiser) and the virgin lieutenant Gorman (William Hope), the combat squad is a cohesive fighting unit comprised of a standard-issue top sergeant (Al Matthews), a calmly heroic Corporal Hicks (Michael Biehn), a highly excitable Private Hudson (Bill Paxton), a sinewy woman warrior, Vasquez (Jenette Goldstein), and a "synthetic" Bishop (Lance Henricksen), who prefers the term "artificial person" and to whom Ripley, once burned by a cyborg, takes an instant dislike.

As the gung-ho marines board their "express elevator to hell," a fast-paced action adventure unspools, awash in gunfire, explosions, and the hysteria of combat. Living up to its title, *Aliens* showcases not a single shape-changing creature but a plurality, expanding the evisceration opportunities exponentially. Blasting the creatures as corrosive acid from their blood eats through the marines' flak jackets, beating back a forward assault from hordes of the creatures scurrying through air shafts, they fight a desperate rear-guard action. During a lull, they come upon a feral girl child, Newt (Carrie Henn), whom Ripley takes under her wing. After a blistering series of firefights and spectacular deaths, the aliens capture the girl. Journeying down into the lowest chambers of an industrial netherworld, Ripley intrudes into the lair of the alien queen, a breeding ground for hundreds of alien offspring. She gathers Newt into her arms and incinerates the pods with her flamethrower and rocket-propelled grenades. Nanoseconds before a nuclear conflagration obliterates the planet surface, Bishop appears in a shuttle craft and plucks the pair from the top of the structure. The survivors return to the mother ship seemingly safe, but as Bishop, Newt, and Ripley disembark, the alien mother rips Bishop in two and takes after Newt. Ripley dons a suit of robotic armor and, again, maneuvers the alien into an open hatch and blasts it into the vacuum of space.

Against the measured, even languorous, unfolding of Scott's *Alien,* Cameron's *Aliens* accelerates fast through low-angle Steadicam movements, jump cuts, and vertiginous point-of-view shots. Especially gripping is the first excursion into alien territory, before a shot is fired or creature spotted, an exemplary demonstration of the "ticking bomb" school of Hitchcockian suspense, a sequence all the more effective for Weaver's fearful alertness and jumpy expectations. But once the first blood is shed and the onslaught begins, Cameron upshifts from cool suspense to supercharged combat action. Unlike *Alien,* the spectatorial experience of *Aliens* is more in the way of an adrenaline rush than nervous anticipation.

Alien³

It is Cameron's Ripley who awakes from hypersleep in *Alien³*. The drip-drip-drip of alien acid has caused the mother ship from *Aliens* to malfunction and eject its emergency escape vehicle onto the planet Fury 161, a desolate penal colony. A computer screen display informs spectators of the death on impact of Hicks and Newt and the "negative capability" of the milk-blooded Bishop. Ripley survives, as yet unconscious, in the prison medical ward tended by a solicitous Dr. Clemens (Charles Dance). The penitentiary is a lice-ridden industrial foundry populated by monkish skinheads, so-called double-Y chromosome types locked up for rape, murder, and millennial Christian fundamentalism, the most verbal and sympathetic of whom is the husky potentate

Dillon (Charles S. Dutton). Needless to say, the tenacious alien swoops down to depopulate the prison, but in such barren and bleak all-male environs the alienated deaths of the nearly indistinguishable inmates (same uniform, same haircut) seem no great loss. Yielding more emotional valence is the revelation midway in the chase that Ripley is carrying an embryonic queen in her uterus. Thus, even if she and the double-Ys succeed in defeating the lone alien splattering the prisoners, Ripley herself faces a fate worse than death. Gestating through the frenzied action is the knowledge that, no matter what the outcome, Ripley is a terminal case. The request she made to Hicks in *Aliens*— to kill her before the alien takes hold—is made again, in earnest, to Dillon.

Nothing if not persistent, the bio-weapons division of the company arrives on Fury 161 to recruit the alien. To the impregnated Ripley, their representative—a Bishop look-alike—holds out the promise of medical intervention and a life of her own. He caps his appeal with a telling below-the-belt temptation: "Children?" But Ripley prefers death to reproduction. With icy determination, she swan-dives backward into a cauldron of molten metal, clutching to her bosom the baby queen, who in mid-dive erupts from her body. The slow-motion descent links the last chapter of *Alien³* with the previous two, echoing both Kane's epochal gut-bust in *Alien* and Ripley's hospital-bed nightmare in *Aliens*. The visual coda is stunning, a horrifying image of aesthetic and thematic closure.

As different from its predecessors as two is from one, three is unapologetically grim and brooding, dark in atmosphere and vision. Though the set design is colorfully hellish, an inferno of red molten metal and yellow chiaroscuro, the third run-through is palpably wearier in tone and timing, less invigorated by the shock of the new. And where the two previous entries are compendiums of slick filmmaking technique, *Alien³* betrays some basic behind-the-camera trouble, a consequence of the multiple rewrites and production difficulties that beset first-time director and MTV auteur David Fincher. (Vincent Ward, director of *The Navigator: A Medieval Odyssey* [1987], a cross between *The Seventh Seal* [1956] and *Back to the Future* [1985], was at the helm of *Alien³* until Twentieth Century-Fox deemed his fourteenth-century sensibility a millennium off.)[9] Moreover, the prolonged dragon hunt that takes up the last third of the film is an utter mess. The industrial noir decor is so underlit and ill designed one can't tell who's doing what to whom and why. Without spatial orientation and tactical information, the frantic chases and topsy-turvy alien point-of-view shots look like the creatures are chasing their own tails. Rather than the claustrophobic terror and spooky disorientation of *Alien* or the rush and exhilaration of *Aliens*, *Alien³* evokes only Fincher's previous work, Madonna's "Express Yourself" music video.

Genre

Separately and together, the three *Aliens* films reflect the chief characteristic of postclassical Hollywood cinema: the breakdown of traditional generic boundaries, the promiscuous cross-pollination among once autonomous breeds. The hybrid genes of the original *Alien* were captured in the advertising tagline ("In space no one can hear you scream"), just as the forthright slogan for *Aliens* announced a fresh generic bloodline ("This time it's war"). The elements in the generic mix become progressively dizzying: horror and science fiction (*Alien*); horror, science fiction, and the combat film (*Aliens*); horror, science fiction, the combat film, and the prison movie (*Alien³*).[10] The popular success of the series—and kindred science fiction/horror/combat genre hybrids such as *The Terminator* and *Predator* (1987)—is emblematic of two phenomena of postclassical Hollywood: first, the equanimity with which contemporary audiences accept violations of the traditional generic order and, second, the transfer of generic allegiances.[11]

Underlying both the tolerance for generic mix-and-match and the shift in generic brand loyalty is the influence of television-trained spectatorship. Even before remote control units and cable narrowcasting accelerated the velocity and multiplied the menu of channel surfing, paleo-televiewers acquired skill in rapid eye movements during the passage from station to station—from, say, the horror of *The Twilight Zone,* to the science fiction of *The Outer Limits,* to the action adventure of *Combat.* Television spawned a generation of genre-wise (and genre-surfeited) spectators, trained experts in the tropes, conventions, and twists of formula programming. Having logged thousands of video hours in front of the small screen before adolescent passage into R-rated theatrical cinema, schooled in the lexicon of genre, zapping between narrative realms, television-age spectators of motion pictures can readily digest several genre menus at a single sitting.

For Hollywood, the legacy of television permitted not just generic bait-and-switch but helped launch a realignment in generic preferences. If conventional wisdom in the entertainment industry gives women the decisive voice in determining a family's living-room viewing options, it bestows upon men, especially young men, the determining influence in motion picture attendance. Classical Hollywood cinema's genres of choice were costume dramas, romantic melodramas, musicals, and westerns, the occasions for family outings and heterosexual courtship. Postclassical studio production is dominated by science fiction, horror, and action adventure, genres just as likely to be the occasion for same-sex outings and loner attendance as dating rituals. As late as the mid-1970s, George Lucas's expensive *Star Wars* project encountered resistance from studios leery of sinking huge sums into what was still considered a marginal genre. Allegedly, the premarket testing for the *Star Wars* title—with its denotation of science fiction ("star") and the combat film ("war")—boded ill for commercial prospects. Only with the juvenilization and masculinization of the theatrical audience for motion pictures did science fiction, horror, and action adventure become staples of motion picture production.[12]

As the series primogenitor, *Alien* has the cleanest, most traceable genealogy. Written by Dan O'Bannon and Ronald Shusett, loosely inspired by the low-budget weirdie *It! The Terror from Beyond Space* (1958), it melded science fiction hardware to a horror framework. A haunted-house-in-space trip with a barely glimpsed monster under the floorboards, it was born of the marriage of technology (the realm of science fiction) and psychology (the realm of horror). In the generic trade-off, horror probably gained more capital than science fiction. After the demise of the Production Code in 1965, the "pure" horror of the classical tradition—the shady implications and suggestive eroticism of Todd Browning or Val Lewton—ebbed commercially. With sexuality unleashed to roam the textual surface, with the Hays Office no longer demanding subliminal insinuations of unholy impulses, monsters from the id were free to occupy ego territory. For the horror film, the freedom from censorship was a mixed blessing. Increasingly, horror became a genre of excess and explicitness: cannibalism (*Night of the Living Dead* [1968]), gross-out (*The Exorcist* [1973]), and serial homicides (the *Halloween* [1978–1989] and *Friday the 13th* [1980–1989] series). Not until AIDS put the fear of sex back into American culture did the classical horror style reemerge—significantly, through the venerable figure of the vampire in films such as *Innocent Blood* (1993), *Bram Stoker's Dracula* (1993), and *Interview with the Vampire* (1994).

But if the horror and science fiction elements are evident enough, the generic roots of the first two *Aliens* are intertwined with a deeper ancestor: the World War II combat film.[13] The spaceship crews of the 1950s derived their style and ethos not from the work of Jules Verne or Fritz Lang but the Army Air Force, an influence displayed most schematically in Howard Hawks's (by way of Christian Nyby's) *The Thing (from Another World)* (1951). Hawks, the director of the definitive World War II bomber film, *Air Force* (1943), took the tropes and truisms of the wartime genre into confrontations with Cold War terrors from beyond space. The generic conventions of the World War II combat film—the cooperative bond between men in groups and the technical divisions of labor among a multiethnic crew—proved remarkably durable and adaptable to postwar menaces. Throughout the 1950s, science fiction cinema turned instinctively to the Strategic Air Command when threatened by invaders from Mars. Only in the late 1960s, when Vietnam had erased the presumption of combat effectiveness and upright morality, might sinister extraterrestrials hover above an Earth whose borders were unprotected by uniformed sentinels with noble motives.

Against this deep background of virtue, competence, and cooperation, the crews of the late 1970s science fiction films are cold, isolated, and hysterical.[14] Nothing is more terrifying in *Alien* than the fact that the common threat of annihilation fails to unite the *Nostromo* crew into a community of common purpose and concerted counterattack. To the death of their comrade Kane, they respond with shock but not grief. The grim burial in space has none of the sense of loss or right-stuff reverence of a John Ford funeral or a Howard Hawks death scene: "Anyone want to say anything?" asks Dallas rhetorically before pushing a button that ejects Kane's corpse into the abyss of space. In the face of danger, they disintegrate. The true enemy lurks within, the synthetic scientist whose loyalties lie not with his comrades, or even the creature, but the company. Yet any member of this crew might be a cyborg.

John Carpenter's *The Thing* (1982), a remake of the Hawks film, depicts the same kind of interpersonal implosion. Radically destructive of the ethos of the original, the second film features a collection of autonomous, angry, unpleasant, and self-interested individuals, as chilly as the stark Antarctic landscape they inhabit. That men could live like this in close quarters—in total isolation, depending on each other for survival and succor—and not develop a fraternal bond defies social reality and dramatic logic. The singularly cynical portrait of military men derives more from a post-Vietnam political perspective than actual experience of the nature of soldierly communion—an outlook typically purveyed by Hollywood directors who have never themselves been inside a barracks or on patrol.

Against the backdrop of combat crew crack-ups in *Alien* and *The Thing*, *Aliens* rehabilitated the World War II combat film and, not incidentally, the U.S. military. Where Scott's *Alien* melded horror and science fiction and expressed Hollywood's post-Vietnam revision, *Aliens* yoked science fiction to action adventure and reflected the military's restoration to public esteem in the Reagan era. The crew of *Aliens* is communal, connected, and combat ready, a unit that would be at home in a World War II combat film. Even the expansion of membership to heretofore marginal groups—blacks, Hispanics, and lesbians—is in line with the progressively open admissions policy of the military squad. The enemy is no longer us—it's them, the creatures in the ventilation ducts and subterranean chambers.

Not that Cameron is a mere jingoist, afflicted with historical amnesia and unfamilair with the generic transformations of the combat genre since 1945.

Appropriately for a tale of posttraumatic stress, *Aliens* owes a good deal of its style and ethos to the Vietnam combat film, the troubled descendent of the World War II prototypes. Led by military incompetents at the service of venal corporate interests, the self-described "grunts," complete with American flag insignia and flamethrowers, reenact a search-and-destroy mission that looks suspiciously like a late-twentieth-century police action. The freak-outs, wild firefights, scrambled video, surly grunts, lower-class ethnicity, macho posturing, even the calculated appropriation of military vernacular, play like a Vietnam-period run-through-the-jungle.[15] Like the military in Vietnam, the marine crew is restricted in the full application of their firepower by rear-echelon motherfuckers ("What are we supposed to use—harsh language?" snaps Hudson). Like the rumors of war on the home front, the fuzzy news of combat arrives via video footage. Transmitted from cameras in the soldiers' helmets, disjointed flashes of gunfire are watched on monitors from afar by a field commander safely ensconced in an armored personnel carrier. The crosscutting from the real scene of action to the video versions is fast, furious, and disorienting, the white noise of a television war.

Aliens also takes as a matter of course the U.S. military's subservience, though ultimate moral superiority, to the company store. As in *Rambo: First Blood, Part II* (1985), it is the corporate civilian and not the military professional for whom the film reserves its deepest hatred. Vietnam-era class antagonisms underscore the linkage. "You're [not] going to let Hicks decide," protests Burke when the chain of command descends upon the corporal. "He's just a grunt . . . Sorry, no offense." "None taken," hisses Hicks.

Alien³ adds another generic overlay: the claustrophobic environs of the prison movie, the narrative of confinement, endurance, and escape. During the Great Depression, the prison movie was a thinly disguised metaphor for life outside the walls of the Big House. In hijacking the conventions of Warner Bros. social-consciousness movies of the 1930s, the prison movies of the past decade are more apt to construct the world behind bars as a fantastical horror landscape, an urban site that, like the inner city, is populated by pathological minorities bent on making life unpleasant for uptown white folk who venture out after hours (cf. the characters played by Tom Selleck in *An Innocent Man* [1989] and Sylvester Stallone in *Lock Up* [1989]). As a social institution, the prison is perverse and punitive not only because it cages its inhabitants but because it segregates them by sex. In *Alien³* Ripley is the alien invader who disrupts the peace of a celibate, all-male environment. Even before the first attack from the creature, she introduces the chaotic element of female sexuality, a force that neither unisex clothing nor close shaves can disguise. Stand-

Alien³ (1992): Ripley (Sigourney Weaver) disrupts the celibate, masculine world of the penal colony.

ing naked and defiant before Clemens, "parading" around the prison interior, she can only discombobulate the monastic social order. Though the sexual assault attempted by the inmates turns out to be redundant (Ripley has already been violated by the creature while in hypersleep), her sexuality is a menace to the men. After sleeping with her, Clemens, his guard down, is garroted by her jealous stalker. Only the threat of death from one alien diverts the men from the lure of sex with the other.

Gender

In classical Hollywood cinema perhaps only the western outdid science fiction in its relegation of women to a peripheral and predictable status. The reason the vintage science fiction weirdies look so ludicrous in retrospect is not that the aliens are so patently cut-rate latex-and-foam fabrications but that the sex roles are imbedded like concrete in the Eisenhower era. In the 1950s the imagination of the future might comprise all sorts of extraterrestrial flora and fauna, but the sexual politics remained determinedly terrestrial and time bound. Two of the stock characters in science fiction cinema—the pilot and the scientific expert—were male-only employment opportunities whose demands for vehicular skill and abstract reasoning disqualified the maladroit and hysterical female from command authority.

At the same time, as a projection of the future, the science fiction narrative might promise variation if not progress. Barred from full admission to the upper echelons of the space crew, women entered as novelty and decoration, sometimes even filling the role of scientific expert in an erotically charged white-coated and horn-rimmed-glasses way. Like Raquel Welch in the biological exploration film *Fantastic Voyage* (1966), the space bimbo filled out a tight-fitting uniform to distract and entice. Though a woman of science, she was destined to lose her composure and succumb to a sheltering masculine shoulder at a crucial moment.

The generic reversal of the space bimbo motif in the person of Ripley, the then-unfamiliar Sigourney Weaver, was the most audacious narrative twist in *Alien:* in this future world, the natural order of things really was upside down. Against all science fiction expectations, the prettiest babe on board is also the shrewdest operator. Killing off the rugged captain in mid-narrative (the manly Tom Skerritt, oozing the right stuff as he makes all the wrong decisions) bordered on generic malfeasance.[16] Rather than cry "Eeek!" and freeze in the face of danger, Ripley becomes the dragon slayer who blows the beast into the vacuum of space. Sexy, strong, and smart, Weaver's Ripley was the connecting thread in the *Alien* series, not a recurrent picaresque hero but a vital link who from *Alien* to *Aliens* maintained a distinct and complex psychological profile as she dominated more and more screen space. Whereas in *Alien* Ripley emerged gradually as the heroine from an ensemble with a high mortality rate, in *Aliens* and *Alien*[3] she is the unchallenged focus of identification, the old-fashioned Hollywood star better lit and lined than her fellows. Of all the roman-numeral sequels, the three *Aliens* comprise the only series focusing on and powered by a female protagonist. Weaver/Ripley is the necessary ingredient in the franchise, the one element in the package without which the science fiction high concept would have fallen to earth.

In *Aliens,* Ripley's aggressive self-sufficiency and ruthless logic is even more pronounced, more of a contrast to the men around her who freak out or freeze in the face of danger. While Ripley thinks one move ahead and takes the reins, the milquetoast lieutenant Gorman sweats and stutters and the panicky audience surrogate Hudson yelps tremulous defeatism in a woozy surfer accent ("Game over, man! Game over!"). Quick-witted and courageous, she makes the tough decisions, initiates dramatic rescues, and assumes natural leadership over the macho squad. The striking element in Ripley's image as a woman warrior is not just her grace under pressure but that her grace under pressure is set in relief against so much male cupidity and incompetence.

Yet despite the distaff Rambo theme of the theater-lobby display kits (featuring a windswept Weaver brandishing fire-breathing weaponry and suited up with crisscrossed ammo belt), Ripley is no Amazon. Tempering Ripley's masculine strength and assertiveness is her maternal devotion to the girl Newt, like herself the sole survivor of an alien visitation. In comforting and protecting Newt, Ripley assumes a less threatening, more familiar female role. Cameron softened her hard edges by making a full-blooded woman out of the bare-bones and rather severe careerist in Scott's *Alien*. Play out the touch of romance between Hicks and Ripley, add android Bishop as manservant, and the surviving *Aliens* trio formed a protean nuclear family, with Mom wearing the pants.

Of course the doctrinal Freudian interpretation of *Aliens* reads the action as an extended meditation on Ripley's fear of motherhood, a fear only overcome through her assumption of maternal stewardship toward Newt ("Mommy!" the girl shouts as the pair come together for a closing embrace).[17] Ripley's opening-act nightmare about the alien embryo erupting from her stomach resembles nothing so much as a difficult birthing. Told by corporate weasel Burke that LB426 is now home to a mining colony settled by families, she is most distressed at the risk to the young ("Children?" she whispers, appalled). In the duel scenes between Ripley and the alien mother, the visual parallel is unmistakable: two queens fighting for their respective offspring. In this light, Ripley's birth-trauma nightmare provided the psychological fuel for her rite of passage through the bowels of the bitch's subterranean lair, a night-sea journey that reenacts the passage through the birth canal, a trip heretofore for knights only, never damsels.

As Ripley fights for her chick, she confronts her own subconscious dread of motherhood. Investing the tough cookie with maternal longings created a kind of gender equipoise, balancing the harsh male proclivity for violence with a softer, feminine nurturing side. The lobby stand-up and iconic publicity picture captures the double play: Ripley, holding firearm aloft, wrapped in munitions, cradles Newt protectively in one arm, at once the woman warrior and the solicitous mother. Newt gives Ripley a culturally permissible way for a woman to fight and kill, not for her own satisfaction or career advancement but for her children. Science fiction cinema may never have produced a more crowd-pleasing moment than Ripley's imperative command to the killer queen: "Get away from her, you bitch!"

Though one undeniable source of the erotic energy of the film is its allur-
ing protagonist, the set design and visual landscape seductively enhance the
sexually charged atmosphere. The architectural motif might be described as
"abstract genital," a style that is alternately penile and uterine, all sharp tumes-
cent shafts, vaginal entrances, and fallopian interiors. As for the creature itself,
he and she is something of a switch hitter. The alien of *Alien* is configured as
a forbidding phallus threatening to penetrate the female. All three of his incarnations—face hugger, chest buster, and dragon jaw—suggest the outline
of the masculine member. The symbol achieves a kind of visual fruition in the
climactic scene aboard the escape pod when the creature rears up tumescently
behind Ripley, who is clad in panties and a skimpy T-shirt. In *Aliens,* however, the creature is female, a queen generating unholy spawn. In *Alien^3,* the
she reverts again to a he, pursuing the female to penetrate and impregnate her.
Vagina dentata and phallic drill, the alien is a cross-dressing monster from the
id whose sexual confusion mirrors the shifting gender dynamics of the series.

To turn from the resourceful, maternal, and victorious Ripley of *Aliens*
to the desperate, vacant, and defeated Ripley of *Alien^3* is to confront another
kind of sex-change operation. Where *Alien* unapologetically affirmed Ripley's strength and tenacity, where *Aliens* developed Ripley's maternal side as a
progressive extension of the well-rounded woman warrior, *Alien^3* can't decide whether it wants to eroticize or de-sex her, to celebrate her for being assertive or chastise her for being uppity. Surely, though, she is punished sadis-
tically for the maternal feelings that developed in *Aliens.* When Ripley comes
to consciousness, she learns of the deaths of Hicks and Newt and indulges a
mother's grief. Still one to go by the book, and fearing the worst, she demands
an autopsy for Newt. To the sounds of bones cracking and organs squishing,
Ripley watches in anguish as her child's body is gutted. During the subsequent industrial-strength funeral scene, Ripley cries, Dillon delivers a depress-
ing sermon, and the shrouded bodies of Hicks and Newt are tossed into a
cauldron of boiling metal. End of family.

As the only woman aboard a planet of rapist/murderers, Ripley is a walking
provocation, even bald and uniformed. However, perhaps to salvage some of
the feminism of the previous installments, she's not only an object of desire
but a subject of one: in the only interhuman sex act of the series, she coolly
propositions and mates with Clemens. But the woman who emerged in *Aliens*
is submerged in *Alien^3:* her unique blend of male and female strengths, macho and maternal, professional confidence and sexual power, cannot save her.

The *Aliens* trilogy would not be a pure product of commercial Hollywood
cinema if it did not express an ambivalence toward the strong woman at its
center. After all, from one vantage, the venerable Hitchcockian formula for

Alien³: The alien face to face with a terrified Ripley.

gripping drama—"torture the women"—defines the narrative project.[18] Recall how in *Alien* the cyborg Ash wraps a bunch of papers into a cylinder and stuffs them into Ripley's mouth, to choke her, to silence her voice. Yet the torment the heroine undergoes in *Alien* and *Aliens* pays off in survival and psychological growth: the crucible of combat restores her sturdy sense of self and saves the lives of her surrogate daughter and husband. In contrast to the poster of the warrior mother advertising *Aliens,* the iconic image from *Alien³* is a Panavision composition of the dragon's head, steel jaws thrust forward, hissing and salivating, face to face with a terrified, whimpering Ripley, looking for all the world like a concentration camp victim threatened by a smirking guard. Like so many of the bankable horror/science fiction series of the 1970s and 1980s, the three *Aliens* could pass for an extended, extraterrestrial stalker film where the killer/rapist ultimately achieves his goal, violating, impregnating, and destroying the too-adventurous, too-assertive female.

The trilogy closes, however, not just by killing the female but by vaporizing her body, obliterating the generative vessel. After all her courage and resourcefulness, suffering and sacrifice, Ripley is left with no reward, no exit, condemned to backflip into a molten inferno. Having faced her demons and fought for life, she must in her last gesture embrace death. For the likes of Ripley, a space in the world, even the imaginary world of the future, is unimaginable. Her alert intelligence and active initiative cannot be contained by marriage, the conventional wrap-up for female-centered narratives, yet neither can she be unleashed to roam free in an uncharted feminist galaxy. *Alien³* depicts the prison of genre more than it knows: it locks out options. Perhaps the nihilistic finale lays bare a piercing critique of a twentieth-century planet Earth inhospitable to independent female life. More likely, it exposes a failure of artistic imagination. As in Ridley Scott's other big box office hit, *Thelma and Louise* (1991), the only conceivable fate for a woman with the right stuff is to be driven off a precipice into oblivion. In the end, the trilogy refuses to liberate Ripley and awake from the repetition compulsion that is its narrative rhythm—from sleep to consciousness to sleep and back again, until finally to death, the big hypersleep.

Notes

1. Among the many studies of 1950s alien invasion films as metaphors for communist attack and infiltration, see Patrick Lucanio, *Them or Us: Archetypal Interpretations of Fifties Alien Invasion Films* (Bloomington: Indiana University Press, 1987), and the "Pods and Blobs" chapter in Peter Biskind, *Seeing Is Believing: How Hollywood Taught Us to Stop Worrying and Love the Fifties* (New York: Pantheon, 1983), pp. 101–159.

2. Robin Wood articulates a contrary view, arguing that "repression of the bisexuality that psychoanalysis shows to be the natural heritage of every human individual and the oppression of homosexuality" is derived from "the flimsy and dubious foundations of biological difference." See Wood, *Hollywood from Vietnam to Reagan* (New York: Columbia University Press, 1986), p. 72.

3. *Demon Seed* is a particularly rich gloss on this gendered reading of computer programming. The sentient computer needs the woman for life: without her, his existence is incomplete; he can be made flesh only by union with the female.

4. The laser disc edition of *Aliens* includes cut footage in which Ripley is shown pictures of the daughter she never knew, a child who has lived and died while Ripley was in hypersleep. There is no intimation of a daughter in *Alien,* and my view is that *Aliens* is the better for the cut footage.

5. A fourth entry with a genetically rebuilt Ripley is in the pipeline.

6. For a provocative analysis of the biological set design of the film, see Harvey R. Greenberg, "Reimagining the Gargoyle: Psychoanalytical Notes on *Alien,*" in *Close Encounters: Film, Feminism, and Science Fiction,* ed. Constance Penley, Elizabeth Lyon, Lynn Spigel, and Janet Bergstrom (Minneapolis: University of Minnesota Press, 1991), pp. 83–103.

7. Director Ridley Scott also bushwacked his own actors: no one in the scene save actor John Hurt knew that they were set up to be covered in blood and entrails.

8. *Cinéfantastique* 9, no. 1 (1979), is a special issue devoted to the design and FX of *Alien*.

9. *Cinéfantastique* 22, no. 6 (June 1992), chronicles the production difficulties attending *Alien³*.

10. This is not to say that science fiction, horror, combat, and prison movies comprise a full accounting of the generic roots of the *Aliens* trilogy. To take the search for genealogy to extremes, trace elements of the familial melodrama, film noir, and the mystery film might be detected as well—and of course any science fiction excursion into a strange frontier inhabited by unfriendly natives can rightly claim first kinship with the American western. Many science fiction critics have noted that the birth of the mature science fiction film coincided with the death of the western, that a Vietnam generation no longer confident about printing the legend of the American past turned America's frontier vision outward to remote galaxies and forward to the future. Interestingly, the late resuscitation of the theatrical western that began with *Dances with Wolves* (1990) and reached an apotheosis with Clint Eastwood's *Unforgiven* (1992) has coincided with a downturn in off-world science fiction cinema.

11. Thomas Schatz, *Hollywood Genres: Formulas, Filmmaking, and the Studio System* (New York: Random House, 1981), Barry K. Grant, ed., *Film Genre: Theory and Criticism* (Metuchen, N.J.: Scarecrow Press, 1977), and Barry Keith Grant, ed., *Film Genre Reader II* (Austin: University of Texas Press, 1995), delineate the conventions of classical Hollywood cinema's genres of choice.

12. On this point, it is worth noting that only in 1992 did a horror film—Jonathan Demme's *The Silence of the Lambs* (1991)—receive an Academy Award for Best Picture. Moreover, although Sigourney Weaver received Academy Award nominations for Best Supporting Actress for *Alien* and Best Actress for *Aliens,* both were a departure in an Academy that routinely overlooks Oscar-caliber work in science fiction, horror, and action adventure while awarding overly generous recognition to performances in films of high serious melodrama and social commentary.

13. See Jeanine Basinger, *The World War II Combat Film: Anatomy of a Genre* (New York: Columbia University Press, 1986).

14. The significant exception is the theatrical version of the 1960s retread created by former World War II bomber pilot Gene Roddenberry, *Star Trek* (1979–1991).

15. For an extended discussion of this trope, see Ellen Draper, "Finding a Language for Vietnam in the Action-Adventure Genre," in *Inventing Vietnam: The War in Film and Television,* ed. Michael Anderegg (Philadelphia: Temple University Press, 1991), pp. 103–114.

16. Subsuming the films under the rubric of horror, Carol J. Clover cites Ripley in remarking that "the emergence of the girl hero" is one of the "remarkable developments in the sex-gender system of horror since the mid-1970s." Clover, *Men, Women, and Chain Saws: Gender in the Modern Horror Film* (Princeton, N.J.: Princeton University Press, 1992), p. 16.

17. William Paul, *Laughing Screaming: Modern Horror and Comedy* (New York: Columbia University Press, 1994), discusses the sexual imagery of *Aliens* and the aesthetics of horror gross-out.

18. This injunction is discussed at length in Tania Modleski, *The Women Who Knew Too Much: Hitchcock and Feminist Film Theory* (New York: Methuen, 1988).

8

Taking Back the *Night of the Living Dead:*
George Romero, Feminism, and the Horror Film

Barry Keith Grant

Near the beginning of George Romero's original *Night of the Living Dead* (1968), Barbara, one of the film's three female characters, sinks into near-catatonic helplessness to become a burden on the other living characters. She remains this way until near the end, when she attempts to help free another woman from the clutches of the zombies, only to be dragged out the window by her now undead brother. In the new *Night of the Living Dead* (1990), written by Romero, no longer can it be said that the character of Barbara, as Gregory A. Waller aptly puts it, "would seem to support certain sexist assumptions about female passivity, irrationality, and emotional vulnerability."[1] Indeed, in the remake, Barbara is the only one of seven characters in the farmhouse to survive the night, and she is an active, assertive character, not only within the diegesis but as a narrative agent as well. This revision warrants closer examination, for it is at once simple yet stunning in its implications.

Romero's broad knowledge of the genre in which he has most often worked is signaled in his films by numerous references to other horror movies, both in dialogue and visual style.[2] In the afterword to his novelization of *Martin* (1978), he explicitly writes that his intention was to "re-vamp" the vampire story.[3]

Night of the Living Dead (1968): the helpless Barbara (Judith O'Dea) is aided by Ben (Duane Jones).

The film's treatment of the vampire makes it clear that, as the pseudo-vampire himself says, "There's no magic"—but there *is* ideology. And clearly, Romero has been particularly concerned about the ideology of gender representation in the horror film, attempting to "revamp" that tradition of the genre as well. Many of his films address this issue, especially the living dead series.

As has often been noted, movies such as Wes Craven's *The Hills Have Eyes* (1977), John Carpenter's *Halloween* (1978), the sequels to both these films, and the seemingly endless *Friday the 13th* and *Nightmare on Elm Street* series—all those horror shows Robin Wood describes as "a single interminable chronicle of blood-letting"[4]—owe much to the original *Night of the Living Dead*. The film inaugurated a cycle of zombie movies that eventually turned what Herschell Gordon Lewis, director of *Blood Feast* (1963) and *2000 Maniacs* (1964), once called the "gore film" into the more ominous-sounding "meat movie" or "splatter film." Romero himself is credited with having coined the term "splatter cinema" to describe those films that revel in physical violence and maiming to the extent that such spectacle becomes their sole raison d'être.[5] And it is, of course, no secret that such movies concentrate their violence upon women.

Night of the Living Dead has had astounding commercial success: made for a paltry $114,000, the film has grossed over $30 million worldwide and become a cult classic.[6] But if it was such a critical and commercial success, the immediate and obvious question is, why should Romero bother to remake it? The cynical view would be that the director is exploiting his own past success, feeding on himself like an ironic variation of his own horrible creatures in a calculated attempt to bolster a sagging career. (None of his other films—particularly those outside the horror genre—have been commercially successful.) But as certain auteurs have returned to their fictional worlds and, over time, deepened their characters and themes—Truffaut with Antoine Doinel, Lang with Mabuse, Coppola with Michael Corleone—so here Romero has returned to his original zombie narrative and fashioned a more politically progressive view than in the original, particularly in terms of the feminist issues raised by the first *Night*'s influence on the subsequent development of the genre.

It is this unfortunate heritage—his own monstrous offspring, so to speak—that Romero increasingly attempts to confront in his living dead movies. In the living dead trilogy—*Night of the Living Dead*, *Dawn of the Dead* (1978), and *Day of the Dead* (1985)—the zombie becomes as crucial a metaphor of social relations for Romero as the prostitute for Godard. *Night*, which David Pirie calls "probably the only truly modernist reading of the vampire myth," has been read variously as a critique of the Nixonian "silent majority," of American involvement in Vietnam, and of the family under capitalism. *Dawn* self-consciously uses the zombie as a conceit for macho masculinism and conspicuous capitalist consumption, "the whole dead weight of patriarchal consumer capitalism," as Robin Wood puts it. (Romero's own description of the film as "a satirical bite at American consumerism" is equally apt.)[7] *Day* shows the extent to which society has collapsed five years later, concentrating the political connotations of zombiedom on the issue of sexual politics. Men in the film are consistently shown to be as much of a threat to life as the zombies that are forever surrounding the band of human survivors.

Romero wrote the screenplay for the new version of *Night*, which was directed by Tom Savini (makeup chief on *Martin*, *Dawn*, *Day*, *Creepshow* [1982], and leading player in *Knightriders* [1981]—all directed by Romero). The original was certainly a "personal" film: Romero co-wrote it based on his original story, and he directed, photographed, and edited it as well. His low-budget horror films that followed the first *Night*—*Jack's Wife* (a.k.a. *Hungry Wives/Season of the Witch* [1973]), *The Crazies* (a.k.a. *Code Name: Trixie* [1973]) and *Martin*—all approach the genre from a similarly subversive perspective, clearly revealing Romero as an auteur before he was officially so dubbed in *Film Comment* by Dan Yakir in 1979.[8] So even though he did not direct the remake of *Night*, Romero's authorship is evident throughout the film.

Surprisingly—especially given Savini's reputation for physically gruesome special effects—the new *Night* downplays graphic violence. Rather, following the trajectory of the trilogy, it consistently foregrounds the dramatic implications of the first version, concentrating on social tensions embodied in relations between living characters. So, for example, the bickering of the bourgeois couple, Harry and Helen Cooper, is now more pronounced, and unambiguously involves physical abuse; and the racial tension raised by the presence of the black hero, Ben, whose racial difference is never mentioned by the other characters, is now more explicit.

But I want to focus here on the rewriting of the character of Barbara. Like her predecessor, the new Barbara initially seems "mousy," as conventionally coded by her tightly buttoned high-neckline blouse, brooch and neckerchief, and the inevitable eyeglasses. She, too, is frightened at the beginning of the film by her brother Johnny's scary stories, and it initially seems as if she, like the first Barbara, will quickly fall into a catatonic stupor. But when implored by Ben to maintain her composure, she quickly rallies herself. Confronted with some approaching zombies, she and Ben dispatch them at the same time, Barbara in fact disposing of the larger of the two with a poker. "I'm not panicking," she coolly tells Ben afterward. "You told me to fight, so I'm fighting." In the course of the narrative, she exchanges her traditional female attire for clothing found in the farmhouse resembling fatigues and combat boots. She emerges as the fittest to survive, and is the only one of the group in the farmhouse alive at the end of the film. Interestingly, according to the original script, Barbara was to have survived the 1968 film as well—albeit reduced to catatonic paralysis.[9] In the remake, she not only survives, but does so by deducing the correct strategy in response to the zombie attacks: neither to defend the house (Ben) nor to retreat to the cellar (Harry), but to flee, since the zombies can easily be outrun. She acts more effectively, in other words, free of the territoriality associated in the film with masculinism.

This change in the character of Barbara should not be surprising, for, although it seems to have gone largely unnoticed, a crucial aspect of Romero's vision almost from the beginning has been his generally positive treatment of women, even a striking empathy with them. Romero's third film, *Jack's Wife*—which he wrote, photographed, edited, and directed—is unambiguously sympathetic toward its female protagonist, a bored housewife experiencing growing dissatisfaction with her patriarchal husband and prescribed lifestyle. Like Fellini's Giulietta, Joan escapes into her imagination, and her fantasies and dreams, to which the viewer is privileged, become indistinguishable from reality. She becomes interested in witchcraft, its appeal for her obviously a fantasy inversion of her real disempowerment. In one of her dreams, Joan imagines her husband Jack leading her around with a dog collar and leash, attacking her in her car, and slapping a newspaper on the window in a deliberate reference to the zombie with the brick who attacks Barbara in the opening scene of *Night*.

Indeed, if there is an agent of horror in the film, it is not the witch Joan, but her husband, who here and in several other scenes is visually coded as the monster. The film thus demythifies witchcraft as supernatural, its ideological project perfectly summed up by the image of Joan buying her witchcraft paraphernalia in a trendy shop and paying for it with a credit card. Her official induction as a witch near the end of the film shows her again being led about on a leash around her neck—witchcraft, that is to say, is just another oppressive ideology (superstition) that prevents this woman from being herself. Romero explicitly describes the film as "feminist," saying of Joan that "She's got everything she could possibly want, except a life."[10]

The clear-headed, unsentimental resourcefulness of the new Barbara in response to the crucible of the undead follows from the treatment of Fran in *Dawn* and Sarah in *Day,* and calls to mind another central aspect of Romero's zombie films: their striking similarity to the adventure films of Howard Hawks and the code of professionalism these films explore. Waller has shown how stories of the undead are about humanity's fitness for survival, although he nowhere links this to the Hawksian theme.[11] Romero himself has explicitly acknowledged the influence of Hawks on his work, and of the 1951 Hawks-produced science fiction/horror film *The Thing (from Another World)* (directed by Christian Nyby) in particular.[12] The Hawksian influence on Romero is pronounced both in his films' plots—the familiar narrative situation wherein a small group is cut off from society and must accomplish a certain dangerous task—and in their mise-en-scène, particularly in the kind of gesture so crucial to the Hawksian universe. Roger's lighting of Peter's tiparillo in *Dawn,* for example, is clearly indebted to similar gestures in Hawks's work: Clift's lighting of Wayne's cigarettes in *Red River* (1948), for example, or the similar interplay between Bogart and Bacall in *To Have and Have Not* (1944).

The much-underrated *Knightriders*—which Romero describes as a personal film and, after *Martin,* his own favorite[13]—is an unabashed homage to the Hawksian code of professionalism. *Knightriders* is about a traveling band of performers who go from town to town engaging in jousting tournaments on motorcycles. The troupe adheres to a rigid moral code that determines both their actions and their social position, the feudal chain of being by which they abide serving as a perfect metaphor for the world of Hawksian professionalism, which is defined in large part by knowing one's limits and abilities. King Billy, the troupe's leader, fights to uphold the code and prevent its corruption by commercialism and egotism. Both temptations are lures to which

Hawksian professionalism in the apocalypse: *Dawn of the Dead* (1979).

the unprofessional rebels, led by Sir Morgan, succumb. Personal grudges and partisan politics rather than the code begin to influence the jousts, and King Billy ultimately keeps the troupe together through his martyrdom, sacrificing himself on the chrome altar of the front grille of an oncoming commercial semi. (This is, of course, corny and melodramatic stuff—the very words Wood uses to describe the comparable work in Hawks's oeuvre, that "completely achieved masterpiece," *Only Angels Have Wings*.) [14]

The world of the living dead films is a brutally Hawksian one, in which the primary task is survival itself. Being able to survive in this world requires a philosophical detachment and existential determination in order to cope with the zombies physically, psychologically, and spiritually. As with, say, the cowboys on the Chisholm Trail in *Red River* or the men in the Arctic in *The Thing*, the characters in the living dead films are cut off from established codes of ethics, forced to survive on an existential precipice even steeper than the mountains surrounding the flyers in *Only Angels Have Wings*. Dr. Grimes's remark on TV in the first *Night* that "the bereaved will have to forego the dubious comforts that a funeral service can give" explicitly establishes this theme, and the films go on to explore both the failure and inappropriateness of such institutions as family, religion, even traditional humanism, to defeat the legions of the undead. This total collapse is shown most powerfully in the opening sequence of *Dawn,* in which a tenement roomful of dying people sequestered by a priest for the giving of last rites becomes a hellish pit of ghoulish violence, and in *Day,* when Sarah unhesitatingly cuts off her lover's arm after he is bitten by a zombie to prevent the infection from spreading.

In the new *Night* Romero clearly has recast Barbara as the film's one true Hawksian professional. The others in the farmhouse are unable to deal with the zombies in a professional manner because of egotism and sentimentality. Tom admits that he could never have shot the first zombie dispatched by Barbara because he was "Uncle Rege," and soon after, as she kills another, Judy screams hysterically, "You shot Mr. Magruder." Barbara coolly demonstrates the necessity of so doing (despite the invitation to sentiment in the shot of a granny zombie) by proving to them that these attackers are already dead: as a zombie comes through the door, she calmly shoots it several times in the chest first, allowing it to keep coming at them as vivid empirical proof of her rational assessment of the phenomenon before hitting it between the eyes. Ben accuses Barbara of "losing it," but she emphatically denies this as she blows away another zombie with the shotgun. "Whatever I lost I lost a long time ago. I'm not planning on losing anything else," she retorts, and then turns the accusation around by telling Ben and Harry that they seem like squabbling children. In the film's dramatic climax, Harry, like Tom and Judy earlier, cannot bring himself to shoot his daughter once she becomes undead even though he knows he must—it is a job that only the true professional can accomplish, and again it falls to Barbara to perform the unpleasant but necessary task.

Romero's treatment of gender in relation to the philosophy of professionalism seeks to resolve the thorny problem for feminism of assessing the value of the Hawksian worldview. Feminist critics have been divided in their opinion of Hawks. Peter Wollen and Robin Wood (even in his later, more politically conscious criticism) clearly articulate the classic auteurist understanding of the relation between Hawks's comedies and adventure films as a dialectic between the "feminine" and "masculine" principles of human nature. The comedies, according to this orthodox view, privilege the emotional life of female characters who are shown to provide a healthy balance to the professionalism of male characters in the adventures.[15] This is precisely the reason Molly Haskell and other early feminist critics also value Hawks's work. As Naomi Wise puts it, "While the men in Hawks' adventure films are professionally skilled . . . , Hawksian women are professional human beings." [16]

Nonetheless, critics as diverse as Claire Johnston and Raymond Durgnat disapprove of these films for the very same reason, finding unacceptable the fact that Hawks's women must constantly prove themselves within a masculine world according to masculine standards. As Johnston notes, the problem with Hawks is that for him "there is only the male and the non-male: in order to be accepted into the male universe, the woman must *become* a man. . . . [S]he is a traumatic presence which must be negated."[17]

By contrast, Romero is considerably more progressive. *Knightriders* shows that it is unnecessary for women to struggle throughout a narrative to demonstrate their professionalism, for it is a fait accompli, a given: after a victorious joust in the troupe's first performance, Sir Rocky removes "his" helmet to reveal that the knight is a woman. Further, nowhere is she shown to have a heterosexual attachment ("I know who I am," she declares at one point, in contrast to Jack's wife); she is simply there, one of the group. Romero is also willing to allow homosexuals into his professional group, as when Pippen, the troupe's master of ceremonies, is unintentionally brought out of the closet and no one thinks twice about it, since his sexual preferences are irrelevant to his professional function within the group. And if Hawks can be seen as an apologist for capitalism by equating it with manliness (most clearly in *Red River*),[18] then Romero's films attack capitalism as consistently as they do the ideology of masculinity. The shots of cash registers in the mall in *Dawn* filled with now useless money, and of bills blowing in the bank entranceway in the zombie-filled streets of Fort Meyers in *Day* are clear comments about the irrelevance of capitalism and materialism to the new morality contemplated by the zombie films.

In fact, it is more often the *men* in Romero's horror films who fail to prove themselves professionally. In *The Crazies,* the first person to become insane is a father, who kills his wife and sets fire to the family house. And in *Creepshow,* the comic-book morality tales of monstrous revenge and poetic justice can be read as the unleashed imagination of a boy against his patriarchal and repressive father in the movie's frame story. This depiction of men as insane oppressors is consistent in the zombie movies. In *Dawn,* Roger becomes so taken with the sporting pleasure of killing zombies that he acts recklessly and, as a result, is fatally bitten. The internecine conflict among the living in *Day* is obviously motivated by the threat to phallic control represented by the presence of the professional woman—she is, in Johnston's words, a "traumatic presence," but significantly, Romero refuses to allow her to be "negated." And in the new *Night,* as before, Harry and Ben lock horns, so to speak ("playing rooster" is how Judy describes it), in a struggle for masculine dominance and territorial control.

Social order quickly collapses—("It doesn't take long for the world to fall apart, does it?" Ben remarks when the farmhouse telephone goes dead)—because of the inability of Romero's male characters to work together. Threatened with violence and dissolution, masculine power oppressively asserts itself in attempts to impose order through authorial control rather than group cooperation. Waller aptly describes the scene in *Dawn* in which the men arm themselves: "The fetishistic objects flash by: high-powered rifles, derringers, revolvers, western-style handguns and holsters, cartridge belts, shotgun shells, and more . . . , the central icons in the so-called male action genres." [19] Social organization and law revert merely to physical power, like Freud's primal horde. The roving band of bikers in *Dawn* is Romero's most explicit image of this masculine power principle, although this is also clear in the new ending he has provided for *Night*.

The territorial battle in the farmhouse between Harry and Ben is a microcosm of the larger social breakdown, as we see toward the end of the film. Radically unlike the first *Night*, Barbara escapes from the farmhouse and, after wandering in the dark wary of approaching zombies, comes upon the local paramilitary unit scouring the countryside for zombies. In the original film, the group appears the next morning and brutally shoots Ben, who has survived the night alone in the cellar but whom they assume (?) is just another zombie. In the new version, these men are shown at first like zombies: in a sudden, startling close-up, the first man is shown wide-eyed, his arm threateningly stiff around Barbara's neck. "What in the name of Jupiter's balls are you doing out here alone, little lady?" he asks. The next morning she awakes (physically and politically) to this barbarism fully institutionalized: some of the men taunt the zombies in a pen, treating them like animals for sport; other zombies are hung for the spectacle of watching them wriggle before they are shot.

This is the debasement of professionalism, its requisite lack of sentiment souring into callousness. Barbara acts as a *corrective* to the narrowness of "masculine" professionalism, rather than, as in Hawks, having to be measured *by* it (in that key Hawksian phrase, to be as "good" as men). The image of a truck selling hot sausages and pork roasted on a spit to hungry participants of the spectacle makes clear the link between zombies and patriarchy, its own monstrousness: like the customers ordering fried chicken in the diner in Hitchcock's *The Birds* (1963), it is an ironic sign of a brutish, insensitive phallic culture.

Crucially, we see the sudden appearance of the zombie hunters and the society they represent from Barbara's horrified perspective. Indeed, the new *Night* adopts the same strategy of narrative viewpoint as the earlier *Jack's Wife,* in which all but a very few shots are motivated from Joan's physical or psychological perspective. Initially the camera adopts Barbara's physical point of view: thus, when the first zombie attacks her in the car in the opening cemetery scene, we are inside, with her, looking out. But then, more importantly, from the moment when she begins to assert her professionalism, we see from her perceptual, or moral, perspective. As soon as Barbara asserts herself, the film dis-

Barbara (Patricia Tallman) emerges as the fittest to survive in the new *Night of the Living Dead* (1990).

penses with shots of her frightened looks at the monsters—that crucial moment in horror films when, as Linda Williams has argued, the aspiring independent woman is punished for attempting to assert her own gaze.[20] So when the now zombified Uncle Rege approaches her from behind, Barbara experiences no horrified discovery; rather, at the last possible moment—and without any indication that she was aware of his presence, so that, perhaps, we are encouraged to expect her to respond with fear and surprise—she wheels about and promptly dispatches him. The viewer is thus prevented from delighting in the voyeuristic spectacle of a frightened and helpless woman.

Yet Barbara *does* look horrified after being "rescued" when, seeing the zombies being hung from a tree and then shot, she says, "We're them and they're us" (a line also heard in both *Dawn* and *Day*). Seen from her point of view, patriarchy is made exceedingly strange, becoming, in fact, repugnant and monstrous. Significantly, the film provides no opportunity to view Barbara undressed before she dons her Rambette costume—as is the case in *Alien* (1979), where it can be argued that the Sigourney Weaver character is recuperated for male pleasure in the concluding shots of her wearing implausibly flimsy space underwear. In refusing to provide the viewer with the dominant male gaze typical of the horror film generally and of the slasher cycle—with its conventional alignment of camera viewpoint and the monster victimizing women—in particular, the new *Night* subverts the form's characteristic sexual politics.[21]

Robin Wood's observation that horror films are progressive to the extent that they refuse to depict the monster as simply evil seems clearly borne out by these films,[22] for even as Romero progressively downplays the Otherness of the zombies, he depicts patriarchy as increasingly monstrous. If the zombies are indeed "nothing but pure motorized instinct," as they are described in *Day,* then the automatic relegation of Fran to a subordinate role by the men in *Day* makes them very much "undead." By contrast, the literal living dead are depicted with increasing sympathy in the trilogy. Beginning as an undifferentiated mass of murderous machines in the first *Night,* they become the pathetic victims of the bikers' crude violence in *Dawn. Day* features Bub, described by Romero as a "zombie with a soul," who in the end uses a gun to kill the macho army captain with at least partial moral approval by both filmmaker and audience. According to Romero, "You have to be sympathetic with the creatures because they ain't doin' nothin'. They're like sharks: they can't help behaving the way they do."[23]

The new *Night* encapsulates the trilogy's depiction of patriarchy, for at the beginning of the film the zombies are the monstrous threat, but at the end it is hysterical masculinity that is truly horrifying. In the conclusion, Barbara returns to the farmhouse the next morning to rescue Ben, followed by some of the men. They let Ben out of the basement to find that, unlike in the original, he has indeed become a zombie, and they shoot him. Barbara, having wandered off alone, discovers Harry, who, wounded but still alive, has crawled into the attic (ironically, given his earlier unyielding commitment to the basement). Perceiving Harry as a horrible patriarch, she shoots him in the head at point-blank range without hesitation. When the men come into the room, she says, "There's another one for the fire," correctly guessing that they will assume Harry also had been a zombie. In the original, Barbara's concluding line belongs to the redneck sheriff instructing his men what to do with Ben's corpse; in the remake, it accompanies a woman's response to patriarchy as defiant as the killing of the salesman in Marlene Gorris's militantly feminist *A Question of Silence* (1982). The new *Night* endorses Harry's fate no less than that of the macho Captain Rhodes in *Day,* who lives just long enough to see his lower body torn off and dragged away by zombies.

The new *Night,* then, attempts to reclaim the horror genre for feminism, for all those female victims in such movies who attempt to resist patriarchal containment. Where, say, R. H. W. Dillard finds the original *Night* to be so effectively frightening because it articulates a fundamental nihilism and negation of human dignity,[24] it is more accurate to say that all four zombie films are so powerful because Romero's undead demand the suspension of normal (bourgeois) values, particularly those of patriarchy. Wood is, I think, exactly right about the apocalyptic yet progressive politics of Romero's zombie films.[25]

My concern here is not simply to validate another male director for classic auteurism, but to read these films, instances of a genre notorious for its brutalization of women, against the grain for their possible value for progressive gender politics. Indeed, Romero's work offers a perfect instance of the exploitation film's potential, as noted by such critics as Pam Cook and Barbara Klinger, for incorporating progressive ideas.[26] When the search team at the beginning of *Day* lands in Fort Meyers, which has become populated entirely by zombies, it is significant that they are shown in front of an empty, now meaningless cinema—for Romero, as an independent regional filmmaker, has managed to make several progressive and commercially viable features while remaining on the margins of the mainstream. (In this sense, *Knightriders* gains additional significance as an autobiographical work about the attempt of a filmmaker to maintain integrity and avoid ideological compromise for commercial reasons.)

"Have we conjured up creatures and given them mystical properties so as not to admit that they are actually of our own race?" Romero has asked.[27] The new *Night of the Living Dead* shows that Romero has put this question to himself, and even if, ultimately, he falls into the trap of defining women in terms that one could argue are still masculinist, he has nevertheless provided one of the most significant feminist perspectives in the history of the horror film.

Notes

1. Gregory A. Waller, *The Living and the Undead* (Urbana and Chicago: University of Illinois Press, 1986), p. 283.

2. Paul Gagne, *The Zombies That Ate Pittsburgh: The Films of George Romero* (New York: Dodd, Mead, 1987), p. 11; John McCarty, *Splatter Movies: Breaking the Last Taboo of the Screen* (New York: St. Martin's Press, 1984), p. 58.

3. George A. Romero and Susanna Sparrow, afterword to *Martin* (New York: Day Books, 1980), p. 209.

4. Robin Wood, *Hollywood from Vietnam to Reagan* (New York: Columbia University Press, 1986), p. 195.

5. See McCarty, *Splatter Movies,* pp. 1, 5.

6. *Dawn of the Dead,* released without an MPAA rating because of its predecessor's cult reputation, still managed to become, like *Night,* one of the most commercially successful American independent features ever made.

7. David Pirie, *The Vampire Cinema* (New York: Crescent Books, 1977), p. 141; Elliott Stein, "*The Night of the Living Dead,*" *Sight and Sound* 39, no. 2 (Spring 1970): 105; Pirie, "New Blood," *Sight and Sound* 40, no. 2 (Spring 1971): 73–75; Wood, *Hollywood from Vietnam to Reagan,* p. 118; Gagne, *Zombies,* p. 87.

8. Dan Yakir, "Mourning Becomes Romero," *Film Comment* 15, no. 3 (May–June 1979): 60–65.

9. John Russo, *The Complete Night of the Living Dead Filmbook* (New York: Harmony Books, 1985), p. 35; Gagne, *Zombies,* p. 25.

10. Yakir, "Mourning Becomes Romero," p. 65; Gagne, *Zombies,* p. 56.

11. Walker, *The Living and the Undead,* p. 18.

12. Gagne, *Zombies,* pp. 7, 11.

13. Ibid., p. 108.

14. Robin Wood, *Howard Hawks* (London: British Film Institute, 1981), p. 17.

15. See Wood, *Howard Hawks,* esp. chaps. 2 and 3; and Peter Wollen, *Signs and Meaning in the Cinema,* rev. ed. (Bloomington and London: Indiana University Press, 1972), chap. 2.

16. Molly Haskell, "The Cinema of Howard Hawks," *Intellectual Digest* 2, no. 8 (April 1972): 56–68; Haskell, "Howard Hawks: Masculine Feminine," *Film Comment* 10, no. 2 (March–April 1974): 34–39; Haskell, *From Reverence to Rape: The Treatment of Women in the Movies* (Baltimore: Penguin, 1974), pp. 208–213; and Naomi Wise, "The Hawksian Woman," *Take One* 3, no. 3 (April 1972): 17.

17. Claire Johnston, "Women's Cinema as Counter Cinema," in *Movies and Methods,* ed. Bill Nichols (Berkeley: University of California Press, 1976), 1: 213; Raymond Durgnat, "Hawks Isn't Good Enough," *Film Comment* 13, no. 4 (July–August 1977): 15–16.

18. Durgnat, "Hawks Isn't Good Enough," pp. 9, 11.

19. Waller, *The Living and the Undead,* p. 310.

20. Linda Williams, "When the Woman Looks," in *Re-Vision: Essays in Feminist Film Criticism* ed. Mary Ann Doane, Patricia Mellencamp and Linda Williams (Frederick, Md.: University Publications of America/American Film Institute, 1984), pp. 83–99. Reprinted in this volume.

21. See Williams, "When the Woman Looks"; and Barbara Creed, "Phallic Panic: Male Hysteria and *Dead Ringers,*" *Screen* 31, no. 2 (Summer 1990): 125–164.

22. Robin Wood, "An Introduction to the American Horror Film," in *The American Nightmare: Essays on the Horror Film,* ed. Robin Wood and Richard Lippe (Toronto: Festival of Festivals, 1979), p. 23.

23. Yakir, "Mourning Becomes Romero," p. 62.

24. R. H. W. Dillard, "*Night of the Living Dead:* 'It's Not Just Like a Wind Passing Through,'" in *Horror Films,* ed. Dillard (New York: Monarch Press, 1976), pp. 55–82.

25. Robin Wood, "Apocalypse Now: Notes on the Living Dead," in *The American Nightmare,* pp. 91–97. Reprinted in Wood, *Hollywood from Vietnam to Reagan,* pp. 114–121.

26. Pam Cook, "Exploitation Films and Feminism," *Screen* 17, no. 2 (Summer 1976): 122–127; and Barbara Klinger, "'Cinema/Ideology/Criticism' Revisited: The Progressive Genre," in *Film Genre Reader II,* ed. Barry Keith Grant (Austin: University of Texas Press, 1995), pp. 74–90.

27. Romero and Sparrow, afterword to *Martin,* p. 210.

9

Gender, Genre, Argento

Adam Knee

While the films of Dario Argento are held in particularly high regard by fans of the slasher film and other related subgenres, his work often forcefully confounds many of the generalizations about relations of gender, power, and spectatorship in the horror genre that have been put forth in film studies. Indeed, so provocative are the spectatorial dynamics of some of Argento's films that Steven Shaviro has recently employed a scenario from *Opera* (a.k.a. *Terror at the Opera* [1987])[1] as a springboard for his critique of the Lacanian accounts of spectatorship that inform much of psychoanalytically oriented film criticism, finding in Argento's work a "counterparadigm for film spectatorship" in its "subversive, complicitous, and irreducibly ambiguous blurring of traditional polarities between male and female, active and passive, aggressor and victim, and subject and object."[2] In an article on the Italian horror film, Leon Hunt concordantly finds *Opera* remarkable for "its extreme play with . . . vacillating positions of identification."[3]

It is interesting that Hunt's discussion and Shaviro's brief, if pivotal, mention of Argento's work and its distinctive qualities are among the very few references to the director in the substantial amount of Anglophone scholarship devoted to the horror film.[4]

Although this inattention undoubtedly stems in part from the relative un-availability of Argento's films, their spotty distribution in both film and video (often in radically reedited form), and their origins (as Italian-produced films) in cultural and industrial contexts somewhat different from those of most English-language horror films,[5] one is forced to suspect that it also arises from the difficulty the works pose for certain assumptions about gender and the gaze in horror. This essay will attempt to examine such difficulty; to explore more closely the distinctive means by which notions of gender, sexuality, looking, and control are articulated in some of Argento's works; and ulti-mately to suggest ways in which the works may hold a potential for broader, more manifold conceptualizations of such notions.

A good deal of recent scholarship on the horror film has in fact fruitfully fo-cused on elaborating the varied figurations of gender and positionings of gen-dered spectatorship in the form, thereby moving away from all-encompassing generalizations about male-identified masculine monsters attacking female victims. Barbara Creed, for example, has argued the centrality of articulations of a "monstrous-feminine" (rather than purely male agents of monstrosity) across the horror genre, as well as claiming an oscillation in possible identifi-cations for both male and female spectators between victim and monster.[6] Perhaps most provocatively, Carol Clover has argued that a true fluidity and uncertainty in figurations of gender (rather than a binaristic alternation be-tween relatively distinct positions) is highly significant to the pleasures in-duced by the various modern horror subgenres she discusses:

. . . each of the horror genres in its own way collapses male and female to the point of inextricability: the slasher through the figure of an an-drogyne, the possession film through the assimilation of male psychic ex-perience to female bodily experience, and the rape-revenge film by ob-vious implication and through a system of intertextual references (above all to *Deliverance*). In each case I have argued against the temptation to read the body in question as "really" male (masquerading as female) or "really" female (masquerading as male), suggesting instead that the ex-citement is precisely predicated on the undecidability or both-andness or one-sexness of the construction.[7]

Clover concordantly suggests that the spectatorial experience for the genre's primarily male audience is a "feminizing" one, requiring a level of identifi-cation with feminine figures in distress and, hence, the contemplation of one's own passivity, humiliation, and penetration. In so doing, Clover explicitly questions the characterization of the male gaze as sadistic in much of feminist film theory, privileging instead a masochistic dimension of male voyeurism.[8]

To the extent that Argento's films consistently foreground ambiguities of gender and sexuality and repeatedly suggest the instability of power relations implied by acts of looking and perceiving, they force us to move toward the kinds of critical positions being laid out by Clover and Shaviro—that is to say, positions that question the rigidity of certain psychoanalytic schema and of certain assumptions about gendered binarisms in the horror film. Admittedly, Argento's works may constitute a special case, existing somewhat outside the subgenres that have been more closely theorized.[9] At the same time, however, Argento's films are most significant in pushing to a palpable extreme certain tendencies Clover detects across a substantial portion of modern horror subgenres, tendencies that are in their essence by no means anomalous, and in thereby suggesting possible directions for both academic film theory and popular generic practice.

In fact, many of Argento's films, while having plot concerns close to those of the American slasher film (a faceless killer commits a series of murders), begin to supercede even the broader parameters for gender conventions laid out by Clover for the slasher film.[10] Clover actually cites a statement from an interview with Argento about the director's preference for female victims as evidence for the overall emphasis on the deaths of women in the subgenre, the special attention that murders of women get, even when male victims are present as well. While Argento's work does tend to have more female victims (two of his films are even set in schools primarily for women), he nonetheless includes quite a few male victims and often dwells on their deaths at some length. Argento's protagonists are themselves fairly evenly split between male and female. Moreover, where Clover sees the killer as being male in most slasher films—albeit a male whose masculinity is profoundly and explicitly compromised—Argento's killers, in their variety and obscurity, tend to frustrate most such generalizations about gender.

Indeed, while Argento tends to visually present his killer as a single hooded and cloaked figure, the killer often turns out to be bi-gendered and multiple-personed, a number of individuals acting as one. The individuals involved in murder are themselves often presented as ambiguous in both their gendered characteristics and their sexual preferences—although the actual identity of the killer is rarely made clear before a film's conclusion, so the spectator is always forced to guess at the killer's sex. In *The Bird with the Crystal Plumage* (*L'Uccello dalle Piume di Cristallo* [1970]), for example, the murderer proves to be a woman acting because of identification with the male perpetrator of a violent attack on her years before, a woman who clearly derives sexual pleasure from her attacks on both her female victims and her male victims. Some of the actions attributed to her, however, have in fact been perpetrated out of love for her by her highly effeminate husband, who is initially misidentified as the killer. In *Four Flies on Grey Velvet* (*Quattro Mosche di Velluto Grigio* [1972]), the murderer is revealed at the film's conclusion to be an androgynous woman who was raised as a boy, while in *Cat o' Nine Tails* (*Il Gatto a Nove Code* [1971]), he is a man with an extra sex chromosome.

Deep Red (*Profundo Rosso* [1976]) offers, in an initially unattributed flashback sequence, a scenario self-consciously modeled on that of *Psycho* (1960, a film widely acknowledged, of course, as an important influence/subtext for much of the slasher genre), in which a young child (whose gender is unclear) is witness to a murder and, we are led to assume, suffers severe psychological difficulty as a result. When we learn that the child who has lived through this incident is in fact an emotionally disturbed gay male friend of the film's protagonist, we automatically assume it is he—the insane, effeminized Norman Bates figure—who has committed the murders. The film's conclusion once again upends our gender- and genre-bound deductions, revealing that, like the effeminized husband in *The Bird with the Crystal Plumage,* the gay male has merely been acting to protect the true murderer, in this case his mother. In *Tenebrae* (*Sotto gli Occhi dell'Assassino,* a.k.a. *Unsane* [1982]), Argento twists the gender and hermeneutic codes surrounding the identity of the killer still further, positing the protagonist's wife as a highly likely suspect, only to introduce clues suggesting the murderer must be a gay male reporter interested in the protagonist, only to have the reporter murdered himself, only to have it finally revealed that the reporter *had* committed the initial murders but the protagonist decided to take advantage of the situation to carry out some revenge killings himself.

In a number of films, Argento keeps us guessing not only as to the killer's sex, but as to his or her *species*. In *Phenomena* (a.k.a. *Creepers* [1985]), for example, an animal becomes a major murder suspect. In *Suspiria* (1979) and *Inferno* (1980), Argento pushes this identity uncertainty and dispersion to its limit by making the agent(s) of death supernatural and never clearly explaining them; in these films killings are variously performed by humans, animals, and, apparently, unearthly beings as well, although groups of female witches do seem to have some authority over what transpires. What is clear in any event is that it becomes difficult simply to attribute the murder and violence in Argento's films to sadistic male agencies—or, for that matter, to males whose masculinity has been somehow qualified, as in many American slasher films. Killers' gendered identities are emphatically rendered complex and obscure, a fact that substantially complicates any traditional understanding of narrative and ocular relations of power in Argento's work while nonetheless foregrounding those relations.

Indeed, the specific power dynamics of a number of Argento's murder scenarios seriously question the nature of generic gendered positionalities. In the scenario cited by Shaviro in *Opera*, for example, the killer ties up the female protagonist—an opera star—and tapes a row of needles into her eyes, thus forcing the female performer into the position of wide-eyed spectator while victims (in some instances male, in others female) are mutilated. Shaviro points out that this yields a "nauseating intimacy and complicity between the female viewer (who is not directly the victim) and the male murderer," as well as a "latent—secretly desirable—erotic thrill" in the female viewer's knowledge that the spectacle is being produced for her and that the scenario thereby resists "being classified according to the conventional binary opposition of sadistic male violence and helpless female passivity."[11] One could also note that, while Shaviro is able to retroactively designate the murderer as male, the killer's gender, sexual preference, and motivation are significantly unclear to the film spectator when the scenario is presented, thereby amplifying the context of instability and uncertainty. The first time one of these murders occurs, moreover, is just after the singer apologizes to her boyfriend for being unable to have sexual intercourse: no sooner does the female performer fail to perform (be passive, penetrated, female) for her boyfriend than she is made to view the killer's performance (in that her eyes are forced open, penetrated), which consists of the forcible penetration (graphically detailed, lest one miss the particular resonance) of her boyfriend's body with a knifeblade.

The Bird with the Crystal Plumage, Argento's first film as director, offers us a scenario strikingly similar in structure and function to that which is repeatedly played out in *Opera*. The film's male protagonist, an American writer on a sojourn in Italy, by chance spots an altercation taking place in an art gallery one evening. He comes forward to assist, only to find himself trapped between two sliding glass doors as a cloaked participant in the evident fight darts out through a rear exit. Like the opera singer, he is forced to watch helplessly, aghast yet fascinated, as an injured, bleeding woman who has been left in the gallery crawls along the floor.[12] The extreme (and, one suspects, erotic) nature of the protagonist's fascination with and attachment to this scene becomes clearer as the film progresses: he repeatedly shows more interest in the details of the investigation than in the amorous attentions of his girlfriend, and he insists on staying in Italy to pursue the case after the chief inspector gives him leave to return to the United States and even after attempts are made on his own life. The writer admits to a developing obsession—particularly with trying to recapture the memory of certain unclear details of the altercation—but he nevertheless finds the investigative adventure liberating: "It's started me writing again. It's broken me loose." (Given Argento's fondness for references to Hitchcock, it is easy to find a comparison here with Jeffries's experience of excitement and liberation as he, too, follows the investigation of an altercation obliquely witnessed in *Rear Window* [1954].)

Pertinent to the issue of ambiguities in gendered identity is the fact that the memory which the writer cannot bring himself to revive, yet which he finds so provocative, is that of the gendered balance of power in the fight he has witnessed: it is only when other immediate evidence makes the conclusion inescapable that he can recall that the woman was the *aggressor* in the fight, the fleeing figure her protective yet victimized husband. In other Argento films as well, the narrative is structured around the protagonist's preoccupation with a violent event with which he or she has become obliquely involved, and resolution is often linked with the protagonist's recapturing of an evasive memory of that event, a veritable primal scene usually characterized by unclarity, blood, violence, and a fascinating sexual ambiguity. Thus, in *Deep Red,* a musician is irresistibly drawn to the scene of a murder he has just unclearly witnessed from a distance, then is likewise drawn into investigating the murder and into trying to recall a crucial hazy detail. In *Tenebrae,* a secondary protagonist likewise finds himself compelled to return to the scene of a vaguely witnessed gruesome murder, only to suddenly realize that, like the writer in *Bird,* he has confused a killer with a victim. And in *Suspiria,* a ballet student dwells upon the memory of the overheard conversation of a murder victim and later finds herself exploring the corridors of the ballet school, where subsequent mutilations take place, with an uneasy fascination. (Indeed, simply undertaking the investigation of an act of aggression implies an effort to resituate polarities of power and looking, to return the stalker's punishing gaze.)

As central as activities of perception and investigation, looking and listening, are to many horror films, they hold a place of singular importance in the films of Argento. The eye itself is particularly privileged, figured as a site of both potential victimization and violation (as in the scenario from *Opera* cited above or a mutilation in *Suspiria* that includes the piercing of a woman's eyes with needles) as well as a potential vehicle *for* victimization: the killer operates through information gleaned from extensive surveillance—indicated in lengthy (and often unusual) point-of-view shots—and he or she is often represented solely through close-ups of his or her eyes. Carol Clover's extremely useful discussion of the eye and the look in horror makes a distinction that is pertinent here between two kinds of gazes in the horror film: an "assaultive gaze," linked with a killer and figured as masculine, and a "reactive gaze," linked with a victim and figured as feminine.[13] Clover argues that, common assumptions to the contrary notwithstanding, it is the latter gaze rather than the former that is privileged within the genre, that the assaultive gaze (even when represented through a point-of-view shot) is often a lacking or faulty one, and that "over and over, horror presents us with scenarios in which assaultive gazing is not just thwarted and punished, but actually reversed in such a way that those who thought to penetrate end up themselves penetrated."[14] The reactive gaze, moreover, is strongly associated through various textual metaphors with the film audience—the receiver of the horror—even though this audience has tended to be primarily male; again Clover explicitly suggests that an important masochistic dimension of the male horror-viewing experience has been overlooked, owing to assumptions about the essential sadism of the male gaze.

Images (including point-of-view shots) that suggest an "assaultive gaze" of sorts are certainly prevalent and foregrounded in Argento's films; the sudden appearance of a pair of *disembodied,* glaring eyes at a woman's window before she is brutally murdered in *Suspiria* would seem a particularly apt example. Yet while the possessor of this gaze is usually done in at the film's conclusion, the gaze itself often seems to have omniscience and power—even superhuman power—for the duration of any given Argento film; this is sometimes in part because, as mentioned earlier, the "killer" *is* in fact either several people or a supernatural force. Although the power of this gaze is not qualified the way the assaultive gaze that Clover describes is, the traditional characterization of this gaze is problematized in other ways. As discussed above, the identity of the agency of the assault is kept largely hidden from the viewer. Rather than a clear, sadistic, male threat, we get an identity that is vague and diffuse, equivocal as to gender, sexuality, and motivation. Ironically, the gaze in Argento becomes so ambiguous in part because the eyes that possess it are so heavily emphasized: in most of the films, the bodily representation of the killer is restricted almost solely to close-ups of eyes and gloved hands, along with a few fleeting long shots of cloaked and hatted figures. What we learn about the killer (before his/her/its final unmasking) is often what is offered in a series of vignettes that punctuate a given film, in which the killer (again, in limited close-ups) gazes at photos of past or future victims or both, assorted deadly cutlery, and possibly some souvenirs of a past traumatic event. When we hear the killer's voice, as we do in some instances, it is so masked as to make gender recognition impossible. Within this context, the eye becomes thematically pivotal as an organ which is itself not intrinsically gendered, but which is at the center of sensory and erotic experience nevertheless.

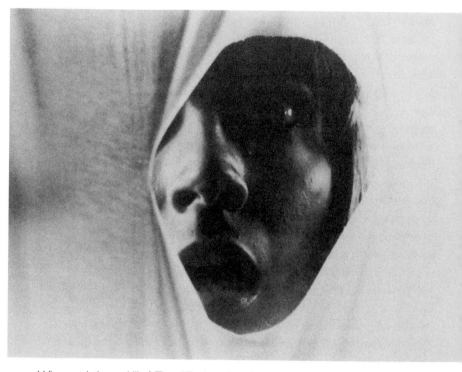

Witness, victim, or killer? The difficulty of reading Argento's images of eyes in *Tenebrae* (1982).

As Argento's images of eyes are difficult to fix or read, especially in gendered terms, so are his point-of-view shots. Hand-held "subjective" camera shots, which appear to be tracking a potential victim, are often revealed after a cut to be from no one's perspective at all. In other instances, such shots are revealed to be from the perspective of a benevolent character. One scene early on in *Tenebrae,* for example, intercuts shaky, hand-held camera shots with more typical stationary shots to show a young woman in a department store, and we briefly hear heavy breathing on the soundtrack. Suddenly, a store detective enters one of the shaky shots and accuses the woman of shoplifting, and it never becomes completely clear whether the subjectively-styled shots have been partially from his vantage point, or from a stalker's perspective, or neither.

In the case of the supernaturally oriented films, it becomes still more difficult to fully understand the perspective offered by presumably "assaultive" point-of-view shots. In one sequence from *Suspiria,* for example, we see a blind man enter an empty plaza with his seeing-eye dog in extreme long shot, as a melody previously associated with a deadly assault plays on the soundtrack. There is a cut to a medium long shot tracking along with the pair as the dog appears to sense a presence, and he and his master stop to listen; the narrative context in conjunction with the moving camera thus vaguely implies the perspective of some presence scrutinizing the pair. Close-ups of the blind man and his dog from an extreme low angle are now intercut with extreme long shots from a number of different perspectives, as well as with shots of the plaza from the dog's and the blind man's "perspective."

The substantial jump in camera distance and angle, in violation of usual continuity editing practices, serves to draw particular attention to the extreme long shots and to suggest again, in conjunction with the general narrative context, that these shots may be from the perspective of one or more predatory figures. One such long shot in particular, a tracking shot taken from behind a row of columns, appears to be from the point of view of a hiding "stalker." Then, two successively closer shots of a gargoyle perched on a building are followed by a previously shown high-angled reverse long shot, and the camera begins to quickly crane forward and down toward and past the man as wings are heard on the soundtrack, strongly implying that the gargoyle has come to life (although pigeons have been visible in the plaza as well). The dog and the man continue to wait and listen, until suddenly the dog jumps up and bites the man's throat, presumably under the influence of some supernatural force.

Gory close-ups of the dog eating his master's flesh are intercut with extreme long shots of the pair, which we again suspect may be from the perspective of some malevolent force—although this hypothesis is complicated when we see two officers noticing the attack and running into the scene from the approximate direction of the camera setup for the preceding long shot. We see the officers enter the scene, however, in a different extreme long shot, this one taken from behind the aforementioned columns and suggesting again, still more strongly, the perspective of a malevolent presence.

While this sequence may not be entirely typical of attack sequences in Argento's films—in that supernatural agents and male victims are both somewhat less common—it is nevertheless highly characteristic in that much of its tension and excitement arise from a confusion over (possible) gazes and perspectives and from a concomitant ambiguity—indeed, a sense of play—in relation to the location and identity of the killer. Which "gazes" here are the "assaultive" ones? From whose perspective(s) are they? This issue is further complicated by the fact that the seeing-eye dog suddenly becomes the attacker and is not here given a clear point-of-view shot himself. The notion of a reactive gaze (a reactive listening?) is itself foregrounded and problematized simply as a consequence of the victim's blindness.

Even in instances where the murder sequence includes the clearer figuration of a generic assaultive gaze, where an attractive young woman is evidently being stalked, such crucial ambiguity in point of view remains intact. In both *The Bird with the Crystal Plumage* and *Tenebrae,* for example, there are instances of stalking sequences where the intended victim is disorientingly framed (with a moving or hand-held camera) from a number of different, evidently "subjective" perspectives, only one of which can be the "real" perspective of the killer. In one astoundingly virtuosic Louma crane shot from *Tenebrae,* a lesbian journalist hears a noise at her window, and the camera then pulls back from outside the window, cranes up outside her house and into her bisexual lover's room, prowls around the room, and then moves back outside and over the roof, subsequently moving down to peer into three more windows on the other side of the house, the last of which is being broken into; editing and slashing then resume, as the two women are dispatched by a razor-wielding unknown party. Clearly, the craning camera's perspective is not simply that of the killer, nor, given its odd and foregrounded specificity, can it be plainly taken as the omniscient gaze of some narrating agency. It serves, rather, as a kind of seductive overture to the paroxysm of violence about to come, a stylistic foreplay to the climactic acts, themselves covered from jarringly unfamiliar perspectives.[15] And the emphasis in this particular instance on both victims' nonheterosexual orientations serves to defamiliarize still further the usual assumptions about the sexuality of stalker attacks in the horror film.[16]

What obtains in all of these sequences is a sense of pleasure and excitement in a pure sensory, perspectival play partially rooted in ambiguity, an emphasis on sensual dynamics that begins to transcend stable gendered generic polarities of active/passive, sadistic/masochistic, stalker/stalked. The cinematic gaze is refigured not specifically because the stalker's vision is somehow qualified, but because the look becomes radically diffused, unmoored from classical subject/object positions. While such ocular ambiguity and instability operate throughout Argento's films, they become particularly important in the stretches of sensory overload within which each murder is embedded. As Shaviro describes it, "Argento's hyperbolic aestheticization of murder and bodily torment exceeds any hope of comprehension or utility, even as it ultimately destabilizes any fixed relations of power."[17] Perhaps nowhere is this aestheticization more evident than in the double-murder sequence that occurs close to the start of *Suspiria,* where the spectator is confronted with an overwhelmingly loud soundtrack of a hybrid electronic/heavy-metal score, women's screams, and blowing wind; an almost surreal, hyperstylized apartment building set, fraught with unexpected angularities and colors; and an astoundingly gory mutilation sequence filmed with unmotivated color lighting on the last IB Technicolor stock available in Italy. At points such as this, Argento's narrative discourse shifts into a register not so much of sadistic spectacle as of sensory overload, of pure sensual immersion.[18]

Indeed, Argento's films are imbued throughout with a sense of visual play and wonder, rich in fascinating images that, as most of those writing on the director have observed, are often allowed to take primacy over their convoluted and improbable narratives. Certainly the subjectively filmed, swooping flight of a raven over the heads of opera spectators in one scene from *Opera* has some narrative importance, but this is subordinated to our engagement with the singularly fascinating variation on the "bird's-eye view" shot presented to us. A very slow tracking shot of an apartment the protagonist has just exited in *Tenebrae,* which continues back from the door until it catches the glint of a metal sculpture, appears still less narratively motivated, yet it too holds strong interest as a visual flourish.

The emphasis on narratives of investigation puts further, often highly reflexive, focus on the image, and, more generally, on processes of perception, of seeing and hearing, and of memory, as well as on the ambiguity and fallibility of all of these. We see (and, sometimes quite significantly, hear) the "point of view" of the protagonist's original experience of an altercation with the stalker, followed by subtly shifted subjective shots of the protagonist's memory of the event as he or she tries to recall a crucial detail. (Argento often uses various optical processes, such as scanning and freeze-frame techniques, to visually suggest these processes of remembering.) In *Deep Red,* we get a clairvoyant's point-of-view image of a murderous scene, while in *Phenomena,* we see the telepathic protagonist's perspective of an insect's point of view, which itself holds clues to a series of murders. The titular image of *Four Flies on Grey Velvet* is a "scientifically" obtained reproduction of the last thing viewed by a murder victim, which ultimately serves as a crucial (if highly enigmatic) clue to the murderer's identity—in a kind of posthumous reversal of the reactive gaze. (That the four flies turn out to have been a single fly, multiply "exposed," suggests again an analogue between human memory and photographic technology.) Investigators scrutinize more traditionally obtained reproductions of past events for clues as well—analyzing taped conversations, for example, in *Bird,* and blowing up a newspaper photograph in *Cat o' Nine Tails.* In the emphasis on such efforts to pin down a highly elusive and mysterious reality through the close examination of various visual and acoustical clues, Antonioni's *Blow-Up* (1966) often becomes as important an intertextual point of reference for Argento as Hitchcock's work is; indeed, as McDonagh points out, the casting of David Hemmings, the star of *Blow-Up,* as the protagonist of *Deep Red* works in tandem with that film's particularly strong emphasis on the perpetual elusiveness of certain kinds of knowledge.[19]

The excitement of Argento's work thus resides in part in ongoing suspense of several kinds, in the interpretive play afforded by various narrative, characterological, and perspectival ambiguities. Where Argento's films crucially differ from the Antonioni film is that their reality does *not* prove forever elusive, only exceptionally strange; generally, an explanation for a given film's mysteries, however fantastic, is ultimately provided. Knowledge is always difficult to achieve here because the supposed norms upon which the investigative assumptions are based prove to have been less than universal; a traditional perspective, a traditional notion of "vision," cannot always be counted upon to yield the truth, to reveal a highly improbable reality. This questioning of any normative perspective is concordant with the literal diffusion of points of view (and point-of-view shots) in Argento's films, the presentation of events from a range of not always clearly defined and often novel vantage points, such as those cited earlier—the sight of killer, victims, and investigator; the hazy memories of the investigator and sometimes of the killer; telepathic visions; animal, insect, and demonic perspectives; vision-impaired human perspectives; oddly angled or oddly placed shots associated with no character whatsoever; and so on.[20]

The norms that repeatedly end up getting thrown into question are those of sanity, of gendered identity, and of sexual desire. Often the truth that has proven so fascinating, yet so difficult to achieve, comes with a dramatic revelation of a sexually traumatic event in the killer's past, or of the killer's present gendered identity, or of his or her previously undetected utter lack of rationality. As visual and auditory perceptions and memories are thrown into doubt, so are assumptions about gender, about sexuality, and about sanity—assumptions about what constitutes a norm, what constitutes the identities of those around us.

Nor do questions of a gendered status quo arise simply in the special cases of the films' killers; variations and fluidity in identity and orientation are not merely written off as the insane aberrations of murderous characters (along the lines of the classical Hollywood paradigm). Rather, with a surprising regularity, Argento constructs a context of sexual ambiguity to function in tandem with his narratives of perceptual uncertainty, to contribute to a broader questioning of traditional notions of center, of norm. Indeed, in historical, cinematic, and generic contexts hardly known for their acceptance of homosexuality and transsexuality, Argento offers us many images of sexual and gender variation which, even when not especially positive, are nevertheless surprisingly neutral; as a result, he establishes a framework within which

The questing David Hemmings in *Deep Red* (1976).

mainstream assumptions may be thrown into doubt. In *Bird,* for example, there is an evidently incidental reference to cross-dressing early on (as the transvestite "Ursula Andress" is accidentally put into an all-male police lineup), and not long afterward there are references to the evident lesbianism of the killer's first victim and the gayness of the man she worked for. *Four Flies on Grey Velvet* features an openly gay private detective who is mockingly portrayed as lisping and effeminate—but who also proves to be a capable (if offbeat) professional and a generally sympathetic secondary protagonist.

In *Deep Red,* Argento makes his questioning of normative assumptions about gender and sexuality far more explicit, as the film's male protagonist (Hemmings) and his female friend are engaged in a debate throughout the film about the veracity of such assumptions—while themselves hardly matching traditional paradigms of "masculine" and "feminine." The female protagonist, played by the somewhat androgynous Daria Nicolodi, repeatedly taunts the male protagonist about his passivity, while often taking aggressive, decisive action herself, in one instance saving Hemmings's life. (Interestingly, Daria, a longtime friend of Dario, appears in quite a number of his films and is sometimes further involved as a writer; she thus serves as a kind of female double for the male director.) Furthermore, the male protagonist's best friend is gay, and it is hinted that the protagonist himself may be gay as well. Argento's films following *Deep Red* continue to be peopled with characters (sometimes, but not always, including the killer) who problematize normative assumptions about gender identity and sexuality: the effeminate male ballet students and "butch" matron of the dance school in *Suspiria; Tenebrae*'s gay male journalist, its lesbian journalist, her bisexual girlfriend, the "pretty," effeminate male assistant of the male protagonist, and the androgynous woman (in fact played by a transsexual) who haunts his memories; the evidently lesbian specialist in electroshock therapy in *Trauma* (1992); and so on.

Thus, as point of view is destabilized and undermined in these films, so are "norms" of gender and sexuality. All traditional positions, former points of identification, are thrown into question, and any strict sense of "otherness," always important to the horror film, thereby becomes diffused as binary distinctions lose their applicability. The pleasure in these texts, it might be argued, resides not so much in a purely sadistic voyeurism (or, for that matter, in a masochistic identification), as in the sense of play, of exploration, such diffusion allows. While it may be problematic to ascribe a progressive function to a series of texts that have so much invested in the detailing of violence toward women, Argento's work nevertheless appears to offer significant alternatives for horror's generic discourse of gender, sexuality, and power.

Indeed, it is in significant measure *by way of* a largely unprecedented violence to bodies female and male that Argento's films articulate their questioning of gendered binarisms: the body in question becomes the body destroyed, markers of difference reduced to meat. The uncut versions of *Deep Red* and *Suspiria,* for example, anticipate the American slasher film in their clinically detailed depictions of various kinds of "body horror"—a man's face smashed into a fireplace mantel, a woman's head slowly severed with her own neckchain, a man eaten by his Doberman, a woman's pulsating heart impaled with a knife in close-up. Many of Argento's subsequent films continue a tendency to jarringly override the sanctity of the body within narrative contexts where, as suggested above, issues of gender and sexuality are already foregrounded; *Tenebrae* and *Opera,* for example, both have various graphic impalings, hatchetings, beheadings, and gougings woven into their textual fabrics.

Judith Halberstam's observations about the way bodily destruction engenders gender deconstruction in Jonathan Demme's *The Silence of the Lambs* (1991) may be instructive here. In describing a graphic autopsy scene in that film, Halberstam notes, "The camera itself has done a kind of violence to whatever humanity remained upon or within the body—this is no longer a body framing an inner life, the body is merely surface, a picture. . . . [T]he corpse is no woman, it has been degendered, it is postgender, skinned and fleshed, it has been reified, turned at last into a fiction of the body."[21] Halberstam notes that the scene anticipates later scenes in which the killer Buffalo Bill, who desires to assume a female identity, is at work on a suit constructed from the skin of his female victims. His grisly activities suggest "the ways in which gender is always posthuman, always a sewing job which stitches identity into a body bag." Thus, while what he does to women is repellant, he nevertheless "challenges the heterosexist and misogynist constructions of humanness, the naturalness, the interiority of gender."[22]

In Argento's work, likewise, uncertainty regarding gender construction is amplified and fortified through the physical destruction of the body. This may be most directly suggested in the director's latest film, which, like *The Silence of the Lambs,* concerns the hunt for a serial killer who retains bodily souvenirs of victims—here, their heads.[23] The detective narrative of *Trauma* turns on the fact that a key witness to a murder misrecognizes a woman's headless body as her mother's body, then proceeds to misidentify what is actually her mother holding her father's severed head as a man masking his face with both of her parents' heads. It is thus that the gender of the killer is initially confused, just as elsewhere in Argento's work; the difference in *Trauma* is the explicitness with which this confusion is linked to a misreading of a number of bodily signifiers (some of them, in this case, literally floating). The film indeed suggests a fluid system of exchange among various heads attached and unattached, initially belonging to men and to women (or can we in fact describe severed heads as being "male" and "female" ?), and among concomitant bodies. The denouement reveals that the killer has herself conceptualized the circulation of severed heads (all of which eventually turn up in a suspect's car trunk) precisely as a system of exchange: the beheadings turn out to be retribution for the accidental decapitation of the killer's baby during its birth, followed by the willful application of shock treatment to make her forget— that is, to destroy part of her history, her identity. The end result of the trauma is that the woman is indeed fully driven out of her head. In the wake of a male doctor's interference with a genuinely female bodily process, heads roll and gendered identities are rendered null, faces in a festering posthuman mass.

What Halberstam identifies as a historical shift in gender representation in the horror film, a "destruction of the boundary between inside and outside,"[24] becomes somewhat translated in the Argento film to a destruction of the boundary between top and bottom, head and body; that which obtains in either event is a pointed questioning of where, precisely, gender resides, a problematizing of the constitution of gender. In its challenging of social norms more generally, Argento's work can at the same time be seen as embodying certain broader, relatively transhistorical cultural tendencies that Marjorie Garber identifies in her recent study of cross-dressing. For Garber, cross-dressing (and our fascination with it) is an index of a fundamental "category crisis"—a failure of boundaries and definitions that is not merely a feature of culture, but rather "the ground of culture itself"; transvestism thus becomes a locus of new cultural possibility.[25] This essay has tried to suggest some of the ways in which such a crisis of category is consistently foregrounded in Argento's films—works immersed in a textual transvestism in the sense that their techniques often express gender indeterminately and blur various fundamental boundaries. In this light, the films' special distinction is perhaps in their ability to render the resultant ambiguity so fascinating, and thus to offer us the possibility for pleasure within the crisis.

Notes

I would like to acknowledge the assistance and advice of two Barrys—Long and Grant—in the writing of this essay.

1. In this essay, I cite the most prevalent English-language titles of Argento's films. I have, wherever possible, attempted to view and discuss (relatively) uncut versions of the films, which in some instances differ significantly from the U.S. releases.

2. Steven Shaviro, *The Cinematic Body* (Minneapolis: University of Minnesota Press, 1993), p. 50.

3. Leon Hunt, "A (Sadistic) Night at the *Opera:* Notes on the Italian Horror Film," *Velvet Light Trap,* no. 30 (1992): 74.

4. Other significant exceptions to this inattention are Maitland McDonagh's in-depth work on the director, "Broken Mirrors/Broken Minds: The Dark Dreams of Dario Argento," *Film Quarterly* 41, no. 2 (Winter 1987–88): 2–13; and *Broken Mirrors/Broken Minds: The Dark Dreams of Dario Argento* (London: Sun Tavern Fields, 1991); and Douglas Winter's interesting overview of his films, "Opera of Violence: The Films of Dario Argento," in *Cut! Horror Writers on Horror Film,* ed. Christopher Golden (New York: Berkley Books, 1992), pp. 268–288.

5. While the generic context of Argento's work is to some extent that of the English-language slasher film—that is to say, while his films have influenced and been influenced by the subgenre and have been a significant part of the subgeneric discourse—their context is also that of the Italian detective thriller known as the *giallo.* For an informative overview of various Italian exploitation genres, see Kim Newman's three-part essay, "Thirty Years in Another Town: The History of Italian Exploitation," *Monthly Film Bulletin* 53, no. 624 (January 1986): 20–24; no. 625 (February 1986): 51–55; and no. 626 (March 1986): 88–91. See also Hunt and McDonagh for discussions of Argento's work in relation to the *giallo.* Hunt describes how Argento's films partake not only of slasher and Italian exploitation conventions, but of "art cinema" conventions as well. Although

it is beyond the specific aims of the present essay, a more complete appreciation of the significance of Argento's work will eventually require that it be viewed in relation to the Italian historical context from which it emerged, as well as in relation to the generic contexts emphasized here. It is immediately suggestive, for example, that a body of works often hinging on themes of violence, social instability, and the powerlessness of agents of government (specifically, police department personnel investigating murders) should have its genesis in an early seventies national context of exceptional social and political turmoil.

6. Barbara Creed, *The Monstrous-Feminine: Film, Feminism, Psychoanalysis* (London: Routledge, 1993), p. 155. Another example of such scholarship is Vera Dika's structurally inflected analysis of the subgenre she terms the stalker film, which takes note of the gendered mix of the form's audiences, its victims, its hero/ines, and its "stalkers." Dika, "The Stalker Film, 1978–81," in *American Horrors: Essays on the Modern American Horror Film,* ed. Gregory A. Waller (Urbana: University of Illinois Press, 1987), pp. 86–101.

7. Carol J. Clover, *Men, Women, and Chain Saws: Gender in the Modern Horror Film* (Princeton, N.J.: Princeton University Press, 1992), p. 217.

8. I allude here to a central debate in feminist film theory, which has engaged the work of, among others, Laura Mulvey, Christian Metz, Kaja Silverman, and Gaylyn Studlar. See Clover, *Men, Women, and Chain Saws,* esp. pp. 205–230, for a discussion of the debate as it pertains to the horror genre.

9 Dika's highly binaristic typology, for example, might well accurately describe the carefully delimited group of films she deals with.

10. Clover, *Men, Women, and Chain Saws,* pp. 21–64.

11. Shaviro, *Cinematic Body,* pp. 49–50.

12. The parallel experiences of the main protagonists of *Bird* and *Opera* can also be viewed in various ways as analogous to the experience of the cinematic spectator. The opera singer's situation in particular appears structured as an allegory for that of the modern horror film spectator, compelled to witness scenes of unspeakable gore, truly pained by the act of looking, horrified yet also complicit. Within such an allegory, the creator of the imagery—the director—becomes as much a criminal aggressor as an artistic entity, and the viewer, at first actively in search of visual pleasure, becomes a largely passive victim. A similar allegory is quite explicitly engaged in *Tenebrae,* which concerns a series of murders closely paralleling those in the work of a mystery novelist (a plot anticipating that of *Basic Instinct* [1992] by a decade). Here the killer even forces pages from a novel down the throat of a victim: the author's work is quite literally implicated in the violence—and, in a surprise twist, the author ultimately carries out some of the violence himself.

13. Clover, *Men, Women, and Chain Saws,* chap. 4.

14. Ibid., p. 192.

15. The sequence involves a level of playful acoustic stylization as well. The crane shot is accompanied throughout by electronic music which, because of its consistent sound quality and loud volume, we interpret as nondiegetic. At the moment the crane shot comes to an end, however, the music is revealed to have been diegetic, as the journalist irritatedly shouts at her lover to lower the volume. Argento thus concludes the crane shot with a number of surprising jolts—at visual and acoustic as well as narrative levels.

16. I by no means intend to suggest here that Argento has managed to obviate the negative implications of this scenario regarding violence toward women; clearly, no matter what the sexual orientation of the female victims and no matter how aestheticized the cinematic form, the attacks can still be read (as film stalker attacks often are) as displaced acts of heterosexual rape—and indeed, in this particular case, as lesbian bashing as well. I do, however, assert, here and throughout this essay, that Argento's work holds a potential for a progressive recasting of the horror genre's gender politics, owing to a distinctive combination of factors, one of these being the nonheterosexual orientations of many characters.

17. Shaviro, *Cinematic Body,* p. 61.

18. The operatic impulses evident in this particular sequence reach their logical culmination in the director's later film *Opera,* set against the literal and figurative backdrop of an opera production.

19. McDonagh, "Broken Mirrors," p. 7. *The Bird with the Crystal Plumage*'s acoustical take on the investigatory themes of *Blow-Up* interestingly anticipates similar conceits in *The Conversation* (1974) and *Blow Out* (1981).

20. One amusing example of this kind of odd, unattributable perspective shot is the view of a recording session from *inside* a guitar being played at the beginning of *Four Flies on Grey Velvet.*

21. Judith Halberstam, "Skinflick: Posthuman Gender in Jonathan Demme's *The Silence of the Lambs,*" *camera obscura,* no. 27 (1991), p. 43.

22. Ibid., p. 51.

23. Like other Argento films, and like other Italian exploitation films generally, *Trauma* is laden with self-conscious references to and borrowings from well-known popular films. While *The Silence of the Lambs* is evidently one influence here, Demme's earlier film *Something Wild* (1986) may be even more heavily referenced.

24. Halberstam, "Skinflick," p. 51.

25. Marjorie Garber, *Vested Interests: Cross-Dressing and Cultural Anxiety* (London: Routledge, 1992), p. 16. See pp. 9–17 for an overview of Garber's premises. Garber also notes that the detective narrative (a central form for Argento) is often constructed around a cross-dressing mystery (see chap. 8).

"Beyond the Veil of the Flesh": Cronenberg and the Disembodiment of Horror

Lianne McLarty

A Plague of Cronenbergs

The critical reactions to the politics of David Cronenberg's horror films have been, to say the least, varied. Robin Wood, for example, has reserved a privileged place for Cronenberg in the "reactionary wing" of the horror genre, particularly because of the pervasive portrayal of the human (sexual/feminine) body as a site of disgust.[1] Similarly, feminist critics have responded with horror at the extent to which these films hinge their monstrous visions on the feminine.[2] Others, however, suggest that Cronenberg's films are adversarial inasmuch as they depict an invasive social order—especially its medical and media technologies—which renders the human body defenseless against its control.[3] In fact, some argue that Cronenberg's horror is directed more at the "patriarchal culprit" and his phallocentric scientific practices than at the monstrous female body.[4]

These contradictory stances on Cronenberg seem to be generated by a similar contradiction at work in his films. While they depict invasive scientific practices that monstrously transform the human body, these films sometimes imagine transformation as a function of the body itself, specifically the sexual/

231

feminine body. A critical Cronenberg appears when the text's focus is on threatening social practices; a very different, indeed a misogynist, Cronenberg appears when the body, particularly the female body, is constructed as the site of the monstrous. Both views of Cronenberg are, to a certain extent, valid, not so much within each film, but at different points in his oeuvre. In short, there is both a reactionary and a progressive Cronenberg.

In the interest of distinguishing between the two, I will begin by establishing the general parameters of contemporary horror, which is said to engage in nightmarish visions of the social world similar to those of the nihilistic strain of postmodern theory.[5] That Cronenberg's films make sense in this context of postmodern horror is said to be a factor in their critique of the social world.[6] What is at issue is whether the postmodernism of these films constitutes an oppositional political stance. I want to argue that Cronenberg's expression of dissatisfaction with the social world is limited to the extent that horror is displaced onto some variant of, in Barbara Creed's words, a "monstrous-feminine." Consequently, the political progressiveness of Cronenberg's films (and postmodern horror in general) hinges on the "figurability" of the feminine.[7]

An apparent shift in Cronenberg's films from a horror located in the (primarily) female body to one located in the male mind—from an embodied to a disembodied horror—seems to carry with it the potential for a critique of social practices inasmuch as the monstrous is disconnected from both the body and the feminine. Cronenberg's more progressive films locate the monstrous in a mind representative of patriarchal social practices rather than in a female body that resists them. It is in this movement from the horrors of the predatory female body (*Shivers* [1975]; *Rabid* [1976]; *The Brood* [1979]) to those of the invaded male mind (*Scanners* [1980]; *Videodrome* [1982]; *The Dead Zone* [1983]) to a depiction of a monstrous, indeed predatory, male mind (*The Fly* [1986]; *Dead Ringers* [1988]) that a critical Cronenberg emerges. The progressive uncoupling of the monstrous and the body dissociates the horror from the feminine and, instead, presents it as a construction of a monstrous patriarchal order.

The Limits of Dissatisfaction: Postmodern Horror and the "Problem" of the Feminine Other

What distinguishes contemporary horror films from a more traditional stage within the genre is that the monstrous threat emerges much closer to home. In post-*Psycho* (1960) / post-*Exorcist* (1973) / postmodern horror the threat is located in the commonplace, and the body is a site/sight of graphic images of invasion and transformation (no doubt generated in part by advances in special effects).[8] Andrew Tudor argues that these "paranoid" visions are symptomatic of a general, post-1960s social uncertainty generated by a rapidly changing world and "escalating disorder"—what he calls "the culmination of the 'age of delegitimization.'"[9] The contemporary horror film is said to articulate postmodern anxieties for "mass audiences, in a manner analogous to the way theoretical postmodernism articulates intimations of instability for intellectuals."[10]

This "delegitimization" of social institutions and the "instability" of subjectivity finds expression in the ways in which these films depict both the monstrous threat and its consequences for protagonists. In contemporary (postmodern) horror, the threat is "not simply among us, but rather part of us, caused by us."[11] Institutions (like the church and the military) that were once successful in containing the monster and restoring order are at best ineffectual (there is often a lack of closure) and at worst responsible for the monstrous. Contemporary horror also tends to collapse the categories of normal bodies and monstrous bodies; it is said to dispense with the binary opposition of us and them, and to resist the portrayal of the monster as a completely alien Other, characteristic of such 1950s films as *The Thing (from Another World)* (1951), *Them!* (1954), and *The Blob* (1958).[12] This tendency to give the monster a familiar face (the monster is not simply *among* us, but possibly *is* us) is tied, in postmodern horror, to the focus on the body as site of the monstrous.

For Noel Carroll, the "person-as-meat" imagery, the "extreme iconography of personal vulnerability," is consistent with postmodernism's declaration of the death of the subject in its "excessive denial of the category of personhood."[13] Pete Boss also accounts for the monstrous consequences experienced by bodies in these films by invoking Jameson's description of a condition "in which the alienation of the subject is displaced by the fragmentation of the subject."[14] Indeed, these images of body invasion and transformation are certainly reminiscent of Baudrillard's "mass," which is both the victim of invasive media images and a monstrous "black hole" that destroys the social.[15]

This description of postmodern horror in which horror happens in the everyday and to our very bodies is certainly applicable to Cronenberg's films. The majority of his films deal with the transformation of the body as a result of scientific or technological experimentation/practices; they exploit a postmodern nihilism that warns of invasive and monstrous technologies. For example, in *Shivers* scientific experimentation produces parasites which, when spread by sexual contact, transform their victims into raw libidinal energy (thus guaranteeing their own propagation); the eponymous "Scanners," a psychic mutation, are produced by medical experimentation (the testing of a drug designed to relieve the negative side effects of pregnancy); and *The Fly* depicts a technology (teleportation) which, in genetically fusing Seth Brundle and a housefly, generates the monstrous postmodern pastiche, Brundlefly.

The fragmentation of Seth's identity is typical of Cronenberg's protagonists; they all suffer an invasion or fragmentation of their subjectivity or both. In *The Brood* Nola seems to fragment into her multitude of monstrous offspring. The minds of the male protagonists in *Scanners, Videodrome, The Dead Zone,* and *Naked Lunch* (1991) are invaded, with the result that they are no longer in control of their own thoughts. Both *The Fly* and *Dead Ringers* throw the subjectivity of their protagonists into question—Seth's humanity literally oozes away, and the Mantle brothers are twins who merge, becoming harder to distinguish psychologically. Cameron Vale's lament in *Scanners,* "I feel so exposed; I can't hear myself," applies to most of Cronenberg's protagonists.

Cronenberg's films, then, exhibit a paranoia toward the social world and profoundly question the stability of human identity within it. They direct dread toward scientific and technological practices and render the Other impossible to disavow by collapsing the boundaries between them and us. Kellner points out that Cronenberg's films, ironically, exhibit features that Wood (perhaps Cronenberg's most vocal detractor) argues are characteristic of progressive horror in that they "do *not* designate the monster as 'simply evil' and 'totally non-human'" but locate its genesis in "existing bourgeois-capitalist society."[16] However, the limits of this postmodern nihilism are indicated by feminist analyses that observe a tendency in contemporary horror to generate paranoia about the social world around constructions of monstrous women. Contemporary horror seems doubly dependent on images of the feminine for its postmodern paranoia: it simultaneously associates the monstrous with the feminine and communicates postmodern victimization through images of feminization. As Barbara Creed observes, the depiction of the male body as womb indicates that the sense of postmodern powerlessness is expressed in "the theme of 'becoming woman.'"[17] This postmodern victimization/feminization is coupled with a tendency to define the monstrous itself as feminine. It is the monstrous births which generate the horror in, for example, Ridley Scott's *Alien* (1979) and *The Brood,* and the female body itself which is site and sight of disgust in *The Exorcist.*[18]

Significantly, this figure of the female victim/monster indicates not that Otherness has disappeared in postmodern horror as "one's own body [is] rendered alien,"[19] but that "traditional concepts of Otherness" have emerged in a "new form."[20] Postmodern horror does not expunge the Other so much as redirect it. And the extent to which its nihilism is dependent on a female victim/monster suggests that the Other of postmodern horror is the feminine itself. When the monster is also the victim, the figurability of the feminine becomes doubly important. It seems that to evoke the feminine is the most economical means of demonstrating postmodern paranoia toward both the social world and its horrific effects on us. It is, however, precisely this feminine Other that dulls postmodern horror's critical edge. Thus, any attempt to sort out the progressive from the reactionary Cronenberg needs to consider not only how he locates the threat in dominant social (scientific and technological) practices, and troubles the traditional tendency to locate the monstrous threat in a clearly demarcated Other, but also how he specifically figures the threat and its monstrous consequences. In short, it needs to consider if the monstrous is coupled with the feminine.

I want to argue that the movement in Cronenberg's films from a horror of the female body to that of the male mind has meant a progressive uncoupling of not only the monstrous and the body, but also the monstrous and the feminine. Films like *Shivers, Rabid, The Brood,* and *Videodrome* depend on a predatory female body in some form—either in the flesh or on video—to give shape to their postmodern horrors. In the latter case, this is coupled with the male mind as a site of invasion. Conversely, *The Fly* and *Dead Ringers* suggest that horror originates in the mind, particularly in its alienation from the body. The monstrous in these films resembles the patriarchal "father" more than the biological "mother," the social world more than the organic body. Read in this way, Cronenberg's films may provide some clue as to what constitutes politically oppositional horror in the age of postmodernism.

"It's the body; the woman's body was all wrong":
The Predatory Female Body

The line quoted above is from *Dead Ringers* (Bev uses it in an attempt to legitimate his threatening medical techniques), but its sentiment is arguably applicable to *Shivers, Rabid,* and *The Brood* as well. Although the original source of the threat in these films is science, it is a science explicitly about reconnecting with, or enhancing, the body. In *Shivers* scientific experimentation is inspired by a desire to get a rational society in touch with the body; in *Rabid* Dr. Keloid's plastic surgery is designed to enhance the body and is also instrumental in saving Rose's life or, at least, in preserving her body; and in *The Brood* Raglan's "psycho-plasmic" therapy encourages patients to express psychic trauma through the body.[21] In these films, science fails when the body is introduced; the science that produces monsters is, in a sense, "embodied," as these films project anxiety about medical technologies onto the body, particularly the feminine body.

In *The Brood* it is specifically the maternal body which produces the horror. Nola's rage (personified by her monstrous children) is the result of her abusive mother and her ineffectual father, who failed to protect her. While Cronenberg's films do not usually concern themselves with "family horror," this film makes the family, and its preservation as patriarchal, a central concern. Interestingly, both mutant families in *The Brood* are constructed as dysfunctional inasmuch as they are female-led: the ineffectual father of Nola's childhood gives way to the totally absent/unnecessary father of the brood. The monstrous children have no father; they do, however, have too much mother. The cycle of abuse is transferred from mothers to daughters: the film concludes with the suggestion that, although the father is successful in rescuing his daughter, he is too late to protect her from the influence of her mother (Candy's arm bears the internal marks of rage as well). The family that produces the horror is one in which the male is, at best, ineffectual and powerless and, at worse, rendered completely irrelevant by a monstrous mother.

Not only is the cause of the horror directed away from the "father" and toward the mothers, but the most monstrous implication of Raglan's therapy is graphically articulated through Nola's aggressive maternal body.[22] Her rage finds outward expression in the brood of mutant children that she produces in a sac on the outside of her body. Each of the brood's murders is directed at a source of Nola's rage: her parents, the schoolteacher she mistakenly suspects is having an affair with her husband, and Raglan himself. Her monstrousness is not only a result of an abusive mother, but is also, as Creed points out, defined precisely in terms specific to her reproductive potential; that is, Nola is a source of disgust because of her ability to give birth parthenogenetically.[23] Nola herself draws attention to this in a scene in which she gives birth to one of the mutant children. Her mouth covered with blood from licking her newborn clean, she articulates her husband's, and presumably the audience's, thoughts: "I disgust you, I sicken you."[24] The mother, then, is doubly horrific: she both causes and is the monster.

In *Rabid* and *Shivers* as well, scientic experiments on women's bodies result in consequences that have much more to do with the female body as a site of disgust than with male science as a source of horror. As in *The Brood,* the horror in *Rabid* is dependent on the monstrous transformation of the female body. Rose develops a vaginalike slit in her armpit, complete with a phallic protrusion, after plastic surgery. She is both a "vampire" (she develops a hunger for human blood) and the original source of a form of rabies that reaches epidemic proportions by the end of the film. That her monstrousness is attached

The Brood (1979): in the birthing scene, horror is directed away from the father (Art Hindle) toward the mother (Samantha Eggar).

to her sexuality is evident in the choice of the actress, Marilyn Chambers, who comes to the film pre-coded as a porn star.[25] It is Rose's aggressive, literally phallic, and ultimately diseased sexuality that defines her as monstrous.

This image of the sexual body as contaminated is also evident in *Shivers:* the parasites are both aphrodisiac and venereal disease; visually, they are both phallic and excremental. Here, again, the sexual body is the ultimate focus of horror. Stripped of inhibition by the parasites and freed from repressive constraints, those infected live out their sexual urges and, by the end of the film, carry their illness to the world beyond the apartment complex. And although the horror here is not specifically a function of the female body, the parasite's original home is *in* a woman, whose sexual promiscuity initially spreads the disease. Again, the threat embodied in science is overshadowed by the body as a site of contamination, transmission, and monstrous transformation.

In short, these films suggest less a horror at social practices that generate monsters than at the potential eruptions of an unpredictable body. It is, more particularly, the projection of evil and revulsion onto the female body that provokes Wood to argue that, along with *Shivers, The Brood* is the "precise

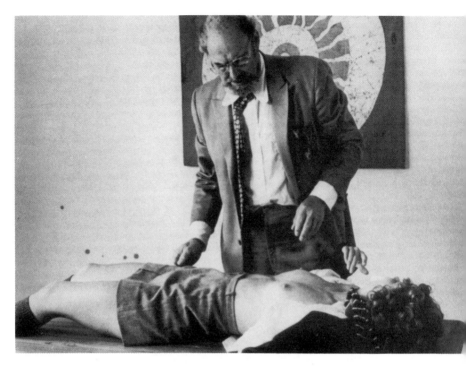

Shivers (1975): the projection of evil and horror onto the female body.

antithesis of the genre's progressive potential" and that the "ultimate dread" in these films is "of women usurping the active, aggressive role that patriarchal ideology assigns to the male."[26] Certainly it is true that while these films do not unquestioningly endorse the patriarchal scientific and technological practices they depict, the very fact that they direct dread toward those practices through some variant of a threatening (feminine) body indicates that horror resides not so much in what is done to the body (by an invasive social world) but in the threat of the body itself. This depiction of a predatory body severs the monstrous from the social.

"The New Flesh": The Invasion of the Male Mind

One of the features distinguishing *Scanners, Videodrome,* and, to a certain extent, *The Dead Zone* from the earlier films is that they move out of the "sphere of sexuality and the family" and "into the corporate world of techno-capitalism."[27] More specifically, these films are about mental horrors. That the practices of this world do pose a persistent threat is central in coding these male protagonists as victims of invasive social forces (rather than unleashed predatory bodies). These films direct dread toward the corporate world and its threat to the mind. It seems that when the focus is on the male mind, the scientific source is a much more pervasive threat and the ultimate subject position is one of victimization.

The source of the threat in *Videodrome* is the multinational corporation Spectacular Optical, which has appropriated the Videodrome technology for its own moralistic ends. Echoing the New Right, one of their followers declares that the world is a cesspool filled with moral degenerates—the implication being that Videodrome will clean it up through mind control. In *Scanners* the corporate threat is represented by Consec, which, under the covert direction of Cameron Vale's evil brother, Daryl Revok, is producing a breed of scanners for the purpose of world domination. Although there is no corporate or technological villain in *The Dead Zone* (Johnny's psychic ability is the result of a car accident), the wider social context of electoral politics is nevertheless alluded to in the figure of Greg Stillson, a presidential hopeful with a right-wing slant and an Everyman appeal.

Unlike the earlier films in which science is simply unlucky and not tied to suspect corporate interests, *Scanners* and *Videodrome* focus on the source of the threat in technology and foreground the corrupt uses to which it can be put. What is of interest here is that *Videodrome,* while it imagines invasive image technology, depends on the feminine tele-body to give shape to the threat. Max is not just invaded by technology; he is specifically invaded by the image of the feminine: Spectacular Optical's plan to use the videodrome signal to penetrate and manipulate human consciousness is executed through the seductive image of Deborah Harry (an apt choice for the female protagonist, Nikky Brand). Indeed, the video signal is associated with female characters from the outset with Max's Girl Friday's video-taped wake-up call. Nikky is also introduced through a video monitor (on the set of "The Rena King Show"), and during the course of the film she becomes increasingly associated with Videodrome itself (when Max plays her a Videodrome tape, she responds, "I was born to be on that show").

The horrific feminine seductiveness of video technology is most poignantly expressed in a scene in which Max's television broadcasts Nikky's lips in extreme close-up and hyperreal, pulsating three-dimensionality. Her erotic enticement to Max—"Come to me, come to Nikky"—results in his being engulfed by the television. Interestingly, it is Max's head, and by implication his mind, which Nikky seems to devour. So linked to video technology is Nikky that her image is as effectively used by Spectacular Optical's adversary, Bianca

Invasive technology is given shape as the feminine tele-body in *Videodrome* (1982).

O'Blivion, to beckon Max toward "the new flesh" by inducing his suicide. Although Bianca's father, Brian O'Blivion, is tied to the image—he exists only in video form—Nikky murders his video image and effectively supplants him as the film's video personality.

Videodrome further depicts the invasion and subsequent transformation of Max's body as a result of this monstrous tele-body. Not only is Max's consciousness invaded by Videodrome-induced hallucinations, but his body is, in effect, transformed into a playback unit for them. Max develops a vaginalike slit in his stomach through which he is programmed by the insertion of a video cassette. Tania Modleski points out that this vision of the victimization of the protagonist by invasive technology is "made to seem loathsome and fearful through the use of feminine imagery."[28] Ironically (perhaps predictably), the victim of seductive (feminine) technology is also the passive, feminized spectactor.[29] *Videodrome*'s self-reflexive concern with the role of media discourse in framing reality and subjectivity is a potentially critical strategy; yet its oppositional potential is diminished to the extent that it figures that monstrous media technology as feminine.

It is important to note that neither *Scanners* nor *The Dead Zone* projects anxieties about the social world onto a "monstrous-feminine" viral- or tele-body, and neither imagines the horrific consequences as a process of feminization (at least overtly). However, like *Videodrome*, they do position their male protagonists as victims of invasive forces. Near the beginning of *Scanners*, Vale is shown tied to a hospital bed, a helpless victim of the voices in his head. The frequent injections that are necessary to keep the voices out serve to foreground his body as the site of invasion. Indeed, Revok went as far as drilling a hole in his forehead to let the voices out. In *The Dead Zone* as well, Johnny's mind has been invaded to the point that he seeks isolation and wears gloves to prevent the visions, which are induced through touch.

This invasion of the male mind and the sense of victimization issuing from it are coupled in these films with the suggestion that when the body does erupt, it is because the mind has been invaded. The bodily effects in *Scanners* are the results of the mental scanning process, which is said to produce nausea, headaches, nosebleeds, and the like. In fact, the special-effects tour de force in *Scanners* is the invasion and subsequent explosion of a male character's head. In *The Dead Zone*, too, the physical degeneration Johnny suffers is brought on by his visions, which are "sucking the life" right out of him. Similarly, in *Videodrome* visions become flesh. Brian O'Blivion explains that the tumor in his head was caused by the hallucinations, just as Max's physical transformations are induced by his mental receptivity to the Videodrome signal. One might say that while Nola's head is in her body, Max's monstrous body is "all in his head."

In these films, then, horror is not a function of the body itself, but rather a result of psychic invasion. In this respect, the horror of the invaded mind indicates a progressive uncoupling of the monstrous and the body. Fear is directed toward what is done to the body via the mind rather than at the body itself. The monstrous is, in this sense, disembodied. What Cronenberg's films up to this point suggest is that the female body is monstrous because it is a female body, while the male body is horrific to the extent that subjectivity is threatened or invaded. This lament for the victimized male—which is, perhaps, merely the regressive flipside of the monstrous-feminine—gives way, however, to an arguably more progressive depiction of a predatory male mind in *The Fly* and *Dead Ringers*.

"Does this look like a sick man to you?": The Monstrous Male Mind

What distinguishes *The Fly* and *Dead Ringers* from other Cronenberg films is that they collapse the distinction between the scientist and the monster. Since the victim/monster is not separated from the scientific cause of the threat, the source of the threat is continually present in the threat itself. These films avoid the tendency to displace anxieties about technology onto the monstrous female body or the victimized male mind. Rather, they hold that mind (in the figure of the scientist/monster) and the social practices it represents up to critical scrutiny. In both films, the horror originates in the minds of male characters whose defining trait is their alienation from the body. The monstrous creations that result express a "will to power" which makes them predatory.[30]

In *The Fly* Seth's scientific practice is dedicated to overcoming the body's restrictions in space. (Significantly, he owes his vision of instantaneous teleportation to the physical response of motion sickness—as a child, he "puked" on his tricycle.) Seth's laboratory apartment, several stories above street level, and his relative isolation there suggests that he exists primarily in his head. Seth is so defined by his mind that in order to avoid thinking about what to wear—about how to clothe his body—he has limited his wardrobe to five sets of the same clothes, an idea he got from Einstein.

It is in Seth's desire to transcend the physical body, and not in the body itself, that the threat originates. While arguably womblike in their shape and function, the telepods are dissociated from the organic.[31] Unlike the organic technology of *Videodrome* (the pulsating, moaning television and the "flesh gun"), this science is associated more with a high-tech world than the human body (Ronnie refers to the pods as "designer phone booths" and "microwave oven[s]"). Brundlefly itself is a product of the computer, the brain behind the tele-pod brawn. Significantly, it is precisely the computer's dissociation from the organic—it cannot tell the difference between Seth's body and the fly's—that creates the monstrous Brundlefly.

The idea that the monster in this film is not of the feminine body born seems to be contradicted by the scene in which Ronnie gives birth to a giant maggot, connecting, as it seems to do, the monstrous with the woman's body.[32] Yet there are ways in which this apparent connection is severed. First, the scene is marked as her dream, a product of her imagination. Further, the phallic look of the maggot associates it more with the father than the mother: its extraction from Ronnie—"There's more, a lot more"—visually resembles Seth's final emergence from his machine when, having fused with one of the pods, his body takes on phallic connotations as he drags more and more of himself out of the tele-pod.

Seth's monstrousness is, if anything, a function of his violent expression of aggression and his will to control; his monstrous transformation is associated with an increase in a traditional masculinity. Significantly, he teleports himself in a jealous rage at Ronnie's absence—she has gone to deal with the "residue

As Seth Brundle (Jeff Goldblum) transforms, his increased sexuality is linked to aggressive masculine behavior in *The Fly* (1986).

of another life" over which Seth has no control. In his descriptions of the effect of the teleportation process, Seth connects it with both power ("surging inside me") and patriarchy ("It makes a man feel like a king"). The hairs that begin to grow on his back are specifically connected to a sense of masculinity underscored by Seth's protests when Ronnie clips them ("Not my hairs!") and by his conviction that they make him more manly.

Seth's increased masculinity is clearly connected to violent, aggressive behavior. The physical prowess Seth displays in his gymnastic routine (he holds his body erect, thus underlining the phallic character of his abilities) is soon replaced by a much more threatening physicality. In a scene of traditional masculine bravado, Seth arm-wrestles in a bar—for the privilege of "taking the lady home"—and subsequently (and graphically) breaks his opponent's arm. Even when Seth's transformation makes him most pathetic, he still poses a threat, particularly to Ronnie. Indeed, his subsequent actions of "kidnapping" her (from the hospital where she has gone for an abortion—an example of his will to control) and attempting to fuse with her to make "the ultimate family" suggest that, in his denial and invasion of her subjectivity, he remains a threat to the end. When Ronnie pleads for him to get help for his condition, he responds by punching the door frame and demanding, "Does this look like a sick man to you?" The implication is yes.

Like Seth, the Mantle twins in *Dead Ringers* are defined by a detachment from the body. The opening scene establishes the twins as mind, unable to accept the body (particularly the feminine body). For them, the body is of interest only as a site for the practice of medical technologies.[33] Their view of sex—"the kind where you wouldn't have to touch each other"—is from the beginning a clinical one: Bev introduces the topic by declaring that he has "made a discovery," and they subsequently propose to have sex with a neighborhood girl as an "experiment." Spurned by the girl ("Fuck off, you freaks"), they retreat to their bedroom/laboratory and conduct "interovular surgery" on an anatomical doll.[34] In other words, they retreat to a body that will not talk back, one contained within medical discourse.

The grotesque gynecological instruments—"evidence," we are told, "of a distorted mind"—which Bev constructs to work on so-called "mutant women" are arguably the central site of the monstrous in *Dead Ringers* and seem the logical extension of the Mantle Retractor (which "may be fine for a cadaver, but it won't work on a living body"). Bev, for example, nearly kills a woman in his attempt to use them. These tools, which are monstrously inappropriate for working on living bodies, represent a physical science that is in fact disembodied. More specifically, this detachment from the body is seen as "deviant" to the extent that it depends on anaesthetized, or preferably dead, women. It is this alienation from the feminine body that constitutes the monstrous threat.

Indeed, Cronenberg connects the practice of this monstrous gynecology with the very issue of representation. The monstrous tools are turned into symbolic gestures: the Mantle Retractor is reproduced as a trophy while Bev's instruments become the basis for an art show.[35] Significantly, there is a framed and prominently displayed drawing of gynecological tools in the twins' university dorm. The medical instruments as well as the "art" inspired by them are coded as representations, and so the film suggests that it is merely a (medical) representation that classifies the feminine as monstrous. Indeed, the very purpose of the monstrous tools specifically, and reproductive technology generally, is to "correct" the female body—that is, to categorize certain female bodies as "deviant" and render them the same as the others.

Thus, despite the compelling assertion that Claire Niveau is "another of Cronenberg's monstrous female freaks" because of her triple cervix,[36] the fact that she is defined as "mutant" by the unbalanced Bev troubles a clearcut classification of her as the monstrous Other. Her body is merely different. It is rather Bev's inability to accept and control her difference that makes him transform her into a monster. Her monstrousness is a product of his mind—as is her "infidelity," the "crisis" that precipitates Bev's decline. His monstrous imagination is perhaps first glimpsed in the scene in which he erroneously thinks Claire is having an affair. In an attempt to offend Claire's supposed lover (in reality, her secretary) and presumably to discredit her, he not only explicitly defines Claire as monstrous, "a mutation," he also contains her within the discourse of his profession. He inquires of the secretary if he has "examined her carefully yet" and clinically instructs him, when doing so, to "lubricate" his finger. In this respect, the monstrous woman is a construct of medical discourse; she is monstrous to the extent that she is *defined* as such. After all, it is an unstable Bev who, in an attempt to defend his life-threatening tools, declares, "It's the body; the woman's body was all wrong." The bondage sex scene is undoubtedly a troubling aspect of this film—yet it also suggests that this image of the bound/controlled woman is a function of their medical practice, as Claire is restrained by surgical tools.

Dead Ringers further suggests that, like gynecological practices, other systems of representation gain their currency out of the image of the abused woman. It is significant that the only time we see Claire at work, she is in makeup preparing to play the role of a victim of violence (her eye has been blackened). Indeed, Claire's opportunity to work comes with humiliation, with her in fact humiliating herself ("I need the humiliation as well as the work"). There is some suggestion that Claire has internalized the patriarchal definition of her. In an attempt to seduce Bev, she suggests that she has been bad and needs to be punished. During the bondage scene she exclaims, "Doctor, I'm cured," and, as if echoing the *Enquirer* headline, moans that without actually reproducing a child of her own, she will never be fully a woman, "just a little girl." The obviousness of the stereotypes (a bad woman needs to be punished, a woman's life is "empty without children"), coupled with Claire's status as actress, seems to suggest that these roles are artificial and cultural rather than natural. It is not insignificant that the Mantles' discourse is undercut at several points when Elly is revealed to be a liar.

These systems of representation (both medical and cultural) not only attempt to speak about the body, but they do so in ways that are suspect. In light of this, it seems that the monstrous threat is not Claire's body in its physical difference but rather the twins' minds in their psychic similarity. As the twins transform from widely respected scientists into drug addicts who can no longer maintain contact with the hospital, they grow more alike. Indeed, what makes them most mentally unbalanced is, finally, what makes them most

The Mantle twins' (Jeremy Irons) monstrous will to sameness is generated by the dread of difference in *Dead Ringers* (1988).

similar: their shared drug addiction. (Elly thinks he can help Bev kick the habit by getting their nervous systems "synchronized.") It is this will to sameness, generated by the twins' "dread of difference," which is monstrous.

The residue of the monstrous-feminine Other seems to be invoked in the choice of names, and particularly in the feminization of Bev. He takes up the traditional female role of remaining home (in his housecoat) while Claire goes off to work. Once his drug addiction takes over, he is isolated in their clinic, "reduced" to watching soap operas. Yet it is arguable that their monstrousness is not tied to their feminine traits but to the Mantles' inability to accept those traits. Significantly, Bev responds defensively when Claire asks why their mother gave them women's names. Thus the film shows that Bev defines as monstrous that which he might recognize but cannot accept in himself.

It is arguable that it is their failure to separate (to accept the difference embodied in Claire), and their increasing isolation in the sameness of one (distorted) mind, that characterizes the monstrous here. The horror of sameness is articulated by the dream Bev has in which he is joined to Elly at the waist by grotesque tissue and then subsequently separated from him by Claire. While Claire's action seems to suggest a horror at separation and difference, the monstrousness of the dream comes more from the union than the separation. It is the bodies of the joined twins that bear the marks of the monstrous. The dream begins with Bev and Claire in bed, and subsequently reveals that Elly is watching. Bev responds by saying "I don't want him to see us," suggesting that it is Elly (in his sameness), not Claire (in her difference), who is responsible for Bev's fear. When he awakes from the nightmare, he jumps out of bed and frantically brushes at his side—the site of sameness in his dream.

It is this horror of sameness that "requires radical surgical measures." Bev's final act can be read as an attempt to carve a separate identity for himself. He eventually tells Claire that the tools are for "separating Siamese twins," and he repeats the line when he begins the procedure. Although he is unable to make verbal contact with Claire, Bev phones her the morning after the murder. This act of "reaching out and touching" Claire in her difference also suggests that his murder of Elly may be read as an attempt (however futile) at separation. In eventually turning the surgical instruments designed for mutant women back onto the twins, *Dead Ringers* suggests that it is monstrous sameness—the inability to accept differences—that is in need of correction.

"Insects don't have politics," or the Question of Opposition

In both *The Fly* and *Dead Ringers,* then, the monstrous is not so much located in the female body as in the male mind, which is alienated from and which attempts to transcend/control that body. This shift in Cronenberg's films from a horror of the (female) body to one of the male mind avoids the tendency of his early work to couple the monstrous and the feminine. While these films succeed in uncoupling the monstrous and the feminine, they are less successful in disrupting the binary thought that characterizes the body as feminine in the first place. Ultimately, *The Fly* and *Dead Ringers,* like all of Cronenberg's films, exhibit a rather traditional opposition between male/mind and female/body. Despite this uncoupling, therefore, the figure of the *feminine as body* persists, even in those films that are primarily about the horrors of the scientific male mind and its attempts to constrain the feminine within its discourses. The centrality of the feminine body (whether predatory or not) in Cronenberg's films indicates that his politics are not adequately accounted for by postmodernism alone.

The adversarial potential of Cronenberg's films in particular, and of contemporary horror in general, is dependent on more than expressions of postmodern paranoia. Cronenberg is important precisely because his films demonstrate that any assessment about the politics of postmodern horror needs to consider the figure of the feminine as crucial. Indeed, Cronenberg's limitations are not so much a function of the narrative conventions of the horror genre, as Kellner suggests, as they are a displacement of paranoia onto the body in general, and the feminine in particular. In progressive horror—for example, *Nightbreed* (1990) and much of the work of George Romero—the horror is not only disconnected from the feminine body specifically, but is located in the practices that construct the body, any body, as monstrous in the first place. Progressive horror need not abandon the body as a site of the horrific. It does, however, need to suggest that the body is monstrous not because of what it is but because of what is done to it.

Cronenberg's films suggest that the oppositional meanings that contemporary horror potentially embodies may not be generated by their postmodernism alone. The postmodern assertion that a breakdown in boundaries has led to an abandonment of "them-and-us" thinking does not make it so in our cultural representations, even within the very texts that ostensibly make such an assertion! Otherness remains a central feature of the horror film, and the embodiment of it in the feminine throws the politics of paranoia into question. Opposition in horror depends on a construction of a monstrous that is not the feminine body but the body politic.

An assessment about the oppositional potential of popular forms has, for some, been rendered irrelevant in a postmodern cultural landscape "far more congested and conflicted than anything envisioned by Bakhtin."[37] The conflict-filled plurality of the contemporary scene indicates that the category of adversarial cultural practice should be rethought since any discussion of opposition necessarily implies a dominant against which such culture reacts. With the disappearance of a dominant in this postmodern heteroglossia, the idea of opposition is said to become outmoded. The popular is a "field of tension which can no longer be grasped in categories such as progress vs. reaction, left vs. right."[38]

From this perspective, postmodern popular forms not only trouble representation, indicating a sensitivity to discourse, but, in recognizing the "conflicted pluralism" that so many discourses constitute, they also struggle to promote themselves over other discourses. Jim Collins identifies this cultural self-promotion as the "discursive ideologies" of popular forms. Postmodern texts, then, are understood as processes of "self-legitimation," not as "vehiculations of a 'dominant ideology.'" In short, they legitimate not a "nonaesthetic, pre-existent" ideology but themselves; they function to "clear a space" for themselves "within a field of competing discourses and fragmented audiences."[39]

The characterization of the popular as such a tension-filled environment constitutes a necessary step for the criticism of a culture that has never been adequately accounted for by paranoid generalizations (such as those of Hork-heimer and Adorno or, more recently, Baudrillard). Yet this kind of post-modernism is restricted by a formalism inasmuch as it tends to privilege the inter-text over the con-text. It fails to see popular representations as media-tions—that is, as representations of something beyond themselves. It fails to situate the popular within a social context and to explore the ways in which culture makes that context meaningful.

What needs to be questioned is not whether the contemporary cultural scene is tension-filled and marked by diversity—it clearly is—but rather the conclusions and consequences for analysis often drawn from this description of the postmodern: that is, that diversity means equivalence, equivalence leads to alternatives, and alternatives render discussions of progressive and reac-tionary representations of the world obsolete. Ultimately, therefore, no one kind of cultural representation is privileged over any other in the postmodern scene. One does not need to resort to cultural pessimism or adopt a conspir-acy theory to recognize that certain representations in contemporary western cultures *are* privileged over others. The simultaneous invisibility and particu-lar kinds of visibility of gays and lesbians, African Americans and women, for example, in mainstream media are cases in point.

The recognition that a notion of a homogeneous (dominant and dominat-ing) mass culture is seriously outmoded does not mean that the categories of progressive and reactionary have become indistinguishable or equally and si-multaneously present. In fact, the existence of contradictory and conflicting discourses within a context that is tension-filled necessitates, rather than oblit-erates, such distinctions. If postmodernism demonstrates a respect for differ-ences, then the difference between a misogynist and a feminist representation is more than a simple matter of alternative discourses. Rather, it is a matter of the difference between how difference is mapped, of how cultural represen-tations respond to and project their images onto the social world.

Popular representations are neither sinister simulacra nor innocent games. They are vehicles through which social reality is figured. Sorting out how cultural products make the social world intelligible is a matter of identifying their role in the hegemonic struggle over meanings, of identifying, in Stuart Hall's words, the "double-stake . . . the double movement of containment and resistance."[40] As Laura Kipnis points out, popular culture is not "an in-strument of domination" but rather an "access to domination, for hege-mony is not given but always in process."[41] The issue, then, is not simply one of a tension among discourses but a struggle over them. Popular representations endorse or challenge more than themselves; they play an increasingly central role in both securing and dislodging oppressive ideologies based on such socially experienced positions as class, gender, race, and sexual orientation. "Insects don't have politics," as Brundlefly claims, but people do.

Notes

I would like to thank Barry Grant for his helpful editorial comments.

1. Robin Wood, "An Introduction to the American Horror Film," in *The American Nightmare,* ed. Robin Wood and Richard Lippe (Toronto: Festival of Festivals, 1979), pp. 7–28; and "Cronenberg: A Dissenting View," in *The Shape of Rage,* ed. Piers Handling (Toronto: General Publishing Co., 1983), pp. 115–135.

2. Barbara Creed, "From Here to Modernity: Feminism and Postmodernism," *Screen* 28, no. 2 (Spring 1987): 47–67; Creed, "Phallic Panic: Male Hysteria and *Dead Ringers,*" *Screen* 31, no. 2 (Summer 1990): 125–146; Marcie Frank, "The Camera and the Speculum: David Cronenberg's *Dead Ringers,*" *PMLA* 106, no. 3 (May 1991): 459–470; and Tania Modleski, "The Terror of Pleasure: The Contemporary Horror Film and Postmodern Theory," in *Studies in Entertainment: Critical Approaches to Mass Culture,* ed. Modleski (Bloomington and Indianapolis: Indiana University Press, 1986), pp. 155–166.

3. Piers Handling, "A Canadian Cronenberg," in *The Shape of Rage,* pp. 98–114; John Harkness, "The Word, the Flesh, and David Cronenberg," in *The Shape of Rage,* pp. 87–97; and Douglas Kellner, "Panic Horror and the Postmodern Body," *Canadian Journal of Social and Political Theory* 13, no. 3 (1989): 89–101.

4. Gaile McGregor, "Grounding the Countertext: David Cronenberg and the Ethnospecificity of Horror," *Canadian Journal of Film Studies* 2, no. 1 (Spring 1992): 43–62; Helen Robbins, "'More Human Than I Am Alone': Womb Envy in David Cronenberg's *The Fly* and *Dead Ringers,*" in *Screening the Male: Exploring Masculinities in Hollywood Cinema,* ed. Steven Cohan and Ina Rae Hark (London and New York: Routledge, 1993), pp. 134–147.

5. See Noel Carroll, *The Philosophy of Horror, or Paradoxes of the Heart* (New York and London: Routledge, 1990); Pete Boss, "Vile Bodies and Bad Medicine," *Screen* 27, no. 1 (January–February 1986): 14–24; and Andrew Tudor, *Monsters and Mad Scientists: A Cultural History of the Horror Movie* (Oxford: Basil Blackwell, 1989).

6. See Scott Bukatman, "Who Programs You? The Science Fiction of the Spectacle," in *Alien Zone: Cultural Theory and Contemporary Science Fiction Cinema,* ed. Annette Kuhn (London and New York: Verso, 1990), pp. 196–213; Julia Emberley, "Metamorphosis," *Impulse* 13, no. 3 (Summer 1987): 18–22; and Kellner, "Panic Horror."

7. Fredric Jameson invokes the concept of "figurability" to access the ways in which opposition can be located, not in formal innovation and self-reflexivity, but at the level of manifest content (representation). The first condition for opposition is to be "visible in the first place, accessible to our imaginations." See "Class and Allegory in Contemporary Mass Culture: *Dog Day Afternoon* as a Political Film," in *Movies and Methods,* ed. Bill Nichols (Berkeley: University of California Press), 2:719.

8. *Psycho* and *The Exorcist* are alternately cited as ushering in contemporary horror by marking a shift in both the narrative concerns and stylistic features of the genre.

9. Tudor, *Monsters and Mad Scientists,* p. 222.

10. Carroll, *Philosophy of Horror,* p. 213.

11. Dana Polan, "Eros and Syphilization: The Contemporary Horror Film," in *Planks of Reason: Essays on the Horror Film,* ed. Barry Keith Grant (Metuchen, N.J.: Scarecrow Press, 1984), p. 202.

12. See ibid. Boss, "Vile Bodies," also argues that traditional categories of Otherness no longer apply and that more recent films blur the traditional distinction between the human and the monstrous.

13. Carroll, *Philosophy of Horror,* pp. 211–213.

14. Boss, "Vile Bodies," p. 23.

15. Jean Baudrillard, *In the Shadow of the Silent Majorities, or The End of the Social and Other Essays* (New York: Semiotext[e], 1983).

16. Kellner, "Panic Horror," p. 101. Cronenberg's films also refuse to affirm the heterosexual couple (and by extension the family) and thereby challenge a persistent tendency of dominant cinema. While this is arguably an oppositional feature of his films, the extent to which this lack of affirmation is generated out of a monstrous overpresence of the female body (as it is in *Rabid, Shivers,* certainly *The Brood* and *Videodrome*) clearly limits the critique.

17. Creed, "From Here to Modernity," p. 60.

18. See Creed, "Horror and the Monstrous-Feminine," *Screen* 27, no. 1 (1986): 44–70 (reprinted in this volume); "From Here to Modernity."

19. Boss, "Vile Bodies," p. 24.

20. Creed, "From Here to Modernity," p. 60.

21. In his discussion of a postmodern Cronenberg, Kellner associates *The Brood* with the "telematic" horrors of *Scanners* and *Videodrome* primarily because of its concern with the mind's effects on the body. Yet *The Brood* is set apart from other telematic horror in its suggestion that, although the mind produces monstrous consequences in the body, the female body produces horrors of its own in the brood of the title. Nola's monstrous body is arguably more predatory than the invaded male minds in *Scanners* and *Videodrome.*

22. See Creed, "From Here to Modernity."

23. Ibid.

24. It is significant that Cronenberg intercuts this scene with Raglan's rescue of Candy; Raglan's self-sacrifice is contrasted with Nola's selfish procreation of the brood and, consequently, herself.

25. This use of a porn star in the lead role has been replayed recently in the made-for-TV movie *The Tommyknockers* (1993) with the casting of Tracy Lords. It also indicates that there are telling connections between some horror films and porn. For a discussion of some of these relations, see Linda Williams, "Film Bodies: Gender, Genre, and Excess," *Film Quarterly* 44, no. 4 (Summer 1991): 2–13; reprinted in *Film Genre Reader II,* ed. Barry Keith Grant (Austin: University of Texas Press, 1995), pp. 140–158.

26. Wood, "Introduction," p. 24.

27. Kellner, "Panic Horror," p. 93.

28. Modleski, "Terror of Pleasure," p. 163. It should also be pointed out that images (literally) of women are also victimized. In one scene Max whips a TV set that alternately projects the images of Nikky and Max's business associate, Masha.

29. Max's emasculated powerlessness is further suggested in the scene in which his gun produces multiple penetrating metal tentacles and fuses with his hand. With his defenses down, he is open to all means of penetration.

30. These monsters are not wholly unsympathetic. They are, however, associated more with control than Cronenberg's other heroes.

31. For conflicting accounts of womb envy in these films see Creed, "Phallic Panic," and Robbins, "More Human."

32. Creed, "From Here to Modernity."

33. This alienation from the body (particularly women's bodies) is also evident in the fact that they not only share women—suggesting a detachment from them—but meet those women in their practice; that is to say, they access the body through intellectual pursuits. Further, they never engage with the more bodily oriented experience of the birth process—as they say, they "don't deliver babies."

34. Like Claire, the little girl sees through the twins, pinpointing their alienation from the body ("I bet you don't even know what fuck is.").

35. Robbins, "More Human," also draws attention to the concern in *Dead Ringers* with discourses. She argues, however, that Cronenberg maintains a separation between Wolleck's art and Bev's surgical instruments. Given the foregrounding of gynecology as representation, however, it seems that art is in fact connected to gynecology through their shared status as representation.

36. See Creed, "Phallic Panic."

37. Jim Collins, *Uncommon Cultures: Popular Culture and Postmodernism* (New York and London: Routledge, 1989), p. 27.

38. Ibid., p. 136.

39. Ibid., pp. 6, 27.

40. Stuart Hall, "Notes on Deconstructing 'The Popular,'" in *People's History and Socialist Theory,* ed. Raphael Samuel (London: Routledge and Kegan Paul, 1981), p. 228.

41. Laura Kipnis, "'Refunctioning' Reconsidered: Towards a Left Popular Culture," in *High Theory/Low Culture: Analyzing Popular Television and Film,* ed. Colin MacCabe (New York: St. Martin's Press, 1986), pp. 31–32.

The Horror Film in Neoconservative Culture

Christopher Sharrett

The relationship of the horror film to issues of social justice and the revolutionary transformation of society was brilliantly described by Robin Wood in a pivotal monograph that argued the essential political progressiveness of the genre for the questions it raises about the social construction of "evil" in western society.[1] Specifically, Wood proposed that the controlling ethic of the horror film makes very problematical the concept of the Other (i.e., that which is deemed by dominant culture antithetical to the Self, which in this civilization embodies the interests of white bourgeois patriarchy and capital). This argument, strongly influential to the critical discourse on the fantastic cinema, valorized the "return of the repressed" element of the horror film that refused the easy dichotomies of normality/abnormality associated with the construction of Self/Other in various popular genres (e.g., cowboys and Indians in the western, cops and gangsters in the crime film, etc.). The very hyperbolic manifestation of the Other in the "monster" of the horror film suggested to Wood an inclination in the genre to undermine assumptions about the Other.

From its inception in the German expressionist cinema and the Universal horror films of the 1930s, the genre seemed to understand the Other as a scapegoat and to refuse to see the monster as aberration to be put down to secure bourgeois normality. The horror films of the 1960s and 1970s became steadily more progressive, constantly challenging the legitimacy of capitalist, patriarchal rule, with the monster no longer metaphysical or the product of a lab experiment gone awry, but instead an emblem of the upheaval in bourgeois civilization itself, a "perfectly ordinary bourgeoise,"[2] thus dissolving further the Self/Other dichotomy. Wood's project is especially useful to current critical studies, since it reminds us of the importance of uniting gender studies to a comprehensive analysis of the social injustice perpetrated by the political economy of late capitalism. Of even greater utility is the sense implicit in Wood that cultural criticism, like all study, must be a preparation for social change rather than a substitute for it. Much of cultural studies within postmodernity insists on a new subjectivism that promotes endless ruminations over spectatorship and the contradictions of the artwork (as if contradiction doesn't inform all experience) apparently as a *political* gesture, losing sight (quite deliberately in many instances) of the limitations of art. Wood is among the radical critics providing a response here, particularly in his sense of the critic's need to apprehend and understand the *essential* ideological nature of the artwork and its status as a cultural product without trying to reinvent it in what often seems a perverse wishdream, and a substitution for implementing a truly radical political program and culture. Nevertheless, Wood's notion of the genre film's political/social context today meets new resistances. Although he is wary of periodization in his analysis (he has never suggested that 1960s Hollywood was a hotbed of radicalism), his general notion that progressive historical moments produce progressive art must be reexamined in light of particular tendencies of the consciousness industry to absorb culture's adversarial impulses. My argument concerning the "neoconservative" aspect of the horror film of the 1980s and 1990s, a tendency seriously challenging the hopes and claims of Wood and like-minded critics, is less about demonstrating culture's reflection of capitalism's various political cycles (that culture always has this function is manifest, and the horror film's relation to Reagan-era sentiments has been touched on in examinations of "slasher" films and similar horror films explicitly about the destruction of women) than it is with a discussion of a cooptation of the horror film's radicalism.[3]

This cooptation is particularly disturbing for its suggestions about the reach of capitalist culture. Inasmuch as the horror film addresses the Other at the primal level of the unconscious,[4] the overturning of the genre's radicalism and the restoration of the Other in fantastic art are evidence of capital's further colonization of consciousness. The sexual politics of postmodern genre cinema can be understood fully only when one focuses on the larger project of the restoration of the Other, itself a component of neoconservative political economy. The relegitimation that this economy undertakes necessarily reinstitutes gender, class, and racial polarization and subjugation while allowing and even advancing discourses that reveal the bankruptcy of such manifestations of capitalist society. More significant, contemporary cultural production demonstrates the importance of reevaluating Gramscian hegemonic conceptions of capital, as sites of resistance are steadily overtaken and placed in the service of capital. In this sense, there is nothing "neo" about the dynamics of capital in the final phase of the twentieth century: capital is merely following a lawful course. The politics of such films as *Near Dark* (1987), *The Silence of the Lambs* (1991), the first three *Hellraiser* films (1985, 1988, 1992), and *Bram Stoker's Dracula* (1992) may be understood in part as emblematic of capital's ongoing attempts at refurbishing its democratic facade by acknowledging the cynicism of the population while simultaneously emphasizing an ersatz liberalism, and by making use of a variety of progressive discourses current in academe that inevitably appear transmutated within the commercial entertainment industry. Understanding this process demands attention to the complexion of neoconservative ideology and its implications for mass culture.

It is apparent that neoconservatism is associated not solely with the terrible reaction of the Reagan-Bush era. The "postliberal" moment that brought Carter and Trilateralism as a response to the legitimation crisis in the wake of Vietnam and Watergate is relevant (as is the continued influence of neoconservatism on the Clinton moment) to understanding finance capital as it dispenses with Keynesian liberalism and the impulse to take the sting out of capitalism by allotting funds to the public sector.[5] The rationales surrounding the neoconservative ethic are too numerous and complex for discussion here; the point is neoconservatism's rather perverse rethinking of capitalist ideology and economic policy in a way that both returns them to laissez-faire formulations while also providing a "postmodern legitimation" of capital.

Such a legitimation has been discovered by Jean-Joseph Goux in his analysis of George Gilder's *Wealth and Poverty,* one of the key tomes of 1980s ideology. Goux discusses Gilder's novel attempt to construct a "theology of capital" that dispenses with the "thrift, sobriety, and asceticism" of Calvinist/Weberian models of capitalism (which emphasize reinvestment) to extol expenditure, excess, and the "prodigality of chance" in a capitalist culture unfettered by Protestant morés or government regulation as it jettisons Keynesian theory.[6] Of course, as bizarre as Gilder and other neoconservative ideologues often sound in relation to "traditional" rationales for capital, Keynesians of the order of John Kenneth Galbraith argued: "Whether we need or even wish the goods produced, their assured production means assured income for those who produce them."[7] It is also worth noting that, according to *Fortune,* many contemporary CEOs take a "progressive" position in the "culture wars," supporting stances anathema to the far right (now deeply entrenched in the Republican Party) such as gay rights and women's rights. Such positions have relatively little consequence to late capital in any event; as capital continues to migrate, decrying "permanent jobs" as it seeks cheaper and cheaper labor, its real enemy is the mass organization. Noam Chomsky notes the parallel between the alliance of German industry with Nazism and that of current corporatism with the American right. While capital often needs scare tactics, ultimately including the battering ram of the state enforcement apparatus against organized resistance, it also depends heavily on a "liberal" patina for its legitimacy. This patina includes not only liberal cultural positions, but even advocacy for limited government monitoring (excessive food and drug "scandals" run the risk of provoking general unrest).[8]

Goux notes the close correlation between Gilder's ideas about prodigality and excess (Gilder actually cites Marcel Mauss and Claude Lévi-Strauss) and notions of sacrifice and expenditure formulated by avant-garde modernists such as Bataille, who proposed wasteful, excessive gestures rather than socialist organizing against the sobriety of capitalist production as an individualist response to capital. There are manifold questions about the political utility of such avant-garde assaults, which have been aimed as often at Marxism as at capital. Gestures of sacrifice and excess, borrowed from romanticizations of primitive economy (potlatch), are challenges to instrumental reason that can be seen as fully absorbed by capital. A number of cultural critics have recently joined Goux in questioning the extent to which the modernist excessive gesture has been transmogrified into an "aesthetic liberation" causing postmodern theory to find easy kinship with dominant culture, as the *jouissance* of excess and "gaming" (i.e., an immersion in the individualism of sign games and textual interpretation divorced from collective political action) indeed become recognizable features of bourgeois life.[9] The neoconservative debunking of traditional readings of capital emphasizing production and reinvestment also debunk, of course, organization and social planning that have also lost favor with sectors of the post-1968 left.

The general dissatisfaction with totalization is one element uniting capital with the bourgeois left, but of consequence for our purposes is the particular contemporary realization of the culture of sacrifice and excess. Missing from Gilder's disingenuous attempt at describing the new playground of capitalist fortuity smiled upon by the gods is the notion of the victim, the scapegoat, a concept better developed by René Girard than Bataille.[10] Girard emphasizes the absolute centrality of the Other to maintain cohesion and a principle of value within the profound contradictions of sacrificial culture, which he suggests encompasses all civilization, irrespective of Bataille's call for sacrifice as adversarial. The climate of "sacrificial excess" saturating the postmodern horror film offers (a) a dominant order that is simultaneously discredited and affirmed,[11] (b) an atmosphere of apparently unfettered sexual expression that offers status to women insofar as they are incorporated into the dominant order, (c) a recognition of a carnivalesque, diverse, chaotic universe that is celebrated at the same time that it is subdued, and (d) a recognition and lionization of the Other only as a preface to its total destruction or incorporation into dominant ideology. A great many works of the past decade partake of the formula; I will suggest the ways by which this mechanism and its ideology are glaring in a few representative horror films.

About halfway through Jonathan Demme's *The Silence of the Lambs,* serial killer Hannibal Lecter, who by this stage has become a mentor to FBI agent Clarice Starling, suggests to her Marcus Aurelius so that she may "see each thing in its nature" and discover that what Buffalo Bill does primarily is "covet." What does he covet? "We covet what we see every day" is Lecter's response, a key admonition to Starling. Indeed, we see less of Marcus Aurelius in this film than Girard's notion that all interchange, all language, all systems of belief spring from the imitative desire to possess what the Other has, to become a double to the Other, to destroy the Other as mimetic desire inevitably degenerates into rivalry and violence.[12] Much has been written about the site of struggle surrounding this film's presentation of gays, but the film's ideology might be more fully illuminated with attention to its logic of scapegoating and mimetic rivalry. The film's attitude toward gay culture and feminism flows axiomatically from its attitude toward *difference,* which must be restored through a sacrificial violence that acknowledges the Other by its obliteration, a strategy that admits both the credulity and the skepticism of the spectator; the "specialness" of the Other and our sympathies with it are acknowledged as its monstrous aspect is confirmed.

While director Jonathan Demme has remarked that he was concerned to depict the origin of serial violence in child abuse and the family structure,[13] the psychopath (both Lecter and his mimetic double, Jamie Gumb) has no real origin in the society that produces him. Although Dr. Chilton's description of Lecter as "monster" is undercut somewhat by Chilton's smarminess and sadism, Lecter is obviously constructed *as* a monster, and an omniscient, all-powerful Ming the Merciless sci-fi character at that, an updating of the impervious invading monsters of 1950s paranoia, whose cages cannot even be approached for fear of contagion (the AIDS climate is manifest here). By the same token, Gumb, or Buffalo Bill, has a pathology described by Lecter as a "thousand times worse than the transsexual." Transgressive sexuality is defined as monstrous, and the definition gains credibility coming from a monster who is also an omniscient father. As the Other is demonized, the authority of patriarchy is bolstered by allowing the daughter the son's position in the Oedipal construct, so as to abolish the female entirely. Perhaps most important, the atmosphere of rivalry saturating the film early on (Clarice and Crawford, Clarice and Lecter, Lecter and Gumb, Clarice and Gumb) is adjacent to the abolition of difference represented by Bill/Gumb, forming a crisis requiring the violent sacrifice of the Other to restore (tentatively) equilibrium. As Girard has argued, there is nothing particularly arcane in this process; while Girard's lack of ideological focus causes him to see this structure as simply endemic to all culture, political analysis shows the utility of sacrificial ideology and its mechanisms to preserving the legitimacy of patriarchy and the class system.

Clarice Starling "covets what [she] see[s] every day"—the badge and pinstripe suit of an FBI agent—as she takes an adversarial position on "the Hoover years" of the bureau, suggesting that the Terrible Father is really out of the picture and the state apparatus healthy and righteous. As much as any popular film of the period, *The Silence of the Lambs* exemplifies bourgeois feminism's refusal of any discussion of class, or of marginalizations that force us to address the necessity of uniting feminism to a critique of political economy. The "therapy" that Clarice undertakes at the feet of Lecter to help her cope with damage caused by the lost father not only ennobles a nostalgia for this lost presence; it restores the father's law within Clarice as she enters the triangle of desire and patriarchal law formed by Lecter, Crawford, and the dead lawman—a construct not unlike that found within the *Star Wars* trilogy. This Girardian triangular desire is located in the male presences of the film. They are Clarice's mediators, who point to the real object of desire, the patriarchal position. The more literal triangle of "three dads" suggests various manifestations of the father: the family, state power, and an elemental patriarchal wisdom and authority embodied in the dead lawman, Crawford, and Lecter.

Clarice's mimetic rival is Buffalo Bill/Jamie Gumb, who in his butchery of women (his nickname recalls the centrality of sacrificial violence in American history and folklore) accedes to the authority of patriarchy, but whose sexual ambiguity forms a challenge to this authority that Clarice must extinguish so that she may enjoy patriarchal embrace. Bill's transvestite dance for the camera, rock music on the soundtrack, constitutes only a fleeting moment of challenge, an instant of postmodern *jouissance* and Bakhtinian carnival that substitutes for resistance. The moment, framed by the rigor and tough-mindedness of Clarice's investigation, necessitates further the destruction of Bill by Clarice.

The particular neoconservatism of the film derives also from a hoary reference: the western. *The Silence of the Lambs* is one of many films of the last decade that reincarnates that genre and its conventions. The older man/young acolyte construct so basic to many westerns is central here (*The Tin Star* [1957] is a point of reference). Not only does Clarice wish the approval of Crawford, she carries with her a powerful mythological legacy in the form of the dead lawman father, a legacy she strives to fulfill as she restores totally the law of the father within herself. "You know the rules" says the Memphis police officer (Charles Napier) as Clarice enters Lecter's quarters. Indeed, Clarice also "covets what [she] see[s] every day": the approbation of phallic power and attendant slice of the pie of patriarchal authority.

To be sure, the postmodern legitimation that the film undertakes allows the burned-out, illegitimate nature of genre art, something that gives the film its progressive moment and credibility. Crawford is manipulative, the medical profession vicious, small-town hicks narrow-minded, family life stifling, the media intrusive and demeaning. That Clarice wends her way through this culture is supposed to suggest an enlightened potentiality. Clarice's lower-class origins make her something like the "man who knows Indians" (much discussed by Richard Slotkin) as she enters Gumb's world; beyond this, her class origins allow no connection at all to her nemesis. The gray, melancholy light of the Middle American landscape, the resonances of tales of the dead gunfighter (the father) and the Plains Indian Wars (Buffalo Bill) reflect the film's sense of the desiccation of popular art and the cultural assumptions supporting it.[14] Such resonances cannot, however, separate the film from the cynical culture that generates it; like that culture, *The Silence of the Lambs* carefully restores the normality of sacrificial violence with its attendant scapegoat mechanism. The film's ending, with its long take of Lecter's disappearance into the Caribbean dusk, is less about the instability of life (cf. the ending to *The Texas Chainsaw Massacre* [1974]) than the inevitability of this violence and the patriarchal law that demands it.

The cooptation of feminism and the restoration of patriarchal normality is manifest in the horror film in ways other than the masculinization of the female hero. Kathryn Bigelow's *Near Dark* turns the mid-1970s convention of the "terrible family" upside down in offering a barbaric vampire clan wholly repugnant and destructive. Unlike the disaffected outlaw clans of *The Texas Chainsaw Massacre* and *The Hills Have Eyes* (1977)—families that embody the "return of the repressed" first in their suggestion of the discarded lower class— this vampire tribe is always separate and distinct from the "normal" family and countryside on which it impinges. When Caleb, the film's farm-boy hero, falls in love with and is temporarily victimized by May (who corresponds to

Near Dark (1987): a postpunk, nihilistic nightworld of vampire hoodlums. (*Left to right,* Lance Henrikson, Joshua Miller, Jenette Goldstein, Bill Paxton)

Ruby of *The Hills Have Eyes*), the film's linchpin is the "rescue" of the idealized, redeemable May from Jesse, Severn, and the rest of her savage family, concurrent with the restoration of Caleb's Norman Rockwell family.[15] The malevolence of clan patriarch Jesse, a figure redolent of any number of Hollywood narratives valorizing the repressive nuclear family, is sufficient to make the image of the clan itself discredit the alternative model of the family caricatured in the clan's rapacious nihilism. The film's particular repressive desublimation is the postpunk, nihilist nightworld of the vampire hoodlums (a kid vampire wears a William Burroughs T-shirt); as in Marcuse's famous formulation, reactionary ideas are framed by apparently adversarial gestures, a safety valve that ultimately gives dominant ideology more legitimacy.[16] The free-form, gratuitous slaughter carried out by the clan partakes of media notions of punk and other youth formations as merely symptomatic of social decay. The punk/redneck aspect of the vampire clan is a reactionary renovation of the Dracula story. The vampire is no longer the parasitical aristocrat but the predatory (because shiftless and anarchical) lower-class element causing trouble for its own.

The operatics of the vampires' demise are unwarranted, since there is virtually nothing in the narrative to motivate sympathy for them, nor is there anything problematic in Caleb's implausible rescue of May. The rescue is, in fact, another reworked "captivity" narrative wherein the white hero rescues the white (in this case also blonde) woman from the savage horde, even as she literally shares their blood and apparently identifies with them, not unlike Debby's situation in *The Searchers* (1956).[17] As in so many westerns, May views her own kind finally as repugnant, preferring the romantic love and normality figured in Caleb. Further, the rescue is by way of clearly demarcating the good sex of the daylight farmland from the bad sex of the turbulent nightworld, where passions are random and tumultuous. May's rescue is yet another assertion of the virgin/whore construction of the female, but particularly instructive here as this image of the female is a rather bald reassertion of a repressive sexual politic while the film's hero dabbles in sexual adventurism. The film further distances the monster from normality by suggesting that although the clan's barbarism represents the deeply entrenched violence of American civilization (vampire patriarch Jesse says he "fought for the South"), their violence is separate and distinct from all other activity of the film. There are no brawls, for example, in the redneck bar they devastate. Despite the Tangerine Dream score, the postpunk/metalhead trappings, and the fleeting rendition of the vampire as "libido unchained," *Near Dark* is a reactionary film allegorizing the threat of lumpenized masses of postindustrial civilization to Middle America. The conventional nighttime setting of the film is less about the domain of the unconscious than it is a pictorial counterpoint to the "morning in America" of rural normality.

The close association of dread and disease with unbridled eros and alternative community is no better evidenced than in the *Hellraiser* films of splatterpunk meister Clive Barker, films also involved with a spectacle of excess simultaneous with a condemnation of transgressive sexuality. At one level the *Hellraiser* films share with the slasher film the simple notion of adolescent sexual curiosity deserving immediate, violent retribution. The *Hellraiser* films are involved, however, in a very tired mythology that places particular emphasis on the sexuality of the female, simultaneously exploiting and condemning it in a construct long implicated in the idealization of the female throughout Western art. The Cenobites, the monsters of these films, are demons representative both of repression (their priestly garb and emphasis on "discipline") and of "desire" (a word used repeatedly by lead Cenobite, Pinhead).

Hellraiser (1988): the myth of Pandora's box in neoconservative culture.

Indeed, the Cenobites, with their tired conflation of sadomasochism (their costumes and accoutrements have a strong S/M motif) with sexuality in general, associate erotic transgression with self-destruction, making these films very central to the AIDS cinema or, rather, that branch of commercial cinema advancing the scapegoating politics of the age of AIDS.[18]

The initial *Hellraiser* is extraordinarily explicit in its agenda. The evil (because sexually aggressive) stepmother has an affair with the randy brother of her unremittingly naive husband. The brother's forays into the nightworld of sexual adventure lead him to an arcane "puzzle box," which, when deciphered and opened, reveals the realm of Leviathan and the demon Cenobites, whose chieftain Pinhead rants on for three films about "the sweet suffering." Eventually Kirsty, the young heroine of the first two films (she is heroic primarily because of her skepticism of sexual profligacy and "knowledge"), learns the secret of the puzzle box and puts a stop to stepmother Julia's appetites, and incidentally closes the door to hell. The puzzle box reworks the Pandora myth (and the Eve narrative) by putting human destiny squarely in the hands of the capricious and too-curious female. Clearly the sexual stepmother Julia fulfills the standard expectations; it is up to Kirsty and the younger generation to convince the world of the Cenobites' power. Sexual curiosity is unequivocally repulsive and destructive, particularly as rendered in the various manifestations of the demon underworld of *Hellraiser*—mutated fetuses and similar genetic monstrosities evoke a horror both of abortion and fecundity. The neoconservative depiction of Pandora/Eve has Kirsty both unleashing the Cenobites and mastering the underworld (she escapes the temptations of "desire").

The degree to which Pinhead has become a superstar icon of this phase of the genre suggests the contradictions of postmodern popular art. Now appearing in a pantheon with Freddy, Jason, and Leatherface (all of whom have largely eclipsed Frankenstein, Dracula, and the Wolfman in the toy and T-shirt market), Pinhead's aristocratic bearing, his ability to rejuvenate himself (the return of the repressed), and his control of the "primal horde" associate him with the Dracula mythology, but his grotesque, sadomasochistic aspect speaks to the media representation of postpunk nihilism that debunks the romance of transgression and resistance. The puzzle box that Pinhead offers us is a key to a zone which, unlike that of Cocteau, offers nothing like inspiration and empowerment for all its dangers. Pinhead's superstar centrality to the apocalyptic *Hellraiser III: Hell on Earth* valorizes rather typically the monster-as-hero, but only by way of further demarcating the Other. While Pinhead finds a new base of operations in a depraved upscale nightspot (the kinkiness of which is again associated with grotesquerie and forebodings of disaster), the sleep of another young ingenue, Joey, is disturbed by images of her dead father, lost in Vietnam. Vietnam is conflated with World War I, as the reclamation of the father is linked to Joey's dream confrontation with Lieutenant Elliot Spencer, a dispirited British infantry officer whose "act of exploration" (the puzzle box) transformed him into Pinhead, the "Black Pope" of Leviathan. The close equation Spencer makes between the wastrel Lost Generation of the post–World War I epoch ("God also fell at Flanders") and the Vietnam aftermath is another attempt, à la *The Exorcist* (1973), to make the devil carry the bag for a variety of political-economic phenomena. For *Hellraiser III,* not keeping the faith brings Armageddon. That the church is also immolated in Pinhead's sardonic passion play pertains as much to the continued fascination with divine retribution in response to the collapse of the covenant as to anarchical sentiment, what Peter Sloterdijk calls "enlightened false consciousness,"[19] the cynicism that replaces class consciousness and critical analysis.

This cynicism proceeds naturally from the particular *frisson* of the horrific landscape the films construct, dependent as it is on elements of Christian mythology. The body is the special locus of horror, always a site of mutilation and the excretory: "Genitalia are disembodied; nude figures take on aspects

Hellraiser: sexual desire and supernatural retribution.

of murder, sacrifice, or voyeurism; humanity is lost in a sea of bodies." [20] The inadequacy of gestures of sacrificial excess proposed by elements of the modernist and postmodernist avant-garde are revealed here, but these gestures are nonetheless central to the films. For example, Pinhead's grisly destruction of J.P.'s nightclub might seem a rebuke of a selfish and indulgent yuppiedom. But Pinhead's first assault is the horrific evisceration of one of J.P.'s groupies, and Pinhead's rebuke is about the hell directly adjacent to sexual gratification. The destruction of the sexually curious reasserts the controlling idea of the entire *Hellraiser* series. While the agenda of the *Hellraiser* films and likeminded elements of the fantastic seems quite explicit in regard to the monstrous repressed serving the role of restoring normality, the larger concern is the extent to which such ostensibly transgressive spectacle, much of which operates outside the bounds of the "good taste" of bourgeois culture, always debunks any politic of resistance.

Another Clive Barker project, *Nightbreed* (1990), suggests the deeply entrenched nature of this ideology. *Nightbreed* shares a good deal in common with George Romero's zombie films and the progressive wing of 1970s horror; the Nightbreed are explicitly linked to the unconscious and are also closely associated with various persecuted minorities (the immediate correlate is the ancient Jews—the Breed even have a "lawgiver"); they face opposition from the state apparatus, local rednecks, and psychiatry (here very much in league with the church, and totally amok in its attempt to stifle the unconscious), yet the rather strict delineation of the Nightbreed along biblical lines (they search for a messiah, fulfilled in the arrival of Boone) and the unremitting tendency to foreground them as comical freaks confounds sympathy for them, precisely because their metaphorical function is undermined. The female Nightbreed are the kind of exotica associated with the nubile court dancers of Bible epics; their sexuality is framed by their grotesquerie, which, although it establishes their "difference" from the straight world and draws our sympathy, nevertheless makes them grotesque (and worse, ludicrous). The women of the normal world are the usual showcased pulchritude, one-dimensional and irrelevant to the narrative. The temporary triumph of Boone and the Nightbreed over the forces of repression recalls the adolescent victors of 1950s science fiction: a fanciful normality is restored that assures the continued battle of good versus evil rather than the impossibility of the dominant order's recuperation.

As self-consciously postmodern in its overbearing allusiveness and montage, Francis Coppola's production *Bram Stoker's Dracula* is a coming-home-to-roost of the horror film's reactionary sentiments developed over the last decade. No single film has incarnated the Other so handily, nor with such unproblematic contempt and revulsion. There is no irony in this being achieved largely through a typical strategy of romanticizing the Other, first by fetishizing and revising the primary source material for the vampire story. In returning to Stoker's novel, the film merely replicates rather than criticizes Victorian morality, but it is an appropriation in service of a contemporary conservatism that pretends a critical distance from ideology. The surfeit of allusions (to *Nosferatu* [1922] and the entire Dracula corpus, to Romanticism, Pre-Raphaelite art, expressionism, Cocteau, to the origins of cinema and "naive" cinematic tricks associated with the earlier fantastique, ad nauseum) is of a piece with postmodern artistic production that affects the notion that self-reflexivity and self-consciousness can still somehow "suspend disbelief," not so much in preventing an apprehension of the work as product of the commercial entertainment industry, but in allowing the most reactionary ideas to pass as if the self-consciousness of the work (with the entire narrative so filled with allusions that its temporality, its historical moment, is meant to appear suspended) provides a disclaimer. The self-reflexivity of *Bram Stoker's Dracula* covers its politics. The spectacularization and visual excessiveness of this product is associated with a particular prodigality—like many contemporary Hollywood films, *Bram Stoker's Dracula* was designed as a "cash machine" whose spin-off market would replicate its ideology in a cascade of junk.

The film opens in 1462, as the cross atop the dome of St. Basil's Cathedral is toppled by Muslim Turks invading Roumania, "threatening all of Christendom." This prelude, particularly noxious given the reemergence of the Muslim world as Other with the "end of communism" (and especially repugnant seen against the backdrop of the current catastrophe in eastern Europe) is Coppola's uniting Stoker's novel to an extraordinarily revisionist account of Vlad the Impaler, the "real" Dracula, who in this narrative is a valiant Prince of the Church, defending "Christendom" from barbaric Islam, his fall occurring only when he tragically renounces God after he returns from impaling Turks to find that his wife Elizabeta is a suicide. In this tawdry *Paradise Lost,* Dracula is angel turned devil; exactly how God transforms Vlad into a vampire is unclear and unimportant, since the film opts for a simplistic equation of Dracula with Satan, with embodied evil. This Dracula is neither debauched roué nor predatory aristocrat.[21] Coppola's version humanizes the vampire solely by making his story a long *Liebestod* of romantic love lost and recovered. Dracula can be humanized only when he is recouped fully into romantic love, monogamy, and Christianity via his pursuit of Mina, seen by Dracula as a reincarnation of his lost wife (an element nowhere in Stoker's novel).[22]

Following the prelude, we are introduced to the vampiric Dracula of nineteenth-century Europe in the standard scene of Harker's visit to Dracula's castle as the Count prepares to buy property in London. This is an aged and very orientalized (the costuming by Eiko Ishoika is heavily featured in the film's publicity material) figure with a Kabuki bouffant, long scarlet gown, and Mandarin fingernails. Coppola was also concerned to emphasize Dracula's repugnant androgyny; he is the "ambiguous host" whose polymorphous nature is intended as destabilizing and unsettling, although solely to underscore the Otherness of the villain. In a single image the Other is constituted as Eastern, effeminate, and aged, eventually a bringer of plagues to the West, a "storm from the East."[23] And we recall that Dracula's burden stems from his renouncing love, the church, the West (his castle, a treasure trove of western culture including Roman statuary and Durer-like self-portraits, is in disrepair, suggesting the debility of the West improperly administered). Always explicit in Dracula's reign of terror in England is the search for romantic love and the desired recuperation of normality. The consistently unnuanced portrayal of Dracula as menace rather than signifier of the essential instability of

The sexual awakening of Lucy (Sadie Frost) necessitates her brutal destruction in *Bram Stoker's Dracula* (1993).

bourgeois life flows out of the jettisoning of psychoanalysis as a framework for characterization. While the Freudian approach to the vampire (that is, the reading that views the Dracula story almost as parody of *Totem and Taboo,* with Dracula the tyrannical father incidentally violating all sexual taboos, including those against homosexuality)[24] seems dated in the wake of much feminist psychoanalytic critical theory, the inattention of Coppola's *Dracula* even to this line of thought is an index of how far the genre has fallen (keep in mind Coppola's film as a prestige project, one of a number that has helped bring the genre into the mainstream).

The association of Dracula with blood diseases—the AIDS allusions could not be more specific—and the lasciviousness of female sexual desire mark the determined conflation of sexuality and apocalypse. Dr. Van Helsing's depiction as eccentric oddball/shaman does nothing to undermine him; on the contrary, this version of the famed vampire killer eschews science for religion as a device for legitimating the character. He tells his medical students that "the name venereal disease—the diseases of Venus—imputes to them divine origin. . . . indeed, they are involved in the sex problem about which the ethics and ideals of Christian civilization have been concerned. In fact, syphilization and civilization have advanced together."[25] Without the intervention of Christianity and romantic love against genital sexuality, humanity is lost. Van Helsing's mobilizing of Holmwood, Morris, Seward, and Harker for "an enormous John Ford shootout"[26] against Dracula is via a destruction of the female, sexualized by Dracula. The "storm from the East" first infects Lucy— the most openly sexual woman of the narrative—through her interest in the graphic illustrations of the *Arabian Nights*. The poisonous influence of the East, evidenced not only in Lucy's erotica but the decor of the early Lucy/Mina scenes, is adjacent to the sexual awakening of the principal female characters. The Pandora's box thematic is visible before the arrival of Dracula; Coppola uses the image of Dracula merely as a device to suggest the wrong turns that sexual curiosity may take, as a montage of Dracula's visage and the storm-tossed Demeter are almost concurrent with Lucy's masturbatory writhings in anticipation of a lover. Coppola's rendering of Fuseli's *The Nightmare* (the wolf-monster Dracula perching on a supine Lucy) is a literalized, uninflected incubus image suggesting a potentiality threatening to the patriarchal order. Dracula's sex with Lucy is preceded by Lucy and Mina's lovemaking during their playful romp in a rain-drenched maze. Lucy's "disease" necessitates her brutal destruction by Van Helsing and company, an evisceration and decapitation played for laughs—a shot of Lucy's bloodied head is followed immediately by Van Helsing slicing a roast beef.

Female sexuality from the film's outset is unequivocally evil, subordinated in the hierarchy of evil only to the incarnated Satan who turned his back on the duties of patriarchal law. From the Brides of Dracula (their hypersexualized characterization is of course by way of *Penthouse,* and the film repudiates this Catholic wish-fantasy by making the Brides insectoid) to Mina's concupiscence with her long-lost prince, horror is rooted in that which transgresses sexuality under patriarchy. Dracula's own "redemption" is a full-blown Passion, with great heaps of Wagner and run-on allusions to fin-de-siècle art, as the Count recites Christ's words on the cross while Mina drives a blade through his heart. A huge church icon of Vlad Dracula floating in heavenly union with Elizabeta/Mina affirms God's victory in reining in his own. There is little in the work of Murnau, of Tod Browning or James Whale, of Val Lewton or Terence Fisher, of any contract director working under the demands of the U.S. or British production codes of the last century, as hackneyed or reactionary as this film. And yet the hypermarketing of the movie, with the rather extravagant discourse about sexuality in its various souvenir books, magazines, and novelizations, affords it, like much neoconservative product, a patina of open, spontaneous, progressive sexual politics. The discourse within these products (about romantic love as enduring, about the thrills and dangers of this same love) merely extends the film's project of replicating rather than deconstructing the sexual politics of Stoker's novel.

I will not attempt here to adumbrate the new conservativism of other elements of the fantastique, but a few observations seem required since critical practice and the cinema itself have long since melded horror and science fiction. Various critics have already noted the apocalyptic dimension to the *Alien, Robocop, Terminator,* and *Predator* cycles, a dimension endemically ahistorical and reactionary that has been part and parcel of American cultural expression since the Puritans, an ideology preferring total annihilation (including self-annihilation) over radical change or even reform.[27] Suffice it to say that these films, like the representative "nontechno" horror I have just noted, are filled with conventions that throw the genres ideologically in reverse while keeping up the postmodern montage and allusionism that seem to make them hip, self-aware, self-reflexive. The new science fiction/horror cycles are deeply implicated in issues of the hegemony of the corporate state as it perfects and consolidates control over technology and modes of production, and of course manipulates gender relations. These films are extremely conscious of various movements (especially feminism) offering resistance to the corporate state and the forms of oppression and repression it imposes (the *Alien* films are notable here and have been analyzed from political and psychoanalytic stances in various locations).[28] The resistance these films propose is atomized and individualistic, usually in the form of the fully masculinized female who internalizes the perspective and means of the oppressor, while female sexuality itself is represented as grotesque and malevolent (again, the *Alien* films are relevant here, including *Alien³* [1992], whose salvific female hero is constructed and circumscribed by an array of Christian apocalyptic ideas not so ambivalently held by hero and enemy alike—annihilation over revolt—but the *Terminator* films also have relevance).

Most disturbing about the depiction of the cityscape in postmodern science fiction/horror is less its use of cyberpunk and *noir* to fetishize the urban crisis than the incorporation of this depiction into the work of contemporary urban analysts, as if these films have anything to offer about the actual vagaries of capital in its abandonment of cities.[29] The *Robocop* and *Terminator* films are not quite as germane to an understanding of the concelebration of the urban apocalypse as *Predator 2* (1990), which shows the true conscience of the commercial industry in conflating the bloodthirsty, unstoppable alien invader (whose head armor resembles dreadlocks) with Jamaican, Colombian, and other Third World "drug posses" whose chaotic gun battle with police opens the film and sets its tone. The Predator is an Other as comprehensive as Coppola's Dracula, if with a different focus. Los Angeles, the postmodern hellscape besieged by crime (not grounded in the social), the Babel whose conscientious and multiethnic enforcement apparatus must do battle with bureaucracy and entertainment media, incarnates a scapegoat in the Predator, who not incidentally is viewed by the bemused Third Worlders as a deity and whose predatory tactics mimic their own. Still more disturbing, the elements mentioned here have at the center of their reaction a profound, rather archetypal hatred of the female.

The hellscape of postmodern science fiction is predicated on the assumption that the family has gone awry (most visible in *Terminator 2: Judgment Day* [1991]), and the female is free in a society not easily determined by male prerogatives. The female must therefore somehow be recuperated into the new, technologically driven order, fortunately still owned largely by men. The *Terminator* films revolve largely around this idea. In the first *Terminator*, Sarah Connor undergoes an Annunciation whereby she learns of her centrality (she bears the messiah) to the cybernetic future and eventually prepares for it by accepting militarization. In *Terminator 2,* the Madonna construct undergoes the schizoid transformation of postmodern narrative. While Sarah is not particularly idealized, she nonetheless has all the trappings of sainthood associated with Christian mythology—her insight is so bizarre she is regarded as crazy and incarcerated, an idea that seems a standard critique of power, but fits handily with postmodernist contempt for psychoanalysis. Yet Sarah's hypermasculinized body (another neoconservative body beautiful that substitutes a narcissistic culture of inversion for political culture), her protection of John, and her battle with the T-1000 finally prepare her for little more than Jean Arthur's position in *Shane* (1953), as Schwarzenegger's cyborg (created and called forth by John Connor) saves the day and bids a self-sacrificial farewell. The female role in cybernetic civilization is necessarily greater than in the previous, industrial epoch; it remains, however, that of facilitator. The disordered family life of the young John Connor might be addressed as the adult John makes society whole again, thanks to his mother's determination to clear the path for the messiah.

If the *Alien* and *Terminator* films show society in distress while the female is recreated as masculinized rejuvenator of the patriarchal order, *Predator 2* goes a more traditional route in associating the female with chaos and decay, while still making use of some of the postmodern science fiction conventions already addressed. The film opens with the Predator's-eye view, as it moves from the overheated jungles of Latin America (the heart-of-darkness site of the first *Predator* [1987]) to the urban apocalypse of L.A. That the jungle directly abuts L.A. is not only about fear of the Hispanic world spilling into Anglo society,

"Pussyface" in *Predator 2* (1990): sex, nature, and the Third World amalgamated as Other. (Production still)

but is another confrontation of Nature against Culture, with Nature here being particularly invasive, corrosive, and uncontrollable. Nature is associated not just with the crazed Latin and Jamaican drug posses, but very directly with the female: Leona, the Hispanic female cop (another masculinized sidekick), is inexplicably spared by the Predator as it discovers her pregnancy. Nothing else is mentioned of Leona's sexuality, and there is nothing else to suggest that the Predator is sympathetic; the moment is merely one more association of the Predator with the female (in fact, with the female sex organs, as they are x-rayed by the Predator). The Predator's body armor is a reification of the armored body omnipresent in postmodern science fiction. Body armor, a key signifier of the fascist state, a guard against "processes of explosion, eruption, implosion," is a barrier to the fluid, chaotic female principle that has upset the patriarchal equilibrium of the postmodern city.[30] Although the Predator has a hypermasculine armored body (women cops also wear armor, or have "armored," muscled bodies), its face grotesquely caricatures female genitalia (at one point policeman Danny Glover calls it "pussy face"). Like the emaciated biomechanical body of the Alien, with its enormous phallic head, the Predator is an apocalyptic, monstrous incarnation of sexuality itself. Genital sexuality embodied in these monsters is, however, essentially female; it is subdued and destroyed by phallic authority whose ambition is to reinstitute repression and "order out of chaos."

At the end of his life Pasolini mourned the fact that "the progressive struggle for democratization of expression and for sexual liberation has been brutally superseded and canceled out by the decision of consumerist power to grant a tolerance as vast as it is false."[31] In his observation of the postmodern scene Pasolini's comment recalls Marcuse and the early admonition of *Dialectic of Enlightenment* that "the triumph of advertising in the culture industry is that consumers feel compelled to buy and use its products even though they see through them."[32] Indeed, the scapegoating of the Other and the attendant false consciousness leaning finally toward despair, abrogation of the political, and self-annihilation occurs with the "inoculation" by dominant culture through capital admitting the critical faculties of the current audience, by revealing the worthlessness of its artifacts, by admitting numerous small acts of evil that the larger evil may remain unexamined.[33] The 1993 Arnold Schwarzenegger vehicle *The Last Action Hero* is instructive, a (failed) "self-reflexive" summer cash machine (termed *Terminator 3: Deconstruction Day* by one critic)[34] that admits to the bankruptcy of commercial narrative, and therefore can ask us to buy it anyway. Jack Slater/Arnold Schwarzenegger can tell his fanboy sidekick, "I need you out there to believe in me." That this bankruptcy is now at such a palpable, material level (and certainly not merely within the fantastic) is instructive for us only as we understand it as another stage in preserving our credulity and acquiescence.

Notes

1. Robin Wood, "An Introduction to the American Horror Film," in *The American Nightmare,* ed. Robin Wood and Richard Lippe (Toronto: Festival of Festivals, 1979), pp. 7–28.

2. Quoted in François Truffaut, *Hitchcock* (New York: Touchstone, 1967), p. 211. While Hitchcock refers here to his conception of Marion Crane, much analysis of *Psycho* (1960) has drawn attention to the parallels between the "Marion story," with its attempts to escape repression and oppression, and Norman Bates. In numerous respects both Marion and Norman are constructed as Other; Marion's transgression of boundaries, her guilt feelings, and the attempted flight from oppression clearly link her story to Norman's.

3. Robin Wood, *Hollywood from Vietnam to Reagan* (New York: Columbia University Press, 1986), chap. 9.

4. Ernest Jones's *On the Nightmare* (New York: Liveright Books, 1971) was for years a springboard text for the psychoanalytic interpretation of the horror film, since reevaluated in the wake of feminist and other more politically informed approaches to psychoanalytic criticism. An important recent example of feminist psychoanalytic criticism challenging aspects of Freud as it approaches the genre is Carol Clover's *Men, Women, and Chain Saws: Gender in the Modern Horror Film* (Princeton: Princeton University Press, 1992). Against Clover's idea that a rethinking of masochism allows the female a site of resistance in the horror film, I would insist that films such as *The Silence of the Lambs* have as their chief agenda the bolstering of a bourgeois feminism that in turn reinforces patriarchy, spectator positioning notwithstanding.

5. A representative example of the introduction of the postliberal moment is Michel Crozier and Samuel Huntington et al., eds., *The Crisis of Democracy: Report on the Governability of Democracies to the Trilateral Commission* (New York: New York University Press, 1974). Conspiratorial approaches to such documents and the organizations that produce them sometimes deflect attention from capital's basic tendency to relegitimate itself. It is also important to note the essential continuity among the "postliberal," "neoconservative," and "neoliberal" (the term commonly attached to the Clinton era) moments: all are attempts at relegitimating bourgeois democracy after episodes of profound crisis while simultaneously deriding and undermining bourgeois democratic institutions and many of the Keynesian economic policies that previously supported them. This is driven chiefly by the lawful supranational reach of late capital and its need to decrease interimperial rivalry over territory and markets by circumventing democratic institutions associated with the nation-state. Trilateralism responded first to the "Nixon shocks" that both undermined the dollar and imposed protectionism over free trade. The "crisis" that most concerned the Trilateralites was an "excess of democracy" born out of various contradictions

of the superstructure (the media's attention to "scandal"). Many of the early documents of the postliberal era were focused on new strategies of cooptation (over coercion).

6. Jean-Joseph Goux, "General Economics and Postmodern Capitalism," *Yale French Studies* 78 (1990): 216. Gilder's book seems compatible in its "prodigality of chance" ethic both with the bourgeois academic fetishization of free play of the signifier and the not-irrelevant prominence of more material "gaming" (lotteries, casinos) as capital's demand for deepened ratios of profit cause it to abandon and pauperize heavily industrialized sectors of the United States.

7. John Kenneth Galbraith, *The Affluent Society* (Boston: Houghton-Mifflin, 1958), p. 119.

8. Noam Chomsky, "Rollback IV: Toward a Utopia of the Masses," *Z Magazine,* May 1995, p. 23.

9. This turn has occurred as radical scholars observe the reactionary, subjectivist slant of some postmodern critical theory and its increased distance from social and political commitments. See, for example, Christopher Norris, *Uncritical Theory: Postmodernism, Intellectuals, and the Gulf War* (Amherst: University of Massachussetts Press, 1992); and Alex Callinicos, *Against Postmodernism: A Marxist Critique* (Cambridge: Polity Press, 1989).

10. See René Girard, *Violence and the Sacred,* trans. Patrick Gregory (Baltimore: Johns Hopkins University Press, 1977). A fuller development of Girard's thesis of the centrality of scapegoating to civilization is *Things Hidden since the Foundation of the World,* trans. Stephen Bann and Michael Meteer (Stanford: Stanford University Press, 1978). To be sure, Georges Bataille understood the contradictions of sacrificial culture. See his "The Psychological Structure of Fascism," in *Visions of Excess: Selected Writings, 1927–1939,* ed. Allan Stoekl (Minneapolis: University of Minnesota Press, 1977).

11. In this thought I am paraphrasing Robin Wood, who suggests that the new conservatism of the contemporary cinema manifests a particular cynicism in many rather disparate films (he cites *Blue Velvet* [1986] and *E. T.* [1975] specifically). Wood remarks: "The explicit or implicit admission (respectively, in the two films cited) is that it is impossible to believe in what is nevertheless being affirmed." Wood, *"Rally 'round the Flag, Boys,* or Give It Back to the Indians," *CineAction* 9 (1987): 8.

12. Girard, *Violence and the Sacred,* pp. 39–67.

13. Amy Taubin, "Demme's Monde," *Village Voice,* February 19, 1991, p. 64.

14. The rebirth and reworking of the western within various genres (against the backdrop of a profound legitimation crisis of Reagan-era America) is developed in Richard Slotkin's *Gunfighter Nation: The Myth of the Frontier in Twentieth-Century America* (New York: Atheneum, 1992).

15. Slotkin argues the importance of the "rescue" motif to American mythology and popular art in *Regeneration through Violence: The Mythology of the American Frontier, 1600–1860* (Middletown, Conn.: Wesleyan University Press, 1972), pp. 123, 134–136. The development of the image of the family in the contemporary horror film is discussed by Tony Williams in his essay in this volume.

16. It seems important today to apply Marcuse's thinking in *One Dimensional Man: Studies in the Ideology of Advanced Industrial Society* (Boston: Beacon Press, 1974) not only to the interrogation of the cooptation of adversarial sexual politics by the culture and

consciousness industries (for example, Madonna, certain advertising art), but also to a wide range of political cooptation within mass culture, whose "leniency" suggests only its hegemony.

17. The "captivity" story is the flip side of the "rescue" narrative discussed by Slotkin in *Regeneration through Violence*, pp. 20–21.

18. AIDS as depicted in cinema and mass culture in general has been discussed by numerous commentators. See, for example, Edward Guerrero's "AIDS as Monster in Science Fiction and Horror Cinema," *Journal of Popular Film and Television* 18, no. 3 (Fall 1990): 86–93. The short-lived journal *Crow* published a fine compendium of films with AIDS-related themes in issue 25 (July 1988). Stuart Gordon's *From Beyond* (1987) is also worth mentioning in this regard, with its clear abhorrence of sexuality and its apocalypticism associated with sexual adventurism.

19. Peter Sloterdijk, *Critique of Cynical Reason,* trans. Michael Eldred (Minneapolis: University of Minnesota Press, 1987), p. 6.

20. Fred Burke's remarks about Barker's illustrative art can be applied to the design of any of the *Hellraiser* films. See Steve Niles and Fred Burke, *Clive Barker: Illustrator* (Forestville, Calif.: Arcane/Eclipse Books, 1990), p. 27.

21. An important ideological reading of Dracula is Franco Moretti, *Signs Taken for Wonder: Essays in the Sociology of Literary Forms* (London: Verso, 1983), pp. 91–94.

22. It might be noted that the film's screenwriter, James V. Hart, authored the screenplay for the Spielberg debacle, *Hook* (1992), a reworking of *Peter Pan* that overturns the rebellion of the "lost boys" against the father in favor of representing Captain Hook as "failed daddy" in the full restoration of patriarchy (in the form of Pan himself). While Spielberg certainly stands out as representative of the extreme reaction of the new Hollywood, his product is, in fact, representative and obviously not aberrant.

23. Francis Ford Coppola and James V. Hart, *Bram Stoker's Dracula: The Film and the Legend* (New York: Newmarket Press, 1992), pp. 38, 23.

24. Gregory A. Waller, *The Living and the Undead: From Stoker's Dracula to Romero's Night of the Living Dead* (Urbana and Chicago: University of Illinois Press, 1986), contains a good critical mapping of the vampire narrative's sexual politics.

25. Coppola and Hart, *Bram Stoker's Dracula*, p. 88. I wonder if this pun is by way of rebuking Dana Polan's "Eros and Syphilization: The Contemporary Horror Film," in *Planks of Reason: Essays on the Horror Film,* ed. Barry Keith Grant (Metuchen, N.J.: Scarecrow Press, 1984), pp. 201–211.

26. Coppola and Hart, *Bram Stoker's Dracula,* p. 3.

27. Scott Bukatman, *Terminal Identity: The Virtual Subject in Postmodern Science Fiction* (Durham, N.C.: Duke University Press, 1993), provides a good overview of most of these cycles and their relevance to the image of the subject within the corporate/technological landscape. The nihilistic reaction of these films, their often "classical" fascism (particularly in regard to the *Terminator* films and similar science fiction about the "armored body") is representative. An overview of the apocalypticism of the postmodern cinema is available in a critical anthology I have edited entitled *Crisis Cinema: The Apocalyptic Idea in Postmodern Narrative Film* (Washington, D.C.: Maisonneuve Press, 1993).

28. There are numerous articles on these films, although *Alien* has received more atten-

tion thus far than the two sequels. Vivian Sobchack, James Cavanaugh, and Judith Newton have made important comments in essays published in *Alien Zone: Cultural Theory and Contemporary Science Fiction,* ed. Annette Kuhn (London: Verso, 1990).

29. Fortunately, Mike Davis's discussion of this issue in his *City of Quartz: Excavating the Future in Los Angeles* (London: Verso, 1990) does not divert him from considering the material conditions of Los Angeles.

30. Klaus Theweleit, *Male Fantasies,* vol. 1, trans. Stephen Conway (Minneapolis: University of Minnesota Press, 1987).

31. Maurizio Viano, *A Certain Realism: Making Use of Pasolini's Film Theory and Practice* (Berkeley: University of California Press, 1993), p. 296.

32. Theodor Adorno and Max Horkheimer, *Dialectic of Enlightenment* (New York: Continuum, 1967), p. 167.

33. Roland Barthes's idea of *inoculation* in his famous "Operation Margarine" essay has continued relevance both to cultural analysis and the "discourse" of state power. See *Mythologies,* trans. Annette Lavers (New York: Hill and Wang, 1972), pp. 41–42.

34. Anthony Lane, "Reality Check," *New Yorker,* July 15, 1993, p. 97.

Part Three

Horror, Femininity, and Carrie's Monstrous Puberty

Shelley Stamp Lindsey

Who, surprised and horrified by the fantastic tumult of her
drives . . . hasn't accused herself of being a monster?

Hélène Cixous, "The Laugh of the Medusa"[1]

What was conventionally the terrain of domestic melodrama—
familial relations and the home—has been adopted by contemporary horror and fantasy films, which engage the terms of domestic drama in order to depict horrors associated with what
Vivian Sobchack calls the "familiar and familial."[2] With their
congruent appeal to melodramatic family structures, the supernatural, and the rhetoric of horror, such films figure the eruption of violence and sexuality into the domestic sphere through
supernatural forces that invade the family home or render its inhabitants monstrous. Domestic space is terrorized in films like
Night of the Living Dead (1968), *The Amityville Horror* (1979), and
Poltergeist (1982), which bring home horrors conventionally re-
hearsed in Transylvania or outer space. Alternately, the nuclear
family itself breeds monstrosity in *Rosemary's Baby* (1968), *It's
Alive* (1974), and *The Omen* (1976), or yields a teen monster
in the midst of a tortured adolescent trajectory in *The Exorcist*
(1973), *Martin* (1978), and *Amityville II: The Possession* (1982).[3]

The family finally *is* monster in *The Hills Have Eyes* (1977) and *Near Dark* (1987). What is striking about these films is not just the familial *context* in which the horror takes place, but the familial *nature* of the horror depicted: perverse social relations breed monstrosity. No longer a place of respite that offers solace from otherworldly terrors, the family is itself the very source of horror.

In first identifying the central role played by the family in contemporary horror, Robin Wood and Tony Williams celebrated the estrangement of familiar social structures possible in the hyperbolized language of horror.[4] Wood's "Introduction to the American Horror Film" provides the critical framework through which most of these horrific domestic narratives have been read, proposing that such films open up an alternative space in which social criticism becomes possible. Wood contends that the sexual repression demanded by patriarchal culture in order to generate neutered, nuclear families returns in horror films "as in our nightmares, as an object of horror, a matter for terror"—the repressed familiar returns as unfamiliar and monstrous.[5]

Usually situated among this body of contemporary films depicting the familiar and familial as horrific, *Carrie* (1976) engages the language of fantasy to represent the terrain of female adolescence. Beginning with Carrie's first menstrual period, her initiation into mature female sexuality, the film traces the development of femininity to its (nearly) successful conclusion. The film is in essence a melodramatic rendering of female puberty where the mousy outcast triumphs (if only temporarily) over popular, better-looking girls by beating them at their own game and winning the Prom Queen's crown. Yet the film surrounds such "familiar" issues with an aura of terror, grafting onto this plot a story of supernatural horror dealing with Carrie's telekinetic powers. Conflating questions of femininity and the supernatural, the film renders Carrie's puberty not simply in the hyperbolic language of melodrama, but in the violent terms of horror, where unarticulated excess is not so much displaced onto the mise-en-scène as it is written on her body.

Wood sees the film as altogether consistent with his view of contemporary horror, arguing that Carrie's supernatural talents are a displaced eruption of the sexual repression enforced by her mother.[6] Reading the film as progressive, Wood maintains that in bringing its world to cataclysm in the end, *Carrie* refuses any hope of a positive resolution to the problems it has introduced around female sexuality. Gregory Waller concurs, including *Carrie* among recent horror films that offer "a thorough-going critique of American institutions and values."[7] In a similar vein, Vivian Sobchack paints Carrie as a pitiable victim of American culture, "as much generated by familial incoherence and paternal weakness as the cause of it."[8] Such accounts stress Carrie's

Carrie (1976): Carrie (Sissy Spacek) being crowned at the school prom.

victimization at the hands of a repressive society, rather than the ways in which Carrie herself is presented as monstrous in the course of the film.[9] While few critics fail to see Carrie as a monster in some sense, most view the havoc she wreaks as a positive rebellion against oppression. They believe she represents nothing truly terrifying and only threatens a repressive society we would all rather do away with anyway.

My argument is precisely the opposite. By mapping the supernatural onto female adolescence and engaging the language of the fantastic, *Carrie* presents a masculine fantasy in which the feminine is constituted as horrific. In charting Carrie's path to mature womanhood, the film presents female sexuality as monstrous and constructs femininity as a subject position impossible to occupy. Above all, I believe, we must consider what most critics have glossed over—the role gender plays in the articulation of horror—since the film repeatedly insists on Carrie's gender and the specific development of *feminine* subjectivity. Through a rereading of *Carrie,* I hope to suggest ways in which horrific family dramas might be opened up to considerations of gender by investigating the particular mix of horror, melodrama, and the supernatural that they engage.

Appropriately, *Carrie* begins in the all-female world of a girl's high school gym class. The camera glides confidently through a locker room of girls frolicking in various stages of undress, apparently oblivious to the camera's eye registering their every bounce and bend in exquisite slow motion. Diegetic sound is replaced by a lyrical musical theme and slowed, steam-filled images sever connections with temporality and materiality: these are ethereal creatures, nymphs at the water pond. Tracking right across banks of lockers, then down an aisle past several girls, the camera finally settles on Carrie, lingering in the shower after others have left, enjoying a moment of solitary pleasure soaping and caressing her breasts and thighs. Amidst streams of soap and water, blood suddenly appears between her legs. Failing to comprehend her first menstrual period and believing she is wounded, Carrie screams in panic, her voice and the roar of the shower abruptly invading the soundtrack. The other girls, gleeful at her terror, begin pelting her with tampons and sanitary pads, taunting "Plug it up, plug it up." We next see the girls in reverse angle from Carrie's position with full motion and diegetic sound restored; no longer nymphs, they now appear as demons hurling tampons and abuse in a swirl of close-up fury. The onset of Carrie's puberty is depicted as a violent departure from the self-sufficient autoeroticism of prepubescence she experiences in the shower, as female sexuality announces itself with a particular violence.

Violence and sexuality are further confused in this sequence through overt parallels to *Psycho*'s shower scene, which evoke associations manifest in Hitchcock's film but so far tacit in *Carrie*.[10] After the camera finds Carrie in a single tracking movement, the scene breaks down into multiple shots, several of which mimic the *Psycho* scene directly: side views of the showerhead spraying water and of Carrie's face up-turned in the stream offer particularly direct quotations. Subsequent shots fragment Carrie's body as torso, legs, breasts, in much the same way that Marion Crane's body is "dissected" in the *Psycho* attack. These intertextual references prompt us to read the sight of blood trickling down Carrie's legs as she herself does; we associate Carrie's menstruation with a bloody attack, with blood flowing from an inflicted wound. However, whereas the violence in *Psycho* is split between victim and attacker, between Marion and Norman Bates, here no such division exists: Carrie's adolescent body becomes the site upon which monster and victim converge, and we are encouraged to postulate that a monster resides within her.

Voyeurism is crucial to both shower scenes as well, as the private pleasure both Marion and Carrie enjoy is framed within a voyeuristic gaze. However, whereas in *Psycho* the viewer's eye is clearly aligned with Norman's inquisitive stare, in *Carrie* no character's look intervenes with the voyeuristic spectacle. Our identification lies directly with the omniscient, roving camera, whose movements are detached from patterns of looking within the diegesis. The scrutiny of Carrie, the vision of horror glimpsed, originates beyond the diegesis in a position of authorial power, as the absence of natural motion and diegetic sound situate the onlooker outside diegetic space.

This position of visual mastery is immediately relinquished following the sight of blood between Carrie's legs, when our identification shifts from the disembodied voyeur gliding boldly through the locker room to an abrupt reverse angle of the other teenagers terrorizing Carrie in a sudden burst of diegetic sound and motion. These two views of the locker room ask us to look twice at the girls, to consider them first as nymphs, then demons. Here in the reverse angle we begin to see a monstrousness lurking beneath the cheesecake curves. So, while Carrie's menstrual blood signals her own monstrosity, the entire locker room of girls is implicated in this horror as well. Indeed, the reverse angle becomes emblematic of the film's final project: to shift the particular horror associated with Carrie onto a larger female population and ultimately to foist a masculine fantasy of femininity onto the female subject. *Carrie's* opening scene depicts the horrors of voyeurism, the horror of what might be seen when the penetrating camera glimpses the sight of sexual difference the male voyeur cannot acknowledge. As Laura Mulvey has so succinctly phrased it, "The look, pleasurable in form, may be threatening in content."[11]

The horror that the female body generates in the male onlooker is familiar to feminist critics of the slasher film, who read the excessive mutilation of women's bodies in these films as a kind of symbolic castration.[12] The horror, as often noted, arises not from woman's "castration," but from the fact that she is *not* castrated.[13] In order to account for this puzzling phenomenon of sexual difference, the male subject constructs a fantasy of female castration, perversely enacted by the slasher. Woman and monster are posed as analogous terms in horror films, Linda Williams notes, because of their shared (and threatening) anatomical difference. "The monster as double for the woman" suggests "a horror version of her own body."[14] Stephen Neale suggests that sexual difference also underlies the horror genre's attempts to negotiate distinctions between the human and the nonhuman or monstrous.[15] Monsters typically disrupt and challenge the presumed homogeneity of human identity by confusing or transgressing boundaries between the human and nonhuman. Like sexual difference, then, the monster introduces a threatening heterogeneity into the category of the human. Nonhuman and nonmale are confused as equivalent threats to human identity; bodily difference becomes, in both cases, the locus of the nonhuman. Construction of the monstrous, Neale suggests, may thus be read as "the product of the displacement of the one instance of hetero-geneity [sexual difference] onto the other."[16] Williams adds that in slasher or stalker films, where the monster remains largely off screen, affinity between woman and monster "gives way to pure identity: she *is* the monster, her mutilated body is the only visible horror."[17]

While questions of *sexuality* have dominated discussions of "familial and familiar" horror films (in particular, the way repressed sexuality erupts as violence in the family), considerations of *gender* are largely confined to the discourse on slasher films, where misogynistic dread of the female body is much more apparent.[18] Gender and gendered sexuality, however, play key roles in *Carrie*'s articulation of the monstrous. Tacit connections between woman and monster, which Williams and Neale find at the core of horror, come to the fore in *Carrie*. Not only is Carrie a *female* monster, but sexual difference is integral to the horror she generates; monstrosity is explicitly associated with menstruation and female sexuality. In the shower scene, where victim and attacker converge on Carrie's body, menstruation and castration are fused in a fantasy of sexual difference permitted by the *generic* confusion of horror, melodrama, and the supernatural.

The shower scene parallel only hints at monstrous aspects of female sexuality; these are soon made explicit when, as a by-product of her first period, Carrie gains telekinetic powers. Hysterical and inconsolable in the shower room, she bursts an overhead light bulb through the sheer force of rage. Michael Bliss unwittingly hits upon the significance of the simultaneous onset of Carrie's supernatural ability and her sexuality when he compares the shower scene to "the significant scenes in *The Werewolf* involving the transfer of the curse."[19] Carrie is indeed the victim of a horror film curse, not quite the curse of Dracula or even the "mummy's curse," but a menstrual "curse" passed down from woman to woman. Menstruation and female sexuality here are inseparable from the "curse" of supernatural power, more properly the domain of horror films.

Prohibitions surrounding first menstruation and menstruating women exist in many cultures and are grounded in fears that during menses a woman is polluted or possessed by dangerous spirits. Hovering on the edge of the supernatural, such women are deemed especially treacherous and subject to taboo.[20] "Exceptional states" like menstruation and puberty foster taboos, Freud believes, because they elicit contradictory, yet equally acute sensations of veneration and dread.[21] Poised between natural and supernatural realms, then, the menstruating adolescent girl occupies a liminal state, an object of both aversion and desire. Equating Carrie's burgeoning sexuality with her new-found telekinetic power, the film hyperbolizes this connection. In *Carrie* what is conventionally uncanny about menstruation and puberty is literalized by the film as a whole, which takes place in the transitory register of the fantastic.

Traits associated with Carrie's menses—explicitly, the onset of sexuality and, implicitly, violence and danger—are displaced onto the telekinetic powers through which she brutally destroys objects outside her body. Her telekinesis signifies the threat that unchecked female desire may pose to society. When Carrie cannot control her rage in the school principal's office, she sends his ashtray into a tailspin; angered by a taunting boy, she sidewinds his bicycle; in her mother's house, she slams windows and breaks a mirror. Ultimately, her supernatural powers grow to such magnitude that she is able to torch her entire Senior Prom.[22] The escalating forcefulness of Carrie's telekinetic ability is matched by her increasingly ardent attraction to Tommy Ross, another byproduct of her emerging sexuality. As Carrie's eroticism moves to objects outside her body, so do her acts of violence, as the aggressive nature of her sexuality is displaced onto destructive telekinetic acts. Telekinesis thus clearly marks Carrie's sexuality as monstrous by acting as a literal inscription of the violence of her desire. Yet although the female body—its fluids, its sexuality, its reproductive power—is clearly the source of horror here, the metaphor of telekinesis represents an attempt to deny the body and its actions. Presented as the ability to move objects with one's mind without physical intervention, telekinesis effectively circumvents the body's agency in the material world.

Following the simultaneous onset of her mature sexuality and supernatural powers, Carrie's subsequent path to womanhood is presented as a treacherous course that must be cautiously navigated by either of the two possible routes she is offered: the sexual repression demanded by her mother, or the promise of femininity volunteered by her gym teacher, Miss Collins. Ostensibly, the film undercuts the repressive asceticism celebrated by Mrs. White while championing the liberating vision of femininity offered by Miss Collins. Indeed, the film goes to great lengths to situate Mrs. White's views in the context of the archaic and horrific. Her dark cape, severe black stockings, and cascading hair mark her Gothic appearance. Against the ranch-style bungalows of the suburban community, her home is a veritable mausoleum lit only by candles and proverbial lightning flashes outside. Miss Collins, on the other hand, braless, physically active, and dressed in shorts and a T-shirt, presents the perfect foil to Mrs.White's deliberately witchlike visage. Promising Carrie a femininity achieved through good posture, lip gloss, and curls, the gym teacher offers the teenager a route to mature womanhood apparently free from the repression enforced by the girl's mother.

Despite these apparent differences, however, the film ultimately endorses Mrs. White's position by equating the two women's aims. Both women are

obsessed with physical punishment and the body, a fact made apparent when the scene of Mrs. White punishing Carrie in the prayer closet is juxtaposed with the scene in which Miss Collins subjects the other girls to a gruelling workout as punishment for their treatment of Carrie in the locker room. The association of these two scenes correlates the sexual sin Mrs. White finds in Carrie (which we are initially encouraged to believe is mistaken) with the blame placed on the other girls. It establishes an analogy early in the film between Carrie's "transgression" and the deviance of a wider female population. Inside the gymnasium, as Miss Collins rants and paces in front of the girls, parallel tracking shots across their faces underscore the universality of their guilt. Outside on the track field the camera again tracks back and forth in front of the girls as they perform calisthenics. Dressed in identical gym clothes and framed at hip and thigh level, the girls are reduced to undifferentiated, anonymous torsos. Early in the film, then, women's deviance is emphasized by establishing a contiguous relationship between Carrie's prayer closet scene and the gym class detention. Although apparently contrasted, Miss Collins and Mrs. White work together in these two scenes to insist upon women's culpability and to establish the female body as site of transgression.

Carrie's teenage contemporaries, Sue and Chris, offer paths through adolescence that parallel the lives of the two older women. Although both girls participate in the locker room assault on Carrie, they are contrasted through the different reactions each has to Miss Collins's detention. Masochistic, Sue is ready to accept her guilt and punishment, while Chris, possessed of excessive sexuality, refuses to concede guilt or suffer punishment and so receives the ultimate retribution—school suspension and loss of her "prom privileges." Chaste and dutiful, Sue reins in her desire so uncompromisingly that she is able to share her boyfriend with Carrie when stricken by a guilty conscience. Chris, whose lip-smacking lust for vengeance is explicitly connected to her sexual appetite, does not allow desire to be overrun by any such ethical sense. If Sue represents a young woman attempting to contain the violent libido Carrie suddenly finds herself in possession of, then Chris, ruled by desire and impulse, represents precisely the opposite.[23] Pushed outside the community after her suspension, Chris eventually unleashes the full force of her lawlessness through a tangled revenge scheme.

Chris, an excessive character prowling the fringes of society, obsessed with sexuality and punishment, is a neat inversion of Mrs. White, while Sue promises to repeat Miss Collins's renunciation of sexuality and the teacher's aggressive

---

(*opposite*) Carrie's monstrosity is a horrific representation of menses and her sexuality.

do-gooder's instinct. Indeed, although Miss Collins initially resists Sue's plan to allow Carrie to take her place at the prom, it provides the culmination of the teacher's tutoring. At the same time, Chris's vengeance fulfills all of Mrs. White's most dire prophesies. These apparent dichotomies are deceptive, however, since the restraint prescribed by Mrs. White is consistently upheld, whether through the "positive" repression practiced by Sue and Miss Collins, or by the menace posed by Chris's volatile sexuality. The bodily repression demanded by Mrs. White is ultimately analogous to the physical makeover promoted by Miss Collins. The culturally sanctioned femininity proffered by the girl's teacher is as repressive as her mother's fundamentalism.

The route to mature femininity Miss Collins offers Carrie, pictured as the road to the Senior Prom, consists of tactful grooming tips on makeup, hair styling, dress, and posture, which eventually allow Carrie to assume Sue's place alongside Tommy on prom night. Carrie's femininity is a posture she assumes by dressing up, putting on, adding to her body. The feminine position Miss Collins holds out, and which Carrie eagerly tries to adopt, stresses her body's external surface, her image. Indeed, all of the scenes associated with the girl's physical transformation are played in front of mirrors so that we do not see Carrie herself, but her reflected image. In the initial scene with Miss Collins in the school washroom, where Carrie is encouraged to scrutinize those aspects of her body which might be enhanced through the addition of color and curl, the teacher says, "See that? That's a pretty girl." Speaking in the third person, she distances Carrie from her own image.

Scenes where Carrie tests shades of lipstick in a drugstore and applies makeup the night of the prom are similarly framed through the girl's mirror reflection, alerting us to the fact that Carrie's "femininity" is a surface alteration designed to mask the true horror of her body. The separation of visual image from physical body that the mirror reflection creates is akin to the effect Carrie achieves by making up. Through the blush, eye shadow, lipstick, and curls she dons, Carrie builds up the surface of her body, as if to cover over what lurks beneath.

Joan Rivière and Michèle Montrelay have described a masquerade of femininity that consists of an exaggerated buildup of the body's surface through makeup, shimmering fabrics, jewels, enhanced color, and elaborate coiffures that catch the eye but ultimately reflect the gaze away from the woman's interior. Accumulating excessive signifiers of femininity, they say, a woman turns herself into a fetish object in order to conceal those aspects of her body disturbing to the male onlooker.[24] The costume Carrie dons on prom night—reflective satin gown, translucent shawl, corsage, loosely curled hair, and face makeup—evokes the array of "so many silent insignias" that Montrelay describes at the heart of masquerade.[25] Extending even beyond such physical alterations to her body, Carrie's "performance" includes assuming Sue's role alongside Tommy at the prom and ultimately appearing on stage as Prom Queen in a drama carefully orchestrated by Chris.

Besides Carrie, Chris is the character most associated with masquerade in the film. Riding in Billy's car before proposing her revenge scheme, she obsessively applies and reapplies makeup, then repeatedly brushes her hair precisely at the moment when her lawlessness has placed her on the perimeter of society. Through this parody of Carrie's own transformation, it becomes apparent that both girls share a need to cover over and conceal aspects of their sexuality marked excessive.

Responding to Miss Collins's initial command to "take care of yourself" and the girls' taunt to "plug it up," Carrie attempts to cover over the monstrosity she believes to be at her core through performance and masquerade. Yet, while these demands are voiced by female characters in the fiction, they satisfy needs of the masculine voyeur who initially glimpsed the horrific sight of sexual difference in the opening shower sequence. As Sarah Kofman puts it, "The good reasons women have for 'veiling' themselves . . . all correspond to men's need for a certain fetishism."[26] Both masquerade and telekinesis perform a similar function in the film, denying Carrie's body, the initial source of horror, and leaving nothing in its place. Just as telekinesis severs the body from physical action, displacing the violence associated with Carrie's desire onto external objects, masquerade separates body from image, interior from exterior. Both strategies attempt to substitute the monstrous female body with a void.

The film's presentation of mature femininity as masquerade and performance insists that the feminine position Carrie tries to adopt is ultimately untenable. Her "innate" femininity, drawn through telekinesis as monstrous and destructive, cannot be suppressed by the culturally sanctioned femininity proffered by Miss Collins, which is explicitly marked as a hopeless charade intended to cover over the natural horror.

Eventually Carrie's masquerade *is* destroyed when Chris unleashes a bucket of pig's blood perched above the prom stage, enacting a perverse inversion of the initial shower scene and returning us to the onset of Carrie's sexuality just at the moment when she seems to have successfully navigated adolescence. Echoes of the earlier shower scene begin as soon as Carrie ascends the stage as Prom Queen. Again, the action is slowed and filmed with a moving camera, while diegetic sound is replaced by the now familiar lyrical theme. For a brief instant Carrie seems to have recaptured the moment of ecstasy witnessed in the shower. Then, suddenly drenched in blood, her interior made exterior, Carrie bleeds from every surface of her body. Equating pig's blood with Carrie's menstrual blood, this inverted shower scene explicitly associates female sexuality with violence, contagion, and death. Her inner monstrosity finally exposed for all to see, and ultimately unable to "plug it up," Carrie becomes an outright monster, unleashing her consummate telekinetic fury on the prom guests.

While Carrie's apocalyptic devastation of the prom is often read as the spectacular (and healthy) return of her repressed sexuality, I believe the sequence demands another reading. In fact, the film maintains that Carrie has *not* repressed her sexuality, having defied her mother's demands and accepted Miss Collins's tutoring, along with Tommy's invitation to the prom. What Carrie *has* attempted to repress is an intrinsic female sexuality associated with the supernatural and the monstrous; the culturally sanctioned "femininity" she adopts is thus marked as a hopelessly failed masquerade. What erupts on prom night in a monumental telekinetic display is not a wholesome sexuality unfairly repressed by the girl's mother, but an absolute monstrousness the film finds lurking at the heart of female sexuality. *Carrie* is not about liberation from sexual repression, but about the *failure* of repression to contain the monstrous feminine.

Carrie's telekinetic wrath is portrayed through split-screen compositions that juxtapose close-ups of her fierce telekinetic gaze on one side of the screen with images of her destructive acts on the other. Ironically, the scene returns to Carrie the gaze that had been granted to the masculine voyeur at the beginning of the film. But it does so in order to suggest the dangers of such a reversal rather than to celebrate Carrie's supernatural empowerment. As Linda Williams notes, the woman's look plays a key role in the traditional construction of horror. It becomes the means by which the female victim registers the monster's threat in the same instant that she recognizes her affinity with the monster as Other. The look—also the means by which the masculine subject initially recognizes sexual difference—is granted to the female subject in order that she might recognize her own monstrosity reflected in the body of the monster. The conflation of woman and monster together on Carrie's body reproduces the woman's look as telekinetic destruction. And despite the emphasis it places on Carrie's sightline, the split-screen process refuses us access to her optical point of view, since both seer and seen are represented on screen at once. She is rendered only as an object of specularity. As in the opening shower scene, where the spectator is assigned a position of visual mastery outside the diegetic space, here the split-screen separates us from Carrie's subjectivity and resigns her to a hopelessly fragmented state. The split-screen presentation of Carrie's vengeance also literally enacts the split between body and action implied by her telekinetic power. Just as telekinesis has functioned from the beginning of the film, this strategy attempts to deny that Carrie's body is the source of horror.

Most important, far from being a rebellion against her mother's sexual repression, the prom-night apocalypse marks the fulfillment of Mrs. White's prophecies and the beginning of Carrie's final regression to her mother's world. Accepting at last her mother's language of cleansing and purification, Carrie does not so much destroy the high school as subject it to ritual purgation through fire and water, using the water hoses and electrical equipment at hand. Arriving home to wash off the layers of blood and makeup that mark her femininity, Carrie regresses further, returning to the amniotic fluid of the maternal womb in the bath, then finally donning a child's white flannel nightgown and falling into her mother's embrace. As intensely oppressive as Mrs. White's views are initially presented to be, it is finally her view of female sexuality that the film upholds, a view linking Carrie's period to "Eve's curse" and equating female sexuality with sin.

Yet even this maternal dyad proves precarious. Muttering "I should have killed you when you were born," Mrs. White flails out with a butcher knife, attempting to stab her daughter and breaking the union to which Carrie has regressed. We learn here that Mrs. White, the sturdiest voice of repression in the film, is herself wracked by fermenting sexuality, as her desire explodes in an immensely phallic display. Assuming the function conventionally performed by the horror film slasher, a character missing from the initial shower scene, Mrs. White executes a familiar punishment. (Mrs. White even resembles "Mrs. Bates," holding the knife high above her head and wearing a high-necked gown.) Refusing to accept such a visible mark of her own inadequacy, Carrie drives a full kitchen's worth of blades into her mother, then brings the house crumbling down around them.[27] Carrie's regression ill fated, the feminine position is now entirely untenable.

In tracing Carrie's torturous path through puberty, the film presents an innate female sexuality, which Carrie experiences as a series of violent telekinetic urges, and offers her two avenues by which she may repress such monstrous desire: the bodily denial endorsed by her mother or the masquerade of femininity offered by Miss Collins. Both scenarios proffer repression and disavowal as the only alternatives to monstrous femininity, and each is marked as equally impossible. Telekinesis (equated with Carrie's innate sexuality) and masquerade (the "solution" advanced by Miss Collins) function equivalently in the film to disavow the horror Carrie's body represents. Severing Carrie's interior from exterior, telekinesis separates body from action, just as masquerade disjoins body and image. By consistently affirming Mrs. White's denial of the body, *Carrie* performs what Kaja Silverman has described as the quintessential gesture of classical film: the displacement of masculine experiences of loss and lack onto the female body, whose anatomical difference marks it safely as Other.[28]

Carrie presents its view of female sexual difference as aberrant and monstrous within a melodramatic context. At the same time as Carrie's body is constructed as the source of horror, the film's melodramatic rendering of her adolescence works to elicit profound sympathy, especially from female viewers. We are encouraged to identify with the teenager frightened by her burgeoning sexuality and unable to sustain the rigid standards of culturally sanctioned femininity, only to find that her attempt to foster a stable sexual identity is deemed impossible. If the feminine position with which we have been encouraged to identify is ultimately untenable, then we as female spectators are implicated in our own attempts to construct a viable subjectivity. By fostering sympathy for Carrie's plight, the film implicates women in its own misogynistic portrait of horror at the feminine.

Following Carrie's colossal destruction of the high school and her ultimate self-annihilation, the narrative shifts markedly from her point of view to Sue's, depicting the other girl's nightmare of visiting Carrie's grave. Rather than being completely destroyed in the end, Carrie is instead relegated to Sue's dream life, a figure of the female unconscious returning to terrorize and impede the now infantile Sue. While the problems of female sexuality have been suppressed by the narrative—Carrie herself is dead and the high school space of adolescence has been consumed in flames—the repressed returns to Sue in her unconscious. Mistakenly hoping that the repression will be complete, Sue's mother can be heard saying over the telephone, "The doctor says she's young enough that she'll forget all about it in time." Yet the film's final image shows Sue waking terrified from a dream, as if to suggest that *Carrie* presents a woman's view of her own monstrosity, that retrospectively the film's fantasy belongs to Sue.

While *Carrie* begins as the aggressive view of the fantasized male subject, through de Palma's authorial camera movement and references to Hitchcock, *Carrie* ends as a woman's nightmare. The shift in point of view that takes place abruptly in the opening locker room sequence—from the omniscient masculine eye to Carrie's reverse-angle view—becomes emblematic of the film's endeavor to shift its perspective from male subject to female subject. Although the film documents the dread of the female body glimpsed by that first male voyeur, it attempts to characterize this fantasy as a woman's.

Leaving us with Sue's dream, *Carrie* suggests that mature femininity, if achieved at all, is a fragile state, constantly undermined by forces beneath its surface that resist containment. While focusing on Carrie's battle to contain her monstrosity, the film also suggests the precarious balance other women attempt to maintain. In shifting the narrative perspective from Carrie to Sue at the end, the film completes the transfer of Carrie's particular horror to the female population as a whole and attempts to displace its masculine fantasy of horror at the female onto the female subject herself. *Carrie* marshals the language of the fantastic in order to present a fantasy of its own, in order to liberalize those aspects of female sexuality the male subject finds so monstrous because so unfamiliar. The fantasy *Carrie* offers is ultimately a paradoxical one: the film enforces sexual difference by equating the feminine with the monstrous, while simultaneously insisting that the feminine position is untenable precisely because of its monstrousness.

Notes

1. Hélène Cixous, "The Laugh of the Medusa," trans. Keith Cohen and Paula Cohen, in *The Signs Reader: Women, Gender, and Scholarship,* ed. Elizabeth Abel and Emily K. Abel (Chicago: University of Chicago Press, 1983), p. 280. Thanks to Julie Clark for drawing my attention to this quotation.

2. Vivian Sobchack, "Bringing It All Back Home: Family Economy and Generic Exchange," in *American Horrors: Essays on the Modern American Horror Film,* ed. Gregory Waller (Urbana and Chicago: University of Illinois Press, 1987), p. 181; reprinted in this volume. Remarking on the conflation of horror and domestic drama, Philip Brophy describes *Amityville II* as "*The Exorcist* meets *Ordinary People*"; see "Horrality—the Textuality of Contemporary Horror Films," *Screen* 27, no. 1 (January–February 1986): 7. Greg Keeler reads *The Shining* in relation to *Kramer vs. Kramer;* see "*The Shining:* Ted Kramer Has a Nightmare," *Journal of Popular Film and Television* 8, no. 4 (Winter 1981): 2–8.

3. In the context of domestic horror, where the figure of the child is so crucial, it is important to stress that *Carrie,* and films like *The Exorcist* and *Martin,* do not deal with child-monsters but adolescents. James Twitchell contributes a great deal to our understanding of horror's family romance in *Dreadful Pleasures: An Anatomy of Modern Horror* (New York: Oxford University Press, 1985), pp. 296–301. Yet he tends to lump children and adolescents together in his discussion of the "downsizing" of monsters in contemporary horror. This obscures the fact that pubescent characters necessarily raise the specter of sexuality.

4. Robin Wood, "An Introduction to the American Horror Film," in *The American Nightmare: Essays on the Horror Film,* ed. Robin Wood and Richard Lippe (Toronto: Festival of Festivals, 1979), pp. 2–28; Wood, "The American Family Comedy: From *Meet Me in St. Louis* to *The Texas Chainsaw Massacre*," *Wide Angle* 3, no. 2 (1979): 5–11; and Tony Williams, "Family Horror," *Movie,* nos. 27–28 (1980–1981): 117–126.

5. Wood, "Introduction," p. 10.

6. Robin Wood, "Yet Another Terrible Child," *London Times Education Supplement,* February 11, 1977, p. 86; and Wood, *Hollywood from Vietnam to Reagan* (New York: Columbia University Press, 1986), p. 154.

7. Gregory Waller, introduction to *American Horrors,* p. 4.

8. Sobchack, "Bringing It All Back Home," p. 183.

9. Others who read the film as progressive include Bruce Babington, "Twice a Victim: Carrie Meets the BFI," *Screen* 24, no. 3 (May–June 1983): 4–18; Michael Bliss, *Brian de Palma* (Metuchen, N.J.: Scarecrow Press, 1983), pp. 50–71; Kenneth MacKinnon, *Misogyny in the Movies: The De Palma Question* (London: Associated University Presses, 1990), pp. 121–138; Paula Matusa, "Corruption and Catastrophe: De Palma's *Carrie,*" *Film Quarterly* 31, no. 1 (Autumn 1977): 32–38; and David Pirie, "*Carrie,*" *Movie,* no. 25 (1977–1978): 20–24. The only analysis I have found that stresses the degree to which Carrie herself is constructed as monstrous is Serafina Kent Bathrick, "Ragtime: The Horror of Growing Up Female," *Jump Cut,* no. 14 (1977): 9–10. MacKinnon provides a summary of other critical responses to *Carrie.*

10. Brian de Palma's films are, of course, notorious for their allusions to Hitchcock. Several de Palma films made after *Carrie* also include references to the shower murder in *Psycho* (1960). *Dressed to Kill* (1980) begins and ends with shower attacks, both fantasized by their victims. *Blow Out* (1981) and *Body Double* (1984) are similarly framed by shower scenes, each part of a low-budget horror film being made within the larger narrative. Remember too that Carrie's adolescence is played out, rather obviously, in *Bates* High School.

11. Laura Mulvey, "Visual Pleasure and Narrative Cinema" [1975], in *Feminism and Film Theory,* ed. Constance Penley (New York: Routledge, 1988), p. 62.

12. Barbara Creed, "Horror and the Monstrous-Feminine: An Imaginary Abjection," *Screen* 27, no. 1 (January–February 1986): 44–70 (reprinted in this volume); Vera Dika, *Games of Terror: Halloween, Friday the 13th, and the Films of the Stalker Cycle* (Rutherford, N.J.: Fairleigh Dickinson University Press, 1990); and Linda Williams, "When the Woman Looks," in *Re-Vision: Essays in Feminist Film Criticism,* ed. Mary Ann Doane, Patricia Mellencamp, and Linda Williams (Frederick, Md.: University Publications of America/American Film Institute, 1984), pp. 83–89 (reprinted in this volume).

13. See Susan Lurie, "The Construction of the 'Castrated Woman' in Psychoanalysis and Cinema," *Discourse* 4 (1981–1982): 52–74; and Lurie, "Pornography and the Dread of Women: The Male Sexual Dilemma," in *Take Back the Night: Women on Pornography,* ed. Laura Lederer (New York: Morrow, 1980), pp. 159–173.

14. Linda Williams, "When the Woman Looks," pp. 87, 89.

15. Stephen Neale, *Genre* (London: British Film Institute, 1980), pp. 21, 60.

16. Ibid.

17. Linda Williams, "When the Woman Looks," p. 96.

18. Further considerations of gender in the slasher film can be found in Carol J. Clover, "Her Body, Himself: Gender in the Slasher Film," *Representations* 10 (1987): 187–228 (reprinted in this volume); Steve Neale, "*Halloween:* Suspense, Aggression, and the Look," *Framework* 14 (1981): 28–29, reprinted in *Planks of Reason: Essays on the Horror Film,* ed. Barry Keith Grant (Metuchen, N.J.: Scarecrow Press, 1984), pp. 331–345;

and Robin Wood, "Beauty Bests the Beast," *American Film* 8, no. 10 (September 1983): 62–65. For a useful discussion of *Carrie's* relation to the stalker cycle in general and to *Prom Night* (1980) in particular, see Dika, *Games of Terror,* pp. 86–87. On the other hand, such recent studies of the horror film as Noel Carroll, *The Philosophy of Horror, or Paradoxes of the Heart* (New York and London: Routledge, 1989), and Andrew Tudor, *Monsters and Mad Scientists: A Cultural History of the Horror Movie* (Cambridge, Mass.: Basil Blackwell, 1989), take no account of gender.

19. Bliss, *Brian de Palma,* p. 52.

20. Janice Delaney, Mary Jane Lupton, and Emily Toth, *The Curse: A Cultural History of Menstruation,* rev. ed. (Urbana: University of Illinois Press, 1988), pp. 28–36.

21. Sigmund Freud, "Totem and Taboo" [1913], in *The Standard Edition of the Complete Psychological Works,* trans. James Strachey (London: Hogarth Press, 1958), 13: 18.

22. In a musical production of *Carrie,* staged during the 1987–1988 Broadway season, the teenager channeled her telekinetic ability more playfully, using it to levitate her lipstick and compact. See Frank Rich, "'I Just Want to Set the World on Fire,'" *New York Times,* May 13, 1988, p. C3.

23. The misogynistic portrait of unrestricted female sexuality that Chris represents (in contrast to Sue) is reproduced in the discussion of the film by David J. Hogan, *Dark Romance: Sexuality in the Horror Film* (Jefferson, N.C.: McFarland, 1986), p. 270: "Though [Carrie] has not *mastered* her sexuality, she makes a conscious effort to put it to *gentle* use. The bitchy Chris is Carrie's converse, almost a caricature of the high school *femme fatale:* blonde hair, wet lips, firm little body, and perpetual come-on attitude—the archetypal cock tease" (emphasis added).

24. Joan Rivière, "Womanliness as a Masquerade" (1929), in *Psychoanalysis and Female Sexuality,* ed. Hendrik M. Ruitenbeek (New Haven, Conn.: College and University Press, 1966), pp. 209–220; and Michèle Montrelay, "Inquiry into Femininity," *m/f* 1 (1977): 83–101. While both outline a similar conception of female masquerade, it is somewhat misleading to collapse their views together here, for each ultimately perceives the process quite differently.

25. Montrelay, "Inquiry into Femininity," p. 93.

26. Sarah Kofman, *The Enigma of Woman: Woman in Freud's Writings,* trans. Catherine Porter (Ithaca: Cornell University Press, 1985), p. 50.

27. The film's use of Christian imagery in this scene and elsewhere—in particular, Mrs. White's peculiar conflation of baroque Catholicism and ascetic fundamentalism—deserves more attention than I can devote to it here.

28. See Kaja Silverman, *The Acoustic Mirror: The Female Voice in Psychoanalysis and Cinema* (Bloomington: Indiana University Press, 1988), pp. 1–41.

13

The Monster as Woman:
Two Generations of Cat People

Karen Hollinger

*. . . it could well be maintained that it is women's sexuality,
that which renders them desirable—but also threatening—to
men, which constitutes the real problem that the horror cinema
exists to explore, and which constitutes also and ultimately
that which is really monstrous.*

Stephen Neale, *Genre*[1]

As Stephen Neale suggests, an intimate relationship seems to
exist among the filmic presentation of the horror monster, the
castration anxiety it evokes, and the cinematic representation of
the female form. The complexity of this relationship has been
suggested by several critics,[2] but its theoretical articulation, how
it works in specific horror films, and its social and historical implications for the positioning of women in patriarchal society
still remain to be more fully examined. A possible step in this
direction involves an inquiry into the filmic presentation of the
monster as woman.

Critics have been slow to investigate the connection between
the representation of the horror monster and that of the female
image because the horror monster traditionally has been presented as male. From classic monster films like *The Cabinet of*

296

Dr. Caligari (1919) through *Nosferatu* (1922), *Frankenstein* (1931), *Dracula* (1931), *The Wolf Man* (1941), *King Kong* (1933), and *The Mummy* (1932) to the contemporary psychopath-as-monster films like *The Texas Chainsaw Massacre* (1974) and *Halloween* (1978) or the monstrous creature-as-phallic-symbol films like *Jaws* (1975), the monster is overtly, even excessively, masculine. A closer look at theoretical approaches to the iconography of the horror monster and that of the female cinematic form, however, reveals striking similarities. The traditional maleness of the horror monster can be explained in Freudian terms as an expression of the connection between the image of the monster and the filmic representation of castration anxieties. It has been proposed that the essential nature of narrative is Oedipal, that it involves the reactivation and eventual management of the castration anxieties for the male subject.[3] If so, the monster film can be said to combine in the figure of its monster the fascination, fear, and anxiety that this reenactment of the Oedipal trauma evokes. Stephen Neale, for instance, argues that the traditional male horror monster mobilizes castration anxieties by his portrayal of the lack that represents castration to the male subject.[4] It is this reenactment of the male Oedipal trauma in the figure of the horror monster that accounts for the male spectator's simultaneous attraction to and repulsion from the monster film and its monstrous central character.

Thus, the monster film is centrally concerned with problems of sexual difference. This concern, according to Neale, acts not to undermine the male spectator's filmic pleasure by using the monster merely to expose the lack upon which castration anxieties are founded, but rather to entertain the spectator by filling this lack.[5] The monster not only represents castration, but also disavows it and provides filmic pleasure for the male viewer by soothing castration fears. The avenues of this disavowal fall into two categories: fetishistic scopophilia and sadistic-investigative voyeurism. The horror monster by his very presence and by the spectacular nature of this presence serves fetishistically to reassure the spectator by masking the castration fear that is the real concern of the film. As Neale suggests, the positioning of the monster as a fetishistic figure of disavowal explains both why so much is made of the details of the monster's construction and why so many of the resources of costume and makeup are expended to make his appearance both spectacular and believable.[6] He must not only frighten but also convince the spectator of the credibility of his existence and appearance if he is to disavow castration as well as symbolize it.

The rhythm of presence and absence that the horror film sets up in regard to the monster's appearance also represents an aspect of this fetishistic avenue of disavowal. The random appearances of the monster throughout the horror film work, as Neale points out, to create a reassuring rhythm of presence and lack that serves to regulate and contain the irrevocable lack, castration.[7] Thus, for the monster to ward off castration anxiety effectively, he must be shown, and if possible even unmasked, in the course of his filmic appearances so that he can visually enact his fetishistic role.[8]

The monster's evocation of castration anxieties can be controlled not only visually by his fetishization, as Neale suggests, but also narratively by plots that involve fetishistic and sadistic-investigative aspects. In fact, the overreacher and discovery plots, two classic forms of monster film narrative,[9] parallel these twin forms of disavowal. The overreacher plot enacts narratively the monster's positioning as a fetishistic figure by setting him up as the embodiment of his creator's lofty and unattainable dreams of reaching a godlike relationship to nature and of creating a perfect human being. Thus, we see inscribed even in the narratives of these monster films disavowal, overvaluation, and fetishistic substitution. An exemplary text in this regard is James Whale's *Frankenstein,* in which Henry Frankenstein's creation of a violent and destructive monster is explained as the result of his desire to assemble a magnificent creature with a superior human brain.

The discovery plot, on the other hand, works to manage the monster and the castration anxieties that he evokes in a slightly different way. Rather than completely disavowing castration through fetishistic substitution and overvaluation, the discovery plot seeks to control the monster by a process of demystification. This narrative movement culminates in the devaluation or punishment of the monster or at least in the acquisition of sufficient knowledge of his mysterious behavior to find a way to deal with his threatening presence.

A comparison of this Freudian description of the filmic presentation of the horror monster and Laura Mulvey's analysis of the iconography of the female form in narrative cinema shows them to be quite similar. According to Mulvey, the figure of the woman, like that of the monster, also mobilizes castration fears in the male subject. She is "the bearer of the bleeding wound," the signifier of the male Other, and the symbol of the castration threat by her real absence of a penis.[10] For Mulvey, the project of narrative cinema as a whole is both to represent this lack and to disavow it in its presentation of the female form, just as the monster film works both to represent and to disavow the threat of the castrated and castrating monster. The two avenues of disavowal for the threat of castration embodied in the filmic image of woman are also sadistic-investigative voyeurism (the investigation of the woman's mystery) and fetishistic scopophilia (the substitution of the fetish object or the turning of the represented figure itself into a fetish through overvaluation).

While a relationship thus seems to exist between the image of woman in cinema and that of the monster in the horror film, the nature of this relationship is obscured by classic monster films, which position women as victims of the monster's aggression. Just as the classic horror monster is commonly defined as male, so the primary object of his desire is almost exclusively female. As Neale points out, patriarchy positions women as subject to men and to their power, and the horror film simply "rehearses and restates this ideology."[11] But, as Linda Williams suggests, beneath this assertion of male power that positions women only as victims there lies a sympathetic affinity and identification between woman and monster. Williams argues that the look of the female victim at the monster in the horror film reveals not only an acknowledgment of her punishment for usurping the male power of the look but also a recognition of her similar status to the monster "in patriarchal structures of seeing."[12]

The positioning of woman as victim in the classic monster film, therefore, functions as a method of masking what is really presented as monstrous and threatening in these works. The fear that lurks behind castration anxieties and the fetishized horror monster can be seen as a fear not of the lack represented by the horror monster but of the potency of female sexuality and the power of woman's sexual difference. Both Neale and Mulvey perceive the threat of the horror monster and of female sexuality to the male in terms of its evocation of a weak, castrated female form. For them, the image of the woman and of the monster recalls for the male spectator his childhood Oedipal trauma during which he came to regard his mother as rendered weak and helpless by castration. It also reactivates the Oedipal fear that he too could be reduced through castration to her situation of powerless deformity and mutilation.

This conception of female sexuality as threatening to the male in terms of its representation of the castrated female's weak and helpless state is called into question by the affinity between woman and monster. If the woman is related to the monster in that they both are seen by patriarchy as representing sexual difference and castration fears, then she is allied not to a representation of weakness but to one of power in sexual difference. For the classic male horror monster, as symbol of the male Other, is not only a castrated victim of male society, but also a powerful, potentially castrating nemesis to the male hero, and he gets his power from the very fact of his dangerous difference from the normal male, from his positioning as "a biological freak with the impossible and threatening appetites that suggest a frightening potency precisely where the normal male would perceive a lack."[13]

The inadequacy of the Freudian rendering of woman as a symbol only of the lack that is castration and nothing more has led revisionist psychoanalytic theorists like Susan Lurie to challenge traditional Freudian notions of the nature of the male Oedipal experience.[14] According to Lurie, the male child's trauma involves not his fear of being castrated and thus reduced to his mother's state of helpless mutilation, but rather a recognition that his mother, although she lacks a penis, is not, in fact, powerless or helpless. The whole notion then of woman as representing castration can be read, according to Lurie, as really a disavowal of this unsettling discovery, as a lie that covers up the male child's recognition of his mother's power in difference. Applying this theory to the monster film suggests that an interpretation with greater explanatory power than those of Neale and Mulvey in assessing the sociohistorical implications of the monster as woman in patriarchal society involves a recognition that the underlying fear that informs these texts and that lies behind the fear of castration is the threat of the potency of nonphallic sexuality. As Williams, building on Lurie's theories, suggests, it is not a recognition of the weakness but of the power in difference that woman, as sexual Other and as a potentially castrating force to the male, represents.[15]

This fear of female sexuality is carefully masked, disavowed, and displaced in the classic monster film with its male monster, fetishistic and investigative plots, and positioning of woman as victim. With the introduction of the female monster, however, this careful cover-up is destroyed because the twin avenues of disavowal no longer disavow. Castration anxieties, the underlying threat of nonphallic female sexuality, and the power in sexual difference explode from the text. Extraordinary means, therefore, must be taken to control and diminish the resulting effects on the traumatized male spectator.

A consideration of the filmic presentation of the female monster demonstrates that her existence threatens to destroy the tight control that the classic monster film imposes on the evocation of castration fears and on the portrayal of the female sexual threat that lies behind castration. From the very beginning of her cinematic career, the female monster's threatening nature was evoked only to be forcefully suppressed. James Whale's *Bride of Frankenstein* (1935) provides an early example of this suppression. The major portion of the film is devoted to a sympathetic rendering of the male Frankenstein monster. He is shown to be a pitiful creature in search of friendship and kindness who kills only when attacked and endures brutally cruel treatment, even visual crucifixion, by his captors. Much is also made in the film of the creation of the female monster, but when she does finally appear, it is only to be quickly disposed of. Despite her wild hairdo and the hissing sound she makes when approached, she is, in fact, not at all a very threatening creature: she clings submissively to Henry Frankenstein, is terrified of the male monster, and is incapable even of protesting when her rejected would-be mate sets out to destroy them both. She seems created only to act as the ultimate victim for the male monster's final demonstration of power. Clearly, however, the female sexual threat in this film, symbolized in the female monster's capacity to reject her mate, is perceived as too dangerous to allow her more than a few moments of screen time.[16]

If the female threat is forcefully controlled in *Bride of Frankenstein* by quick and total destruction, it is allowed to demonstrate its overwhelming power in Jacques Tourneur's *Cat People* (1942). Tourneur, a director noted for his subtle visual suggestion of horror,[17] allows his female monster to triumph over all male efforts to control her. Attempts are made to utilize the traditional monster film's methods of disavowing the female sexual threat, but they are exposed here as pitifully inadequate to control the horror of the female monster. Irena (Simone Simon), the cat woman, is pursued by two men, each of whom represents one avenue of disavowal. Oliver Reed (Kent Smith) is a non-threatening male presence who tries to control Irena's sexual threat by converting her into a fetishistic figure, placing her in the cult of the beautiful and sexually provocative, but unknowable and untouchable woman. Oliver describes their relationship as involving his being drawn to Irena by the force of her sexual attraction, which holds him against his will. He confesses: "I'm drawn to her. There's a warmth from her that pulls at me. I have to watch her when she's in the room. I have to touch her when she's near, but I don't really know her. In many ways we're strangers."

In direct contrast to Oliver's passive fetishism and embodying the sadistic-investigative avenue of disavowal is the aggressive sexual threat represented by the psychiatrist Dr. Judd (Tom Conway). He sets out actively to counter Irena's dangerous sexuality with the force of his phallic presence. His aggressive sexuality is symbolized in his walking stick, which contains within it a hidden sword. The sword connects him visually to another phallic power in the film, King John of Serbia, whose statue Irena keeps in her apartment. As she tells Oliver, the legendary King John rescued her village by driving out evil invaders who had led the villagers to witchcraft and devil worship. Since Irena's statue portrays King John with a panther impaled on his sword, a connection is made between the devil worshipers, whom Irena describes as having escaped King John's invasion by fleeing to the mountains, and the cat women, whom she later mentions to Dr. Judd under hypnosis. The image of a primitive, evil matriarchy threatening to male power is thus suggested. As Dr. Judd relates Irena's description of the cat women, they are "women who in jealousy or passion or out of their own corrupt passions can turn into great catlike panthers. And if one of these women were to fall in love and if her lover were to kiss her, take her into his embrace, she would be driven by her own evil to kill."

Irena believes herself related to these evil creatures, and Dr. Judd sets out to disprove this belief. The conflict between Irena's determination to cling to her conviction that she is, in fact, a cat woman and Dr. Judd's attempts to "cure" her becomes a struggle for power and domination. Dr. Judd initially attempts to gain control over Irena by mastering her secrets, investigating her while she is under hypnosis. After their first session together, he taps his little black notebook and tells her that although she remembers nothing of what she has revealed to him, he has it all at his command. Later, when they meet again at the zoo, she asks how he knew where to find her, and he answers with a look of mastery that makes her visibly uncomfortable, "You told me many things." Dr. Judd's attempts to control Irena do not stop with his investigation of her psyche. They culminate in his sexual advances, their kiss, and her transformation into a panther. In the resulting battle, the shadowy forms of the panther and the phallic walking stick/sword are seen in violent conflict. The panther, although wounded, is still victorious: Dr. Judd is killed, and the walking stick/sword is later discovered to have been broken in the battle, half of it left embedded in Irena's body.

If Dr. Judd's active attempts to exert male control result only in his death, Oliver's passive reaction to Irena's sexual threat leads him to a different fate. He turns to a seemingly asexual union with his female friend and co-worker, Alice (Jane Randolph), who describes their relationship in this way:

> I know what love is. It's understanding. It's you and me and let the rest of the world go by. It's just the two of us living our lives together happily and proudly, no self-torture and no doubt. It's enduring and it's everlasting. Nothing can change it. Nothing can change us, Oliver. That's what I think love is.

There is no sexuality here. Alice offers Oliver a safe, secure, and nonthreatening affection, but it is also presented as an asexual one. As they stand over Irena's dead body in the film's concluding scene, Oliver comments to Alice, "She never lied to us," reconfirming the horrible reality of Irena's sexual threat. It is a real threat to Oliver, and one that must never touch his ideal relationship with Alice, a relationship that is safe in its asexuality.

Although Irena's threatening sexuality is managed at the film's conclusion through her violent destruction, it is never brought under the sway of male dominance. Both Oliver and Dr. Judd fail to control her, and she is left to destroy herself by deliberately opening the gate to the panther's cage in the zoo and exposing herself to its attack. Acting in accord with the patriarchal standards that she has internalized, Irena punishes herself for a sexual nature that

Alice (Jane Randolph, *right*) finds her robe ripped by the claws of passion in *Cat People* (1942).

she has come to see as evil. This self-induced punishment, however, does not diminish the power of her sexual difference, and Tourneur's film remains a strong statement of female power in difference, which is controlled only by the woman's internalization of patriarchal standards.

Tourneur's version of *Cat People* thus illustrates the forceful expression of the female threat to the male in the character of a female monster. A consideration of this film makes it tempting to see the female monster as defying the usual filmic avenues of disavowal and expressing a threat beyond narrative control. A comparison of Tourneur's film with Paul Schrader's 1982 remake, however, demonstrates clearly that the female monster, in fact, can be controlled by a strong, even brutal evocation of phallic power. Schrader's film, in its crudely explicit narrative presentation of horror, acts as a reassertion of the phallic control that Tourneur's subtle, visually and thematically suggestive style intentionally eschews.

The project of Schrader's *Cat People* is much like that of the male child who finally has come to see his mother's nonphallic power and wants desperately to disavow it. Schrader's film works to represent the female as a weak, castrated figure and to reaffirm her submission to the phallic dominance of the male.

This reaffirmation involves the transformation of the original film's representative of failed phallic power, Dr. Judd, into a much more threatening male monster who can assert the force of the male sexual threat even in death. This figure is Irena's brother Paul (Malcolm McDowell), another cat person who in his panther form is responsible for many brutal murders. He brings Irena (Natasia Kinski) to live with him, hoping that an incestuous relationship with her, another cat person, will prevent his transformation into a panther.[18]

Thus, Irena is introduced in this film not as a powerful sexual threat, but as a potential victim to Paul's threatening sexuality. This portrayal is immediately established in the film's opening scenes depicting primitive tribal ceremonies in which young women are offered as sexual partners to male panthers. A comparison of this representation of the origin of the cat-people legend to that presented in the Tourneur version is informative. Whereas in the original the cat women are seen as powerful witches and devil worshipers who escape King John's male domination by fleeing to the mountains, in Schrader's version they become ritual sacrifices to the lust of male panthers. Irena's connection to these primitive female victims is made visually by the transition from these opening scenes to her arrival in New Orleans to meet Paul. A dissolve superimposes a close-up of Irena's face as she searches through the airport for her brother over the face of one of these female sacrificial victims.

Throughout the film, in scenes depicting his postcoital attacks on his sexual partners, Paul's strength is contrasted to Irena's weakness. Even in death, Paul maintains significant power. He is killed while in his panther form not by Irena or Oliver (John Heard), her zookeeper lover, but by Alice (Annette O'Toole), Oliver's female co-worker, who represents the asexual nonthreatening femininity characteristic of her counterpart in the original version. Male power in Schrader's as in Tourneur's film thus is at least partially subdued by a voluntary female renunciation of sexuality, but Paul is not really completely subdued. After his death, his corpse in its panther form is subjected to an autopsy by Oliver. When the carcass is opened up, a noxious gas is released that affects Oliver so strongly that he is sent to a hospital to recover, and the panther's body disintegrates, leaving behind only a green slime associated earlier in the film with Paul's transformations from one physical form into another. The suggestion is made that even after his death Paul remains a threatening creature capable of inflicting bodily harm on others and of escaping any attempts to understand and thus to control him. Irena, on the other hand, does not demonstrate a very powerful or threatening nature. She is shown only once with blood on her mouth after an apparent attack on a rabbit. While the phallicly potent Paul rips off a zookeeper's arm and devours unsuspecting

In her panther form, Irena refrains from attacking Oliver (John Heard) in *Cat People* (1982).

female sexual partners, Irena can only stalk rabbits. A castrated cat, she is reduced to small acts of viciousness.

When she does finally accept her sexual power and have sex with Oliver, she takes on her panther form but then refuses to attack him; instead, she goes off into the night to find another victim. Even though Irena is shown in her panther state, the details of her animal brutality are not presented. She does kill in order to return to her human form, but she murders the custodian of Oliver's cabin; he is, significantly, an old man well past the age of sexual potency. Thus, the force of her threat to the sexually active male is reduced. The actual attack itself is not shown. In contrast to the graphic portrayals of Paul's victims' mutilations, Irena's victim is simply shown in what appears to be a nonmutilated state. He could as easily have died from fear as from Irena's attack. Irena is not seen again until she has returned to her human form and awaits Oliver in his cabin. The visual presentation of this scene is significant. The shadows from the cabin's window screens cast a cagelike pattern on Irena. She seems to have willingly sought out her own imprisonment. Her lover has sought her out as well, and she begs him to kill her. When he refuses, she asks that he use his phallic power to return her to her animal state so that she can be freed from the torment of her sexual potency. He agrees, ties her to the bed in his cabin, and performs his rites of transformation.

Extraordinary means are here taken to reaffirm the power of male sexuality and to minimize the female sexual threat. In order to accomplish this reaffirmation, the nonthreatening male in the film is converted into a benevolent sexual despot. He provides for the weak female a way out of the horror of her sexual potency; she can find salvation if she submits to his mastery. The final scene in the film recapitulates this theme as Oliver stands outside a panther's cage and allows the cat (by implication, Irena in her animal form) to eat from his hands through the bars. The zookeeper shows kindness and concern but remains completely in control. The panther growls but finally can only submit to his dominance. It is a scene that shows the threat of female power effectively subdued and the final triumph of the male complete.

A comparison of Tourneur's film to Schrader's indicates that the filmic evocation of the female sexual threat through the figure of the female horror monster involves a complex formulation related not only to the psychic needs of its male spectators and to the internal requirements of the textual systems of the films themselves, but also to the social conditions under which the films were made. Tourneur's 1942 film speaks to a patriarchy secure in its control of female power yet on the brink of the wartime initiation of women's challenges to that control. It, therefore, rehearses and restates in symbolic form a reassuring confidence in women's internalization of patriarchal standards and of images of female power as evil. This symbolic restatement of the patriarchally correct positioning of women in 1942 also involves a strong expression of women's potential power in difference and the threat it poses to a male-defined hegemony. This expression could be tolerated by a society that still felt sure of male social dominance.

By 1982, however, when Schrader became attracted to the notion of redoing *Cat People,* women had made so many threatening advances against male power that the patriarchal assumption of women's internalization of its cultural standards and codes no longer could be confidently entertained. It became necessary to reassert male dominance in the only other way possible, through the use of force. Thus, in a period of growing assertion of female power against patriarchal hegemony, Schrader's film acts as a historically conditioned response to Tourneur's version. It attempts to master through generic variation the evocation of the female sexual threat in the original film and to reassert crudely, but effectively, the phallic control that is only subtly suggested in Tourneur's work. In both films, however, the presence of the female monster brings to the surface of the text the underlying threat of female sexuality and of the power of sexual difference that shapes it.

Notes

1. Stephen Neale, *Genre* (London: British Film Institute, 1980), p. 61.

2. See, for instance, ibid., pp. 43–45 and 60–61; Linda Williams, "When the Woman Looks," in *Re-Vision: Essays in Feminist Film Criticism,* ed. Mary Ann Doane, Patricia Mellencamp, and Linda Williams (Frederick, Md.: University Publications of America/ American Film Institute, 1984), pp. 83–99 (reprinted in this volume); and Margaret Tarratt, "Monsters from the Id," in *Film Genre Reader II,* ed. Barry Keith Grant (Austin: University of Texas Press, 1995), pp. 330–349.

3. See, for example, Janet Bergstrom, "Alternation, Segmentation, Hypnosis: Interview with Raymond Bellour," *camera obscura,* nos. 3–4 (1979): 71–104; and Teresa de Lauretis, *Alice Doesn't: Feminism, Semiotics, and Cinema* (Bloomington: Indiana University Press, 1984).

4. Neale, *Genre,* pp. 43–44.

5. Ibid.

6. Ibid., p. 45.

7. Ibid., p. 44.

8. Hence the opposition that Jacques Tourneur encountered when he was determined in *Cat People* only to suggest visually the existence of the monster rather than to present it explicitly. This visually suggestive style of horror filmmaking violated the positioning of the monster in its traditional fetishistic role.

9. The existence of these two classic horror plots was suggested by Noel Carroll, "Nightmare and the Horror Film: The Symbolic Biology of Fantastic Beings," *Film Quarterly* 34, no. 3 (Spring 1981): 16–25.

10. Laura Mulvey, "Visual Pleasure and Narrative Cinema," *Screen* 16, no. 3 (Autumn 1975): 7.

11. Stephen Neale, "*Halloween:* Suspense, Aggression, and the Look," *Framework* 14 (Spring 1981): 28.

12. Williams, "When the Woman Looks," p. 85.

13. Ibid., p. 87.

14. Susan Lurie, "Pornography and the Dread of Women," in *Take Back the Night: Women on Pornography,* ed. Laura Lederer (New York: Morrow, 1980), pp. 159–173. Williams first applied Lurie's ideas to the woman as victim in the horror film in "When the Woman Looks," pp. 89–90.

15. Williams, "When the Woman Looks," pp. 89–90.

16. Elsa Lanchester plays two roles in the film: as Mary Shelley in the prologue and later as the female monster. Shelley is presented in the prologue as an angelic Victorian woman who has demonstrated her suppressed wickedness by writing a naughty book. This positioning of the woman anticipates Tourneur's *Cat People,* in which it is suggested

that the female monster is finally controlled by her own internalization of patriarchal standards.

17. For a discussion of Tourneur's suggestive visual style, see Paul Willemen, "Notes toward the Construction of a Reading of Tourneur," in *Jacques Tourneur*, ed. Claire Johnston and Paul Willemen (Edinburgh: Edinburgh Film Festival, 1975), pp. 16–35.

18. While Paul's desire to prevent his transformation into a panther could be seen as adding a redeeming dimension to his character, his motivation does not seem to involve a struggle between good and evil within his nature, but only a desire to save himself from the unpleasantness and danger of his transformations. He expresses no real regret for the mutilations he has committed in his panther state or concern for his victims. He presents his situation to Irena entirely in the context of his own needs, and he appears untroubled by the fact that he is asking her to sacrifice herself to his sexual desires.

14

Here Comes the Bride:
Wedding Gender and Race in *Bride of Frankenstein*

Elizabeth Young

James Whale's 1935 *Bride of Frankenstein* is such a fixture in American popular culture that its most memorable image—of a woman in a long white dress with a wacked-out, white-streaked Nefertiti hairdo and wild, glazed eyes—has become the standard currency, requiring no explanation, for parodies ranging from *The Rocky Horror Picture Show* (1975) to *Far Side* cartoons.[1] Enshrined in popular culture, it ranks, too, as a favorite with film critics. Devotees of the horror film term it "a masterpiece," "a nearly perfect feature," and "the last word in monster movies; glittering and intelligent, frightening and humorous, with the right touches of both whimsy and the Gothic macabre."[2] Recent film historians praise its formal construction, asserting that the film is "close to flawless" in its "acting, direction, photography, set design, editing and overall presentation."[3] And a third strand of criticism focuses on the film's comic possibilities, celebrating it as "one of the world's first camp classics."[4]

What these various accolades leave untouched, however, is the way in which this very funny horror film is about some very serious issues. For even as it appears to escape into a genre of fantasy—in this case, Gothic horror—*Bride of Frankenstein* refracts a series of social anxieties involving gender, sexuality, and race.

Feminist criticism and social history enable us to locate in the film a series of complex, and at times contradictory, narratives of historically situated power relations. To begin with, the film's complex gender dynamics, which consistently take the form of a triangle involving two men and a woman, seem at first to enact the exchange and erasure of women, whether this triangle is configured Oedipally or—in a more capacious explanatory frame—as an instance of the "traffic in women." But the film also challenges the static parameters of such triangular models, both by transforming the competitive force of male rivalry into a subversive mode of male homoeroticism and by undermining its apparent demonization of women with a final, fleeting moment of female power. The film's gender triangles, that is, interrogate even as they illuminate explanatory frames of feminist theory, emerging as highly unstable structures in terms of both gender and sexuality.

We can evaluate the film's potentially transgressive treatment of gender, however, only through a more precise assessment of its relation to its historical moment, the 1930s. In *Bride of Frankenstein,* I will argue, the monster appears as a marker of racial difference, and his sexualized advances to the film's women encode racist American discourse of the 1930s on masculinity, femininity, rape, and lynching. This focus on race radically revises an initial feminist reading of the film's discordant gender moments—and the limited explanatory paradigms on which they rest. The film stands, in other words, as one complex instance of the relationship between race and gender in Depression-era U.S. culture and as a testing ground for the feminist theory that would seek to explain such relationships.

The complexity of these relations, moreover, both responds to and comments critically upon directions in feminist film theory. Recent feminist criticism of the horror film, like feminist film theory generally, has developed powerful psychoanalytic interpretations, focusing, for example, on the explanatory force of male anxieties about castration and about the maternal body.[5] Although such readings are useful, they often lack historical specificity and can be inattentive to what Paula Rabinowitz has recently termed "the relationships between the intrapsychic process of subjectivity and the social formations of sex, gender, class, and race."[6] The following reading of *Bride of Frankenstein* takes as its central contention the interdependence of these social formations and, in so doing, attempts to dislodge feminist film theory's myopic focus upon the white male gaze and spectator. For the axes of gender and race crosscut each other by the film's end, suggesting an ideological complexity with important implications for our understanding of both film and feminism.

Given the many versions of the Frankenstein story, it may be useful to begin with a discussion of *Bride of Frankenstein* and its textual parents. In Mary

The creature (Boris Karloff) attacks the scientist's bride (Mae Clarke) in *Frankenstein* (1931).

Shelley's 1818 novel *Frankenstein,* several speakers relate the disastrous relationship between an ambitious young scientist, Victor Frankenstein, and his unnamed, monstrous creation. After a series of murders by the monster, the book ends with the death of Frankenstein, and possibly of the monster, near the North Pole. Whale's first Frankenstein film, *Frankenstein* (1931), simplifies this plot, focusing on the moment of the monster's creation, his murder of a child, his attack upon the scientist's bride, Elizabeth, and his death in a fire; in contrast to the ending of the book, here the scientist and his bride emerge unscathed.

A sequel to the earlier film, *Bride of Frankenstein* draws upon another episode in the Shelley novel, that of the creation of a female mate for the monster. *Bride of Frankenstein* opens with a framing device, a discussion among Lord Byron, Percy Bysshe Shelley, and Mary Shelley about the Frankenstein story. To orient new viewers, the character of Mary Shelley summarizes the plot of the first film, but with an important revision: rather than perishing in the mill burning that concluded the previous film, the monster (Boris Karloff), it seems, is still alive. The film then segues into its new story, in which the monster wanders the countryside. Pursued by a group of angry townspeople, he is caught and imprisoned. Escaping, he finds solace with a blind hermit who plays music and teaches him to speak, but he is again discovered and must flee for his life.

Meanwhile, Dr. Frankenstein (Colin Clive), happily reunited with Elizabeth (Valerie Hobson), falls under the spell of his former teacher, Dr. Praetorius (Ernest Thesiger), who wants to create a female mate for the monster but needs the expertise of Frankenstein (now renamed Henry). The two stories intersect when Dr. Praetorius encounters the monster in a crypt, where the doctor is grave-robbing for his experiments, and the monster is hiding from the crowd. Praetorius instructs the monster to abduct Elizabeth, after which Henry, fearing for her safety, lends his skills to the scientific project. The climax of the film is a creation scene in which the two men bring a female form to life. After animation, however, the bride (Elsa Lanchester) recoils from the monster's advances; he, in rage and despair, blows up the castle, himself, Dr. Praetorius, and the bride. Alone among the film's characters, Henry and Elizabeth escape, and they look tearfully back upon the exploding castle in the film's final moment.[7]

What gender arrangements underlie this plot? Its original source, Mary Shelley's *Frankenstein,* has been one of the proof-texts for contemporary feminist literary criticism, with various interpretations focusing, for example, on the novel's complex thematics of maternity, its self-reflexive commentary upon female language and authorship, and its implicit evocation of the relation between gender and imperialism.[8] We may begin to untangle the role of gender in Whale's film by turning to one of the many feminist approaches to the novel, Mary Jacobus's "Is There a Woman in This Text?" which concentrates on the moment in Shelley's *Frankenstein* in which the male scientist and his male creature argue over the creation of a female monster. Jacobus reads this scene—from which the plot of *Bride of Frankenstein* will emerge and expand—as dependent on an asymmetrical gender triangle constituted by a woman and two rivalrous men. Locating this triangle model in relation to Freud, as both an evocation and a critique of Oedipal rivalry, she suggests that it "characteristically invokes its third (female) term only in the interests of the original rivalry and works finally to get rid of the woman."[9]

An initial look at *Bride of Frankenstein* confirms the salience of this model, for the film—which Jacobus touches on briefly—repeatedly stages gender as a disappearing act, whereby once two men are together, the lady vanishes.[10] From the first, Dr. Praetorius acts as the elder figure of authority to whom Henry is involuntarily drawn, in a rivalrous relation that is founded, and continually dependent, on the exclusion of Elizabeth. When Dr. Praetorius first arrives at the Frankenstein manor, Henry and Elizabeth are tearfully huddled together on Henry's bed; Henry asks Elizabeth to leave the room, and a long shot charts her disappearance from the frame as the two men embark on their conversation. In the next scene, the two men retire to Dr. Praetorius's chambers—"You must see *my* creation," Dr. Praetorius exhorts—leaving Elizabeth behind entirely. Once they are there, women become merely the hypothetical term of a future undertaking, as Dr. Praetorius urges that "together, we create his mate." Later, after Elizabeth has been kidnapped at Dr. Praetorius's instructions, he allows Henry to telephone her. Again, Elizabeth only appears in order to disappear, for what the camera marks as salient about the scene is the two men clustered together at the mouthpiece.

Disembodying women metaphorically, the film also dismembers them literally, as the narrative of the bride's creation graphically demonstrates. When Dr. Praetorius and his ghoulish assistant go grave-robbing, the camera shows two male figures suspended above a female corpse; later, Praetorius and Frankenstein begin their experiment by conversing over a female heart in a jar. All this is preparation for the film's climactic scene, in which the two scientists animate the female monster; at this moment, the camera frames them in medium shot on opposite sides of her mute, bandaged form. Reading this moment against the first scene between Henry and Praetorius, we can see that the bride's appearance fills the same function, structurally, as Elizabeth's earlier disappearance. Both are silent catalysts for the furthering of relations between the film's male protagonists, with the bride providing a more visceral example, different in degree but not in kind, of the treatment of Elizabeth.

Indeed, for all the apparent contrast between them, Elizabeth and the monster's mate are two of the film's female doubles—a twinning that the very title of the film ambiguously encodes.[11] For just who is the bride of Frankenstein? Frankenstein, of course, is Henry's surname, and *his* bride is Elizabeth; indeed, because it is not clear exactly when in the film the two marry, Elizabeth is perpetually Frankenstein's bride.[12] Yet in the creation scene, Praetorius triumphantly baptizes the female monster as "the Bride of Frankenstein." There are, then, not one but two brides of Frankenstein—or perhaps even more than two, for the film's title phrase, "bride of Frankenstein," omits the definite article, as if to suggest the endless repeatability of this most common female role.

The relation between Elizabeth and the bride in turn forms part of a broader circulation of female roles in *Bride of Frankenstein,* because, as the film's audience was well aware, the actress Elsa Lanchester plays both bride and Mary Shelley.[13] In the film's first scene, Lanchester as Mary Shelley sits demurely on a drawing-room couch, embroidering carefully, dressed in a long, white gown, and flanked by her husband, Percy Shelley, and Lord Byron. Her angelic persona serves contradictorily both to promote and to defuse her narrating powers; she occupies the important position of author, but here only as the conduit for a story passing between two men. Lanchester's later appearance extends the assumption of powerlessness that underlies this position, as the bride lies mute between a second pair of men, Praetorius and Frankenstein. She who seemed ostensibly to be the creator, Mary Shelley, is, at the end, reduced to man's creation; she, too, is "of Frankenstein," if not his wifely property then his artistic and scientific achievement. In the film's gender system, Mary Shelley, Elsa Lanchester, Elizabeth Frankenstein, and the monster's mate are all Mrs. Frankenstein. And as the maleness of the marital patronymic suggests, this is a role in which women become not only interchangeable but no one at all.

This analysis of the film's gender dynamics considerably expands the explanatory rubric of Oedipal rivalry with which we began, for it suggests that *Bride of Frankenstein* offers not only a psychoanalytic paradigm of male rivalry and female erasure but also the performance of a more capacious and complex system of gender exchange. Indeed, the film's gender triangles as we have traced them suggest the continuing relevance of a founding model of contemporary gender theory, Gayle Rubin's formulation of the "traffic in women," in which the exchange of women, which is enacted in psychoanalytic modes, serves fundamentally to consolidate gendered social structures.[14] As we have seen, *Bride of Frankenstein* encodes such circulation on a variety of registers: the women within its plots pass between a series of husbands and monsters, disappearing and reappearing as they spill beyond the confines of an Oedipal triangle. As the film's title highlights, in a system of male exchange, women's identity is most fully marked by their value as commodities, their status as property—marital, scientific, creative, authorial—passing between men.

Yet *Bride of Frankenstein* also suggests the stresses under which the "traffic of women" itself operates. For although the film triangulates and traffics in its women, its narrative also gestures toward a series of challenges implicit within this gender paradigm. We may begin to locate these sites of contradiction by returning to the film's title, which not only marks the instability of the term "bride" but also highlights the ambiguity of *male* identity within the film, for "Frankenstein"—in Shelley's novel, the name of the doctor—here signifies both scientist and monster. If this slippage among male names suggests generally that male identity in the story is unfixed, then a second look at the film's opening tableau provides a fuller set of clues to the complexities of the film's presentation of men. At times during this scene, the camera frames Mary Shelley between her husband and Lord Byron, enacting in visual terms her intermediate status between them. Yet at other moments the triangle is reconfigured visually, when the camera separates Mary Shelley off to one side and focuses on the two men; in these shots, Lord Byron leans against Percy Shelley with his arm draped over the other man's shoulder. This opening sequence offers a suggestive frame for the workings of the film's gender triangles, as it oscillates between an overt mode of female exchange and the implicit homo-erotic connections that, with a new focus of the camera lens, can be seen to underlie it. The scene suggests, in short, that in order to assess the contradictions within the film's presentation of gender, we will need to attend more closely to what it is that might pass sexually between men.

In work that builds on Gayle Rubin's, Eve Kosofsky Sedgwick has argued that, in patriarchal culture, sexual ideology must negotiate uneasily between two very similar arrangements: homosociality, the constant affirmation of shared interests between men, which, in a patriarchal society, works to consolidate male power; and homosexuality, the overt, erotic expression of sexual desire between men, which is of great subversive potential within such a system and therefore must, by its logic, be brutally suppressed. Women serve, then, not merely as a medium of exchange in the homosocial system but also as a desperate cover-up, a means of channeling suspicion of homosexuality into heterosexual appearances. In such a homophobic culture, any threat of exposing the potential homoeroticism that underlies male homosociality constitutes a challenge to the whole system of exchange.[15]

If *Bride of Frankenstein*'s opening presentation of Byron and Percy Shelley helps to highlight this threat, within the film's Frankenstein plot, each successive gender triangle is even less stable and suggests a progressive falling away from an "acceptable" homosociality into an overt homosexuality. We have already seen how Dr. Praetorius's arrival activates a scene of male rivalry with Dr. Frankenstein. But the moment also serves to consolidate a sexualized relation between the two men: Praetorius is, after all, enticing Henry away from his marital bed and inviting him to his own apartment. If Praetorius is Henry's rival as scientist, that is, he is also Elizabeth's rival as lover. Moreover, Praetorius's physical appearance and behavior are ambiguously marked; film historian Vito Russo argues that the character appears "odd, sissified," and carries connotations of homosexuality.[16] We may locate this "oddness" more precisely in the stereotypically gay attributes of a later scene, when Praetorius is shown dining alone in a crypt with a skull set before him, a bottle of wine next to him, a long cigarette in his hand, and an insouciant expression on his face. At this moment, the doctor appears in the visually coded form, here rendered campily, of the homosexual as decadent aristocrat.

Like Praetorius, the monster stands outside of normative male sexuality, but his form of male sexual "confusion" has far more serious consequences for the film's gender triangles. The monster, like the cultural stereotype of the homosexual man, is an "unnatural" creation, an analogy to which the film gives form in significant ways.[17] When the monster learns to speak, for example, he indiscriminately links the word "friend"—his only term for an affective bond—with the hermit who first befriends him; then, in the scene just discussed, with Dr. Praetorius; and finally with his future female mate. He has no innate understanding that the male-female bond he is to forge with the bride is assumed to be primary or that it carries a different sexual valence from his relationships with the two men: all affective relationships, with women and men, are as easily "friendships" as "marriages."

In the face of such sexual instability, the film struggles to reassert heterosexual ideology anew, most pointedly in the final creation scene. The imagery of this birth scene is specifically and hyperbolically phallic, from the long shaft that elevates the bride to the roof, where she will receive lightning conducted from the storm raging outside; to the men's excited shouts of "It's coming up" as she is raised; and finally to the orgasmic quality of the lightning hitting the bed. The camera work, which Albert J. LaValley terms "extravagant, almost unhinged," lends an air of manic instability to the proceedings.[18] For the first time, Praetorius and Frankenstein are framed not with a level camera but in diagonal medium shots; rapid crosscutting from shaft to body to men further disorients the eye, as if to confirm formally the volatility of the film's presentation of gender. At this point, in short, the creation of the female form is essential to quiet what are increasingly unfixed gender designations.

In this context, the bride's rejection of the monster has disastrous repercussions. When the bride first comes to life, she stands neatly flanked by the two men: the covertly homosocial, rather than overtly homosexual, order seems restored, and she need only acquiesce to the monster's (heterosexual) invitation. But instead, she recoils from his advances, shrieking not once but twice. At the bride's second rejection, she actually falls out of the left-hand side of the frame, as if her act is so chaotic as to destabilize the camera itself. Given this catastrophic rejection, the monster's insistence that he and Praetorius die together marks the recognition that at least two of the male identities in the film cannot be reconstituted for normative heterosexuality. To be sure, order is nominally restored at the film's end: it is the heterosexual couple, Elizabeth and Henry, who remain alive. But given the instability that has preceded their happy coupling, it is doubtful that the system as a whole now looks so smooth; at the very least, the violence with which such eruptions must be suppressed has been exposed. As D. A. Miller argues in reference to the sensation novel: "Reconstituted in a 'sensational' account of its genesis, [a heterosexual] norm

Bride of Frankenstein (1935): the bride (Elsa Lanchester) flanked by the men.

risks appearing *monstrous:* as aberrant as any of the abnormal conditions that determine its realization." [19]

If the bride's rejection of the monster forms the climax to the film's narrative of homosociality, it also signals a key reversal in *Bride of Frankenstein*'s presentation of female powerlessness. At first glance, the female monster seems to behave in a manner fully congruent with the female passivity that the "traffic in women" demands. As Karen F. Hollinger describes, "She clings submissively to Henry Frankenstein, is terrified of the male monster . . . and seems created only to act as the ultimate victim for the male monster's final demonstration of power." [20] Yet the bride's apparent passivity is, in fact, a compensatory behavioral cover for what her very presence suggests: that she stands as an index of male anxiety about, rather than indifference to, women and their bodies. After all, the bride's composite female form translates the idea of the social construction of woman into an essentialist nightmare, whereby women are *literally* constructed, assembled horrifically from female body parts. The violence of this process suggests that beneath the film's fantasy of male parthenogenesis, there is something in whole female bodies to be feared, which Hollinger identifies as "the underlying threat of female sexuality and of the power of sexual difference that shapes it."[21] Despite her secondary status as a creature of male fantasy, the monster betrays the fear that all female bodies are in fact unspeakably monstrous—and in this monstrosity, unspeakably powerful.[22]

If such an analysis provides the bride with only the most indirect agency, as a demonized figure of repressed sexual power, then the moment when she first refuses the monster stands as a more overt instance of female authority. As Jacobus notes, this moment is one of sexual autonomy, as the bride refuses "to mate in the image in which she was made."[23] Moreover, in the film's imagery of doubling, whereby the bride consistently represents a more extreme version of Elizabeth, her shrieks enact an inchoate refusal of the female coming-of-age narrative that the other woman has assumed—a narrative conveniently telescoped, in the bride's case, to the only two events deemed essential for women: birth and marriage. Finally, we should note that when the bride just says no to being the monster's first lady, her rejection is significant specifically as an act of speech—one whose authority is implicitly twinned, via the double casting of Elsa Lanchester, with the authorship of Mary Shelley. After all, Shelley, who not only speaks but writes, sets the story in motion with a female signature. Reading backward, we can see Mary's opening words as forming the story that gives voice to the bride's scream; reading forward, we can see the bride's scream as the most visceral and impassioned version of the "angelic" Mary's story. Together, that is, the bride's scream and Mary's speech offer a rejection of the systems of circulation that would disembody, dismember, exchange, and erase them in a moment—suggested only to be suppressed—when the female goods get together and refuse to go to market.[24]

Gender relations in *Bride of Frankenstein,* I have argued thus far, are simultaneously conventional and disruptive. The film at first seems to stress a rigidly restrictive paradigm in which women pass interchangeably between men. At the same time, however, the narrative hints at two implicit fissures in this theoretical ground, through its presentation of the homoeroticism that guides its male characters and of the monstrous power that informs the bride's shriek of refusal.[25] This reading of the film renders dynamic certain features of feminist theory, suggesting the interrelation between psychic and structuralist models of gender exchange, between issues of gender and sexuality, and between female powerlessness and female agency. What we now need to ask, however, is how these theoretical paradigms operate in precise relation to *Bride of Frankenstein*'s particular cultural moment of the mid-1930s. How can we read this film historically—and how, in turn, will a historical reading of *Bride of Franken-stein* revise our initial assessment of the film?

First, recent assessments of the 1930s suggest that the era resists any easy initial characterization in terms of both gender and sexuality. On the one hand, despite the massive social effects of the Depression, the period seems not to have brought significant disruptions of conventional gender arrangements; as Susan Ware suggests, the roots of the Feminine Mystique of the 1940s and 1950s are clearly visible in the preceding decade.[26] Yet the decade did see some gradual changes in women's status, including continued entry into the labor market, participation in a variety of political movements, and some visibility at high levels of government.[27] Yet if relations between genders were fundamentally unchanging during the era, relations within genders were slowly altering in terms of the ideological construction of same-sex desire. John D'Emilio and Estelle Freedman suggest that in the 1920s and 1930s, discussion of homosexuality was taking new, and newly anxious, forms. In this period, a variety of discursive forms—books like *The Well of Loneliness,* blues songs like "Sissy Man" and "Bull Dagger Woman," the psychiatric language of "inversion"—brought the newly "invented" category of "the homosexual" to the public eye from a variety of perspectives. Even as scientific definitions codified homosexuality in strictly negative and punitive terms, other modes, like the blues song, offered a more diverse sexual vocabulary. As D'Emilio and Freedman put it, "The resources for naming homosexual desire slowly expanded."[28]

What was the relation of film to this ambiguous social matrix of gender and sexuality? The 1930s were famously a "golden age" for Hollywood, not only in film's new formal sophistication or its popularity with Depression audiences but also, for women, in its on-screen presentation of strong female actresses like Katherine Hepburn, Bette Davis, and Rosalind Russell. As Ware interprets it, such stars and the roles they played both reflected and fostered new images of women in the culture at large, in a constitutive model of culture that we may apply similarly to *Bride of Frankenstein,* despite its apparent distance from lived gender relations.[29] Reading allegorically, we can see the film's systems of exchange as schematic, if parodic, representations of the most conventional workings of gender in the era; its almost—but not quite—total suppression of female agency, meanwhile, acts as commentary upon the very real anxieties about the role of women in the 1930s. Finally, the homoeroticism of the film's plots similarly echoes and shapes contemporary images of masculinity, with the male creature literally incarnating the monstrous connotations of homosexual "inversion."

If such an interpretation can only proceed metaphorically, with the film allegorizing the tensions of its era, then the history of *Bride of Frankenstein* as an artifact of mass culture offers more specific connections between the work and its cultural moment. *Bride of Frankenstein* was made five years after the establishment of the infamous Hollywood Production Code and less than a year after Will Hays, responding to public pressure, created the Production Code Administration to enforce it. Because the first *Frankenstein* had already been the subject of a bitter censorship battle over its goriness, the makers of *Bride of Frankenstein* were undoubtedly aware of the need to restrain overt displays of brutality and violence—as well as of sexuality, adultery, and anything that threatened the so-called sanctity of marriage and the home.[30] In this context, then, we can understand the film to be battling against a specific and highly publicized set of constraints that sharply delimited representational possibilities for both horror and gender.

As the film is in tension with the overt gender prescriptions of the Production Code, so too the history of *Bride of Frankenstein*'s prerelease editing hints at its negotiation of contemporary gender norms. In addition to customary editing, the film went through a substantial last-minute cut after being shown briefly in previews. It was trimmed at this point from ninety to seventy-five minutes, and among the later changes was the omission of a grim scene in which Praetorius experiments on a live woman, dissecting her until she awakens and screams for mercy. The ending was also altered at the last minute to omit the suggestion, present in the film's final shooting script, that the female monster's heart might be that of Elizabeth.[31] The question of the filmmakers' intentions in making such changes aside, we may infer that the omitted material would have made too explicit the brutal asymmetry of power relations between the sexes. Had the film even briefly suggested that the bride's heart came from Elizabeth, for example, it might have exposed the fragility of the romantic fiction cloaking the "traffic in women." Indeed, such a suggestion would have implied that the customary emotional danger of romance—a woman's broken heart—might be the visceral, literal result of association with men.

If we turn from the history of the film's production to that of its consumption, a related series of social concerns, involving normative masculinity, come into view. *The New Republic,* for example, in favorably comparing *Bride of Frankenstein* with *The Cabinet of Dr. Caligari* (1919), praised its art as the kind "that gives the healthy feeling of men with their sleeves rolled up and working, worrying only about how to put the thing over in the best manner of the medium—no time for nonsense and attitudes and long hair."[32] Here the film's art is ostensibly rescued from an effeminized realm—obliquely rendered as "attitudes and long hair"—and reclaimed, strenuously, for the terrain of real men, those who work "with their sleeves rolled up." Yet in the light of the film's homoeroticism—and particularly, given Praetorius, its aesthetics of decadence—this assertion of normative masculinity appears rather anxious, as though the review claims the film's "maleness" not in spite of but because of considerable evidence to the contrary. A second example, from *Time*'s April 1935 review of the film, further emphasizes the link between *Bride of Frankenstein* and contemporary sexual ideology as it affected both women and men: "In private life also Miss Lanchester is the wife of Henry VIII (Charles Laughton). Although he is known for his plump effeminacy, she is mannish in dress."[33] Here, a compulsion to spot real-life "inversions" (the effeminate man, the mannish woman) coincides with commentary upon a film about monstrous creatures with "unnatural" desires. In fact, we need only look at the story of James Whale to note the proximity of the film's themes to its era, for according to Vito Russo, Whale was ostracized professionally for being openly gay in homophobic Hollywood. Whale's directorial signature reminds us not only of the historical link between camp sensibility and gay male culture but also of the explicit social consequences of being perceived as sexually "unnatural." In the film's negotiation of contemporary sexual ideologies, the realities of the Gothic could be as distant as its parodically Romantic, mittel-Europa setting—or as close as the editor's scissors, the reviewer's pen, or the director's chair.[34]

This reading of *Bride of Frankenstein*'s historicity, which suggests the film's mediation of gender norms and anxieties in the 1930s, is, however, itself incomplete, for it treats gender in isolation from other social phenomena of the 1930s, particularly the volatile and contested ground of U.S. race relations. If gender and sexuality were only implicitly in flux during this era, the Depression's impact on race relations was immediately felt in at least one arena—that of lynching. The first half of the decade saw an increase in the lynching of black men. The well-known Scottsboro case (1931), in which an all-white Southern jury sentenced a group of young black men to death for allegedly raping two white women, offered a legally sanctioned version of the tradition in which black men were brutally murdered for their supposed crimes against whites. Antilynching activist Jessie Daniel Ames suggested in a 1942 report that lynching in the early 1930s was distinguished not only by its frequency but also by the barbaric nature of the individual crimes. Although such crimes were vigorously protested by black activists as well as by some white liberals, such protests were often thwarted. In 1934, for example, the NAACP renewed its long-term lobbying for a national antilynching bill, but the bill was defeated the following year, 1935—the year, that is, of *Bride of Frankenstein*'s release.[35]

Moreover, the representation of race in film was itself a highly contested issue throughout the 1930s. The decade was framed by the release of films that featured black characters in demeaning stereotypes, from *Hearts of Dixie* (1929), which introduced the figure of Stepin Fetchit, to *Gone with the Wind* (1939), whose black characters formed a nostalgic romanticization of "happy slaves" in the antebellum South. Other films with black characters—*Hallelujah* (1929), *Imitation of Life* (1934), *So Red the Rose* (1935), *Green Pastures* (1936), *Prisoner of Staten Island* (1936)—also caricatured black life, and the period as a whole has been characterized as the era offering only servant roles for black actors.[36] But black writers and activists consistently fought against such images, not only challenging the showing of overtly racist films—like D. W. Griffith's epic, *The Birth of a Nation* (1915), which underwent a mid-decade revival— but also influencing the production of films. The NAACP was able to temper some of the more egregious racial content of *Gone with the Wind* during filming; the film also met with black protest upon its release.[37] Hollywood filmmakers also nervously accommodated conservative standards for the representation of race: battle scenes between blacks and whites in *Rhodes of Africa* (1935), for example, were cut so as to minimize direct racial confrontations, and the liberalism of the antilynching film *Fury* (1936) was tempered by a focus on a white victim.[38] Such self-censorship against both Left and Right suggests that the apparent uniformity of black servant roles on screen in fact served as an ideological screen for the volatility of Depression-era race relations.

Given this contemporary struggle over both lived and filmic race relations, *Bride of Frankenstein*'s monster takes on new significance as a creature marked not only by an undifferentiated "otherness" but also specifically by behavioral and visual codes associated with blackness. In a 1944 article on images of black men in film, Lawrence Reddick cited the stereotypes of irresponsible citizen, social delinquent, vicious criminal, and mental inferior.[39] Within this cluster of stereotypes, one—that of the black "brute"—carried particular force, perhaps because it exposed the fears domesticated by valorizing the figure of the black servant. From *Birth of a Nation* onward, as Donald F. Bogle describes, black men were depicted as "subhuman and feral . . . nameless characters setting out on a rampage full of black rage."[40] Delinquency, criminality, inferiority, subhumanity—these attributes fully converge in *Bride of Frankenstein*'s monster. Indeed, in an era when Hollywood hesitated to depict black characters committing violence, the film's monster—for all his apparent distance from "reality"—may more fully emblematize the iconography of U.S. racism than any other film, more openly mimetic, could have in this era.

If the monster's behavior implicitly links criminality with contemporary images of black violence, so too does his physical appearance gather force from racist stereotypes. His large, black-clad, awkward form embodies the racist association of blackness with subhumanity, as does his facial appearance, which makeup artist Jack Pierce apparently designed "to give the monster a primitive, Neanderthal appearance" by sloping "the brow of the eyes in a pronounced ape-like ridge of bone."[41] This confluence of racist stereotypes appears elsewhere in films of this era, for we might think of the monster as cousin to that most famous of demonized movie characters, the one who not only appears "ape-like," but in the form of an actual ape: King Kong, who became, as Thomas Cripps puts it, "a mythic figure, part 'bad nigger' and part universal victim of exploitation."[42]

In *Bride of Frankenstein*, too, the monster appears as victim, in this case as a fugitive whose repeated escapes from mob pursuit resonate with contemporary accounts of lynching. The first Whale *Frankenstein* film concludes with an extended sequence about the monster's flight from a crowd of angry townspeople, whose pursuit of him is figured with all the visual markers—barking dogs, fiery torches, angry shouts—of a lynch mob. *Bride of Frankenstein* confirms and extends the force of this imagery, presenting the monster in a condition of continual flight from a murderous mob. Captured partway into the film, he is strung up on a tree as an angry cluster of men surrounds him. This visual moment is so shockingly reminiscent of the imagery of lynching that, as with the monster's "blackness," the film here radically rewrites boundaries between the "fantasy" of horror film and the "realism" of other cinematic genres. Indeed, *Bride of Frankenstein* is able to take up contemporary racism not despite its Gothicism but by virtue of it. In contrast to films like *Fury,* whose obvious topicality set sharp limits on their content, it may be that *Bride of Frankenstein* could articulate a lynching plot more vividly through fantasy than could be represented through realism.

The generic conventions of film horror in fact provide unusual insight into lynching, as the film suggests in its presentation of the metaphorics of monstrosity. Not only does the pursuit of the monster suggest a lynching narrative, but the very composition of his body offers a grisly echo of the consequences of lynching. Composed of the mutilated and dismembered parts of corpses, the monster emblematizes the frequent mutilation and dismemberment of lynching victims. That the monster's parts were stolen from graves emphasizes this connection, for the corpses of lynching victims were similarly desecrated, as in the case of George Armwood, who "was mauled and mutilated before he was lynched . . . and whose body was then burned and further desecrated." Continuing with the news that "whatever fragments of his corpse remained in his coffin may have been dug up," this newspaper story offers a plot whose ending—dismemberment—is the monster's own beginning.[43]

Finally, another newspaper report of lynching from the same era suggests an uncomfortable circulation between horror films and acts of lynching as viewer "spectacles": "The lynching site was located across the street from a picture show where a horror film was playing. A number of women emerging from the theater saw the Negro hanging from the tree and fainted."[44] This account literalizes the close connection between the movie theater and the setting for lynching, which physically neighbor each other as they offer similar sights of terror. In its evocation of the connection between U.S. racism and Gothic monstrosity, *Bride of Frankenstein* manifestly participates in this representational slippage. Even as it dilutes its horror with comedy and situates it in a zone of apparent "fantasy," the film yet more strongly invokes— indeed, has more license to invoke—the imagery, narrative, and formal conventions of contemporary U.S. lynching.[45]

Keeping in mind this link between the horror of lynching and the horror of the monster movie, we can read *Bride of Frankenstein* initially as intervening in lynching discourse in order to present the plight of the monster sympathetically. Counterposed to the unjust pursuit by the frightening lynch mob are the actions of the kind hermit, blind to the monster's appearance, who teaches him language, literally enacting "color-blind" liberalism. Such sympathy further emerges in the iconography of Christian martyrdom that surrounds the monster throughout the film. When the old man comforts the monster to sleep, a crucifix remains brightly lit above their heads even after the shot fades to black. With the monster recognizably coded as a black fugitive, this religious symbolism translates, via *Uncle Tom's Cabin,* into the Christian abolitionist narrative of slave humanity, misery, and redemption.

If the monster is figured sympathetically as a martyred black fugitive, he is also, however, a *male* fugitive, a gendering that transforms both his character and the film as a whole. In the history of U.S. race relations, lynching was commonly connected with fraudulent rape charges, a false charge that formed, in Angela Davis's words, "one of the most formidable artifices invented by racism."[46] In the racist iconography that sustained such accusations, the most common cultural image was that of a black man, "a monstrous beast, crazed with lust," assaulting a white woman.[47] As Jacqueline Dowd Hall has shown, such accusations not only imprisoned white and black women in sexual stereotypes but also served as a powerful means of controlling black men, who were mutilated and killed in the thousands of lynchings following the end of the Civil War.[48]

By the 1930s, the myth of the black rapist so permeated Hollywood film that the explicit representation of rape—something the Production Code in any case severely restricted—was not required in order for its ideological threat to be registered. Again, *King Kong* provides one version of this over-determined racist cultural fantasy, in the film's memorable image of the fair, blonde Fay Wray dangling helplessly in the brutish paw of the dark male gorilla.[49] In the logic of racial representation, the very explicitness of this image seems enabled by the film's extreme distance from mimesis, its adherence to the safely nonrealist fantasy of science fiction. By contrast, in films set closer to home, the proximity of U.S. racism presumably proscribed such explicitness, even as it made the imagery of interracial rape yet more available on the slimmest of connotations. In *Gone with the Wind,* for example, as Sedgwick has noted, the scene in which an ex-slave attempts to rob Scarlett depends for its effect on the imagery of rape.[50]

Bridging the ideologically explicit fantasies of *King Kong* and the more muted historical "realism" of *Gone with the Wind,* both *Bride of Frankenstein* and its predecessor, Whale's *Frankenstein,* bear the traces of the racist connection in U.S. culture between race and rape. In one sequence in the earlier film, the monster enters Elizabeth's room on her wedding night and corners her behind the locked door; the camera cuts away to the other people in the house hearing her screams. When they break into her room, her white dress is disheveled and she lies across one corner of the rumpled bed moaning desperately, "Don't let it come here." Although the monster's crime is officially the penetration of the room, not the woman, his actions are framed precisely according to the stereotype of interracial rape. The next scene of the film implicitly realizes the disastrous consequences of such rape, when an angry young father displays to the crowd the body of his little girl, whom the monster has killed by accident. Reading these two scenes together, it is as though the body of the girl, utterly victimized and now dead, metaphorizes the fatal effects for white women of contact with black men. By the end of this sequence, the black man has become the archetypal rapist. If not actually dead, the white woman is, as Hall puts it, "the quintessential Woman as Victim: polluted, 'ruined for life,' the object of fantasy and secret contempt."[51]

Bride of Frankenstein deploys this powerful stereotype of interracial rape through its narrative. The monster's resuscitation of a drowning girl appears, to the two men who come upon him, as an imminent sexual violation, as does his abduction of Elizabeth while she is resting in her bedroom. Again, the scenes do not require explicit sexual content for the overdetermined imagery of interracial rape to take hold, for as Valerie Smith notes, "The fiction of a black male perpetrator automatically [sexualizes] a nonsexual crime."[52] But the perpetrator, in this case, is also a victim, in an overlay of iconographic forms—rapist and martyr—that sets the film in conflict with itself. Indeed, in both Frankenstein films, the monster embodies a paradox, the sympathetic lynch-mob target who is also, possibly, a demonic rapist. But because the monster's status as innocent victim is transformed if he seems to pose a "genuine" sexual threat, ultimately the force of this second, gendered metaphoric persona—black male rapist—is so great that it overrides the first, undercutting any claims to compassion.

In this context, relations between the monster and other men, and between the bride and the monster, require rereading. Because cultural stereotypes of interracial rape presumed female victims and male attackers, the film's insistence upon the monster as would-be rapist serves to highlight his heterosexuality and consequently to alter the terms of his involvement in the film's homoeroticism. As male, the monster is allowed into some of the homoerotic bonds that are determined through the exclusion of women, particularly those with Praetorius; indeed, with his indiscriminate "friends," his inability to grasp normative gender codes, the monster manifests this homoeroticism too overtly for the stability of the film's sexual plots. As a *black* man, however, the monster is also, contradictorily, defined against these same men as a figure of monstrous heterosexuality. And having incarnated both these threats—the excessively homoerotic white man and the excessively heterosexual black man—the monster's presence is too explosive for him to survive. Hence he effects the explosion that closes the film, a suicidal act that literalizes the self-canceling effects of embodying sexual and racial contradictions.

The racial coding of the bride as white victim works similarly to undermine previous interpretations, for it recasts what incipient subjectivity we might have identified in her—as monstrous, sexual nay-sayer—in racial terms. She seems clearly to be figured as "white": her skin is very fair, she is dressed in a long white gown similar to those worn by both Mary Shelley and Elizabeth, and her physical gestures echo visually the repulsion felt by Elizabeth in both films' protorape scenes. Given this racial costuming, the bride's shrieks take on new meaning. Not simply a plea for female subjectivity or a revelation of a homosocial dynamic, they metaphorically encode a rejection by the white woman of the black man's sexual advances. That is, in questioning the coercive power of the white man—and the homosocial bonds that ratify it—the bride also defines and flees the heterosexuality of the black man. In this context, moreover, the bride's death at the end of the film not only recalls but brings to fruition the sequence in the first *Frankenstein* film in which the monster's attack on Elizabeth is followed by the death of the little girl. For if Elizabeth herself survives, the fate of the monster's mate, like that of the little girl, more pointedly signals the underlying consequences for a white woman of being sullied—indeed, beneath the white dress, "blackened"—by contact with the black man, a degradation so great that it must lead to death.

A reading of *Bride of Frankenstein* through multiple historical frames, then, helps us to see that gender, sexuality, and race inextricably implicate one another in this film. Attention to the interdependent historical paradigms of race and gender relations shows that bonds between men in the film are located on two axes, sexual and racial, which contradict each other. Similarly, interracial rape here acts, as Smith has theorized, as a "border case" that splits potential allegiances between race and gender,[53] a splitting that means that the film's model of female identity can gain its authority only through a racist assertion of whiteness. In their very interdependence, moreover, the film's narratives of power relations are indelibly marked by contradiction rather than closure. Even though Henry and Elizabeth survive and the monsters die at the end of *Bride of Frankenstein,* this ending hardly resolves the film's knot of contradictions. Rather, in a film in which death is the precondition for life, we might take the destruction of the monster and his mate as a sign that they—like the ideological fears they incarnate—will have been dismembered here only to be remembered elsewhere, reanimated in life and animated on screen.

This reading of *Bride of Frankenstein,* as we can now summarize it, comments critically upon three related registers of feminist inquiry. First, in its stress upon the interdependence of power relations within the film, this interpretation confirms that a "gender reading" is not only incomplete but seriously inaccurate when gender, race, and sexuality are artificially separated from one another. Moreover, it is only when we see the contours of the horror genre as surprisingly "realistic," however nonmimetic, that the film's ideological narratives, including those of gender, come into view. Finally, this assessment of the film implicitly suggests that "theory" and "history" are mutually constitutive realms of inquiry, with race and gender operating simultaneously as theoretical paradigms and as historical frameworks. This interrelation between theory and history brings me, at last, to the question of feminist film theory. For *Bride of Frankenstein*'s narratives, as I have sketched them, not only amplify what have been the central concerns of feminist film theory—the meaning of the filmic gaze and of the act of spectatorship—but also radically restructure these concerns to suggest their historical contingency.

Following Laura Mulvey's groundbreaking article, "Visual Pleasure and

Narrative Cinema," feminist film theorists have suggested that narrative cinema is structured by the "male gaze," which both symbolizes and ratifies male power; in this voyeuristic system, which is constructed in psychoanalytic terms by castration anxiety, women merely "connote to-be-looked-at-ness."[54] *Bride of Frankenstein* rehearses such visual objectification throughout, with the camera enclosing each woman (Mary Shelley, Elizabeth, the bride) in an act of cinematic framing that enacts the film's narrative frame-up of women. Not simply a general rehearsal of the male gaze, however, the film suggests the particular congruence between the all-powerful roles of scientist and director. As Dr. Frankenstein constructs a human form, so too does the filmmaker, with the camera's gaze, create film narrative; women's bodies serve as sites of experiment for both figures. God, scientist, father and mother, Dr. Frankenstein's survival at the film's end thus mimics the continuing presence and ultimate power of the camera. In this triumph, he bespeaks what Constance Penley has explicated as cinema's desire to function as a "bachelor machine," an apparatus obsessed with, among other themes, voyeurism and reproduction. Reproducing life by animating corpses, Frankenstein is thus both camera and directorial eye—roles in which, as Penley describes it, the producer of the bachelor machine "submits to a fantasy of closure, perfectibility, and mastery."[55]

The idea of a "fantasy" of closure, however, suggests the permeability of this structure, and indeed, as the film destabilizes the "traffic in women," so too does it call into question the primacy of the male gaze. For the moment when the bride shrieks is also one in which she gazes: in the first moment of her creation, a close-up shows her looking directly back at the camera, disrupting the cinematic economy that usually presents women as objects *of* looking. In the context of film monstrosity, moreover, this look would seem to reverse what Linda Williams has identified as the visual crux of the cinematic confrontation between women and male monsters, namely a moment of doubled self-recognition, whereby what the woman sees is really her *own* monstrosity, reflected back, Medusa-like, in the figure of the monster.[56] Here, by contrast, because the figures of woman and monster are a priori collapsed into one another in the figure of a female monster, the bride's look may suggest a wry awareness of her own monstrosity, a suggestion that if women are, in the visual economy of the gaze, always already monsters, then at least the female monster can stare back. In other words, if, in the eye of the camera, the bride already looks *like* a monster, then at least she can look back, with transgressive force, *as* a monster.

This celebratory reading of the bride's gaze is however, premature, for—as with its gender narrative—the film's relation to the gaze, both male and fe-

The bride's horrified gaze in *Bride of Frankenstein.*

male, is racially coded as well. In its refraction of U.S. race relations, *Bride of Frankenstein*'s cinematic gaze frames and demotes the figure of the black man (the monster) as well as that of the white woman (Mary Shelley, Elizabeth, the bride). Our first glimpse of the monster, for example, is a close-up that fetishizes two body parts—his hand, disembodied, and then his gray, demonized face—before depicting his murder of an innocent villager. That is, the "bachelor machine" is also a color wheel: its punitive, self-authorizing control extends, in racial terms, over nonwhite as well as nonmale objects. But race does not simply *intensify* the gaze, making a "male gaze" an even more oppressive "white male gaze"; it alters it. For the monster's death, juxtaposed with Elizabeth's survival, seems to suggest that the camera's gaze can accommodate a white woman less anxiously—or to different effect—than a black man. Indeed, if we see the bride as Elizabeth's double, then it appears that the film's women, unlike its black man, can begin actively to reject the entrapment of the gaze, but only by asserting their racial "purity." With race as fulcrum, the bride's visual "No!" appears less subversive than sinister, for it confers upon her the agency of a monstrous gaze only at the expense of de-monizing—and ultimately helping to destroy—her monstrous mate.

This contradictory visual narrative has consequences for feminist film the-ory, not only because it specifies the parameters of the male gaze, but also be-cause it helps us to question the biases of film theory itself. For insofar as feminist film theory continues to rely on psychoanalytic categories, it will suffer from the limitations of their ahistoricity. As Jane Gaines puts it, film theory "based on the psychoanalytic concept of sexual difference . . . is unequipped to deal with a film which is about racial difference and sexual-ity."[57] *Bride of Frankenstein*'s unusually full rehearsal of the iconography of lynching and interracial rape also allows us to locate one specific factor in film theory's shortsightedness. For as Gaines notes, "In the context of race relations in U.S. history, sexual looking carries with it the threat of actual rather than symbolic castration."[58] As a film about the issues that surrounded castration in this era—race, rape, lynching—*Bride of Frankenstein* translates castration anx-iety from a metaphorical register of the cinematic apparatus to a zero-degree reminder of the historical realities of U.S. racism. Rather than simply catalyz-ing the apparent mastery of the camera, castration anxiety in this film is also one of the material monsters—no less real for being rendered through the genre of horror—that undergirds its plot.

This same critical impasse between psychoanalytic and materialist explana-tory models also informs any claims we might make about this film and spec-tatorship. In recent years, feminist film critics have turned increasingly from film texts to film spectators, in part as an attempt to revise the static deter-minism of male-gaze formulations. This new emphasis on "the female spec-tator" has nonetheless continued to reproduce the same theoretical disjunc-ture between psychoanalytic models that metaphorize the act of spectatorship at the level of the individual, and historical models that materialize it at the level of the larger culture. As Jacqueline Bobo writes, "When the female spec-tator is usually spoken of and spoken for, the female in question is white and middle-class."[59]

How, by contrast, can we analyze *Bride of Frankenstein* with attention to what Linda Williams calls "the historical female spectator"?[60] We have seen how the bride's spectatorial moment undermines its subversive potential, not simply because it hovers too close to a visual reification of female monstros-ity—a conclusion we might reach through a psychoanalytic approach to male anxiety and visual fetishization—but more materially because of its relation to the iconography of race. For insofar as the bride's gaze posits a resisting fe-male spectator, that spectatorial community is divided by a color line rather than united by a gender bond. In the context of the 1930s, an era when theaters forced black moviegoers to sit in separate sections from whites or to come in by a back door, such a demarcation could well be absolutely literal. For those who were excluded from theaters that categorically refused to admit black viewers at all, racial rather than sexual difference might well provide the founding condition for an experience of film spectatorship—or the racist denial thereof. When black viewers did have full access to the film, the act of spectatorship was by no means homogeneous. Recounting her experiences viewing films such as *Gone with the Wind* and *Birth of a Nation,* for example, bell hooks has articulated a model of resisting spectatorship among black viewers: "Our gaze was not passive. The screen was not a place of escape. It was a place of confrontation and encounter."[61]

From the monolithic entrapment of the "male gaze" to the heterogeneity of the act of spectatorship, where, finally, does this discussion of *Bride of Frankenstein* leave feminist film theory? That film criticism's reliance upon psychoanalytic categories has constrained its theoretical models seems clear, for it is only when we translate the film's visual problematics to a more historical register that film theory can accommodate the complex interweaving of race and gender in this work. Whether psychoanalysis need *inevitably* function in this fashion, however, is less certain.[62] Historical and psychoanalytic conceptions of the way film gazes upon monsters might fruitfully critique each other. Indeed, in historicizing its premises and claims, feminist film theory might usefully contextualize psychoanalysis itself, as a narrative constituted in a particular historical era, not coincidentally almost the same moment as the founding of cinema itself. Whatever methodological strategies underpin it, the point is that without attention to the many forms of difference that structure films such as *Bride of Frankenstein,* feminist film theory risks, itself, becoming monstrous.

A scene early in *Bride of Frankenstein* shows Dr. Praetorius demonstrating to Frankenstein his failed experiments: a series of miniature people—king, queen, archbishop, mermaid, and so on—sealed in little glass jars. To Frankenstein, such figures are fantastically irrelevant. So too many forms of popular culture like the horror film, ostensibly antimimetic, appear: sealed-off toys, remote from history. Yet films like *Bride of Frankenstein* are deeply implicated in their historical moment, accommodating complex and contradictory narratives of gender, sexuality, and race. We might reread the politics of genre, then, to include horror as an important mediation of a variety of social tensions. We might, in turn, use such readings to interrogate feminist scholar-

ship—and particularly, in this case, feminist film theory—to ensure its continued attention to sexual difference as a complexly contingent and historicized
phenomenon, one whose contours often resist large claims, but instead must
be mapped on a terrain of shifting allegiances and conflicts with race and
other forms of difference.

If, finally, *Bride of Frankenstein* seems to reinforce many aspects of dominant U.S. culture, I would suggest that the story is still incomplete. For the plot
of Dr. Frankenstein and his monsters, rather than assuming any fixed representational form, is constantly being rewritten and reinvented, not only in
film but throughout popular culture.[63] And in this glut of Frankenstein stories, one man's monster—or one woman's bride—is another's occasion for
kitsch, parody, or camp. *Bride of Frankenstein*'s protean history as a cultural artifact suggests the ways in which visual pleasure in narrative cinema may, in
fact, be extraordinarily carnivalesque, participatory, and resistant to closure—
which is a lesson, finally, that the film itself helps to show us. After all, it is no
accident that the frame that opens *Bride of Frankenstein,* that of Mary Shelley's
conversation with Percy Shelley and Lord Byron, has no parallel scene at the
end of the film. If it is Mary Shelley who has the first word on the monster
and his mate, it is the film's spectators—heterogeneous and unbridled—who
have the last.

Notes

*I would like to thank William A. Cohen, Catherine Gallagher, Laura Green, Karen Jacobs,
Simone Davis Szamosi, and the editors of* Feminist Studies *for their assistance with various versions of this essay.*

1. For an introduction to the remarkable presence of the Frankenstein story in popular culture, see Donald F. Glut, *The Frankenstein Legend* (Metuchen, N.J.: Scarecrow
Press, 1973); and Glut, *The Frankenstein Catalog* (Jefferson, N.C.: McFarland, 1984). On
the history of Frankenstein plays and films, see Albert J. LaValley, "The Stage and Film
Children of *Frankenstein:* A Survey," and William Nestrick, "Coming to Life: *Franken-
stein* and the Nature of Film Narrative," both in *The Endurance of Frankenstein,* ed.
George Levine and U. C. Knoepflmacher (Berkeley: University of California Press,
1979), pp. 243–289 and 290–315, respectively; William K. Everson, *Classics of the Horror
Film* (Secaucus, N.J.: Citadel Press, 1974), pp. 36–61; and Steven Earl Forry, *Hideous
Progenies: Dramatizations of Frankenstein from Mary Shelley to the Present* (Philadelphia:
University of Pennsylvania Press, 1990).

2. Glut, *Frankenstein Legend,* p. 132; Radu N. Florescu, *In Search of Frankenstein*
(Boston: New York Graphic Society, 1975), p. 193; Chris Steinbrunner and Burt Gold-
blatt, *Cinema of the Fantastic* (New York: Saturday Review Press, 1972), p. 106.

3. Michael Brunas, John Brunas, and Tom Weaver, *Universal Horrors: The Studio's Classic Films, 1931–46* (Jefferson, N.C.: McFarland, 1990), p. 120.

4. Martin F. Norden, "Sexual References in James Whale's *Bride of Frankenstein*," in *Eros in the Mind's Eye: Sexuality and the Fantastic in Art and Film*, ed. Donald F. Palumbo (Westport, Conn.: Greenwood Press, 1986), p. 150.

5. See, for example, Karen F. Hollinger, "The Monster as Woman: Two Generations of Cat People," *Film Criticism* 13, no. 2 (Winter 1989): 36–46; Barbara Creed, "Horror and the Monstrous-Feminine: An Imaginary Abjection," *Screen* 27, no. 1 (January–February 1989): 44–70; and Linda Williams, "When the Woman Looks," in *Re-Vision: Essays in Feminist Film Criticism*, ed. Mary Ann Doane, Patricia Mellencamp, and Linda Williams (Frederick, Md.: University Publications of America/American Film Institute 1984), pp. 83–99. All three of these essays are reprinted in the present volume.

6. Paula Rabinowitz, "Seeing through the Gendered I: Feminist Film Theory," *Feminist Studies* 16, no. 1 (Spring 1990): 168.

7. For detailed summaries of *Frankenstein* and *Bride of Frankenstein*, see Brunas, Brunas, and Weaver, *Universal Horrors*, pp. 26–27 and 119–120.

8. For influential examples of these approaches, see respectively, Ellen Moers, *Literary Women* (New York: Doubleday, 1974), pp. 90–112; Sandra M. Gilbert and Sandra Gubar, *The Madwoman in the Attic: The Woman Writer and the Nineteenth-Century Literary Imagination* (New Haven: Yale University Press, 1979), pp. 213–247; and Gayatri Chakravorty Spivak, "Three Women's Texts and a Critique of Imperialism," *Critical Inquiry* 12, no. 1 (Autumn 1985): 243–261. For an overview of feminist criticism of *Frankenstein*, see Catherine Gallagher and Elizabeth Young, "Feminism and *Frankenstein*: A Short History of American Feminist Criticism," *Journal of Contemporary Thought* 1, no. 1 (1991): 97–109.

9. Mary Jacobus, "Is There a Woman in This Text?" *New Literary History* 14, no. 1 (Autumn 1982): 119.

10. Norden also identifies a series of triangles in the film involving two men and a woman. See "Sexual References," p. 141.

11. The film's working title until just before its release was *The Return of Frankenstein*, a hesitation due at least in part to the ambiguities of the title *Bride of Frankenstein*. See Everson, *Classics*, p. 45; and Brunas, Brunas, and Weaver, *Universal Horrors*, p. 119.

12. Everson attributes this confusion to the film's extensive last-minute reediting, which may have damaged continuity. See *Classics*, p. 45.

13. In Elsa Lanchester's words, "I think James Whale felt that if this beautiful and innocent Mary Shelley could write a horror story such as *Frankenstein*, then somewhere she must have had a fiend *within*." Quoted in Brunas, Brunas, and Weaver, *Universal Horrors*, p. 116.

14. Gayle Rubin, "The Traffic in Women: Notes toward a 'Political Economy' of Sex," in *Toward an Anthropology of Women*, ed. Rayne Rapp Reiter (New York: Monthly Review Press, 1975), pp. 157–210.

15. Eve Kosofsky Sedgwick, *Between Men: English Literature and Male Homosocial Desire* (New York: Monthly Review Press, 1985), esp. pp. 1–27.

16. Vito Russo, *The Celluloid Closet: Homosexuality in the Movies* (New York: Harper

& Row, 1981), p. 51. Norden also notes the connotations of Praetorius's homosexuality. See "Sexual References," p. 143.

17. Both Vito Russo and Robin Wood make a connection between monstrousness and sexual "unnaturalness." See Russo, *Celluloid Closet,* p. 49; and Wood, "An Introduction to the American Horror Film," in *Planks of Reason: Essays on the Horror Film,* ed. Barry Keith Grant (Metuchen, N.J.: Scarecrow Press, 1984), p. 172.

18. LaValley, "Children," p. 272.

19. D. A. Miller, "*Cage aux folles:* Sensation and Gender in *The Woman in White,*" *Representations* 14 (Spring 1986): 119.

20. Hollinger, "The Monster as Woman," p. 40.

21. Ibid., p. 45.

22. Other feminist film critics of the horror film specify that what is at issue in the genre is male anxiety about maternity. As Barbara Creed puts it, in the horror film "the maternal figure is constructed as the monstrous-feminine." See "Horror and the Monstrous-Feminine," p. 50; see also Williams, "When the Woman Looks," pp. 89–90. From Dr. Praetorius's boast to Henry that he grew his creatures "from seed" onward, *Bride of Frankenstein* indeed gives voice to a set of compensatory male strategies—those of Frankenstein, Praetorius, even the monster—for producing offspring. The fact that what the men produce is not another man but a woman suggests the difficulty of eliminating the figure of a woman altogether from this scenario of three men and a baby.

23. See Jacobus, "Is There a Woman in This Text?" p. 135.

24. I paraphrase here from Luce Irigaray: "But what if these commodities refused to go to market? What if they maintained 'another' kind of commerce, among themselves?" See "Commodities among Themselves," in *This Sex Which Is Not One,* trans. Catherine Porter (Ithaca, N.Y.: Cornell University Press, 1985), p. 196.

25. In his survey of U.S. horror films, Robin Wood argues for a similar political multivalence in the genre as a whole. See "Introduction," pp. 191–192. For other assessments of film horror, see Andrew Tudor, *Monsters and Mad Scientists: A Cultural History of the Horror Movie* (Oxford: Basil Blackwell, 1989); and S. S. Prawer, *Caligari's Children: The Film as Tale of Terror* (New York: Oxford University Press, 1980).

26. Susan Ware, *Holding Their Own: American Women in the 1930s* (Boston: Twayne, 1982), p. 199.

27. See ibid; Sara Evans, *Born for Liberty: A History of Women in America* (New York: Free Press, 1990), pp. 197–218; and William Chafe, *Paradox of Change: American Women in the Twentieth Century* (New York: Oxford University Press, 1991), pp. 22–118 and 121.

28. John D'Emilio and Estelle Freedman, *Intimate Matters: A History of Sexuality in America* (New York: Harper and Row, 1988), pp. 288–289.

29. See Ware, *Holding Their Own,* esp. p. 173: "Hollywood, not Hull House, guaranteed women's popularity in the decade." Relevant discussions of 1930s films include Andrew Bergman, *We're in the Money: Depression America and Its Films* (New York: New York University Press, 1971); Robert Sklar, *Movie-Made America: A Social History of American Movies* (New York: Random House, 1975); and Warren Susman, "The Culture of the 1930s," in *Culture as History: The Transformation of American Society in the Twentieth Century* (New York: Pantheon, 1984), pp. 150–183.

30. Censors in Kansas City cut *Frankenstein* in half, only to be countermanded by an

order from the state governor. As pointed out in Brunas, Brunas, and Weaver, *Universal Horrors*, p. 27, the censorship controversy almost certainly boosted revenues for the film. Recent discussions of the Production Code include Gregory D. Black, "Hollywood Censored: The Production Code Administration and the Hollywood Film Industry, 1930–1940," *Film History* 3, no. 1 (March 1989): 67–89; Leonard J. Leff, "The Breening of America," *PMLA* 106, no. 3 (May 1991): 432–445; and Stephen Vaughn, "Morality and Entertainment: The Origins of the Motion Picture Production Code," *Journal of American History* 77, no. 1 (June 1990): 39–65.

31. Glut, *Frankenstein Legend*, pp. 127, 131.

32. Otis Ferguson, review of *Bride of Frankenstein*, *New Republic*, May 29, 1935, p. 75.

33. Review of *Bride of Frankenstein*, *Time*, April 29, 1935, p. 52.

34. On Whale's homosexuality in the context of Hollywood culture, see Russo, *Celluloid Closet*, p. 50; on his approach to the film's humor—what we might now identify as his camp style—see Brunas, Brunas, and Weaver, *Universal Horrors*, pp. 120–121; James Curtis, *James Whale* (Metuchen, N.J.: Scarecrow Press, 1982), pp. 118–119; and Norden, "Sexual References," pp. 149–150.

35. Jessie Daniel Ames, *The Changing Character of Lynching: Review of Lynching, 1931–41, with a Discussion of Recent Developments in the Field* (1942; reprint, New York: AMS Press, 1973), p. 2. For a detailed account of lynching in the first half of the 1930s, see Robert L. Zangrando, *The NAACP Crusade against Lynching* (Philadelphia: Temple University Press, 1980), esp. pp. 98–138.

36. As Donald F. Bogle puts it, "No other period in motion-picture history could boast of more black faces carrying mops and pails or lifting pots and pans than the Depression years." *Toms, Coons, Mulattoes, Mammies, and Bucks: An Interpretive History of Blacks in American Films*, rev. ed. (New York: Continuum, 1989), p. 36. For specific accounts of these films, see Thomas Cripps, *Slow Fade to Black: The Negro in American Film, 1900–1942* (New York: Oxford University Press, 1977), pp. 263–308; and Daniel J. Leab, *From Sambo to Superspade: The Black Experience in Motion Pictures* (Boston: Houghton Mifflin, 1975), pp. 83–118.

37. For a detailed account of black media protest in this era, see Leonard Archer, *Black Images in the American Theatre: NAACP Protest Campaigns—Stage, Screen, Radio, and Television* (Brooklyn: Pageant-Poseidon, 1973), pp. 183–224. On *The Birth of a Nation*, see Archer, pp. 195–196; on *Gone with the Wind*, see Archer, pp. 205–208, and Leab, *From Sambo to Superspade*, pp. 199–201.

38. On *Rhodes of Africa*, see Leab, *From Sambo to Superspade*, p. 103; on *Fury*, see Leab, p. 106; Cripps, *Slow Fade to Black*, p. 295; and Bergman, *We're in the Money*, pp. 120–122.

39. Lawrence Reddick, "Of Motion Pictures" (1944), reprinted in *Black Films and Filmmakers: A Comprehensive Anthology from Stereotype to Superhero*, ed. Lindsay Patterson (New York: Dodd, Mead, 1975), p. 4.

40. Bogle, *Toms, Coons, Mulattoes, Mammies, and Bucks*, p. 13. See also Joseph Boskin, "Sambo and Other Male Images in Popular Culture," in *Images of Blacks in American Culture*, ed. Jessie Carney Smith (Westport, Conn.: Greenwood Press, 1988), pp. 257–272; and Paul Hoch, *White Hero / Black Beast: Racism, Sexism, and the Mask of Masculinity* (London: Pluto Press, 1979), esp. pp. 43–64.

41. Glut, *Frankenstein Legend*, p. 100.

42. Cripps, *Slow Fade to Black,* p. 278. On *King Kong* (1933) as a racial allegory, see also Hoch, *White Hero/Black Beast,* pp. 48–49. For a related perspective on the historicity of U.S. film monsters, see Wood, "Introduction," esp. pp. 168–169.

43. "Lynch Victim's Corpse May Have Been Dug Up," *Birmingham News,* November 29, 1933, reprinted in Ralph Ginzburg, *100 Years of Lynchings* (Baltimore: Black Classic Press, 1962), p. 203.

44. "Suspect Hanged from Oak on Bastrop Public Square," *New Orleans Tribune,* July 10, 1934, reprinted in ibid., p. 220.

45. This interpretation of *Bride of Frankenstein*'s relation to race is indebted to critics of Shelley's *Frankenstein* who have read the novel as a response to contemporary fears about class upheaval. See, for example, Chris Baldick, *In Frankenstein's Shadow: Myth, Monstrosity, and Nineteenth-Century Writing* (Oxford: Clarendon Press, 1987), esp. pp. 10–29; Paul O'Flinn, "Production and Reproduction: The Case of *Frankenstein,*" in *Popular Fictions: Essays in the Literature and History,* ed. Peter Humm, Paul Stigant, and Peter Widdowson (London: Methuen, 1986), pp. 196–221; and Franco Moretti, *Signs Taken for Wonders: Essays in the Sociology of Literary Forms* (London: Verso, 1988), pp. 83–108.

46. Angela Davis, "Rape, Racism, and the Myth of the Black Rapist," in *Women, Race, and Class* (New York: Random House, 1981), p. 173.

47. George T. Winston (1901), quoted in Jacqueline Dowd Hall, "'The Mind That Burns in Each Body': Women, Rape, and Racial Violence," in *Powers of Desire: The Politics of Sexuality,* ed. Ann Snitow, Christine Stansell, and Sharon Thompson (New York: Monthly Review Press, 1983), p. 334.

48. Hall, "The Mind That Burns," p. 335.

49. Cripps, *Slow Fade to Black,* p. 278, notes that the German title of the film was *King Kong und die Weisse Frau* ("King Kong and the White Woman"), a change that foregrounds the connotations of interracial rape.

50. Sedgwick, *Between Men,* p. 10.

51. Hall, "The Mind That Burns," p. 335.

52. Valerie Smith, "Split Affinities: The Case of Interracial Rape," in *Conflicts in Feminism,* ed. Marianne Hirsch and Evelyn Fox Keller (New York: Routledge, 1990), p. 276.

53. See ibid., esp. p. 272.

54. Laura Mulvey, "Visual Pleasure and Narrative Cinema," *Screen* 16, no. 3 (Autumn 1975): 11.

55. Constance Penley, "Feminism, Film Theory, and Bachelor Machines," in *The Future of an Illusion: Film, Feminism, and Psychoanalysis* (Minneapolis: University of Minnesota Press, 1989), p. 58.

56. Williams, "When the Woman Looks," esp. pp. 85–89. See also Mary Ann Doane, *The Desire to Desire: The Woman's Film of the 1940s* (Bloomington: Indiana University Press, 1987), pp. 123–154.

57. Jane Gaines, "White Privilege and Looking Relations: Race and Gender in Feminist Film Theory," *Cultural Critique* 4 (Fall 1986): 61.

58. Ibid., p. 70.

59. Jacqueline Bobo, quoted in Janet Bergstrom and Mary Ann Doane, "The Female Spectator: Contexts and Directions," *camera obscura,* nos. 20–21 (May–September 1989): 9.

60. Linda Williams, "Feminist Film Theory: *Mildred Pierce* and the Second World War," in *Female Spectators: Looking at Film and Television,* ed. E. Deidre Pribram (London: Verso, 1988), pp. 12–13.

61. bell hooks, "Liberation Scenes: Speak the Yearning," in *Yearning: Race, Gender, and Cultural Politics* (Boston: South End Press, 1990), p. 4. See also Jacqueline Bobo, "*The Color Purple:* Black Women as Cultural Readers," in *Female Spectators,* pp. 90–109; and Manthia Diawara, "Black Spectatorship: Problems of Identification and Resistance," *Screen* 29, no. 4 (Autumn 1988): 66–76. On forms of theater segregation in this era, see Leab, *From Sambo to Superspade,* pp. 94–95.

62. See, for example, Michael Rogin, "'The Sword Became a Flashing Vision': D. W. Griffith's *The Birth of a Nation,*" *Representations* 9 (Winter 1985): 150–195; Kaja Silverman, "White Skin, Brown Masks: The Double Mimesis, or with Lawrence in Arabia," *Differences* 1, no. 3 (Fall 1989): 3–54; and esp. Elizabeth Abel, "Race, Class, and Psychoanalysis? Opening Questions," in *Conflicts in Feminism,* ed. Marianne Hirsch and Evelyn Fox Keller (New York: Routledge, 1990), pp. 184–204.

63. For examples of this reinvention, see Glut, *Frankenstein Catalog,* which is subtitled *Being a Comprehensive Listing of Novels, Translations, Adaptations, Stories, Critical Works, Popular Articles, Series, Fumetti, Verse, Stage Plays, Films, Cartoons, Puppetry, Comics, Satire and Humor, Spoken and Musical Recordings, Tapes, and Sheet Music Featuring Frankenstein's Monster and/or Descended from Mary Shelley's Novel.*

15

King Kong: The Beast in the Boudoir—
or, "You Can't Marry That Girl, You're a Gorilla!"

Harvey Roy Greenberg

I have elsewhere explored weird cinema's depiction of the monster as abused child. This essay studies the beast as personification of an angst-ridden adolescent.[1] Since my discussion focuses so exclusively upon the psychosexual difficulties of male monsters, a note of explanation is due to female readers.

There have been only a handful of memorable feminine creatures—one principally remembers the heroines of *Cat People* (1942), *Dracula's Daughter* (1936), *Attack of the 50-Foot Woman* (1958), and *Bride of Frankenstein* (1935) (although she only makes a cameo appearance). Perhaps moviemakers have believed that public taste would be as much offended by lady as child monsters, or chauvinistically held the purity and innocence of woman sacrosanct.

In any case, most female monster movies to date have portrayed what *men* find fearful about the feminine (like the eponymous Fifty-Foot Woman, archetype of the castrating harpy who stomps through the dreams of impotent male movie maniacs). This may be a far cry from what women would deem loathsome or pitiable in themselves. Female producers and directors—there are still precious few of either—might presumably be more in touch with their sex's unique possibilities for monstrousness.

Contemplating the fate of the Oedipus complex, Freud theorized that the uproar of the Oedipal stage subsides when the boy is able to renounce sexual designs upon his mother. Rather than compete with his father, he identifies with him, secure in the knowledge that he, too, will find in his maturity a love object as fulfilling.

During the latency stage—approximately age six through ten—the boy is at relative peace emotionally. He uses his respite from the sensual itch to acquire intellectual and social skills in the company of like-minded buddies. If girls are thought of at all during this period, it is with a conflation of disinterest and dislike. But as the sap rises, the pubescent boy undergoes a disquieting metamorphosis, radically stretching his physical dimensions and developing primary and secondary sexual characteristics. These changes threaten the cornerstone of emotional stability—the image of one's body—and can be experienced with as much distress as if they were being inflicted upon the adolescent by some inimical outside force rather than occurring as a result of a natural internal process.

Alarmed by his burgeoning biology, exhilarated and disequilibrated by his nascent strength, the adolescent may verge on panic like Dr. Jekyll, helpless before the appearance of Hyde; or may tremble like the Wolf Man at the rising of the moon. Anxiety is sharpened by the return of repressed fantasies, at least partly derived from childhood sexual notions with disturbingly perverse or sadistic components. The Oedipus complex is resurrected, this time in a mature physique.

Two centuries prior to Freud, the French *philosophe* Diderot asserted in *Rameau's Nephew:* "If the little brute were left to himself and kept in his native ignorance, combining the undeveloped mind of a child in the cradle with the violent passions of a man of thirty, he would wring his father's neck and sleep with his mother." [2] Diderot's uncannily accurate reflection describes the source of the male adolescent's central anxiety: awed by his newfound aggressive capabilities, repelled by his incestuous feelings for his mother, he dreads the loss of his father's guidance plus an even heavier retribution, if the secret aim of his sexuality is discovered and the deadly competition of nursery days rejoined.

Propelled by his riotous hormones, the adolescent commences working through his lurid fantasies, transferring his yen for his mother to real, live girls—those same scary enigmas shunned like lepers throughout the comfortable latency years. As he tries to puzzle out the riddle of maternal sexuality, he is torn between lofty idealization and lascivious degradation of women (a neurotic version of this splitting is found in the "Madonna-Whore complex"). [3]

In his daydreams, the pubescent male is a chivalrous, chaste rescuer of maidens in distress from villains who represent his Oedipal rival as well as his own "animal" aspect, or he is a superstud plowing through acres of obligingly spread thighs, or, closer to the truth, an inept klutz forever banging his nose into a girl's eye on first kiss. He looks into the mirror, hoping to see Lothario or Lochinvar, Paul Newman or Paul McCartney. Instead, staring back is a pimply, half-formed apparition as appalling as the Creature from the Black Lagoon.

We will not, therefore, be surprised to find the dilemmas of puberty cunningly reinvented in weird cinema (a genre, one notes, always popular with adolescents), with the monster symbolizing the adolescent intruder on the Oedipal scene, hell-bent on ripping Mom untimely away from Dad. It is commonplace for the monster to carry off a scantily clad woman who just happens to be the girlfriend of the handsome hero, as well as the daughter (or chief assistant) of a famous elderly scientist. Under the Oedipal rubric, monster (teenager) wants girlfriend (mother) of hero (father) all to himself. But at another level, the hero as adolescent disavows *his* Oedipal itch for incestuous monkeyshines by slaying the evil creature, then returning the heroine in good order to her real or symbolic dad before wedding her prim and proper.

Not infrequently, the heroine is snatched out of her bedroom by the monster. Dracula and Frankenstein's creature were among the first of these Oedipal beasts in the boudoir, followed by a legion of deformed nocturnal Casanovas. Frankenstein's monster-"son" kidnaps his "father's" wife-to-be from the wedding chamber until the the latter can resolve Junior's Oedipal fix by furnishing him with a ready-made bride of his own. Karloff even looked like a caricature of an adolescent bursting out of his clothes. When he clomps off with Valerie Hobson tossed over his shoulder, the latter screaming like a banshee until she faints dead out, one recalls an uproarious Sid Caesar pantomine of a youngster at his first prom, staggering across the floor in an elephantine jitterbug as he hurls an imaginary girlfriend through the air.

What the monster would do with the girl if he had a chance to keep her is anyone's guess including his own, given the obscure nature of his desire and genital apparatus—which accurately reflects the adolescent's uncertainty about the mechanics of sex and the ambivalence of his feelings toward his love object.

But happily for the howling heroine, our monster never gets the opportunity to penetrate the sexual murk. Hardly does he have a chance to bed down the heroine in cave or tomb, when the Oedipal avengers—square-jawed hero, scientist father—backed up by a Superego horde of cops, National Guard, or Air Force, demolish the creature and restore the heroine to her human lover.

Just as there have been few actual child monsters, actual adolescents turning into monsters are in equally short supply throughout weird cinema. *I Was a Teenage Frankenstein* (1958) devolved around mad scientist Whit Bissell's botched reconstruction of a youngster who had been dismantled in an auto wreck. In the more promising *I Was a Teenage Werewolf* (1957), a demented school psychiatrist blows the lid off the Id of a troubled predelinquent by giving him "regression serum" to put him in touch with his primitive aggressive impulses. Predictably, the cure is worse than the disease; psychopathy yields to lycanthropy with the usual dire consequences. The moral of the tale seems to be: stay away from the shrink if you've got hangups, or you'll end up wolf-meat!

The hero of *The Wolf Man* (1941) and the heroine of *Cat People* are both afflicted with the adolescent's alienation, the painful sense of—as one patient put it—"being alone and afraid, in a world I never made." But arguably the most impressive Hollywood monstrosity to recapitulate the psychosexual issues of human puberty remains the eponymous protagonist of RKO's 1933 epic, *King Kong*. Besides embodying a Brobdignagian teenage Romeo, Kong also reads as a symbol of Natural Man, seeking his lost freedom amidst urban blight and economic oppression. Of which, more presently.

King Kong opens in New York of the Depression. The people cry out for bread and circuses. Breadlines abound, and for circuses, there is the dime escape of Hollywood. Carl Denham, a "Bring 'Em Back Alive!" entrepreneur, is about to embark on his latest jungle spectacular, a production so shrouded in secrecy that even the trusted captain and the thickheaded first mate, Jack Driscoll, have not been told the destination.

The expedition cannot sail until Denham nails down an ingenue. The director is no more sanguine than his crew about bringing a woman along, for none of his other films ever needed a heroine:

> *Denham:* Isn't there any romance or adventure in the world without having a flapper in it? . . . I go out and sweat blood to make a swell picture, and then the critics and exhibitors all say, (*mockingly*) if this picture had a love interest, it would gross twice as much. All right, the public wants a girl, this time I'm goin' to give 'em what they want . . . I'm goin' out to get a girl . . . even if I have to *marry* one!

—a fate presumably worse than death. Denham's threat becomes more understandable if he and his crew are interpreted as a gang of latency-age boys who were doing fine until the girls had to barge in and ruin everything. One is reminded of Rick Blaine's decision in *Casablanca* (1943) to renounce the untrustworthy Ilse Laszlo for the masculine solidarity of the trenches.

Denham ventures into the city's lower depths and discovers his heroine, Anne Darrow, near a mission for destitute women. She has just been caught snitching an apple, so the director's first business with her is a rescue operation. He pays off the irate grocer, treats her at a diner to "sinkers" and coffee, then proposes to lift her from tap-city obscurity to stellar heights. Befitting an adolescent's love object, Anne is eminently rescuable, down on her luck, a diamond on a dustheap, with her freshness slightly tarnished by the effluvium of a fallen woman.

She hesitates for a second over Denham's offer, thinking he wants her as his mistress—and the script delicately hints she would have been willing to let him be her Sugar Daddy. But, in the conventions of the "conscious" movie, it is necessary that the shining myth of Anne's purity be maintained, consistent with the "Madonna" side of the adolescent's ambivalent attitude toward feminine sexuality. So with gruff chivalry Denham swears, "You've got me wrong, I'm on the level . . . *no* funny business, just trust me and keep your chin up!"

One believes him, for there is no passion in the man for anything but flying in the teeth of danger to display his courage to the gawking public. A classic counterphobic and possibly a closet homosexual to boot, Denham regards woman as a weak but potentially dangerous vessel. He is comfortable with her as long as she can be treated either as a desexualized buddy or a mere block of talent to be shoved about dumbly before his camera.

The brawny first mate, Driscoll, is similarly leery of Anne's charm. The big lug gets their relationship off to a romantic start by accidentally slugging her, a tried and true Hollywood formula—Boy Meets Girl, Boy Hits Girl—grounded on the ancient Tinseltown assumption that initial enmity between the sexes is a sure sign of true love. Jack then delivers himself of sentiments that one would expect either from a gorilla or an unsocialized teenager:

Anne: I guess you don't think much of women on ship.

Jack: Naw—they're a nuisance . . . you're all right . . . but women can't help bein' a bother, just made that way, I guess . . .

In a scene filled with suggestions of what is to come, Denham finds Anne and Jack on deck. Anne fondles a tiny monkey. "Beauty and the Beast, eh?" says Denham sardonically. Jack, already in thrall to Anne's beauty, is *identified* with her plaything, a miniaturized Kong!:

Denham: (taking Jack aside): I've got enough troubles without a love affair to complicate things.

Jack: Love affair? You think I'm goin' to fall for anyone?

Denham: (cynically): Pretty tough guy! Beauty gets ya—that's the idea of my picture—the Beast was a tough guy, too. He could lick the world, but when he saw Beauty, she got him . . . he went soft, he forgot his wisdom, and the little fellows licked him . . . think it over, Jack!

Denham resents Beauty's intrusions into his virile art, and has objectified his mistrust of woman into a cautionary fascist fable of the decline and fall of the Nietzschean *Ubermensch* at the hands of the mediocre mob, his might sapped by mawkish sentiment. He takes Driscoll's crush on Anne as a personal threat, a ruinous acting out of his script in advance.

The misogyny of the preadolescent boy is based on his fear of being similarly unmanned by his dependency upon his mother. There is much preadolescent about Denham's philosophy, with its implicit misogyny, its ruthless justification for the rule of the strong over the "little guys." "Thou goest to thy woman," Nietzsche is reputed to have said; "Take thy whip!" Some wag remarked that had that impotent neurotic ever taken up his whip, his woman would have beaten him over the head with it! One intuits an analogous impotence in Denham, hidden by his macho bravado.

As they sail on to the mysterious island Denham says contains an ancient wonder "no white man has ever seen," the producer shoots preliminary rushes of Anne shrieking into the wind, staging in his mind's eye the reprisal for her disturbing allure:

Denham: You're amazed, you can't believe it . . . it's horrible, Anne, but you can't look away . . . there's no chance, no escape . . . but perhaps it will be better if you can scream! . . . scream, Anne, scream for your life!!

The ship docks in a foggy cove, cribbed from Gustave Doré, to the accompaniment of the muffled throb of drums and distant chanting: "*Annikanna Annikanna Kongkong!!!*" In the morning, Denham's party surprises a village of Hollywood blackamoors capering in stylized boogie-woogie before a colossal wooden gate, while the women deck out a nubile maiden in the local wedding regalia—shells and feathers. "Aw, they're up to some of their heathen tricks," growls Driscoll. "*Ana saba Kong!*" angrily shouts the native chief, halting the festivities. The captain translates that "the girl there is the bride of Kong . . . the ceremony is spoiled because we've seen it!"

The chief spies Anne and offers to buy the "golden woman" on the spot as a gift for Kong, at the going exchange rate of six native girls for one white woman ("Yeah," interjects Driscoll, that irrepressible honky, "blondes *are* scarce around here!"). When the chief is turned down, the natives grow restless and the company retreats back to the ship, Denham leading the way with his hands thrust into his pockets, whistling ostentatiously in a caculated display of adolescent braggadocio.

That night, Driscoll meets Anne on deck and clumsily opens his heart:

Jack: Don't laugh, I'm scared for ya—I'm sort of scared of ya, too. [*Vide supra!*] Anne—I, er, uh . . . I guess I love you!

Anne: Why, Jack, I thought you hate women . . .

Jack: I know—but you aren't women . . . say, Anne, I don't suppose, er, I mean, well you don't feel anything like that about me, do ya?

They clinch decorously. Driscoll, the muscle-bound, red-white-and-blue hero, chaste as a clam, stammers out his declaration of love like an amorous schoolboy, and only a few moments later the blacks spirit Anne away to become the bride of Kong!

It is integral to the exuberant racism of *King Kong* that the Negro should be portrayed as the degraded repository of the white man's forbidden impulses; indeed, psychoanalysis speculates that this projection is characteristic of ethnic and racial prejudice. It is always the other guy, the swarthy foreigner with his strange speech and natural sense of rhythm, who indulges in the dirty, delicious deeds denied us in the name of higher civilization.

According to this debased view of other lands and peoples, one of "our" women must be worth six of theirs. And although "their" men are capable of the most heinous aggression, one of "our" men can still take on and whip half a dozen of theirs in a fair fight. (I remember standing outside the Renel Theatre in Philadelphia after watching John Wayne wipe out half the Japanese Empire in *Sands of Iwo Jima* [1949], seriously debating with my friends how many Japs were equal to one Marine.) Kong, then, is the epitome of the white man's daydream of the brute black, the heartless, mindless foreigner, feasting on violence and rapine. We discern in his persona the raw sexuality which the ingenuous, racist bumpkin Driscoll has repressed, and which Anne has aroused.

Until now, the pace of the film has been leisurely. Viewer curiosity has been piqued, but there has been little to arouse anxiety. But immediately after Driscoll breaks through his inhibitions and forsakes the homoerotically inflected gang mentality of boyhood, Kong bursts upon the scene, the lid is blown off the Id, and one marvelous disaster after another spills across the screen, a cascade of splendid catastrophes ignited by Kong-Driscoll's fumbling passion. For sexuality and aggression, Eros and Thanatos, are imperfectly fused in the immature psyche of the adolescent male.

Anne's first encounter with Kong is redolent with rape imagery. The bolt of the enormous gate towering over the village is drawn back, and the natives lash her wrists to two posts set into a massive altar. Their ebony hands claw at her fair white flesh in lascivious chiaroscuro. They leave her spread invitingly before Kong's advance. The gate is shut, a mighty phallic bolt driven home. The chief raises his staff (!) and intones an incantation in Wilshire Boulevard Swahili. I transliterate to the best of my limited ability:

Chief: Kora kanay—Kong! Otaravey yama—KONG!! Wasaba kanamaka!! Otaravey rama—KONG!!!

Anne screams, tentatively, in terms of her potential decibel level. The chief raises his staff again. Half-naked minions strike a huge brass gong, and then crashing through the jungle he comes, Anne's demon lover. Making straight for the altar, he leers down at her, his great eyes rolling, his thick lips peeled back in a titanic snarl—and Denham's shipboard fantasy of Anne's punishment is consummated. Her gaze is drawn inexorably up, up toward the hairy colossus— *"You're amazed, you can't believe it . . . it's horrible, but you can't look away . . . scream, Anne, scream for your life!"*

And she does, with every conceivable ruffle, flourish, and furbelow a scream permits, so that in recollection it seems as if all her vocalizations hereafter consist of one prolonged scream. Kong plucks her up in his paw and thunders back into the bush with Driscoll and the others in hot pursuit. She has become a metaphor of woman swept away against her conscious will by the dark sensuality of the man-beast. Her taking by Kong is rich in associations with bacchanal and Dionysian revel.

Driscoll and Kong are two tough customers gone soft under Beauty's sway. Both will compete for Anne Darrow's hand. Kong must lose despite his superior strength and size, as the adolescent Oedipal monster who has intruded into a human, implicitly parental romance. But as I have intimated, at another level Driscoll and his simian adversary are also two sides of the *same* adolescent ego. For Kong may be read as Driscoll's naked ape, Driscoll's unconscious pubescent lust.

Boy meets girl, and boy's ape is unchained to roar and ruin. Then ape meets girl, and ape undergoes a curious, tender transformation. Throughout the ensuing carnage the public will see Kong only as the beast incarnate, slouching toward Manhattan. Yet in Anne's company, Kong dwindles away

The beast acts out the male adolescent's rescue fantasy of an idealized beloved in *King Kong* (1933).

into a clumsy knight errant, more interested in battle to protect his lady fair than making love to her (after all, she fits in the palm of his hand, and he has problems with the language).

It is immediately apparent that he intends her no real harm. He abuses her once, almost by accident. In an expurgated sequence he rips off her clothes, but contents himself merely with pawing her and sniffing at his fingers, like a teenager who won't wash his hands after a session of heavy petting, to preserve the lingering female scent.

Although I admit a certain lack of expertise in primate analysis, I believe Kong really delights in her company, wants the best for her as a Jane to his Tarzan, a comfort to his lonely jungle life. In his good faith it is inconceivable to him that she sees him only as an ugly monster. He is, I think, confused by her incessant screaming whenever he draws near, and not a little hurt by the ingratitude that prompts her to run away every time he turns his back to defend her. In sum, King Kong has been reduced to a blown-up version of the moonstruck Driscoll, wooing Anne like a fumbling adolescent, fearful of rejection, terrified by the mysterious longings she has stirred.

Kong now proceeds to rescue Anne from one danger after another—some real, others invented by his addled brain—with alarming consequences to person and property. In fact, the remainder of the film is essentially a prolonged acting out of the rescue fantasy central to the adolescent's asexual relationship with an idealized beloved. Of course, while Kong is engaged in shielding Anne from prehistoric behemoths, Driscoll rushes around madly in all directions to save her from Kong!

Jack finds her hidden away in Kong's cliffside apartment. He throws down a vine, and as the two dangle precariously Kong reels them up. They let go and plunge into the sea; the action in this scene and elsewhere in the film has an unsettling dreamlike quality. Distances are oddly distorted, foreshortened or stretched. Jack and Anne surely fall no more than a score of feet, yet it seems as if they drop through the endless abyss of nightmare into a pellucid sea, to awaken upon a serene beach with Kong faded into the mists of sleep.

The respite is brief. Kong descends from his cliff to recover his lost prize—and, naturally, to rescue Anne from Jack! The native village is smashed like kindling before Kong can be subdued by gas grenades. Denham's script is now in effect directing itself. The producer is completely unmoved by the chaos around him. Arch-imperialist and colonialist, he can only exult at the spectacle of his fortune rising from the natives' ruin and Kong's enslavement:

Denham: We came here to get a moving picture—we found something worth more than all the movies in the world . . . the whole world will pay to see this—he's always been King of his world, but we'll teach him fear! We're millionaires, boys!!!

Dissolve to Denham displaying Kong at inflated prices to a Gotham audience. Kong is manacled and collared to a cruciform restraint reminiscent of a similar shackling of the creature in *Frankenstein* (1931) (the monster as a Jesus-like scapegoat). "He was a King and a God," declaims Denham to the rubes (for all their society duds), "but now he comes to civilization, merely a captive—on show to satisfy your curiosity!"

Denham hustles in Anne and Driscoll, the latter nearly as uncomfortable in his tux as Kong is in his chromed steel chains, both sacrifices on Beauty's altar. "Get 'em together, boys," says Denham to the paparazzi, "They're going to be married tomorrow!" For every light on Broadway, there's a broken heart. The flashbulbs pop, and Kong, anguished by this latest threat to his lost

King Kong: The Beast on display, sacrificed on Beauty's altar.

lady love ("Watch out, he thinks you're attacking the girl!"), bursts his bonds and embarks on another misbegotten rescue, this time in Metropolis—shades of Frankenstein's disrupted nuptials!

Kong brings to the Big Apple his own unique brand of urban renewal that would set the style for hundreds of monsters yet unborn. Critic X. J. Kennedy astutely observed that Kong's demolition of New York real estate may have reflected the inchoate cravings of many an oppressed city dweller "to turn on the machines and kick hell out of them." [4] One recalls that *King Kong* is a film of the Depression, that Denham's voyage was undertaken to give the impoverished masses a fantasy escape from their bitter economic plight. The American dream had soured overnight. I submit that many viewers, obscurely blaming their hardships on the shady practice of the bankers and brokers of Wall Street, took an unconscious pleasure as Kong, innocent country boy at heart, wreaked revenge on the Babylon of the East.

He bashes his way out of the theater, clambers up Anne's hotel, and grabs her out of the bedroom. After laying waste to the Third Avenue El, he takes her to a tryst atop the Empire State Building—one notes with a pang of nos-

The giant ape does battle with the Air Force atop the Empire State Building in
King Kong.

talgia that in 1933 the landmark skyscraper is gracefully unmarred by its TV
tower.

Now that Kong has rescued her according to his lights, the unconscious
movie demands that she in turn be rescued from him and restored to her
fiancé. Denham conceives his most brilliant PR coup, summoning up the
U.S. Air Force to eliminate Kong before the eyes and ears of the world. "Oh
boy, what a story!" cry the newsmen, as Kong, the quintessential victim of media exploitation, goes down before the blazing guns. He appears at his most
human in his final agony. Cupping Anne in his palm, he looks down at her
tenderly, replaces her delicately on the parapet, and pitches forward into the
canyons of Manhattan. Untouched as usual by pity for the maimed or dead,
human or otherwise, Denham pronounces Kong's epitaph with relish for the
headlines: "It wasn't the airplanes . . . it was Beauty killed the Beast!"

The picture ends with the Beast laid to rest and Jack Driscoll domesticated,
off camera. One imagines that his marriage to Anne will be as uninspired and

as forgettable as his wooing. Addressing the Driscoll-Kong equation from a psychodynamic viewpoint, one concludes that Driscoll has worked through his fear and reactive sadism toward women, passed through adolescence, and forged a viable if tepid sexual adaptation. Yet the rampant vitality of Kong's fatal passion is not so easily forgotten. Denham has it that Beauty killed the Beast, that every man dies a little if he opens his heart to love.

But who really killed Kong Kong? Surely not his *amour fou* for Anne, but Denham himself! Out of his greed and misogyny, Denham composed his fable of Superman's undoing, then orchestrated it to his immense profit. It was Denham who brought Anne to tempt Kong on Skull Island. It was Denham who insisted on seizing Kong, the better to vaunt his schoolboy courage when he could have departed in peace. Finally, it was Denham who called out the machines to assassinate the noble animal.

Denham's public forced a woman upon him, and he exacted a callous revenge as price. If you want a woman, he has implied, then you must endure the consequences of the mischief she will surely provoke—shades of Sam Spade, Rick Blaine, Howard Hawks, Sam Peckinpah—generations of macho heroes and moviemakers. Denham's closing lines reflect his inhumanity and unregenerate preadolescent fascism. Money and fame are only unsatisfactory props for the damaged ego of such a base creature. For it is Denham, the real beast of *King Kong,* who has been permanently unmanned by his contempt for Beauty, while Kong's tragic love affirms the inherent beauty of his fallen spirit.

Notes

1. On the monster as abused child, see my "Where Do Monsters Come from, Daddy?" in *The Movies on Your Mind* (New York: Saturday Review Press/E. P. Dutton, 1975), pp. 206–219. For analyses of horror movies similar to the present essay, see Walter Evans, "Monster Movies: A Sexual Theory," *Journal of Popular Film* 2, no. 4 (Fall 1973): 353–365, reprinted in *Planks of Reason: Essays on the Horror Film,* ed. Barry Keith Grant, pp. 53–64 (Metuchen, N.J.: Scarecrow Press, 1984); Evans, "Monster Movies and Rites of Initiation," *Journal of Popular Film* 4, no. 2 (1975): 124–142; Frank D. McConnell, "Song of Innocence: *The Creature from the Black Lagoon,*" *Journal of Popular Film* 1, no. 2 (Winter 1973): 15–28, reprinted in McConnell, *The Spoken Seen: Film and the Romantic Imagination* (Baltimore and London: Johns Hopkins University Press, 1975); and Margaret Tarratt, "Monsters from the Id," 2 pts, *Films and Filming* 17, no. 3 (December 1970): 38–42; and no. 4 (January 1971): 40–42, reprinted in *Film Genre Reader II,* ed. Barry Keith Grant (Austin: University of Texas Press, 1995), pp. 330–349.

2. Denis Diderot, *Rameau's Nephew; D'Alembert's Dream* (London: Penguin, 1966), p. 47.

3. For my analysis of the Madonna-Whore complex in the detective film and else-where, see "*The Maltese Falcon*—Even Paranoids Have Enemies," in *The Movies on Your Mind,* pp. 53–78.

4. X. J. Kennedy, "Who Killed King Kong?" in *Focus on the Science Fiction Film,* ed. William Johnson (Englewood Cliffs, N.J.: Prentice-Hall, 1972), p. 108.

The Stepfather: Father as Monster in the Contemporary Horror Film

Patricia Brett Erens

Can a commercial psychological thriller modeled after Hitchcock's *Psycho* (1960) offer a progressive reading for contemporary women? Can such a film draw upon the exploitative elements of the genre and simultaneously serve as a radical reformation of the same? *The Stepfather* (1987), an independent production directed by Joseph Ruben, brings together many of the major themes current in recent horror films, especially antifeminist sentiments circulating in contemporary popular culture. However, Ruben and screenwriter Donald E. Westlake resolve the generic conflicts in a new and important way.

The plot relies upon many of the character types and narrative moves that have become familiar to contemporary thriller audiences, dating back to John Carpenter's *Halloween* (1978). This is hardly surprising when one notes that Ruben's previous credits include *The Pom Pom Girls* (1976), *Joyride* (1977), *Our Winning Season* (1978), and *Dreamscape* (1984). The story centers on Jerry Blake (Terry O'Quinn), who having murdered his previous

wife and children, is now remarried to a young widow, Susan (Shelley Hack), and is living in a quiet Seattle suburb where he sells real estate. Jerry and Susan seem the ideal couple. Only Susan's sixteen-year-old daughter Stephanie (Jill Schoelen) mars the image of the perfect family. Getting into one scrape after another, Stephanie not only has failed to come to terms with the loss of her real father, but she also detects something disturbing about her stepfather, which she confides to her therapist, Dr. Bondurant (Charles Lanyer).

Like other recent films, most specifically *Blue Velvet* (1986), *The Stepfather* addresses the dark side of family life and small-town America. More unusual is the fact that the film takes a feminist position, foregrounding patriarchal power but positing the maternal order in opposition to the destructive elements of patriarchy.

Partway through the film, after an argument with Stephanie concerning the good-night kiss she gives her boyfriend, Jerry decides to rid himself of this family as he has done in the past "when they disappointed him." This leads to the dramatic climax—Jerry's assault on Susan and his prolonged attack on Stephanie. In the final struggle Susan, although badly wounded, uses a pistol to shoot Jerry, while Stephanie delivers the final stroke with Jerry's knife. The film ends in the family yard as Susan and Stephanie, fully recovered, enter their home arm in arm.

This ending, along with much that precedes it, serves to valorize women's maternal role and the strong female bonding that exists between mothers and daughters. Such valorization is an exception in mainstream cinema, both past and present. In those films where such bonding does occur (for instance, in *Stella Dallas* [1937]), the narrative works toward the removal of this female threat to patriarchal power by the reassertion of the heterosexual couple (as in the wedding scene in *Stella Dallas*). Such is not the case with *The Stepfather*.

Through an analysis of *The Stepfather* and specifically of the ways in which the film offers many of the pleasures associated with the pre-Oedipal stage—bonding with the mother, feelings of plenitude and unity—I propose to demonstrate how the work offers new forms of cinematic pleasure for women in a genre notorious for its exploitation of women and the female body. As a further consideration, I will also discuss the ways in which the screening situation itself calls upon the memories of the pre-Oedipal period and stimulates the reemergence of repressed desires for the mother (for male as well as female viewers), which are amply reimagined in this work.

In his essay on the American horror film, Robin Wood concludes that indeed the monster has now become *the American family* and that the elements so carefully repressed in American life—sexuality, and particularly female and childhood sexuality—have all returned to haunt us.[1] According to Wood, the older construct of the monster was simply our repressed fears projected onto a grotesque figure of terror. However, as he notes, since *Psycho,* the horror film has become both American and familial and the monster has taken on a new guise.

Wood sets out several elements that define the new genre, including the image of "the terrible house"; women as the ultimate object of the protagonist's animus; the release of sexuality presented as perverted, monstrous, and excessive; the ambivalence toward the family; and the theme of "the double." All of these are important themes in *The Stepfather.*

Houses (both those of Blake's first and second marriages) function not simply as the scenes of the crimes, but also as claustrophobic spaces within which desires and tensions are exacerbated. The Blake household, once the domain of the mother, has now become subject to the law of the father. As Stephanie complains, Jerry has taken over *their* home. Where once the family seemingly romped with free abandon, they now sit stiffly at the dinner table, heads bowed in prayer. With the arrival of Jerry, domestic space becomes filled with tensions, secrets, fears, furtive gazes, rivalries, and uncontrollable emotions—which will eventually erupt in a murderous massacre.

"The terrible house" is closely related to ambivalent attitudes toward the family. Much is made in the movie about the perfect family—families from television dramas and sitcoms like *Father Knows Best, Leave It to Beaver, Mr. Ed,* and *The Waltons.* In TV wonderland, parents and children work together with perfect trust and love, without any deep-seated problems. Those problems which do emerge are quickly resolved (certainly within the half-hour or hour time slot). Life is clean, beautiful, and perfect. Unfortunately for Jerry, life does not always imitate television. Stephanie has become a problem student and does not have the warm feelings for him that he has tried to cultivate. Stephanie also poses other difficulties. Her wish to go away to boarding school (a wise decision, according to her therapist) is seen by Jerry as a breakup of the family unit. Further, her movement into sexual adulthood also threatens to destroy the stable self-sufficiency of father-mother-daughter. For Jerry then, his new family, the means whereby he seeks to achieve the perfection of his ideal family, is both a loved object and a hateful disappointment, producing ambivalent feelings that he cannot reconcile.

The other themes cited by Wood, such as women as the ultimate object of the protagonist's animus, appear self-evident. Although not all of his victims are female, Jerry's primary animus is turned against Susan and Stephanie; the murders of Dr. Bondurant and Jim Ogilvie (his former brother-in-law) are principally protective measures to avoid detection or thwart an attack. Jerry's response to Stephanie's budding sexuality reflects a form of "sexual disgust" that Wood finds prevalent in many recent horror films. What is unique about *The Stepfather,* however, is that the film's structuring devices do not lock us into Jerry's subjective point of view. Hence we are distanced from his reactions to female sexuality (sexuality as perverted and monstrous), which allows us to critique his emotions rather than forcing us to identify with them. This difference sets *The Stepfather* sharply apart from other works in the genre, as I will detail below.

No film better critiques the family institution than *The Stepfather.* Like *Blue Velvet,* the film opens with an idyllic view of small-town America. In *The Stepfather,* the opening shot is a high-angle view of a town street, filled with autumn leaves at the height of their beauty. This sight could occur anywhere in the USA. But even before Ruben rudely demystifies this vision, there is a feeling that something is amiss. As in *Blue Velvet,* the discordant feeling emanates from intense colors that look patently artificial and undermine our belief in what we are shown. Such a reaction seems to illustrate Hitchcock's dictum that "things are not always what they seem." And sure enough, in *Blue Velvet* the credit sequence is soon followed by a disquieting scene depicting an older man in the throes of a seizure, ending with an equally disturbing track into the grass that reveals swarms of slimy insects.

In *The Stepfather,* we move from the autumnal exterior to a bloody interior as Jerry washes, dresses, takes on a new identity, and calmly walks past the aftermath of his massacre, straightening toys and overturned chairs as he leaves. In both films the message is clear—behind the doors and underneath the calm exterior, there is passion, struggle, and death.

This message, of course, is not totally new. In the seminal work *Psycho,* Hitchcock dispelled a belief in the innocence of American rural life and the happy family, and no contemporary psychological thriller is without indebtedness (and in many cases direct reference) to this work. *The Stepfather* is no exception. The similarities are numerous. In both films we have a psychotic multiple-murderer who holds conversations with an imaginary parent. (In *The Stepfather* Jerry alternates between the punishing father and the abused son.) In both works the victims are women (and in *The Stepfather,* there are children as well), knifed in an angry and bloody symbolic rape. Like *Psycho, The Stepfather* includes a psychiatrist who helps explain the protagonist's pathology. Likewise, both narratives contain a private investigator working on his own, who becomes another of the murderer's victims.

Visually and symbolically *The Stepfather* utilizes several familiar icons from the earlier work. Most prominent is the house itself, a large wooden structure that seems to typify postwar America in the way that *Psycho*'s Gothic mansion typified a previous era. Like Bates, Blake (note the similarity) is associated with birds. Jerry works for the American Eagle Realty Company, a name that resonates with predation, national pride, and patriarchal power. A large stuffed bird also appears behind Jerry's head during the Thanksgiving dinner scene. Jerry's private space, like Norman's in *Psycho,* is located in the cellar—a symbolically subterranean region where he keeps his power tools, builds birdhouses (replicas of the homes he sells), and vents his anger; there repressed and buried memories reemerge. The two men also demonstrate a penchant for disguises, although they function differently in each work. Perhaps the most obvious reference to *Psycho* is the shower sequence (can any shower scene ever be neutral or innocent again?) which precedes Jerry's attack on Stephanie. Like the original, this scene features a nude woman and the requisite overhead shot.

However, whereas many current homages to Hitchcock films, such as *The Bedroom Window* (1987, with references to both *Rear Window* [1954] and *Vertigo* [1958]), do little more than restate the original without the complex artistry of the master, *The Stepfather* reworks all of the major players and themes to state a new premise about American life, one which I propose works both as an expression of male hostility and fear, resulting from the social gains made by women in the last twenty years, and as an affirmation of female bonding which has emerged as a viable alternative for many women during the same two decades. No doubt the latter has also exacerbated the former. On a deeper level, *The Stepfather* also provides one of the clearest articulations of cinema's relationship with the pre-Oedipal stage expounded in the writings of Jacques Lacan and Gilles Deleuze and applied to film studies by Christian Metz, Charles Altman, and Gaylyn Studlar.

Following the prologue in which Jerry Blake so calmly leaves the scene of his crime, the film moves forward a year. We are introduced to a pretty and pert Stephanie and her equally attractive mother in a playful scene where the two take turns pelting each other with leaves. The game ends as they roll in a bed of leaves. Both appear wrapped up in and totally happy with one another. The romp is soon interrupted with the arrival of Jerry, setting into play not the classic Oedipal conflict wherein the daughter sees herself as a rival for the father's affections, but rather a struggle for the love and attention of the mother. Susan's willingness to drop Stephanie when Jerry arrives home leaves Stephanie feeling resentful and abandoned.

What immediately makes *The Stepfather* distinct from *Psycho* is the development of Stephanie's character as a parallel to Jerry's. Here we have the theme of "the double"—Stephanie/Stepfather. In this regard the two form two sides of one coin, echoing themes from Hitchcock's *Shadow of a Doubt* (1943), which is also set in small-town America. In *Shadow,* Uncle Charlie arrives in town, a secret murderer of wealthy widows and a psychotic misogynist beneath his charming manner. By film's end, his niece, Charlie, who had admired and identified with her uncle, has come to learn the truth not only about her uncle, but also about her own dark instincts. Like him in spirit, she is nonetheless recuperated into the film's narrative, safely married off to the town's detective, who will, we suppose, keep her in check and protect her from herself. Some of these themes are also at work in *The Stepfather*. And if there is any doubt of Ruben's intentions, he dissolves from a close-up of Jerry to our first view of Stephanie, reminiscent of a similar dissolve from Joseph Cotten to Teresa Wright in the beginning of *Shadow*.

As Stephanie meets with her therapist, Dr. Bondurant (the *good* doctor), or in conversations with her mother and her best friend, Karen, we learn that she wants her mother for herself, has succeeded in splitting her father ideal into good father (her real father, significantly named Maine)/bad father, and also harbors hostile feelings toward her stepfather.

The conflict here is thus between pre-Oedipal desire as exemplified by Stephanie and post-Oedipal desire as exemplified by Jerry. Reversing *Psycho*, the film presents the pre-Oedipal wishes of Stephanie to bond with her mother as healthy, while the post-Oedipal behavior of Jerry, usually taken as normal, ultimately reveals sadism and psychosis. In some ways Stephanie can be compared to the Teresa Wright character in *Shadow of a Doubt*, but she does not desire Jerry as Charlie had wanted her uncle. (A comparison of each daughter's attitude toward her mother adds to the emotional divergence between the two works.) The conflict between Stephanie and Jerry thus takes on a broader significance than is initially apparent. The degree to which their opposing psychic drives are developed as a subtext in the film, together with the emergence of strong pre-Oedipal themes, mark *The Stepfather* as an important departure from most Hollywood films, which are concerned almost exclusively with Oedipal issues.

From Stephanie's perspective, the film's ending seems almost too good to be true. With Jerry now safely dead, along with the film's only other attractive and possibly eligible males, Stephanie has her mother all to herself. Having jointly accomplished the murder, the two now inhabit the house alone. In the final shot, Stephanie wrecks Jerry's wooden birdhouse, sawing through the tall cylindrical post, toppling this symbol of the American dream from its pedestal. With this stroke Ruben has destroyed the American home with its male head of household, leaving it impotent on the ground. Likewise, he has reconstituted the family couple as two women, seemingly sufficient unto themselves (certainly safer). In one image, Ruben has represented men's worst fears and perhaps many women's fondest hopes.

It is also important to note that in depicting the mother-daughter relation-ship, Ruben gives it an amazing degree of mutual respect and equality, despite the age difference. The two nurture one another and are able to talk honestly. This relationship is in stark contrast with the aspirations of Jerry, who enjoys being the man of the house, making the decisions, and taking charge. Ruben emphasizes his need for order and control and his desire for perfection, the kind of perfection that leaves little room for messiness (pelting leaves) or change and growth (Stephanie's sexual maturity and eventual separation).

Thus in reshaping *Psycho,* and to a lesser degree *Shadow of a Doubt,* Ruben and Westlake have totally reversed the dynamics and implications of the orig-inal. Whereas in *Psycho* Norman manages to kill the female protagonist, Mar-ion, whose sexuality touches off an uncontrollable murderous desire, in *The Stepfather* Jerry is inadequate to the task and is himself knifed by Stephanie. Notably, it is Stephanie's emerging sexuality that throws Jerry into a psychotic fit and leads to his decision to kill both mother and daughter. The fact that a virginal heroine is able to save herself from attack has been a common plot device since *Halloween.* But in most horror films the survivors form a hetero-sexual couple. *The Stepfather* breaks this pattern in a bold, clearcut way.

Also of importance is the figure of the psychiatrist. In *Psycho* he serves as the voice of authority, providing audiences with access to the truth, however limited or subverted his monologue may appear. Here, however, along with all other male authority figures, he is eliminated, to be replaced by a female.

On a deeper level, *The Stepfather* seems to speak for the reemergence of the repressed pre-Oedipal feelings between mother and child, especially between mother and daughter. The young male child's mandate to separate from the mother and to assume the cultural and physio-psychological aspects of the fa-ther are well documented in Freud's description of the Oedipal stage. How-ever, at a later stage the male can reinvest his desire in a new female partner. The female child, however, equally encouraged to separate from the mother, is expected to shift her sexual attraction to the opposite sex. Little encourage-ment is given for female bonding or for close relationships between women (although they almost always exist), no doubt due to men's fear that they will ultimately result in male exclusion. One need only think of the demeaning perception on the part of many men of female gatherings or the persistent depiction of female friendship in so many movies as a competition between women for the affections of a male.

The Stepfather not only valorizes the mother-daughter bond but also gives new emphasis to the importance of the pre-Oedipal stage—Lacan's Imagi-nary Order wherein the child is at one with the mother and makes no distinction between the two bodies. This is in contrast to the post-Oedipal stage—the Symbolic Order wherein the male child identifies with the language and the law of the father and takes his place in culture while the female child enters culture with the burden of lack. As formulated by Lacan, the transition from the Imaginary to the Symbolic begins with the Mirror Stage (technically the end of the pre-Oedipal stage), in which the child is able to distinguish itself from its mother's body and thus to constitute itself as a separate individual. It is significant that in the final episodes of *The Stepfather,* Stephanie has locked herself in the bathroom. As Jerry, wielding a butcher knife, attempts to break down the door, his pounding shatters the full-length mirror inside the bathroom. Stephanie uses a piece of shattered glass to strike out and wound Jerry. Symbolically she has used the mirror to rebel against male authority and to cripple male power.

In addition to the relative importance of each parental figure in each stage (mother/pre-Oedipal vs. father/post-Oedipal), the two stages also embody a distinction in terms of sexual desire. Gaylyn Studlar has drawn upon the writings of Gilles Deleuze to set out the elements of desire that fuel the pre-Oedipal and post-Oedipal stages—most particularly masochism, which is associated with pre-Oedipal desires for union with the mother, and sadism, which is linked to post-Oedipal desires for dominance and control.[2] Concomitant with these desires is the sought-for source of gratification, namely genital sex, which is associated with sadism, and pregenital sex, an aspect of masochism, which seeks a symbiotic bond with the mother, the first source of pleasure. At this stage, the mother is perceived as a symbol of plenitude, not castration (as happens later).

Susan is represented as the oral mother of the pre-Oedipal stage. We see her either in the kitchen preparing food, in the bedroom performing sex, or in nurturing conversations with Stephanie. Susan thus symbolizes the source of masochistic pleasure connected with the pre-Oedipal stage.

Jerry, on the other hand, reflects the sadistic tendencies related to the post-Oedipal period. His need to dominate the household, to control each situation, and to maintain a sense of order (a word he uses frequently) drives him to seek the perfect family, to make them a part of his perfect world, a world utterly in his control.

Extending Studlar's formulations to a larger canvas, the canvas of the movie screen, leads to an analysis of the ways in which the filmgoing experience replicates the experience of the pre-Oedipal stage. As many critics have pointed out,[3] film viewing stimulates regression on the part of the spectator (brought on by the darkened room, the lack of sensory stimuli, and the large screen upon which a viewer may project private fantasies), especially to an early oral stage in which the child feels at one with the mother (replicated by a viewer's easy identification with characters on the screen) and willingly gives up the self to passive pleasures. Further, as Charles Altman points out, film "sets up an Imaginary relationship between the film spectator and the world which he sees mirrored on the screen. . . . The mirror approach recaptures the extent to which the film viewer, like the child in the mirror stage, can make sense and unity only by at first accepting a lie, which then calls for correction."[4]

Studlar expounds on these ideas in her discussion of the "dream screen" and its relationship with masochism:

Masochistic fantasy is dominated by oral pleasure, the desire to return to the nondifferentiated body state of the mother/child, and the fear of abandonment (the state of nonbreast, nonplenitude). In a sense, these same wishes are duplicated by the film spectator who becomes a child again in response to the dream screen of cinema. This dream screen affords spectatorial pleasure in creating the first fetish—the mother as nurturing environment. The spectator in the cinematic dream screen regresses to a state that Baudry says is analogous to the oral period. Like the fetish objects that follow, the dream screen restores the sense of wholeness of the first symbiotic relationship as it restores the unity of the undifferentiated ego/ego ideal. It functions like a "good blanket" reuniting the spectator/child with the earliest object of desire that lessens the anxiety of the ego loosened from body boundaries.[5]

Yet despite these arguments, traditional classical cinema has always worked to resolve the Oedipal situation by the establishment of a heterosexual couple as the narrative closure. Few if any films posit the pre-Oedipal as a possibility unless the protagonist has lapsed into psychosis (as in de Palma's *Sisters* [1972] or *Psycho* itself). On the other hand, obviously the supposed resolution of Oedipal conflicts comes with a price—a series of repressions, above all of desire for the mother. *The Stepfather* resolves this conflict in a new and radical manner.

If we apply Kaja Silverman's reading of Lacan, the Mirror Stage coexists with the Symbolic Order and is mutually consonant.[6] As such, it need not be repressed for healthy functioning. Thus in *The Stepfather* we are offered two desiring subjects: Stephanie poses one extreme in her desire for the mother and her rejection of the father as an intrusion into this relationship, while Jerry poses an alternative in his frightening identification with the law of the father, his desire to dominate both Susan and Stephanie, and his function as an obstacle between mother and daughter. In the film as in life, this has destructive consequences.

In this manner *The Stepfather* reveals what previously films have repressed, namely the desire for the mother. Unlike *Psycho,* where this desire leads to psychosis and destruction, in *The Stepfather* it is treated as natural and normal. In fact, it is Jerry's inability to come to terms with these forces which lead to his destruction, and in this film he rather than Stephanie is the psychotic. One surmises that in the narrative's unforeseen future, Stephanie will go on to form heterosexual relationships with men, but without having to forego the nurturing relationship with her mother.[7]

All of this places the mother in a much more dominant position than those formulations of cinema based on Oedipal narratives, which emphasize the need to separate from the mother and to distinguish what is male from what is nonmale, making sexual differences the major feature of the plot.

Thus in *The Stepfather* the mother is restored to her rightful place, or not dismantled in the first place. The final scene at last brings down Jerry's birdhouse, a symbol of the structures that have confined women in their roles as cooks, cleaners, and caretakers, subject to the law of the father. It is noteworthy that Stephanie uses Jerry's power tool to destroy the construction. It is to be assumed that Susan and Stephanie will create a new social order, one no longer conceived in hierarchical terms but closer perhaps to a nurturing society, which Adrienne Rich calls "synocentric" culture.[8] Whatever it will be, it will no longer be "a man's world."

Notes

1. Robin Wood, "An Introduction to the American Horror Film," *The American Nightmare: Essays on the Horror Film,* ed. Robin Wood and Richard Lippe (Toronto: Festival of Festivals, 1979), pp. 7–28.

2. Gaylyn Studlar, "Masochism and the Perverse Pleasures of the Cinema," in *Movies and Methods,* ed. Bill Nichols (Berkeley: University of California Press, 1985), 2: 602–621.

3. Jean-Louis Baudry, "The Apparatus," *camera obscura,* no. 1 (Fall 1976): 105–126; Charles F. Altman, "Psychoanalysis and Cinema: The Imaginary Discourse," *Quarterly Review of Film Studies* 2, no. 3 (August 1977): 257–272; Robert Eberwein, "Reflections on the Breast," *Wide Angle* 4, no. 3 (Summer 1981): 48–53; Christian Metz, *The Imaginary Signifier,* trans. Celia Britton, Annwyl Williams, Ben Brewster, and Alfred Guzzetti (Bloomington: Indiana University Press, 1982); and Studlar, "Masochism," among others.

4. Charles Altman, "Psychoanalysis and Cinema: The Imaginary Discourse," in *Movies and Methods,* 2: 522–523.

5. Studlar, "Masochism," p. 614.

6. Kaja Silverman, *The Subject of Semiotics* (New York: Oxford University Press, 1983), p. 161.

7. Of interest here is the process that Freud identified as "the negative Oedipus complex," discussed at length in Kaja Silverman, *The Acoustical Mirror: The Female Voice in Psychoanalysis and Cinema* (Bloomington: Indiana University Press, 1988). As Silverman points out, in *The Ego and the Id* (1923) Freud states that the complete Oedipus complex is actually twofold, both positive and negative, and while the male child may indeed see himself as his father's competitor for the love of the mother, he may simultaneously display "an affectionate feminine attitude to his father and a corresponding jealousy and hostility towards his mother." Such ambiguity likewise applies to female sexual development. Silverman quotes from "The Evolution of the Oedipus Complex in Women," *Psychoanalysis and Female Sexuality*, ed. Hendrik M. Ruitenbeek (New Haven: College and University Press, 1966), pp. 40–41. Having entered "the negative Oedipal" phase, the young girl "wants to conquer the mother for herself and to get rid of the father." Such emotions are not unlike those of Stephanie in *The Stepfather*.

Silverman further notes (p. 120) that, early on, Freud stressed "the continuity rather than (as might be expected) the discontinuity between the little girl's love for her mother" and the "lengthy duration of the little girl's erotic attachment to her mother." Silverman argues for the importance of taking up Freud's notion of "the negative Oedipus complex," which was later supplanted by other paradigms. The value for women, I believe, is that "the negative Oedipus" formulation provides a space wherein female heterosexual attachments (to the father or to other males) can exist without the concomitant necessity of rejecting the mother, and that it offers a more complex view of female sexual desire. It also allows for female maternal bonding to exist within the Symbolic Order rather than exclusively in some utopian paradise that is commonly associated with the pre-Oedipal phase.

The above theories are also relevant to the findings of Nancy Chodorow in *The Reproduction of Mothering: Psychoanalysis and the Sociology of Gender* (Berkeley: University of California Press, 1978), wherein she demonstrates not only that the bonding between mothers and daughters goes well beyond the pre-Oedipal stage, but also that, in the main, daughters never entirely break with their mothers. She also asserts that while Freud felt that separation from the mother was an essential part of masculine development, it need not be the norm for females.

8. Adrienne Rich, *Of Woman Born: Motherhood as Experience and Institution* (New York: Norton, 1976), chap. 4.

Burying the Undead: The Use
and Obsolescence of Count Dracula

Robin Wood

*"Oh my God, what have we done
to have this terror upon us?"*

Bram Stoker, *Dracula*

The immense cultural significance of Count Dracula (and associated vampire mythology) cannot be doubted; it is attested to
by the fictional persistence of the Count within our culture and
especially underlined by the fact that there have been at least
five major film versions of Bram Stoker's 1890 novel: those by
F. W. Murnau (1922), Tod Browning (1931), Terence Fisher
(1958), Werner Herzog (1979), and John Badham (1979). In addition, a distinguished television version with Louis Jourdan appeared in 1978—not to mention minor versions, sequels, spin-
offs, and related movies on vampire themes. It is not far-fetched
to claim that Count Dracula offers himself as a privileged focus
for any inquiry into the possibilities of liberation within Western civilization.

Dracula mythology has various historical sources and literary
precedents, but its major cultural importance clearly begins
with Stoker's novel. As a figure of popular myth in Western cul-

ture, Dracula is the product of Victorian sexual repressiveness; over ninety years later, we are still trying to exorcise him.

My objective in the following essay is to explore the implications of this situation through a consideration of the differences and similarities between Stoker's novel and the films of Murnau and Badham, respectively the earliest and the most recent major film treatments, as well as the two most distinguished, challenging, and intelligent of the lot. Specifically, I shall begin by establishing the most important variants in the three versions; then I will take a closer look at Stoker's novel; and finally I will return to the two film versions to identify what seems to be their essential contribution to the Dracula mystique.

The clearest way of setting forth the major variants is to examine in turn each of the five main characters. In Stoker's novel, Renfield is explicitly insane, an inmate of Dr. Seward's asylum; in Murnau's film, he is the estate agent who sends Jonathan to Transylvania and plans Dracula's invasion of civilization; in Badham, he is Dracula's servant/assistant from the outset. The novel explains why Dracula chooses Renfield as an assistant and is able to manipulate him: he is zoophagous and hence prone to vampiristic tendencies; but Stoker does not account for the basis of his carnivorous appetites nor define precisely what they might entail. Murnau provides no explanation whatsoever, and while this might seem to be a weakness, it can be argued to be a strength; for what Dracula (called Nosferatu) represents is something that already exists—albeit in a feebler form—at the heart of civilization.[1]

Of all the five major characters, Jonathan undergoes the least change (perhaps because he is the least interesting, the obligatory "leading man" whose function is taken for granted). The first part of Murnau's film follows the first part of the novel quite closely; Badham denies Jonathan even the quasi-heroic status of the trip to Transylvania and the personal confrontation with Dracula in his castle. Whereas Stoker wants Jonathan read as the conventional "noble hero" and Badham reduces him to a conventional nonentity, Murnau emphasizes his impotence before the terrible forces, creating Dracula as Jonathan's repressed double through a complex and systematic use of mirror images. His precise relationship to the woman changes somewhat from work to work: in Stoker they are engaged, and marry during the course of the novel; in Murnau they are married from the outset; in Badham they are only engaged, and never marry. Only Badham suggests that they indulge in premarital intercourse, thereby significantly weakening the connotations of Dracula as the product of sexual repression, a change of emphasis crucial to the meaning of the film: the opposition becomes that of the ordinary guy vs. the sexual superman.

Much more complex, in this comparativist respect, is the figure of Van Helsing, for here the crucial changes involve the novel's three central characters, and one quickly realizes that a change in one necessitates a modification of the others, so intricate and essential are the interconnections.

In the novel, Van Helsing is one of the three major characters; he and Dracula battle for possession of the woman (the outcome viewed as her damnation/salvation). Murnau, however, demotes Van Helsing to an amiable old fuddy-duddy who lectures on Venus's flytraps but achieves nothing whatever; Badham preserves the central conflict in Stoker but totally transforms, or reinterprets, the implicit attitudes and sympathies.

As for the female protagonist, here we have first to clear up some confusing name changes—the reason why hitherto I have referred to the heroine as "the woman" rather than by a name. In Stoker, Lucy is the weaker girl who becomes vampirized by Dracula and begins to prey on others; Mina—the major character of the two—is at first engaged to Jonathan and subsequently marries him; Dracula assaults her, and the men have to struggle to rescue her from his power. Murnau reduces Lucy to insignificance (all but eliminating her from the film) and changes Mina to Nina, making her the vampire's antagonist and destroyer (the reason, obviously, for the demoting of Van Helsing). Badham—confusingly—reverses the two names, seemingly a result of his decision to make the first, weaker woman Van Helsing's daughter (in the novel, Van Helsing, like Dracula, is not related to anyone): Van Helsing is Dutch, and Lucy is not a Dutch name, but Mina could be short for Wilhelmina. The facility of this name change, however, may also point to the recognition that, despite the way in which Stoker insistently *contrasts* the characters, the women are to some degree interchangeable—or two aspects of a composite figure.

The distinction in characterization between the two women is simple and obvious—and carried over from Stoker to Badham fairly consistently. Stoker's Lucy is a lightweight, frivolous figure—"girlish," as the term is popularly used; his Mina is stronger, more solid, more intelligent, more determined. Yet both are repeatedly described as feminine ideals (though sexually mature women, both are called "little girls" by their menfolk), so to see them as two sides of the same coin is entirely appropriate. Taken together, they can be seen as exemplifying a deep-seated Victorian unease about womanhood which (as the Badham version demonstrates) our culture has still not resolved nearly a hundred years later. Stoker's Lucy embodies the more obvious Victorian ideal of what a woman should be: helpless, rather silly, irresistibly pretty, in urgent need of the protection and leadership of a good, strong, noble man. Yet there lingers the constant sense that a woman who is strong, intelligent, clear-sighted (but still, of course, irresistibly pretty—or here should one say "beautiful"?—and still, somehow, totally dependent on the male) would be even better. But what to do with such a type? She scarcely needs that male protection and thereby constitutes an implicit threat to male supremacy. By actually *improving* on the ideal, she raises problems.

In any case, all the three versions have one crucial recognition in common: it is the woman that the work is really about.[2] This is especially clear in the Badham film (wherein much of the fascination lies in its efforts to cope with feminism), but it is equally true of the novel, or at least its second half, to which Mina is absolutely central and in which Dracula appears only intermittently. A similar claim can be made for the Murnau film, where, as we have seen, Nina is raised to the status of the vampire's true antagonist.

Before leaving the female roles, I should indicate one further important difference between Stoker and Badham. In the novel, Mina has no parents and Lucy's are very minor figures. Dr. Seward, head of the asylum, is one of Lucy's three suitors, the other two (a British lord and a rich American—shades of Henry James!) being dropped from (as far as I know) all the film versions but the Louis Jourdan television adaptation. It is the Badham version that, very interestingly, makes Mina Van Helsing's daughter and Lucy Dr. Seward's—the paralleling of the two women echoed in the paralleling of the two fathers, with the weak woman having the strong father and vice versa.

Dracula himself also undergoes striking transformations from version to version. In the book, he is an old man when Jonathan encounters him in Transylvania, and is rejuvenated in England by fresh blood. But he is never as grotesque as Max Shreck (Murnau) nor as romantically attractive as Frank Langella (Badham): the two films "exaggerate" him in precisely opposite directions. It should also be pointed out that, after the Transylvania prologue, Dracula virtually disappears from the surface action of the novel, reappearing only in occasional fleeting glimpses. There is nothing in the novel corresponding to Murnau's account of Dracula's journey, nor to the scenes between Dracula and Lucy in Badham's version. To account for this situation, let us turn now to a consideration of the implications of Stoker's narrative technique.

Obviously the diary/journal/letter format employed by Stoker makes for an extremely cumbersome and frequently implausible narrative. How fortunate that so many of the characters keep diaries, and of such inordinate length and detail, often reporting entire conversations verbatim—or entire speeches in broken English by the interminable Van Helsing! How do they find the time, patience, and inclination, with so many extraordinary things going on around them? About the mid-point of the book, furthermore, there comes a time when, for the narrative to continue, it becomes necessary for all the characters to read each other's diaries, so that they may catch up with the reader, in the intervals of congratulating each other (their other major occupation) on their extraordinary goodness and nobility. The insistence on goodness and nobility is itself significant, far exceeding the requirements of Victorian courtesies: one way of describing the book today might be to say that it is about the price at which all that goodness and nobility must be bought.

Also significant, I think, is that the diary form is a means of excluding from any apparent control over the narrative the two most powerful presences of the novel: Count Dracula himself and Bram Stoker. The author, who conceived Dracula, must absolve himself of all responsibility and guilt for that conception; with his (superficial, profoundly hypocritical) commitment to the "good" and the "noble," he must never be seen to describe Dracula himself, in his own person, and above all must never appear to enter into the Count's mind. The corollary is that Dracula must never be allowed a voice, a discourse, a point of view: he must remain the unknowable, whom the narrative is about, but of whom it simultaneously disowns all intimate knowledge. All the presented discourses are those of the good and the noble; it is only through their voices that their author must be seen to speak. It is up to the reader to supply the discourse of Dracula, from the manifold hints the book offers.

Another important aspect of this disowning of Dracula has to do with his foreignness. The remoteness and inaccessibility of his Transylvanian fastness are repeatedly stressed. The first pages of the novel introduce the motif of the crossing of bridges—a piece of symbolism vividly taken up by Murnau and his screenwriter ("And when he had crossed the bridge, the phantoms came to meet him"). The book also has Jonathan cross the "Mittel Land" into regions where language ceases to be recognizable or clearly identifiable. The only intermediaries between Dracula and civilization are those upon whom he depends for transport: the Szgany, gypsies, traditionally regarded as outside civilization, deeply suspect and dangerous, and possessors of magical powers. Dracula himself is descended from Attila and the Huns, the traditional enemies of the civilized world. He is also, of course, associated insistently with the animal kingdom, especially nocturnal animals such as wolves and bats.

The other attribute given to Dracula and Transylvania is that they are dreamlike and are, in fact, the characters' dreams, the nightmares of the good and noble, who at various points in the book are said to rub their eyes in the expectation of waking up. It is worth mentioning here that, according to the testimony of their creators, all three of the archetypal works to which virtually all our horror literature and cinema can be traced back—*Frankenstein* (1818), *Dr. Jekyll and Mr. Hyde* (1886), and *Dracula* itself—had their origins in nightmares. As Bram Stoker's nightmare, then, Count Dracula cannot be so easily disowned, just as we, living in the post-Freudian age, cannot be so innocent about nightmares as was possible for Mary Shelley, Stevenson, and Stoker.

The monstrous figures from our dreams are our images of our repressed selves, and thus Transylvania, by extension, becomes the land of the unconscious, an interpretation which is thoroughly confirmed by Stoker's imagery. There is the whole nightmare-like account of Jonathan's journey to the castle at the opening, with its wolves and mysterious lights hovering on the verge of impenetrable darkness; and consider this, from near the close, as the party returns to Transylvania to hunt Dracula down: "It is a wild adventure that we are on. Here, as we are rushing along through the darkness, with the cold from the river seeming to rise up and strike us; with all the mysterious voices of the night around us, *it all comes home*. We seem to be drifting into unknown places and unknown ways; into a whole world of dark and dreadful things" (emphasis added).[3] For all the emphasis on "unknown" places, "it all comes home": the sense of terrible familiarity, combined with the sense of helplessness suggested by "drifting," must be read not only in terms of the repetition of past experience, but as referring to the familiarity of nightmares, the familiarity of a disowned self that insists upon recognition.

Approached from such a psychoanalytic perspective, and in terms of not only his novelistic but also his various cinematic incarnations, the meanings he has accrued since 1890, Dracula becomes a remarkably comprehensive amalgam of our culture's sexual dreads. But first I should deal briefly with one interpretive problem (actually, it seems to me a nonproblem and can be settled quite simply).

The question has been raised as to whether *Dracula* is really about sexuality and sexual repression, or whether it is instead about the human fear of death, compensated for in the vampire's immortality (an aspiration that must, however, be chastized at the close). The simple answer is that if it is about the former, it must be also about the latter; and one can appeal here to the Freudian theory of the conflict between the Pleasure Principle and the Reality Principle. We are born with the Pleasure Principle—the naive expectation of the immediate and unqualified satisfaction of our desires—and our development grows out of the collision between this and the Reality Principle, the realization that our desires cannot all be totally and immediately gratified. The ultimate, irresistible reality, the ultimate and final interruption of pleasure, is plainly death. If Dracula, then, is to embody the potential triumph of the Pleasure Principle, he must be potentially immortal. Further, it is important to distinguish between different kinds of "reality" that impede the untrammeled functioning of the Pleasure Principle. Death is a metaphysical reality; we cannot change it. But many of the so-called "realities" that get in the way of the satisfaction of desire are social realities, that is to say not "realities" at all but products of a specific cultural situation, ideological constructs, hence susceptible to challenge and change. It is to these "realities" (to all that Marcuse, following Freud, defines as "surplus repression") that Dracula provides one of the supreme challenges in our art and entertainment.[4]

What, then, gives the figure of the vampire Count such comprehensive potency? In light of the Victorian England that conceived and nurtured this monster (though perhaps things have not changed as much as we would like to think), the answers seem to be:

1. *Irresistible power, physical strength; supernatural magnetic force*—easily translatable into imagery of sexual potency. For this was a time when the fact of sexuality was regarded as in itself a great pity, even within the sanctification of marriage.

2. *Nonprocreative sexuality.* For the Victorians, the sole legitimate *aim* of sex was procreation; if one equates Dracula's blood-sucking with sexual pleasure (made horrifying in order to be designated as evil and disowned), it is clear that, whatever it is, it is not going to produce offspring. (The heavily signified *contagion* of vampirism is a very different thing.)

3. *Promiscuity or sexual freedom.* Though Dracula is shown to have a passion for particular women and to value some women over others, his attachments are clearly not exclusive. He transgresses against the principle of monogamy— for Victorians, the only legitimate *form* of sexuality.

4. *"Abnormal" sexuality.* However we interpret the blood-sucking, it is clearly other than "normal" copulation (for Victorians, the only legitimate *method* of sexuality). The stunning climactic moment in the novel when the men break into the bedroom to find Mina with the Count is eloquently suggestive here: Dracula has gashed open his chest and Mina is kneeling on the bed and sucking his blood, while her husband lies in a trance beside her. The suggestion of fellatio is obviously very strong; one can easily apply the same principle in reverse to Dracula's sucking of women.

These components of the Dracula mystique are strongly established and fairly obvious. Two others are all but suppressed in the novel but are hinted at sufficiently to be regarded as present there and are more fully developed in (respectively) the Murnau and Badham versions:

5. *Bisexuality.* Dracula's attraction to blood, although generally focused on women, crosses the boundary of gender: when Stoker's Jonathan cuts himself shaving, Dracula wants to "suck" him. This homosexual element is played up

strongly in Murnau's film—not surprisingly, given the director's homosexuality—in Dracula's nocturnal visit to Jonathan's bedchamber. True, the vampire is interrupted and diverted by Nina's telepathic communication (and henceforth she, not the male, becomes his obsessive goal). Yet the bedchamber scene is played, unmistakably, for its potential perverse sensuality, with Jonathan prostrate on the bed (his attitude suggests a kind of desperate surrender) and the monster advancing and enfolding him with a lascivious longing.

6. *Incest.* In the book this remains ambiguous and uncertain, but Stoker describes one of the three female vampires who haunt Dracula's castle (and have presumably been vampirized by him) as bearing a striking physical resemblance to him: we must, I think, take her as a close relative, probably a sister. The Badham version takes up the incest hint strongly, transferring it to father and daughter: Mina's attempted seduction of Van Helsing in the vaults beneath the graveyard, which is "answered" by her father's plunging a phallic stake into her.

The violation of one further taboo—perhaps the one that still arouses the most horror and resistance—is suggested in the novel but has not, as far as I know, been taken up in any film version except the Jourdan television film:

7. *Child sexuality.* All of Lucy's victims are children; the strong suggestion is not only that she (the Victorian child-woman) likes children, but, even more shockingly, that the children have enjoyed the experience and want more.

It should be added that the novel (which is probably more "perverse" than any film version has dared to be, despite—or perhaps because of—its insistent dedication to the cause of the good and the noble) symbolically enacts in its "good" characters, under cover of the most admirable intentions, something of the "forbidden" that Dracula represents: after Lucy has been sucked by the vampire, all three of her suitors, and later Van Helsing himself, give their blood to her in transfusions. Not only can this be read in terms of all three (or four) men "having" her, it also realizes the novel's suppressed but quite insistent homosexuality, the men mingling their blood with each other's. (We know now that Stoker was himself homosexual, which on the one hand supports this reading and on the other highlights the oppressiveness of the novel's surface, its "conscious" level of meaning: its dedication to the good and the noble of Victorian society is not merely oppressive but self-oppressive.)

The simplest way of looking at the novel is to see it as resolving into the classic Freudian struggle between the Superego (Van Helsing) and the Id (Dracula) for possession of the Ego (Mina). It is the product of a culture wherein Superego and Id can never possibly be reconciled and where no compromise is conceivable: one must annihilate the other. Within the Freudian terms themselves, such an account must be immediately qualified: Superego and

Id are not simply different, diametrically opposed forces, but are intimately related, closely involved with one another. According to Freud, all energy derives from the Id; in the course of human development, some of this energy becomes siphoned off (through the processes of repression) and converted into the *repressive* energy of the Superego; the psyche's warring elements have a single origin. This is dramatized throughout horror (and other) fiction in the figure of the double—a figure too complex to be reduced to a single generalized meaning, but which always carries overtones (at least) of the Superego/Id dichotomy.

Such a meaning lurks just beneath the narrative surface of Stoker's novel and is reproduced (in one form or another, the form depending on the changes I outlined earlier) in the various film versions. Why, we must ask, must Van Helsing be foreign—the only foreign character of any consequence beside Dracula himself? Because the good and noble British (and the American) cannot cope with Dracula—to cope with him requires access to knowledge that would threaten their innocence, and that innocence must be preserved at all costs. Van Helsing has possession of that knowledge; the novel also gives him connections as close to Dracula as Budapest.

But Van Helsing is related to Dracula not only in being foreign. The two characters are linked by one very striking physical characteristic: both are described as having bushy eyebrows that meet over their noses. Above all, Van Helsing is given one of the most remarkable and revealing Freudian slips in literature.[5] The passage comes the morning after Dracula and Mina have been discovered together in the bedroom; the men are discussing, in Mina's presence, the means of trapping Dracula in his London hideout (it is Jonathan's narration):

> So I started up crying out: "Then in God's name let us come at once, for we are losing time. The Count may come to Piccadilly earlier than we think."
>
> "Not so!" said van Helsing, holding up his hand.
>
> "But why?" I asked.
>
> "Do you forget," he said, with actually a smile, "that last night he banqueted heavily, and will sleep late?"
>
> Did I forget? shall I ever—can I ever! Can any of us ever forget that terrible scene! Mina struggled hard to keep her brave countenance; but the pain overmastered her and she put her hands before her face, and shuddered whilst she moaned. Van Helsing had not intended to recall her frightful experience. He had simply lost sight of her and her part in the affair in his intellectual effort. When it struck him what he had said,

he was horrified at his thoughtlessness and tried to comfort her. "Oh, Madam Mina," he said, "dear, dear Madam Mina, alas! that I of all who so reverence you should have said anything so forgetful." (p. 276)

It is not only the relish evident in Van Helsing's gloating words ("last night he banqueted heavily, and will sleep late"), but the fact that they are spoken "with actually a smile" that suggest the character's vicarious *enjoyment* of what Dracula has done. With Mina present to hear, the words become a reenactment of her violation, illuminating the close relationship between exaggerated "reverence" and the desire to rape. The relationship between repressor and repressed, Superego and Id, can never be pure, never one of simple and absolute opposition.

But the Superego/Ego/Id account leaves undiscussed what I have already signaled as the crucial issue of the novel and both film versions: the centrality of the woman to the fiction, whether Mina, Nina, or Lucy. The ultimate horror of the novel is horror at the possibility of the arousal of female sexuality. The virtuous Victorian woman was, after all, supposed not to enjoy sex but to endure it, perhaps praying to pass the time and distract her mind from the inherent disgustingness of the operation. Sexuality is also energy, power, activity: sublimated, it is the source of all creativity, pleasurable work, achievement. If women became sexual beings, who knows where it might all end? Only two options could be permitted: women must be either asexual, passive, and pure, or sexual and degraded. Stoker enlists Mina as an accomplice in her own continued repression: she is horrified at her own "contamination" by Dracula, and actually makes the men, including her adoring husband, promise to cut off her head and drive a stake through her heart if they cannot prevent her from becoming a vampire.

Stoker's mise-en-scène for the final climax is expressively magnificent (if horrifying in ways quite beyond anything of which we can assume him to have been conscious): Dracula destroyed by the three younger men under Van Helsing's supervision, as Mina watches from a hill, secure within a circle drawn by pieces of holy wafer, the woman surveying and assenting to her own castration. The problem Mina represents is posed, as I suggested earlier, by her actually improving on the Victorian ideal of insipid and submissive girlhood: she has, as Van Helsing says at one point, "the mind of a man" (p. 221); she participates in the male knowledge and abilities of writing, typing, and shorthand; she is strong and determined. So, above all, she must be shown to submit voluntarily to the patriarchal order, to the (supposedly) benign domination of all these good and noble, strong and brave, and above all manly men. The purpose of this submission is revealed on the book's very last page in a brief, perfunctory, yet crucial epilogue: the child, male of course, who bears the names of all the virtuous male figures. Stoker makes it explicit that the child is born on the anniversary of the death of the American suitor Quincey Morris; he does not make explicit (though the reader cannot but recall) the far more significant fact that this is also the anniversary of the destruction of Dracula.

As for patriarchy, its rights, and its true source of strength and endurance, there is a marvelous giveaway in Mina's own journal—the irony clearly inadvertent on the part of both character and author, but no less telling for that: "Oh, it did me good to see the way that these brave men worked. How can women help loving men when they are so earnest, and so true, and so brave! And, too, it made me think of the wonderful power of money! What can it not do when it is properly applied" (p. 332). It is a passage to delight the heart of any Marxist-feminist—the economic base of male dominance so nakedly exposed. Elsewhere, Mina's husband puts it even more brutally: "Judge Moneybag will settle this case, I think" (p. 312).

There remains to consider briefly some of the significant variants worked on these themes in the two film versions.

In Murnau, the first, and still the greatest, adaptation, all of the changes are guided by a sure creative intelligence. (I have elsewhere analyzed the film at length and will not repeat the details of my interpretation here.)[6] What is most fascinating is the most drastic change, the promotion of Nina to status of chief antagonist. The use of Nina throughout the film is amazing: Stoker's implication that Jonathan and Dracula represent alternative husbands for her is greatly developed, and the decision is made hers. The intercutting of the journeys of Jonathan and Dracula is among the film's finest inspirations (and a sequence that makes nonsense of Bazin's extraordinary assertion that "in neither NOSFERATU nor SUNRISE does editing play a decisive part").[7] Through the editing, the two men are exactly paralleled as Nina's two husbands; Nina sits by the shore (among gravestones in a cemetery in the dunes) looking out to sea, ostensibly for Jonathan, whose mode of travel is by land; in the sleepwalking scene she exclaims, "He is coming! I must go to meet him!" after a shot, not of Jonathan, but of the vampire's ship.

Nina herself, emaciated and bloodless, ambiguously resembles both vampire and Christian martyr; at once Nosferatu's destroyer and potential mate, her ecstasy and terror are both religious and sensual. The film's background is of course German Expressionism, with its characteristic awareness of repressed forces but its simultaneous viewing of them as horrifying, bestial, and overwhelmingly powerful. Nina's sacrifice of herself again enlists the woman in

Nosferatu (1922): the vampire as the repressed forces within the impotent protagonist.

the battle for patriarchy, but the nature of the sacrifice is profoundly ambiguous, and the price of victory is her own destruction, so that patriarchy is left empty, without the ratification of the adoring woman to venerate the brave, strong, pure men. Unlike Stoker's novel, therefore, Murnau's film cannot possibly move toward the birth of the child "whose bundle of names links all our little band of men together" (p. 352). Indeed, the film casts grave doubt on the virtues of courage, strength, and purity, Jonathan becoming completely impotent at all points when he is confronted with the vampire, who in turn symbolizes his repressed self.

We may turn, then, to a film in which Dracula receives a totally different embodiment, and ask how far, in fact, have we progressed in the last half century? Badham's movie has been gravely underestimated, by critics and public alike: in many ways it is quite remarkable, and as an interpretation of the novel extremely audacious. *Sight and Sound,* in one of its inimitable capsule reviews, went so far as to call it a straightforward adaptation that did not try to interpret, an observation that must go down in history as one of the most startling critical aberrations of all time.[8] For a start, this appears to be the first

The romantic passion between the Count (Frank Langella) and Lucy (Kate Nelligan) is compromised by the trappings of Dracula mythology in *Dracula* (1979).

Dracula movie with a happy ending (of sorts) and the first in which it is Van Helsing, not Dracula, who is transfixed through the heart with a stake (minor details that presumably escaped the *Sight and Sound* reviewer). Its key line is perhaps Van Helsing's earlier "If we are defeated, then there is no God"; they are defeated.

The film is very much preoccupied, in fact, with the overthrow of patriarchy in the form of the Father, Van Helsing, of whom God the Father is but an extension. The ending is the triumph of not merely Dracula (who, progressively undaunted by garlic and crucifixes in the course of the film, finally flies off, burnt, battered, but still alive and strong, into the sunlight) but of Oedipus, who, having carried off the woman, kills the father and flies away. The film makes clear that Lucy is still his, even though she cannot join him until the sequel (which, in view of the poor box office response, will now never be made). Indeed, the editing suggests quite strongly that it is Lucy who gives Dracula the strength to escape. It would be nice simply to welcome the film on those terms and leave it at that. Unfortunately, the matter is not so clearcut, and the film seems to me, though very interesting and often moving, severely flawed, compromised, and problematic. Its chief effect, perhaps, is to remind us that we live in an age not of liberation but of pseudo-liberation.

The film's problems are again centered on the woman, now Lucy (the superb Kate Nelligan), and on the difficulties of building a positive interpretation on foundations that obstinately retain much of their original connotations of evil. The result is a film both confused and confusing. In response to our popular contemporary notions of feminism, Lucy's strength and activeness are strikingly emphasized and contrasted with Mina's weakness, childishness, and passivity. Dracula insists that Lucy come to him of her free choice: the film makes clear that he deliberately abstains from exerting any supernatural or hypnotic power over her, as he did over Mina. The film thus ties itself in knots in first presenting Lucy as a liberated woman and then asserting that a liberated woman would freely choose to surrender herself to (of all people) Dracula. Badham wants to present the Dracula/Lucy relationship in terms of romantic passion, a passion seen as transcending everyday existence; yet he cannot free the material of the paraphernalia of Dracula mythology, and with it the notion of vampirism as evil. With its romantic love scenes on the one hand, and the imagery that associates both Dracula and Lucy with spiders on the other, the film never resolves this contradiction.

Although it pays a lot of attention to the picturesque details of Victoriana, Badham's movie seems far more Romantic than Victorian in feeling and owes a lot to a tradition that has always had links with Dracula mythology: the tradition of "*l'amour fou*" and Surrealism. It is a tradition explicitly dedicated to liberation, but the liberation it offers (lacking any theories of feminism or of bisexuality) proves usually to be very strongly male-centered, with an insistent emphasis on various forms of *machismo*. From *Wuthering Heights* (1847) through *L'Age d'Or* (1930) to Badham's *Dracula,* "*l'amour fou*" is characteristically built on male charisma to which the woman surrenders. The film's emphasis on heterosexual romantic passion actually diminishes the potential for liberation implicit in the Dracula myth: the connotations of bisexuality are virtually eliminated (Dracula vampirizes Renfield purely to use him as a slave, not for pleasure, and he does so in the form of a bat; Jonathan's visit to Transylvania is foregone, so there is no possibility of any equivalent for the castle scenes in Murnau); and the connotations of promiscuity are very much played down, with Dracula vampirizing other women almost contemptuously, his motivation centered on his passion for Lucy. Under cover of liberation, then, heterosexual monogamy is actually reinstated.

More sinister (though closely related) is the film's latent fascism. Dracula and Lucy are to be a new King and Queen; the "ordinary" people of the film—Jonathan, for example, and Mina—are swept aside with a kind of brutal contempt. Between them, Dracula and Lucy will create a new race of superhumans who will dominate the earth. Dracula's survival at the end—with Lucy's complicity—is a personalized "triumph of the will," the triumph of the superman over mere humans.

What Badham's film finally proves—and it is a useful thing to have demonstrated—is that it is time for our culture to abandon Dracula and pass beyond him, relinquishing him to social history. The limits of profitable reinterpretation have been reached (as Frank Langella's Dracula remarks, "I come from an old family—to live in a new house is impossible for me"). The Count has served his purpose by insisting that the repressed cannot be kept down, that it must always surface and strive to be recognized. But we cannot purge him of his connotations of evil—the evil that Victorian society projected onto sexuality and by which our contemporary notions of sexuality are still contaminated. If the "return of the repressed" is to be welcomed, then we must learn to represent it in forms other than that of an undead vampire-aristocrat.

Notes

1. Only the Browning version tries to "rationalize" Renfield by having him—instead of Jonathan—go to Transylvania, where he is vampirized by the Count.

2. The recognition is not shared, at least to the same extent, by the Browning and Fisher versions.

3. Bram Stoker, *Dracula* (New York: Penguin, 1979), p. 333. Subsequent references to the novel are from this edition and appear parenthetically in the text.

4. Herbert Marcuse, *Eros and Civilization: A Philosophical Inquiry into Freud* (Boston: Beacon Press, 1966), p. 37.

5. I use the term somewhat loosely, perhaps, since no actual verbal error or substitution of one word for another takes place. Yet the essence of the "Freudian slip" is certainly here: the speaker's words betray a significant slip between conscious and unconscious intention.

6. See my essay "The Dark Mirror: Murnau's *Nosferatu*," in *The American Nightmare: Essays on the Horror Film,* ed. Robin Wood and Richard Lippe (Toronto: Festival of Festivals, 1979), pp. 43–49.

7. André Bazin, "The Evolution of Film Language," in *The New Wave,* trans. Peter Graham (Garden City, N.Y.: Doubleday, 1968), p. 30.

8. "Film Guide: *Dracula,*" *Sight and Sound* 48, no. 4 (Autumn 1979): 268.

18

Daughters of Darkness:
The Lesbian Vampire on Film

Bonnie Zimmerman

. . . they all know she's there.
and no one goes out after dark.
they tuck their daughters into bed,
   and lock their doors.
they say, we should have killed her back then,
when we first knew.

and their daughters lie awake in their beds,
and smile.

Karen Lindsey, "Vampire" [1]

The return of the vampire—tall, dark, and irresistibly male—
has not yet revived interest in a surprising phenomenon of the
1960s and early 1970s: the lesbian vampire film. Although the
archetypal vampire in this culture is Dracula, often accompanied by submissive brides and female followers, lesbian vampires
have a long and worthy history in literature, legend, and film.
Two sources for the lesbian vampire myth have been used extensively by filmmakers. One is the Countess Elizabeth Bathory,
a sixteenth-century Hungarian noblewoman who was reputed
to have tortured 650 virgins, bathing in their blood in order
to preserve her youth. The second source is Joseph Sheridan

LeFanu's *Carmilla* (1871), an intensely erotic novella recounting the story of the Countess Millarca Karnstein, who lives through the centuries by vampirizing young girls.

One of the earliest classic vampire films, Carl Dreyer's *Vampyr* (1932), is a very free adaptation of *Carmilla,* purged of all suggestions of lesbian sexuality. *Dracula's Daughter* (1936) includes a muted lesbian encounter between a reluctant vampire-woman and a servant girl, suggesting an important class dynamic to the lesbian vampire myth. When the seducer is another woman, she must derive her power from her class position rather than her sex. *Blood of Dracula* (1957) combines this class element with the classic stereotype of the schoolgirl-teacher lesbian relationship: the socially dominant teacher (who herself is not a vampire), through scientific experiment, turns her powerless student into a blood-sucking monster.

Several other films prior to 1970—*La Danza Macabra* (1964), *La Maschera del Demonio* (also called *Black Sunday,* 1960), and *I Vampiri* (1956)—also feature female vampires who exhibit greater or lesser degrees of interest in their own sex. Two films based on *Carmilla*—Roger Vadim's *Et Mourir de Plaisir* (*Blood and Roses* [1960]) and *La Maldición de los Karnstein* (*Terror in the Crypt* [1964])—exploit particularly well such conventions of the Gothic horror genre as historical settings, mysterious castles, and aristocratic characters, as well as the dream sequences of surrealism, to draw us into their fantasy landscapes.

Although, like all vampire films, these pre-1970 examples express a nostalgia for death and a subtle "juxtaposition of erotic and macabre imagery,"[2] after 1970 filmmakers began to explore the explicit connections between sex and violence, not only in a heterosexual context but in a lesbian one as well. One impetus for these films was certainly the desire to capitalize on the market for pornography, since the lesbian vampire genre can allow nudity, blood, and sexual titillation in a "safe" fantasy structure. The English company Hammer Films (responsible for the Christopher Lee Dracula series as well) based its exploitation trilogy—*The Vampire Lovers* (1970), *Lust for a Vampire* (1970), and *Twins of Evil* (1971)—on the ubiquitous *Carmilla.* These Hammer films connect the proven conventions of the genre—a Gothic girls' school, black magic, moonlit lakes, and period costumes—with modern expectations of sex and blood. A final *Carmilla* of the period was *La Novia Ensangretada* (1972).

On the other hand, *Countess Dracula* (1971), *La Noche de Walpurgis* (1970), and *Blood Ceremony* (1973) were each inspired by the legend of the Countess Bathory. *Countess Dracula,* another Hammer film, is particularly interesting in that the vampire countess attempts to consume the personality and body of her own daughter, a suggestive parallel to the version of mother-daughter relationships popularized by Nancy Friday's book *My Mother, My Self* (1977) and Ingmar Bergman's *Autumn Sonata* (1978).

Finally, a number of films developed lesbian themes independent of either Carmilla or the Countess Bathory. American-International graduate Stephanie Rothman is moderately sympathetic to lesbianism in *The Velvet Vampire* (1971), although she stops short of allowing her women full expression of their attraction.[3] She also introduces a feminist twist: the vampire halts in her pursuit of the female victim to attack a rapist. Jean Rollin's *La Frisson des Vampires* (1970), on the other hand, is a striking articulation of the male fantasy of the "butch" lesbian, complete with metal chains and black leather boots. It also makes explicit a theme that is implicit in most of these films and in our culture as a whole: that lesbians and homosexuals are narcissists capable of making love only to images of themselves. Hammer's vampires seduce young women who are strikingly similar to themselves; Rollin's lesbian is finally reduced to sucking the blood from her own veins.

This brief filmography suggests that lesbian vampire films use many of the stereotypes that have been attached to lesbianism at least since the nineteenth century: lesbianism is sterile and morbid; lesbians are rich, decadent women who seduce the young and powerless. But the fact that the lesbian vampire myth returned with such force and popularity in the films of the early 1970s suggests to me that an additional factor may have been added by the specific historical developments of the 1960s and 1970s: feminism and public awareness of lesbianism.

The lesbian vampire, besides being a Gothic fantasy archetype, can be used to express a fundamental male fear that female bonding will exclude men and threaten male supremacy. Lesbianism—love between women—must be vampirism; elements of violence, compulsion, hypnosis, paralysis, and the supernatural must be present. One woman must be a vampire, draining the life of the other woman, yet holding her in a bond stronger than the grave. David Pirie, excusing the negative stereotype of the female vampire (which, he notes, appears at exactly the time women were challenging such degrading images), argues that "the function of the vampire movie is precisely to incarnate the most hostile aspects of sexuality in a concrete form."[4] But it is necessary to ask why and in what form hostile sexuality gets incarnated in the lesbian vampire film.

The male vampire has been used to suggest that heterosexuality is sometimes indistinguishable from rape: the recent *Dracula* (1979) with Frank Langella crudely overemphasizes this identification. The function of the lesbian vampire is to contain attraction between women within the same boundaries of sexual violence, to force it into a particular model of sexuality. By showing the lesbian as a vampire-rapist who violates and destroys her victim, men alleviate their fears that lesbian love could create an alternate model, that two women without coercion or morbidity might prefer one another to a man.

Although direct parallels between social forces and popular culture are risky at best, the popularity of the lesbian vampire film in the early 1970s may be related to the beginnings of an international feminist movement, as a result of which women began both to challenge male domination and to bond strongly with each other.[5] Since feminism between 1970 and 1973 was not yet perceived as a fundamental threat, men could enjoy the sexual thrill provided by images of lesbian vampires stealing women and sometimes destroying men in the process. The creators of those images—like the pornographic filmmakers who appeal to male fantasies with scenes of lesbianism—must have felt secure enough in their power and that of their primary male audience to flirt with lesbianism and female violence against men. It is suggestive that lesbian vampires no longer populate the screen (not even to relay the myth's normative message to women: if you value your neck, stick with your man). Today men do not want to see themselves as the victims but the perpetrators of sexual violence; they want to see women subdued and violated by men, not other women. The explicitly male sexual threat of Dracula is the message for the 1980s.

The myth of the lesbian vampire, however, carries in it the potentiality for a feminist revision of meaning. The Karen Lindsey poem that prefaces this essay tells us that sexual attraction between women can threaten the authority of the male-dominated society. The lesbian vampire film can lend itself to an even more extreme reading: that in turning to each other, women triumph over and destroy men themselves.

One film that is considerably ambiguous about the lesbian vampire and thus lends itself particularly well to a feminist interpretation is *Daughters of Darkness* (*La Rouge aux Lèvres* [1970]), a Belgian film directed by Harry Kumel. I saw this film shortly after its release in this country; the audience consisted of aficionados of soft porn, followers of the new wave intrigued by the presence of Delphine Seyrig, and a large contingent of lesbians curious about the film's advertised display of lesbianism. My analysis of *Daughters of Darkness* is intended to raise some questions about the meaning of the archetype and the possibilities of interpreting hostile images from a feminist perspective. It is certainly limited by the fact that these lesbian vampire films are simply not around any longer and available for careful study. But I hope that my ideas stir some discussion and a revival of interest in this lost genre.

The Countess Bathory (Delphine Seyrig) manipulates the young heterosexual couple in *Daughters of Darkness* (1970).

Daughters of Darkness opens in Ostend, off-season, where a newlywed couple—immaculate, handsome, a veritable Barbie and Ken—have stopped on their way to England to break the news of their marriage to his family. They epitomize the perfect heterosexual couple, except that he turns out to be a sexual sadist and his "mother" is really an aging homosexual lover. The other visitors at the hotel are a beautiful countess who appears only at night and her devoted female companion. She is, of course, the Countess Bathory (Delphine Seyrig), who after a thirty-year absence has returned to the Ostend hotel as young and fresh as ever (diet and lots of sleep, she explains, have prolonged her youth). While her assistant distracts the newlywed husband, the Countess seduces his willing bride. (She is fed up with her husband's overt sadism, preferring the subtleties of a bite on the neck.) The vampire assistant is killed—it is not clear how—by the husband, who then confronts his bride and the Countess. In the midst of their altercation, the two women conveniently shatter a crystal bowl over his hands, exchange a look that is equally erotic and hungry, then quickly clamp their lips to his wrists: *la rouge aux lèvres*—blood on the lips. The new lovers drive off into the sunrise, only to end in a fiery automobile crash which, in accordance with traditional vampire lore, ends the Countess's reign by impaling her on a tree branch. But the Countess's spirit immediately transmigrates into the body of the young bride, who then returns to the hotel to seduce another willing victim.[6]

Kumel places *Daughters of Darkness* solidly within the Gothic horror tradition through his use of the empty hotel (equivalent in effect to the mysterious castle), aristocratic characters, and an evocative use of color: the Countess, with her bleached white hair and silver lamé gowns, suggests the glamor of death, the assistant in solid black reminds us of night terrors, the blood-red of violent sexuality marks the dissolves between scenes. At the same time that the film evokes the atmosphere of the vampire genre and carries its message that woman-bonding is unnatural and dangerous, it also, as critics have noted, suggests the radical potential of the myth.

Pirie notes that "the overall framework of ideas [in the film] is not just sexual but political," limiting its political stance, however, to that of a class analysis of bourgeois decadence and alienation.[7] However, *Daughters of Darkness* can be given a feminist reading that uncovers a "lucidly antimale" as well as antibourgeois political stance.[8] The "antimale" bias inherent in the lesbian vampire myth can be expressed and seen as a justification for women's suppression, but it can also be interpreted by feminists as a justified attack on male power, a revenge fantasy, and a desire for separation from the male world. The following analysis of *Daughters of Darkness* further explains these ideas.

The lesbian vampire myth, to begin with, is a variation of the classic triangle: man and female vampire battling for possession of a woman. Pirie notes that lesbian vampire films such as *Daughters of Darkness* often incorporate the motif of the honeymoon (the honeymoon also appears in some heterosexual vampire films and in satires of the horror genre, such as *The Rocky Horror Picture Show* [1975]). I would suggest that this is because the honeymoon, traditionally, is a transitional period during which the husband asserts his power and control over his bride, winning or forcing her into institutionalized heterosexuality. For the husband, then, the honeymoon period provides fear and anxiety: will he prove potent enough, both sexually and socially, to "bind" his bride to himself and the marriage structure? Bondage and discipline in *Daughters of Darkness* is used as a highly appropriate symbol of the husband's fledgling power over his bride (while in *La Frisson des Vampires* male power is mocked by the lesbian vampire's chains). The virgin-bride, linked to the institution of heterosexuality by socialization rather than by experience, is particularly vulnerable to the blandishments of a sinister sexual force. Women must be forced into marriage, into "normal" womanhood, since, left to their own designs, they might be as easily attracted to a "perverse" form of sexuality, whether extramarital, diabolical (possession by the devil), or lesbian.

It is essential in a film that explores this male fear of heterosexual inadequacy that the point of view be firmly and unambiguously male. The male viewer or reader must be able to step in imaginatively to take over when the situation has reached the appropriate level of sexual arousal, thus potentially spiraling out of control. The heterosexual context of the film must be very clear; lesbianism must be presented as an aberration. This is the function of the lesbian interlude in a pornographic film: the male viewer, excited by the promise of stepping in to separate two women and thus prove his superior prowess, is able to affirm both his sexual potency and his masculine superiority at the same time.

When the lesbian is also a vampire, he has an added explanation for the attraction one woman might have for another. It is not he who is inadequate; he is competing with supernatural powers. A man who offers his woman life through his sexual potency (symbolized by sperm) cannot compete with the vampire who sucks away her life (symbolized by blood). Instead, he must destroy the vampire—the lesbian—who threatens male power through sexual attacks on women. For, in fact, whether the woman vampire is lesbian or heterosexual, her real object of attack is always the male.

This is the message contained within the fantasy structures of the lesbian vampire genre. But in *Daughters of Darkness,* heterosexuality is of a decidedly ambiguous character. The only male in the film is unsympathetic and hardly a character men might care to identify with, since he is himself sexually aberrant, the kept man of an elderly transvestite. Furthermore, because of his own homosexuality, he is particularly vulnerable in relation to his bride and thus abuses his male "privilege" of establishing control over his woman. His sadism and murderousness are outside the conventions of Gothic fantasy since he himself is not a vampire: he is a simple killer. And he is an ineffective one as well, since he ends up the victim of the vampires, one of whom is his own bride. Although the purpose of the lesbian vampire myth is to provide a way for men to soothe their sexual anxieties, *Daughters of Darkness* accentuates that anxiety instead.

Furthermore, Delphine Seyrig is a very atypical lesbian vampire. She is a mature woman, unlike many other lesbian vampires who appear young and themselves vulnerable. This, in addition to her off-screen celebrity, gives her an aura of authority. She is never shown nude and is thus not vulnerable to male prurience as most lesbian vampires are. In the film she is the sexual and political equal of the male character, if not his superior. She is never shown actually attacking the young bride; there are no bites on the neck, no bared fangs.

Instead, we see Seyrig sitting with a distracted look on her face, her hand gently stroking the hair of her original assistant. Or we see her hand wander slowly toward the bride, more to protect her from her husband than to threaten her. She is portrayed as being a sophisticated, intelligent, motherly, and fascinating woman. If there were any lingering doubts as to her benignity, Seyrig inclines toward a camp interpretation that dissipates some of the Gothic atmosphere. Altogether, we might be tempted to doubt that any supernatural means were necessary to entice the young woman were we not shown the two vampires sucking the husband's blood. In this rivalry between man and vampire for possession of the bride's body and soul, the vampire's power seems both superior to and more desirable than the man's.

Finally, the ending of the film emphasizes the power of woman and the attractiveness of lesbianism. The spirit of the Countess immediately occupies a new body once it is deprived of the old, suggesting that lesbianism is eternal, passing effortlessly from one woman to another. No attempt of man or God can prevent the lesbian from passing on her "curse." The effect of this transference is not at all horrifying, but rather amusing, almost charming, especially to a lesbian viewer. The stiff-faced beauty queen, whom we have seen as innocent bride, passive masochist, and fascinated victim, is now the powerful, immortal lesbian vampire. Any woman, this suggests, can be lucky enough to be a lesbian.

I am not arguing that *Daughters of Darkness* in itself is a feminist film, although Kumel seems to be manipulating our expectations of the genre. As an academic and film historian, he must certainly have been aware of his effects, especially since it is reported that he would not have made the film without Seyrig, because of whom many of the negative aspects of the lesbian vampire are mitigated. But it is when the viewer is herself a lesbian and feminist that the film takes on a kaleidoscope of meaning. It shows lesbianism as attractive and heterosexuality as abnormal and ineffectual. It carries a subtle message justifying man-hating that casts in a political light the traditional fear-of-woman theme inherent in vampire mythology. It gives the last laugh to Countess Bathory and not to the vampire hunters. It is filmed with style and humor, not with horror and violence. It suggests that women have good reasons for turning away from sadistic men to other women and even justifies, to a limited extent, the elimination of men.

It suggests finally that the lesbian vampire theme—although originally misogynistic and antilesbian—can be revised and reinterpreted, thus opening it to use by feminists.[9] The myth has been used to attack female autonomy and bonding and to express male fear of women. A feminist reading of *Daughters of Darkness* suggests that feminists can transform this myth (as we are transforming the patriarchal myth of witchcraft, for example). The many daughters of Carmilla and the Countess Bathory still lie awake in their beds smiling, waiting for the kiss of the revitalized lesbian vampire.

Notes

1. Karen Lindsey, "Vampire," *The Second Wave*, 2, no. 2 (1972): 36.

2. David Pirie, *The Vampire Cinema* (New York: Crescent Books, 1977), p. 100.

3. See Dannis Peary, "Stephanie Rothman: R-Rated Feminist," in *Women and the Cinema,* ed. Karyn Kay and Gerald Peary (New York: E. P. Dutton, 1977), pp. 179–192. I have not seen Rothman's films, but, on the surface, Peary's argument for Rothman as a feminist seems to me to be overstated.

4. Pirie, *The Vampire Cinema,* p. 100.

5. Sharon Russell, in private correspondence, suggests also that "there is some increase in [the] number of films dealing with witches during periods when women's roles increase in importance." These relationships need further study. See Russell's "The Witch in Film: Myth and Reality," *Film Reader* 3 (1978), pp. 80–89, reprinted in *Planks of Reason: Essays on the Horror Film,* ed. Barry Keith Grant (Metuchen, N.J.: Scarecrow Press, 1984), pp. 113–125.

6. Werner Herzog's *Nosferatu* (1979) uses the same transference device: after the original vampire dies, his victim immediately takes on the same physical characteristics.

7. Pirie, *The Vampire Cinema,* p. 113.

8. Parker Tyler, *Screening the Sexes* (New York: Holt, Rinehart and Winston, 1972), p. 115. As is typical of this book, Tyler's observation is brilliant and totally undeveloped.

9. Another delightful revision of the vampire image is Sue Fink's and Joelyn Grippo's "Leaping" (music and lyrics by Sue Fink), as sung by Meg Christian on *Face the Music,* Olivia Records LF913B.

19

From Dracula—with Love

Vera Dika

Bram Stoker's Dracula (1993) is, paradoxically, very much Francis Ford Coppola's Dracula, and the title itself is the first clue in this system of contradictions. By including the name of the novel's author in his work, Coppola refers us back to the "original," but does so precisely at the close of the twentieth century, in an era that has been called Postmodern and where the original is often hopelessly muted.[1] The title also takes us back to the nineteenth century, a time before the proliferation of Dracula interpretations, parodies, and pastiches—and, interestingly, to a time before the century-long evolution of the horror genre on film. In this way we are returned to the beginning, to the past; but when we look at the film itself, we are not presented with the original at all. Instead, the film reveals a wholly new work and conception, one that will take Dracula to a new stage in its interpretation of woman, of blood, and of the monster.

By turning to the original, then, Coppola takes not only Dracula, but the horror genre itself, back to a symbolic ground zero. And from this position there is an additional strategy, to "authenticate," that is, to include more historically accurate material into the work. *Bram Stoker's Dracula* shares this tendency with some recent films, especially those that have attempted to revive the western genre. In *The Last of the Mohicans* (1992), for example, a similar attempt is made to take the western back to its source, the 1826 James Fenimore Cooper novel in which the basic conventions of the genre first appear. And in both *Bram Stoker's Dracula* and the western films (e.g, *Tombstone* [1994], *Geronimo* [1993], and *Posse* [1993]) there is a seeming attempt to present previously excluded historical detail: just as in *Tombstone,* for example, we are given a more accurate portrayal of the shoot-out at the OK Corral, so in *Bram Stoker's Dracula* there are scenes that refer to Vlad the Impaler, the historical figure on whom the fictional Dracula is purportedly based.

It would then seem that, in 1993, to revive an old story is an attempt to present it in all its purity, its freshness. On closer inspection, however, it becomes apparent that what we are witnessing is not an attempt merely to revitalize the original or to re-present history, but rather to retell it. The inclusion of historical "accuracy," in the end, is only a reshaping of that material into a new story, a new myth. Unlike Modernist attempts to "de-mythify" established generic forms, what results here is a Postmodern "neo-mythification," if you will. Gone is the pretense of dislodging the ideological "real" from behind fictional material (as in Robert Altman's *McCabe and Mrs. Miller* [1974], for example) or, variously, the compulsion to "re-mythify," to merely resuscitate a past form. Instead, what we arrive at in Coppola's work is the construction of a Postmodern Dracula, one in which representation itself comes into high relief and where gender takes on a new focus. Although there have been other retellings of Stoker's story, such as the "women's lib"–inspired *Dracula* by John Badham (1979), in Coppola's work the book's devastated victim, Mina, becomes the film's heroine. In addition, she shares this position with the Count himself, now a character remodeled to support the changed dynamic.

The horror genre has evolved through a number of stages across its history on film. The most significant shift, however, has been in the representation of the monster. The earlier classical monsters, such as Dracula or Frankenstein, or even the science fiction monsters of the 1950s, such as the Thing, have been replaced in more recent years by the psychological deviant. Beginning with Alfred Hitchcock's *Psycho* (1960) and moving through such films as *The Texas Chainsaw Massacre* (1974), *Halloween* (1978), and *Friday the 13th* (1980), the monster is presented less as a supernatural creature and more as a man (only occasionally as a woman) whose unknowable and unfathomable mental perversion leads him to stalk, to kill, often numerous victims. A significant film in this evolution is *Henry: Portrait of a Serial Killer* (1990), a work in which the conventions of cinematic realism are utilized in a chilling and openly repulsive presentation of senseless murder. So significant is this contemporary shift that, for critics like Noel Carroll, the presence of a psychological deviant as the central menace, instead of a traditional monster, is enough to disqualify a work from belonging to the horror genre altogether.[2] For Coppola, then, to roll back this later development within the horror film, to return us to one of the most influential monsters of all time, and to do so now in a style quite opposed to that of realism, is so relevant in its conceptualization and its realization that I will use it as a starting point in the discussion of *Bram Stoker's Dracula*.

Coppola uses Bram Stoker's novel as a source and, more than any previous rendition of *Dracula*, includes characters, lines of dialogue, situations, and, most importantly, the journal format of the novel to structure his film. For this reason, a multiple perspective emerges, as the voice of the film is generated from varying points of view, including those of Jonathan Harker, Mina Harker, Dr. Seward, and Dr. Van Helsing. In the novel, these multiple perspectives interweave to create the effect of enveloping doom, as different voices describe their perceptions, encounters with the monster, and, later, the plan for his ultimate demise. In the film, the journal format instead serves to fracture the notion of subjectivity. It no longer becomes a matter of multiple, more-or-less valid views of the monster, but rather a decentering of these now secondary characters. Unlike the novel, the character who ultimately emerges as hero in *Bram Stoker's Dracula* is Dracula himself; but this time he is not alone in this hero position—his woman, Mina, is with him.

According to Carroll, the monster of the horror genre has the distinct characteristic of being "interstitial," that is, he has a borderline quality, a categorical incompleteness.[3] He can be both alive and dead, as is Dracula; both animal and vegetable, as is the Thing; or both organic and mechanical, as is the Alien. This categorical impurity causes the feeling of revulsion, which is the characteristic emotion, according to Carroll, of the horror genre. As categorically impure, the classical monster is also capable of being a shapechanger: mist at one moment, a bat or rat at another. Dracula, in particular, embodies this tendency, as does his association with such unclean elements as dirt, vermin, and blood, not to mention death. He is what Julia Kristeva, in *Powers of Horror,* describes as the "abject"—that which, like filth, death, and decay, must be cast away in order for life to continue.[4]

But in *Bram Stoker's Dracula,* the monster is also a handsome young man, played by Gary Oldman. Although Badham's *Dracula,* starring Frank Langella, presents a devastatingly attractive Count who seduces his willing victims, he is never a lover in the real sense. In *Bram Stoker's Dracula,* the monster is now rendered as an ardent lover who is passionately loved in return by the beautiful Mina. And it is precisely here that the most significant distinction between the novel and the film can be cited. As Carroll has noted, the horror genre's emotion of revulsion is one that is created by the reaction of the characters to the monster.[5] They respond with horror and fear because of the disgust that the monster inspires in them, and in our identification with these characters, we participate in that revulsion. In stories not of the horror genre, however, as in the fairy tale, the response to the monster is quite different. *Beauty and the Beast* is a good example, for here the monster's ugliness is met by Beauty with tenderness, acceptance, and then love. So even in horror films like Badham's version of *Dracula,* where Mina's initial response to the handsome Count is desire, her ultimate reaction to him has to be, and is, revulsion and fear. In *Bram Stoker's Dracula,* however, the defiled monster is consistently adored by Mina. With only a minor hesitation at first, Mina loves Dracula across the entirety of the film with a passion and intensity that is meant to transcend even death.

So, while the monster of *Bram Stoker's Dracula* is often represented to comply with the classical model, he is also made to incorporate some contradictory elements. He may be a shape-changer, dead, soulless, and associated with vermin, but his makeup and costuming are fashioned to underscore a new set of elements. When we first meet Dracula in the film, he is Kabuki-like. With an ancient, furrowed face and white hair rising in Oriental swirls, the Count enters the room uncharacteristically clothed in a sumptuous red silk robe. Certainly this is the color of blood, but now the rich hue and shimmering texture of the material has a vibrancy that connotes life and sexuality (quite unlike the fetid black clothes worn by previous Draculas) rather than defilement and death. A similar transformation is rendered in Dracula's demeanor, beautifully rendered by Oldman. No longer is this the frigid, acrid stiffness of the Count in F. W. Murnau's *Nosferatu* (1922) or the lascivious glare of Bela Lugosi's *Dracula* (1931) or even the smarmy sexuality of Frank Langella's monster; here, instead, we encounter a face and demeanor of deep longing, of tremendous loss. And, as Dracula gazes at the photograph of the young Mina, the very image of his lost wife, there is revealed an unfathomable love and a determination to find her anew. In this way, *Bram Stoker's Dracula* is more a love story than it is, strictly speaking, a horror film.

A similar type of transformation has been accomplished by Coppola's film in its representation of women and of blood. For Kristeva, menstrual blood and, by extension, women are seen as abject by society. The female is associated with filth and defilement, that which must be cast away from the symbolic system. For this reason, woman can become synonymous with evil.[6] In literature, this fear of the wound—of female genitalia and female genital function—has been incorporated, according to another theory, now by Sigmund

Bram Stoker's Dracula (1993): Dracula (Gary Oldman) in his Oriental guise.

Freud, into stories that inspire dread, fear, and loathing. In his essay "The Uncanny,"[7] Freud argues that this emotion has its source in things once familiar to us, to what was "homey," or *heimlich,* but is now repressed. He claims that within this familiarity, this comfort, lurks the opposite emotion, the *unheimlich,* or "uncanny," the dread of our first home, of the womb, of our mother's genitalia. And for the male, it also includes the fear of the mother's imagined castration and, potentially, his own.

This composite of fears and images is clearly evidenced in Bram Stoker's Victorian novel as well as in the repression they inspire. The blood that Dracula craves, and from which we recoil, the "blood of life," derives its power from the ancient fear of menstrual blood. In Stoker's story, the female "wound" is displaced upward, from the genital area to the neck, and the act of sucking is at once a perversion of sexual intercourse and of lactation as well. Mother's milk and menstrual blood, as corporeal excrement, are the abject.[8] And by extension, the women in Stoker's novel, primarily Lucy and Mina, are ultimately bitten, defiled. But their resplendent purity, meekness,

The fear of female sexuality as represented in *Bram Stoker's Dracula*.

and nobility (as the Victorian ideal), which define their perfect position as victims, are only a cover for the fear that female sexuality inspires. And this fear is only barely disguised in Stoker's titillating story, one that has, because of this potent psychological dynamic, intrigued audiences now for over one hundred years. The threat of the female, in her perceived "hideous" lasciviousness, festers close to the surface of the novel and gives it its compelling disgust, a disgust that is only partially deflected onto the living corpse of the Count himself. In a play of opposing tensions, Dracula is at once the fetid corpse and the mild infant, suckling his mother's milk, while the woman, as the mother, is defiled, and defilable, abject.

It is here that Coppola's film takes a very different attitude to the established composite of elements. The central women in his film, Lucy and Mina, are no longer merely victims. Instead, they are sexually aggressive and desiring females in a way that has rarely been presented on film before. Lucy, Dracula's "victim"—the "devil's concubine," as she is referred to by Dr. Van Helsing—is first presented as a "pure and virtuous girl," but one with a healthy appetite for sex as well as an active imagination. At first it is merely a willful game, but after she is "bitten," Lucy writhes, moans, and stalks her men (once walking directly toward the camera, toward that dominant male gaze) in a near parody of the masculine fear of the sexually voracious female. This is the woman as sexual monster, predatory, wanton, requiring performance and satisfaction from her partner. Her function within the film is to bring to its active surface, to make almost confrontational, what had been the thinly disguised but driving central force of the original novel, namely, the fear of female sexuality.[9]

Mina is represented somewhat differently, but only by degrees. Although she gives herself willingly to the Count, she does not do so in simpering submission (so as to facilitate an act of rape, as do the women in both *Nosferatu* and Badham's version of *Dracula*), but in the kind of open desire that joins sexual passion with love. In fact, she is one of the few females in the history of film to be so wanton in her sexual display and not to be severely punished for it by the end of the film. Mina begins the film as the "good girl," and only becomes "bad" later. She emerges as the heroine, who, unlike the Mina of Stoker's novel, is not in need of her men to save her from the clutches of the monster. Instead, Mina "embraces" the monster, loving him so completely that she frees him from his curse with her own hand. She decapitates him, freeing herself as well. Their love is eternal, beyond both life and death.

The question of love beyond death, of loss, of holding on somehow to those who have passed out of this life is a crucial one for our times. On a cultural level, it certainly refers us to AIDS, the silent plague that has destroyed too many lives too soon. The notion of a blood disease and of the plague, however, has been, from the beginning, associated with Dracula. In Stoker's novel, Dracula is a polluting force, spreading death and defilement through the blood (Mina even says, "There is a poison in my blood, in my soul, which may destroy me"[10]), and in *Nosferatu,* the Count is specifically credited with the spread of the Black Death. In Coppola's film, Dracula's infection is again termed a blood disease, but now it is updated and presented specifically as a venereal disease. Dr. Van Helsing lectures on this issue at the university as close-ups of red blood cells swim languidly over the surface of the screen. But AIDS bears another resemblance to Coppola's Dracula, and does so in a way not addressed by any of the earlier versions of the story. Both in our current reality and in the film, the disease is spread through passion, desire, love. (It must be remembered that the Dracula of old did not love; nor did Norman Bates, the Alien, or the Thing.) The idea that love, or desire, should cause defilement and one's own death is, in lived reality, a hideous perversion of the human sexual act—a situation so horrendous that, although this film attempts to dramatize the conflict, it is, in the last analysis, an almost inappropriate, or inadequate, response to the terrifying truth.

But this is not necessarily a failing of the film. Much like the 1950s science fiction films discussed by Susan Sontag in "The Imagination of Disaster," the inadequacy of the cinematic attempt to fully resolve lived fears (in the case of the 1950s, the fear of world annihilation by the Bomb) is precisely the attribute within the films that makes those fears palpable, manageable to the viewer. Sontag argues that the quality of these low-budget science fiction films, which were generally artistically unsophisticated and unintentionally hilarious, was essential in creating this effect. These films did, however, dramatize scenes of far-reaching disaster, but did so in a way that was diminished and assimilable, thus making thinkable the unthinkable.[11]

Coppola's *Dracula* seems to pay homage to this tradition, now putting an emotional distance between itself and its reference to AIDS as well as to its other distressing elements, with the artificial sets, unlikely casting, and throwaway lines of dialogue. One could claim that the high plasticity of the sets and the arch acting style recall the 1931 version of *Dracula;* but more so, they recall that 1950s science fiction cycle of B films, the low budgets of which allowed for only the most obviously fake backdrops and special effects as well as often inexperienced actors. Although Keanu Reeves, who plays Jonathan Harker, is a star, he somehow fits this bill. Reeves still carries with him the goofy, surfer persona garnered from films like *Bill and Ted's Excellent Adventure* (1989). This, along with his youthful status as a representative of Generation X (as are all of the young actors in the film) and his offhand delivery of lines, allows Reeves to take the role of Harker to a slightly ironized plane. The dialogue often has a similarly distanced tone. When speaking of Lucy, now a vampire, Dr. Van Helsing flippantly remarks, "We'll drive a stake through her heart and then cut off her head." This line is taken directly from Stoker's book and has been repeated in Dracula renditions across the century, but the attempt at humor here somehow falls flat. It serves only to rupture the fiction, at once acknowledging the history of that statement and the absurdity of it, as well as allowing us a certain distance from the drama.

For Coppola, *Dracula's* central metaphor as a blood disease refers to AIDS, and its central tension of love in relationship to death and loss is a devastating one. But here, as in those science fiction films of the 1950s, we are allowed to experience this mingling of elements at a remove, not only made palpable as entertainment but foregrounded for our contemplation. In addition, while *Bram Stoker's Dracula* raises to its manifest surface the fear of woman, of blood, and of AIDS, it must be noted that the emotional effect of this film is atypical of the horror genre. The ultimate effect is not revulsion; instead, woman, blood, and even the monster are presented, often in contradiction to earlier renditions, with the added connotation of life. And in the end the film's elements coalesce, promoting a response to both life and death as one of liberation and voluptuous acceptance.

This notion of the liberation of sex and violence has a history in art, especially in the work of the Surrealists, and can be helpful in the understanding of Coppola's work. The stated intention of the Surrealists was to liberate the unconscious, the libido, into the content of art. In both painting and literature, they often used the method of psychic automatism in an attempt to map the movement of the mind and to encourage the violent clash of improbable pairings and combinations. Through these clashes, especially in the expression of both Eros and Thanatos, sex and death, the individual was seen as free, capable of liberating desire from the constraining and limiting effects of culture. But this liberation was not played out on the world of the flesh, of the real. Nor was it simply a retreat into fantasy, as was the work of the Symbolists (who propelled the inner world onto a slightly altered representational space, creating hallucinogenic, decadent surfaces but not altering the internal unity of the work). Rather, it was an incursion into the "marvelous," the fragmented, combustive world of the unconscious. The charged world of the marvelous embodied "an impassioned fusion of wish and reality, in a surreality where poetry and freedom were one."[12] Beauty was to be convulsive, and everyday reality supplanted. Although coming to us in a very different era, Coppola's *Bram Stoker's Dracula* bears an interesting relationship to Surrealism.

But before we can deal directly with Surrealism in Coppola's film, it is essential to note the director's stated intention. Far from seeing Surrealism as his inspiration, Coppola cites quite another art historical influence. In the production notes for *Bram Stoker's Dracula,* Coppola claims that many of his stylistic choices were meant to reference Symbolist painting, since this was the major art practice contemporaneous with Stoker's novel.[13] The influence of Symbolism is certainly evidenced in the presentation of the film as a delirious dream, and then supported by the sumptuous visual conception: the swirling composition of the sets and the camera movement, the design and color of the costumes, and the often heady transition of shots. Images superimpose one on the other, underscoring the screen as a pictorial plane rather than as a lived scene, and images dissolve into others based on visual similarities and meanings. A close-up of an eye, for example, dissolves into the rounded bottom of a glass as it fills with the nineteenth-century hallucinogen of choice, absinthe. Bubbles rise through the liquid, as the letters spelling out "sin" reflect from behind its frothy surface. The invitation is one of lascivious surrender.

But the languid surface of such images is not the total effect of the film. Instead, the film is experienced as fragmented in terms of story (by Hollywood standards), decentered in terms of character, and artificial in terms of sets and acting. A link to Surrealism can be cited in the film's tendency for combustive combinations and for the disruption of its internal continuity. The experience of watching *Bram Stoker's Dracula* is often one of shocks and jolts, since the film's narrative transitions do not always have conventional Hollywood invisibility and linearity. The story is told from varying points of view through the journal format; violent camera movement propels us at high speed from the monster's point of view into the depth of the image, intensified by the high volume and sumptuousness of the musical score. These are just some of the elements that tend to eject viewers from a conventional illusory stance toward the fiction and to confront them with disjunction and hyperbole. The similarity to Surrealism is also linked to the film's major focus: not only the violent and sensual pairing of sex and death, but the ultimate co-mingling of that union. It is the liberation of desire that is at issue here, and one that is set in the world of the marvelous, of the supranatural. But it is also a world of representation, specifically of cinematic representation, that we are confronted with. How else to explain the shadow play of silhouetted cut-out soldiers in battle, the obvious rear-projected scenery outside Harker's train window, or the scenes of early cinema itself, also contemporaneous with the release of Stoker's novel (1897)?[14]

So, although it is important to cite similarities to Surrealism, it is also important to note significant differences. In the last analysis, *Bram Stoker's Dracula* is not so much a liberation of the psyche as it is an attempt at liberating the psychological limits imposed on the psyche by the representations of culture. And in this sense it is quite a Postmodern endeavor, one that sets us securely in our own era and not that of Bram Stoker. In fact, this concern with the image and with the generic assumptions rendered by film has been a major impetus in much of Coppola's work over the years.

Many of Coppola's films have maintained a close relationship to the major film genres. Even in the early days of his career, Coppola directed a low-budget horror film, *Dementia 13* (1963), for Roger Corman at AIP, and later, a musical, *Finian's Rainbow* (1968), for Warner Bros./Seven Arts. *The Godfather* (1972) and its sequels (1974, 1990) draw heavily on the gangster genre, as does *The Conversation* (1974) on the hard-boiled detective story. But genre is not utilized equally in all these works. As his career evolved, Coppola has increasingly concerned himself not merely with a play of established forms, but with a studied comment on the social, political, and cultural concerns that have been elucidated through the genre film. *The Godfather* films, for example, attempted a critique of capitalism, utilizing the struggle of the criminal for success as its central metaphor. Of course, this comparison between crime and capitalism is implicit in the classical gangster genre as a whole, but in Coppola's trilogy, it is fashioned to occupy a more central and explicit focus.

After *Apocalypse Now* (1979), however, Coppola's work began to evidence a radical departure from the realism of *The Godfather* movies, moving instead to the high plasticity of *One from the Heart* (1982) and to the stylistic pronouncements and artificialities of *Rumble Fish* (1983) and *The Outsiders* (1983). This tendency toward abstraction, and away from psychological or representational realism, is one that is continued in *Bram Stoker's Dracula*. For a filmmaker who, since *The Godfather*, has tried to straddle the divide between high art and popular culture, *Bram Stoker's Dracula* succeeds where *One from the Heart* fails. Now popular audiences, and at least some critics, responded favorably to the flamboyant visual effects and to the horror-film-inspired format.[15]

From a more scholarly perspective, however, these two elements must be seen as being not only sufficient but at the very center of the film's importance. In fact, it is through the sensuous surface of the film, in conjunction with the structure of the story, that not only meaning is created but experience as well. In *Bram Stoker's Dracula,* Coppola goes back to his own early history, to *Dementia 13,* and to a classic novel of the horror genre. This time, however, he utilizes the elements of the original Dracula and then recasts it in contemporary terms. As in his later Postmodern works, Coppola transposes the images generated by popular culture, especially those rendered so vividly in generic film works, and reshapes them, giving them new meaning. In *Bram Stoker's Dracula,* the monster is a lover, woman is openly sexual, and death is not a boundary to the power of love. The film that has resulted can best be described as a "neo-mythification" because the issue here is always one of representation: its limitations, its look, and now the addition of a representational renewal. There is no claim here to having exposed an ideological real: the "truth" about the meaning of blood, for example, or of woman, or of the monster. Neither has there been, as in high Modernist work, an attempt to somehow make the viewer aware of the systems of the film's own making, to "demystify" the illusion of the fiction itself. Instead, blood, woman, and the monster have been repositioned here and given a new meaning. The Dracula story has been retold, but always with an eye to the horror genre as a representational system, one palpably made up of costumes, sets, lines of dialogue, camera movement, and images.

Bram Stoker's Dracula seems also to have a personal significance for Coppola. It is a film in which "the voice of the author" (a term that has lately fallen out of fashion) is in evidence. Like the Surrealists who returned to the notion of subjectivity after the more impersonal formal concerns of Cubism, this Dracula can be seen as a father's cry, an outraged plea, to God, to life, for the tragic loss of his son, Gio, who was decapitated in a boating accident. The decapitations proliferate in this film (ironically, however, they have appeared in Coppola's work before: the cook in *Apocalypse Now*, for example, and the infamous horse's head in *The Godfather*), as the artist enacts a kind of repetition compulsion to live and relive the traumatic event. As the end credits of the film roll, poignant lyrics accompany it; they foreground the pain of loss for the author, but also for the members of the audience:

> Once I had the rarest rose
> that ever deigned to bloom.
> Cruel winter chilled the bud
> and stole my flower too soon.
> Oh, loneliness, oh, hopelessness,
> to search the ends of time.
> For there is in all the world,
> no greater love than mine.

The lyrics are certainly consistent with the themes within the film, but they can also be seen to carry a personal meaning. This is a song of love beyond death. It touched the heart of the author, and it now addresses the emotions and memories of those in the audience who have suffered similar losses. The film ends with the hope of conquering death through love and, perhaps, even loving one's own death:

> Now the floor of heaven gave
> the stars of brightest gold.
> They shine for you, they shine for you,
> they burn for all to see.
> Come into these arms again,
> and set this spirit free.

Francis Ford Coppola has taken Bram Stoker's nineteenth-century novel, one steeped in the mystification of defilement for the sin of sexual desire and the fear of sexual difference, and transformed it into a work of innovative and affirmative exultation. Never before has a horror film embodied such hope in the conquering power of love beyond death.

In loving memory of Tom Hopkins

Notes

1. Fredric Jameson, "Postmodernism and Consumer Society," in *The Anti-Aesthetic: Essays on Postmodern Culture,* ed. Hal Foster (Port Townsend, Wash.: Bay Press, 1983), pp. 115–125.

2. Noel Carroll, *The Philosophy of Horror, or The Paradoxes of the Heart* (New York: Routledge, 1990), p. 38.

3. Ibid., p. 31.

4. Julia Kristeva, *Powers of Horror: An Essay on Abjection,* trans. Leon S. Roudiez (New York: Columbia University Press, 1982).

5. Carroll, *Philosophy of Horror,* p. 17.

6. Kristeva, *Powers of Horror,* p. 70.

7. Sigmund Freud, "The Uncanny," in *Studies in Parapsychology,* ed. Philip Reif (New York: Collier, 1963), pp. 16–62.

8. Kristeva, *Powers of Horror,* p. 71.

9. The works of Cindy Sherman, especially her early photographs "Untitled Film Stills" (1977–1983), portray women in stereotypic ways. The recontextualization of these images within an art gallery setting, however, as well as their allusive relationship to pop cultural images, allows us to look at them *as* representations. Similarly, in *Bram Stoker's Dracula,* Lucy recalls a long line of dangerous women, from Irena in *Cat People* (1942) to Alex in *Fatal Attraction* (1987). But in the context of Coppola's film, this image dislodges itself, forcing a confrontation with its flamboyant excess and its lascivious threat.

10. Bram Stoker, *Dracula* (New York: Penguin, 1979), p. 392.

11. Susan Sontag, "The Imagination of Disaster," in *Film Theory and Criticism,* 3d ed., ed. Gerald Mast and Marshall Cohen (New York: Oxford University Press, 1986), p. 465.

12. René Passeron, *The Encyclopedia of Surrealism* (London: Somogy, 1975), p. 261.

13. Francis Ford Coppola, *Bram Stoker's Dracula: The Film and the Legend* (New York: Newmarket Press, 1992), p. 70.

14. It is not easy to explain or excuse the opening sequence of *Bram Stoker's Dracula,* with its represented clash between Christianity and Islam, a clash that vilifies the latter and exalts the former in its purity of purpose. This sequence seems to feed on the worst of contemporary hatreds and fears, a fact that threatens the opening of the film with a reactionary politic. I do not wish to overstate my point, but a slight vacillation in this clash should be noted. The image of Islam in Coppola's film is not consistently maintained as an evil force, the way that it is, for example, in *Raiders of the Lost Ark* (1981) or *True Lies* (1994). Instead, in *Dracula,* the aggrieved Count soon destabilizes this conflict by his rejection of Christianity and his continued allegiance to the Cross. On a symbolic level, then, the opposition between "good" and "evil" as embodied by the conflict between Christianity and Islam falls away. Dracula places himself in a realm that is beyond these conflicts, one that is of his own making, or more precisely, one of myth.

15. See Vincent Canby, "*Bram Stoker's Dracula,*" *New York Times,* November 12, 1992, p. C13; and Caryn James, "Dangerous Liaisons Are All the Rage," *New York Times,* November 22, 1992, sec. 2, p. 13.

20

The Place of Passion:
Reflections on *Fatal Attraction*

James Conlon

Let us not be disturbed by an argument that seeks to scare us into preferring the friendship of the sane to that of the passionate.

Plato, *Phaedrus*[1]

Given the infinity of human desire, and the equally infinite possibilities for human misery, it is difficult to know what to do, according to which ethics to live.

Unfortunately, the ethical options, at least the basic ones, are not nearly as infinite. In his novel *Madame Bovary,* Flaubert has two of the more established ethical options engage in a late-night debate. The local priest offers the traditional religious option: no human desire will be left unfulfilled, if only one sacrifices now and places faith in the ultimate graciousness of an infinite god. The local pharmacist offers a less ancient—and less risky—option: the drugs of science. These promise not exactly fulfillment but, at least, a modification of misery. Both priest and pharmacist produce texts and arguments to validate their options.

However, these texts and arguments prove quite incapable of answering the questions of Emma Bovary, over whose self-poisoned body they debate. Her lover had swayed her by proclaiming that her only duty was to passion, "to feel what is great and love what is beautiful."[2] But believing him ended up destroying her. The ethical guidance she needed was practical and emotional: How much passion should a life contain? What place should it be given in human life?

This is certainly not a modern question. It is, for example, at the heart of Plato's entire philosophy, from his ethics to his aesthetics. Nowhere is his answer to this question more dramatically presented than at the climax of the *Symposium*. There he makes it clear that passion has no place. It can only bring untruth, pain, and destruction. The drunken, erratic passion of Alcibiades is contrasted with the steady revealing power of Socrates' reason. There is no contest. Passion, like the artists who inspire it, must be forever banished if any human happiness is to be achieved.

Plato's answer to the place of passion has dominated the history of ethics. In fact, Nietzsche claims it *is* the history of ethics. "All the old moral masters are agreed on this: *il faut tuer les passions*."[3] Nietzsche's own attempts to revolutionize philosophy focus on transforming the place it assigns passion. His own ideal, in sharp contrast with Socrates, is the Greek god Dionysus, whose value is directly tied to the "great and terrible passions" he can permit himself.[4]

Throughout history, then, the question of the place of passion has attracted all manner of philosophical and literary answers. Flaubert, however, gives the question a particularly modern form by raising it in the context of adultery, of a specific reaction to domestic life. I want to examine a contemporary text that proceeds along similar lines—Adrian Lyne's film *Fatal Attraction* (1987). Whether it proves an ethically useful text, in the way that the *Symposium* or *Madame Bovary* do, can be answered only in the reading of it.

The plot of the film is uncomplicated. Dan Gallagher (Michael Douglas) is an attorney living in New York with his wife, Beth (Anne Archer), and his six-year-old daughter, Ellen. While his family is out of town, he meets Alex Forrest (Glenn Close), a successful editor. They spend the weekend together, sharing a bed and their favorite opera, *Madame Butterfly*. Alex would like this sharing to continue, but Dan insists on treating it as a one-time sexual fling. At first, Alex reacts to this rejection with a suicide attempt in the romantic tradition of *Madame Butterfly*. But when she learns she is pregnant, she turns her anger outward instead of on herself. She begins an increasingly violent series of attacks on Dan's family until, in self-defense, Beth is forced to kill her.

The film has been characterized repeatedly as a "thriller" in the "Hitchcockian tradition." This is a helpful categorization only if there is no misunderstanding of what that tradition entails. Hitchcock is acknowledged as a master technician adept at scary editing and strange plot twists. But Hitchcock's deeper mastery—like all artists—is of the human soul. He knows those hidden things that thrill and frighten it. I believe *Fatal Attraction* is definitely in *this* Hitchcockian tradition. It is frightening to watch, not because it jars with unexpected cuts, but because it gives visual form to those most elusive of fears—the ones we cannot deny but cannot quite accept either.

As the film ended the first time I saw it, I overheard a man say to his companion, "Well, so much for fooling around." At first glance, it might seem the film is just another cautionary tale about the dangers of casual sex. In the age of AIDS, the cost of not knowing who one's sexual partner is has become increasingly high. This film seems to add one more fearsome possibility to these costs: one might end up sleeping with a maniac.

At second glance, it might seem the film is a reactionary tale about feminism. The liberated, independent, assertive woman is really a time bomb, hooked to a biological clock, and ready to explode. *Ms.* magazine argues that Alex is portrayed as a feminist "sent around the bend by the failure of her doomed vision."[5]

I do not deny that these glances reveal some of the levels on which the film operates, but they do not seem to me to reach deep enough. In restricting the film to current rather than perennial fears, they do not account for how thoroughly afraid the film makes us. Yes, casual sex is dangerous, but it is an avoidable danger, like cocaine. And if independent women seem threatening, they are so only to the insecure. But the fear felt in this film seems more fundamental, less avoidable, than these. It seems, rather, to be a fear about passion itself, about its powers and possibilities in human life.

The film opens on an ordinary domestic scene. Dan, in underwear and earphones, is doing paperwork on the sofa. His daughter, cuddled next to a dog, is watching a silly show on television. Beth is in the bathroom getting ready for an evening party. Though this certainly is not an idealized scene of domestic bliss, there is something engaging and pleasurable about its ordinariness, about the steady, mutual living a family shares.

This steadiness is interrupted by the phone, and Dan stubs his toe answering it. It is a minor disturbance, a friend of Beth's asking what she is wearing to the party. However, it prefigures Alex's later phone calls and the major disturbances they will cause. By means of the phone, Alex can inject herself, at any time, into the heart of Dan's domestic life—into an evening with friends, into his bedroom. Given the weekend they experienced together, Alex feels she has a reasonable claim to be there. Dan finds her claim surprising, utterly unreasonable, and potentially destructive of the family he cherishes. The tension of the film revolves around their argument, around the validity of Alex's claim to a place in Dan's life.

Alex Forrest (Glenn Close) threatens the domestic security of the Gallaghers (Michael Douglas and Anne Archer) in *Fatal Attraction* (1987).

The facts are not disputed: Dan and Alex spent a weekend together. The length of time, of course, is not really relevant. Romeo and Juliet spent less time than a weekend together. What is relevant is the meaning of the weekend, how it is interpreted. Dan wants to treat it as a fantasy that can be entered and left without repercussions and remembered later with fond, private smiles. Alex enters the weekend with similar expectations.

An "innocent" drink after a business meeting leads them to an "innocent" dinner. Alex, clearly more adept at sexual intrigue than Dan, suggests that dinner lead to an "adult" night together, a night without strings. When she develops strings, he feels wronged because she hasn't played by the "rules." But, as Alex points out, his moral indignation is self-serving and misplaced. As adults should know, rules against involvement are far too simplistic for the intricacies and possibilities of passion.

But why does Alex change her mind about the weekend? That she is lonely and desperate for love is obvious enough—and understandable. But Dan, too, is desperate—albeit, quietly—and Alex pushes him to acknowledge this. As they share dinner in her apartment, Dan is listing the details of his family life: He's been married nine years and has a six-year-old daughter. "Sounds pretty good," Alex says; but while Dan is proudly agreeing, she asks, "If it's so good, what are you doing here?" Doesn't he realize the contradiction involved in praising the fullness of his life in her kitchen, after sleeping in her bed? Dan himself is jarred by her question, criticizes it as out of place, and evades it. He will evade it again when she asks it in the subway station. But the viewer cannot. Is Alex "just a weekend," as Dan insists, or an attempt to fill a rather substantial hole in the center of his being?

To begin to answer this, we must turn to Beth, who is, at least in theory, already the center of his being. Beth is a housewife—as good a one as can be imagined. Her interests seem exclusively focused on creating a home—not just a place that is efficient and comfortable but a genuinely nourishing and enjoyable place to be. She worries about meals, reads to their daughter, offers Dan backrubs and brandy, and makes his friends hers. The weekend with Alex is only available because Beth is hunting for a suburban home that will free her family from the frenzy of New York. She is someone who can thoroughly deliver the domestic riches Dan so obviously savors.

But such a home can be dull. For this reason, parties are slotted into the domestic routine. However, it is at a party that Dan meets Alex. Their conversation is brief but filled with the excitement of two people who find each other intriguing and are unlikely to see each other again. This scene, with its stirring of sexual possibilities, shifts immediately to the domestic bedroom. Here, too, there are sexual possibilities but without the edge of excitement. Beth reminds Dan that, before he undresses, he must walk the dog. And when he comes back from that task with the vestiges of desire still on his face, he finds Ellen cuddled in bed with her mother. Beth is apologetic but suggests that such restrictions are the price of home and family.

Dan's sex with Alex the following night is in even more dramatic contrast with this marital sex scene. With Alex there is no casual undressing, no neat folding of clothes, no practical prioritizing about what should be done before what. There is just the total urgency of passion, of flesh desperate for the closest avenue to flesh. They couple and cling at the kitchen sink, clothes off only as far as the essentials.

It is crucial to understand this powerfully evoked contrast. Alex is not just a variation on something Dan already has in his life. Rather, she offers something fundamentally different, something that Beth does not generate.

This is not to claim that Beth is just another frigid film wife. Part of the complexity of the film is that Beth herself is enticing and sensuous. Nowhere is this more studied than in the second domestic bedroom scene. As we saw her do before the publishing party, Beth is putting on lipstick in preparation for another weekend event. However, Alex has happened in the meantime, and Dan feels the need to appreciate the kind of sensual experience Beth offers. Dan—and the camera—reflectively contemplate Beth's beauty, bathe in the muted glow of her skin. Though there is touch here, it is a tender, affectionate touch. The desire Beth generates is equal to Alex but radically different. Nietzsche would call it "Apollonian" and contrast it with the Dionysian. It is the desire for the safe and giving warmth of her, not a purging heat; her body as a home, not an adventure. (Though—interestingly—the film interrupts even this desire with friends at the door!)

Beth, then, is a desirable woman. She is not presented in any way as a drag on Dan's life. Rather, she enriches it with a crucial dimension. So crucial that Dan takes it as complete, that—given Beth—nothing else crucial is missing from his life. Alex will not allow him this illusion. Passion is missing and he feels its absence keenly, otherwise he would not be with her. As passion, then, she demands a place in his life; she demands respect.

That Dan—and the audience—automatically fight this respect seems to me related to the history of passion in Western thought. Ever since Plato's poignant arguments, moralists have encouraged killing the passions. Therefore, it is not surprising that audiences encourage killing Alex. She is identified with what has been labeled least human about us, what we should be most humiliated by. Beth is Dan's pride, a "higher" love; Alex is his shame.

This traditional, hierarchical evaluation of human desires is, I think, mistaken. Because no thinker I know has fought this mistake more perceptively, more painfully, than Thoreau, I want to use him—need to use him—as a guide in analyzing exactly what passion is and then in assessing its worth.

In the remarkable first sentence from the "Higher Laws" chapter of *Walden,* Thoreau describes a personal moment of passion: "As I came home through the woods with my string of fish trailing my pole, it being now quite dark, I caught a glimpse of a woodchuck stealing across my path, and felt a strange thrill of savage delight, and was strongly tempted to seize and devour him raw; not that I was hungry then, except for the wildness which he represented."[6] That Thoreau does not act out his temptation to "seize and devour" and that Dan and Alex do does not alter the underlying similarity of their passions.

Two things seem essential in Thoreau's account. The first is the nature of the object he desires. It is definitely not a woodchuck or food to eat. The specific object is merely representative of that which underlies it. To seize and devour the woodchuck is to acknowledge and possess in some way what is more basic than its individual life or form—wildness itself. Therefore, passion is not a physical but a metaphysical hunger. What it seeks is not an itch scratched but union with the being that underlies individual beings.

Second, it is not just the metaphysical aspect of the object that characterizes passion but the manner in which that object is sought and possessed. The term "passion" is the opposite of "action." Action, in its ordinary sense, implies something chosen and propelled by the self, the ego. Passion implies being chosen—beyond personal decision, beyond societal and practical concerns, beyond calculations of pleasure and pain. It is a union with something more vast than the self, unmediated by any categories of reason.

Only the foolhardy would deny that passion, as Thoreau conceives it, is an incredibly dangerous force, vulnerable to all kinds of abuse. But this danger has caused it to be condemned as fundamentally negative. Thoreau struggles to correct this condemnation: "I found in myself, and still find, an instinct toward a higher, or, as it is named, spiritual life, as do most men, and another toward a primitive, rank and savage one, and I reverence them both. I love the wild not less than the good."[7]

I am identifying Alex with the second of Thoreau's instincts—the wild. Her name (Forrest) and the location of her apartment in a wholesale meat district, with open fires and people carrying raw parts of animals through the street, are—perhaps—overdone; but she is unquestionably intriguingly wild! She can react to mild flirtation with a vicious stare, move quickly from sex to dance, stop the elevator between floors, and turn Dan's cruel heart attack hoax into one of her own. She is a passionate, exciting, dangerous woman. I believe, with Thoreau, that she deserves more respect than Dan—or the moral tradition—is willing to give her.

Surely, one reason for Dan's refusal to respect Alex is that he is not used to this kind of woman. None of the above actions could be imagined coming from Beth. Also, he is not quite in Alex's league. It isn't just that he stumbles on his pants as he carries her to the bedroom, he stumbles conversationally. He never seems adequate to the multiple levels of her discourse or the quickness of her logic. He seems much more comfortable bowling than examining the emotions of Madame Butterfly. Alex always seems ahead of him, deeper than he can fathom. However, the fundamental reason he rejects her is, as Alex states on the tape, that he is afraid of her, afraid of women—at least undomesticated ones. So, after their night together, he slips off sheepishly before she wakes, more out of fear of her personality than any deep marital commitment.

But . . . wait a minute, viewers will object, you are acting as if Alex is a perfectly sane, well-balanced woman. Clearly, she is not; she is "sick." Reviewers have been particularly graphic about Alex's mental state. She is "a glamorous nut case," "a lovelorn psycho," "loony," "ga-ga," "berserk," and so on. Such virulence should make us nervous—and attentive. Madness, as Foucault and Szasz have tried to teach us, is predominantly a social phenomenon that reveals at least as much about the labeler as the labeled. If Alex is mad, in what, exactly, does her madness consist? As she calmly tells Dan: "I had a wonderful time last night. I'd like to see you again. Is that so terrible?" Is it?

I have argued that it is too simplistic to see the situation between Alex and Dan as stereotypical female misunderstanding of male intentions (to him it's a fling, to her it's forever). In definite ways, Alex knows Dan's mind better than he does. When he jumps up to leave right after they make love, Alex is angered by his insensitivity but also by his confident ignorance of her importance to him. Significantly, Beth understands this quite well. When Dan finally tells her about Alex and attempts to dismiss it as "just a weekend," she attacks him exactly as Alex had. It is not Alex who is out of touch with reality here!

But then Alex slits her wrists—a sure sign of madness! This is the only time in the film that Alex embraces the romantic, Madame Butterfly scenario of the wronged but still subserviently loving woman. There is a madness here! But it is not her suicidal behavior that has attracted the severe diagnosis of reviewers. Rather, it is her refusal to play the culturally accepted role of the jilted heroine.

Surely, her initial behavior, though embarrassing to Dan in front of his secretary, is hardly "demented." She surprises him at his office, apologizes for her "Madame Butterfly" behavior, and invites him to the opera. When he refuses, she offers a "stiff-upper-lip" handshake in a gesture of resigned termination. Dan, however, bypasses the handshake and takes her in his arms. The close-up of Alex's face in this embrace is full of longing possibilities. As so often in the film, sexual roles are reversed here, and Alex is left with the question: "When does no really mean no?" Viewed without sexual stereotypes, Alex's initial behavior seems to be quite the opposite of crazy.

But things change radically when she discovers she is pregnant with Dan's child. Though he offers to pay for an abortion, she has decided to keep the child and hopes he will welcome it, even become involved in its life. It is only after Dan angrily rejects this proposal for a family that Alex's more "insane" actions begin. She trashes the family station wagon, "cooks" their pet rabbit, kidnaps Ellen, and attempts to kill Beth. The essence of her madness, then, is related to the fact that the family she proposes is so automatically denied. What is so insane about her proposal, her envisioned family?

The morning of Dan's sheepish retreat from their passionate lovemaking, Alex calls him and urges him to spend Sunday with her. He tries to excuse himself with the demands of domestic life: he has work to do and the dog to take care of. But Alex persists: she's a great cook, loves animals, and "will be a good girl" so he can get his work done. In essence, she is arguing that she is

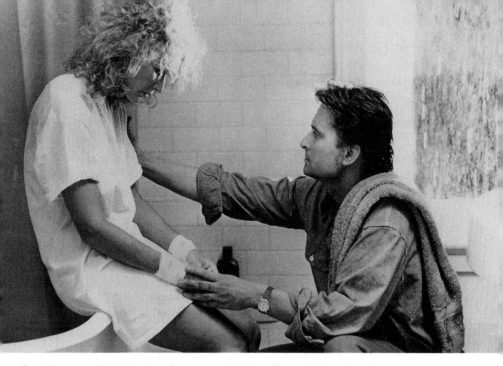

Fatal Attraction: Alex's "madness" says as much about Dan as it does about her.

not only a source of passion but also of domestic pleasure. And, in fact, their weekend does manage both: a passionate Saturday night is followed by a Sunday walk in the park with the dog, a mutually cooked spaghetti dinner, and *Madame Butterfly* on the stereo.

Thus, to Alex, their weekend isn't "just a weekend"; it is concrete proof that a union of the passionate and the domestic is not sheer fantasy. When she finds she is pregnant, she pursues Dan as the most realistic—perhaps, at thirty-six, the last realistic—chance for making this dream a reality.

Dan sees this dream as not just unrealistic but insane. It isn't the strength of his commitment to Beth that motivates him so much as his unarticulated conviction that home can never be the place for passion. Passion and the kitchen sink are utterly incommensurable. A homestead can exist only as long as wildness is kept outside of it, at its boundaries.

Alex's "insane" actions, then, are not maniacal vengeance against Dan but distorted reactions to his unquestioned belief that passion and home are antithetical. Her trashing the car and cooking the rabbit are attacks on a concept of family that excludes her from it; her kidnapping of Ellen and attempt to kill Beth are desperate attempts to include herself in it.

But the film relentlessly argues the irrationality of such an inclusion. The initial sex between Alex and Dan is visually identical with their later struggle to kill each other. It is the same kitchen setting, the same intertwining chore-ography, even the same panting soundtrack. Passion leads inevitably to mur-der; it cannot be extricated from death. Passion will destroy domestic secu-rity, just as surely as domesticity will smother it. There is no possibility of union, no having it both ways. One must choose. Either/or. Passion or home.

The wrenching violence of the choice seems accurately reflected in the in-tense physical violence of the final scene. Dan has locked the doors for the evening and is fixing tea. Beth is upstairs getting ready for a bath. As she wipes the steam from the mirror, Alex appears in it. It is, of course, a well-worn cinematic—and psychological—cliché that one never knows whom one will see as one looks in a mirror. Obviously, too, both the passionate and the do-mestic woman are abstractions—constructs of male desire. But still, the audi-ence is as jarred as Beth to see Alex in the mirror with her—both in white—two sides of the same soul.

Even in her deranged state, Alex remains consistent: if Beth weren't so selfish and stupid, she would see the inadequacies of the domestic life she has created for Dan. Killing Beth is the only way of removing the major obstacle to the family Alex envisions and believes Dan needs. In this hope, she lunges at Beth with a knife and they struggle.

But it is Dan who must determine the outcome. He finally hears Beth's calls for help and runs upstairs. Since he was never able to take Alex's vision seri-ously, there is no doubt about his choice. Screaming, he charges Alex, knocks her into the bathtub, and strangles her under water. The vehemence of his hands on her throat—by now, the audience's hands—has gone quite beyond self-defense. It is motivated by a bitter and angry hatred. But make no mistake, it is not Alex whom he hates and wants so violently dead; it is his own passion.

Passion, however, is notoriously tenacious. As Dan sits panting on the side of the tub, Alex rises out of the water, knife in hand, and is shot through the heart by Beth. It is as if both of them, husband and—especially—wife, must kill that part of themselves that inherently undermines domestic tranquility.

One of the fundamental ethical convictions of our culture, a belief central to its plan for human happiness, is that marriage is the proper place for pas-sion. Only in marriage can passion achieve its natural fulfillment. Though marriage is a difficult ethical ideal, it is the only one able to deliver both the powers of passion and the securities of home.

Few have analyzed the historical development of this cultural conviction with as much intelligence as Denis de Rougemont in his classic *Love in the Western World*. His conclusion is as categorical as it is disturbing: "Passion and marriage are essentially irreconcilable. Their origins and their ends make them mutually exclusive. Their co-existence in our midst constantly raises insoluble problems, and the strife thereby engendered constitutes a persistent danger for every one of our social safeguards."[8] *Fatal Attraction* reaches the exact same conclusion. The attraction that is fatal, it argues, is not primarily that between Alex and Dan but between domesticity and passion. They cannot coexist. One must choose between them. And, because passion is the more dangerous of the two, the correct choice is obvious. Because passion cannot be domesticated, it must be eliminated. In arguing thus, the film critiques a cherished cultural hope and calls for the sacrifice of an intense part of ourselves.

The film began with an attempt to find the perfect home. Now that Alex is definitely excluded from it, that home can be a reality. Dan watches the police drive off and then embraces Beth. The last shot of the film focuses on their family portrait atop a dresser. It is a lingering shot—and gives us ample time to worship the icon enshrined on this altar. However, the violence of the previous scene has not yet faded from our emotional sight, so we see, as in a double exposure, both the family icon and the blood spilt in sacrifice to it. This is a very scary picture.

Notes

1. Plato, *Phaedrus,* in *The Collected Dialogues,* Bollingen Series 71, trans. R. Hackforth, ed. Edith Hamilton and Huntington Cairns (Princeton, N.J.: Princeton University Press, 1961), p. 492.

2. Gustave Flaubert, *Madame Bovary,* trans. Francis Steegmuller (New York: Modern Library, 1950), p. 163.

3. "It is necessary to kill the passions." Friedrich Nietzsche, *Twilight of the Idols,* in *The Portable Nietzsche,* ed. and trans. Walter Kaufmann (New York: Viking Press, 1968), p. 486.

4. Friedrich Nietzsche, *Will to Power,* trans. Walter Kaufmann and R. J. Hollingdale (New York: Vintage Books, 1968), p. 530.

5. Laurie Stone, "The New Femme Fatale," *Ms,* December 16, 1987, p. 79.

6. Henry David Thoreau, *Walden* (New York: Signet Classic, 1980), p. 142.

7. Ibid., p. 143.

8. Denis de Rougemont, *Love in the Western World,* trans. Montgomery Belgion (Princeton, N.J.: Princeton University Press, 1983), p. 277.

21

Birth Traumas: Parturition
and Horror in *Rosemary's Baby*

Lucy Fischer

Before you were born darling
I carried you on my lap the prince
    of whales and I huffed and I puffed
through the great acline making our own
        mountain from testaments of wet love
Love's labor to skin to blood
    to cellular surprise

Summer Brenner, "Blissed Raga" [1]

nausea. vomit. muscle strain . . .
afraid of what it will / won't be
anxious. it's got to look like him
it's got to look like me. be healthy. be live. be all right

Wanda Coleman, "Giving Birth" [2]

Multiple Births

Contemporary popular culture has delivered us multiple em-
bodiments of childbirth. In the supermarket, the slick cover of
Working Mother presents a radiant television personality who is

"Pretty and Pregnant." *Newsweek* flaunts a responsible expectant couple purchasing Mass Mutual Insurance. *Parent* pictures a postpartum Madonna gazing wondrously at her infant—nursing now, but planning to use Gerber Baby Formula. In the local video store, the self-help aisle is stocked with reassuring instructional tapes: *Your First Baby* and *Childbirth Preparation.* The neighborhood bookshop features *Pregnant and Lovin' It,* a guide to "one of the greatest, most pleasurable events of . . . life."[3]

The popular cinema of past decades has proffered alternate views of maternity. *It's Alive* (1974) opens with a woman in labor, trying to quell a premonition that something is dreadfully wrong. The sequence ends with bloodied doctors evacuating a delivery room where they have inadvertently birthed her murderous monster. This eerie scenario is extended in the film's two sequels: *It Lives Again* (1978) and *It's Alive III: Island of the Alive* (1987). In *The Brood* (1979) a female mental patient incubates heinous fetuses in external belly sacs; *Embryo* (1976) and *Eraserhead* (1978) pursue the theme of malevolent extrauterine conception.

Our reflex is to keep these diverse impressions of childbirth separate: to deem some idyllic and others grotesque, some accurate and others apocryphal, some objective and others subjective, some natural and others perverse. But work on horror suspects such binary oppositions, recognizing realism in the bizarre. Caryn James sees the genre as evoking "universal" terrors; Dennis L. White notes its roots in "the common fears of everyday life."[4]

Some scholars have claimed veracity for horror in the *psychological* domain, seeing its diegetic dementia as but a transmutation of "normal" consciousness. Thus, the *doppelgänger* is viewed not only as a supernatural fiction, but as a metaphor for the perennially divided human self.[5] Other critics have found horror's "validity" in the *political* sphere: it is claimed that Robert Weine created a harbinger of Nazi Germany; that George Romero crafted a bourgeois American Nightmare; that Don Siegel created a parable of the red menace.[6] For some writers, horror articulates cultural tensions. Dana Polan finds domestic strife in *The Howling* (1980), and Serafina Bathrick decodes sexual fears in *Carrie* (1976).[7] Hence, in psychic or in social registers, horror constitutes an expressionistic "allegory of the real."[8]

It is from this perspective that I will view Roman Polanski's *Rosemary's Baby* (1968)—a movie that heralds both the birth of horror and the horror of birth in the modern cinema.[9] Though the film is certainly an odious fable of parturition, it is also a skewed "documentary" of the societal and personal turmoil that has regularly attended female reproduction. While for Rhona Berenstein the film reflects the "horrifying status of motherhood in Ameri-

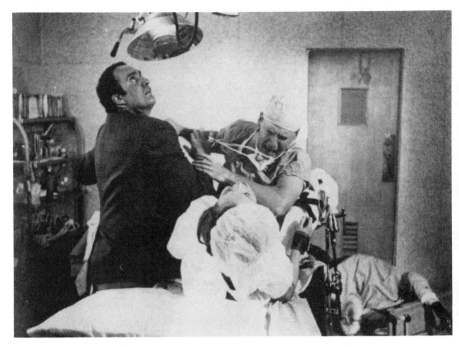

Monstrous parturition in *It's Alive* (1974).

The horror of parthenogenesis in *The Brood* (1979).

can patriarchal culture," I will read the film against that grain, for its utterance of women's private experience of pregnancy.[10]

> *Last night I dreamed I gave birth to a monster. Are you that menacing creature I saw in my dreams? My monster, myself. . . .* Maybe it's Rosemary's baby in there.

Phyllis Chesler, *With Child* (emphasis added)[11]

The "Gynecological Gothic"

Rosemary's Baby is the story of Rosemary and Guy Woodhouse (Mia Farrow and John Cassavetes), newlyweds who rent an apartment in the Bramford, a Victorian high-rise reputed to have been haunted by witches.[12] Guy, an actor, is consumed with his career. Rosemary, a traditional homemaker, wants to start a family. Once the Woodhouses move in, their eccentric elderly neighbors, Roman and Minnie Castevet (Sidney Blackmer and Ruth Gordon), insinuate themselves into the couple's life. At first, Guy resists them, while Rosemary urges him to socialize. But after a dinner party (in which Roman claims a certain influence in the theater world), Guy seems bent on befriending the Castevets. Soon he expresses his willingness to have a child. Gradually, Rosemary becomes wary of the Castevets: she wonders why the previous tenant barricaded a door leading to their apartment; she hears strange chants emanating through their adjoining wall; a young female guest of the Castevets suddenly commits suicide; Minnie gives Rosemary a foul-smelling amulet to wear.

Rosemary becomes pregnant and, despite her reservations, allows Minnie to advise her—to administer herbal medicines and to enlist the services of Dr. Abraham Sapirstein (Ralph Bellamy). Rather than thrive, Rosemary sickens and fears that something is amiss. When her friend Hutch (Maurice Evans) warns her that the Castevets are demons, he mysteriously dies, willing her a volume on witchcraft through which she learns the terrible facts. She tries, frantically, to escape the clutches of the Castevets, who have ensnared Guy with the promise of stage stardom. When Rosemary seeks refuge with her own obstetrician, Dr. Hill (Charles Grodin), he thinks she is crazed and calls Dr. Sapirstein and Guy to retrieve her. Rosemary flees and gives birth to a baby in her home, but the infant is taken from her and she is told it is dead. As the film ends, she follows the sound of a baby's cry to the Castevets' apartment where a coven is celebrating the arrival of the devil-child. Though at first repulsed, Rosemary soon approaches the cradle to comfort the infant.[13]

Significantly, Rosemary gains access to her child through a door that conjoins the Woodhouse and Castevet abodes—a geographic proximity that has doomed her pregnancy. This trope of *contiguity* will also inform my methodology, as I read the film in the "space" of various neighboring cultural discourses on childbirth: the sacred, the mythic, the obstetrical, the psychiatric, the therapeutic, and the artistic. By juxtaposing such diverse textual "locales," I will outline their complex boundaries. For as Stuart Hall has noted, the study of popular culture "yields most when it is seen in relation to a more general, a wider history."[14]

One might say that the true subject of the horror genre is the struggle for recognition of all that our civilization represses or oppresses.

Robin Wood[15]

False Labor

As multifarious visions of childbirth have proliferated, so have competing discourses, each seeking to explain and contain it. Despite this vocality, the dialogue has disempowered woman or relegated her to virtual silence. Religious thought elides her from the birth act (as in Eve's appearance from Adam's rib, Athena's creation from the forehead of Zeus, or Aphrodite's formation from the phallus of Uranus). Traditional obstetrics denies the parturient woman agency, configuring her as passive patient. Psychiatry "damns her with faint praise" for successfully achieving maternal maturity by sublimating her penis envy.

No wonder that in this plethora of voices many sense a mutism. Iris Marion Young is not "surprised to learn that discourse on pregnancy omits subjectivity" and that "the specific experience of women has been absent from most of our culture's discourse about human experience."[16] Myra Leifer corroborates this insight: "Although for many years researchers have been interested in the effect of the trauma of birth on the newborn . . . strikingly less attention has been given to its impact upon the mother."[17] It is important that Leifer (writing in 1980) uses the term "trauma"; for in the decades immediately preceding, voluntary, middle-class pregnancy was regarded more romantically. As E. Zajicek remarks, "In the 1930s and 1940s, when views of women were more obviously stereotyped . . . it was considered important for them to experience only the rewarding, fulfilling aspects of pregnancy and motherhood." Any deviance from this was regarded as "a sign of maladjustment."[18] Even a current manual promises expectant women a purely "joyful" pregnancy, urging them to "be free of fear and full of confidence."[19]

The feminist movement of the 1970s spurred a reconsideration of parturition in two contradictory ways. On the one hand, reproduction was further glorified by the proponents of woman-centered, natural childbirth. Suzanne Arms deems this the "most profound, personal experience a woman can have" and claims that if the woman finds it "dangerous, risky, painful and terrifying," it is only because the male medical system has made it so.[20] On the other hand, the era saw a lifting of taboos concerning childbirth. In a satiric attack on the Lamaze method, Nora Ephron complains that it "never crossed [her] mind that [she] would live through the late 60's and early 70's in America only to discover that in the end what was expected of [her] was a brave, albeit vigorous squat in the fields like the heroine of *The Good Earth*."[21] On a darker note, Adrienne Rich admits that pregnancy is not only an exquisite phenomenon, but one characterized by "anxiety, depression, [and] the sense of being a sacrificial victim."[22] While the bleak side of parturition represents just another rival discourse, its admission stands as a corrective to more ubiquitous and sanguine views.[23] Released in 1968, *Rosemary's Baby* announces this discursive disturbance, and the film's malign mise-en-scène bespeaks a return of the repressed.

In considering the film, we might first examine the work's chilling atmosphere (the threatening Bramford, its repugnant tenants, the rumors of savagery, the nightmare imagery). As Diane Waldman has noted, the narrative has all the earmarks of the Gothic mode (the naive young heroine, her opaque husband, the awesome mansion, the supernatural events).[24] As such, it might well be dismissed as mere phantasmagoria, but it is more challenging to query the film's relevance to childbirth lore. (James Twitchell finds all horror related to themes of "sex and reproduction.")[25]

In 1945, Freudian psychiatrist Helene Deutsch acknowledged maternity's disquieting aspects, despite her conviction that it was woman's sublime calling. In one passage, she spoke of pregnancy as having an "abnormal psychic charge" and employed the term "horror" to characterize delivery. She resorted to the same phrasing to describe women with postpartum problems: "Something has happened during childbirth to disappoint [them] and fill them with *horror*."[26] More recently, in Liefer's interviews with primiparous women, subjects related the "horror stories" they had heard.[27]

Such tales are not entirely fictional. As Ann Dally has stated, "Throughout history, until recent times, motherhood was always close to death." This obtained for the newborn, in periods of high infant mortality. (In England and Wales of 1885, 14 to 16 percent of babies died during their first year.) But childbirth was also "one of the greatest hazards that adult women had to face."[28] Included in the chamber of maternal horrors was puerperal fever, which reached epidemic proportions between the seventeenth and nineteenth centuries. Most ghoulish was its transmission by doctors, who, unaware of sepsis, went directly from dissecting cadavers to delivering babies. As Julia Kristeva remarks: "Here is a fever where what bears life passes over to the side of the dead body."[29] Another potential medical crisis was obstructed labor, for which physicians used tortuous tools to extract (or decapitate) the baby. Sheila Kitzinger describes such a delivery scene (evocative of a sequence in the film *Alien* [1979]): "A long . . . labour may be terminated by rupture of the uterus and death of the baby and mother, and to those helping it must look really *as if the baby has burst up out of the womb*" (italics added).[30]

Beyond such parallels between the macabre and childbirth, what else can we read from the supernatural aura of *Rosemary's Baby?* Rich speaks of female reproduction as conventionally assigned "malign occult influences," as being "vulnerable to or emanating evil."[31] Kitzinger talks of parturition as a "ritual state" necessitating the intervention of shamans, priests, and priestesses.[32] Both associate pregnancy with "possession." For Kitzinger, this means "being taken over by an unknown and even hostile stranger";[33] for Rich, it connotes domination by labor's painful contractions. Both remark on the uncanny sense of "doubling" and "splitting" in reproduction—the former at conception; the latter at delivery.[34] Hence, pregnancy is a "liminal" or "marginal" state.[35] Kristeva extends this discussion, noting the link between maternity and sacred defilement: "Because of her parturition and the blood that goes with it, *she* will be 'impure.'"[36] While such characterizations are clearly pernicious, Grete Bibring wonders whether, by banishing "magical and superstitious customs surrounding pregnancy," science has "removed certain concepts and activities which . . . help in organizing and channeling the intense emotional reactions of the pregnant woman."[37]

But what of *Rosemary's Baby*'s specific references to witchcraft? What social or psychic echoes reverberate here? It is necessary to recall the history of childbirth, prior to the ascendancy of the male physician, when care of the pregnant woman was entrusted to a midwife—often a poor, older, peasant woman with little standing in the community. Frequently, such individuals were thought to bear evil spirits, capable of inducing female fertility or male impotence.[38] Consequently, midwives were often accused of witchcraft and were cited in the *Malleus Maleficarum,* the primary reference volume of the era. As Thomas Rogers Forbes writes: "Because midwives so often were in bad repute, even an innocent practitioner might be accused of witchcraft if the delivery had an unhappy outcome."[39] When the birth was successful, midwives might still be charged with selling an infant's soul to the devil. In the *Compendium Maleficarum* of 1626, Guaccius writes: "When [witches] do not kill the babies, they offer them (horrible to relate) to the demons in this execrable manner. After the child is born the witch-midwife . . . pretends that something should be done to restore the strength of the baby, carries it outside the bedroom, and elevating it on high [offers] it to the Prince of Devils."[40]

In recent years, feminists have challenged liturgical discourse, reclaiming the figure of the midwife-witch. By rereading it, they have seen her as the repository of patriarchal fears of female strength and as a scapegoat for the emergent obstetrical profession. As Rich notes: "Men gradually annexed the role of birth-attendant and thus assumed authority over the very sphere which had originally been one source of female power and charisma."[41]

In this light, it is tempting to recast Minnie Castevet as an ersatz modern midwife, shrouded in misogyny. From her first entrance into the Woodhouse apartment (when she asks if Rosemary will have children), she is concerned with her neighbor's reproductive life, and when Rosemary becomes pregnant, it is Minnie who administers homeopathic potions (filled with "snails and puppy-dog tails"). Like the ancient midwife, she must transfer her power to a male physician (Abe Sapirstein), who, nonetheless, relies on her expertise. Significantly, rumors of the Bramford's haunting center on the Trench sisters' cannibalism toward babies. The historical roots of the midwife-witch are consonant with Minnie's naturalistic presentation, a touch that caught critics off guard. Robert Chapetta complains that the demons in Polanski's film are "not frightening, but an absurd lot, rather like a small far-out California religious sect."[42]

Hysterical Pregnancy

Although some unsettling elements of the film are explained by the actual linkage of witchcraft and childbirth, it is equally fruitful to place them within a *psychological* frame. For much of what passes for Rosemary's demented musings are consonant with representations of women's ordinary experience of parturition. The birth process starts with conception, and in *Rosemary's Baby* the primal scene is overlain with terror. One night Guy reveals his sudden desire to father a baby, whereupon he choreographs a candlelight dinner. The meal is interrupted by the arrival of Minnie, who brings her special "chocolate mouse." Though Rosemary dislikes its "chalky undertaste," Guy urges her to eat it. (Significantly, Kristeva finds a link between culinary and maternal defilement: "Dietary abomination" has "a parallel . . . in the abomination provoked by the fertilizable or fertile feminine body.")[43]

Within moments of eating, Rosemary collapses and Guy carries her to bed. Rosemary suffers a perverse delirium: she sails on a ship; Guy rips off her clothing; Rosemary gazes up at religious paintings; she walks through flames; a monster's hand maims her; hags tie her down and paint her body; she begs the Pope for forgiveness. "This is not a dream," she shouts; "this is really happening!" The next morning, when Rosemary notices scratches on her skin, she asks Guy what has transpired. He says that, despite her faint, he had not wanted to "miss baby night," and confesses that sex had been fun in a "necrophilic sort of way."

This warped rape fantasy reverberates with cultural clichés of woman's sexual position. With female eroticism conceived as "the embodiment of guilt," it is logical that Rosemary seeks the Holy Father's blessing.[44] That she is unconscious during intercourse mocks woman's "designated" coital stance: passive and undemanding. That Guy is uninvolved with her impregnation evokes primitive beliefs that human males are removed from procreation. Finally, the devious denouement of Rosemary's pregnancy assigns her blame. It is *she* who has most wanted a child. (Even in her drugged stupor, she pleads to "make a baby.") It is *she* who has arranged to live in the Bramford (despite its chilling reputation). It is *she* who has pushed intimacy with the Castevets. (Guy originally warned: "If we get friendly with an old couple . . . we'll never get rid of them.") Thus, the New Eve is charged with Original Sin.

Louise Sweeney found viewing *Rosemary's Baby* "like having someone else's nightmare."[45] In truth, dreams have long been linked to the horror genre, and Noel Carroll sees the form as fraught with "nightmare imagery."[46] Significantly, researchers have also noted the importance of dreams to pregnancy. Deutsch deems the nine-month period a quasi-oneiric state, since women must attend to an abstract being. She also finds women prone to reverie in this condition and records some patient dreams that are reminiscent of Rosemary's. Certain fantasies occur in water (conjuring the amniotic fluid); others offer scenarios of harassment: "In such dreams wild beasts chase the dreamer, or a sharp claw or tooth is plunged into some part of her body. She tries to flee, but her persecutors run after her from behind while she faces another danger in front."[47]

As Rosemary's pregnancy progresses, its baroque narrative constructs a distorted projection of quotidian experience. Almost immediately, she is consumed with angst: she is uneasy when Dr. Hill requests a second blood sample; she develops insomnia upon hearing the Castevets' voices next door. When Rosemary visits Dr. Sapirstein, she reveals that she fears an ectopic complication. Though, within the diegesis, there is an unearthly rationale for Rosemary's

\s, her state of mind is not untoward. Leifer notes a "growing sense of anxiety" accompanying pregnancy, along with a feeling of "emotional liability."[48] In the past, such nervousness was often regarded as hysterical, and its admission was discouraged. Recently, however, scholars have seen such tension in a positive light as "a significant reflection of the developing maternal bond."[49] Rosemary, however, is almost paranoid—understandable given the assumptions of the plot. Again, we find that pregnant women can approach this state. As Leifer notes: "Women commonly beg[in] to view the outside world as potentially threatening. They bec[ome] more cautious in their activities, fear[ing] that they might be harmed or attacked."[50] For Leifer, this is not a pathological symptom but a protective stance that reflects "realistic concerns" for safety.

The premise of *Rosemary's Baby* is that the heroine gestates a devil-child; but worries of an abnormal fetus are common. Deutsch mentions the "painful idea that [the baby] will be a monster, an idiot, a cripple."[51] And Leifer reports: "Women typically . . . vividly imagine a variety of deformities that they had either read about or seen."[52] Some women perceive the fetus as a foreign being: Deutsch admits that it can be seen as a "parasite" that "exploits" the maternal host.[53] Interestingly, a 1968 pregnancy manual uses this precise language, characterizing the "tiny parasite of a fetus" as appropriating the body of its "mother-host" for "his own purposes."[54] Even the cool discourse of modern science casts the fetus in an eerie light. Three years before the release of *Rosemary's Baby*, Lennart Nilsson published his shocking, groundbreaking photographs of embryos in *Life* magazine.[55] As ontogeny repeats phylogeny, the embryo is seen to resemble an aquatic being (what Summer Brenner calls "the prince of whales"). Genetics catalogs the fetus's sequential organ development, informing us when it acquires what. (We are reminded that, for Carroll, monsters suffer from "categorical incompleteness.")[56]

While women have been told to purge such disturbing thoughts (to deny pregnancy's "chalky undertaste"), Leifer argues for their validity: "These concerns often represen[t] realistic apprehensions about a variety of unknown events."[57] Patriarchy has its own reasons for eliding female ambivalence. While man has traditionally imagined the *mother* as "abject"—associated as she is with menstrual blood and infantile excrement[58]—he rejects the thought that she might find abjection in *him* (the beloved child). Such inversion constitutes a narcissistic wound to one who refuses to see the Other in himself.

Along with a case of the "nerves," Rosemary suffers illness, a fact that brings to the surface cultural confusion about the status of pregnancy. On the one hand, history has amassed a compendium of medical disorders that collectively mark the state a "disease"—from eclampsia to toxemia, to varicose veins, to morning sickness. Yet with the threat of physiological harm abated, women have challenged institutionalized paternalism, claiming recognition for the pregnant woman's health, strength, and fortitude.

Ironically, while physicians have made the parturient woman an Imaginary Invalid, they have often disregarded her justified complaints. In *Rosemary's Baby,* the heroine's discomforts are consistently minimized, as though "pain, like love, [were] embedded in the ideology of motherhood."[59] Guy ignores her ailments, and Dr. Sapirstein implies that they are psychosomatic. In 1939, a study showed nausea to entail the repudiation of femininity; in 1943, another found queasiness prevalent in women "who had an unconscious desire not to be pregnant."[60] Though Guy and Dr. Sapirstein have devious reasons for slighting Rosemary's grievances, most doctors and husbands ostensibly do not.

Following the trajectory of documented pregnancies, Rosemary's discomfort and fear temporarily lessen at the moment of "quickening." As Leifer notes: "The almost universal reactions to this event [are] immense relief . . . and a new feeling of confidence."[61] However, when Rosemary shouts "It's alive!" the contemporary audience is struck by the intertextual irony of her words.

As Rosemary's term continues, she becomes appalled by her pallid and wasted appearance. While her condition results from demonic poisoning and stands in *inverse* relation to the usual plenitude of pregnancy, some expectant women dread their corporeal transformation. Leifer claims that many regard their swelling bodies as "ego-alien" and view them in fantastic terms: "The rapidly growing abdomen continued to evoke anxiety, and women reported feeling like Alice in Wonderland, upon taking the magic pills; growing and growing with no end in sight . . . losing control over their bodies."[62] For Walter Evans such metamorphosis is central to horror: "The key to monster movies is mysterious psychological and physical change directly associated with secondary sexual characteristics."[63]

Consumed by her fears of possession, Rosemary refuses to see friends, tracing the pregnant woman's alleged "increased self-preoccupation and . . . decline of emotional investment in the external world."[64] Virginia Wright Wexman and Diane Waldman see Rosemary not only as carrying a child but as becoming infantilized.[65]

As Rosemary's worries multiply, she grows leery of Guy's involvement with the Castevets: she is puzzled by the scratches he has made on her body; she searches for cult markings on his shoulder; she is perplexed that he can no longer return her gaze; she wonders why he is suddenly a popular actor, whose "break" comes at the expense of another's welfare. While Rosemary's doubts are explained supernaturally, such behavior can occur in ordinary circumstances. "Anxiety about losing one's husband . . . was expressed by more than half of the women [questioned]."[66]

For these myriad reasons, expectant women may feel a loss of control, a challenge to their physical and spiritual autonomy. For Zajicek, pregnancy is "a period of emotional stress" with a "high potential for psychiatric breakdown." Women seek external support out of a desire "to be cared for and protected"—a fact that mirrors Rosemary's unwise turn to Minnie Castevet.[67] The film chronicles this dependency, as Rosemary passively "transfers" stewardship of her pregnancy to others. Though she has wanted a child, it is Guy who orchestrates conception. One friend sends Rosemary to Dr. Hill; then Minnie reroutes her to Dr. Sapirstein. Since the latter is a "front," Minnie engineers Rosemary's care behind the scenes. Both Guy and Dr. Sapirstein attempt to keep Rosemary ignorant, cautioning her against reading. In a drugged delivery (fraught with childbirth "amnesia") Rosemary's baby is stolen from her in recompense for Guy's Faustian pact.

An alternate title for the film might read: *Whose Baby Is It Anyway?*

I can't remember the birth. Cold white rooms, cleanliness
the color of nothing. Sometimes a woman dreams that she's
given birth to a litter of piglets attached to her breasts like
pink balloons. When I look in the crib there is no baby . . .

Maxine Chernoff, "A Birth"[68]

Postpartum Document

The arrival of Rosemary's child is one of the most ghastly scenes in the film. Pursued by Guy and Dr. Sapirstein from Dr. Hill's office, she returns to her apartment, where she falls on the floor in the throes of labor. A hallucinatory sequence unfolds in which a coven of witches gag her, tie her down, sedate her, and deliver a male child whom they steal away. On one level (divested of the occult), the scene can be read as a dramatization of old-fashioned home birth—with a female midwife present. The feigned death of Rosemary's child stands in for the infant mortality that obtained until the modern era. (In justifying his evil sacrifice to the Castevets, Guy even asks Rosemary: "Suppose you had had the baby and lost it—wouldn't it have been the same?") On another tier, the birth scene superimposes upon that historical site the malevolent mythology of witchcraft—the notion of midwives as Satanic, as swiping babies for the devil. On a final plateau, the vignette subjectively replicates woman's experience of traditional hospital birth—of being physically re-strained, anesthetized, and summarily separated from her baby. Diane di Prima portrays such an event in her poem "Nativity":

> Dark timbers of lost forests falling into my bed.
> My hairs stirring, not asleep. Did they fetter me
> with cat's paw, rock root, the beard
> (of shame) of woman? They fettered me
> w/ leather straps, on delivery table. I cd not
> cry out. Forced gas mask over mouth,
> slave. I cd not
> turn head. Did they fetter me
> w/ breath of a fish? These poison airs? I cd not
> turn head, move hand, or leg
> thus forced. They tore child from me. Whose?[69]

A woman interviewed by Leifer recalls postpartum stress that is also compa-rable to Rosemary's: "The next day . . . all my fears came to the fore. I was so tired, and in a very strange state . . . [E]very time I heard a baby crying, I thought it was mine and that nobody was responding to his screaming . . . I began to feel really paranoid, very persecuted, that maybe they didn't bring him in because something was wrong with him. Then I began to think that maybe the baby had died that night, and I got into a whole fantasy about that."[70] Though Rosemary suspects that her "dead" child is living (and not that a live one is dead), her sense of disorientation approaches this. She be-comes alarmed when she hears a muffled infant's wail next door, and when one of Minnie's friends saves the milk extracted from the maternal breast.

Even Rosemary's response to her demon-child suggests a new mother's contradictory emotions. Bibring finds frequent "disturbances in the earliest attitudes of the young mother toward her newborn baby." Deutsch remarks that many women first view their newborn as a "rejected alien object."[71] Rosemary's vacillation between love and hate should not surprise us in a genre structured by the "conflict between attraction and repulsion."[72] Such a magnetic field sustains the tension of *Rosemary's Baby,* which acknowledges parturition as a bliss and a blight.

Like most social groups, the Castevets' coven harnesses guilt to prod Rose-mary toward parental bonding. "Aren't you his mother?" they ask; "Be a mother to your baby." Maternal "instinct" triumphs; ambivalence is quashed. On the one hand, this ending can be seen as oppressive. Even in the hands of

Pressured by the coven, Rosemary accepts her loathsome progeny in *Rosemary's Baby* (1968).

the devil, the dominant (Christian) ideology of mothering obtains.[73] From another perspective the denouement is progressive. Rather than reject the devil-child (the virtual anti-Christ), Rosemary accepts it, distancing herself from the Catholic Madonna.[74] This ending so displeased Ray Bradbury that he authored another: "I went back to see *Rosemary's Baby* the other night. I had to go back . . . Sitting there in the dark watching, I felt the same sense of dissatisfaction. The truth is I simply do not believe or accept the end of *Rosemary's Baby*."[75] In his script, Rosemary carries her newborn to a church, confronting the Almighty with his "son"—harking back to the biblical connection between Lucifer and God.

It seems significant that, as Rosemary rocks the cradle, we never fully glimpse her infamous baby, who remains forever offscreen.[76] On one level, this scopic denial foregrounds Carroll's notion that monsters are "inconceivable."[77] But, on another, it addresses horror's appropriation of the quotidian. In accepting her loathsome progeny, Rosemary acknowledges her *own* demons—the fears of motherhood that society wants hushed. Thus, in some respects, Rosemary's baby is her double, reminding us of Marcia Landy's observation that "the monster's transformation is associated with reproduction, like a woman."[78] In her diary, Phyllis Chesler calls her fetus "my monster, myself" querying: "What if you're born . . . with my anger, my excesses?"[79] Dana Polan notes an introspective trend in contemporary *grand guignol,* which "now suggest[s] that the horror is not merely among us, but rather part of us."[80]

If *Rosemary's Baby* assumes a certain "banality" to horror, it replays that thesis on the level of style. With the exception of the dream/hallucination sequences, the work is crafted with conventional cinematic verisimilitude: long-shot/long-take format, standard lenses, location shooting, continuity editing, credible costume and decor. For Marsha Kinder and Beverle Houston, *Rosemary's Baby* "create[s] the impression that never . . . were things so clearly seen, so concrete, so 'real.'"[81]

This dialectic aspect of pregnancy is evident in Margaret Atwood's short story "Giving Birth," where a parturient woman (Jeannie) is "shadowed" by an invisible lady who accompanies her to the hospital. While Jeannie takes an optimistic view of pregnancy, her alter-ego voices reservations:

> . . . there is another woman in the car. She's sitting in the front seat, and she hasn't turned or acknowledged Jeannie in any way. She, like Jeannie, is going to the hospital. She too is pregnant. She is not going to the hospital to *give* birth, however, because the word, the words, are too alien to her experience . . . Jeannie has seen her before, but she knows little about her except that she is a woman who did not wish to become pregnant, who did not choose to divide herself like this, who did not choose any of these ordeals, these initiations. *It would be no use telling her that everything is going to be fine.* (italics added)[82]

> *A pointing finger always accompanies the classic text: the truth is thereby long desired and avoided, kept in a kind of pregnancy for its full term, a pregnancy whose end, both liberating and catastrophic, will bring about the utter end of the discourse.*

> —Roland Barthes, *S/Z* (emphasis added)[83]

Afterbirth

Early on in *Rosemary's Baby* we learn that the Woodhouse and Castevet apartments were once a single residence that was later subdivided. The Woodhouses now live in the "back rooms" of the original lodging. Significantly, at the film's conclusion, Rosemary opens the barricaded door that conjoins the two habitations. Sensing that her attendants are sequestering her child, she goes to her hall closet and removes the rear shelves. Like Alice, she peers through a hole into her neighbor's caballic abode.[84] Grasping a knife, she traverses the space—leaving home for a Satanic Wonderland. (As Julia Kristeva has noted, abjection involves an ambiguity of "borders.")[85]

Clearly, Rosemary's trajectory has implications beyond the physical, for it replays (in navigational terms) the thematic project of the film. While contemporary discourse (be it patriarchal or feminist) has often idealized childbirth and suppressed its disturbing terrain, the film negotiates the geography that connects these ideological quarters. In journeying to the Castevets' suite, Rosemary links woman's conscious and unconscious pregnancies, her ecstatic and despondent views, modern and ancient medical practices, scientific and mystical beliefs, realistic and supernatural portrayals. In unleashing the horrific, Rosemary has un-"shelved" the Maternal Macabre—has reclaimed its "back rooms," has forced it out of the cultural and cinematic "closet."

In 1968, many middle-class expectant mothers were enrolled in uplifting Lamaze classes where they dutifully viewed graphic movies of labor and delivery. (On the same page as Andrew Sarris's *Village Voice* critique of *Rosemary's Baby* is a notice for a screening of an instructional childbirth film.)[86] Here is how Margaret Atwood depicts such a session in "Giving Birth":

They have seen the film made by the hospital, a full-colour film of a woman giving birth to, can it be a baby? "Not all babies will be this large at birth," the Australian nurse who introduces the movie says. Still, the audience, half of which is pregnant, doesn't look very relaxed when the lights go on. ("If you don't like the visuals," a friend of Jeannie's has told her, "you can always close your eyes.")[87]

Such Lamaze devotees may well have avoided Polanski's thriller, fearing the distress it could engender. Retrospectively, however, one wonders *which* women were most "prepared" for parturition: the women who saw the horror film or those who saw the documentary?

Notes

1. In Laura Chester, ed., *Cradle and All: Women Writers on Pregnancy and Childbirth* (Boston: Faber and Faber, 1989), p. 40.
2. Ibid., p. 69.

3. *Working Mother,* June 1989; *Newsweek,* May 14, 1990; *Parents* 43 (Fall 1968); Lindsay R. Curtis and Yvonne Caroles, *Pregnant and Lovin' It* (Los Angeles: Price/Stern, 1985), p. 4.

4. Caryn James, "The High Art of Horror Films Can Cut Deep into the Psyche," *New York Times,* May 27, 1990, p. 15; Dennis L. White, "The Poetics of Horror: More Than Meets the Eye," *Cinema Journal* 10, no. 2 (Spring 1987): 16.

5. C. F. Keppler, *The Literature of the Second Self* (Tucson: University of Arizona Press, 1972).

6. Siegfried Kracauer, *From Caligari to Hitler: A Psychological History of the German Film* (1947; reprint, Princeton, N.J.: Princeton University Press, 1974); Robin Wood, *Hollywood from Vietnam to Reagan* (New York: Columbia University Press, 1986), esp. pp. 70–134; Bruce Kawin, "The Mummy's Pool," in *Planks of Reason: Essays on the Horror Film,* ed. Barry Keith Grant (Metuchen, N.J.: Scarecrow Press, 1984), p. 74.

7. Dana Polan, "Eros and Syphilization: The Contemporary Horror Film," in *Planks of Reason,* ed. Grant, pp. 202–208; Serafina Kent Bathrick, "Ragtime: The Horror of Growing Up Female," *Jump Cut,* no. 14 (March 1977): 9–10.

8. Dana Polan coined this term for me in a discussion of the paper, but let me elaborate on its use. Allegory is commonly understood to be an extended narrative that carries a second meaning along with the surface story. As Gay Clifford points out in *The Transformations of Allegory* (London: Routledge and Kegan Paul, 1974), pp. 11, 25: "Allegorical action often takes the form of a . . . quest, or a pursuit" exposing a "credible and realistic hero to a journey through an extraordinary allegorical world." Often, as in the case of *Frankenstein* or *The Trial* (both cited by Clifford), though the diegetic universe is fantastic, it invokes a real social order (the perils of technological invention in *Frankenstein;* moribund and irrational bureaucracy in *The Trial*). It is in this sense that I apply the term to *Rosemary's Baby.* While on one level Rosemary's journey proceeds as a hyperbolic fiction, on another it charts the psychological and historical "realities" of quotidian pregnancy. According to theorists, allegory can either apply to the process by which an author creates a fiction or to the strategy by which a critic reads it. It is this latter sense I invoke, and make no claims for allegorical intentionality on the part of Ira Levin or Roman Polanski.

9. Noel Carroll, *The Philosophy of Horror, or Paradoxes of the Heart* (New York: Routledge, 1990), pp. 2, 107.

10. Rhona Berenstein, "Mommie Dearest: *Aliens, Rosemary's Baby,* and Mothering," *Journal of Popular Culture* 24, no. 2 (Fall 1990): 55.

11. Phyllis Chesler, *With Child: A Diary of Mothering* (New York: Thomas V. Crowell, 1979), pp. 36, 33.

12. "Gynecological Gothic" was used by Penelope Gilliatt in her review of *Rosemary's Baby:* "Anguish under the Skin," *New Yorker,* July 15, 1968, pp. 87–89.

13. The film is based on Ira Levin's 1967 novel of the same title (New York: Random House).

14. Stuart Hall, "Notes on Deconstructing 'The Popular,'" in *People's History and Socialist Theory,* ed. Raphael Samuel (London: Routledge and Kegan Paul, 1981), p. 230.

15. Robin Wood, "An Introduction to the American Horror Film," in *Planks of Reason,* ed. Grant, p. 17.

16. Iris Marion Young, "Pregnant Embodiment: Subjectivity and Alienation," *Journal of Medicine and Philosophy* 9 (1984): 45.

17. Myra Leifer, *Psychological Effects of Motherhood: A Study of First Pregnancy* (New York: Praeger, 1980), p. 117.

18. S. Wolkind and E. Zajicek, *Pregnancy: A Psychological and Social Study* (London: Academic Press, 1981), pp. 32, 35.

19. Curtis and Caroles, *Pregnant and Lovin' It*, p. 4.

20. Suzanne Arms, *Immaculate Deception: A New Look at Women and Childbirth in America* (Boston: Houghton Mifflin, 1975), pp. xiii, 23.

21. Nora Ephron, "Having a Baby after 35," *New York Times Magazine,* November 26, 1978, p. 88.

22. Adrienne Rich, *Of Woman Born: Motherhood as Experience and Institution* (New York: Norton, 1986), p. 153.

23. Marcia Landy helped focus the discussion on the issue of discourse and suggested the usefulness of Michel Foucault's *The History of Sexuality,* vol. 1, trans. Robert Hurley (New York: Pantheon, 1978).

24. Diane Waldman, "Horror and Domesticity: The Modern Romance Film of the 1940s" (Ph.D. diss., University of Wisconsin, Madison, 1981), pp. 308–325.

25. James B. Twitchell, *Dreadful Pleasures: An Anatomy of Modern Horror* (New York: Oxford University Press, 1985), p. 66.

26. Helene Deutsch, *The Psychology of Woman* (New York: Grune and Stratton, 1945), 3:135, 251.

27. Leifer, *Psychological Effects,* p. 45.

28. Ann Dally, *Inventing Motherhood: The Consequences of an Ideal* (New York: Schocken, 1983), pp. 26, 31.

29. Julia Kristeva, *Powers of Horror: An Essay on Abjection,* trans. Leon S. Roudiez (New York: Columbia University Press, 1982), p. 159. Kristeva's work and its relation to the horror film is also discussed in Barbara Creed, "Horror and the Monstrous-Feminine—An Imaginary Abjection," *Screen* 27, no. 1 (January–February 1986): 44–71 (reprinted in this volume).

30. Sheila Kitzinger, *Women as Mothers* (New York: Random House, 1978), pp. 85–86.

31. Rich, *Of Woman Born,* pp. 163–164.

32. Kitzinger, *Women as Mothers,* p. 71.

33. Ibid., p. 78.

34. See also Young, "Pregnant Embodiment," p. 46.

35. Kitzinger, *Women as Mothers,* p. 67.

36. Kristeva, *Powers of Horror,* p. 99.

37. Grete L. Bibring, "Some Considerations of the Psychological Process in Pregnancy," *Psychoanalytic Study of the Child* 14 (1959): 113–121.

38. See Deutsch, *Psychology of Woman,* p. 206; and Rich, *Of Woman Born,* pp. 135–138.

39. Thomas Rogers Forbes, *The Midwife and the Witch* (New Haven: Yale University Press, 1966), p. 5. See Barbara Ehrenreich, *Witches, Midwives, and Nurses: A History of Woman Healers* (Old Westbury, N.Y.: Feminist Press, 1973), p. 13.

40. Quoted in Forbes, *Midwife and the Witch,* p. 128.

41. Rich, *Of Woman Born,* p. 129.

42. Robert Chapetta, "*Rosemary's Baby,*" *Film Quarterly* 22, no. 3 (Spring 1969): 38.

43. Kristeva, *Powers of Horror,* p. 100.

44. Rich, *Of Woman Born,* p. 164.

45. Louise Sweeney, "Polanski's Satanic Parody," *Christian Science Monitor,* June 22, 1968, p. 6, western edition.

46. Noel Carroll, "Nightmare and the Horror Film: The Symbolic Biology of Fantastic Beings," *Film Quarterly* 34, no. 3 (Spring 1981): 16.

47. Deutsch, *Psychology of Woman,* p. 233.

48. Leifer, *Psychological Effects,* p. 31.

49. Ibid., p. 47.

50. Ibid., p. 49.

51. Deutsch, *Psychology of Woman,* p. 151.

52. Leifer, *Psychological Effects,* p. 47.

53. Deutsch, *Psychology of Woman,* p. 131.

54. H. M. Liley and Beth Day, "The Inside Story of Your Baby's Life before Birth," *Expecting,* special issue of *Parents* 43 (Fall 1968).

55. Lennart Nilsson, "Drama of Life before Birth," *Life* 58, no. 17 (April 30, 1965): 54–71.

56. Carroll, *Philosophy of Horror,* p. 33.

57. Leifer, *Psychological Effects,* p. 47.

58. Kristeva, *Powers of Horror,* pp. 57–173. See esp. pp. 115–116 and 99–100.

59. Rich, *Of Woman Born,* p. 157.

60. Wolkind and Zajicek, *Pregnancy,* pp. 77, 76.

61. Leifer, *Psychological Effects,* p. 78.

62. Ibid., pp. 34, 35.

63. Walter Evans, "Monster Movies: A Sexual Theory," in *Planks of Reason,* ed. Grant, p. 54.

64. Leifer, *Psychological Effects,* p. 43.

65. Virginia Wright Wexman, "The Trauma of Infancy in Roman Polanski's *Rosemary's Baby,*" in *American Horrors: Essays on the Modern American Horror Film,* ed. Gregory A. Waller (Urbana: University of Illinois Press, 1987), p. 34; Waldman, "Horror and Domesticity," p. 310.

66. Leifer, *Psychological Effects,* pp. 49–50.

67. Wolkind and Zajicek, *Pregnancy,* p. 60; Leifer, *Psychological Effects,* p. 54.

68. Maxine Chernoff, "A Birth," in *Cradle and All,* ed. Chester, p. 93.

69. Diane di Prima, "Nativity," in ibid., p. 107.

70. Leifer, *Psychological Effects,* p. 59.

71. Bibring, "Some Considerations," p. 14; Deutsch, *Psychology of Woman,* p. 251.

72. Carroll, "Nightmare and the Horror Film," p. 17.

73. Waldman, "Horror and Domesticity," pp. 314–315.

74. Berenstein, "Mommie Dearest," pp. 68–69.

75. Ray Bradbury, "A New Ending to *Rosemary's Baby,*" in *Focus on the Horror Film,* ed. Roy Huss and T. J. Ross (Englewood Cliffs, N.J.: Prentice-Hall, 1972), p. 149.

76. Though we do not see the baby in this sequence, there is an earlier moment (after Rosemary has first approached the cradle) when she is horrified by the child's ap-

pearance and asks, "What have you done to his eyes?" Later, when she learns that her son is the devil's child, she shouts, "It's not true," and her image is superimposed with a shot of the creature's eyes. These eyes are possibly her child's or those of the devil; it is unclear.

77. Carroll, *Philosophy of Horror*, p. 21.

78. Marcia Landy, *British Genres: Cinema and Society, 1930–1960* (Princeton, N.J.: Princeton University Press, 1991), p. 411.

79. Chesler, *With Child*, p. 101.

80. Polan, "Eros and Syphilization," p. 202.

81. Beverle Houston and Marsha Kinder, "*Rosemary's Baby*," *Sight and Sound* 38, no. 1 (Winter 1968–1969): 18.

82. Margaret Atwood, "Giving Birth," in *We Are the Stories We Tell*, ed. Wendy Martin (New York: Pantheon, 1990), p. 139.

83. Roland Barthes, *S/Z: An Essay*, trans. Richard Miller (New York: Hill and Wang, 1974), p. 62.

84. Wexman also makes the comparison to *Alice in Wonderland* in "The Trauma of Infancy."

85. Kristeva, *Powers of Horror*, p. 69.

86. Andrew Sarris, "*Rosemary's Baby*," *Village Voice*, July 25, 1968, p. 37.

87. Atwood, "Giving Birth," p. 139.

Selected Bibliography

Ayscough, Susan. "The Sexual Politics of David Cronenberg." *Cinema Canada,* no. 102 (December 1983): 15–18.

Bathrick, Serafina Kent. "Ragtime: The Horror of Growing Up Female." *Jump Cut,* no. 14 (1977): 9–10. [*Carrie*]

Bell-Metereau, Rebecca. "Woman: The Other Alien in *Alien.*" In *Women Worldwalkers: New Dimensions of Science Fiction and Fantasy,* edited by Jane B. Weedman, pp. 9–24. Lubbock: Texas Tech Press, 1985.

Bellour, Raymond. "Hitchcock, the Enunciator." *camera obscura,* no. 2 (Fall 1977): 69–94.

———. "Psychosis, Neurosis, Repression." *camera obscura,* nos. 3–4 (Summer 1979): 105–132. Reprinted in *A Hitchcock Reader,* edited by Marshall Deutelbaum and Leland Poague, pp. 311–331. Ames: Iowa State University Press, 1986.

Berenstein, Rhona. "Frightening Women: An Introduction to Classic Horror's Marketing Strategies." *Framework* 5, nos. 2–3 (Fall 1992): 337–349.

———. "Mommie Dearest: *Aliens, Rosemary's Baby,* and Mothering." *Journal of Popular Culture* 24, no. 2 (Fall 1990): 55–73.

———. *Attack of the Leading Ladies: Gender, Sexuality, and Spectatorship in Classic Horror Cinema.* New York: Columbia University Press, 1995.

Bergstrom, Janet. "Enunciation and Sexual Difference." *camera obscura*, nos. 3–4 (Summer 1979): 33–70. [*The Birds*]

———. "Sexuality at a Loss: The Films of F. W. Murnau." *Poetics Today* 6, nos. 1–2 (1985): 185–203.

Berks, John. "What Alice Does: Looking Otherwise at *The Cat People*." *Cinema Journal* 32, no. 1 (Fall 1992): 26–42.

Bisplinghoff, Gretchen. "Codes of Feminine Madness." In *Film Reader 5*, pp. 37–40. Evanston, Ill.: Northwestern University, 1982. [*Repulsion*]

Brown, Royal S. "*Dressed to Kill:* Myth and Male Fantasy in the Horror/Suspense Drama." *Film/Psychology Review* 4, no. 2 (Summer/Fall 1980): 169–182.

Bundtzen, Linda K. "Monstrous Mothers: Medusa, Grendel, and Now *Alien*." *Film Quarterly* 40, no. 3 (Spring 1987): 11–17.

Byers, Thomas B. "Kissing Becky: Masculine Fears and Misogynist Moments in SF Films." *Arizona Quarterly* 45, no. 3 (Autumn 1989): 77–95.

Clover, Carol. "Getting Even: Rape and Revenge in *I Spit on Your Grave* and *The Accused*." *Sight and Sound* 2, no. 1 (May 1992): 16–18.

———. *Men, Women, and Chain Saws: Gender in the Modern Horror Film*. Princeton: Princeton University Press, 1992.

Cobbs, John L. "*Alien* as an Abortion Parable." *Literature/Film Quarterly* 18, no. 3 (1990): 198–202.

Cohen, Keith. "*Psycho:* The Suppression of Female Desire (and Its Return)." In *Reading Narrative: Form, Ethics, Ideology*, edited by James Phelan, pp. 147–161. Columbus: Ohio State University Press, 1989.

Conlon, James. "Silencing Lambs and Educating Women." *Post Script* 12, no. 1 (Fall 1992): 3–12.

Cook, Pam. "Exploitation Films and Feminism." *Screen* 17, no. 2 (Summer 1976): 122–127.

Creed, Barbara. "Dark Desires: Male Masochism in the Horror Film." *Screening the Male: Exploring Masculinities in Hollywood Cinema*, edited by Steven Cohan and Ina Rae Hark, pp. 118–133. London and New York: Routledge, 1993.

———. "From Here to Modernity: Feminism and Postmodernism." *Screen* 28, no. 2 (1987): 47–67. A shortened version appears as "Gynesis, Postmodernism, and the Science Fiction Horror Film." In *Alien Zone: Cultural Theory and Contemporary Science Fiction Cinema*, edited by Annette Kuhn, pp. 214–218. London and New York: Verso, 1990.

———. *The Monstrous-Feminine: Film, Feminism, Psychoanalysis*. London: Routledge, 1993.

———. "Phallic Panic: Male Hysteria and *Dead Ringers*." *Screen* 31, no. 2 (Summer 1990): 125–146.

Dadoun, Roger. "Fetishism in the Horror Film." *Enclitic* 1, no. 2 (1979): 39–63. Reprinted in *Fantasy and the Cinema*, edited by James Donald, pp. 39–61. London: British Film Institute, 1989.

de Lauretis, Teresa. *Alice Doesn't: Feminism, Semiotics, Cinema*. Bloomington: Indiana University Press, 1984.

Deutelbaum, Marshall, and Leland Poague, eds. *A Hitchcock Reader.* Ames: Iowa State University Press, 1986.

Dika, Vera. *Games of Terror: Halloween, Friday the 13th, and the Films of the Stalker Cycle.* Rutherford, N.J.: Fairleigh Dickinson University Press, 1990.

———. "The Stalker Film, 1978–81." In *American Horrors: Essays on the Modern American Horror Film,* edited by Gregory A. Waller, pp. 86–101. Urbana and Chicago: University of Illinois Press, 1987.

Diski, Jenny. "Sitting Inside." *Sight and Sound* 5, no. 4 (April 1995): 12–13. [*Rosemary's Baby*]

Doane, Mary Ann. "Technophilia: Technology, Representation, and the Feminine." In *Body/Politics: Women and the Discourses of Science,* edited by Mary Jacobus, Evelyn Fox, and Sally Shuttleworth, pp. 163–176. New York: Routledge, 1990.

Draper, Ellen. "Zombie Women When the Gaze Is Male." *Wide Angle* 10, no. 3 (1988): 52–62.

Eisenstein, Alex. "*Alien* Dissected: Anatomy of a Monster Movie." *Fantastic Films* 13 (1980): 51–63.

Erens, Patricia. "*The Seduction:* The Pornographic Impulse in Slasher Films." *Jump Cut,* no. 32 (1987): 53–55, 52.

Evans, Walter. "Monster Movies and Rites of Initiation." *Journal of Popular Film* 4, no. 2 (1975): 124–142.

———. "Monster Movies: A Sexual Theory." *Journal of Popular Film* 2, no. 4 (Fall 1973): 353–365. Reprinted in *Planks of Reason: Essays on the Horror Film,* edited by Barry Keith Grant, pp. 53–64. Metuchen, N.J.: Scarecrow Press, 1984.

Frank, Marcie. "The Camera and the Speculum: David Cronenberg's *Dead Ringers.*" *PMLA* 106, no. 3 (May 1991): 459–470.

Gans, Herbert J. "*The Exorcist:* A Devilish Attack on Women." *Social Policy* 5 (May–June 1974): 71–73.

Garrett, Greg. "Objecting to Objectification: Re-Viewing the Feminine in *The Silence of the Lambs.*" *Journal of Popular Culture* 27, no. 4 (Spring 1994): 1–12.

Giacci, Vittorio. "Alfred Hitchcock: Allegory of Ambiguous Sexuality." *Wide Angle* 4, no. 1 (1980): 4–11.

Grant, Barry Keith. "The Body Politic: Ken Russell in the 1980s." In *Fires Were Started: British Cinema and Thatcherism,* edited by Lester Friedman, pp. 188–203. Minneapolis: University of Minnesota Press, 1993.

———, ed. *Planks of Reason: Essays on the Horror Film.* Metuchen, N.J.: Scarecrow Press, 1984.

Greenberg, Harvey R. *The Movies on Your Mind.* New York: Dutton/Saturday Review Press, 1975.

Guerrero, Edward. "AIDS as Monster in Science Fiction and Horror Cinema." *Journal of Popular Film and Television* 18, no. 3 (Fall 1990): 86–93.

Halberstam, Judith. "Skinflick: Posthuman Gender in Jonathan Demme's *The Silence of the Lambs.*" *camera obscura,* no. 27 (1991): 37–52.

———. *Skin Shows: Gothic Horror and the Technology of Monsters.* Durham, N.C.: Duke University Press, 1995.

Heldreth, Leonard G. "The Beast Within: Sexuality and Metamorphosis in Horror Films." In *Eros in the Mind's Eye,* edited by Donald Palumbo, pp. 117–125. Westport, Conn.: Greenwood Press, 1986.

Hogan, David J. *Dark Romance: Sex and Death in the Horror Film.* Jefferson, N.C.: McFarland, 1986.

Horwitz, Margaret M. "*The Birds:* A Mother's Love." *Wide Angle* 5, no. 1 (1982): 42–48. Reprinted in *A Hitchcock Reader,* edited by Marshall Deutelbaum and Leland Poague, pp. 279–287. Ames: Iowa State University Press, 1986.

Hutchings, Peter. "Masculinity and the Horror Film." In *You Tarzan: Masculinity, Movies, and Men,* edited by Pat Kirkham and Janet Thumim, pp. 84–94. London: Lawrence and Wishart, 1993.

Jancovich, Mark. *Horror.* London: Batsford, 1992.

Kane, Joe. "Beauties, Beasts, and Male Chauvinist Monsters." *Take One* 4, no. 4 (March–April 1973): 8–10.

Kavanagh, James H. "'Son of a Bitch': Feminism, Humanism, and Science in *Alien.*" *October,* no. 13 (Summer 1980): 91–100. Reprinted in *Alien Zone: Cultural Theory and Contemporary Science Fiction,* edited by Annette Kuhn, pp. 73–81. London and New York: Verso, 1990.

Klinger, Barbara. "*Psycho:* The Institutionalization of Female Sexuality." *Wide Angle* 5, no. 1 (1982): 49–55. Reprinted in *A Hitchcock Reader,* edited by Marshall Deutelbaum and Leland Poague, pp. 332–339. Ames: Iowa State University Press, 1986.

Kristeva, Julia. *Powers of Horror: An Essay on Abjection,* translated by Leon S. Roudiez. New York: Columbia University Press, 1982.

Kuhn, Annette, ed. *Alien Zone: Cultural Theory and Contemporary Science Fiction Cinema.* London and New York: Verso, 1990.

Laurie, Susan. "Pornography and the Dread of Women: The Male Sexual Dilemma." In *Take Back the Night,* edited by Laura Lederer, pp. 159–173. New York: William Morrow, 1980.

Lenne, Gerard. "Monster and Victim: Women in the Horror Film." In *Sexual Strategems,* edited by Patricia Erens, pp. 31–40. New York: Horizon Press, 1979.

McConnell, Frank D. "Song of Innocence: *The Creature from the Black Lagoon.*" *Journal of Popular Film* 1, no. 2 (Winter 1973): 15–28. Reprinted in *The Spoken Seen: Film and the Romantic Imagination,* edited by Frank McConnell, pp. 135–146. Baltimore and London: Johns Hopkins University Press, 1975.

Modleski, Tania. "The Terror of Pleasure: The Contemporary Horror Film and Postmodern Theory." University of Wisconsin at Milwaukee, Center for 20th Century Studies, Working Paper, no. 8 (Fall 1984). Reprinted in *Studies in Entertainment: Critical Approaches to Mass Culture,* edited by Tania Modleski, pp. 155–156. Bloomington and Indianapolis: Indiana University Press, 1986.

———. *The Women Who Knew Too Much.* New York and London: Methuen, 1988.

Mulvey, Laura. "Visual Pleasure and Narrative Cinema." *Screen* 16, no. 3 (Autumn 1975): 6–18.

Naureckas, Jim. "*Aliens:* Mother and the Teeming Hordes." *Jump Cut,* no. 32 (1986): 1, 4.

Newton, Judith. "Feminism and Anxiety in *Alien.*" *Science Fiction Studies* 7, no. 3 (1980):

278–304. Reprinted in *Alien Zone: Cultural Theory and Contemporary Science Fiction,* edited by Annette Kuhn, pp. 82–87. London and New York: Verso, 1990.

Norden, Martin F. "Sexual References in James Whale's *Bride of Frankenstein.*" In *Eros in the Mind's Eye: Sexuality and the Fantastic in Art and Film,* edited by Donald F. Palumbo, pp. 141–150. Westport, Conn.: Greenwood Press, 1986.

Pannill, Linda. "The Woman Artist as Creature and Creator." *Journal of Popular Culture* 16, no. 2 (Fall 1982): 26–29.

Paul, William. *Laughing Screaming: Modern Horror and Comedy.* New York: Columbia University Press, 1994.

Peary, Dannis. "Stephanie Rothman: R-Rated Feminist." In *Women and the Cinema,* edited by Karyn Kay and Gerald Peary, pp. 179–192. New York: Dutton, 1977.

Penley, Constance, Elizabeth Lyon, Lynn Spigel, and Janet Bergstrom, eds. *Close Encounters: Film, Feminism, and Science Fiction.* Minneapolis and Oxford: University of Minnesota Press, 1991.

Price, Theodore. *Hitchcock and Homosexuality.* Metuchen, N.J.: Scarecrow Press, 1992.

Robbins, Helen W. "'More Human Than I Am Alone': Womb Envy in David Cronenberg's *The Fly* and *Dead Ringers.*" In *Screening the Male: Exploring Masculinities in Hollywood Cinema,* edited by Steven Cohan and Ina Rae Hark, pp. 134–147. London and New York: Routledge, 1993.

Rodowick, D. N. "The Difficulty of Difference." *Wide Angle* 5, no. 1 (1982): 4–15.

———. *The Difficulty of Difference.* New York: Routledge, 1991.

Russell, Sharon. "The Witch in Film: Myth and Reality." *Film Reader 3,* pp. 80–89. Evanston, Ill.: Northwestern University, 1978. Reprinted in *Planks of Reason: Essays on the Horror Film,* edited by Barry Keith Grant, pp. 113–125. Metuchen, N.J.: Scarecrow Press, 1984.

Shaviro, Steven. *The Cinematic Body.* Minneapolis: University of Minnesota Press, 1993.

Sloan, Kay. "Three Hitchcock Heroines: The Domestication of Violence." *New Orleans Review* 12, no. 4 (Winter 1985): 91–95. [*The Birds*]

Sobchack, Vivian. "Child/ Alien/ Father: Patriarchal Crisis and Generic Exchange." *camera obscura,* no. 15 (1986): 7–34. Reprinted in *Close Encounters: Film, Feminism, and Science Fiction,* edited by Constance Penley, Elizabeth Lyon, Lynn Spigel, and Janet Bergstrom, pp. 3–31. Minneapolis and Oxford: University of Minnesota Press, 1991.

———. "Revenge of *The Leech Woman:* On the Dread of Aging in a Low-Budget Horror Film." In *Uncontrollable Bodies: Testimonies of Identity and Culture,* edited by Rodney Sappington and Tyler Stallings, pp. 79–91. Seattle: Bay Press, 1994.

Spoto, Donald. *The Dark Side of Genius: The Life of Alfred Hitchcock.* Boston and Toronto: Little, Brown, 1983.

Steffan-Fleur, Nancy. "Women and the Inner Game of Don Siegel's *Invasion of the Body Snatchers.*" *Science Fiction Studies* 11, no. 2 (July 1984): 139–153.

Tarratt, Margaret. "Monsters from the Id." 2 pts. *Films and Filming* 17, no. 3 (December 1970): 38–42; no. 4 (January 1971): 40–42. Reprinted in *Film Genre Reader II,* edited by Barry Keith Grant, pp. 330–349. Austin: University of Texas Press, 1995.

Taubin, Amy. "Killing Men." *Sight and Sound* 1, no. 1 (May 1991): 14–18.

Tharp, Julie. "The Transvestite as Monster: Gender Horror in *The Silence of the Lambs* and *Psycho.*" *Journal of Popular Film and Television* 19, no. 3 (Fall 1991): 106–113.

Twitchell, James B. *Dreadful Pleasures: An Anatomy of Modern Horror.* New York: Oxford University Press, 1985.

Ursini, James, and Alain Silver. *The Vampire Film.* New York: A. S. Barnes, 1975. Revised as *The Vampire Film: From Nosferatu to Bram Stoker's Dracula.* New York: Limelight, 1993.

Waller, Gregory A. *The Living and the Undead: From Stoker's Dracula to Romero's Night of the Living Dead.* Urbana and Chicago: University of Illinois Press, 1986.

Weiss, Andrea. *Vampires and Violets: Lesbians in Film.* New York: Viking, 1993.

Wells, Paul. "The Invisible Man: Shrinking Masculinity in the 1950s Science Fiction B-Movie." In *You Tarzan: Masculinity, Movies, and Men,* edited by Pat Kirkham and Janet Thumim, pp. 181–199. London: Lawrence and Wishart, 1993.

Wexman, Virginia Wright. "The Trauma of Infancy in Roman Polanski's *Rosemary's Baby.*" In *American Horrors: Essays on the Modern American Horror Film,* edited by Gregory A. Waller, pp. 30–43. Urbana and Chicago: University of Illinois Press, 1987.

Williams, Linda. "Film Bodies: Gender, Genre, and Excess." *Film Quarterly* 44, no. 4 (Summer 1991): 2–13. Reprinted in *Film Genre Reader II,* edited by Barry Keith Grant, pp. 140–158. Austin: University of Texas Press, 1995.

———. *Hard Core: Power, Pleasure, and the Frenzy of the Visible.* Berkeley: University of California Press, 1989.

Williams, Tony. "Feminism, Fantasy, and Violence: An Interview with Stephanie Rothman." *Journal of Popular Film and Television* 9, no. 2 (Summer 1981): 84–90.

Wood, Robin. "Beauty Bests the Beast." *American Film* 8, no. 10 (September 1983): 63–65. Reprinted as "Returning the Look: *Eyes of a Stranger.*" In *American Horrors: Essays on the Modern American Horror Film,* edited by Gregory A. Waller, pp. 79–85. Urbana and Chicago: University of Illinois Press, 1987.

———. "Cronenberg: A Dissenting View." In *The Shape of Rage,* edited by Piers Handling, pp. 98–114. Toronto and New York: General Publishing/New York Zoetrope, 1983.

———. *Hitchcock's Films Revisited.* New York: Columbia University Press, 1989.

———. "An Introduction to the American Horror Film." In *American Nightmare: Essays on the Horror Film,* edited by Robin Wood and Richard Lippe, pp. 7–28. Toronto: Festival of Festivals, 1979. Reprinted in *Hollywood from Vietnam to Reagan,* by Robin Wood, pp. 70–94. New York: Columbia University Press, 1986. Also in *Planks of Reason: Essays on the Horror Film,* edited by Barry Keith Grant, pp. 164–200. Metuchen, N.J.: Scarecrow Press, 1984.

———. "Neglected Nightmares." *Film Comment* 16, no. 2 (March–April 1980): 25–32.

———. "Return of the Repressed." *Film Comment* 14, no. 4 (July–August 1978): 25–32.

———, and Richard Lippe, eds. *American Nightmare: Essays on the Horror Film.* Toronto: Festival of Festivals, 1979.

"Writers on the *Lamb*: Sorting Out the Sexual Politics of a Controversial Film." *Village Voice,* March 5, 1991, pp. 49, 56, 58–59.

Young, Elizabeth. "*The Silence of the Lambs* and the Flaying of Feminist Film Theory." *camera obscura,* no. 27 (September 1991): 5–35.

Notes on Contributors

RHONA J. BERENSTEIN is Assistant Professor in the Film Studies Program at the University of California, Irvine. She is the author of *Attack of the Leading Ladies: Gender, Sexuality, and Spectatorship in Classic Horror Cinema* (1995). Her work on horror has appeared in such journals as *Framework, CineAction, Film History,* and *Journal of Popular Culture.*

CAROL J. CLOVER is Professor of Rhetoric (film) and Scandinavian (medieval studies) at the University of California, Berkeley. Her books include *The Medieval Saga* (1982) and *Men, Women, and Chain Saws: Gender in the Modern Horror Film* (1992).

JAMES CONLON teaches in the Philosophy Department at Mount Mary College in Milwaukee, Wisconsin. His writing on philosophical themes in film has appeared in such journals as *Post Script, Journal of Popular Film and Television,* and *Journal of Aesthetic Education.*

BARBARA CREED teaches in the Department of Fine Arts, Melbourne University, Parkville, Victoria, Australia. The author of *Horror and the Monstrous Feminine: Film, Feminism, Psychoanalysis* (1993), she has published widely in the areas of film and feminist theory.

VERA DIKA teaches film studies in the Department of Film and Television at both the University of California, Los Angeles, and the University of Southern California. She is the author of *Games of Terror: The Films of the Stalker Cycle* (1991). Her film criticism has appeared in such publications as *Art in America, Artforum,* and the *Los Angeles Times.*

THOMAS DOHERTY teaches American studies at Brandeis University in Waltham, Massachusetts. He is the author of *Teenagers and Teenpics: The Juvenilization of American Movies in the 1950s* (1988) and *Projections of War: Hollywood, American Culture, and World War II* (1994).

PATRICIA BRETT ERENS, Professor of Film Studies at Rosary College, River Forest, Illinois, is the author of *The Jew in American Cinema* (1984) and editor of *Sexual Stratagems: The World of Women in Film* (1979) and *Issues in Feminist Film Criticism* (1990).

LUCY FISCHER is Professor of Film Studies at the University of Pittsburgh. She is the author of *Jacques Tati: A Guide to References and Resources* (1983) and *Shot/Countershot: Film Tradition and Women's Cinema* (1989) and editor of a critical volume on *Imitation of Life* (1991).

HARVEY ROY GREENBERG, M.D., practices psychiatry and psychoanalysis in Manhattan and is Clinical Professor of Psychiatry at the Albert Einstein College of Medicine at Yeshiva University in New York City, where he teaches medical humanities and adolescent psychiatry. He is the author of *The Movies on Your Mind: Film Classics on the Couch* (1975) and *Screen Memories: Hollywood Cinema on the Psychoanalytic Couch* (1993), and his work has appeared in a wide variety of periodicals.

KAREN HOLLINGER teaches film and literature at Armstrong State College in Savannah, Georgia. She coedited (with Virginia Wright Wexman) *Letter from an Unknown Woman* for the Rutgers Films in Print series and has published articles on film and literature in *Film Criticism, Literature/Film Quarterly, Quarterly Review of Film and Video, Journal of Film and Video,* and *Studies in Short Fiction.*

ADAM KNEE is former Program Coordinator in the Department of Communication at the New School for Social Research in New York City, where he currently teaches. He has taught film history and theory at New York University and Penn State University, and his writing has appeared in *Wide Angle, Film Quarterly, Minnesota Review,* and the anthology *Screening the Male: Exploring Masculinities in Hollywood Cinema,* edited by Steven Cohan and Ina Rae Hark (1993).

SHELLEY STAMP LINDSEY is an Assistant Professor at the University of California, Santa Cruz, where she teaches film history and theory. Her work has appeared in such publications as *Screen, Quarterly Review of Film Studies, Journal of Film and Video,* and *cinemas.*

LIANNE MCLARTY is Director of the Film Studies Program at the University of Victoria, British Columbia, Canada. She has published on experimental film in *Cine-Tracts* and *Take Two: A Tribute to Film in Canada,* edited by Seth Feldman (1984). She is also a member (along with Alison Hearne and Lynne Hissey) of Femamatic, a feminist critical collective ("We slice, we dice, we theorize.")

CHRISTOPHER SHARRETT is Associate Professor of Communication at Seton Hall University. His work has appeared in *Cinéaste, Film Quarterly, Persistence of Vision, Journal of Popular Film and Television, CineAction,* and elsewhere. He has edited *Crisis Cinema: The Apocalyptic Idea in Postmodern Narrative Film* (Maisonneuve Press, 1993).

VIVIAN SOBCHACK is an Associate Dean and Professor of Film and Television at UCLA School of Theater, Film and Television. She is author of *Screening Space: The American Science Fiction Film* (1987), *The Address of the Eye: A Phenomenology of Film Experience* (1993), *An Introduction to Film* (1980, with Thomas Sobchack), and has edited two anthologies, *The Persistence of History: Cinema, Television and the Modern Event* (1996) and *Meta-Morphing: Visual Transformation and the Culture of Quick Change* (1999).

LINDA WILLIAMS is Professor of Film Studies and Women's Studies at the University of California, Irvine. She is the author of *Hard Core: Power, Pleasure, and the Frenzy of the Visible* (1989) and *Figures of Desire: A Theory of Analysis of Surrealist Film* (1989). Her articles have appeared in *Cinema Journal, Film Quarterly,* and elsewhere.

TONY WILLIAMS is Associate Professor of English at Southern Illinois University in Carbondale, where he teaches film and literature. He is the author of *Jack London: The Movies* (1992) and *Hearths of Darkness: The Family in the American Horror Film* (1996) and the coauthor (with Lawrence Staig) of *Italian Westerns: The Opera of Violence* (1975) and *Vietnam War Films* (1994). His essays have appeared in such journals as *CineAction, Movie, Jump Cut, Science Fiction Studies,* and *Wide Angle.*

ROBIN WOOD is the author of *Hitchcock's Films* (1965), *Ingmar Bergman* (1969), *Claude Chabrol* (with Michael Walker, 1970), *Personal Views* (1970), *Hollywood from Vietnam to Reagan* (1985), and *Hitchcock's Films Revisited* (1989). He teaches at Atkinson College, York University, Toronto, and is a member of the *CineAction* editorial collective.

ELIZABETH YOUNG is Assistant Professor of English at Mount Holyoke College in South Hadley, Massachusetts, where she teaches film, feminist theory, and American literature. Her articles on horror films have appeared in *camera obscura* and *Feminist Studies* and are part of a larger work in progress on feminist theory and Frankenstein films.

BONNIE ZIMMERMAN is Professor of Women's Studies at San Diego State University, where she teaches courses on literature, theory, and humanities. Her publications on lesbian literature and critical theory include *The Safe Sea of Women: Lesbian Fiction 1969–1989* (1990).

Index

**Boldface page numbers indicate
photographs.**

abjection, 8, 35–65, 390–391, 421, 427
action films, 139, 189–190
Adorno, Theodor, 249
adventure films, 139, 189–190
After Many Years, 33n
Age d'Or, L', 377
AIP (American-International Pictures),
    381, 397
Air Force, 190
Alice in Wonderland (Carroll), 422, 427
Alien, 47–51, 53, 55–56, 58–59, 61–63,
    66, 71, 86, 91, 112, 113, 181–199,
    209, 234, 269, 276, 390, 394, 418
Aliens, 66, 86, 91, 92, 98, 110, 112, 113,
    181–199, **186, 197**
Alien series, 7, 9, 181–199, 269, 276
Alien³, 181–199, **193,** 269
Allan, Elizabeth, 121
Allen, Woody, 2, 96
All of Me, 101

Altered States, 48, 159
Altman, Charles, 357, 361
Altman, Robert, 389
American Gothic, 169
American-International Pictures (AIP),
    381, 397
American Werewolf in London, An, 66
Ames, Jesse Daniel, 321
Amityville Horror, The, 78, 146, 152, 279
Amityville II: The Possession, 152, 279
Amityville 3-D, 152
Andrew, Dudley, 147–148
Antonioni, Michelangelo, 223–224
Ape Man, The, 1
Apocalypse Now, 398, 399
Argento, Dario, 9, 88, 213–230
Aristotle, 182
Arms, Suzanne, 417
Arvidson, Linda, 33n
Attack of the 50-Foot Woman, 2, **3,** 77, 338
Atwood, Margaret, 426–427
audience, 7, 9, 66–113, 117–142
Audrey Rose, 150

Author! Author!, 154–155
authorship, 70, 164, 202, 312, 398
Autumn Sonata, 381

Bacall, Lauren, 204
Back to the Future, 160, 163, 188
Back to the Future series, 183
Badham, John, 10, 364–367, 370, 375–378, 389, 390, 394
Bad Seed, The, 161
Bakhtin, Mikhail, 248, 258
Barker, Clive, 261, 264, 275
Barrowclough, Susan, 112
Barry, John F., 127–128, 140
Barrymore, John, 132–133, 134–135
Barthes, Roland, 276, 426
Basic Instinct, 229
Bataille, Georges, 38, 40, 56, 256–257, 274
Bathory, Countess Elizabeth, 379, 381, 387
Bathrick, Serafina Kent, 294, 413
Baudrillard, Jean, 233, 249
Baudry, Jean, 361
Bazin, André, 374
Beauty and the Beast, 20, 21
Bedroom Window, The, 357
Behind the Green Door, 101
Belle et la bête, La. See *Beauty and the Beast*
Bennett, Constance, 135
Bennett, Joan, 135
Berenstein, Rhona, 7, 9, 413–415
Berger, John, 33n
Bergman, Ingmar, 96, 111, 381
Bibring, Grete, 418, 424
Bigelow, Kathryn, 7, 259
Bill and Ted's Excellent Adventure, 395
biographical films, 139
Birds, The, 42, 61, 65, 79, 88, 90, 93, 208
Bird with the Crystal Plumage, The, 215–218, 222–223, 225, 229, 230
Birth of a Nation, The, 322
Bissell, Whit, 341
Black Cat, The, 129–130

Black Sunday, 380
Blade Runner, 66, 182
Bliss, Michael, 284
Blob, The (1958), 4, 233
Blood and Roses, 380
Blood Ceremony, 380
Blood Feast, 109, 201
Blood of Dracula, 380
Blood Splash, 169
Blood Splattered Bride, The. See *Novia Ensangretada, La*
Bloodsucking Freaks, 41
Blow Out, 82, 107, 112, 230, 294
Blow-Up, 223–224
Blue Velvet, 274, 354, 356
Body Chemistry, 7
Body Double, 68, 78, 294
body horror, 35–65, 68–69, 79–80, 87, 96–101, 105, 201, 226–228, 231–252
Bogart, Humphrey, 204
Bogle, Donald F., 322, 335
Boogeyman, The, 169
Boss, Pete, 233
Boys from Brazil, The, 157
Bradbury, Ray, 425
Brakhage, Stan, 34
Bram Stoker's Dracula, 10, 11, 190, 255, 265–269, **267**, 388–400, **392, 393**
Brenner, Summer, 412, 421
Bride of Frankenstein, The, 2, 9, 124, 127, 130, 300–301, 309–337, **317, 329,** 338
Briggs, Joe Bob, 67, 104, 107
Brood, The, 232, 234–238, **237,** 251, 413, **414**
Brown, Rita Mae, 7, 84
Browning, Tod, 190, 268, 364, 378n
Brueghel, Pieter, 158
Buckets of Blood, 75
Buffy, the Vampire Slayer, 7
Bukatman, Scott, 275
Burke, Fred, 275
Burke, Kathleen, **131**–132
Busby, Marquis, 129
By Reason of Insanity (Stevens), 173

Cabinet of Dr. Caligari, The, 5, 6, 296–297, 320, 413
Caesar, Sid, 340
Cameron, James, 113, 183, 185, 191, 195
camp, 87, 179–180, 309, 315, 321, 332, 335, 386
Campbell, Joseph, 35
Candyman, 5, 10
Carmilla (LeFanu), 380–381, 387
Carpenter, John, 71, 81, 94, 201, 352
Carradine, John, 2
Carrie, 9, 40, 42, 44, 146, 151, 161, 162, 275–295, **281, 286,** 413
Carroll, Noel, 10, 233, 295, 307, 390, 391, 420, 421, 425
Casablanca, 341, 350
Cassavetes, John, 153
Castle, William, 1
castration, 7, 22–23, 30, 32, 35–36, 42, 44, 56, 59, 61, 94–96, 176, 283, 297–300, 310, 328
Cat o' Nine Tails, 216, 223
Cat People (1942), 9, 41, 61, 301–304, **303,** 306–308, 338, 341, 400
Cat People (1982), 9, 41, 61, 303–308, **305**
Cavanaugh, James, 276
censorship, 334–335. *See also* Production Code Administration
Chambers, Marilyn, 237
Chaney, Lon, 18, 19
Changeling, The, 161
Chapetta, Robert, 419
Chernoff, Maxine, 423
Chesler, Phyllis, 415, 426
Children of the Damned, 161
Chodorow, Nancy, 363
Chomsky, Noam, 256
Christian, Meg, 387n
Christian, Roger, 185
Christine, 149
City Lights, 33
Cixous, Hélène, 279
Clarke, John, 166
Clarke, Mae, 142

class and horror, 4, 6, 10–11, 173–175, 250, 258, 310, 330, 336
Clifford, Gay, 428
Clift, Montgomery, 204
Close Encounters of the Third Kind, 146, 157–158, 161
Clover, Carol J., 8, 11, 138, 166–171, 173, 177, 178, 179, 198, 214–215, 218–219, 229, 273n
Cocteau, Jean, 263, 265
Code Name: Trixie. See Crazies, The
Cohen, Larry, 107, 108, 164
Coleman, Wanda, 412
Collins, Jim, 248
Colossus: The Forbin Project, 182
Combat (TV series), 189
combat film. *See* war films
comedy, 101, 139, 161
Confessions of a Serial Killer, 173
Conlon, James, 10
conventions of horror, 1–8, 17–24, 27, 31–33, 35–65, 66–113, 121–122, 141, 143–163, 189–193, 199
Conversation, The, 230, 397
Cook, Pam, 211
Coontz, Stephanie, 173
Cooper, James Fenimore, 389
Coppola, Francis Ford, 10, 202, 265–268, 388–391, 393–400
Corman, Roger, 397
Costello, Dolores, 134
costume drama, 189
Cotton, Joseph, 358
Count Dracula, 364, 371
Countess Dracula, 380
Craven, Wes, 108, 111, 164, 173–174, 201
Crawford, Joan, **21**
Crazies, The, 202, 207
Creature from the Black Lagoon, 40
Creed, Barbara, 8, 214, 232, 234, 236, 334, 429
Creepers. See Phenomena
Creepshow, 202, 207

Cries and Whispers, 96
crime films, 253
Cripps, Thomas, 323
Cronenberg, David, 9, 231–251
Cruising, 41, 81, 94, 101
Cubism, 398
Curse of the Cat People, 173
Curtiz, Michael, 135–136
cyberpunk, 269

Dadoun, Roger, 54, 59–60, 65
Dally, Ann, 417
Dances with Wolves, 199
Danza Macabra, La, 380
Daughters of Darkness, 382–387, **383**
Davies, Marion, 142
Davis, Angela, 324
Davis, Bette, **21,** 319
Davis, Mike, 276
Dawn of the Dead, 164, 200–212, **205**
Day of the Dead, 200–212
Day the Earth Stood Still, The, 161, 162
Dead Ringers, 232, 234–235, 241–242,
    244–247, **246,** 252
Dead Zone, The, 232, 234, 238–241
Death of Richie, The, 151
Debord, Guy, 165
Deep Red, 216, 218, 223–226, **225**
de Lauretis, Teresa, 54, 65
Deleuze, Gilles, 357, 360
Deliverance, 91, 111, 214
De Luca, Michael, 180
Dementia 13, 397, 398
D'Emilio, John, 319
Demme, Jonathan, 199, 226, 230, 257
Demon, 92
Demon Seed, 157, 182, 198
de Palma, Brian, 27–29, 34, 66, 68, 88,
    95, 98, 104, 107, 112, 292, 294, 361
de Rougemont, Denis, 410–411
Derry, Charles, 5, 7
Dervin, Daniel, 64
detective films, 351, 397
Deutsch, Helene, 417, 420–421, 424
Diary of the Dead, 169

Dickstein, Morris, 108
Diderot, Denis, 339
Dietrich, Marlene, 133
Dika, Vera, 10, 11, 229, 295
Dillard, R. H. W., 210–211
Dilly, Les, 185
Di Prima, Diane, 424
Disclosure, 8
Doane, Mary Ann, 17, 33n
Doctor X, 119–120, 135, 140
Doherty, Thomas, 7, 9
Don't Go in the House, 173, 180
Doré, Gustave, 343
Douglas, Kirk, 152
Dr. Jekyll and Mr. Hyde (1931), 20, 40,
    126–127, **126,** 136–137
Dr. Jekyll and Mr. Hyde (1941), 20, 40
Dr. Jekyll and Mr. Hyde (Stevenson), 369
Dracula (1931), 20, 22, 24, 58–59, **61,** 66,
    121, 123, 124, 125, 129, 297, 340, 364,
    378n, 389, 390, 391, 395
Dracula (1958), 364, 378n
Dracula (1979), 10, 364–367, 370, 373,
    375–378, **376,** 381, 389, 390, 394
Dracula (Stoker), 10, 265–269, 364–378,
    388–394, 396–399
Dracula's Daughter, 338, 380
Drake, Francis, 121
Draper, Ellen, 141
Dreamscape, 352
Dressed to Kill, 27–31, **28,** 32, 34, 40, 41,
    75, 77, 81, 82, 101, 294
Dreyer, Carl Theodore, 66, 380
Du Maurier, Daphne, 135
Durgnat, Raymond, 206

Eastwood, Clint, 199
Ebert, Roger, 31–32, 109
Ellis, John, 5, 133
Embryo, 157, 413
Engels, Friedrich, 171
Enoch Arden, 16–17, 33n
"Enoch Arden" (Tennyson), 33n
Entity, The, 2
Ephron, Nora, 417

epic films, 8, 265
Eraserhead, 413
Erens, Patricia Brett, 9
E.T.: The Extra-Terrestrial, 146, 157, 159, 162, 274
Et Mourir de Plaisir, 380
Evans, Walter, 5, 422
Everson, William K., 141, 333
Everything You Always Wanted to Know about Sex . . . , 2
Every Woman Has a Fantasy, 101
Evil Dead, The, 41, 113
exhibition, 67, 69, 71–72, 117–142
Exorcist, The, 40, 44, **45**, 66, 146, 149, 150, 162, 165, 190, 232, 234, 251, 263, 279, 293n
exploitation films, 31–32, 66–68, 106, 108, 201, 211, 228, 230
Eyes of Laura Mars, The, 76, 77, 82, 94

fairy tales, 71, 135
family horror, 9, 143–163, 164–180, 279–280, 284, 293n, 352–363
Fantastic Voyage, 194
Far Side, The (comic), 309
Fatal Attraction, 10, 400, 401–411, **404, 409**
Father Knows Best (TV series), 355
Fellini, Federico, 203
Ferguson, Otis, 320
Fetchit, Stepin, 322
fetishism, 22, 35–65, 96, 288, 297–299, 307
film noir, 199, 269
Fincher, David, 188
Finian's Rainbow, 397
Fink, Sue, 387n
Fischer, Lucy, 10
Fisher, Terence, 268, 364, 378n
Flaubert, Gustave, 401–402
Flowers in the Attic, 165
Fly, The (1986), 232, 234–235, 241–244, **243**, 247
Fog, The, 71, 86
Foladare, Maury, 140

folklore, 35, 70–71, 75, 99, 103
Forbes, Thomas Rogers, 418
Forbidden Planet, 182
Ford, John, 191
Foucault, Michel, 164, 407–408
Four Flies on Grey Velvet, 216, 223, 225
Fox, Sidney, 142
Frankenstein (1931), 24, 66, 117–118, 123, 124, 137, 142, 297, 298, **311**–312, 323, 325, 334–335, 340, 347, 389
Frankenstein (Shelley), 311–312, 314, 336, 369, 428
Frankenstein Meets the Wolf Man, 128–129
Frankfurt School, 106
Freaks, 20, 22
Freddy's Dead: The Final Nightmare, 168, 172, 176, 179
Freedman, Estelle, 319
Frenzy, 111
Freud, Sigmund, 22, 23, 35, 47–48, 49–53, 55, 59, 60–61, 65, 68–69, 71, 92, 100, 162, 167–169, 177n, 208, 267, 273n, 284, 297–300, 312, 339, 359, 363, 369–370, 371–372, 391–392
Friday, Nancy, 381
Friday the 13th, 31–32, 69, 77, 84, 90, 101, 150, 166, 170, 171, 389
Friday the 13th—A New Beginning, 170
Friday the 13th Part 2, 77, 86, 170
Friday the 13th Part III, 80, 81, 170
Friday the 13th, Part VI: Jason Lives, 170–171
Friday the 13th, Part VII: The New Blood, 171
Friday the 13th Part VIII: Jason Takes Manhattan, 170–171, 175
Friday the 13th—The Final Chapter, 170
Friday the 13th series, 71–72, 77, 78, 81, 94, 164–165, 170–171, 190, 201
Frisson des Vampires, La, 381, 384
From Beyond, 275
Fury, 322, 323
Fury, The, 146, 151, 152–153
Fuseli, Henry, 5, 268

Gaines, Jane, 140, 330
Galbraith, John Kenneth, 255–256
gangster films, 125, 138, 139, 253,
  397–398
Garber, Marjorie, 228, 230
Garbo, Greta, 133
Gatto a Nove Code, Il. See *Cat o' Nine Tails*
gaze, 8–10, 15–34, 89–91, 100–101, 104,
  141, 167, 208–210, 218–222, 282–
  283, 297, 299, 310, 327–330, 393
German expressionism, 6, 253, 374
Geronimo (1993), 389
ghouls, 39, 41
giallo, 228n
Giant Claw, The, 55–56
Giger, H. R., 185
Gilder, George, 255–256, 274
Girard, René, 256–257, 258, 274
Gish, Lillian, 33n
"Giving Birth" (Atwood), 427
Godard, Jean-Luc, 202
Godfather, The, 397, 398, 399
Godfather, The, Part 2, 397
Godfather, The, Part 3, 397
Godfather series, 397–398
God Told Me To, 92
Gone with the Wind, 322, 325, 331
Good Earth, The (Buck), 417
Gordon, Stuart, 275
Gorris, Marlene, 210
Gothic horror, 5, 7, 309, 321, 380–381,
  384, 385, 417
Goux, Jean-Joseph, 255–256
Graduate, The, 69
Gramsci, Antonio, 166
Grant, Barry Keith, 179
Great Santini, The, 153–154
Greenberg, Harvey R., 5, 9, 107
Green Pastures, 322
Griffith, D. W., 16–17, 33n, 322
Grippo, Joelyn, 387n
Guaccius, 418–419

Halberstam, Judith, 226–227
Hall, Jacqueline Dowd, 324–325

Hall, Mordaunt, 123
Hall, Stuart, 249, 416
Hallelujah, 322
Halloween, 27, 32, 71, 72–74, 76–77, 78,
  80, 81, 83–**84,** 86, 94, 100, 150, 170–
  171, 177n, 201, 297, 352, 359, 389
Halloween II, 78, 80–81, 82, 170
Halloween III: Season of the Witch, 149
Halloween series, 71–72, 81, 164–165,
  190, 201
Hammer Studios, 380–381
Handel, Leo, 139
Hannah, Daryl, 4
Hardy, Phil, 141
Harry, Deborah, 239
Hart, James V., 275
Haskell, Molly, 206
Hawks, Howard, 190, 191, 204–208, 350
Hays, Will, 320
Hays Office, 190. *See also* Production
  Code Administration
Hearts of Dixie, 322
Heath, Stephen, 22
He Knows You're Alone, 2, 31, 78, 81,
  82, **93**
Hell Night, 76, 78, 79, 81, 84, 86, 104
Hellraiser, 261, **262, 264**
Hellraiser III: Hell on Earth, 263–264
Hellraiser series, 255, 261–264
Hemmings, David, 223–224, **225**
Henry: Portrait of a Serial Killer, 176, 389
Hepburn, Katharine, 319
Herring, Henry, 34
Herzog, Werner, 364, 387n
Heung, Marina, 155, 162n
Hide in Plain Sight, 154
Hills Have Eyes, The, 41, 71, 164, 201,
  259, 280
Hills Have Eyes, The, II, 201
Hitchcock, Alfred, 34, 65, 66, 71, 72, 75,
  87, 90, 97, 102, 104, 111, 112,
  196–197, 218, 223, 273n, 282, 292,
  352, 356, 357, 389, 402–403
Hobart, Rose, 127
Hobson, Valerie, 340

Hoffman, Dustin, 154
Hogan, David J., 295
Hollinger, Karen F., 9, 317–318
Hollowgate, 169
Homicidal, 2
Hook, 275
hooks, bell, 331
Hooper, Tobe, 67, 72
Hopkins, Miriam, **126,** 127, 137, 142
Horkheimer, Max, 249
Horror of Dracula. See Dracula (1958)
Houston, Beverle, 426
Howling, The, 413
Hunger, The, 41
Hungry Wives. See Jack's Wife
Hunt, Leon, 213
Hurd, Gail Anne, 110
Hush . . . Hush, Sweet Charlotte, **21**
Hyams, Leila, 142

identification. See spectatorship
I Dismember Mama, 173
Imaginary Order, 57, 359–361
Imitation of Life (1934), 322
Incredible Shrinking Man, The, 2, 56
Incredible Torture Show, The, 41
Inferno, 216
Innocent Blood, 190
Innocent Man, An, 192
Interview with the Vampire, 190
Invaders from Mars (1953), 161
Invasion of the Body Snatchers (1956), 4, 5, 48, 161, 413
Invasion of the Body Snatchers (1978), 48
Invisible Man, The, 130–131
Irigaray, Luce, 334
Island of Dr. Moreau, The (Wells), 131
Island of Lost Souls, **131**–132
I Spit On Your Grave, 77, 79, 96, 109n
It! The Terror from beyond Space, 190
It Lives Again, 413
It's Alive, 76, 107, 149, 164, 279, 413, **414**
It's Alive III: Island of the Alive, 413
I Walked with a Zombie, **6,** 10
I Was a Teenage Frankenstein, 341

I Was a Teenage Werewolf, 341

Jack's Wife, 2, 202, 203–204, 207, 208
Jacobus, Mary, 312, 318
James, Caryn, 413
James, Henry, 367
Jameson, Fredric, 162–163, 233, 250n
Jancovich, Mark, 6
Jason Goes to Hell: The Final Friday, 171
Jaws, 56, 79, 90, 297
Jesse James Meets Frankenstein's Daughter, 2
Joe, 150
Johnston, Claire, 206–207
Jones, Amy, 7, 84
Jones, Ernest, 273n
Jourdan, Louis, 364, 371
Joyride, 352
Judgment Night, 11
Juno, Andrea, 106, 108

Kaplan, E. Ann, 89
Karloff, Boris, 124, 136, 340
Kawin, Bruce, 11, 34
Keeler, Greg, 154
Kellner, Douglas, 162, 234, 251
Kelly, Mary, 60–61
Kennedy, X. J., 348
Kenton, Erle C., 131
Killing Kind, The, 173
Kinder, Marsha, 426
King, Stephen, 8
King Kong (1933), 5, 6, 9, 20, 21, 22, 40, 66, 123, 126, 135–136, 140, 297, 323, 325, 336, 338–351, **346, 348, 349**
Kipnis, Laura, 249
Kitzinger, Sheila, 418
Klein, Melanie, 34
Klinger, Barbara, 211
Knee, Adam, 9
Knightriders, 202, 204–205, 207, 211
Kofman, Sarah, 289
Kramer vs. Kramer, 154–155, 161
Kristeva, Julia, 8, 35–65, 390, 391, 418–419, 427, 429
Kubrick, Stanley, 147, 149, 182

Kumel, Harry, 382, 384, 386
Kuzui, Fran Rubel, 7

Lacan, Jacques, 22, 51, 52–53, 55, 57, 162, 213, 357, 359–360
Lady in a Cage, 173
Laemmle, Carl, 117–118
Lambert, Mary, 7
Lanchester, Elsa, 132, 142, 307n, 313–314, **317,** 318, 321, **329,** 333
Landy, Marcia, 426, 429
Lang, Fritz, 190, 202
Langella, Frank, 367, **376,** 378, 381, 390
Last Action Hero, The, 272
Last House on the Left, The, 111
Last of the Mohicans, The (1992), 389
Last of the Mohicans, The (Cooper), 389
Laughton, Charles, **131**–132, 321
LaValley, Albert J., 316
Leatherface: The Texas Chainsaw Massacre III, 171
Leave It to Beaver (TV series), 355
Lee, Christopher, 380
LeFanu, Joseph Sheridan, 379–380
Lehman, Peter, 4
Leifer, Myra, 416–417, 420–422, 424
Lenin, Vladmir Ilyich, 164
lesbian vampire films, 2, 10, 379–387
Levin, Ira, 428
Lévi-Strauss, Claude, 52, 53–54, 256
Lewis, Herschell Gordon, 201
Lewton, Val, 190, 268
Lindsey, Karen, 379, 382
Lindsey, Shelley Stamp, 9
Little Shop of Horrors (1986), 110
Lock Up, 192
Lords, Tracy, 251
Lucas, George, 182, 189
Lugosi, Bela, 124, 391
Lurie, Susan, 23, 299–300, 307n
Lust for a Vampire, 380
Lyne, Adrian, 402

Macabre, 69
Madame Bovary (Flaubert), 401–402

Madonna, 188, 274
Maldición de los Karnstein, La, 380
Maltin, Leonard, 151
Manhunter, 173
Maniac, 169
March, Fredric, **126,** 127, 136–137
Marcus, Steven, 97, 99, 111
Marcuse, Herbert, 260, 272, 274, 370
Marcus Aurelius, 257
Mark of the Vampire, 121, 128, 129
Marnie, 173
Marsh, Mae, 33n
Marsh, Marian, 132, 134–135, 142
Martin, 200, 202, 204, 279, 293n
masochism, 97–98, 105, 118, 138n, 167–168, 176–177, 178, 273, 360
masquerade, 134, 288–290, 295
Massey, Anna, 27
Masson, Jeffrey, 169
Matinee, 1
Mauss, Marcel, 256
McCabe and Mrs. Miller, 389
McCarthy, 125, 138
McConnell, Frank, 4
McDonagh, Maitland, 223
McGrath, Patrick, 169
McLarty, Lianne, 9
meat movies, 41, 69, 76, 201, 233. *See also* slasher films; splatter films
melodrama, 9, 17, 118, 125, 143–163, 199, 269, 279–282, 284
Member of the Wedding, The (McCullers), 21
Meschera del Demonio, La. See *Black Sunday*
Metz, Christian, 16, 165, 229, 357
Miller, Alice, 169, 178
Miller, D. A., 316–317
mirror stage, 57–58, 360
Mitchell, James E., 119–120
Mitchell, Juliet, 61
Modleski, Tania, 106, 113, 127, 168, 199, 240
Monolith Monsters, The, 161
Monster and the Girl, The, 2

Montrelay, Michèle, 288–289, 295
Moore, Mary Tyler, 154
Most Dangerous Game, The, 135
Motel Hell, 76, 109
Mother's Day, 77
Mr. Ed (TV series), 355
Mr. Mom, 55
Ms. 45, 77
Mulvey, Laura, 8, 15–16, 22, 141, 229,
    283, 298–300, 327–328
Mummy, The (1932), 125, 136, 297
Mundorf, Norbert, 120
Murders in the Zoo, 138–139
Murnau, F. W., 10, 34, 268, 364–368,
    370–375, 391
musical films, 139, 189
My Mother, My Self (Friday), 381
My Secret Life (anon.), 97
mystery films, 125, 139, 199
Mystery of the Wax Museum, 123, 130, 135

Naipaul, V. S., 43
Naked Lunch, 234
narcissism, 23, 25, 27, 42
Navigator, The: A Medieval Odyssey, 188
Neale, Stephen, 5, 7, 165, 283–284,
    296–300
Near Dark, 7, 255, 259–261, **260,** 280
Nelligan, Kate, 377
Newton, Judith, 276
Nietzsche, Friedrich, 343, 402, 406
Nightbreed, 10, 248, 264–265
Nightmare on Elm Street, A, 76, 84–85,
    108, 110
*Nightmare on Elm Street, A, Part 2: Freddy's
    Revenge,* 113, 172
*Nightmare on Elm Street, A, 3: Dream War-
    riors,* 175–176
*Nightmare on Elm Street, A, 4: The Dream
    Master,* 172, 176
*Nightmare on Elm Street, A, 5: The Dream
    Child,* 176
Nightmare on Elm Street series, 71–72,
    164–165, 170–172, 173–176, 179,
    183, 201

Nightmare, The (Fuseli), 5, 268
Night of the Living Dead (1968), 6–7, 10,
    164, 190, 200–212, **201,** 279, 413
Night of the Living Dead (1990), 200–212,
    209
Night of the Living Dead series, 200–212
Nilsson, Lennart, 421
Noche de Walpurgis, La, 380
Nocolodi, Daria, 225–226
Nosferatu (1922), 10, 18, 20, 22, 34, 66,
    265, 297, 364–368, 370, 373–**375,**
    391, 394
Nosferatu (1979), 10, 387
Novia Ensangretada, La, 380
Nyby, Christian, 190, 204

O'Bannon, Dan, 190
Oedipal theory, 34, 51–54, 56–59, 62,
    98, 156, 165, 169, 178, 297, 310,
    339–340, 354, 357–363
Old Dark House, The, 121, **122**
Oldman, Gary, 10, 390, 391, **392**
Omen, The, 40, 66, 150, 279
One from the Heart, 398
On Golden Pond, 154–155
Only Angels Have Wings, 205
Opera, 213, 217–218, 223, 226, 229, 230
Ordinary People, 146, 154–156, 161, 162
Orphans of the Storm, 33n
Other, The, 150
Our Winning Season, 352
Outer Limits, The (TV series), 189
Outsiders, The, 398

Paramount Studios, 126, 131, 136, 138n
Parasite Murders, The. See Shivers
Parents, 165
Parsons, Louella O., 123
Pasolini, Pier Paolo, 272
Patch of Blue, A, 33n
Paul, William, 199n
Peary, Dannis, 387n
Peckinpah, Sam, 350
Peeping Tom, 24–27, **26,** 28, 31
Penley, Constance, 2, 328

People under the Stairs, The, 10, 173, **174**
Perils of Pauline, 88
Peter Pan (Barrie), 275
Peterson, Kristine, 7
Pet Sematary, 7
Pet Sematary II, 7
Phantom of the Opera, The (1925), 18–20, **19**, 21–22
Phenomena, 216–223
Philbin, Mary, 18
Pieces, 169
Pierce, Jack, 323
Pink Flamingos, 101
Pirie, David, 202, 381, 384
Plato, 41, 401–402, 406
Play Misty for Me, 77
Poe, Edgar Allan, 88
Poison Ivy, 7
Polan, Dana, 275, 413, 426, 428
Polanski, Roman, 413, 419, 427, 428
Poltergeist, 56, 146, 151–152, 162, 279
Poltergeist II: The Other Side, 171–172
Pom Pom Girls, The, 352
pornography, 67–70, 76, 96, 101, 111, 112, 178, 251, 380, 382, 385
Posse, 389
postmodernism, 9, 231–235, 247–252, 253–276, 388–389, 397–398
Predator, 189, 270
Predator 2, 269–272, **271**
Price, Michael, 124
primal scene, 47–48, 50, 66
Prisoner of Staten Island, 322
prison movies, 189, 192, 199n
Production Code Administration, 190, 320, 325, 335
Profundo Rosso. See *Deep Red*
Promise of Red Lips, The. See *Daughters of Darkness*
Prom Night, 31, 295
Psycho, 2, 4, 27–29, 30, 31, 34, 40, 41, 42, 63, 69, 71, 72, 74–75, 76, 77, 80, 81, 85–87, 94, 96–98, 101, 102–103, 109, 110, 167, 170, 173, 216, 232, 251, 273n, 282–283, 291, 294, 352, 355, 356–357, 359, 361–362, 389, 394
Psycho II, 101
Psycho IV: The Beginning, 168, 173
Psycho series, 71–72

Quattro Mosche di Velluto Grigio. See *Four Flies on Grey Velvet*
queer reading, 10, 315–316, 334, 335, 379–387
Question of Silence, A, 209

Rabelais, François, 59
Rabid, 232, 235–237, 251
Rabinowitz, Paula, 310
race and horror, 4, 9, 10–11, 173–175, 250, 255, 310, 321–332, 344
Race with the Devil, 11
Raiders of the Lost Ark, 400
Rambo: First Blood, Part II, 192
Rankin, Ruth, 136
rape revenge films, 2, 77, 214
Rear Window, 218, 357
Rebel without a Cause, 162
Reddick, Lawrence, 322
Red River, 204, 205, 207
Reeves, Keanu, 395
Reflection of Fear, 40
repression, 4–5, 46, 92, 109, 144, 152, 155, 169–170, 198, 253, 280–281, 339, 354–355, 372–374, 378
Revenge of the Nerds, 161
Rhodes of Africa, 322
Rice, Anne, 7
Rich, Adrienne, 362, 417–419
Ricoeur, Paul, 148
Rivière, Joan, 288, 295
RKO Studios, 140, 341
Robocop, 182, 269
Robocop 2, 183, 269
Rocky, 177n
Rocky Horror Picture Show, The, 101, 309, 384

Roddenberry, Gene, 199
Rodowick, David, 167
Rollin, Jean, 381
Romero, George A., 9, 108, 164, 200–212, 248, 265, 413
Rosemary's Baby, 10, 40, 66, 78, 143, **145**, 147–149, 153, 157, 279, 412–431, **425**
Rosemary's Baby (Levin), 428
Ross, T. J., 5, 6
Rothman, Stephanie, 7, 108, 381, 387n
Rouge aux Lèvres, La. See Daughters of Darkness
Ruben, Joseph, 352, 356, 358–359
Ruben, Katt Shea, 7
Rubin, Gayle, 314, 315
Rumblefish, 398
Russell, Chuck, 175
Russell, Rosalind, 319
Russell, Sharon, 387n
Russo, Vito, 315, 321, 334

sadism, 105, 118, 138n, 167–168, 176, 178, 360
Sands of Iwo Jima, 344
Sardou, Victorien, 88
Sargent, Epes W., 127–128, 140
Sarno, Joe, 112
Sarris, Andrew, 34, 427
Saunders, John Monk, 142
Savini, Tom, 165, 202–203
Scanners, 232, 233–234, 238–241, 251
Schallert, Edwin, 123
Schoell, William, 67, 80, 83, 91
Schrader, Paul, 303–304, 306
Schreck, Max, 367, **375**
Schwarzenegger, Arnold, 272
science fiction, 2, 4, 9, 50, 66, 71, 143–163, 181–199, 269–273, 275, 325, 389, 394–395
Scott, Ridley, 113, 187, 191, 195, 198, 198n, 234
Searchers, The, 261
Season of the Witch. See Jack's Wife

Sedgwick, Eve Kosofsky, 315, 325
Seventh Seal, The, 188
Sex and the Vampire. See Frisson des Vampires, La
Seymour, Michael, 185
Seyrig, Delphine, 382, **383**, 385–386
Shadow of a Doubt, 357–359
Shadow of the Werewolf. See Noche de Walpurgis, La
Shane, 270
Sharrett, Christopher, 9, 11, 165
Shaviro, Steven, 213–214, 217, 222
Shayne, Robert, 175
Shelley, Mary, 310–312, 314, 318, 333, 336, 369
Sherman, Cindy, 400
Shining, The, 66, 71, 151–154, **153**
Shivers, 232, 233, 235–237, **238**, 251
Shoot the Moon, 146, 155
Showalter, Elaine, 102
Shusett, Ronald, 190
Siegel, Don, 4, 413
Silence of the Lambs, The, 199, 226–227, 230, 255, 257–259, 273n
Silverman, Kaja, 105, 112, 165, 168, 229, 291–292, 361, 362
Siskel, Gene, 109
Sisters, 164, 361
Six Weeks, 154
Skal, David J., 126
Skerritt, Tom, 194
slasher films, 8, 41, 44, 66–113, 150, 152, 166–167, 173, 178–179, 209–210, 213–215, 216, 226, 228n, 229, 254, 261, 283, 284, 291, 294, 295. See also meat movies; splatter films
Sloterdijk, Peter, 263
Slotkin, Richard, 259, 274, 275
Slumber Party Massacre, 7, 76, 84, 85, **95**
Smith, Paul, 168
Smith, Valerie, 326, 327
Sobchack, Vivian, 9, 276, 279, 280
Soble, Alan, 112n
Socrates, 402

Something Wild, 230
Sontag, Susan, 394–395
So Red the Rose, 322
Sotti gli Occhi dell'Assassino. See *Tenebrae*
special effects, 67, 87, 143, 150, 164–166, 168, 177n, 182, 184, 297, 395
spectatorship, 5, 7, 15–34, 36, 40, 43–44, 57–58, 66–113, 117–142, 165, 166–177, 179, 183–184, 189–190, 213–230, 254, 273n, 296–300, 310, 327–328, 330–331, 354, 360–361, 385, 391, 394–395
Spielberg, Steven, 90, 275
splatter films, 41, 66, 201. *See also* meat movies; slasher films
Splatter University, 104, 109
Staiger, Janet, 121–122, 179
stalker films. *See* slasher films
stardom, 131–137
Starman, 146, 157, 159
Star Trek series, 182, 199
Star Wars, 161, 165, 189–190
Star Wars series, 258
Stefano, Joseph, 173
Stella Dallas, 354
Stepfather, The, 9, 352–363, **353**
Stepfather series, 165
Stevens, Shane, 173, 180
Stevenson, Robert Louis, 369
Stoker, Bram, 265–269, 364–378, 388–390, 392–394, 396–397, 399
Stoller, Robert, 102
Strait-Jacket, 77
Strangler, The, 173
Streep, Meryl, 154
Stripped to Kill, 7
Stripped to Kill II, 7
Studlar, Gaylyn, 133–134, 229, 357, 360–361
sublimation, 144
Sunrise, 374
surrealism, 35, 377, 396–397, 398
Suspiria, 216, 218–223, 226
Svengali, 132, 134–135, 141

Sweeney, Louise, 420
Symbolic Order, 35–65, 360
Symbolism, 396
Symposium (Plato), 402
Szasz, Thomas B., 408

Taboo, 69
Taking Off, 150
Talalay, Rachel, 179
Tangerine Dream, 261
Tarratt, Margaret, 4
technological horror, 181–183, 231–241, 269–270, 275
Tenebrae, 216, 218, **220**, 222–223, 226, 229
Tennyson, Alfred, Lord, 16
Terminal Island, 7
Terminator, The, 158, 182, 189, 269–270, 275
Terminator 2: Judgment Day, 182, 269–270, 275
Terror at the Opera. See *Opera*
Terror in the Crypt, 380
Terror Train, 31
Texas Chainsaw Massacre, The, 32, 41, 67, 71, 72–75, **73**, 76–77, 78, 79–80, 83–85, 109, 110, 164, 171, 259, 297, 389
Texas Chainsaw Massacre, The, Part 2, 74–76, 77–79, 85–86, 91, 94–95, 102, 104, 109, 171
Texas Chainsaw Massacre series, 81, 92
Thelma and Louise, 198
Them!, 4, 161, 233
They Came from Within. See *Shivers*
Thing, The (from Another World) (1951), 48, 56, 61, 190, 191, 204, 205, 233, 389, 390, 394
Thing, The (1982), 48, 56, 61, 191
Thoreau, Henry David, 406–407
Tin Star, The, 259
To Have and Have Not, 204
To Love a Vampire. See *Lust for a Vampire*
Tombstone, 389

Tommyknockers, The, 251

Toolbox Murders, The, 169

Tootsie, 101–102

Tourneur, Jacques, 301, 303–304, 306, 307n, 308

Trauma, 226–227, 230

Trespass, 11

Trial, The (Kafka), 428

True Lies, 400

Truffaut, François, 202, 273n

Tudor, Andrew, 4, 8, 233, 295

Turner, George, 124

Twentieth Century-Fox, 183, 188

20,000 Leagues under the Sea, 182

Twilight Zone (TV series), 189

Twins of Evil, 380

Twitchell, James B., 5, 6, 70, 108–109, 293n, 417

2,000 Maniacs, 201

2001: A Space Odyssey, 143, 147–149, 182–183

Tyler, Parker, 387n

Uccello dalle Piume di Cristallo, L'. See *Bird with the Crystal Plumage, The*

uncanny, the, 55, 92, 100, 392

Uncle Tom's Cabin (Stowe), 324

Unforgiven, 199

Universal Studios, 5, 124, 129, 253

Unsane. See *Tenebrae*

Vadim, Roger, 380

Vale, V., 106, 108

Vampire Bat, The, 135

Vampire Lovers, The, 380

vampires, 9–10, 23, 39, 41, 59–60, 66, 69, 124, 141, 190, 200, 202, 260–261, 265–269, 275, 364–378, 380–382, 386

Vampiri, I, 380

Vampyr, 20, 110, 380

Van Sloan, Edward, 117–118, 137

Velez, Lupe, 142

Velvet Vampire, The, 7, 381

Verne, Jules, 190

Vertigo, 34, 357

Videodrome, 98, 232, 234–235, 238–241, **240,** 251, 252

Village of the Damned (1960), 161

Virgin Spring, The, 111

voyeurism, 16–17, 22, 25–26, 42, 328

Wagner, Richard, 268

Waldman, Diane, 128–129, 417, 422

Waller, Gregory A., 200, 208, 280

Waltons, The (TV series), 355

Ward, Vincent, 188

Ware, Susan, 319

war films, 8, 125, 139, 189–192, 199

Warner Bros. Studios, 135, 192, 397

Wayne, John, 204, 344

Weaver, James, 120

Weaver, Sigourney, **193,** 194–195, **197,** 199, 209

Weine, Robert, 413

Weird Woman, 1

Welch, Raquel, 194

Well of Loneliness, The (Hall), 319

werewolves, 39, 66

West, Mae, 83n

western films, 139, 189, 193, 199, 253, 261, 274, 389

Westlake, Donald E., 352, 359

Wexman, Virginia Wright, 422

Whale, James, 124, 268, 298, 300, 309, 311, 312, 321, 323, 325, 333, 335

Whatever Happened to Baby Jane?, **21,** 66

White, Dennis L., 413

White, Miriam, 34

White Zombie, 10, 124, 141

Williams, Linda, 8, 92, 111, 178, 209, 283–284, 290, 299, 300, 307n, 328, 330

Williams, Tony, 9, 11, 280

Wise, Naomi, 206

witches, 35, 39, 387n, 418–419, 423–424

Wizard of Oz, The, 172

Wolfen, 66
Wolf Man, The, 1, 7, 297, 339, 341
Wollen, Peter, 206
Wood, Robin, 4, 9, 10, 67, 71, 106, 107,
   110, 144, 164, 198n, 201, 202, 205,
   206, 210, 211, 231, 234, 237–238,
   253–254, 274, 280, 334, 354–356, 416
Wray, Fay, 135–136, 141–142, 325
Wuthering Heights (Brontë), 377

Yakir, Dan, 202
Young, Elizabeth, 9
Young, Iris Marion, 416

Zajicek, E., 416, 423
Zillman, Dolf, 120
Zimmerman, Bonnie, 10
Zombie Flesheaters, 41
zombies, 39, 41, 141, 200–212, 265